Contemporary Europe and the Atlantic Alliance

D1196449

Contemporary Europe and the Atlantic Alliance
A Political History

L.H. GANN and PETER DUIGNAN

First published 1998

2 4 6 8 10 9 7 5 3 1

Blackwell Publishers Ltd
108 Cowley Road
Oxford OX4 1JF
UK

Blackwell Publishers Inc.
350 Main Street
Malden, Massachusetts 02148
USA

British Library Cataloguing in Publication Data

A CIP catalogue record for this book is available from the British Library.

Library of Congress Cataloging in Publication Data

Gann, Lewis H., 1924–
    Contemporary Europe and the Atlantic alliance : a political
history / L.H. Gann and Peter Duignan.
        p.   cm.
    Includes index.
    ISBN 0–631–20589–6 (alk. paper). — ISBN 0–631–20590–X (pbk. :
alk. paper)
    1. Europe—Politics and government—1945–   2. North Atlantic
Treaty Organization.   3. National security—Europe.   I. Duignan,
Peter.   II. Title.
D843G266 1997
320.94—dc21   97–3886
                                                                    CIP

Typeset in 9¹/₂ on 10¹/₂ pt Garamond
by Graphicraft Typesetters Ltd, Hong Kong
Printed in Great Britain by T.J. International, Padstow, Cornwall

This book is printed on acid-free paper

Contents

Maps

Preface

In 1945 much of Western Europe lay prostrate. Whole cities had, in large part, been reduced to rubble; millions of people had lost their homes or their lives; tens of millions were refugees. World War II left a legacy of misery, hatred, and an inheritance of defeat for all European countries except Britain, the Soviet Union, and a handful of neutrals. No expert predicted a rapid recovery. Many philosophers, poets, historians, and novelists looked toward the future with gloom. Western civilization, or at least the bourgeois order, had supposedly come to the end of its tether.

This melancholic mood, however, bore no relation to what actually happened. Western Europe achieved the most rapid recovery in its history. There was not just a German *Wirtschaftswunder*, but a whole series of seeming economic miracles. Western Europe entered a new age of prosperity – "30 golden years." At the same time, democracy revived on the European continent. Indeed, the Western democracies produced an array of political talent drawn from the ranks of the moderates – Christian democrats, progressively minded Tories, social democrats, Labourites, acting in informal concert on many major issues.

Notwithstanding many forecasts to the contrary, the US abandoned its traditional isolationism, and joined with the Western European countries in reconstructing Europe (Marshall Plan) and defending the West in NATO (1949) and a variety of other organizations designed for economic, political, and military support. (These included the United Nations Relief and Rehabilitation Association or UNRRA, set up in 1943; the General Agreement on Tariffs and Trade or GATT, initiated in 1947; and the North Atlantic Treaty Organization, created in 1949.) A new transatlantic community (the Atlantic Community) came into being which profoundly affected life in many different fields. While the European continent was divided by an "Iron Curtain," the main Western European countries joined to form the European Economic Community (the EEC, later known as the European Union, EU), which was formed in 1957 and became operative in 1958. This is the story that we have told in our book *The Rebirth of the West: the Americanization of the Democratic World, 1945–1958*.

The present work has a somewhat different focus. It covers a longer time span: from the year in which the EEC began to function to the present. The secondary literature on the subject is immense. Our footnotes are not therefore exhaustive, but are merely intended to give general guidance to the reader. Our work once more concentrates on the Atlantic partnership, that is to say the United States and its main Western European allies. Our work is one of synthesis, multidisciplinary in character, suitable – we trust – for upper division undergraduates, for general readers interested in contemporary history, and also for specialists who wish to see their own work in a wider perspective. We deal primarily with parties, politics, and politicians within the principal countries of the Western alliance, their social development, and the interaction between the various Western states.

In designing our work, we faced once more the difficult choice of which countries to include and which to leave out. We have concentrated on the relations between the US and the member states of NATO and the European Economic Community. Such a limitation invites obvious criticism. Prague, for example, is as much a Western city as Vienna – why then omit Czechoslovakia? (Even in a purely geographical sense, the Czech capital lies well to the west of the Austrian capital.) But a long period of communist domination did impose certain features in common on the member states of the Warsaw Pact (established 1955 as a military alliance between the Soviet Union and its Eastern European satellites). We have therefore left out the countries formerly under communist domination until such times as they rejoined the West. We likewise excluded Greece, Turkey, and Israel. All three have strong links to the West, but they are all primarily part of the eastern Mediterranean and are involved with the Middle East.

In our treatment, we have compromised between a thematic and a chronological approach. We have separate chapters on transnational organizations such as NATO, and transnational issues such as the student revolution of the 1960s and the Cold War. But, at the same time, we have placed emphasis on the main nation-states comprised within the NATO alliance, their politics, social condition, and interaction with one another. This approach may occasion dissent from those who believe that the age of the European nation-state is passing, that the future belongs, on the one hand, to a European superstate, and, on the other, to its regions. The EU's member states have indeed ceded important functions to Brussels (headquarters of the EU). Similarly, the regions have become important in once highly centralized states such as France and Spain. But political loyalties still mainly center on the nation-states. European hikers mostly sew their own respective colors on their backpacks – not the dark blue colors of the EU complete with a circle of golden stars. European soccer crowds always cheer for their own respective national teams. More fundamentally, the essentials of sovereignty remain with the EU's individual member states in the sense that any one of them could secede from the European Union without being prevented from doing so by armed force, as were the Southern states during the American Civil War and the Catholic cantons in the Swiss *Sonderbundskrieg* during the nineteenth century.

We should like to thank the Director of the Hoover Institution and our colleagues there for their help. We are also indebted to the Institute for Advanced Study, Princeton, where we did part of our work. Above all, we should like to express our gratitude to all those who have commented on, or read, our manuscript as a whole or in part. They include Martin Anderson, Sam Barnes, Dennis Bark, Bruce Bueno de Mesquita, John H. Bunzel, Angelo M. Codevilla, Robert Conquest, Gerald A. Dorfman, John B. Dunlop, Robert Hessen, Tony Judt, Henning Köhler, James A. McAdams, Edwin Meese III, Norman M. Naimark, Agnes Peterson, Richard F. Staar, Barry Weingast, and Hans Peter Widmaier. We should also like to express our gratitude to our successive secretaries, Theory (Margaret) Berger and Harold Farmer. We stand indebted alike for their patience, hard work, and their counsel. Our appreciation also goes to the staff of Blackwell Publishers, especially Tessa Harvey and Sue Ashton, for their help in editing the manuscript and seeing it through the press. All errors which remain in this book are, however, purely our fault.

L.H. Gann
Peter Duignan
Stanford, CA
December 1996

On 17 January 1997, my co-author, L.H. Gann, died suddenly in Palo Alto, California. Unfortunately he won't see this last book of ours in print, nor will he be able to finish a new book he had just started on German history from Bismarck to Kohl.

Peter Duignan
Stanford, CA
February 1997

Acknowledgments

The authors and publisher are grateful to the following for permission to use maps in this volume. *The Washington Post National Weekly Edition* for permission to use Map 8, "NATO looks ahead", 31 July–6 August 1995; *The New York Times* for permission to use Map 12, "The Bosnian settlement", 17 November 1996; and Houghton Mifflin, Boston, for Map 13, which is taken from *Present Tense: the United States since 1945*, by Michael Schaller, Virginia Scharff and Robert D. Schultzinger (Boston: Houghton Mifflin, 1992), p. 588.

The publishers apologize for any errors or omissions to the above list and would be grateful to be notified about any corrections or omissions that should be added to this book.

PART I

Setting the Stage: Politics in the Atlantic Community, Late 1950s to the Early 1970s

Introduction to the Politics

When World War II ended, Western Europe was in a parlous state. Experts vied in the pessimism of their forecasts, and this with good reason. The world had witnessed unparalleled destruction and bloodshed in what had been the greatest clash of arms in history. Persecution and mass murder had occurred on a scale, and with methods, that would have horrified Genghis Khan. War had left a legacy of misery and despair that might have turned to massive violence thereafter. Sooner or later, said the pessimists, a Fourth Reich would emerge in Germany from the ruins of the Third. Or, other forecasters predicted either in hope or in fear, Western capitalism was destined to perish of its own internal contradictions; Soviet communism represented the wave of the future.

But, as we have pointed out in an earlier volume, *The Rebirth of the West*, the prophets of gloom all proved mistaken. By the late 1950s, Western Europe was more prosperous than it had ever been in its previous history. The main Western European states had joined in the European Economic Community (EEC, formally set up in 1957, effective as from 1958). The US had abandoned its traditional isolationism, and joined in the formation of the North Atlantic Treaty Organization (NATO, set up in 1949) to defend Western Europe against Soviet expansion, to control West Germany, and to keep the US involved in Europe. Western Europe and North America had become linked through countless ties of a cultural, economic, and military kind. West Germany had been legitimized and integrated into the Western alliance, and Germany's neighbors, especially France, were relieved.

Economists talked about the *Wirtschaftswunder*, the economic miracle experienced alike by West Germany and its Western European neighbors. But even more startling was the political miracle. In stark contrast to the 1930s, Western politics were now dominated by moderates — moderate social democrats, moderate Labourites, moderate Tories, moderate Catholics. Not that revolutionary aspirations had disappeared. In Italy and France, the communists remained powerful, with widespread support among the workers. But nowhere in Western Europe did the communists ever come close to seizing power. Neither had right-wing extremism disappeared from Western politics. Fascist sympathizers remained in Italy, Nazi sympathizers in both Germanys, Pétain sympathizers in France. But the old right was marginalized. Racism Nazi-style had been discredited by the shameful record of the Third Reich and its accomplices. Anti-semitic remarks would still be heard in country clubs as well as bar-rooms. But anti-semitism had ended as an effective political force in Western Europe and the US. Similarly, anti-Catholicism had ceased to be a potent political force in Protestant countries, and anti-Protestantism in Catholic countries, except in a few holdouts such as Northern Ireland.

As agriculture declined in relative importance, the political power of great landowners and farmers diminished. The nobility did not disappear. Powerful families still held great estates in Britain; the various diplomatic corps continued to boast of members whose names had for long filled the pages of *Burke's Peerage* and the *Almanac de Gotha*. In republics as in monarchies, titles continued to carry a social cachet. Upper-class Germans and Americans loved a lord as much as did true-born Englishmen. But the aristocrats' traditional stake in the military and in higher administration starkly diminished; scions of the nobility increasingly made their name in new service industries such as public relations, in the arts – or what passed as such.

Within the conservative parties leadership usually fell to businessmen and professionals. (Lord Home was the last of the great aristocrats to become British prime minister, 1963–4.) Even General Dwight Eisenhower (US president 1952–60) came from a modest background. As the welfare state placed an ever-increasing tax burden on its citizens, skilled, even semi-skilled, workers acquired an increasing stake within conservative organizations. So did white-collar workers (especially those employed in the private sector rather than the public sector). But through all shifts and changes moderation ruled supreme. The politics of moderation went with a tightening of transnational links through the spread of consumerism; the growth of tourism into a major service industry; the diffusion of patents and translations; the development of informal and formal networks in international commerce, banking, science, academia, labor unions, the military, and the entertainment industry. Class-based voting declined in every major Western country.

In all the Western states, moreover, politics experienced a generational shift. The postwar leaders of the Western world had mostly reached their respective age of majority before World War I, at a time when Western Europe stood at the height of its global power. (Churchill had been born in 1874, Adenauer in 1876, de Gasperi in 1881, Truman in 1884, de Gaulle and Eisenhower both in 1890. At the battle of Omdurman in 1897, Churchill had actually ridden in the cavalry charge against the Muslim enemy armed only with a lance – as had his crusading ancestors centuries before.) These men differed politically. But they were all shaped by certain common experiences (including World War I and the Great Depression), and all shared certain assumptions concerning both the best way to run a family and to govern a country.

During the 1960s, a new generation stepped into the upper ranks of politics. To these men and women World War I, the Slump (and also the Spanish Civil War) were mere memories. They took for granted the post World War II recovery, the Cold War, and US predominance within the Western alliance. Many of them would later become critics of the welfare state which their elders had created, though this was not apparent at the time. (Margaret Thatcher started as joint parliamentary secretary at the British Ministry of Pensions and National Insurance, a major welfare agency, in 1961. Helmut Kohl assumed the presidency of the CDU (Christian Democratic Union) in the *Land* of Rhineland-Palatinate in 1965; Ronald Reagan was elected to the governorship of California in 1967.) The new leaders even included a king. In Spain, King Juan Carlos was sworn as monarch six years before General Francisco Franco died (1975), thereby terminating the longest-lived personal dictatorship in European history. All these new politicians later became the leaders of their respective countries; all of them were conservatives; none of them would have been judged fit to govern by the establishments of their respective countries in their grandparents' time. (Thatcher was a woman, and would have been excluded by her gender; Reagan had started his career as an actor in derring-do movies; Kohl had served as an advocate within the management group for chemical industries in Rhineland-Palatinate, a respectable job but not an occupation suitable for the leader of a conservative party in Wilhelmine Germany.)

Perhaps the greatest shift came in the US. John F. Kennedy's election to the presidency meant that Irish Catholics had made it to the top – but not only the Irish. (Eleven Ulstermen, that is, Scottish-Irish Protestants from Ireland had previously made it to the presidency.) Kennedy only won by a paper-thin majority. His opponent, Vice-President Nixon – a man whom his best friends would not have described as a charismatic personality – got as much of the white Protestant vote as Eisenhower had done. Nevertheless, Kennedy succeeded. His victory was due to getting an overwhelming majority of votes among Catholics, Jews, blacks, and blue-collar workers (many of them white "ethnics"). Older America was outvoted for the first time by a majority of the "hyphenates" (Irish-Americans, Italian-Americans, etc.), who had been told for two centuries that they were only on approval in an America ruled by WASPs. Kennedy's rise to the presidency symbolized a remarkable social shift, as Catholics strikingly improved their social and economic position in the US – and equally so in Britain, West Germany, Switzerland, and Holland.

There were many other challenges to the accustomed order. For instance, ecology became part of the "new politics" – symbolized by the publication of Rachel Carson's book *Silent Spring* in 1962. Its thesis was not novel, but the book effectively publicized long-standing concerns. (The last of the traditional London pea-soup fogs of Sherlock Holmes fame occurred in 1952; thereafter, the old-fashioned pollution occasioned by coal dust and the smoke of countless fireplaces was eliminated except in communist countries where pollution and environmental degradation increased.) From the 1960s onward, clear skies – in the public mind – ceased to be associated with factories standing idle by reason of wartime destruction or a world slump. Instead, clear skies and clean streams became – at least in theory – a social entitlement. Ecological concern ceased to be limited to the correction of existing abuses, but thereafter became future-oriented. (In 1971, for example, Congress ended a program to build an American supersonic transport (SST), in part because of fears regarding possible damage to the ozone layer surrounding the globe.) At the same time, the development of nuclear power, heralded with optimism during the early 1950s, became a matter of bitter controversy.

In 1963, a year after the appearance of Carson's book, Betty Friedan published *The Feminine Mystique*. She did not thereby originate gender politics; "the woman question" had already been earnestly debated in the nineteenth century by radicals such as August Bebel, the German Social Democratic leader, and many others. But, by the 1960s, gender politics acquired increasing resonance: more women entered the labor force; women began to move into managerial and technical jobs hitherto closed to them; contraceptive devices became available to all who wanted them and were publicized in the most respectable of ladies' journals. Advocates of women's rights thereafter joined the advocates of other constituencies – homosexuals, lesbians, racial and ethnic minorities – who claimed for their groups equal and, later, often both preferential and deferential treatment.

There were the new politics of youth, stimulated by the Vietnam War. The new youth movement resembled in some ways the old youth movement which had begun toward the end of the last century: it was international in character, and it appealed to a minority of college-educated youngsters. All over the Western world these youthful men and women claimed to be the moral reference group and the moral role model for society at large. The movement's adherents, however, formed a minority even among college students, themselves a minority in the US. (A poll found in 1969 that 72 percent of the country's 6.7 million students had never joined a demonstration; another poll reported that only 12.8 percent called themselves "revolutionaries" or "radical dissidents.")[1] Hostility to "hippies," "peaceniks," and "pinkos" abounded on many college campuses (especially in religious institutions and junior colleges). Many young Americans took pride in styling themselves "cowboys," committed to what they regarded as traditional American values. But, unlike the leftists, "cowboys" rarely wrote for the press; they did not appear on TV; their activities did not arouse interest among professors. The leftist minority, by contrast, never wanted for publicity: strikes and demonstrations were adjudged supremely newsworthy by the media. Militants thereby managed to weaken or disrupt academic institutions in many parts of the country.

There were wider cultural changes which affected politics. Whereas the Old Left had idealized the urban worker, the New Left lauded peasants and those rural pursuits of which the militant campus youth had no first-hand experience. Blue jeans worldwide replaced the proletarian cloth cap; rock music took the place of old-fashioned marching songs; the unstructured "demo" replaced the disciplined rallies of old, with their stewards and their brass bands. Men's fashions became more colorful, and pornography more acceptable than hitherto. For all their egalitarian appeal, the most successful of protest artists became multi-millionaires. (Their contingent included the Beatles, who sang for high fees in praise of the simple life, and actors such as Jane Fonda, bosom friend of the Vietcong.) Jet set society mightily expanded, with its pop singers, painters, authors, and actors who vied in elevated sentiments and conspicuous consumption. Television became a major force in politics, and politicians all over the Western world learned from actors how to improve their public appearance. By contrast, the radio – the favorite instrument alike of Churchill, Hitler, Roosevelt – lost some of its former importance to television, except in the more backward parts of the globe.

Television, again, was not a recent invention. The first high-definition TV program had been telecast in 1936 by the BBC (British Broadcasting Corporation). The transmission began with a song whose lyrics began:

A mighty maze of mystic rays
Is all about us in the blue.

The BBC, however, did not trust its brainchild. The BBC looked upon itself as an agency for improving the mass of people rather than as an instrument of entertainment. Moreover, Sir Charles Reith, the BBC's head, instinctively distrusted the new people who came into television from the movies, the music hall, and the theater. (This was a time when radio announcers in the BBC studio still wore dinner jackets when reading news bulletins over the air.) The politicians at first were also indifferent to the new medium – even Winston Churchill who did well on the screen in his old age. During World War II, television in Britain shut down as all the technicians were needed for war work.

It was the US that pioneered the mass production of TV sets after hostilities had ended. (By 1950, only 11 percent of American families possessed a set; by 1960, 88 percent did so.) Television accordingly replaced radio as the chief political medium. Richard M. Nixon made extensive use of the screen, but John F. Kennedy proved an even greater master. The television debates between Vice-President Nixon and his young Democratic challenger clearly went in Kennedy's favor, and influenced the 1960 presidential election accordingly. In continental Europe, General de Gaulle – for all his vaunted traditionalism – also proved a great showman on TV.

1 William Manchester, *The Glory and the Dream: a Narrative History of America, 1932–1972*, New York, Bantam Books, 1975, p. 1167.

In Britain, the first of the great political performers on TV was Sir Harold Macmillan (Conservative prime minister, 1957–63). By habit a careless dresser with an unkempt moustache, he owed his appearance as an Edwardian man-about-town to the television producer's art. But genuine enough were Macmillan's charm, wit, and skill as a raconteur, practiced in exclusive London clubs and dinner parties. He soon came to understand that "a television audience could not be addressed like a public meeting, but it could and should be treated like an intimate dinner companion."[2]

Politics also altered in a more subtle fashion. As the state assumed an ever-growing number of tasks, politicians were expected to be knowledgeable on an ever-growing array of problems. No one had expected Bismarck, Cavour, or Lincoln to have opinions on global warming, acid rain, developmental aid to Third World nations, AIDS, and suchlike. Modern politicians, by contrast, were expected to be universally instructed – and, unsurprisingly, failed the test. Hence there was political disillusionment; an increasing percentage of voters in many countries stayed away from the polls. The power of central governments seemed to weaken in a variety of ways. There were challenges from regional movements among Basques, Catalans, Welsh, Scots, Lombards, and others. Powerful occupational groups (such as the British trade unions or French farmers' associations) bade defiance to central authorities. Nevertheless, the rule of the moderates continued – Tories, Labourites, social democrats, Christian democrats, social liberals and their like, between them, dominated Western politics (except in the Mediterranean periphery, in Greece, Portugal, and Spain, where democratic government was safely established only after a considerable time lag).

There was, however, a long-term shift from the left to the center in national politics. On the face of it, this is surprising, for after World War II prospects seemed bright for socialism. Nationalization of certain key industries was acceptable to many conservatives as well as socialists. Communist parties occupied a powerful position in France and Italy respectively. Militant youths of all nationalities widely favored leftist parties. The "soft," as opposed to the "hard," left was well entrenched in the prestige media, in literary associations, universities, and the mainline churches (especially in transnational bodies, such as the World Council of Churches which increasingly identified itself with the Third World against Western capitalism). Literary intellectuals inclined to the left. Western scholars overwhelmingly came to accept the world's communist systems as permanent features in the world's political landscape. (Even West German academics largely became convinced that communism in East Germany was irreversible.)

Nevertheless, the communist parties in Western Europe could not expand their electoral base: their leadership remained too inflexible, too dogmatic; the "Peoples' Democracies" and the Soviet Union too unattractive as paradigms to be imitated. The moderate left, by contrast, gained strength. Within the major Western countries, the production of raw materials – fuel and food – declined in relative importance; so, in the long haul, did manufacturing, while an increasingly large proportion of the employed were to be found in the service sector. This shift also affected voting patterns. Within parties such as the SPD in Germany or Labour in Britain, the working classes lost in relative importance. Instead, the leftist parties increasingly relied on people in the so-called "helping professions" – teaching, nursing, social work – particularly on workers in the public sector.

2 Michael Cockerell, *Live from Number 10: the Inside Story of Prime Ministers and Television*, London, Faber, 1988, p. 63.

The decisive part in this drama was played by the German Social Democratic Party (SPD), the oldest and largest of modern socialist parties. When World War II ended, socialist leaders persecuted by the Nazis returned from exile or from concentration camps. The SPD was determined to learn from the errors of Weimar, but the party drew the wrong conclusion from its past débâcle. Social Democrats believed that the "social market" capitalism promoted by the Christian Democrats under Konrad Adenauer would inevitably undergo a terminal crisis. The party also expected a new wave of German nationalism and hoped to profit from this upsurge, rather than be swept away by the tide – as in 1933. Finally, the SPD felt convinced that Germany would somehow soon be reunited.

The party did extremely well in *Land* (federal states) and city elections. It was the SPD which governed West Berlin during the perilous days of the Berlin blockade, an experience that profoundly affected the party's fortunes. In national politics, however, the party's original assumptions proved to be widely mistaken. The SPD kept losing national elections in a country thoroughly satisfied with postwar prosperity and social peace. The party moreover learned from the experience of socialist mayors and socialist *Ministerpräsidenten* in charge of *Land* governments, practical men who successfully engaged in coalition politics. The SPD could also draw on a long and intellectually distinguished tradition of theoretical revisionism, represented in the past by Eduard Bernstein (a late nineteenth-century German Social Democrat), and in the present by Carlo Schmidt. Men such as Willy Brandt, mayor of Cold War West Berlin, and Herbert Wehner, an ex-communist distinguished by Stalinist ruthlessness, supplied the tactical skill required to secure the adoption of the so-called Godesberg program.

The Godesberg program was accepted in 1959, the year in which Castro seized power in Cuba, and de Gaulle attained the presidency in France. Unlike these latter two events, the Godesberg program did not make an international splash. But its long-term effects may have been even greater. A great socialist party, an organization of crucial importance to Europe, abandoned socialism as traditionally defined. The party ceased to be bound by socialist dogma; class war went by the board; the SPD had become a frankly reformist party, a *Volkspartei*, an organization willing to win by appealing to voters of any kind.

The shift in France took longer. French socialists had ingloriously led a coalition government (1956–7), but war in Algeria prevented thoroughgoing domestic reforms. The socialists, moreover, were split on every conceivable issue: the Algerian conflict, the European Defence Community, relations with communists, attitudes toward the US. The socialist SFIO (*Section française de l'Internationale ouvrière*) largely disintegrated; political clubs proliferated, a process which in France so frequently accompanied popular disillusionment with established parties. It was François Mitterrand who secured decisive change. Making his name in a political club, the *Convention des institutions républicaines*, he secured leadership of the *Parti socialiste* (PS) in 1971, determined to gain the presidency at the expense of socialist purity. French socialism became as "presidentialized" as the French Republic; Mitterrand absolutely dominated the party, and henceforth his own version of moderate reformism would prevail.

The socialist parties of Italy, Spain, Portugal, and Greece subsequently watered down their respective socialist constitutions. Even the communist parties in Italy and France softened their stand, especially so in Italy. (Here communists gained respectability by heading honest and competent municipal governments in cities such as Bologna. By contrast, major coalition partners, especially the Christian Democrats and Socialists, were demoralized by pervasive connections with crime syndicates.)

The greatest holdout of democratic socialism was Great Britain. The Labour Party in 1945 had won a great electoral victory, a success not duplicated in France, Germany, or Italy. Labour acquired an emotional stake in welfarism and nationalization, a sense of uplift inherited from the non-conformist chapel in which so many Labour people used to worship. It was with deep emotion that the Welsh mining MPs had sung *Cwm Rhondda* as they marched through the division lobbies in the House of Commons to nationalize their pits. Able revisionists, such as Anthony Crosland or Douglas Jay, might criticize traditional party doctrine in theory; innumerable compromises were made in practice. But public ownership of the means of production remained a moral ideal, as well as an assumed badge of modernity. As Labour politician Barbara Castle put it, Russia's nationalized Sputnik now circling round the earth, tracked at every stage by Britain's publicly owned radar telescope at Jodrell Bank, represented typical symbols of this modern age. It was only in the early 1980s that the Labour Party in Great Britain dropped socialism in theory as well as in practice.

The political decline of socialism went with a progressive weakening of socialism's intellectual tradition. After World War II, socialists had dominated much of Western thought. Socialist historians, such as Christopher Hill and Eric Hobsbawm, produced new, interesting, and challenging work. Marxist economists, such as Paul A. Baran and Paul M. Sweezy, claimed to be at the cutting edge of research into macroeconomic problems and consistently produced bad analyses. But socialist academics thereafter seemed incapable of creating major new intellectual syntheses; socialist theoreticians proved even less capable than their conservative colleagues of predicting long-term changes in the real world.

A few examples of mistaken assumptions must suffice. During the 1960s and 1970s, most theoreticians (including many conservative ones) had assumed that the future of the global economy would belong to the world's corporate giants. Communist planners in particular had put their trust in large-scale enterprise such as coal mining and steel-making, with huge armies of labor, organized in a hierarchical fashion. But far from decaying, the petty bourgeoisie in the capitalist countries remained a powerful force. It was often the small entrepreneurs, more flexible, more adaptable than the dinosaurs of capitalism, who pioneered the new industries. Neither socialist nor conservative fore-casters had foreseen the long-term shift from olden-day heavy industries to science-based industries. (The British in World War II had pioneered both the first proto-computer and penicillin, but it had never occurred to Labour planners in the 1940s and 1950s to put public money on a large scale into improving and mass-producing such products as against coal, iron, and steel.) Socialist theoreticians had equally failed to predict the new urban problems derived from the massive immigration of foreign workers; the perilous diffusion of drugs; the social disruption linked to the construction of poorly run public housing schemes located in high-rise buildings.

Socialists (but not socialists only) had likewise placed undue hopes in the beneficence and efficiency of the state. All over the Western world, the power of the state had increased, as had the proportion of the gross national product (GNP) transferred from the pockets of private citizens to public treasuries. In countries such as Austria, Britain, France, and Italy, the state had indeed assumed an important part in the ownership or control of major industries. Planners also had used the state to shift money and other resources from the "rich" to the "poor," and from "rich" to "poor" regions, such as the Italian South. But contrary to traditional socialist predictions, state-run industries did not generally fare well. In Italy, in particular, state enterprises gave rise to massive corruption, equalled in scope by private gangster capitalism (*mafiosi*) or the kind practiced by the BCCI (Bank of Credit and Commerce International) shut down by the Bank of England and other regulators in 1991. Throughout the Western world, socialist intellectuals had assumed that they were living through the last stages of late capitalism, *Spätkapitalismus*. But for all its deficiencies, capitalism did not decay. "Real existing socialism" of the Marxist–Leninist variety did much, much worse, east of the Elbe, even though communism's internal contradictions as yet remained partly hidden by the Iron Curtain and the largest propaganda machine in history.

In the end it was not Western capitalism but the Soviet Union which perished of its own contradictions. The Soviet hegemony in East Central Europe faltered; the Cold War ended; and in 1991 the Soviet Union collapsed. According to revisionist scholarship, the keys to history were class, race, and gender. However, these issues had only played a secondary role in the great transformation. For better and for worse, nationalism and religion remained mainsprings of politics in the post-communist successor states. As it solved old difficulties, the new order created new problems. But at least the great East–West confrontation had ended; democratic aspirations were in the ascendant. The world had good reason for gratitude.

2

US Politics: Kennedy to Nixon

Introduction

After the end of World War II America bestrode the world. Having been just one among seven great powers before war broke out in 1939, the US emerged from war as the world's mightiest country in 1945. The US's primacy continued even after the Western European countries, Japan, and the Soviet Union had recovered from wartime destruction. By the end of the 1950s, the US was the world's leading industrial producer state, the chief agricultural producer, and the world's greatest trader. The US led in most scientific and technological pursuits, in the number of patents registered and Nobel Prizes gained annually. The US held a dominant position in scientific and technological research; the US excelled in the social sciences and the humanities. The US worker remained the world's most productive. The US had pioneered a great number of service industries; no other country could beat the US in its ability to adapt inventions and discoveries to industrial mass production. The US economy continued to grow at a substantial rate. The US inflation rate was negligible (about 1 percent in 1960). The US had the world's most favorable trade balance (it was only after 1975 that the US suddenly had to cope with an overall trade deficit). The US had the world's highest gross national product per head of population. The US provided for its people the world's highest average living standard. Americans owned more cars, refrigerators, radios, and television sets than the people of any other country. Supposedly a selfish nation, America contributed more to private charities than any other country.

The gap between the US and its chief allies did begin to close. Nevertheless, US primacy was indisputable. The US dominated the NATO alliance. US aid had played an essential part in Western Europe's postwar recovery, and in the movement toward closer economic and political union. The US was by far the world's strongest naval power; the US possessed more nuclear weapons than the rest of the world. The US successfully withstood Soviet threats against West Berlin where the Soviet attempt in 1948 to blockade the city had led to the most impressive demonstration of air power in history. A whole city was supplied with its necessities by planes. US military might had also successfully defended South Korea against communist aggression. The US was a global power and armed accordingly.

Immigrants from all parts of the world continued to flock to the US to find freedom and opportunity. Americans had pioneered, or at least played a major part in, the arts of mass production, mass distribution, the standardization of industrial products, and the special skills required for conveniently packaging an enormous number of consumer products. In America the consumer was king as nowhere else in the world. Americans enriched the economies of other countries by massive technological transfers, such as the "Atoms for Peace" program which helped to diffuse nuclear technology. The US provided more foreign aid than any other state. The US also profoundly affected popular culture all over the world. All modern fairy-tales were of American origin: Bambi, Donald Duck, Mickey Mouse. The music of Irving Berlin, Bing Crosby, and Frank Sinatra, the humor of Danny Kaye and the Marx Brothers, gave pleasure to audiences all over the globe. American movies and, later on, US television programs were appreciated in some of the world's most unlikely places. English, especially its American version, became the world's *lingua franca*. Americans played a leading rule in the world economy as investors, as purveyors of new technology, new methods of business and management. Not surprisingly enthusiasts spoke of "the American Century," the "American High."[1]

There was also stunning demographic growth. Between 1950 and 1960, the American population increased from 151,300,000 people to 179,300,000 – the greatest decennial jump for half a century. The numerical increase amounted to 28,000,000, more than the population of Sweden, Norway, Denmark, and The Netherlands combined. Expansion went with an internal shift of population. Both black and white country folk left the rural areas in the Old South, looking for jobs in the Southern cities and, increasingly, in the industrial areas of the North. Migration was speeded by the mechanization of farming; it weakened the traditional Southern power structure in which great landowners had possessed a commanding say. The Western and Southwestern states likewise gained as newcomers found new homes in the Sunbelt, especially Arizona and California. New industries opened in the West; new colleges opened their doors; existing institutions such as Stanford University (a superior finishing school before World War II) grew into a major university. Between 1930 and 1960 California's population more than tripled (from 4,408,260 to 15,717,204), a shift of resources that no European country could remotely match. Before World War II, the West had played a subordinate role within the US economy, heavily dependent on Eastern money, and on the production of raw materials. Thereafter, the importance of the West continued to increase, as against the Atlantic seaboard states and the so-called Eastern Establishment. The economy of the West (especially California's) was transformed as agribusiness, shipbuilding, aviation, steel, electronics, and high-tech industries came into their own. No politician thereafter could ignore the West. New York and Chicago were equalled or exceeded in importance by Los Angeles. (John F. Kennedy in 1960 and Richard M. Nixon in 1968 both secured the great majority of the states west of the Mississippi in their respective bids for the presidency.)

Equally striking was the altered pattern of growth. As Theodore H. White, a political commentator of the period, put it, "just as the census of 1890 had announced the passing of the frontier, the census of 1960 announced the passing of the great city."[2] For half a century, great American urban centers had dominated American culture; big city

1 For a statistical analysis, see Ben J. Wattenberg, *This USA: an Unexpected Family Portrait of 194,067,296 Americans Drawn from the Census*, Garden City, NY, Doubleday, 1965. Also see Peter Duignan and L.H. Gann, *The Rebirth of the West: the Americanization of the Democratic World, 1945–1958*, Oxford, Blackwell, 1992, p. 108ff, p. 179ff; William L. O'Neill, *American High: the Years of Confidence, 1945–1960*, New York, Free Press, 1986.
2 Theodore H. White, *The Making of the President, 1960: a Narrative History of American Politics in Action*, New York, Atheneum, 1988 (originally 1961), p. 216, and its successor, *The Making of the President, 1968: a Narrative History of American Politics in Action*, New York, Atheneum, 1969; Michael Barone, *Our Country: the Shaping of America from Roosevelt to Reagan*, New York, Free Press, 1990.

machines had played a major part in American politics. Big cities, of course, continued to remain important, but from 1960 onward, city cores increasingly relinquished citizens to the suburbs. (The exceptions were Los Angeles, itself a collection of suburbs held together by freeways, and the cities of the South – Houston, Dallas, Birmingham – situated in the part of the US that was a generation behind the rest.)[3] The demographic losers included also small towns and the countryside. Family farms were abandoned; village stores closed their doors. Fewer workers produced more and more crops. By contrast, the suburbs continued to expand. They no longer depended in the main on railroads, and on ports, as the older cities had done. Instead, suburbanites drove by car to work, to school, and to the shopping mall. For long distance journeys, the traveler went by plane rather than by rail or by boat. The aviation and automobile industries played a vital part in the US economy, and in years to come, the auto worker would be idealized as farmers had once been lionized. Teamsters acquired enormous power within the labor unions, whereas railroad men ceased to be of major significance. Suburbs in turn needed freeways, motels, and supermarkets. The new suburbs were built on credit. By using credit cards and other credit facilities, ordinary consumers suddenly were enabled to gain credit on easy terms for building houses, buying cars, acquiring refrigerators, thereby obtaining a privilege once confined to wealthy merchants and noblemen.

The construction of surburbia was itself an immense achievement. It required a national exertion greater than that needed in clearing the original wilderness. Housing and construction became the US's greatest single industry; by 1960 one-quarter of all houses occupied by Americans had been built in the preceding decade – an effort that no other nation could remotely match. The political consequences of these demographic shifts were momentous. Farmers, once the most powerful occupational group in the US, had lost their supremacy in US politics; the small town ceased to be the arbiter of political and moral values. Traditional industries – coal mining, shipbuilding, steel manufacturing – declined in relative importance; high-tech industries diversified. The blue-collar workers remained powerful in politics but, contrary to Marxist theoreticians, the proletariat acquired neither cohesion nor class consciousness. Employment opportunities for unskilled and semi-skilled labor diminished; highly skilled and supervisory labor merged with white-collar workers. From being mere auxiliaries in the army of labor, white-collar workers became its chief contingent. The service industries acquired ever-increasing importance and ultimately dominated the economy. American politics, indeed, life in general, would increasingly be dominated by suburbia.

Some liberal intellectuals, then and thereafter, were apt to deplore the change. Indeed, America's most bitter critics were Americans; no foreigner could quite match in intensity the American intellectual's critique of his or her own country. Surburbanites supposedly were greedy, selfish, and philistine. They were "Organization Men" who had sold their souls. They were sheeplike, easily manipulated by "Hidden Persuaders." They were conformists. They lived in ticky-tacky little houses all the same. They were sexist and racist to the core. They were over-indulged and spoiled. Whereas old-style leftists had censured capitalism for under-paying the worker, the new-style censors blamed capitalism for seducing the workers by consumerism and ill-earned affluence. Suburbanites, the charge sheet continued, might therefore well build their own form of American fascism: pleasant in theory perhaps, but ugly in reality.

3 Kenneth T. Jackson, *Crabgrass Frontier: the Suburbanization of the United States*, New York, Oxford University Press, 1985.

Some criticisms were well founded in part – a point that conservatives liked to ignore. There was indeed poverty aplenty, though poverty differed enormously in kind and impact.[4] There was a world of difference between a penniless Mexican immigrant struggling along with the help of his kinfolk, a once prosperous alcoholic cast into misery by his weakness for liquor, an elderly worker thrown out of employment because there was no longer a demand for the products of his industry, and a married middle-class graduate student manipulating the welfare system for his own benefit. Poverty was, moreover, hard to measure. (Official statistics took no account of transfer payments in kind, such as food stamps or health care and housing subsidies; by definition, moreover, statistics could not measure indirect income derived from gifts or services supplied by friends and family members, or from the "second economy" which escaped the attention of census takers and tax gatherers.) The fact remains that poverty, although declining, persisted; its very existence offended socially conscious Americans, and those who believed that all social evils could be ended by social planning.

All the same, the dramatic misfortunes forecast by so many left-wing critics of the US, including distinguished intellectuals such as Bertrand Russell, Thomas Mann, and Jean-Paul Sartre, bore no relation to reality. Neither Nazism, fascism, nor communism ever gained a substantial foothold in the US. American women, then as now, led the struggle for feminine emancipation; no other country in the world equalled the US in feminine militance. For all its ethnic dissensions, the US by far remained the world's greatest immigrant country. There was a striking decline in prejudice against once-despised outgroups of every kind – Jews, Mexicans, blacks, "Oakies," and also Catholics. Intermarriage between members of different religious, national, and racial groups increased. Despite successive race riots, much publicized in the media worldwide, the US was by far the world's most successful multiracial society – far more than other multi-ethnic states such as the Soviet Union, Yugoslavia, Burundi, Cyprus; the list is long. In America there was no warfare between Jews and Arabs, Serbs and Croats, Greeks and Turks, Protestant Irish and Catholic Irish, Eritreans and Amhara. Few Americans permanently left their country: Latins did not wish to settle in Cuba; few Jews went to Israel, few blacks departed for Africa. By the 1970s, names such as Goldberg, Nader, Tsongas, Kissinger, Hayakawa, Brzezinski had become household words without the ethnic, religious, or racial hatred or scorn that such or similar names had once evoked.

Given the striking shift in the ethnic composition of US immigrants from mainly European to primarily Asian and Latin American newcomers, there was surprisingly little resistance on the part of American nativists or labor unions to this flood until "Prop 187" passed in California in 1994. (Between 1965 and 1990, 14 million new-comers arrived legally, of whom about 85 percent were non-European. The number of undocumented aliens in the US is unknown but probably amounts to 4 or 4.5 million.) The Americans' relative lack of hostility to this shift is historically unprecedented, both in the US and the world at large. Not that prejudice has evaporated. But from the 1950s onward, open and covert restrictions have declined on the socioeconomic mobility of American minority groups. A Catholic thereafter became president; a Greek-American vice-president; a German-Jewish American, and a Polish-American respectively secretary

---

4 According to the Bureau of the Census figures released in 1992, the proportion of Americans classed by income as "poor" stood at 17.3 percent in 1965, 11.2 percent in 1974, 15.2 percent in 1983, and 14.2 percent in 1991. The poverty rate by race stood as follows in 1991: blacks 32.7 percent, Hispanics 38.7 percent, Asians 13.8 percent; whites 11.3 percent.

of state (both spoke English with accents!); a black American, a Lebanese-American, and a Japanese-American were elected US senators. Olden-time Jewish immigrants may have exaggerated when they called the US *die goldene medinah* (the golden state); Germans may have been too optimistic when they had styled America as *das Land der unbegrenzten Möglichkeiten* (the land of unlimited opportunities). But, overall, the US offered more chances to more people than any other country.

The US was also one of the world's most stable states, despite its ethnic diversity, physical mobility, and widespread crime. Lenin had once called for the workers to be armed; in the US alone Lenin's slogan was turned into reality. Ordinary citizens owned firearms by the tens of millions. Violence, however, rarely spilled from the private enterprise of crime to the public realm of politics. Neither were there any regional independence movements in the US after the end of the Civil War; in this respect the US was quite different from countries such as the Soviet Union, Spain, or Nigeria. Overall, Americans prized their political institutions and held on to them – unlike so many continental Europeans. Compare a nonagenarian American in 1959 with, say, a nonagenarian German from Bavaria and a nonagenarian Frenchman. The Bavarian oldster would successively in his lifetime have owed allegiance to a Bavarian king, a German *Kaiser*, a *Reichspräsident* under the Weimar Republic, a *Führer* in the Third Reich, and a *Bundespräsident* in the German Federal Republic. A Frenchman of the same age would in turn have lived under an Empire, the Third Republic, General Pétain's *Etat français*, the Fourth Republic, and the Fifth. An American, by contrast, would have been subject to the same constitution – the world's oldest. Americans might be contemptuous of particular politicians, or even politicians in general. But Americans revered the Constitution and the Bill of Rights; no major political movement ever professed to change their legitimacy, and even enemies of democracy pretended to speak in the Constitution's name. Immigrants accepted the Constitution's legitimacy as much as old-timers; there were bitter quarrels on how the Constitution should be interpreted, but there was uniform agreement concerning its public acceptability. Class war doctrines did not flourish in the US; immigrants had come to seek their fortune as individuals, not as members of some collectivity. Under the Constitution, Americans to this day prize freedom from government interference. More than any other people, Americans regard freedom as more important than equality, and are least inclined to regard the reduction of income inequalities as a task that government should shoulder.

The Constitution established the division of powers between the executive, the legislature, and the judiciary; the Constitution also provided for a division of functions between the central and state governments. Ever since Roosevelt's New Deal, the central authority had gained in power; nevertheless, power remained widely dispersed in a manner incomprehensible to foreigners. (There were in the 1970s, for example, 40,000 different police forces in the US.) Americans voted more often, in national, state, and local elections than the citizens of any other country. There was a great army of unpaid activists. (During the 1960 presidential election, for instance, some 4,000,000 volunteers were busy organizing rallies, ringing doorbells, mailing envelopes.) Each presidential, each gubernatorial candidate had to create or rebuild a personal organization – this in a country where people moved often, and over great distances. The American system thereby accommodated flux in a way which no European system could rival.

The US also gave temporary places of prominence to an extraordinarily large number of people, and provided for political alliances of the strangest kind. Such alliances might join different ethnic groups, different occupational groups, activists concerned with particular ideologies or religions. Class played its part in American politics but American politics were never class politics pure and simple – not surprisingly so in a country where there was a great deal of social, occupational, and geographical mobility, and where class divisions were always fluid. American labor unions were seldom radical; neither were associations of particular immigrant groups. Demands for radical change derived in the main from universities and the literary intelligentsia rather than from the working class. All political parties in the US were themselves coalitions, with a fluctuating membership, and a scanty headquarters staff.

No major US party could remotely compare in organization and discipline, say, with the German Social Democratic Party or the Italian Christian Democratic Party – in our opinion a positive good that Americans have cause to relish. Nevertheless, the two-party system firmly remained in place. True enough, the role and organization of parties changed as communications improved, and as politics had to rival mass entertainment. Radio, later television, enabled voters to look at and listen to leading politicians at home, instead of going to a public meeting, or stopping at the local railway siding during a candidate's "whistle stop tour." National party conventions became less import-ant, as conventions increasingly became exercises in public relations which melded the razzle dazzle of a carnival with serious speech making. Delegates at national conventions lost the bargaining power they had once possessed; candidates – the argument went – thereafter increasingly ran as individuals, emphasizing their personal qualities rather than their party allegiance. During the 1950s, two Democrats, Sam Rayburn, the speaker of the House, and Lyndon B. Johnson, the Senate majority leader, had effectively led the Congress. They had no successors in a Congress (until Representative Newt Gingrich in 1994) where leadership became fragmented, and where sophisticated polling techniques, access to television, and funds directly supplied by political action committees and local sources combined to strengthen the individual member's position as against his or her party's. The "Yellow Dog Democrat" (allegedly willing to vote even for a yellow dog, if such were his or her party's choice) disappeared from the political scene; so did his or her Republican equivalent. A good television manner became a major asset.

Nevertheless, parties stayed crucial in politics. The national party organizations in particular increased their respective revenues, improved their professional skills, and strengthened their administrations. Each party's national committee provided presiden-tial candidates with legal advice, strategic counsel, assistance in public relations, political information, and financial help. The national party organization played an even larger role in congressional elections by contributing money and campaign services to congressional candidates as well as political advice. The parties continued to broker divergent interests, and they did so with surprising success. Hence the US managed to avoid fragmentation into a multiplicity of parties, despite the country's heterogeneous composition. Third parties therefore failed to hold their own, even though they might temporarily benefit one or the other of the major parties by splitting existing voting blocks.

US politics of the period conjure up the over-used term "Establishment." These men supposedly consisted of an inner ring of East Coast bankers with names like Harriman and Rockefeller; victorious generals such as Marshall and Eisenhower; senior State Department officials; heads and trustees of great universities and foundations. They were Protestant, white, Anglo-Saxon males (WASPs) educated at places such as Groton, and Choate, Yale and Harvard, or perhaps West Point. They supposedly shared membership in the same clubs; their surnames never ended in a vowel; they spoke with similar accents; they were subject to the same prejudices. The stereotype holds a modicum of truth. The US never had a Jewish, black, or Mexican president; Kennedy was the first Catholic to hold presidential office. But overall political and social influence was far more widely distributed in the US than legend suggests. From World War II, moreover, the social base of the power élites expanded. These élites were far from unanimous in their political orientation. And men such as Eisenhower, Nixon, or Lyndon B. Johnson all rose to presidential office from humble backgrounds in a manner unknown in Britain until Edward Heath stepped into the premiership in 1970.

Sociologically, the US Establishment did not resemble a single pyramid, but rather a set of interlocking rings to which periodically were joined new links. American politics depended on gaining the assent of the West's largest electorate. (In the 1960 election 68,832,818 Americans voted, or 64.5 percent of the 107,000,000 Americans old enough to participate.) Hence "to become known, to be identifiable to voters in terms of their own gut reactions, is perhaps the most expensive and necessary condition of American Presidential politics."[5] But even the most skillful electoral campaigns could not prevent Americans from increasingly "splitting their ticket" – to a much greater extent than anywhere in Europe. The constitutional separation of powers was thus paralleled by the electoral separation of power which commonly pitted a Congress dominated by one party against a presidency held by another. The US was too large, too diverse, too unruly to be run according to one ruling ideology.

No matter who occupied the White House, politicians had to deal with several hardy perennials. During most of its existence, the US had been an isolationist or neutralist country. World War II fatally weakened the neutralist spirit; the Cold War, the Marshall Plan, the NATO alliance and the US–Japan security treaty spelled the end of old-time isolationism, but the isolationist impulse would periodically revive. Its main impulse would no longer come from the Middle West, from farmers, and from ethnic minorities, but from the radical intelligentsia. The second great political controversy concerned the role of the state in the economy and in public welfare. Americans overwhelmingly rejected state ownership of the means of production. But the regulatory, interventionist welfare state grew apace – no matter which party held office. Both Democratic and Republican policy-makers had an essential part in its expansion, a point all too often forgotten by conservatives.

The growth of the welfare state in turn entailed the end of old-fashioned patronage politics. There was no longer scope for the wardheeler able to fix a ticket, provide food parcels and a bag of coal for a poor family, or get some low-paid municipal job for a deserving youngster. Not that agencies such as Tammany Hall should be despised in retrospect. At the heyday of Tammany Hall, New York was physically a safer place than it is now. But Tammany Hall could not hold out against middle-class reformers entrenched in permanent civil service machines, even though the total cost of administration vastly increased. Americans, being a legalistic though not necessarily a law-abiding people, have traditionally put their trust in laws and law courts. Reluctant to accept the public ownership of farms and factories, Americans reformers have preferred to control industry by indirect means. Elected officials, judges, and bureaucrats between them thus built an intricate system of regulations. This subjected industry and commerce to a degree of control which would have been unacceptable even during the halcyon days of the New Deal. The constitutional division of powers between the executive, legislature, and judicature entailed unending debate in which arguments shifted in accordance

5 White, *The Making of the President, 1960*, p. 33.

with political change. While Franklin D. Roosevelt held office, liberals extolled the presidency, and cursed the Supreme Court as a reactionary bastion. By the time Nixon was in office (1968), the position was reversed. Liberals praised judges and reviled the "Imperial Presidency;" it was now the conservatives' turn to laud the executive, and condemn the judges for meddling in politics. Yet by comparison with politics in countries such as Italy, Spain, or even France, US politics were consensual to an extent that few of the participants realized.

Above all, Americans remained a religious people: a much larger percentage of Americans attended Church or synagogue than Germans, French, or British people. Religion remained a major determinant in politics, as Catholics and Jews were far more apt to vote for the Democratic Party than the Republicans, whereas the reverse generalization held true for Protestants. All hyphenate Americans (such as Irish-Americans or German-Americans), but especially Catholics, radically improved their socioeconomic position. By 1974 Catholics, on the average, earned more than members of any other Christian denomination (followed in the Northern cities, in descending order, by Episcopalians, Presbyterians, Methodists, Lutherans, and Baptists), a state of affairs unthinkable to olden-time defenders of WASP supremacy.[6] Catholics also increased their demographic share of the US population. (Between 1947 and 1987 the proportion of Catholics went up from 20 percent to 28 or 29 percent, whereas Protestants declined from 69 percent to 59 percent, and Jews from about 5 to 2 percent.) The "GI Bill" gave all veterans, including Catholics, a chance to enter into the élite professions and move out of the working class. There was indeed a steep decline from regular weekly attendance at a place of divine worship (from 49 percent in 1958 to 41 percent in 1977), but thereafter church attendance remained fairly steady; the great majority of Americans continued to assert the importance of religion in their lives. Hence there was no room in American politics for anti-clericalism of the French or Spanish variety. No matter what his or her private convictions, no American politician would ever downgrade religion.[7] Whether religious or not, moreover, American politicians of whatever stripe – left-wingers as much as right-wingers – widely inherited from the Protestant churches a peculiar pastoral style which blended self-righteousness with a real or pretended sense of guilt. In this, as in so many other respects, the US remained a peculiar country. (The French, for example, could not believe the moralistic reaction to Kennedy's sex life or Nixon's Watergate.)

Like so much else in America, the role of religion underwent far-reaching changes in politics. In the olden days, there had been bitter struggles between different denominations. Protestant fundamentalists, for instance, and Catholics had been at daggers drawn. Indeed, the controversy over prohibition had religious as well as ethnic aspects, as righteous Anglo-Saxon Protestants meant to get even with beer-swilling Germans, whisky-drinking Irish, and wine-sipping Italians. By the 1960s, such confrontations had been largely forgotten. The European immigrants and their descendants had been largely assimilated; the recent immigrants from Europe were usually skilled or managerial people,

6 Andrew M. Greeley, *The American Catholic: a Social Portrait*, New York, Basic Books, 1977, pp. 54–65.
7 For details, see the issue "Religion in America," *The Gallup Report*, April 1987, no. 259. To be exact, by 1986, 55 percent of all respondents claimed that religion was very important in their private lives; 30 percent said it was fairly important. Corresponding figures in 1952 had been 75 percent and 20 percent, see especially p. 13.

well qualified and well able to speak English. Traditional white "ethnic" neighborhoods changed in character. Successful people of any racial or ethnic provenance were likely to move to the suburbs; the mainline churches therefore drew an ever-increasing part of their membership from suburban congregations. The role of religion in US politics likewise altered. Instead of contending with one another, the mainline churches established friendly interdenominational ties. New cults made their appearance in abundance. There was a new rift, one that divided liberals from conservatives within almost every single denomination. Liberals prevailed within the mainline Protestant churches and most Jewish congregations. Conservatives were strong within the fundamentalist Protestant groups and some of the new sects. But every denomination experienced that essential division over lifestyles and fundamental cultural assumptions which profoundly altered the shape of American politics in years to come.

The Democrats: John F. Kennedy and Lyndon B. Johnson

The Democratic Party is the world's oldest among existing political parties. "No Communist, Socialist, Liberal, Nationalist or Conservative party anywhere on the globe matches its long-lived vitality."[8] In its modern form, the party was shaped by Franklin D. Roosevelt who built a disparate coalition into what appeared the natural ruling party of the US. From the days of President Roosevelt to the time of President Bush, far more Americans identified themselves as Democrats than as Republicans; this generalization held true even during the Reagan years when the Democratic Party seemed in disarray.[9]

Roosevelt's New Deal made a profound impression among progressives in Europe – an alternative to communism. But the Roosevelt coalition was too hard for foreigners to understand; it contained people who had nothing in common: poverty-stricken white Southerners, suburban reformers with a conscience, labor union stalwarts, liberal intellectuals, big city machine politicians and their assorted retinue, and European immigrants from countries such as Ireland, Italy, and Poland. The party had a strong Catholic component. There were Jews, militant atheists, followers of Karl Marx, but also a substantial contingent of businessmen and farmers (especially those apt to profit from public contracts and subsidies), state employees and teachers with a stake in the expansion of public services, blacks, and Mexicans. The Democratic Party's central organization was as sketchy as the Republicans'. Likewise, the Democrats had no regnant ideology. Political scientists in Europe spilled a great deal of ink in trying to explain why the US never developed a leading working-class party such as the Labour Party in Britain or the Social Democrats in Germany. The Democratic Party never challenged the free enterprise system; neither did Democrats claim to represent one particular class. They did, however, pursue a reformist program which enormously expanded regulations, welfare, the number of persons employed in public services, and the proportion of the American GNP used for public services. The Republicans thereafter did not much diverge from the pace set by the Democrats. (By 1977, after eight years of Republican administration, 48 percent of the federal budget was spent on health, education, and income security,

8 White, *The Making of the President, 1968*, p. 63.
9 To be exact, the proportion as between Republicans, Democrats, and Independents respectively stood as follows. In 1937: 34, 50, 16; 1960: 30, 47, 23; 1972: 28, 43, 29; 1980: 24, 46, 30; 1990: 32, 40, 28; *The Gallup Poll Monthly*, January 1992, p. 11.

as opposed to 30 percent when President Nixon had taken office. Indeed, by the end of 1977, the amount of money spent cumulatively on public welfare by the federal, state, and local governments, since the so-called War on Poverty had begun under President Johnson, was estimated at $300 billion, more than the estimated cost of fighting World War II of $288 billion.)[10]

Federal power grew enormously during the era of Democratic ascendancy. Growth was promoted by innumerable judicial decisions, the expansion of the public services, the delegation of law-making power to designated agencies, the ever-expanding volume of regulations which in turn required lawyers and other public servants for their elucidation and application. Without having planned to do so, the Democratic Party set the agenda for a Keynesian, state-intervention program. Overall, the Democrats (and to a lesser extent, the Republicans), accomplished what the old Socialist Party of the US had intended to accomplish before World War II. Nobel Prize laureate Milton Friedman and his wife, Rose Friedman, have summarized this remarkable transformation by showing in detail how the 1928 platform of the Socialist Party was largely put into practice by avowed critics of socialism.[11] The Socialist Party, a moderate and reformist body led by Norman Thomas, had reached the height of its power in the late 1920s and early 1930s when its voting strength had reached just under 1,000,000. While lacking an ideology, the Democrats shared certain attitudes. They were optimists; they believed in progress. The "New Deal," the "Fair Deal," the "New Frontier," the "War Against Poverty" would all make the US a better country. The US should, and indeed could, be improved – both materially and morally. Reforms at home went with reform abroad; US aid to the Third World would transform the world. No task was too hard for American idealism – it would transform both the US and the entire globe. The Democrats therefore stood also for activism in foreign politics: the US would resist communists and tyrants and spread democracy and economic development all over the world. Hence Democrats turned out to be the interventionist party. In 1917, the US had entered World War I under Woodrow Wilson, a Democratic president to fight the Kaiser; in 1941, the US became involved in hostilities against Japan and Germany under Roosevelt; Harry Truman committed the US to NATO, intervened in Greece, and fought the Korean War; it was Kennedy and Johnson who attempted to resist the communist assault against South Vietnam.

The Democratic coalition, however, underwent profound change over time. Family farms diminished in importance all over the US. Hence the farming vote declined both for progressive farmers in the Middle and smallholders in the South. Big city machines likewise lost in importance, though this was a long drawn-out process. By the early 1960s machines still dominated politics in metropolitan centers such as New York, Chicago, and Philadelphia. For a time, this strategy still worked. In the 1950s, the Kennedy family and Democratic National Chairman John Bailey largely controlled New England; trade union leader Walter Reuther and Governor G. Mennen Wilson could "deliver" Michigan; Mayor Richard J. Daley was king in Chicago and therefore Illinois.

By the end of the 1960s, the structure of Democratic politics had been totally transformed. The big city boss, able to provide local jobs, patronage, and favors, could not

10 Martin Anderson, *Welfare: the Political Economy of Welfare Reform in the United States*, Stanford, CA, Hoover Institution Press, 1978, p. 72.
11 Milton and Rose Friedman, "The Tide is Turning," appendix A in Peter Duignan and Alvin Rabushka, eds, *The United States in the 1980s*, Stanford, CA, Hoover Institution Press, 1980, pp. 3–30.

compete with the new welfare bureaucracies, centrally run and financed by the tax-payers. Traditional ethnic neighborhoods changed as successful people migrated to the suburbs. The Democrats henceforth could no longer be certain of Polish, Italian – even of Irish – support. Great organizations such as Tammany Hall decayed. Tammany Hall had once governed New York. But by 1960 already, Tammany's boss Carmine DeSapio controlled only one of several boroughs, and even within this borough (Manhattan) he was under intense pressure from earnest middle-class reformers. Labor unions remained powerful, and were sturdy supporters of the Democratic Party. But, overall, their power likewise diminished. (Between 1955 and 1962 already, the percentage of workmen belonging to the unions dropped from 24.4 to 22.2 percent. This process would con-tinue, as the proportion of blue-collar workers in the labor force went down, while white-collar workers – managers, professionals, salesmen, office workers – would increase in number.)

Not that ethnicity ceased to count. A number of reliable ethnic blocs remained, even though generalizations are always dangerous, and no single ethnic community ever voted as a solid unit. Jewish Americans had preferred the Democratic Party ever since Roosevelt's day. (*Diese velt, jene velt und Roosevelt* – this world, the next world, and Roosevelt – went a Yiddish pun. "They [the Jews] live like Episcopalians and vote like Puerto Ricans," according to a political wisecrack.) The Democrats could rely on the vote of Puerto Ricans (US citizens by birth and concentrated in big cities like New York). The Demo-crats also obtained a majority of Mexican votes in the West and Southwest. (This group would become increasingly important, as more Latinos came to the country, and as newcomers slowly took up citizenship.)

The most solid Democratic bloc, however, were the blacks. Black Americans, once supporters of Lincoln's Republican Party, largely switched their allegiance to Roosevelt during the days of the New Deal. Blacks had looked to the federal power for ending slavery; they would continue to do so for supporting integration, enforcing civil rights legislation, and expanding social services. Blacks overall had vastly improved their econ-omic condition since the days of the New Deal, but the black community consistently contained the largest percentage of poor people (followed by the Hispanics). There was also a major geographical shift. Whereas in 1910 something like 90 percent of all American blacks had lived in the states of the Old South, by 1960 nearly one-half lived in the North and West, predominantly in the great metropolitan centers. Blacks voted predominantly in big city states which carried the largest blocs of electoral votes within the nation.

Black support henceforth became increasingly important to the Democrats, as the great majority of blacks continued to vote the Democratic ticket, and as an increas-ing proportion of black voters went to the polls. The black condition thereafter both declined and improved. In the inner cities there was a rapid increase in unemployment, single-parent households, illegitimacy, drug consumption, and serious crime. None of these afflictions was confined to one particular race, but blacks suffered in particular. Well-to-do blacks moved out of the cities into the suburbs, but the inner-city blacks were thereby left to their own devices. Civic breakdown in the inner cities was linked to the partial breakdown of the black family. (Between 1950 and 1990 the percentage of black families headed by single women rose from 17.2 to 56.2.) Black poverty diminished over this period in terms of real income. But poverty persisted, and concern for poverty remained in particular a Democratic Party issue. On the other hand, the black middle class rapidly grew in numbers and political power. (By 1992, Douglas

Wilder, a black politician, had gained distinction as governor of Virginia, once a key state of the Confederacy. Black mayors headed the biggest American cities. Some 6,600 elected black officials held office at various levels of government.) The main beneficiaries of this transformation were the Democrats.

This shift could not have occurred had racism been an unchanging element in the American political economy, an assumption widely shared by committed liberals. Neither does "white racism" account for many other variables; for instance, the striking disparities between established institutions in their ability to integrate the races. The armed forces and professional athletics do far better in this respect than high schools and colleges in racially mixed neighborhoods. Yet white soldiers and white athletes are not noticeably more tolerant than white school teachers. Similarly, analyses of US politics and society that hinge on white racism do not account for the way in which black West Indians in the US have done better, on average, than black Americans.[12]

Nevertheless, race continued to play a major role in US politics, albeit linked mostly to other social issues. The old alliance between the Democratic Party and white Southern voters crumbled, as did the once little questioned commitment to the Democratic Party of white workers in the North. Whites, especially working-class voters, resented affirmative action programs, racial quotas, and court-ordered school busing. The Democratic Party became identified by many working-class whites with blacks, infidels, and the liberal-left fringe groups. There was equal dislike for those progressive intellectuals – students, pastors, professors, journalists – who claimed to constitute the nation's moral role model and reference group. The clash was dramatized when, in 1972, an unelected Illinois delegation led by the Rev. Jesse Jackson denied seating to Richard Daley's delegation at the Democratic National Convention, thereby slamming the door on those white "ethnic" voters whom Daley represented in particular. Henceforth the Democratic Party labored under a major handicap.

Noteworthy also was the role of the intelligentsia. During the nineteenth and the beginning of the twentieth century, savants, writers, artists, and their like had normally supported the Republican Party, the party of Lincoln, the party of reform. The alienation of the Republican Party from the intellectual mainstream began during the days of Theodore Roosevelt; alienation deepened during the era of Franklin D. Roosevelt. Teachers, journalists working for prestige publications, pastors in mainline Protestant churches, men and women employed in the public services, especially welfare agencies – an ever-increasing army – were apt to vote for the Democrats. Especially important were the college professors. Their numbers, and the size of their student audiences, increased enormously as universities grew in number and size. (Between 1960 and 1980 the total budget for US colleges and universities increased from $7 billion to $62 billion in 1980 and $130 billion in 1989.)[13] College and university faculties between them came to make up one of the largest occupational groups in the country.

There was an even more astonishing increase in size of their student audiences. After World War II the student population began to rise, in part as a result of the generous "GI Bill" which provided tuition for veterans, including countless men and women who would not have been able to afford a university education in prewar days. Overwhelmingly, they were hard workers; their presence on the campuses transformed the character

12 For a general book on the subject, see Thomas Sowell, *Ethnic America: a History*, New York, Basic Books, 1981.
13 Martin Anderson, *Impostors in the Temple*, New York, Simon and Schuster, 1992, p. 28.

of US higher education. By 1960, about 3.3 million students attended colleges and universities, already the largest student body on earth. Then came growth of an even more spectacular kind – thanks to the baby-boomers. During the 1960s, the student body went up to about 8.5 million, and by 1975 it had soared to 11.2 million, almost half the eligible youth in the US. By 1968 this huge campus population outnumbered farmers by almost three to one, coal miners by fifty to one, railway workers by nine to one. Students were the country's largest working group with a single interest.

Students and their professors were, of course, a variegated lot. There were conservative as well as liberal professors, conservative as well as liberal students. But all statistics agree that teachers in the social sciences and the humanities at any rate mainly voted for the Democratic ticket, and described themselves as liberals rather than as conservatives.[14] American universities influenced the Atlantic world – both for better and for worse. There was an active interchange between US and European institutions; intellectual isolationism lessened on both sides of the Atlantic; both radicals and conservatives learned from their opposite numbers beyond the Atlantic.

The same generalization applied to the media and entertainment industry whose foremost stars acquired enormous influence as role models on both sides of the Atlantic community. Well-paid, smart, and glamorous, self-indulgent rather than self-disciplined, valuing self-expression rather than civic virtue, liberal intellectuals became a power in the land. Not only were professors, singers, actors, and students vocal and visible, but their work time was far more flexible than that of operatives and employees tied to an 8–5 schedule. The "new class" had thus far more time at its disposal for teach-ins, sit-ins, and demonstrations than did ordinary workers. Hence the "new class" exerted an influence quite out of proportion to its numbers. It included a host of new protest groups spawned by the New Left: feminists, ecologists, militant homosexuals, proponents of ethnic studies, black and Chicano nationalists. These activists formed new organizations such as the "Peace and Freedom Party," but they were too divided among themselves to form an effective bloc of their own and the main beneficiary of their energy was the Democratic Party. The new following, however, could no longer be controlled by party bosses of the traditional kind; new generations of militants responded to the appeal of television, of "demos" and teach-ins. They were well educated, vocal and knowledgeable about administrative and legal procedures. During the 1960s, therefore, campus denizens would come to predominate over farmers and factory workers within the Democratic Party.

It was John F. Kennedy who most skillfully responded to this profound transformation. His Irish ancestors had migrated to the US; their families had made good. (His maternal grandfather had been mayor of Boston; his paternal grandfather a saloon keeper active in politics.) John F. Kennedy had a fine war record in the US navy (an important political consideration for an electorate containing millions of veterans from World War II and the Korean War). Kennedy was rich, well spoken, Harvard educated, energetic, photogenic, quick witted, married to a glamorous wife. He exuded optimism and vigor.

14 For detailed statistics, see, for example, "Politics of the Professoriate," *The American Enterprise*, July–August 1991, p. 86ff. In area and ethnic studies, the proportion of self-described liberals, middle-of-the-roaders, and conservatives was respectively 76, 22, and 2 percent. In humanities, literature, history, philosophy, religion, and theology, the proportion was 76, 9, and 15 percent. In social sciences, anthropology, political science: 72, 14, and 14 percent. In psychology: 68, 17, and 15 percent.

He had a sense of humor. He was supported by a powerful clan. He was superbly good at television – indeed, European statesmen studied his performance as a paradigm. He was a Catholic, a point in his favor not only with Irish-Americans, but also with Spanish-Americans, Polish-Americans, Italian-Americans and other ethnic minorities who had until then suffered social discrimination because of their religion. Kennedy was propelled into politics by his father Joseph Kennedy, an ex-bootlegger rewarded for political services to President Roosevelt by the ambassadorship to Great Britain. Joseph wrecked his political career by his isolationism, and by forecasting in 1940 a British defeat. John dropped Joseph's political legacy. Yet he retained all the advantages derived from membership of a powerful political clan. (Both father and son ruthlessly pursued women, but their adulteries went unreported in the media.) None of the stereotypes commonly applied at the time to European "ethnics" clung to Kennedy. He was a man of culture, anglophile by inclination; he had truly arrived.[15]

Kennedy campaigned as a hawk. A practicing Catholic, brought up in an atmosphere bitterly hostile to communism, he was a "Cold Warrior" by conviction, with special sympathy for fellow Catholics living freely in Western Europe, and those oppressed behind the Iron Curtain. As Kennedy put it, the conflict between East and West pitted freedom under God against Godless communism. This language appealed to the bulk of Americans: anti-communism was an electoral asset among non-communist leftists, among Catholics, and Protestant fundamentalists. Kennedy's denunciations of communism particularly appealed to the millions of refugees who had come from Eastern Europe, followed later by countless more from Cuba, Vietnam, and Cambodia. Kennedy gained equal approval for his stern insistence on military power. US confidence had been shaken in 1957 by the Soviet success in launching Sputnik; Kennedy thereafter accused the Eisenhower administration (quite mistakenly) of having permitted a "missile gap" to develop between the US and the Soviet Union.

Kennedy also appealed to the "new class" of the college-educated. Kennedy's book *Profiles in Courage* had won a Pulitzer Prize. He was superb at talking to journalists (who never reported, for instance, his countless marital infidelities). He and his wife, Jacqueline, equally understood the language of artists and professors, and knew how to gain their esteem. Kennedy shared the intellectuals' preoccupation with self-evaluation and self-promotion. He shared in part their infatuation with the Third World (a mood represented by men such as Chester Bowles, later appointed ambassador to India). "Third Worlders" had a naïve trust in the Third World which supposedly represented the cause of global morality, and was assumed to hold a casting vote between East and West. According to Third Worlders, the newly independent countries of Asia and Africa also constituted a new economic frontier, to be developed with Western aid for the benefit of mankind. JFK created the Peace Corps and appointed his brother-in-law Sargeant Shriver as its head. It would be a bold professor, indeed, who publicly contradicted such views on a prestige campus.

Kennedy, however, did not take such prejudices too far. (He described himself as an idealist without illusions.) He did not pick a particularly liberal team. None of Kennedy's Cabinet appointees were dreamers except Arthur Schlesinger, Jr. But Kennedy carried conviction with an extraordinarily wide coalition. He was the perfect candidate to bridge

15 For John F. Kennedy, see Nigel Hamilton, *JFK: Reckless Youth*, New York, Random House, 1992 (the first volume of a planned trilogy). Arthur Meier Schlesinger, Jr, *A Thousand Days: John F. Kennedy in the White House*, Boston, Houghton Mifflin, 1965.

the "Old Politics" of smoke-filled saloons with the "New Politics" of the television studio and lecture room. Even so Kennedy only won by a hair's breadth in one of the closest elections in US history (49.7 percent of the vote went to Kennedy, 49.5 percent to Richard M. Nixon, the opposing candidate, Eisenhower's former vice-president). Given the extent of electoral fraud in places such as Chicago, the real result may have been even more evenly matched in an election decided far more by religious and cultural than by economic issues. (Catholics and Jews mainly voted for Kennedy, Protestants for Nixon.) Kennedy, however, gained nearly all the Western states; he won in New England; he did well in the Middle West, though the Democrats no longer commanded a united South.

Once installed in the White House, Kennedy proved a great public relations expert. Under Truman and Eisenhower the presidency had been supremely unglamorous; it would revert to dullness under Johnson. The Kennedys, by contrast, briefly brought a sense of style to the White House. At Jacqueline Kennedy's behest, invitations to the White House went to poets, actors, and musicians. (John F. Kennedy's favorite tune, by contrast, reputedly was "Hail to the Chief.") Professors and major journalists were made equally welcome. (J.F.K., in particular, relied on academicians from Harvard for appointment to the executive branch and for research and technical advice.) He created the illusion of the White House as a princely court (Camelot) where arts and letters were appreciated, and academic talent honored. Kennedy was also the darling of the press corps who did not object to Kennedy's habit – not uncommon among men in his family – of combining private lechery with the public profession of stern principles.

Kennedy's reputation was tragically enhanced by the manner of his death. The war hero who had survived naval combat in the Pacific fell to an assassin's bullet in Dallas, Texas (1963). The findings of the Warren Report into the president's death were widely though unjustly impugned: the president supposedly had been killed at the behest of assorted conspiracies hatched, according to taste, by Fidel Castro, Lyndon Johnson, the Mafia, the CIA, or the military–industrial complex. Kennedy died young, and for long remained embedded in the American conscious as the embodiment of youthful idealism: a paradigm for politicians to come. Kennedy stood for all that most college-educated Americans prized at the time. He supported social legislation at home and aid to poor countries abroad. He promoted the Alliance for Progress in the Western Hemisphere, and also the Peace Corps. He sympathized with the anti-colonial movements in Africa as much as with oppressed blacks in the American South. He spent heavily on the exploration of space, supposedly mankind's new frontier. (When the US mission reached the moon in 1969, the US had spent $25 billion – more than the gross national product in one year of Belgium, a substantial industrial power in its own right.) He was equally admired abroad. (In Britain, Kennedy easily beat all other contenders for popularity gaining 60 percent of the "vote" among all respondents, and 79 percent among the young, whereas Castro only rated 4 percent even among this group.)[16] The Kennedy years were marked by prosperity: the US emerged from a temporary slump, and the "golden years" continued until the 1970s, quite irrespective of which party held the presidency.

16 Kennedy's nearest contenders were Harold Macmillan and Pope John XXIII in a poll to determine the "greatest man" of the 1960s, a poll held in 1969. See Paul Barker and John Harvey, "The Way We Weren't," *New Statesman and Society*, 28 August 1992, pp. 18–20. Their study suggests that the impact of the "revolutionary 1960s" was much less than journalists assumed.

For all his reputation as a liberal, however, Kennedy was conservative by the standards of a later generation. When Kennedy took office, a militant civil rights campaign had begun to get underway. The campaign would become radicalized under Kennedy's successor, and change the face of America. Kennedy's response was moderate. He proposed a civil rights bill, but his proposals did not go very far. (The bill enforced in 1964 through Johnson's tactical skill was tougher than the original one.) Kennedy favored social legislation, as his predecessors had done, but the massive growth of the welfare state came under Johnson and Nixon. Kennedy's fiscal policy was orthodox. Before his death, the House approved a multi-million dollar tax cut which deliberately raised short-term budgetary deficits in order to enhance popular buying power, and thereby stimulate the economy.

In foreign politics Kennedy was a hawk, albeit a hesitant hawk, unwilling to admit that in war the enemies of one's enemy are classed as friends. Kennedy spent heavily – and wisely – on defense at a time when Soviet power seemed more formidable than ever. Kennedy gained his most brilliant success when he forced the Soviet Union in 1962 to remove their nuclear missiles from Cuba. But Kennedy's victory was marred by error and hesitancy. In his election campaign, Kennedy had taunted the Eisenhower administration for permitting a missile gap to develop between the US and the Soviet Union – but there was no gap. Kennedy persistently exaggerated Soviet strength, and thereby dealt excellent diplomatic cards to Nikita Khrushchev, the Soviet leader. Having taken power, Kennedy failed either to stop or to support properly an invasion of Cuba, organized by Cuban exiles with the help of the CIA. Planning should have been left to the armed services not the CIA, a body totally unfitted for such tasks.[17] To permit the invasion to go forward without the support of US air power was worse – the decision ensured certain failure for the insurgents. As a result, Cuba stayed a communist bastion which outlived the Soviet Union. (However, Cuba's very existence as a communist bastion may have unintentionally weakened the Soviet Union by forcing Moscow permanently to support at heavy expense one of the most corrupt and ill-managed of its client states.) Kennedy also unilaterally withdrew US intermediate-range ballistic missiles (IRBM's) from Western Europe. No counter-weight was left to Soviet weapons in the SS-4, SS-5, and similar categories. Kennedy thereby initiated a policy of studied inconsistency combined with intermittent failures to consult the US's Western European allies which would plague NATO relations thereafter. The Kremlin also may have been confused. As former German Chancellor Helmut Schmidt put it in a trenchant critique, "I do blame the Russians for many things, but I find it difficult to blame them when they say that they cannot read the Americans clearly enough."[18]

Kennedy's foreign policy had other weaknesses. Under pressure from his own *nomenklatura*, the East German communists, and Peking, Khrushchev permitted the East Germans to build the Berlin Wall, as well as massive frontier fortifications which shut off East Germany from West Germany. Kennedy gained fame for his speech at the Wall

17 For an analysis of its weakness, see Angelo Codevilla, *Informing Statecraft: Intelligence for a New Century*, New York, Free Press, 1992. For a critical account of Kennedy's foreign policy, see Michael R. Beschloss, *The Crisis Years: Kennedy and Khrushchev, 1960–1963*, New York, Edward Burlingame, 1991.
18 Helmut Schmidt, "Leadership in the Alliance," in Walter Laqueur and Brad Roberts, eds, *America in the World 1962–1987: a Strategic and Political Reader*, New York, St Martin's Press, 1987, p. 116.

in 1963 in which he declared *"Ich bin ein Berliner"*, but otherwise made little use of the subject in intensifying the Cold War against the Soviets and their allies. Kennedy supported the Republic of Vietnam (South Vietnam) against subversion, guerrilla war, and military infiltration directed by the Democratic Republic of Vietnam (North Vietnam, a communist state). In doing so, Kennedy assisted a sovereign state recognized by the US and other Western and neutralist countries. As Kennedy put it, "The Free World must increasingly protect against and oppose communist subversive aggression as practiced today most acutely in South East Asia."[19] Kennedy would surely therefore not have abandoned Vietnam had he escaped assassination. Kennedy hated to be regarded as a weakling. He himself had earlier charged the Eisenhower administration with indecisiveness. Bitter passions had been roused after World War II by the question of "who lost China?" Kennedy, much concerned with his future place in American history books, would equally have dreaded being charged with the loss of South Vietnam.

Kennedy's *modus operandi*, however, was peculiar. Determined to repel the enemy, he tripled the number of US military advisers in Vietnam. But he failed to make the best of indigenous support. The most determined anti-communist leader in South Vietnam was Ngo Dinh Diem (chief of state since 1955), referred to by Johnson as the Churchill of South East Asia. Diem was a ruthless autocrat, but the Vietnamese communists regarded him as by far the most dangerous of their opponents. Diem was overthrown and killed by a military conspiracy. Though Kennedy had not foreseen Diem's assassination, he knew in advance of the plot, and made no attempt to prevent it. It was as if the British government had been appraised of a plot against de Gaulle, but had failed to inform the general, hardly behavior designed to reassure an ally, and hardly in tune with that higher morality which Kennedy liked to invoke.

Kennedy's accession to office gave a new impetus to the anti-colonial cause. President Roosevelt had regarded Western colonialism as a threat to world prosperity and to world peace alike. The State Department looked to a policy of accelerated reform whereby the colonial regimes would become accountable to an international authority in which the US would have a commanding voice. Anti-colonialism appealed to liberal academics and liberal church people. But there was no powerful ethnic lobby prepared to take up the anti-colonial cause. (Jewish-Americans then remained preoccupied with Israel; black Americans primarily with their own emancipation.) Kennedy's accession to office once again gave promise of an overhaul in US politics. Kennedy regarded anti-colonialism as a weapon in the Cold War, even as an influence which would ultimately endanger the Soviet empire itself. In unfriendly hands, the African coasts would threaten Western communication. African produce would be increasingly important both for military and peaceful purposes. Anti-colonialism should be linked to foreign aid as an instrument for spreading prosperity and civil rights to the furthest corners of the globe.

But Kennedy's policy involved the US in serious contradictions. NATO's cohesion depended on the goodwill of the colonial powers. (The French, in particular, resented real or alleged US sympathy for the Algerian independence movement.) Kennedy's policy was even more ambivalent regarding Portugal, a NATO ally. The US provided clandestine financial support in 1961–2 for Holden Roberto, head of the FNLA (*Frente Nacional de Libertação de Angola*), one of the independence movements which carried on

---

19 Cited in James T. Patterson, *America in the Twentieth Century*, San Diego, Harcourt Brace Jovanovich, 1989, p. 385. For Kennedy's views on colonialism, see Peter Duignan and L.H. Gann, *The United States and Africa: a History*, Cambridge, Cambridge University Press, 1984, p. 284ff.

guerrilla warfare against the Portuguese, and which had slain thousands of Portuguese settlers in Angola. This was scarcely loyal behavior toward a US ally whose grant of air and sea bases in the Azores provided an essential link in NATO defense by enabling US troops rapidly to deploy in Europe, and by providing a staging point for supplying Israel and other US allies in the Middle East. Clandestine US aid to the guerrillas did not even give any leverage to future US diplomacy in Angola, as the FLNA turned out to be the wrong partner, and victory went to the MPLA (*Movimento Popular de Libertação de Angola*), a pro-communist body allied to the Soviet Union and Cuba. Despite his failures, however, Kennedy and his enthusiasts endowed the presidency with romantic expectations which no Founding Father had anticipated, and no successor could meet.

Kennedy's assassination shocked both America and the world at large. For the US it was a major crisis, marked by innumerable conspiracy theories. Kennedy was a man with many contradictions – intriguer and patriot, lecher and idealist, waverer and man of action. Death turned him into an American martyr – forever handsome and full of promise. Kennedy's death also unexpectedly propelled his vice-president Lyndon Johnson into the presidency, like Truman after Roosevelt's death. Johnson was everything Kennedy was not: a Southerner, a strict Protestant brought up in the Texas hill country, used in childhood to see around him poverty of a kind that Kennedy could hardly imagine. In backwoods cabins there was no electricity, no running water, no flush toilets, no radio. By the time a farmer's wife was in her thirties, she would be stooped, her neck aching from ever-lasting exertion. Disease was rife, and cash scarce. Not that Johnson came from the ranks of the very poor. (His father was a local politician come down in the world, but famous for his honesty; his mother was a school teacher.) But Johnson was determined to make good where his father had failed – and Johnson was well equipped to succeed.[20] Tough, able, intelligent, domineering, endowed with boundless physical energy, vain, egotistical, a born fixer, he was one of the ablest politicians the South had seen. Whine or wheedle, buy or bully, Johnson would get his way. Johnson possessed that indefinable gift of being able to ingratiate himself with men and women of the most diverse backgrounds. Southern hillbillies, WASP bankers, Jewish intellectuals, Irish saloon politicians – Johnson could talk them over. Tall, gangling, with a mobile face and a Southern drawl, he provided that populist touch desperately needed by the Democratic Party in its fight to retain the allegiance of white Southerners. Full of folksy wisdom – some phoney – Johnson would never be accused of Yankee guile or liberal guilt.

Robert A. Caro, most eloquent of Johnson biographers, presents him as essentially an amoral man, yearning for power. Johnson was not above stealing votes, brightening for public consumption his skimpy combat record in World War II, or making the most opportunistic political alliances. But Johnson was more than just a power-hungry "pol." Though born in the bleak West Texas hill country, in an environment where racial prejudice was an accounted virtue, Johnson genuinely wanted to bring civil rights to blacks and help the poor, white or black. Memories of rural poverty stayed with Johnson as long as he lived; they gave an intensity to his work for the welfare state which Kennedy's more fashionable supporters could not match. This commitment went with

20 Robert A. Caro, *The Years of Lyndon Johnson, vol. 1: The Path to Power*, New York Vintage Books, 1990; Robert A. Divine, ed., *Exploring the Johnson Years*, Austin, Texas, University of Texas Press, 1981. For a general political survey, see Barone, *Our Country*.

a sense of inferiority toward Kennedy's smart, metropolitan entourage. Installed in the White House, Johnson was determined to prove to doubters all and sundry that he would prove a worthy successor in Camelot.

Johnson, however, took office under a cloud. The Kennedy family disliked him. Johnson's alleged want of sympathy for the poor aroused the displeasure of militant students, especially those who had never experienced the slightest hardships in their own lives. The smart set detested his shiny suits, bar-room stories, crude table manners, his burps, and his domineering ways. Johnson was supposedly cool toward good causes, especially civil rights. He suffered from a sense of inferiority, even illegitimacy, having arrived at the presidency through a tragic assassination. Yet Johnson would have made a great president at a quiet time. In the 1964 presidential elections he shattered Barry M. Goldwater, the Republican challenger. (He gained every state except Arizona, Louisiana, Mississippi, Alabama, Georgia, and South Carolina, the bulk of the old Confederacy.) Johnson thereafter passed the most comprehensive civil rights legislation since Reconstruction. Restraints on employment, segregated schooling, and other instruments of racial discrimination were rendered inoperative, and the US as a whole acquired a genuinely free market in labor, real estate, and education. Southern blacks registered as voters in rapidly increasing numbers as a result of civil rights legislation, and rewarded the Democratic Party by their electoral support. Europeans could sympathize with a man who strove for civic equality, and thereby deflected incessant Soviet propaganda designed to show the capitalist US as the world's main bastion of racism.

Having promised Congress, on taking office, that he would run the country with the utmost thrift and frugality, Johnson enormously expanded the social welfare services (including, for example, food stamps). For better or for worse, Johnson turned out to be one of the most outstanding architects in building the US welfare state. (Between 1960 and 1970, the percentage of federal outlays devoted to social welfare expenditure went up from 28.1 to 40.0 percent of total expenditure.) Johnson's "War on Poverty" was "the most ambitious attempt to redistribute income ever since the United States had begun."[21] Expansion would continue into the Reagan years, as welfare lobbies multiplied, and attained a powerful momentum of their own.

Johnson also showed considerable ability in foreign affairs: he successfully managed a crisis over Panama; and he proved skillful at handling as prickly a character as de Gaulle. But Johnson had no feel for foreign ways, or for alien ideologies. His nemesis was the Vietnam War which he had neither started nor knew how to end. We shall merely confine ourselves here to stressing a few major points. Johnson stepped up the war in an unprecedented manner. (Between 1957 and 1964 a total of 23,300 military forces were deployed in Vietnam, with 269 killed in combat. By 1968 the total had risen to 536,100 and 14,617 respectively.)[22] The Vietnam War ceased to be an encounter fought by regulars, and turned into an encounter fought by conscripts. Such a war needed an ideological motivation, with issues starkly defined. Johnson could have beaten the anti-communist drum, called for a declaration of war against North Vietnam, and outright victory. Had he done so, he might have had an enthusiastic response in a country where communists were hated.

21 Anderson, *Welfare*, p. 16. For a general history, see Walter I. Trattner, *From Poor Law to Welfare State: a History of Social Welfare in America*, New York, Free Press, 1989.
22 Patterson, *America in the Twentieth Century*, p. 414, gives a full list. The total loss of American personnel amounted to 47,328 killed and 303,600 wounded.

But Johnson would not put the case for the war and he did not want to declare war; he was out of his depth both as a war leader and a propagandist. The rules of engagement imposed on US forces in Vietnam tied the military hand and foot. Had similar rules of engagement been adopted in World War II, the Germans and Japanese would assuredly have won. Johnson constantly, and ignorantly, interfered with ongoing operations; his lack of judgment in this respect exceeded the German Führer's in World War II. As a politician Johnson never tried to seize the commanding heights of morality. There was little attempt to exploit the massive murder campaigns carried out by the communists in North Vietnam, South Vietnam, and Cambodia – to publicize communist atrocities, or expose communist mendacity. There was no welcome for returning Vietnam veterans who were widely exposed to insults, abuse, and even job discrimination on campuses. There was little effort to broadcast details concerning the brainwashing techniques and the torture employed against US prisoners of war in communist hands. On the contrary, wives of prisoners, such as Vice-Admiral James B. Stockdale's spouse, met with official discouragement when they tried to do so. It was at the wives' initiative that the horrors inflicted on Americans achieved due publicity in the US. By contrast, leftist poets, singers, and actresses such as Jane Fonda and Shirley MacLaine could visit Hanoi, lend their respective names to the communist cause, and thereby incite the anti-war movement and depress the spirit of US prisoners in enemy hands. Almost entirely neglected was the fighting record of the South Vietnamese forces whose casualty list was much longer than the Americans' (an estimated 250,000). South Vietnamese soldiers – dead or alive – remained un-persons in the US.

The explanation is simple. Johnson would neither declare war nor pay for the war by raising higher taxes, but kept adding to the national debt by his "War on Poverty" and by the war in Vietnam, a disastrous expedient in the long run. Johnson moreover dreaded setting off what he regarded as an ultra-right reaction, anti-communist hysteria on a national scale followed by a new McCarthy witch-hunt. An anti-communist backlash, in his view, would have endangered the "War on Poverty" at home. New perils would be created overseas, as the Soviet Union would renew pressure on West Berlin and other neuralgic points, and the People's Republic of China might intervene in Vietnam, or assail Taiwan. Better to force the enemy to the negotiating table by those methods of military gradualism that Johnson's political advisers considered the height of sophistication. Such methods, however, were bound to fail in what was essentially both an ideological war and an Asian nationalist war against white imperialism, points that Johnson, essentially a negotiator, was unable to comprehend. Johnson, like his presidential predecessor and successor, never understood Hanoi's ideological motivation and nationalist resistance, its determination to win an unconditional victory. Johnson's very strengths – his pragmatism, his skill as a negotiator, his self-confidence in interfering with the generals' decisions on the ground to gain political points – turned out to be grave disadvantages. So did his remoteness from European affairs at a time when the European left denounced the Vietnam War, and when even European NATO-supporters feared the diversion of US strength to South Asia. US military efficiency declined in Europe as top-ranking specialists and long-serving noncoms were posted from Europe to South East Asia. Morale declined within the US army in Europe; drug usage and drunkenness increased, and so did crime.

In a more general way, the war divided Americans as no war had split them during the twentieth century. Lifelong friendships broke asunder; families were severed. Worse still, the Vietnam War, unlike World War II, imposed a disproportionate burden on blacks and blue-collar workers. In World War II, no taint of draft dodging clung to the middle class as a whole. (George Bush, a "hawk" in later politics, and George McGovern, a "dove," had both served with distinction as combat pilots.) In the Vietnam War, a substantial part of the American bourgeoisie opted out of the service (as did part of the French bourgeoisie in the Algerian War). There were innumerable ways of dodging the draft, by service in the Peace Corps, VISTA, by enrolling for graduate training. These and other options all required a college education, or at least the equivalent training. Legends to the contrary notwithstanding, it is not true that the underclass paid the bulk of the blood toll. As in World War II and the Korean conflict, junior infantry officers, pilots and other specialists suffered particularly heavy casualties; these were mainly drawn from the middle class. Nevertheless, a man with talent, money, or proper family connection, a person most likely drawn from the middle class, could avoid service far more easily than a trucker's or a mechanic's son. Once drafted, a worker's son was more likely to serve in Vietnam than a professor's, a parson's, or a businessman's, and more likely to fight in a combat unit.

It was also white workers who paid the highest price for racial integration. A college student living in a residential unit on campus was less likely to be mugged than an elderly shopkeeper in a decaying neighborhood, yet the professor was apt to censure the ordinary citizen's preoccupation with rising crime as overt or covert racism. Well-off progressives called for integrated public schools, but were apt to send their own children to a private boarding school. Rioting middle-class students terrorized the universities and exchanged blows with young policemen drawn from the ranks of blue-collar workers and with conservatives on campus. Middle-class literati denounced the petty bourgeoisie and "racist" white workers with peculiar venom. America began to suffer from a concealed class war, and the Democratic Party was the chief loser.

Johnson was particularly ill suited to deal with these problems. Temperamentally, Johnson was light-years away from young militants with their anti-Americanism and cult of self-awareness and self-pity. But Johnson also alienated old-timers. In the view of Theodore H. White (in *The Making of the President*), Johnson considered the Democratic Party as much personal property as his ranch, and displayed customary niggardliness with regard to its upkeep. In 1966 Johnson slashed the budget of the Democratic National Committee to the bone, eliminating even the vital voter-registration division, a decision that the party would bitterly regret. Federal patronage for politicians almost dried up. White middle-class radicals increasingly gained positions of power; machine politicians were on their way out. Stumped by his party's problems, Johnson announced in March 1968 that he would not seek another term, and retired to his ranch near Johnson City, Texas.

Within the Democratic Party, Robert Kennedy was Johnson's most likely successor, representing both the "new class" and the Kennedy clan's claim to leadership. Historians still argue whether Robert Kennedy, with his militant rhetoric, could have reestablished the old alliance of blue-collar workers, Catholics, Jews, Chicanos, blacks, and white liberals. But he never got the chance; he was assassinated by a crazed Jordanian immigrant, Sirhan Sirhan, and leadership fell to Hubert H. Humphrey, Johnson's vice-president, a moderate liberal, but in general a supporter of the "New Class" within the Democratic Party. The Democratic Convention at Chicago occasioned widespread rioting, as militant students planned to provoke the police by stoning and taunting the "pigs" who charged into the crowd, on national TV. These events must be seen in perspective. Despite wild talk concerning an impending revolution, despite Black Panthers,

Weathermen, Brown Berets, and other revolutionary groups, the US never remotely faced an insurrectionary situation except on campuses, where radicals knew they were safe. The country was prosperous; unemployment remained low; students expected to get good jobs; most of their parents did well. Mayor Daley of Chicago received a huge number of sacks of fan mail from citizens who liked to see hippies and radicals beaten up during the 1968 Democratic Convention. But, in political terms, the "law and order" issue benefited the Republicans.

By contrast, liberal intellectuals, youthful militants, feminists, and radical dissenters of whatever stripe were deeply offended. They remained a minority within the party but were crucial for a Democratic victory in a national election. "Without their help as fund raisers, publicists, and precinct workers a Democrat did not become President of the United States."[23] The Democratic Convention in 1972 tried to regain their allegiance by adopting a quota system which benefited blacks, women, students, as against traditional Democratic leaders, including labor union officials, urban machine politicians, congressional members, and spokesmen of white ethnic groups. According to defenders of this and other reforms, activists turned the Democratic Party from a loose confederation into a national mass party; power moved from state party leaders toward the national organization; women and minorities at last received their due: the donkey was pulled out of the ditch![24] In fact, however, the left-wing activists were unrepresentative of Democratic voters at large; their success merely represented a partial victory gained by one of several competing élites. The excesses of the New Left broke apart the Democratic Party. The Democrats continued to do well in local and state elections where bread-and-butter issues outshone ideology. But in the national struggle for presidential office, the Democratic Party remained weakened for years to come.

The Republican Party

According to its critics, the Republican Party has historically functioned as the mouthpiece of privilege. But, in fact, Republicans traditionally saw themselves as harbingers of progress. It was the Republican Party that abolished slavery, and thereby smashed the Southern system of ethno-castes. It was the Republican Party that wrote the first civil service laws, passed the first legislation to control trusts, control railways, protect the consumer, ensure soil conservation. It was the Republican Party that traditionally held the loyalty of black Americans, and of American intellectuals. "Its men of state and diplomacy were, as often as not, thinkers and scholars; it is doubtful whether any president, even Wilson or the second Roosevelt, made the White House so familiar a mansion to writers and artists as did Theodore Roosevelt."[25]

From the first decade of the present century, the Republican Party began to turn inward, toward nativism and neutralism. The blunt remarks against "rum, Romanism

23 William L. O'Neill, *Coming Apart: an Informal History of America in the 1960s*, Chicago, Quadrangle, 1971, p. 388.
24 Caroline Arden, *Getting the Donkey out of the Ditch: the Democratic Party in Search of Itself*, New York, Greenwood Press, 1988.
25 White, *The Making of the President, 1968*, p. 60; Franklin L. Burdette, *The Republican Party: a Short History*, New York, Van Nostrand, 1972; George H. Mayer, *The Republican Party, 1854–1966*, New York, Oxford University Press, 1967.

and rebellion" (made by a Protestant clergyman in support of the Republican ticket in 1884) once more became popular within the party's ranks. Isolationism remained popular, particularly among Middle Westerners of German or Scandinavian origin, and among Irish-Americans. (It was only in World War II that isolationism went into disfavor, in part owing to the efforts of Wendell Willkie, a much underrated progressive of German descent who ran against Roosevelt in 1940.) After World War II, the Republican leadership overrode isolationist opposition within the party. Isolationists included "China Firsters" who believed that cosmopolitan Easterners had betrayed China to the communists, and thereby lost a historic opportunity for opening China to Christianity and US commerce. Instead, the Republican leadership backed a policy of "Europe First," the Marshall Plan, and NATO.

The election of General Eisenhower to the presidency (1952) symbolized both the victory of Republican internationalism, and also the appeal of a man whose candidacy transcended party allegiance. Eisenhower was a remarkable man. He had the supreme gift of being able to conceal his intellectual superiority. He gave the impression of being an amiable company chairman, fond of golf, addicted to pious generalities, indifferent to intellectual pursuits. (According to one of the countless Eisenhower jokes of the time, Eisenhower's physician had forbidden him to read, lest the general should excessively strain his lips.) The reality, of course, was quite different – as should have been obvious to anyone who had seen Eisenhower, in World War II, subordinate to his will men such as General George Patton, General Charles de Gaulle, and Field Marshall Lord Montgomery, equally able, arrogant, and endowed with a supreme gift for showmanship. Eisenhower, moreover, was good at delegating authority.

This skill had served him well as a military leader. He carried it over to the White House, where he filled key offices with capable people, and then allowed them to handle problems in their own way. This leadership style was also applied to diplomacy, albeit with less success, with Secretary of State John Foster Dulles, and his brother, CIA director Allen Dulles, enjoying a good deal of independence. For all his well-cultivated image of a farm boy, Eisenhower worked extremely hard, adhered to highly efficient staffing principles, and maintained firm control over his team – all behind a screen of military gobbledegook that concealed his intentions.

In domestic policies, Eisenhower was, in every sense of the word, a centrist. He initiated little legislation of his own, but oversaw an improved highway and seaway system. He also gave firm support to the ongoing struggle for civil rights, both in regard to legislation and the school integration case at Little Rock, Arkansas. (He despatched federal troops there to enforce a 1954 ruling of the Supreme Court against racial segregation in public schools.)

As regards foreign policy, Eisenhower continued his predecessor's policy of containing communism, by diplomacy where possible, by a strong military posture where necessary. The defeat of isolationism within the Republican Party was a matter of crucial importance within the Atlantic Community. (Isolationism would not revive until the Soviet Union's future breakup.) Organizationally, however, the Republican Party remained remote from European conservative bodies. US trade unionists, clergymen, scholars established links between their own organizations and their opposite number in Europe – not so the US party organizers, Republican or Democrat. The Republican Party – like the Democratic Party – had no precise European equivalent. It worked as a loose coalition of state and local organizations; elected committees in cities and counties each sent two members to the Republican National Committee which helped to run presidential campaigns, with much initiative left to individual presidential candidates. According to legend, the Republican Party spoke above all for the Eastern Establishment – great bankers, lawyers, businessmen, and foundation heads. These men traced their ancestors to the Protestant countries of Northern Europe; they had gone to the same exclusive prep schools, studied at Ivy League colleges, married only among themselves, and despised the rest of Americans, secure in their plush leather and polished brass wealth. They were particularly influential in foreign policy. No matter which party governed, it was the Eastern Establishment which supposedly provided the counsel required for running the American empire.

This picture is much overdrawn. The US was far too large and variegated to support such an Establishment. There were powerful cliques of wealthy people, many of them Easterners with liberal sympathies. They belonged to old-established Anglo-Saxon families, people with manners and money. They regarded public service as a duty for the well-bred, especially in foreign affairs. But they did not run the US. Presidents such as Eisenhower and Nixon came from a relatively humble background. So did influential men such as John J. McCloy (at various times president of the World Bank, High Commissioner for Germany, chairman of the Council of Foreign Relations, the Ford Foundation, and the Chase Manhattan Bank, named with some exaggeration by John Kenneth Galbraith "chairman of the American Establishment").[26]

Neither did Establishment people run foreign policy. The State Department, after World War II, drew recruits from an ever-widening reservoir of men (and, in time, of women). Presidential advisers on foreign policy were a variegated lot, not particularly distinguished by their social origins. (Eisenhower took advice from George Humphrey, an Ohio entrepreneur, John F. Kennedy from his brother Robert, Lyndon Johnson from Abe Fortas, a Jewish lawyer, Richard Nixon from Henry Kissinger, a history professor, son of a school teacher, who had come to the US as a refugee from Nazi Germany.)

As regards membership, the Republican Party, like the Democratic Party, could rightly claim to be a *Volkspartei*; its supporters comprised a substantial number of workers as well as farmers, businessmen, and bankers. (There was also a minority of blacks who still upheld the "Party of Lincoln.") The Republican Party was by no means the party of private enterprise pure and simple; but overall Republican voters would be more likely to identify themselves as aggrieved tax-payers than as aggrieved workers. Above all, the Republican Party represented mainly Protestant America. A voter's religious and regional background played a greater part in determining his or her party allegiance than social class. It was only from the 1960s that the emphasis shifted. The Republican Party thereafter attracted an increasing number of people who had once voted for the Democrats – white "ethnics," including Catholics, white Southerners, small entrepreneurs (especially those in high-tech industries). Republicans from the Western states became increasingly influential. There was also a new contingent of intellectuals, including free-market theoreticians such as Milton Friedman, and policy-makers such as Kissinger, James Schlesinger, George Shultz and Caspar Weinberger, whose ability would match Harvard professor Arthur Schlesinger's, and John Kenneth Galbraith's on the Democratic side. At the same time, the Republican Party, more than the Democrats, emphasized anti-communism, and commitment to those "traditional values" assailed by feminists, gays,

26 Kai Bird, *The Chairman John J. McCloy: the Making of the American Establishment*, New York, Simon and Schuster, 1992; Thomas Alan Schwarz, *America's Germany: John J. McCloy and the Federal Republic of Germany*, Cambridge, MA, Harvard University Press, 1991.

and militants of many other stripes. Rum and Romanism no longer seemed objectionable – but rebellion more than ever.

Old Eastern wealth within the party was represented by Nelson A. Rockefeller (elected governor of New York state in 1958). According to traditional standards, Rockefeller should have led the Republican Party by right of family, wealth, connection, and temperament. Rockefeller had been born to a great fortune; his very name was popularly associated with riches, an American Croesus. Rockefeller enjoyed undisputed acceptance by the oldest and most distinguished families in America, acceptance that always escaped the Kennedys. The Rockefeller Foundation financed every good cause known to American philanthropy; it was matched by numerous other bequests that perpetuated Rockefeller's name in medical and other research.

Rockefeller was a stout campaigner, cheerful and outgoing, always ready to shake hands or slap backs. He was a meticulous organizer. He had a social conscience. His concerns embraced rights for the aged, the poor, the sick. Not that he questioned capitalism. Rockefeller was a firm believer in free enterprise, in thrift and hard work, but in his view private enterprise required government support. As governor, he was the biggest spender in the country. (In his ten years as governor, spending in the state budget almost quadrupled.) Rockefeller enormously expanded the state university system; he promoted the construction of houses and hospitals; the state capital expanded; rivers were cleaned; he supported minimum wage laws, civil rights laws, consumer protection, control of narcotics. Rockefeller also was a strong advocate of the NATO connection and of strong national defense; indeed, he bitterly criticized Eisenhower for not adequately meeting the Soviet threat. Rockefeller's outlook was in no way parochial. (Before attaining the governorship, he had held a variety of national offices under the Roosevelt and Eisenhower administrations respectively.) He was a man of culture (he had founded the Museum of Primitive Art in New York), and he was much more likely to impress European statesmen than a provincial such as Johnson or Barry M. Goldwater.

But Rockefeller also had problems as a candidate. Party loyalists resented the way in which he regarded the New York Republican Party as his own Grand Ducal fiefdom. Moralists called him a wife-stealer (a divorced man himself, Rockefeller married a divorcee, not an acceptable decision at the time). Advocates of frugality in government derided his record as a lavish spender. In a more fundamental sense, power was shifting from the North East to the West, from old wealth to new, from long-established WASP clans to families of more recent provenance. (Senator Joseph McCarthy's witch-hunt against real or alleged communists in high places was not merely an exercise in "red-baiting." For the first time, "new" Americans – Irish-descended McCarthy, and his assistant Roy Cohen, a Jewish American – accused the traditional Establishment of being "un-American".) Having made numerous tactical mistakes, Rockefeller failed to secure his party's nomination. It was a decisive defeat for the Republican Party's liberal wing.

Rockefeller would have been thoroughly at home among Tory magnates in England, but not so his equally "liberal" rival George Romney (elected governor of Michigan in 1962). Romney represented the Republicanism of the Middle West, as advocated by progressively minded farmers and industrialists. (Romney himself was a farmer's son who had made a fortune by turning American Motors, then a moribund corporation, into a prosperous enterprise.) Romney would have appealed to Lincoln. He stood for the emancipationist heritage. (In one election he gained 30 percent of Michigan's black vote, an unprecedented success for a Republican.) He cooperated with the labor unions. He abounded in good works. A Mormon by conviction, he represented traditional small-town morality: he neither cursed, drank, nor fornicated; he kept the Sabbath holy; he considered the Constitution of the US a divinely inspired document. Indeed, for two years in his youth George Romney had preached as a Mormon evangelist in the streets of England and Scotland. These were welcome qualifications for those strict, religious-minded Americans who believed that the US was being destroyed by the war protesters' "three A's": "acid," abortion, and amnesty. Romney looked presidential, silver-haired and dignified. But, like Rockefeller, he was regarded as a "left winger" within his party; he was not well informed either on national or international issues; above all, he dithered on the Vietnam War. Not surprisingly, he missed the chance of becoming the US's first Mormon president.

A third contender was Senator Barry Goldwater. Goldwater is now remembered as one of the US's most discredited presidential candidates: no primary candidate for presidential office ever lost an election by so overwhelming a margin. (In the presidential election of 1964, Johnson gained 61 percent of the vote as against 38 percent for Goldwater.) As James Reston, a leading columnist at the time, put it, "Barry Goldwater not only lost the Presidential election yesterday but the conservative cause as well. He has wrecked his party for a long time to come."[27] To his opponents, Goldwater was the archetypical reactionary, bigot, "red-baiter," warmonger, racist. According to Martin Luther King, the Goldwater campaign showed signs of Hitlerism. According to historian Richard Hofstadter, Goldwater's conservatism represented a paranoid style in American politics. Edmund G. Brown, then governor of California, thought that only "Heil Hitler" was missing from the Republican Convention. The real Goldwater was rather more complicated. His grandfather, a Jewish immigrant, had started Phoenix's largest department store. Barry Goldwater, raised as an Episcopalian, served in the Air National Guard, was elected mayor of Phoenix, Arizona, and later senator (1952). Goldwater represented the new suburban frontier of an expanding West. (Between 1949, when he had become mayor, and the late 1980s, the population of Phoenix alone rose from about 100,000 to more than 2,000,000.) He was an unabashed patriot for his home state. He had done well in the military (an army air force officer during the war, he rose to the rank of air force general after years of part-time service). He disliked the Eastern Establishment. He was by temperament a *frondeur*, a nay-sayer in Congress where the Republicans had for so long labored in opposition.[28] He was renowned for his personal honesty – the kind of man who would rather be right than president.

More importantly, Goldwater represented conservatism of a new kind. US conservatives then were an assorted lot, with little in common. They comprised Catholics brought up in the tradition of St Thomas Aquinas, Protestant fundamentalists, protectionists who longed to impose heavy duties on foreign imports, isolationists who objected to US membership of NATO. Other conservatives included Southern racists, moralists who pined for the days of Prohibition, Ivy League Republicans who looked down on the populace, traditionalists who idealized the memory of Burke and Disraeli; there were also rural romantics who prettified the Old South, and mistakenly equated *ante bellum*

27 Cited in R. Emmett Tyrrell, Jr, *The Conservative Crack-Up*, New York, Simon and Schuster, 1992, p. 146.
28 Edwin McDowell, *Barry Goldwater: Portrait of an Arizonan*, Chicago, H. Regnery, 1964. His own writings include *Why Not Victory?*, New York, McGraw-Hill, 1962; *The Conscience of a Conservative*, New York, McFadden Books, 1964, *With No Apologies*, New York, Morrow, 1979.

plantations with feudal fiefdoms in medieval England. The conservative movement also had a paranoid fringe who – according to taste – blamed for the world's ills either International Jewry, the Papacy, or the British monarchy. Whatever their background, conservatives were apt to look with dismay toward a menacing future.

Goldwater was different. He began his career as a conventional small businessman. His support mainly derived from small entrepreneurs, not from old wealth which preferred men such as Rockefeller. But Goldwater was much more than a defender of small business. He helped to shift the focus of American conservatism. Goldwater would have no truck with anti-semites, foes of the Papacy, or isolationists. Goldwater's brand of conservatism supported NATO without question. He was a cultural optimist, not a pessimist. He bitterly opposed communism but, unlike so many other foes of communism at the time, Goldwater felt sure that the West could win. Modern readers easily forget the political pessimism that so widely beset anti-communists of an earlier vintage. They hated the Soviet Union, but were enormously impressed by its military might, the success of Soviet propaganda and disinformation campaigns, the sophistication of its espionage networks, and the extent of its foreign contacts in high places. The bulk of anti-communists at the time at best hoped to "contain" communism. Goldwater, by contrast, looked to communism's ultimate destruction: "Why Not Victory?" is the title phrase of a Goldwater book. In this respect Goldwater stood a world apart from Nixon or Johnson, neither of whom could envisage communism's downfall, within a generation.

Goldwater, moreover, drew support from a new conservative counter-culture which attracted former leftists as well as traditional right-wingers. This counter-culture derived intellectual support from free-enterprise economists such as Milton Friedman, anti-Stalinist historians such as Robert Conquest, and gifted polemicists such as William Buckley (founder of *National Review*, established in 1955). There was likewise backing from the so-called neo-conservatives, many of them Jewish, many of them former socialists. Foremost among them were intellectuals such as Irving Kristol, a co-editor of the London-based *Encounter*, and Norman Podhoretz, editor of *Commentary*. The neo-conservatives considered capitalism to be both morally and functionally superior to socialism, but insisted that capitalism required a moral foundation based on religion. In this respect they agreed with the religious right, made up mainly of fundamentalists who began to play an active part in politics from the 1970s, convinced that the US would go the way of Sodom, unless Americans changed their ways. The new conservatives remained divided into many groups, but there was cooperation of sorts. The conservative movements set up new institutions such as the Heritage Foundation, the American Enterprise Institute, and the Intercollegiate Studies Institute. Conservatives from 1960 on acquired a leading say in the Hoover Institution at Stanford University. Conservatives founded new journals such as *National Review, Policy Review, National Interest*, and *Academic Questions*. The Republican Party was intellectually invigorated. By the early 1960s, there was established a new conservative counter-culture, ready to oppose the counter-culture of the left.

Goldwater gained a number of distinguished recruits for his cause, including three subsequent presidents: Richard Nixon, Ronald Reagan, and George Bush. But at the time Goldwater could not transmute conservatism into a mass movement. He came across as a stern, rigid, honorable man, but he lacked the skills either of the conciliator or of the demagogue. The average American did indeed dislike communism; there was a huge market for anti-communist tracts. (John A. Stormer's philippic *None Dare Call It Treason* went through six printings in a single year.) But the ordinary voter did not personally feel threatened. Intellectual critiques of the welfare state made few converts at a time when the state was held in high regard on both sides of the Atlantic as an instrument for assuring social justice. Goldwater's presidential campaign suffered as Democratic campaigners successfully depicted him as a fanatic who would not hesitate to start a nuclear war ("In your guts you know he's nuts," in the words of a Democratic slogan). Goldwater himself was no racist. But in fact the 1964 election was racially divisive. (Goldwater obtained about 38 percent of the vote. Of this percentage, 24 percent were conservative white Republicans; about 14 percent were white racists who disliked blacks, and voted for George Wallace in 1968. Johnson, by contrast, received 61 percent of the vote: 51 percent came from moderate whites, including Democratic loyalists and disaffected Republicans, 10 percent from blacks.) In the 1964 election only Goldwater's native Arizona and the main Southern states voted for him – an undiluted disaster for Republicans, and for Democrats the greatest triumph in their history.

Centrist Republicans thereafter looked for salvation to Richard M. Nixon (1913–94) who had almost scored a draw against Kennedy in the 1960 presidential election. Nixon campaigned against Hubert Humphrey, a moderate liberal, Johnson having withdrawn from the race in 1968 because of pressure from anti-war activists such as Congressman Allard Lowenstein. Nixon and Johnson therefore never ran against one another. Yet they had a surprising amount in common. Both had tremendous energy and enormous drive. Both were ruthless campaigners who aroused deep personal loyalties and deep hatreds. Both were egotists who expected their respective followers to sacrifice themselves for their overlord's greater glory. Both belonged to that new and younger age cohort, born just before the outbreak of World War I, which now replaced the leaders of Eisenhower's generation. Both were brought up in small towns; both went to provincial colleges. (Johnson graduated from the South West Texas Teachers' College; Nixon obtained his education at Whittier College, but later went to Duke University Law School.) Both were good tacticians, brought up in a harsh Protestant ethic, determined to win, at any price. Each saw himself as the spokesman for the "forgotten Americans" (Nixon's phrase), by whom they meant working and lower middle-class people. After reaching the heights, both Johnson's and Nixon's respective careers plunged into disaster.

But there were also great differences. Johnson was flamboyant in the best Texas fashion; Nixon cold, introspective, and reserved. Johnson was a provincial – the butt of jokes made by the Kennedys and their entourage. Nixon became a successful New York lawyer, at home with old wealth. Unlike Goldwater, Nixon understood both Wall Street and Main Street, both essential to the Republican Party. Whereas Johnson was gregarious, Nixon was a loner – as Tom Wicker put it for the *New York Times*: "His own strategist, campaign manager, writer, and fund raiser."[29] Whereas Johnson troubled little about foreigners, Nixon took them seriously. (Konrad Adenauer counseled that the US should stay in Vietnam, lest Washington should lose credibility worldwide; de Gaulle, by contrast, advised a cautious US withdrawal.) Johnson trusted only to experience, and read little. Nixon's knowledge of history was wide, and he wrote well. (His book on leadership will probably be read longer than the rest. For Nixon, characteristically, the essence of leadership was "to change the national mood or to take an unpopular issue and make it popular.")[30]

29 Cited in Stephen E. Ambrose, *Nixon: the Education of a Politician, 1913–1962*, New York, Simon and Schuster, 1987, p. 653.
30 Richard Nixon, *Leaders*, New York, Warner, 1982, p. xiii.

More important was a temperamental difference in outlook. Johnson, last of the "New Dealers," retained the optimism of Franklin D. Roosevelt's days. Nixon was a pessimist, a man apt to distrust his friends as well as his enemies. He was also the first Republican president who condemned what he regarded as the US Establishment – a viewpoint utterly strange to men such as Eisenhower or Ford. For Nixon there was something wrong with the ruling élite, more particularly that "new class" of college-educated Americans aspiring to leadership in the arts, the media, the judiciary, the educational system. He disliked what he regarded as their softness, indecisiveness, self-pity, self-righteousness, and intolerance. As Nixon saw it, the "new class" and their ill-bred children at college despised ordinary Americans. The "new class" mismanaged the Vietnam War abroad and the "War against Poverty" at home. Above all, Nixon derided what he considered the "new class's" moral obtuseness with regard to communism. As Nixon put it later, many years after having left office:

> Those on the left who sneer at the anti-Communist cause are callous to the great suffering inflicted on innocent human beings . . . Communism has produced a legacy not of progress but of poverty . . . It has killed 40 million people in the Soviet Union, 50 million in China, hundreds of thousands in Eastern Europe, 3 million in Southeast Asia, 1 million in Afghanistan, and untold others in the scores of so-called Communist Wars of national liberation.[31]

Communism's moral depravity, Nixon felt, was perfectly obvious to ordinary Americans. But lacking firm moral standards of its own, the "new class" was incapable of justly appreciating the communist peril both abroad and at home. Unfortunately, however, the new élite was firmly entrenched, and could hardly be replaced. Hence Nixon looked to the US's future with foreboding: statesmen and patriots could slow down its relative decline, but could not end the retreat from greatness. Nixon thus drew on the skills of Henry Kissinger, a German-Jewish intellectual, a Harvard professor, and one of Rockefeller's original protégés. Kissinger was an outsider – he never lost his heavy German accent – but his very position as an outsider turned out to be an asset at a time when insiders seemed to have failed. Kissinger was devious and opinionated, but also an excellent diplomatist and tremendously learned. Kissinger drew heavily on European history, a field in which he was an expert. Kissinger in particular admired statesmen such as Metternich and Castlereagh who had rebuilt the European balance of power after the Napoleonic Wars. He likewise sought to emulate the makers of the Westphalian Peace (concluded in 1648 to end the Thirty Years' War between Protestants and Catholics in Central Europe, the treaty laid down the principle *cuius regio eius religio*: subjects had to conform to their respective ruler's religion). As a scholar, Kissinger came to understand the importance of ideology in history. As a diplomatist, he undervalued it. Not in his wildest dreams could he imagine that the US would have infinitely more staying power than the Soviet Union, and that the Soviet regime would collapse under its own weight in Kissinger's own lifetime. In this particular respect, the *realpolitician* gravely departed from *realpolitik*.[32]

31 Richard Nixon, *In the Arena* . . . , New York, Simon and Schuster, 1990, p. 307.
32 For Kissinger, see Walter Isaacson, *Kissinger: a Biography*, New York, Simon and Schuster, 1992; Robert D. Schulzinger, *Henry Kissinger: Doctor of Diplomacy*, New York, Columbia University Press, 1989; Henry Kissinger, *Diplomacy*, New York, Simon and Schuster, 1994; *White House Years*, Boston, Little, Brown, 1979.

What did Nixon achieve? As a strategist, he was outstanding. From the revolution-aries' standpoint, 1968 proved the year of global reaction. In France, there was the revolution that never was. Gaullist rule was consolidated. In the US, the Republicans won, even without support from the whites in the old Confederacy. (The Republicans won by a small majority: 31,770,222, or 43.4 percent of the voters, opted for Nixon; 31,267,744, or 42.7 percent, cast their ballots for Humphrey; and 9,906,141 or 13.5 percent for George Wallace.) Nixon thereafter greatly increased his majority, gaining 47.2 million votes in the 1972 election, as against 29 million votes for Humphrey. Nixon won 60.7 percent of the vote, the third highest percentage in modern US history. (The Democratic Party, by contrast, seemed in disarray, prisoners to those "special interests" favored in the Democratic Party's new quota system to benefit women, minorities, and youthful leftists.) For Nixon, this was an astonishing achievement at a time when the great majority of Americans still defined themselves as Democrats (46 percent, as against 27 percent Republicans, according to 1968 Gallup polls), and when commentators even spoke of a "Kennedy dynasty." This victory was masterminded by Nixon. It was he who conceived the overall strategy; he recruited the key staff who worked with him; he plotted the tactics and made every campaign decision. There was no king-maker behind Nixon. "He had able advisers, but he called the shots."[33]

As commander-in-chief, Nixon strove for a "peace with honor" which would safe-guard South Vietnam's independence, "Vietnamize" the war, and allow US land forces gradually to disengage from South East Asia. This strategy, on the face of it, was not unreasonable. The South Vietnamese army increased in efficiency. The Tet offensive was smashed in 1968, thereby largely eliminating the Viet Cong communists' ability to carry out guerrilla warfare in South Vietnam. In 1972 the South Vietnamese, with American support, defeated a major offensive conducted by conventional North Viet-namese forces fielding strong armored formations.

The Vietnam War remains bitterly controversial, despite the long years that have elapsed since its termination. To many Americans the conflict appears both immoral and, in retrospect, unwinnable. Here we shall merely point out that the main political assumptions of the anti-war movement in the US turned out to be mistaken. The communist movements in Asia no more represented the cause of the popular masses than they did anywhere else. Contrary to academic orthodoxy, the Kuomintang regime in Taiwan turned out to be far more competent and successful than the communist regime on the Chinese mainland. Within Vietnam, the communists likewise failed to make a success of their domain. The war was provoked by Hanoi – not by Saigon. It was not South Vietnamese troops which invaded the North, but North Vietnamese forces which penetrated into the South – Hanoi would never consent to withdraw them. Despite South Vietnamese corruption, South Vietnam was a more prosperous country than North Vietnam and, relatively speaking, a freer one. The conflict in South Vietnam was not a national independence struggle supported by all South Vietnamese patriots; the war was waged under purely communist leadership for the sole purpose of imposing a communist dictatorship in South Vietnam potentially masked by an appeal to nationalism and reunification. The Viet Cong guerrillas in the South were sustained by Northern help, and in all essentials directed from Hanoi. The war was won not by popular partisans but by regular forces, mainly recruited in North Vietnam. The communist victory did not bring prosperity and freedom but misery and tyranny.

33 Martin Anderson, "Richard Nixon's Place," *The Christian Science Monitor*, 5 March 1990, p. 18.

According to the opponents of the war, the Vietnam conflict was not merely immoral, but also militarily unwinnable. The war demoralized not merely the American people, but also the American army, as drug usage increased, racial tensions grew ever more bitter, and entire frontline units went on the military equivalent of strikes by refusing to engage in combat. This was hardly surprising, given the hateful nature of the South Vietnamese regime whose incompetence by itself rendered nugatory all attempts to "Vietnamize" the war, despite the unthinking "can-do" optimism displayed by American military leaders. These arguments, however, do not explain why the US should have won every major military engagement in Vietnam. Neither do they account for the way in which the US did build a successful South Korean army, though all the criticisms made by the US left against South Vietnam had previously been advanced, almost verbatim, against South Korea and its supposedly fascist leadership under Syngman Rhee.

Not that the Americans did not make plenty of mistakes of their own. In 1963 President Ngo Dinh Diem, the most powerful political personality, was displaced from power and killed – with US connivance. Concerned to steal the communists' thunder, the Americans in the early 1970s promoted land reform, with untoward result. As in many other countries, an ill-considered land reform reduced agricultural productivity. The landowners departed from the villages to the town, taking along their political, entrepreneurial, and organizational skills. Land reform discouraged financial investment in the countryside. Land reform inhibited the development of a vigorous rural capitalism, as the new owners could not freely sell their holdings, and thereby profit from a genuinely free land market. Rural society was destabilized.

There was indeed incompetence and corruption aplenty in South Vietnam, but the South Vietnam army's history as yet remains to be fairly written. Its losses were much heavier than those of the US forces; its defeats are remembered, its exploits forgotten. Its morale declined as the US Congress refused further US support – this at a time when the South Vietnamese forces had increasingly become mechanized, and therefore more dependent than ever on ammunition, equipment, fuel, and spare parts from the US. Without constant supplies, the South Vietnamese forces ceased to be operational; the very success with which the Americans had taught their own tactics (for instance, the deployment of artillery and helicopters on the battlefield) now worked against the Americans' pupils.

The Nixon administration, however, faced serious long-term problems. The dual wars against poverty and the communists in Vietnam brought inflation, a particularly cruel form of taxation that favored debtors over creditors, people in employment against those on fixed incomes (between 1967 and 1981 the real value of a dollar dropped from 100 to 37 cents). Inflation went with budgetary deficits (the 1968–9 budget was the last balanced budget put together by US law-makers; thereafter, deficits continued to rise). The US also suffered increasingly from foreign (especially German and Japanese) competition in fields once considered typically "American" (the last year in which the US had a trade surplus in cars was 1967). The golden postwar years were coming to an end – this at a time of social dislocation, rising black militance, student insurrections, and disappointed hopes concerning the war against poverty.

The Nixon administration thus had no hope of winning the domestic war over Vietnam. The "hawks" declined, and the "doves" continuously gained in power. North Korean aggression against South Korea had been undisguised; the Korean War therefore had occasioned little opposition in the US. By contrast, the North Vietnamese assault against South Vietnam was well camouflaged. The communists continued to cultivate the legend that the *nomenklatura*'s was the people's cause. The communists unsparingly used terror as an indispensable instrument of policy, as witnessed by the "Boat People" thereafter. But the bulk of self-styled progressives, both in the US and the world at large, refused to accept the evidence, or indeed found justification for communist killings. In academia and much of the media, the Vietnam War increasingly appeared a crime against humanity, committed by the US against an inoffensive people struggling against colonialism. The supposedly criminal nature of the US's war reflected the evils of Western capitalism as a whole. The leftist intelligentsia's hostility to US intervention merged with the counter-culture, student discontent at the draft, popular distrust concerning the management of the war, and the selective secrecy which enshrouded its conduct. This malaise kept increasing. Whereas the US public had overwhelmingly backed US intervention in the Korean War, support for the Vietnam War began to dwindle. (The turning point came in 1967.)[34]

Nixon was out of his depth. Indeed, no president in the twentieth century ever aroused as much hatred in the US as Nixon. Not only the progressive intelligentsia, but also for many middle-of-the-roaders, even some right-wingers, Nixon became an arch scoundrel, representing the worst in his party and his country. For his own part, Nixon, by the early 1970s, saw himself as a man beleaguered, isolated, defamed by an ever-hostile press, flayed by ever-hostile clergymen, professors, and TV anchorman. Leaks appeared to threaten the innermost secrets of US warmaking and US diplomacy. The White House was besieged by demonstrators, and secret documents were published by the press. Not surprisingly, Nixon fell into a mood of near-paranoia. It was in this atmosphere that Nixon's administration engaged "plumbers"; it was in this climate of fear that the Watergate break-ins took place. Then followed those official cover-ups which ruined the Nixon administration, and led to the president's resignation in 1974.

Yet Nixon, on the face of it, should have been applauded by the liberal left. It was Nixon who ended American involvement in Vietnam. It was Nixon who made striking concessions. (Originally, the US insisted that complete withdrawal of American troops from South Vietnam must be accompanied by the total withdrawal of North Vietnam regular forces. But in 1974 Kissinger secretly conveyed to Hanoi's representatives in Paris proposals for a ceasefire which dropped this demand.) The Americans would then have done well to accept requests on the part of the South Vietnamese Joint General Staff for a new program of ARVN (Army of the Republic of Vietnam) expansion and the provision of more powerful weapons. This request, however, was rejected. The peace agreement concluded in 1973 left South Vietnam in a vulnerable condition because all American troops had to be withdrawn, while 160,000 North Vietnamese soldiers would continue to stay in South Vietnam.

It was a grave defeat for Kissinger, but Kissinger's negotiations with North Vietnam were undercut by massive US domestic opposition to the war. As Raymond Aron, a leading French intellectual, put it "the liberals, the Democrats, the Kennedy faithful overwhelmed the executors of their own heritage. They forgot their responsibilities and the peace programs which they themselves had proposed. They became, knowingly or not, partisans of peace at any price."[35] Disillusioned by the war, determined also to

34 In 1965, just under one-quarter of respondents in public opinion polls thought that intervention was a mistake. By 1973, about 60 percent thought that intervention had been mistaken.
35 Raymond Aron, "Kissinger, Vietnam, and Cambodia," *Policy Review*, Summer 1980, no. 13, p. 165.

regain its former role in foreign policy, the Congress thereafter refused further support for Saigon.[36] Isolated and demoralized, South Vietnam was defeated by a mechanized campaign that would have done credit to General Heinz Guderian and other German experts in *Blitzkrieg*.

American idealists had hoped that the killing would stop, once US involvement ended. These expectations went unfulfilled. The Vietnamese communists intensified terror against real or suspected opponents; nearly two million Vietnamese therefore fled from their native land, often under the most appalling conditions. Laos turned into a communist dictatorship (1975). In Cambodia the communist Khmer Rouge seized power in the same year and turned their country into a Killing Field. Unexpectedly, there was also warfare between the communist successor states, as Vietnam invaded Cambodia, and as fighting broke out between Vietnam and the People's Republic of China (1979). Whereas the capitalist states of South East Asia made rapid economic advance, the communist states lagged behind in a manner unforeseen by their admirers in the US academy.

In US politics, the anti-war movement merged with the youth revolt on the campuses (a subject discussed in chapter 9). The commanding heights of morality, formerly held by the anti-communists, now passed to the peace lobbies and the new grievance élites. The war delegitimized the old Establishment, both among those who demonstrated for peace, and those who had fought in the war. As Kissinger pointed out, men such as McGeorge Bundy, Dean Acheson, John McCloy, who had first backed intervention, were the first to lose their nerve – this at a time (1968) when the bulk of the US electors still described themselves as hawks. Dubious, in particular, was the record of Robert S. McNamara (Secretary of Defense 1961–8). Formerly head of the Ford Motor Company, later President of the World Bank, McNamara was the most established of Establishment men. Yet he proved a failure in whatever capacity he served. An arid quantifier, he thought in terms of statistical abstractions. A theoretician among theoreticians, he was a principal architect of that "no-risk, no-win" strategy which demoralized the US armed forces. Worse, he continued to support the war in public while in private he had lost all hope of victory – this for narrow party advantage. Worst of all, he no longer believed in that moral justification for which he expected men to die.

The war thus left bitterness unequalled in US politics since the US Civil War. Controversy remained unresolved. Was the "domino theory" nonsense? Did US intervention in fact prevent other dominoes from falling (for instance, Indonesia, where an attempted communist takeover in 1965 was crushed with much slaughter)? Could the war have been effectively "Vietnamized" had the South Vietnamese after 1973 been adequately supplied with arms, ammunition, fuel, and spare parts? The North Vietnamese, after all, had also suffered horrendous casualties. The administration's fear of Chinese intervention was never justified at a time when Beijing had come to look on Moscow as its main enemy – not Washington, not Saigon. Within the US the debate continued, though largely excluding the million refugees from Vietnam whose political importance in the US never remotely equalled that of the exiles from Cuba. Even at their best, the South Vietnamese (especially the urban middle class) could never match the discipline, dedication, and, above all, the ruthlessness of the North Vietnamese. The war, therefore, was lost, and within the US distrust of government rose in a way unequalled during any preceding years of the twentieth century.

36 In 1973 the Congress passed the War Powers Act over Nixon's veto, thereby preventing in practice any resumption of hostilities on the US's part.

The US's NATO allies regarded the Vietnam War as a dangerous diversion of US military effort. But the Europeans warmly backed Nixon when he tried to deal directly with the People's Republic of China and the Soviet Union. In 1972 Nixon visited Beijing, hoping thereby to gain increased leverage for the US in international politics at a time when Moscow and Beijing were at daggers drawn. Nixon's decision was courageous, but right-wingers feared that Taiwan was thereby being abandoned. In a more general sense, they objected to legitimizing the regime of Mao Zedong, the greatest mass killer since Stalin. Others expressed apprehension that the visit might unfavorably affect US relations with Japan and South Korea. But from the standpoint of *realpolitik*, Kissinger's policy of playing off the two major communist powers against one another was sound. Indeed, widely held fears that the People's Republic of China might have intervened in the Vietnam War seem unrealistic in retrospect, given the extent of hostility between Moscow and Beijing at the time. Thereafter, Nixon also traveled to Moscow where he was warmly welcomed by the Soviet government which was anxious to avoid a *rapprochement* between Washington and Beijing at Moscow's expense. The SALT I treaty, designed to stop the numerical buildup of the Soviet strategic rocket forces, was signed. This and subsequent arms limitation agreements with the Soviet Union worked to the US's military disadvantage. But they met with almost universal support within the US, and might have been expected to enhance Nixon's popularity with the liberal left.

Nixon's most important foreign policy success, however, was gained in the Middle East. In 1973 Israel became involved in the so-called Yom Kippur War against its Arab neighbors. As in 1948, 1956, and 1967, the Israelis once more proved militarily superior, but this time it was touch and go. Israel was diplomatically isolated, with the Soviet Union in the Arab camp. Given the opposition's strength, Israel might have been destroyed, but for Nixon's willingness to provide diplomatic support and weaponry. (All of the US's allies stood aloof, except Portugal which had provided bases in the Azores, used to supply the Middle East.) Moscow made ready to intervene by sending Soviet troops and nuclear arms into the Middle East; Washington ordered a nuclear alert. The Soviet Union drew back in what was the most serious confrontation since Cuba. Nixon can reasonably claim to have been one of the Jewish people's most influential friends in modern times. But, unfortunately from Nixon's standpoint, none of these accomplishments translated into votes.

In domestic affairs Nixon should also have pleased the liberal left. He sturdily refused to accept support from the racist right. To the Friedmanites' horror, he tried to cope with continuing inflation by temporarily instituting controls on prices and wages. (As a young lawyer in World War II, Nixon had served with the Office of Price Administration; he thereafter had professed himself thoroughly unhappy with this experience.) The welfare state substantially expanded under Nixon who added new features of his own, such as the "Family Assistance Plan." Nixon also considered himself an environmental president (for example, he proposed in 1972 the Pure Air Tax Act). Nixon was also an "affirmative action" president. (In 1968 the Office of Federal Contract Compliance first issued guidelines alluding to "goals," "timetables," and "representation," all of which were then further strengthened, with new and onerous obligations on employers.) It was also Nixon who established the Environmental Protection Agency (EPA, 1970). At the same time, the US lost its initial predominance in nuclear weaponry. (The Soviet Union attained parity in strategic arms by the early 1970s, but thereafter continued its buildup, determined to gain numerical superiority.)

Nevertheless, Nixon was remembered by his liberal critics as a reactionary. In part, he was the victim of circumstances. It was during his presidency that the golden years of postwar prosperity ended. Sometime about 1973 the steady upward movement of US family incomes faltered. The Bretton-Woods system of fixed exchange rates collapsed. Oil prices rapidly rose – not altogether because Arab oil sheikhs had suddenly become greedier than hitherto, but because foreign oil producers wished to make up for the inflation of Western currencies (especially the dollar), and for the low prices charged during the 1960s. Inflation, in turn, derived from the unexpectedly high expense of the Vietnam War, the US refusal to pay for the war by higher taxation, the rising level of welfare expenditure throughout the Western world, and excessive expansion of the US money supply.

These could not be laid at Nixon's door. But Nixon, for all his ability, lacked an adequate understanding of the intangible side of politics. He came across as what he was in fact – a cold, calculating man, willing to sacrifice his most loyal supporters for the sake of political advantage. He chose men poorly. (His vice-president, Spiro Agnew, was forced to retire for dubious financial transactions. Nixon himself was discovered by the IRS to owe a great deal of money in back taxes, not good publicity for a politician who pretended to speak for the oppressed US tax-payer.) But the worst was the legacy of distrust left by the Vietnam War and Watergate. As a former air force officer put it in retrospect, "when the purpose of a war is unclear or seriously in doubt, when the government that can take you off the street and send you to fight . . . does not have the courage either to win the war or to abandon it, then the demand for lives to sacrifice is not honorable."[37] After Vietnam and Watergate, the legislature ceased to trust the executive to carry out the laws. The executive did not trust the legislature to keep essential secrets. The press did not trust officials, as the prizes in the profession now went to investigative journalists in search of real or alleged abuses. Distrust began to seep into the citizens' perception of their governing institutions as a whole. It was a striking change from the 1950s when Americans had expressed confidence in their ruling bodies. For all his abilities, Nixon inflicted grave damage on his party, damage which Ronald Reagan would later partially repair. Worse still, Nixon – the sworn advocate of law and order – turned out to be a law-breaker. His breach of faith would bedevil US politics for years to come.

Yet, in retirement, Nixon accomplished what was perhaps his most surprising feat – he rebuilt his reputation. America loves a repentant sinner, and Nixon played the part. He admitted his faults – most of them. He published books, lectured to distinguished audiences, talked to high-placed foreigners, even cultivated TV anchormen. He became an elder statesman who counseled succeeding presidents. All his life Nixon had hated the media, and the media had hated Nixon. The Watergate scandal had proved a media boon, and propelled to fame and fortune two young reporters, Bob Woodward and Carl Bernstein, who became role models for the investigative journalists of the future. But then Nixon beat the media at their own game. When he died in 1994, the media managers' obsequiousness astounded even the cynics – Richard Nixon had the last laugh!

37 Jack Du Vall, "Another '68 Grad Looks at the Draft Issue," *Christian Science Monitor*, 29 September 1992, p. 18.

3

West German and Austrian Politics, 1959–1974

West Germany

The Federal German Republic came into existence in 1949, just ten years after the outbreak of World War II. Seemingly, the new state was born under an unlucky star: the German economy was only beginning to recover; widespread damage remained; worse still were the moral ravages of war. Germany's name had become hateful abroad owing to Hitler's murder campaign against the Jews and countless other atrocities; the Germans were widely looked upon with distrust. Within Germany itself, there was a legacy of anger and betrayal: Germany had suffered enormous casualties; one-third or so of the former Reich had been lost to Poland and the Soviet Union; about one-fifth of West Germany's population came to consist of refugees forced to start again with nothing.

Germany, moreover, was a divided country. By the 1960s, it was not only communists and communist sympathizers who found much to praise in the German Democratic Republic (the GDR, also founded in 1949). Even as sophisticated a student of German society as Ralf Dahrendorf, a man without the slightest sympathy for communism, found much to like in the new socialist state. It was "naïve and dangerous" to believe, he wrote in 1965, that the GDR merely rested on Soviet bayonets. The GDR had very real achievements to its credit: a comprehensive welfare state and a newly found legitimacy. As Dahrendorf put it:

> The DDR [GDR] is the first modern society on German soil ... While the "reliable" core of the political class of the DDR would certainly be threatened by any change toward greater liberalism, it would be wrong to underestimate the lasting effects of its values: a mentality of upward social mobility and achievement, confidence in the state, in planning, not market rationality ... The syndrome of equal opportunities, permanent discussions, privilege-free access to élite positions, and pronounced publicness of life is characteristic here ... Today the regime of the DDR is quite legitimate in terms of the assent, or at least the absence of active dissent on the part of its citizens ... The two Germanies are moving increasingly far apart ... no centripetal force is recognizable ... which might enforce reunification inside, by internal social forces.[1]

Given such misconceptions, it is not surprising that the division of Germany therefore came to be seen widely as permanent. According to a standard work published in 1986, just three years before the GDR collapsed, "the German question is now taking new

1 Ralf Dahrendorf, *Society and Democracy in Germany*, Garden City, NY, Doubleday, 1969, pp. 401–10.

forms – one in which the criterion is not, for the foreseeable future, that of German reunification but that of an autonomous relationship between the two German states independent of what is happening in East German relations."[2]

By contrast, the Federal Republic (FRG) aroused a surprising degree of criticism both at home and abroad, despite the fact that East Germans continued to seek refuge in the West, often at desperate risk to themselves. In the eyes of communists and their friends, the FRG formed a revanchist bastion of Western monopoly capitalism dependent on Washington, or, more properly speaking, on Wall Street. West Germany, however, also had many non-communist critics. "Take away Prussia, and what is left?" had once been asked contemptuously by Walter Rathenau (a Jewish Prussian of the Weimar Republic, and later assassinated by ultra-nationalists). "Only a *Rheinbund* (Rhenish League created by Napoleon as a French satellite) plus a Catholic and clerical republic."[3] For many Social Democrats, this description seemed to fit the FRG to perfection. For German nationalists of the old school, Adenauer, the FRG's first chancellor, and ex-mayor of Cologne, represented Rhenish separatism at its worst – not just clericalism, but also the anti-Reich legacy of those Cologne archbishop-electors who had traditionally sought an alliance with France at the Holy Roman Empire's expense.

To much of Germany's "soft left," strongly represented within the ranks of the literary and academic intelligentsia, the FRG appeared even worse: it embodied Philistinism, corruption, outworn family values, out-of-date regional loyalties, obscurantism, and class prejudice. If a historian in some future century were to reconstruct West German society after World War II, using only literary sources of the time, he or she would surely conclude that West German democracy was a sham, that a despicable ruling class was lording it over ignorant "proles." The average West German voter would have appeared as *Stimmvieh* (voting cattle) represented by such fictional characters as Lieschen Müller, a lady of peculiar stupidity much derided at literary gatherings.

But there were also serious concerns. What would happen to democratic legitimacy, once prosperity waned? Democracy was said to have only shallow roots in German soil; hence a Fourth Reich might well emerge from the ruins of the Third. The West German élites wanted self-assurance after World War II, and also lacked cohesion. If Hugh Gaitskell, Harold Wilson, Harold Macmillan, and Edward Heath had all met at a British dinner party, they could easily have chatted about many things – especially about Oxford. Balliol College, New College, Jesus College would alone have provided for them a common frame of reference. But, as Dahrendorf points out, what could Konrad Adenauer, Erich Ollenhauer, and Erich Mende (at one time, leaders of the Christian Democrats, the Social Democrats, and the Free Democrats, respectively) have talked about had they casually gotten together at a social occasion? Adenauer had spent part of the war years in hiding, Ollenhauer exiled in London as secretary of an émigré organization, Mende at the front winning the Knight's Cross of the Iron Cross. In Germany at the time, those at the top of society were "essentially strangers to each other."[4]

2 Philip Windsor, "German Disunity," in Richard Mayne, ed., *Handbooks to the Modern World: Western Europe*, New York, Facts on File, 1986, p. 313. For a similar assessment, see F. Stephen Larrabee, "From Reunification to Reassociation: New Dimensions of the German Question," in F. Stephen Larrabee, ed., *The Two German States and European Security*, New York, St Martin's Press, 1989, esp. p. 29.
3 Cited in Paul Gottfried, "Über den deutschen Nachkriegskonservatismus," *Criticón*, May–June 1985, p. 113.
4 Dahrendorf, *Society and Democracy in Germany*, p. 257.

The new state, moreover, lacked a common focus. London, Paris, Lisbon, Stockholm, Copenhagen were alike in being the cultural, economic, and political capitals of their respective countries. Bonn seemed to its detractors a Rhenish Canberra – a provisional capital only, a pleasant, modest city situated on the left bank of the Rhine, looking toward the West – not a national center. The FRG, to make matters worse, continued to suffer certain restrictions on its sovereignty and – like the Weimar Republic – the FRG was the child of defeat. The FRG was peculiar in another sense. Traditional German historiography had either been Prussophile or Austrophile, championing either the mission of Prussia or of Austria-Hungary to unify the various German states before the creation of Bismarck's Second German Empire in 1871. Both Austrophiles and Prussophiles had paid scant attention to the "Third Germany" which finally prevailed in its new dress as the Federal German Republic.

Yet the FRG turned out to be the most successful state in German history. The story deserves to be recapitulated.[5] From 1948 onward Germany underwent an economic miracle – a *Wirtschaftswunder*. The bombed cities were rebuilt. German industries and agriculture revived. By the 1960s, West Germany had once more become Europe's leading economic power outside the Soviet Union. Equally astounding was Germany's political miracle. Contrary to widespread expectations, democracy revived and its opponents languished. Notwithstanding numerous contemporary assumptions to the contrary, Germany possessed parliamentary and constitutional traditions, including a legacy of vigorous local government. These traditions were taken over by the founding fathers of the new republic, who sought to avoid Weimar's errors. The Basic Law avoided a powerful presidency elected by popular vote – no more Hindenburgs, and no more Hitlers! The federal presidency became mainly a ceremonial office. The constitution emphasized the division of powers, and especially stressed federalism. Regionalism had always played a crucial role in Germany's history; after the collapse of the Third Reich, regional authorities had continued to operate under allied occupation. Regionalism was socially acceptable; indeed, it was almost a social advantage to speak correct German with a regional accent. The reconstituted *Länder* embodied these regional traditions. The *Länder* also furnished opportunities for local initiative as well as for public careers. (Willy Brandt, Helmut Schmidt, Helmut Kohl – all of them to become federal chancellors – started their political careers in West Berlin, Hamburg, and Rhineland-Palatinate respectively.) The *Länder* were represented in a powerful Second Chamber, the *Bundesrat*. Regionalism was further strengthened by self-government within the *Bezirke* (local authorities with considerable local powers). There was likewise a supreme court with extensive jurisdiction, yet another brake on real or potential abuses. The electoral system discouraged that multiplication of small parties which had weakened the Weimar Republic. The First Chamber, or *Bundestag*, elected the federal chancellor, but there were detailed provisions to avoid those deadlocks that had plagued Weimar. There was no more talk of a unitary Reich. Bismarck would neither have sought nor secured election to the *Bundestag*. Instead, the governing parties were those whose predecessors had been

5 The most recent and most extensive history of the Federal German Republic in English is Dennis Bark and David Gress, *A History of West Germany*, vol. 1: *From Shadow to Substance, 1945–1963*, vol. 2: *Democracy and its Discontents, 1963–1988*, Oxford, Blackwell, 1989 (revised and greatly expanded edition, 1993). Other works include John Ardagh, *Germany and the Germans: an Anatomy of Society Today*, New York, Harper and Row, 1987, and Gordon Craig's masterful *The Germans*, New York, Putnam, 1982.

outsiders in the Imperial *Reichstag* – Catholics, Social Democrats, and left-wing liberals. It was the governing parties of the Weimar Republic which ruled the FRG. Prussia as a state had been eliminated by the victorious allies in 1947 and would never again dominate German politics. (Even when the East German *Länder* were reconstituted after the collapse of the GDR, Prussia was not revived.)

Contrary to many expectations, the FRG met with no serious internal challenges. The welfare state, inherited from the Weimar Republic, and first legally enshrined in its constitution, kept growing apace. By the early 1960s, the mass of refugees from the East had been absorbed. The Nazis had discredited themselves by military disasters and countless atrocities. A millenarian creed that exalted strength and victory could not cope with weakness and defeat. Worse still, from the Nazis' point of view, the great bulk of party officials did not live up to their heroic self-image. Far from dying in the ditch, they mostly disclaimed knowledge of, or responsibility for, the horrors which had disgraced the Third Reich. The Nazi Party had identified itself with Young Siegfried, the dragon-slayer of German mythology. Now Siegfried hid his sword in the attic, insisted that he had always liked dragons, and sued for his pension rights! Nazi Germany's military downfall had been so obvious that there would be no legend of a Germany "undefeated on the field of battle," as there had been after World War I. A great many Nazis never paid the penalty for their crimes, as documented in works such as Tom Bower's well-named book *Blind Eye to Murder*.[6] But there would be no Fourth Reich.

The communists did no better. Before the Nazis took over, the *Kommunistische Partei Deutschlands* (KPD) had been a powerful force, complete with its own combat formations, committed to fighting the class war to the bitter end. But in 1933 the Nazis' opponents all surrendered without firing a shot. (The only serious threat to Hitler's dictatorship thereafter came from the army.) The communists' prestige further suffered when the *Wehrmacht* invaded the Soviet Union, and even communist German soldiers were disillusioned by what they saw. Once the war was lost, Germany lost about one-third of its former territory to Poland, the Germans were expelled, and the Soviet Union took the blame in German eyes, not the Western allies. (Something like 12,000,000 Germans were driven from East Prussia, Pomerania, Silesia, and the Sudetenland; another 3,000,000 fled from East Germany to West Germany. As a result, something like one-fifth of West Germany's population thereafter consisted of "expellees," mostly penniless, all compelled to make a new start.)

As Norman Naimark, a modern American historian, shows in his ongoing research, the Soviet occupation of East Germany in 1945 was a nightmare. West Germans regarded themselves as fortunate to fall under British or American rule; in East Germany there was murder and rapine. The Soviet soldiers' dreaded command to women – *Frau komm* – did more to blacken the Soviet Union's reputation than all the Nazis' propaganda had done. The Soviet-occupied zone was first plundered by the Soviets, and then misgoverned by the Soviets' East German allies. Three million people – one-sixth of East Germany's population – fled to the West before the Berlin Wall was built in 1961 and East Germany was cut off. There were leftist intellectuals aplenty in West Germany. But their hostility to the FRG, and the extensive disinformation campaign carried out by the communists and their allies left the ordinary German voter unaffected. (FRG voters perceived industry as the most important political pressure group in West Germany,

6 Tom Bower, *Blind Eye to Murder: a Pledge Betrayed: America and Britain and the Denazification of Post-war Germany*, London, Granada, 1983.

followed by the Catholic Church, then by political parties. Intellectuals were not even mentioned by the various respondents in an opinion poll taken in the early 1960s.)[7]

The FRG was far more stable than the Weimar Republic had ever been. The Weimar Republic had suffered from excessive rivalry of numerous parties. (Between 1919 and 1933 20 different governments had held office.) The FRG, by contrast, had learned from Weimar's mistakes, and yet had taken over the best traditions of its predecessors (including well-established social services). Politics in the FRG centered on three main parties, all firmly committed to democracy. These were the CDU (Christian Democratic Union), the SPD (Social Democratic Party), and the FDP (Liberal Democratic Party, the smallest of the three.) Under article 21 of the West German Basic Law, the political parties were charged with "participating in the formation of the people's will." They were respected, as they had not been in the days of Weimar; they were also well organized and well financed. (From 1959 the parties began to receive massive subventions from the state coffers, in addition to membership contributions and other forms of income.) Each of the major parties had its own bureaucracy, its own auxiliary organizations, and research institutions. During the 1990s, the established parties would incur much criticism and lose numerous members – a subject to which we shall return. Nevertheless, the three main parties all made democracy work at a critical period in German history. They also helped to integrate West Germany by transcending the regionalism inherent in the FRG's federal system.

Neither did the FRG face any threat from the military. The *Reichswehr's* commitment to the Weimar Republic had been strictly conditional; the *Bundeswehr*, by contrast, was totally loyal. No matter what German critics might assert, or foreigners might fear, the new *Bundeswehr* was fully integrated into the state. For the first time in history there was a new German army, powerful and efficient, yet totally subject to civilian authority, a democratic army, serving a democratic people – this was the true miracle of twentieth-century Germany.

In the Kaiser's army, junior officers were expected to teach civics to recruits as well as drill, so as to instill a proper spirit of dynastic loyalty in their men. "Grenadier Cohen," sternly asks a junior lieutenant in his civics class, "Why should a German soldier gladly sacrifice his life for his Imperial Majesty, the German Kaiser, and his Royal Majesty the King of Prussia, and the beloved German fatherland?" "Lieutenant, sir," answers the Jewish soldier as he smartly stands to attention, "You are absolutely right, sir. Why should he?" The soldier's question would be asked many times again. The *Bundeswehr* was the first German army in history which demanded commitment to the democratic institutions of the *Bundesrepublik*. The *Bundeswehr* also insisted on a new system of *innere Führung*, self-directed and internalized discipline. This was accounted politically fitting for citizens of a democratic state, suitable also in a military sense for a modern army where maximum responsibility would fall on junior leaders in charge of small units and on individuals. Left-wing critics feared that the *Bundeswehr* might once again revert to militarism. Right-wing critics feared lest *innere Führung* would disrupt all discipline, and would be unable to stand up to the highly disciplined East Germany *Nationale Volksarmee* (NVA), smartly drilled to perform a Soviet- (not German-) style goose step. But in the end it was the NVA's morale that collapsed in 1989 – not the *Bundeswehr's*.

---

7 Josef Othmar Zöller, *Rückblick auf die Gegenwart: die Entstehung der Kanzlerdemokratie*, Stuttgart, Seewald Verlag, 1964, p. 33.

Henceforth its officers became a specialized managerial group without the olden-time privilege and glamor. An ambitious young man of modest social background wanting to go to the very top would best succeed by going either into politics or business. It was business values (Deutschmark nationalism) that prevailed in the new state, not old-fashioned militarism.

The political culture of the FRG was more *weltoffen* (open to the world, open to the West) than the Weimar Republic had ever been, despite Weimar's cosmopolitan veneer. Weimar had been hated by all and sundry; the FRG met with no opposition from any major party, newspaper, or trade union. There was none to revile the national flag (black–red–gold). What a change from the Weimar Republic when reactionaries of all stripes had castigated these same colors – black for the priests, red for the reds, yellow for the Jews! The Federal German Republic was truly a part of the West, linked to its Western European neighbors and to the US by countless ties – through migration, political and economic associations, military cooperation, trade, banking, industry, science, technology, scholarship, and tourism. All public opinion surveys agreed that the great majority of West Germans became satisfied with their institutions, and would continue to remain so.

The founding father of the new state was Konrad Adenauer, the first federal chancellor. It was Adenauer who, more than any other man, placed his personal imprint on the new republic. As chancellor alone he wielded great powers. (The Federal Chancellor, *Bundeskanzler*, served as head of the executive, appointed his ministers, and ran the government. The *Bundestag* could not remove him by a vote of no confidence unless the opposition could provide a successor with majority support.) On the face of it, Adenauer seemed much too old for the job in a country in which, during the Nazi era, youth had been exalted to the point of hysteria. (*Jugend, Jugend, schmettern die Heldenfanfaren.*) "youth, youth, the hero trumpets roar," according to the Hitler youth anthem.) When Adenauer became chancellor in 1949 he was 73, by which time most men have drawn their old-age pension. To his opponents he appeared as a survivor from the Weimar Republic, a political has-been. (At the start of the Nazi era, he was removed from his job as chief mayor of Cologne for political unreliability; after World War II, the British discharged him from the same post for alleged incompetence. Both dismissals later proved unexpected political boons.) Adenauer stayed in office for fourteen years, longer than any democratically elected European statesman of his time. Adenauer's political longevity – longer also than Adolf Hitler's – was itself a miracle. Adenauer was old and looked old, a grandfather in politics. He spoke with a high-pitched voice in a *Kölsch* (Cologne) accent; his speeches sounded flat, like a company chairman's address to his stockholders. He was a practicing Catholic and a good family man (with three children from his first marriage, and four from his second). He liked classical poetry and was fond of growing roses. In short, Adenauer appeared an archetypal representative of the provincial German bourgeoisie that so many German intellectuals liked to mock.

Yet Adenauer was Germany's greatest modern statesman – a West German who looked to the West.[8] He had shrewdness, a dry sense of humor, cunning, and a streak

---

8 For the origins of the new state, see, for instance, Bark and Gress, *History of West Germany*; Peter H. Merkl, *The Origin of the West German Republic*, New York, Oxford University Press, 1963. For relations between Erhard and Adenauer, see Daniel Koerfer, *Kampf ums Kanzleramt, Erhard und Adenauer*, Stuttgart, Deutsche Verlags-Anstalt, 1987; and Henning Eöhler, *Konrad Adenauer: eine Politische Biographie*, Frankfurt, Prophyläen, 1994.

of ruthlessness. At his best, he ruled in a patriarchal fashion, almost like a latter-day grand-duke. Konrad Adenauer lived modestly, in Rhöndorf, near Bonn. Unlike so many Germans of his generation, Adenauer was not intimidated by uniforms, honors, or titles; he had, moreover, an immense capacity for work – remarkable even in Germany. In a country still trying to comes to terms with its past, Adenauer, like Kurt Schumacher or Willy Brandt on the oppositional benches, had nothing for which to apologize politically; they were all untainted by the Nazi stain. Above all, the old man (*der Alte*) knew what he wanted, and usually got his way.

Adenauer succeeded above all in foreign politics. He was resolved to integrate West Germany into Western Europe and NATO. In Adenauer's view, nothing could be more dangerous for Germany than to seek once more to play East against West, or to look for a perilous neutrality. *Westintegration* should have absolute priority over reunification. It was under Adenauer that West Germany joined the European Economic Community and NATO; indeed, West Germany became the most "European" of European states, with its sovereignty partly impaired through allied occupation and its military ties. Nevertheless, European integration received overwhelming popular support which – far from diminishing – continued to rise.

As regards relations with particular countries, Adenauer was particularly resolved to establish that close Franco-German relationship for which he had already striven after World War I. (Adenauer had then sought to separate Rhenish Prussia, mainly a Catholic region, from Prussia, and turn it into a separate *Land*.) After de Gaulle's return to power, Adenauer established a close personal relationship with de Gaulle. This culminated in Adenauer's last major achievement: the Franco-German friendship treaty of 1963. (Relations with Britain remained more distant. Britain was the Social Democrats' favorite country, not the Christian Democrats'.) As regards the Soviet Union, Adenauer believed that Moscow's position would ultimately weaken, owing to rising discontent within the Soviet Empire, and also to the Sino-Soviet split. Adenauer's hostility toward communism did not, however, prevent him from establishing in 1955 normal relations with the Soviet Union as a great power.

But the key to Adenauer's foreign policy was the American alliance. Helmut Schmidt (German chancellor from 1974 to 1982) once jokingly remarked that "the Americans are as they are – but they are the only Americans we have got." These were exactly Adenauer's sentiments. Nothing could substitute for the US nuclear shield, not even de Gaulle's favors. Adenauer and his family, moreover, got on well with Americans as people. (The second Frau Adenauer was a cousin of Mrs John McCloy, wife of the US High Commissioner in Bonn.) The US was an essential factor in the new German equation, and – as Adenauer put it to McCloy – demilitarization and neutralization would alike become impossible, once West Germany was safely ensconced within the NATO alliance. Adenauer also played a major role in shaping the governing party, the Christian Democratic Union (CDU), allied to the Christian Social Union (CSU, a Bavarian party). The CDU defined itself as moderately conservative and traditionalist. In fact, the CDU was a newcomer, only having come into existence after World War II. In German terms, its program was novel. The CDU's earliest manifesto, the "Ahlen Program" issued in 1947, had been leftist, strongly influenced by Catholic social thought. Under Adenauer's inspiration, the CDU increasingly moved to the center–right, seeking to combine a free-market economy with welfarism – a line taken by the CDU's chief economic expert Ludwig Erhard and the Freiburg School of economists. In a sense, the CDU was revolutionary: the first great self-styled conservative party that was pro-Western and pro-capitalist.

The CDU's conservatism would not have been recognized as such by German rightists of an earlier vintage – be they Hapsburg monarchists, Prussophiles, "conservative revolutionaries," or chauvinists of the kind who had once supported the Pan-Germans or other ultra-nationalist movements. The CDU also differed from the old Center Party, its closest model. While the Center had constituted a Catholic lobby during the Weimar and the Imperial era, the CDU tried to appeal to Christians of all denominations, even unbelievers. ("The CDU – neither Christian, nor democratic, nor a union" went the oppositional taunt.) But the CDU's departure from the old Center Party's vocation as a Catholic minority lobby was perhaps the most important political shift in modern German political history. In a sense, the CDU was novel, a true *Volkspartei*, transcending social class. At the same time, the CDU emphasized traditional social values, family-centered and regional. (It was at the CDU's behest that West German abortion laws were much stricter than those adopted in East Germany.) The CDU believed in welfarism and a Western alliance; otherwise, the party lacked a rigid ideology. To its critics, especially those on the right, the CDU had elevated political opportunism into a cardinal virtue. The CDU was a catchall party, providing a home for liberals, conservatives, Catholics, Protestants, towns, country folk, former Nazis and their erstwhile victims. The CDU capitalized on postwar prosperity, "Deutschmark nationalism." But, more importantly, it was the CDU's very pragmatism that appealed to millions of voters sickened by bitter experience of ideology-based politics, whether of Nazi or communist provenance.

The CDU's close associate, the CSU, particularly stressed Bavarian ways. As Emile Durkheim, a founding father of sociology, had already observed more than a century ago, "Catholic Bavaria is, of all Germany, the country that has always lived a life of its own and has been most jealous of its autonomy."[9] For the first time in German history there was a powerful conservative movement that enjoyed wide popular support, was parliamentary in outlook, pro-West and pro-capitalist. Until German reunification, the CDU/CSU's popularity, moreover, would increase rather than diminish, unlike the popularity of the pro-Republican parties during the Weimar era. (In 1949 the CDU/CSU share of the electoral vote amounted to 31.0 percent, as against 29.2 percent for the Social Democratic Party (SPD). By 1976, the CDU/CSU's percentage had risen to 48.6, as against 42.6 for the SPD.)[10]

In the FRG, as in the German Democratic Republic (GDR), the traditional élites had ceased to govern as a matter of right. A Pomeranian nobleman such as Hans-Joachim von Merkatz was a rarity in a Bonn cabinet. On the contrary, the overwhelming majority of West German political leaders had derived from modest circumstances. Whereas Friedrich Ebert, the first president of the Weimar Republic, had been widely reviled for his lowly social origins, no West German would have dreamt of censuring Heinrich Lübke, a federal president, simply for having been born the son of a village shoemaker. (Lübke rather was the butt of jokes that made fun of his poor English.) The workers were integrated into the new order: most federal and *Länder* governments of whatever political complexion contained at least one labor union man or some other workers' representative. Workers' children, especially Catholic ones, made their way to colleges and

9 Emile Durkheim, *Suicide: a Study in Sociology*, New York, Free Press, 1965, p. 207.
10 Karl W. Deutsch and D. Brent Smith, "The German Federal Republic: West Germany," in Roy C. Macridis et al., eds, *Modern Political Systems: Europe*, Englewood Cliffs, NJ, Prentice-Hall, 1978 edn, p. 266.

universities with greater ease than before; social distance between the classes strikingly diminished compared with prewar days. Bonn was not Weimar.

When the war ended, religion remained an important issue. In Germany, the Catholic population had traditionally been more rural in composition than the Protestants, less well educated in an academic sense, under-represented in the higher ranks of the army, civil administration, business, and diplomacy. (As late as 1952, the German bishops issued a complaint at the exclusion of Catholics from the post of West German ambassador to the Vatican. It was insulting to assume that Catholics would not properly represent German interests in dealing with the Pope.) But, as time went on, Catholics improved their relative economic and educational standing, as they did in Britain, Holland, Switzerland, and the US. Indeed, many of the new West German industries moved to new centers such as Munich. Postwar migrations altered existing settlement patterns. In political terms, moreover, there was a decisive shift. Whereas Catholics had been a minority in the united Reich, they enjoyed almost numerical parity in the FRG – an advantage that they would only lose again with German reunification in 1990.

The CDU's history reflected these changes. Despite its initial resolve to be more than just a Catholic lobby, the CDU initially depended mainly on the support of Catholics, especially practicing Catholics. (Of regular churchgoers, 57 percent of Catholics preferred the CDU in 1956; only 32 percent of regular church-going Protestants did so. For "others" the figures were much lower still.) The CDU's party élite was two-thirds Catholic at the time, drawn overwhelmingly from south and western Germany. Of these élite members, 35 percent had been arrested or jailed by the Nazis; 22 percent derived from the working class; 74 percent from the middle class; only 4 percent from the aristocracy. (The SPD élite at the time, by contrast, contained no Catholics at all: 35 percent were Protestants, 65 percent either professed no religion or provided no data; 48 percent derived from the working class and 28 percent from the middle class; 26 percent had been arrested or imprisoned by the Nazis, 33 percent were returned emigrés.) The CDU élite was well educated (70 percent had gone to a university, as opposed to 35 percent for the SPD élite in 1956).[11] The CDU, moreover, drew much of its support from an extensive network of Catholic associations including the *Bund katholischer Unternehmer* (an employers' association), the *Katholische Arbeiterbewegung* (a workers' association), *Katholische Jugend* (youth group), *Katholischer Frauenbund* (a woman's movement), and others.

As time went on, the CDU, however, increasingly ceased to be a Catholic "confessional" organization, and turned into a *Volkspartei*, claiming to represent every major section of the population. In fact, its main appeal was to the middle classes, although the CDU has always retained substantial support among white-collar and blue-collar voters.[12] (Indeed, during the first free elections in East Germany in 1990, the CDU turned out

11 For the social composition of the new élites, see Zöller, *Rückblick auf die Gegenwart*, pp. 307–12. A substantial work on the subject as a whole is Werner Conze and M. Rainer Lepsius, eds, *Sozialgeschichte der Bundesrepublik Deutschland: Beiträge zum Kontinuitätsproblem*, Stuttgart, Klett-Cotta, 1983.

12 In 1958, 59 percent of independent farmers supported the CDU, but only 3 percent supported the Social Democrats. Comparable figures for civil servants were 43 as against 11; for employers and self-employed, 40 as against 8; white-collar workers, 37 as against 20; housewives, 36 as against 20; free professions, 33 as against 5; rural laborers, 31 as against 19; unskilled workers, 28 as against 32; skilled workers, 26 as against 38. See Karl W. Deutsch and Rupert Breitling, "The German Federal Republic," in Roy C. Macridis and Robert E. Ward, eds, *Modern Political Systems: Europe*, Englewood Cliffs, NJ, Prentice-Hall, 1963 edn, p. 365.

to be the blue-collar worker's favorite choice.) Adenauer could claim much of the credit for this transformation and for the CDU's striking success. In particular, the *Bundestag* election of 1957 was for him a personal triumph. The CDU's record as a governing party seemed exemplary, especially in foreign policy; the CDU, moreover, "Americanized" its electoral campaign, employing an American expatriate familiar with new polling and advertising techniques. The CDU/CSU received an absolute majority.

From 1959, however, Adenauer lost his grip; *Kanzlerdemokratie* ("chancellor democracy," based on Adenauer's personal standing) weakened. In 1959, Adenauer failed to secure the candidacy for the federal presidency – an unexpected defeat, and, in a sense, a political turning point. In the 1961 elections, his majority declined in the *Bundestag*. (CDU representation fell from 281 to 241 seats. The SPD representation rose from 169 to 190 seats, the FDP's from 41 to 67.) Combined, the two oppositional parties would now be able to outvote the CDU. *Der Alte wird alt* (the old man is getting old) went a popular comment, as Adenauer's political campaigning became increasingly inept. (During the Berlin crisis of 1961 he saw fit to rail at West Berlin mayor Willy Brandt for his illegitimate birth, thereby losing many votes.) Indeed, the crisis occasioned by the building of the Berlin Wall (1961) was a traumatic experience for the CDU government, as Bonn's chosen allies seemed to lack resolution, whereas Brandt gained in stature by his firmness and dignity. In an indirect way, the election of John F. Kennedy had also weakened Adenauer's position: compared to the youthful and photogenic American, Adenauer seemed a relic. The new administration in Washington, moreover, no longer backed Adenauer with the matter-of-fact assurance that its predecessors had done.

German–American ties loosened in certain other respects. Germans widely disapproved of the Vietnam War – either because they equated US involvement with "dollar imperialism," or because they feared a decline in NATO's military capability. As German prosperity solidified, German emigration to the US diminished to a trickle. German language teaching declined in US high schools and colleges. Moreover, the German youngsters who reached the age of majority during the 1960s had no memories of the postwar misery, of the Marshall Plan, of the defeated Germans' intense desire in 1945 to be occupied by Americans rather than Russians. On the other hand, the US and West Germany remained important partners in trade. Even the "new politics" created new transatlantic images, as ecologists, feminists, and the German New Left in general derived inspiration from the US youth culture, with its rock music, youth fashions, and youth jargon. (A host of words such as "junkie," "dealer," "cool," passed into German.) More importantly, West Germany remained the US's chief ally in Europe, while even the most francophile within West Germany's "political class" continued to regard the US as Germany's principal partner.

In 1963, Adenauer departed from the chancellor's office, to be replaced by Ludwig Erhard. Erhard, in theory, should have made a great chancellor. He had gallantly served in World War I as a sergeant. He had a head for economics. His democratic credentials were impeccable: he had been dismissed from his former job by the Nazis. He could rightly claim to be the chief architect of the *Wirtschaftswunder* after World War II, the man who had done more than any other to free the West German economy from outworn restrictions and regulations. He was kindly, pleasant, and conciliatory. As a vote-getter, he actually did better in the 1965 elections than Adenauer had done in 1961.[13] He was entitled to be called *Herr Professor*, a distinct advantage in Germany where the

13 Koerfer, *Kampf ums Kanzleramt.*

academicians retained social prestige at a time when the generals' had much declined. He was also a Protestant. (Protestants also stepped into other positions of prominence, with Gerhard Schröder replacing Heinrich von Brentano as foreign minister, and Kai-Uwe von Hassel moving into the ministry for defense.)

Yet Tacitus's cruel description of an obscure Roman emperor also applied to Erhard: *omnium consensu capax imperii, nisi imperasset* (by everyone's consent he would have been a great ruler, if only he had never ruled). Erhard got on badly with Adenauer, who continued to intrigue against him. (Adenauer retained the chairmanship of the CDU until 1966.) There were difficulties within the cabinet and, in 1966, the existing coalition between the CDU and the Free Democratic Party (FDP) collapsed. Not that Erhard was unable to point to some political successes. (For instance, he established diplomatic relations between the FRG and Israel.) But he was forced to yield to pressure from US president Lyndon Johnson for additional financial contributions from the FRG for Atlantic defense at a time when the FRG suffered from a recession. The FDP would not participate in a government containing Franz Josef Strauss, a key figure in the CSU. Increasingly, the CDU regarded its former hero as an electoral liability.

The FDP suddenly occupied an unexpectedly important position – all the more surprising since the FDP was not a united party, and since its electoral support was limited. (In 1961, the FDP gained 12.89 percent of the vote; this percentage would decline to 9.5 in 1965.) The FDP's main support derived from Protestants, from people without a religious affiliation, and from anti-clericals. The FDP continued two separate traditions: those of the German Democratic Party, a progressive body, with a long-standing liberal tradition derived from south-west Germany, and the moderately conservative German People's Party, both of Weimar days. The liberals within the FDP were represented by Theodor Heuss, a scholar and a gentleman, deservedly chosen to be the FRG's first president. The conservatives' spokesman was Erich Mende (who later switched to the CDU). Thereafter, the FDP increasingly moved leftward, calling for a conciliatory *Ostpolitik*, *détente* with Germany's eastern neighbors, improved relations with the GDR, and the abrogation of the Hallstein Doctrine. (According to this doctrine, the FRG was the sole legitimate custodian of sovereignty for the whole of Germany because only the FRG's government had been freely elected by the German people. Countries recognizing the GDR in future would thereby commit an unfriendly act against the FRG.)

Negotiations between the FDP and the CDU regarding the future of their coalition broke down. Erhard was forced out of office, and the chancellorship fell to Dr Kurt Georg Kiesinger, a former prime minister of the *Land* of Baden-Württemberg. Kiesinger had once been a member of the Nazi party, but after the war he redeemed his record; he was, moreover, a man of great political flexibility. If a coalition with the FDP proved impractical, why not a "Grand Coalition" with the SPD?

On the face of it, such an arrangement seemed unlikely. The SPD had been refounded after World War II by Kurt Schumacher. Schumacher was a Prussian of Prussians: tough, dour, and courageous. Badly wounded in World War I, Schumacher barely survived a Nazi concentration camp in World War II. Schumacher was a German patriot who looked to German reunification, hated the communists, but also looked askance at the Western allies. He regarded Adenauer as a Rhineland "separatist" and, worse still, as the Western allies' willing tool. (*Der Kanzler der Alliierten*, the Allies' Chancellor, went the taunt.) Schumacher died in 1952, succeeded in the party's leadership by Erich Ollenhauer. Ollenhauer was Schumacher's very opposite: a fox, not a lion, conciliatory, and anxious to appeal to a much wider public than Schumacher. The SPD's nationalism softened;

nevertheless, the SPD and the CDU remained divided by a gulf. The CDU was primarily a Catholic party; the SPD mainly Protestant. The CDU professed to be Christian and the SPD Marxist. The CDU was a recent party, a political parvenu. The SPD prided itself on being the world's oldest socialist party, with luminaries such as Karl Marx, Friedrich Engels, August Bebel, Karl Liebknecht, and Rosa Luxemburg among its pioneers. To old-timers, moreover, the SPD was something more than a party – a political church dedicated to building a better world.

There were other differences. The CDU had a strong rural component; the SPD was overwhelmingly urban. (It was for this reason that the Nazis had been able to penetrate Protestant rural areas with comparative ease; they encountered greater opposition in the Catholic countryside where the Center Party was strongly entrenched.) The SPD had traditionally been strong in working-class areas; with its disciplined hierarchy, the SPD could make a good claim to represent the best of the old Prussian tradition with its commitment to duty, work, and punctuality. In organizational terms, the SPD relied on a mass membership (estimated at 600,000 in 1957); the CDU had far fewer members (250,000 in 1957). The CDU drew a much larger percentage of its income from private contributions, especially from business; whereas the SPD relied mainly on membership fees. Above all, the SPD considered itself for long as a class party. As Kurt Schumacher had insisted, "the SPD is, and will remain, a poor people's party."[14]

During the late 1950s and thereafter, these generalizations ceased to hold good. The social distance between Catholics and Protestants declined, as did the social distance between classes. There were far-reaching changes within the Catholic church, as Pope John XXIII insisted on a variety of reforms, and on a more conciliatory approach toward socialists and communists. (In 1964, the Pope, for the first time in history, received an official SPD delegation.) The SPD broadened its social appeal, as did the CDU. There were changes even within the CSU, the most conservative body within the CDU/CSU alliance. Alois Hundhammer, spokesman for the rigid old-line Catholics, lost the party's chairmanship to Franz Joseph Strauss. Strauss seemed an unlikely protagonist of liberalization. A powerful man, physically as well as politically, he was feared for the ferocity of his polemics, and for his commitment to rearmament. (Between 1956 and 1962 he served as minister for defense.) Strauss was a German Gaullist. Not for him the evils of "Genscherism," the policy of Atlantic cooperation promoted by Hans-Dietrich Genscher, the leading politician of the Free Democratic Party. By training a lawyer, Genscher served as minister of the interior under Brandt's SPD–FDP coalition, later as foreign minister, and thereafter under Helmut Kohl, the longest-serving foreign minister in modern German history (1974–92), and an architect of German reunification. Strauss, by contrast, wanted to assert above all Germany's interests (according to his critics, he meant Bavaria's). Hence Strauss detested Genscher's preference for alphabet-soup international organizations such as the UN and the CSCE. In fact, Genscherism always prevailed. (Strauss was forced out of ministerial office by the so-called *Spiegel* affair in 1962 involving a gross violation of press freedom.) But it was under Strauss that the CSU ceased to be primarily a confessional party. (For all his professed anti-communism, Strauss also helped in making massive loans available to the GDR, professedly for Germany's national interest.)

There were also changes within the SPD. By the late 1950s and the early 1960s, the SPD could, by no stretch of the imagination, be described any longer as a poor

14 Cited in Zöller, *Rückblick auf die Gegenwart*, p. 167.

people's party. West German society was becoming more affluent than ever before; the refugees from the Eastern territories had largely been absorbed. Hence the *Bund der Heimatvertriebenen*, the refugees' political organization, ceased to play a major political role – although, at the height of its influence, the league had been able to secure 27 seats in the *Bundestag*. The SPD's traditional appeal – with its peculiar blend of neutralism, German nationalism, and class consciousness – clearly had not worked, and neither had a distinctively Marxist program. Hence power within the party increasingly shifted to the revisionists. They counted among their number the so-called Grand Dukes (*Landesfürsten*), men who played the leading role in the politics of specific *Länder* and big cities. Used to forming coalitions with other parties at a local level, the Grand Dukes were quite prepared to do the same in Bonn.

The resultant transformation of the SPD entailed bitter controversy between the reformers, men such as Carlo Schmid, one of the SPD's most gifted theoreticians, and Schmidt's fellow academician, Wolfgang Abendroth, a Marxist. (He and his "circle" were later excluded from the SPD.) The revisionists won, and the Godesberg program of 1959 committed the SPD to a strictly reformist line: doctrinaire Marxism was dropped; the SPD ceased to be a class party. When the congress ended, the delegates once more joined in the old fighting song, *"Brüder, zur Sonne zur Freiheit"* ("Brothers, forward to the sun and liberty"), but the anthem was never sung again at the party's official occasions. Radicalism, of course, did not die within the ranks of the SPD. It would be revived again by groups such as the *Jusos* (young socialists), by activists in local branches, but the new radicalism found its main support among the youthful and the highly educated, not the industrial workers. As a party, the SPD turned to total acceptability. The SPD thereafter could claim to be a *Volkspartei* with as much justification as the CDU.

Not that all went well with the SPD. More than the CDU, the SPD was beset by ideological struggles, not surprising within a party which had a special appeal to school teachers and professors. Divisions between traditional Marxists and revisionists were replicated between those which split the Old Left from the New Left. The SPD, moreover, had difficulties in understanding sea changes in German public opinion: in this sense, the SPD was far more conservative than the CDU. After 1948, the SPD failed to recognize the broad public support for the social market economy, despite two serious electoral defeats suffered by the SPD in 1953 and 1957 respectively. The SPD again misread German public opinion when they opposed German backing for NATO. (Even after the collapse of the Warsaw Pact, a study made by the Allensbach Institute indicated that 51 percent of all respondents within the Federal Republic desired a retention of NATO membership, as against 34 percent who advocated neutrality.) The SPD was equally slow in grasping the Germans' commitment to European unification. (Again, the SPD would drag its feet on German unity when the German Democratic Republic collapsed in 1990 and Germans on both sides of the border clamored for immediate unification.) The SPD, far more than the CDU, was a party which usually had to catch up with public opinion.

Fortunately for its own future, the SPD contained within its ranks a great many politicians of outstanding ability, many of them trained in the rough and tumble of municipal politics. Willy Brandt, the SPD's new leader (1964) made a perfect representative for the party's new line. Whereas Kurt Schumacher, the SPD's first head after World War II, had been a fervent German patriot, Brandt had fled from Nazi Germany in 1933, settled in Norway, married a Norwegian wife, and for a time adopted Norwegian citizenship. Brandt was a keen supporter of the European Community, the very opposite of a German nationalist. He was handsome and popular; he deliberately modeled himself on John F. Kennedy, and rivaled Kennedy's success with women. In appearance a kindly patriarch, he dealt as ruthlessly with his friends as with his enemies. (In 1964, as mayor of West Berlin, he succeeded Erich Ollenhauer as party secretary, and continued to occupy the post until 1987.) Superbly good at handling the media, Brandt acquired international acclaim. (Brandt's honors included the Nobel Peace Prize, awarded to him in 1971, the presidency of the Socialist Internationale, and a string of honorary degrees.) He ended his career as an elder statesman and a recognized member of what might be called Leftist High Society – a distinction that none would have associated with Schumacher.

Brandt, however, also possessed more solid qualifications for high office. During 1957–66, a critical period, he served as governing mayor of West Berlin; his anti-communist credentials were impeccable. It was Brandt who had played a major part in persuading the Americans to reinforce their West Berlin garrison during the 1961 crisis.[15] Brandt was converted to a more conciliatory line toward the East by his disillusionment with the inadequate Western response toward the construction of the Berlin Wall. At the same time, Brandt understood the average German voter's caution and skepticism. In 1965, Brandt thus appropriated for his own party the unadventurous CDU slogan *keine Experimente* (no experiments), a line that would reappear with an anti-Community connotation in Germany during the last stages of the GDR. Coalitions between the SPD and the CDU, moreover, had already operated in individual *Länder*, especially in embattled West Berlin.

In 1966 Brandt and Kiesinger formed a "Grand Coalition" that briefly united the SPD, the CDU, and the CSU in an ill-assorted partnership. Brandt became vice-chancellor and foreign minister, thereby gaining the two most prestigious jobs after the chancellorship. The Grand Coalition caused a political uproar, especially on the SPD's left. But, in a sense, the Grand Coalition provided also a kind of personal legitimization for Brandt and Kiesinger alike: the ex-émigré and the ex-Nazi vouched for one another as members of the same team. Above all, the SPD had become fully respectable in the eyes of middle class people, a governing party with all a governing party's perks and prestige. The respectability factor is hard to overestimate in German politics. (Gann remembers the reminiscences of his mother, a Jewish banker's daughter from Frankfurt and a staunch liberal. His mother's cook urged his mother in 1933 to vote for the SPD instead of the middle-class German Democratic Party. She cast her vote according to the cook's recommendation but would not tell any of her own friends. Thirty years later, such reluctance would have seemed inconceivable.) On the contrary, the SPD made substantial inroads into the ranks of middle-class voters, and also of Catholics and women. The party's membership further increased (reaching 960,000 in 1976). The SPD strengthened its hold on many local governments, and by the late 1960s controlled all major metropolitan areas. Above all, the SPD did well nationally (obtaining in the 1969 election 42.7 percent of the vote as against 39.3 percent in 1965. Corresponding figures for the CDU/CSU were 47.6 percent and 46.1 percent respectively; for the FDP, 9.5 percent and 5.8 percent).

Like the Socialist Party in France and the Labour Party in Britain, the SPD increasingly drew on the votes of white-collar workers, especially teachers, and employees in

---

15 Koerfer, *Kampf ums Kanzleramt*, p. 547. Barbara Marshall, *Willy Brandt: eine Politische Biographie*, Bonn, Bouvier Verlag, 1993. Dieter Dowe, ed., *Partei und soziale Bewegung: Kritische Beiträge zur Entwicklung der SPD seit 1945*, Bonn, Dietz Verlag, 1993. For a masterly discussion of *Ostpolitik*, see Timothy Garton Ash, *In Europe's Name: Germany and the Divided Continent*, New York, Random House, 1993.

the public service of the *Länder*, and local governments. (From the 1960s onward, the importance of the working-class vote declined as manufacturing diminished as a share of the gross domestic product, as industries increasingly replaced workers by machines, and as Turks and other foreigners – most of them non-citizens and non-voters – took over many traditional working-class jobs.) The SPD, moreover, did well with young voters, including women, whose chances for promotion in the party rank were greater in the SPD than in the CDU. (In Germany, the disproportion between young and older men was even greater than in any other Western European country, given the exceptionally high losses incurred by the *Wehrmacht* in World War II.) The youthful voters, of course, were as divided as their seniors. A minority took part in the student revolutions of the 1960s, the campaign against the Vietnam War, and the campaigns against nuclear weaponry. The ultra-militants questioned parliamentary democracy and put their faith in a utopian revolution. By contrast, the great majority of German youth did not trust an ill-defined revolutionary future. Neither did they look back to the Nazi past – now ancient history to men and women born after 1945. To many of these young men and women, the SPD's moderation made a strong appeal, as the SPD shifted its emphasis from the class struggle to the fight for a humane society which would secure the rights of women, minorities, and "guest workers," improve the condition of the "Third World," take care of the environment, and strive for social justice. Brandt made himself an effective spokesman for these new politics. Young and well-educated voters no longer cared that Brandt had returned to Germany in 1945 wearing a Norwegian military uniform. The SPD had come a long way from its traditional nationalism.

In 1967 the Hallstein Doctrine was dropped. German public opinion, or what passed for such, increasingly accepted the permanence of Eastern European frontiers, even of the GDR's permanent existence. Brandt's own formula in this regard was *Wandel durch Annäherung* (transformation through *rapprochement*). West Germans, according to Brandt, could best bring about changes in East Germany, and improve the East Germans' condition, by establishing closer ties with the GDR, even by paying overt or covert subsidies in return for concessions concerning "human rights" and for increased facilities accorded to West Germans wishing to see friends and relatives in East Germany. (By its linkage to West Germany, East Germany also secured *de facto* membership to the EC.) West German hard-liners denounced this policy as one of paying blackmail, even as surrender on the installment plan. Communist hard-liners in East Germany, by contrast, condemned this policy as a strategy of *Aufweichung* (softening) socialism. But Brandt's policy had a wide appeal, both to those who accepted peaceful coexistence with East Germany, and those who wished to speed its demise. In addition, Brandt specially appealed to leftist intellectuals who – almost alone in Germany – objected to German reunification on moral grounds. In their opinion, socialism in East Germany should be preserved because it was morally superior to capitalism, however badly Honecker's socialism might work in practice. Germany, moreover, had morally lost the right to be a united country – after Auschwitz, Germany did not deserve to be a united state.

We shall refer again to these controversies in chapter 12. We merely wish to point out at this stage that the construction of the Berlin Wall in 1961, the creation of a fortified frontier zone through Germany, the ending of most legal emigration from East to West Germany, gave a breathing space to the GDR. The brain drain to the West largely ended. The Soviet occupation of Czechoslovakia in 1968 seemed to leave no doubt that Moscow would hold on to its own, come hell or high water. The East German authorities further improved their espionage network in Western Germany, with agents in the highest ranks of the West German Establishment. Some of them were discovered. The very extent of these revelations created a sense of uncertainty in West German politics, a malaise perhaps even more useful to the East German authorities than the information obtained from corrupt or unsuspecting West German politicians.

Not surprisingly, Brandt's line appealed not only to "peaceniks" but also to businessmen with a stake in inter-German trade, to humanitarians who wished to better the lot of ordinary East German citizens, and also to hard-minded "Gaullists" within the CDU, including Franz-Josef Strauss, leader of the CSU and a staunch anti-communist by repute. From the late 1960s onward, the Federal Republic massively subsidized the East German regime – through the sale of political prisoners from East to West (nearly 34,000 of them by the end of the late 1980s), through "family reunion" projects allowing elderly East Germans to emigrate to West Germany, through loans, through road and rail fees, credits, fees for waste disposal, and other devices. By the late 1980s, these amounted to the princely sum of 8.3 billion Deutschmarks. Even the churches were drawn into this traffic. By paying blackmail, the Federal Republic thereby helped to stave off East Germany's looming bankruptcy.

Nevertheless, the logic of facts seemed incontrovertible to the advocates of *Ostpolitik*. A conciliatory *Ostpolitik* appeared essential for a conciliatory *Westpolitik*. West Germany had no reason to welcome a total economic collapse in East Germany. For the future, West Germany needed to establish a commercial stake east of the Elbe (an object accomplished). Germany needed to expiate its Nazi past and rebuild confidence in East Central Europe (likewise achieved). For the time being at any rate, the two Germanys would have to coexist; after all, none of West Germany's neighbors wanted German unification. The German Democratic Republic seemed firmly established. Few predicted at the end of the 1960s that the Soviet empire would only last another 20 years. On the contrary, it was the US which appeared in trouble – torn by the Vietnam War. The anti-war movement in the US and the anti-war movements in Europe mutually reinforced one another. The Vietnam War also had other unintended consequences: the withdrawal of experienced officers, non-commissioned officers and men from Germany to Vietnam led to an erosion of leadership and morale in the US forces in Germany. The US soldiers' purchasing power fell as a result of inflation. GI Joe no longer seemed ten foot tall, as he had in 1945; all too often he earned instead pity or resentment.

Ostpolitik, therefore, made a substantial appeal far beyond the ranks of the SPD. *Ostpolik* went with *Westintegration*, as in 1968 the EEC customs union was all but completed. The SPD made further gains in a controversy over proposed constitutional changes providing the government with increasing emergency powers. A compromise was adopted in 1968; this ensured the right to strike and the enjoyment of basic liberties even during an emergency. The CDU–SPD coalition, however, steadily weakened, as CDU members believed that their party had already made too many concessions to the SPD, while leftists accused the SPD of having sold out to the Establishment. The 1969 elections further strengthened the SPD which won 224 seats, as against 242 for the CDU/CSU, and 35 seats for the FDP. The SPD therefore changed course. Brandt secured the support of the FDP for a "social–liberal" coalition between the SPD and the FDP, with Brandt as the first Social Democratic chancellor in postwar Germany.

Brandt as an individual and the SPD as a party reached the peak of popularity in 1972 when the SPD, for the first time in the Federal Republic's history, became the most powerful party with 45.8 percent of votes cast in the general election. For the first time in postwar West German history, the CDU was excluded from government. After two weak chancellors, Erhard and Kiesinger, the chancellor's office once more achieved central importance – all the more so as Brandt had the chancellery (*Bundeskanzleramt*) reorganized. But Brandt's first priority remained foreign policy. In this regard, Brandt had relatively good cards, given the economic strength provided to the FRG by its capitalist enterprise. In 1970, West Germany's share of the world trade in manufacture was not much less than that of the united Wilhelmine Reich at the height of its power – 19.8 percent as against 22.4 percent. West Germany lost less time in strikes than the US or the other major Western European countries. Germany's consumer price index had risen less than that of its competitors.[16] Overall, the West German economy remained resilient, despite a heavy burden of taxation, and despite massive state intervention in the economy.

Brandt thus felt convinced that he could afford both to expand aid to the Third World, and continue concessions toward the East based on economic strength. Brandt was the first West German leader to pay an official visit to the GDR. It was a trip much praised at the time, though fraught with unforeseen long-term consequences for the SPD when the GDR was about to collapse, and Brandt's conciliatory stance would be held against him and his party by the East German electorate. Brandt also played a major part in securing a new four-power agreement on West Berlin whereby the Soviets fully accepted the position of the Western powers (the US, France, and Britain) in a divided city. In 1970 the FRG concluded a non-aggression pact with the Soviet Union; an agreement was concluded between the FRG and Poland in the same year. *Ostpolitik* continued, despite resultant friction with the US, made worse by the relative deterioration of the US economic position, and by the collapse of the Bretton Woods Agreement.

Brandt proved a brilliant showman. But he was unable to hold on to power. As an ex-mayor of West Berlin, he had made his career in a city whose budget was heavily financed by the West German taxpayer – not a good training in financial orthodoxy. Brandt identified his future with that of the left wing within the SPD. He might not personally approve of the young leftists' utopian dreams, but he felt convinced that, overall, their influence would infuse the SPD with much-needed enthusiasm. Brandt was particularly impressed with the "anti-fascism" of a new generation that looked with disdain at their parents' Nazi past, and claimed moral credit for having been born after the demise of the Third Reich. According to Helmut Schmidt, Brandt's chief critic within the SPD, it was the left wing that triumphed at the SPD's party conference at Hanover in 1973. As Schmidt saw it, the conference had been "an important stage in the decline of the SPD, mainly because the party chairman failed forcefully to oppose leftist errors and prevent fatal decisions."[17]

The leftists' power was all the more resented by the moderates, owing to the leftists' growing influence in the media, in publishing, in academia, and in secondary education (West Germany experienced the same rift between the values of the traditional working class and those of the "new class" now apparent in every Western country). In West Germany the rift became even greater given disagreement over *Ostpolitik*. Increasingly, Brandt's

16 Tables on pp. 283 and 285 in Michael Balfour, *West Germany: a Contemporary History*, New York, St Martin's Press, 1982. For Brandt's own assessment at the time, see Willy Brandt, *Koexistenz-Zwang zum Wagnis*, Stuttgart, Deutsche Verlags-Anstalt, 1963.
17 Cited in Bark and Gress, *A History of West Germany*, vol. 2, p. 263. See also David P. Conradt, Gerald R. Kleinfeld, George K. Romoser and Christian Søe, eds, *Germany's New Politics*, Tempe, Arizona, German Studies Association of the US.

policy seemed to change from *Wandel durch Annäherung* (change through *rapprochement*) to *Annäherung ohne Wandel* (*rapprochement* without change), as Brandt, his followers, and indeed many CDU supporters accepted the permanence of Germany's division.

Brandt stayed in power until 1974 (the year that also saw President Nixon's resignation and President Pompidou's death). The immediate occasion for Brandt's departure from office was one of the many spy scandals that disgraced the FRG, and made West Germany appear supremely vulnerable. East Germany maintained a huge espionage organization in West Germany. East German spies infiltrated into the most sensitive positions. They included Günter Guillaume who advanced to serve as one of Brandt's close associates. On being convicted as a spy, he was sentenced to 16 years' jail, but was released in exchange for eight Western agents and a total of 3,000 exit permits for GDR citizens – the spy affair at least achieved something of value."[18] Germany had suffered from the oil shock. But despite such scandals and new economic challenges, the FRG had once more become a great power, with a prosperous economy, the strongest military forces in Europe outside the Soviet Union, yet with political and parliamentary institutions as stable as any in the world. Public opinion polls on controversial subjects must admittedly be treated with some caution. Nevertheless, polls do provide illustrative evidence on the way politics work. And all polls agreed: West Germans were overwhelmingly satisfied with their country's democratic system, and West Germany's West European and transatlantic bonds. It was an outcome that few would have anticipated at the FRG's foundation.

Austria

Austria, after 1945, resumed its independence which it had lost during the Third Reich. (Hitler had annexed Austria in 1938, and split the country into *Gaue* (districts); hence, the very name of Austria had disappeared from the map.) By the end of World War II, the Austrians had had enough of the *Anschluss* (union with Germany). The Austrian State Treaty (1955) assured Austria's future neutrality and independence. Independent Austria for the first time acquired full legitimacy in the eyes of its people, and Austrians increasingly regarded themselves as members of a distinct nation, separate from Germany. (In 1945, shortly after the war had ended, cabarets once more started to open among the ruins. One showed a sweet young *Dirndel* (peasant girl) wearing a scarf inscribed "Austria". Her hair tousled, her frock slipping, her blouse half undone, she grinned as she sang a hit tune of the time, 'I didn't want to do it, he made me do it.") The new Austria faced a difficult situation, having suffered a series of disastrous "brain drains." Hitler had exiled or murdered the Jews. During World War II, Austrian soldiers had faced heavy losses in battle. After the war had ended, numerous Austrians went to Germany and Switzerland to find jobs. Nevertheless, Austria recovered with surprising speed, and perfected a "Swiss" type of economy – with high-precision engineering, tourism, and financial services.[19]

The Second Austrian Republic also gained what the First Republic (1918–38) had lacked – political stability. During the 1930s, Austria, like Spain, had experienced bitter civil strife between Catholics and socialists. Then came the *Anschluss*, then catastrophe.

18 Karl-Heinz Janssen, "Offizier im besonderem Einsatz," *Die Zeit*, 29 April 1994.
19 Anton Pelinka, "Austria," in Gerald A. Dorfman and Peter J. Duignan, eds, *Politics in Western Europe*, Stanford, CA, Hoover Institution Press, 1991, pp. 324–49.

Thereafter, Austrians worked out a series of remarkable compromises. Conservative Catholics, organized in the ÖVP (*Östereichische Volkspartei*), agreed to cooperate with their erstwhile enemies, the socialists, grouped in the SPÖ (*Sozialistische Partei Östereichs*). Between them, they agreed on one of the most far-reaching nationalization programs initiated in any Western country; yet private business continued alongside nationalized industries, and steadily expanded. The "red–black" alliance was cemented by what might be called Austria's three "p"s. The *Proporzystem* shared out jobs in the public sector in a proportionate fashion among members of the main party. *Protektion* (personal patronage, inherited from imperial days) solidified into party-centered nepotism. *Parität* allowed for wage settlements to be achieved by bargains between government, employers, and workers. According to its critics, the system made for mediocrity. Vienna's olden style intellectual supremacy in the German-speaking world failed to revive – all the more so as the capital was partially cut off from its natural hinterland by the Iron Curtain. The Republic's bureaucracy became even more powerful than the civil service of imperial days. (Austria was the world's only republic where senior officials joined in the title of court councillor, *Hofrat* – a republic of *Hofräte*.) Politics were further complicated by a federal arrangement which split the small country into separate *Länder*, just as in West Germany, a much larger country. Nevertheless, federalism at least imposed some brakes on the central power, and thereby formed yet another part of the Austrian compromise.

The system worked. The SPÖ's and ÖVP's internal development replicated the SPD's and CDU's in West Germany. The ÖVP became less outspokenly Catholic. The SPÖ ceased to be a workers' party, and increasingly appealed to members of all classes (especially the young and the well educated, workers in public employment, and voters interested in the "new" issues of feminism and ecology.) Equally important was the personality factor. The SPÖ's most important postwar leader was Bruno Kreisky (party chairman from 1967 to 1983, federal chancellor from 1970 to 1983). Kreisky's long tenure of power was itself paradoxical. Kreisky was a Jew – not a political advantage in a country in which anti-semitism as yet remained stronger than in West Germany, and which had shown less willingness than West Germany to come to terms with the Nazi past. Yet Austrians accepted Kreisky almost as a monarch – Bruno I, as he was jokingly called. More surprising still, Austrian workers and socialist intellectuals alike identified themselves with a leader who had little in common with either. Kreisky was descended from the Jewish *haute bourgeoisie*, part of that liberal, urban upper class that had played such a major part in the economic and cultural life of olden-day Vienna, Prague, and Budapest. Kreisky had survived the Third Reich as a political exile in Sweden. (Nineteen members of his family had perished in the Holocaust.) At the end of World War II he returned to Austria, and quickly made his way in the SPÖ. He did so by dint of tactical skill as well as intellectual ability. (A writer in his own right, he published extensively on labor relations, unemployment, international affairs, and also published a massive political autobiography.)[20] Unlike Olof Palme, the Swedish social democratic leader, Kreisky was not an ideologue. Unlike Brandt, Kreisky formed no part of the socialist *Schickeria* (the international smart set). He was a man of solid bourgeois tastes, solidly married, solidly dressed in made-to-measure suits, solidly read in the German classics. But, as a superb tactician, able to win the confidence of the most diverse factions within his party, it was Kreisky, more than any other, who turned the SPÖ from a socialist into a social democratic body. He represented, not so much Austro-Marxism,

---

20 Bruno Kreisky, *Im Strom der Politik, Erfahrungen eines Europäers*, Berlin, Siedler Verlag, 1988.

but Austro-Keynesianism. (He managed to get numerous international firms to open branches, or shift their headquarters to Vienna. He stimulated economic development with massive deficits which remained to plague his successors.)

Kreisky was a paradox in other ways. Kreisky, a Jew, turned out to be one of Israel's most highly placed critics in the West. The German-speaking Jewish *haute bourgeoisie* had traditionally rejected Zionism, regarding themselves as Germans above all. In Kreisky's own words, "my parents' respective families had been rooted in Austria for a century. They had supplied judges, attorneys, physicians, and merchants. My roots are in Austria ... What should I do in Palestine where all is strange to me ... ?"[21] No sympathy, therefore, for Zionists! Kreisky instead sided with the Third World whose influence continued to grow in the Socialist Internationale. Kreisky sought for dialogue with the PLO (Palestine Liberation Organization). He censured Israel for practicing its own form of apartheid, and denigrated Menachem Begin's government in Jerusalem as semi-fascist – without, however, clarifying that Israel had remained at war with the Arabs since its inception, and had fought three successive wars for its very existence.

Whatever the merits of Third Worldery, Kreisky style, Austria did well in international affairs. In 1955 the four allied powers had agreed to withdraw their troops in exchange for an Austrian State Treaty which committed Austria to neutrality. At the same time Austrians emphasized their own national culture as a means of sustaining their new found national identity. (As angry Germans put it, Austrians persuaded the world that Beethoven had been an Austrian and Hitler a German.) But the wartime allies had themselves been the first to assert that Austria had been an accomplice to Nazi aggression. Austrians could hardly be censured for taking the "Big Four" at their word. Austria thereafter took an important part in international organizations, especially the Socialist Internationale and the UN.

To sustain their international position and their sense of nationhood, Austrians cultivated memories of Austria's former imperial splendor, with copious (though not wholly inaccurate) references to the Habsburgs' relative tolerance toward ethnic minorities. Austria, a Western country, was supposed to be peculiarly well fitted to act as a bridge from West to East (in fact, Vienna lies geographically east of Prague). There was a new cultural concoction for tourists which oddly blended the operatic glitter of *Die Fledermaus* with *The Sound of Music*, alpine scenery, Schönbrunn palatial splendor, the trot of *Fiaker* (hackney coaches), zither chords and candlelight. But whatever the validity of such invented traditions, Austrians did come to feel themselves to be members of a disjunct and separate nation. (Even Austria's third party, the *Freiheitliche Partei Östereichs*, softened its former pro-Germanism.)

Austria thus got on particularly well with the GDR. ("Three German states, two social systems, one culture.") Both Austria and the GDR felt apprehensive about West Germany – more powerful, more prosperous than the former two, and a magnet for skilled and enterprising immigrants alike from East Germany and Austria. Both Austria and the GDR claimed for themselves the convenient status of history's victims (the former penalized by Prussian militarism, the latter by German fascism). The GDR and Austria thus cooperated in a variety of ways. (For instance, Austria helped the GDR to expand its iron and steel industries.) But whereas the GDR would falter, Austria would prevail. There would be no second *Anschluss*.

21 Interview with *Jeune Afrique*, 20 May 1975, in Bruno Kreisky, *Das Nahost-problem?*, Vienna, Europa Verlag, 1985, p. 26. We are indebted also to Kurt Leube, a friend of the former chancellor.

4

French Politics, 1958–1974

On 13 May 1958, Prime Minister Pierre Pimflin formed the last government of the Fourth Republic in France. On the same day, élite units of the French army and militant settlers in Algeria rose against *le système* which threatened to put an end to *Algérie française*, and to haul down the tricolor in Algeria. General Charles de Gaulle became head of state. His first words on assuming authority were about "the degradation of the state."[1] This was the disease he dreaded most and that he meant to cure.

For the moment, France seemed the sick man of Europe. No great Western state after World War II had ever been as divided internally as France during the Algerian crisis – not even Britain during the Suez disaster of 1956, nor the US during the Vietnam War. The French army had been forced to withdraw from Indo-China after a long and bitter war (1946–54). Then a rising had begun in Algeria (1954). In purely military terms, France had largely won the struggle by 1958 – but politically the war was lost. French society was rent asunder; so were the armed forces, the civil service, and public corporations. On paper, France was part of NATO. But the bulk of her armed forces were tied down in Algeria, and French armed might in Europe counted for little. Because of this the US insisted on rearming West Germany and making it the center of NATO's defense. The very authority of the French state seemed to be crumbling; and the Fourth Republic had become *la mal-aimée* (the ill-beloved).

The Fourth Republic and its politicians did not entirely deserve their bad reputation. It was they who had presided over the astonishing recovery of the French economy after World War II, over industrial and agricultural modernization, the demographic rejuvenation of France, an extended welfare state, the expansion of French education, and the integration of France into NATO and the European Economic Community. (Contrary to a widespread misconception, the rate of economic expansion was actually even greater during the most troubled years, 1948–58, than in the subsequent Gaullist decade.)[2] It was the Fourth (and later the Fifth) Republic that successfully stuck to a series of ambitious investment programs. "If there is one single reason why the road, rail and social infrastructure of France in the 1990s compares so favorably with British conditions, it is . . . 'the thirty glorious years' . . . of sustained investment between 1945 and 1975."[3]

1 Cited in Ted Morgan, *The French: Portrait of a People*, New York, Putnam, 1969, p. 244. See also John Ardagh, *The New French Revolution*, New York, Harper and Row, 1969; Vincent E. McHale, "France," in Gerald A. Dorfman and Peter J. Duignan, eds, *Politics in Western Europe*, Stanford, CA, Hoover Institution Press, 1991, pp. 57–88.
2 *New York Times*, 8 December 1967, cited by James Chace and Elisabeth Malkin, "The Mischiefmakers: the American Media and De Gaulle, 1964–1968," paper presented at the Centennial Conference on De Gaulle and the Construction of Europe, 12–14 October 1990.
3 Peter Hennessy, *Never Again: Britain 1945–1951*, New York, Pantheon, 1993, p. 379.

The Fourth Republic's political achievements were equally impressive. In 1945 France formally resumed her place as one of the victorious powers. (France was allocated – at British behest – her own zone of occupation in vanquished Germany.) France had been beaten by the Germans in 1940; and memories of defeat and collaboration remained engraved in the national memory. But the Fourth Republic played an active part in Western European politics, and a leading role in the formation of the European Coal and Steel Community (ECSC, 1952) and the European Economic Community (EEC, operational 1958). The Fourth Republic resisted all domestic challenges from the French Communist Party, even though this was one of the most powerful communist parties outside the Soviet bloc, highly disciplined, well organized, with an enormous clientage system, and covert as well as overt links to the French Establishment. The old right – anti-Protestant, anti-Jewish, anti-republican – had been discredited, but not crushed, by collaboration with the Nazis. France continued to be a class-conscious country in which politics were apt to pass from father to son. (A middle-class technician or engineer whose father was a worker would be almost twice as likely to vote for the left as one whose father had himself belonged to the middle class.)[4] But class divisions began to weaken, as workers as well as bourgeois people began to buy cars, refrigerators, and TV sets, and as education improved for the poor. France remained highly centralized, as it had been under previous regimes; but at least some attention began to be paid to the cultural diversity of regions such as Brittany, Alsace, and Corsica.

France stayed bitterly divided by ideology. Nevertheless, the traditional cleavage between clericals and anti-clericals narrowed. The Third Republic had been *laïque* (lay-minded) in inspiration; very few Catholics ever managed to serve as cabinet ministers under the Third Republic. Catholics, however, including priests, had an important share in the Resistance during World War II; thereafter, Catholics played a major part in French politics. Admittedly, the main Catholic party, the *Mouvement républicain populaire* (MRP) never managed to develop into a powerful Christian Democratic party of the German or Italian kind. However, anti-clericalism ceased to be a major force in politics – as did anti-semitism.

De Gaulle inherited from the technocrats of the Fourth Republic national economic planning, major changes in transportation – even the nuclear bomb. The Fourth Republic had to cope with all manner of difficulties, including the most powerful and the most rigidly Stalinist communist party in Western Europe. Yet to its credit, France lapsed neither into communism nor fascism. There was much talk of the parliamentary instability engendered by the Fourth Republic, as ministry followed upon ministry. But the same men held office again and again in different permutations. In this sense, there was neither discontinuity nor lack of experience at the top. Only the prime ministers moved in rapid succession, whereas the number of ministerial changes in Paris was actually less than in London during the same period.

It was an astonishing achievement for a country whose international reputation during World War II had sunk so low that President Roosevelt had contemplated placing liberated France under allied military government – a humiliation that de Gaulle never forgot. Moreover, the Fourth Republic had to cope with many other problems not of its own making. There was a long legacy of political dissension and instability. Thus a senior citizen born in France in 1890 would, by 1960, have lived through three different regimes: the Third Republic (1870–1940), Marshall Pétain's collaborationist *Etat Français*

---

4 William Safran, *The French Polity*, New York, Longman, 1985, p. 32.

(1940–45), and the Fourth Republic. The senior citizen's septuagenarian grandparents, born in 1830, would have seen four regimes: the July monarchy headed by a king, the Second Republic, the Empire of Napoleon III, and the Third Republic. Their real or invented past, with their changing quarrels and changing mystiques, continued to shape the present.

France remained an over-administered country whose people had traditionally looked to the state for a great variety of services and subsidies. Respect for the French state found expression in its people's love of official decorations, an affection that exceeded, if anything, the Germans'. (Decorations kept multiplying. By the time of the Fourth Republic there were 84 different kinds, ranging from the Postal Service Medal for industrious mailmen to the Grand Cross of the Legion of Honor. At the battle of Verdun in World War I, a posthumous decoration of valor had even been awarded to a carrier pigeon on completing a desperate mission.) France was a country in which government inspectors watched their colleagues, and *concierges* (janitors, caretakers) traditionally watched their fellow citizens to help the police. But France was also a land whose citizens traditionally took pride in their wit, discernment, disputatiousness, and skill at tax evasion. France was not an easy country to rule.

Admittedly, the shifting coalitions of moderate parties that governed the Fourth Republic did well enough domestically. But they could neither win nor end the Algerian War. By 1958 the French settlers and part of the army in Algeria were themselves in revolt; the motherland was hopelessly divided. The bulk of the militant right and the moderate republicans looked to General de Gaulle, though for very different reasons. De Gaulle had saved France in 1940 when he proclaimed continued French resistance against the Germans and defiance to the German's French collaborators. In 1944 Free French troops under de Gaulle's command had been the first to march into liberated Paris. Now, at the height of the Algerian War, de Gaulle was expected to save France again.

De Gaulle in Power

No modern Frenchman has aroused more passionate controversy than de Gaulle. (He was the only West European statesman during the postwar period subjected to several assassination attempts, all from the extreme right.) To his admirers, de Gaulle was the savior of France, the man who shaped the French Fifth Republic (as Konrad Adenauer had shaped the German Federal Republic), one of the great state-builders of the twentieth century. De Gaulle earned praise for having saved France from the Germans during World War II, from the communists during the immediate postwar years, from fascists during the Algerian imbroglio – tall, commanding, regal in bearing, a true king but not a tyrant. To his critics, de Gaulle was a villain. Representative L. Mendel Rivers, a Democrat from South Carolina, called him "the most ungrateful man since Judas Iscariot betrayed Jesus Christ."[5] These would have appeared charitable sentiments to the settler militants and *paras* (paratroopers) who in 1961 staged a rising in Algeria against de Gaulle's government. Having originally promised that France would never abandon Algeria, the General had forsworn his trust. Why should French soldiers be censured for rising against the French government? Had not Muslim soldiers bravely fought for

5 Alistair Horne, *A Savage War of Peace: Algeria, 1954–1962*, New York, Penguin, 1987, p. 380.

France – to be treacherously abandoned to their enemies? Had not de Gaulle himself rebelled against Vichy? As the paratroopers clambered into the trucks that carried them into detention, they defiantly sang an Edith Piaf number, then a popular favorite, *"Rien, je ne regrette rien"* ("There's nothing I regret.") But then neither did de Gaulle. There were trials, convictions, executions; the militant right was smashed, Algeria given up (through the Evian agreement concluded in 1962); the settlers were abandoned and so were the Muslim soldiers and civil servants who had fought for France. The Fifth Republic was never seriously challenged thereafter. The Algerian ulcer was lanced; France was ready to return to play a major part in European affairs – as de Gaulle had intended.

De Gaulle was a man who believed in principled inconsistency. While out of office, he had constantly denigrated political parties, their divisiveness, and ambitions, indeed their supposed "omnipotence." The constitutional amendment of 1962, instituting the direct election of the presidency, was meant precisely to reduce the parties' importance. Yet de Gaulle presided over a highly efficient and disciplined party of his own, and the Gaullists continued to dominate those right-wing coalitions that ran the Fifth Republic for many years. As head of state, de Gaulle considered himself the representative of that true France that had persisted for untold centuries. Nevertheless, the men and women who had rallied to him in 1940, and many of those who later served him in high office, included outsiders of every kind: there were among them adventurers and eccentrics, numerous foreigners (mostly soldiers in the Foreign Legion), and people of mixed cultural backgrounds whom old-line conservatives would have denounced as *métèques* (half-breeds). De Gaulle used them all as long as they proved useful. He did so without hesitation, for he saw himself as an uncrowned king. His bearing was regal; he towered over a crowd intellectually as well as physically – *le Grand Charles*. He was a national figure far more even than General Eisenhower, the only other general to attain presidential powers in a Western country after World War II.

De Gaulle was the supreme showman in Western politics after World War II. He gave to France what the country desperately wanted after prolonged humiliation abroad and strife at home: color, dignity, drama. As Stanley Hoffmann, an American historian, points out, a brief television speech, delivered by the general wearing his old uniform, brought to a swift end the military putsch in Algeria in 1961. Even more stunning was the *mise en scène* of de Gaulle's "disappearance" in 1968. His opponents thought that the supposedly perilous combination of student riots and workers' strikes had put an end to the old man's career. Instead, de Gaulle came back from a quick trip to the French forces in Germany, sure of the military's loyalty, a Jupiter returned to proclaim law and order to a country now profoundly hostile to revolution. Yet he never sought dictatorial powers and always warned his compatriots against the dangers of despotism.

Above all, de Gaulle was a pedagogue and an intellectual. His speeches, carefully learned by heart, were models of clarity. He could write wittily and well. His military studies, his *Mémoires de guerre* (1954–9), were not ghost-written. The General himself would surely have felt at ease under the *ancien régime*, both in a great *salon* and in the *palais royal*. There were many other anomalies. De Gaulle, a Catholic born and bred, never tired of expressing respect for the traditional values of the French family; yet it was he who gave French women the vote. De Gaulle eloquently proclaimed the virtues of the nation state against soul-less Eurocrats; nevertheless, in European affairs, it was de Gaulle who turned out to be a *fédérateur malgré lui* (a federalist despite himself) in helping to shape the EEC's agricultural policy. De Gaulle vetoed Britain's admission to the EEC in 1963; but he collaborated with Britain in projects such as the Concorde (a commercial jet plane project initiated in 1967). His vision of France emphasized the heroic virtues; yet it was de Gaulle who presided over the growth of the French consumer society. De Gaulle never tired of criticizing American power; all the same, his own military policy only made sense within an alliance that ultimately depended on the US nuclear deterrent. De Gaulle lambasted the US political and cultural impact on Europe; nevertheless, de Gaulle's constitution for France, with an elected presidency (adopted by a popular referendum in 1962), greatly profited from the American example disguised by Gaullist showmanship. De Gaulle, like Churchill and Roosevelt, had first made his name in public by using the radio. Unlike Churchill, however, de Gaulle switched to the new medium of TV with astonishing ease. As he put it, "they [the French opposition] have the newspapers, I have television."[6]

For all the General's complexities, his basic assumptions were straightforward enough. His father had been headmaster of a Jesuit school; Charles's love had been the army. He looked to France and her grandeur; he saw the world naturally divided into nation states. (He never spoke of *Europe des patries*; his favorite phrase was *Europe des états*.) The French state had been humiliated in World War II. De Gaulle made sure that its prestige would survive even when her fortunes had reached their nadir. (It was only with British help that France was accorded a seat at the Security Council of the UN in 1945.)

As de Gaulle saw it, France was dangerously threatened from without. The least of her foreign problems was British rivalry; more serious were the complications that would arise from a future German reunification. The Soviet Union posed a potential military threat, made worse by the adherence of the French communists to Moscow's cause. Above all, there was the American challenge. De Gaulle's prejudices with regard to the US were not comparable to the visceral dislike of the US evinced by Jean-Paul Sartre, and indeed by the bulk of the contemporaneous French intellectual establishment. De Gaulle simply wanted a greater say for France within Western councils. (On taking power in 1958, he unsuccessfully asked for a reorganization of NATO under a tripartite directorship, with France, Britain, and the US as members. During the Cuban crisis he was further disillusioned by US reluctance to consult its allies fully.)

Of course, de Gaulle understood perfectly well that American support, and American nuclear might, were essential for the defense of Western Europe. Yet, for de Gaulle, the American connection posed grave problems. These derived in part from the Americans' perceived moralism and unreliability. (The US, for instance, had not only abandoned but indeed condemned their French, British, and Israeli allies during the Suez crisis of 1956.) De Gaulle, and many other French politicians, equally denounced what they regarded as Washington's hegemonic claims, the Americans' "Messianic" complex, their political naïveté, and, above all, their industrial supremacy, embodying the enormous strength of an inept giant. (De Gaulle's return to power in 1958 coincided with the implementation of the Treaty of Rome, the opening of the French economy to world competition, and the increased penetration of French markets by US corporate enterprise.) France and the US were also divided by other cultural misperceptions: the bulk of French intellectuals knew little and cared less about American history; France, moreover, was the only major European country that had supplied but a handful of immigrants to the US – on the contrary, France was itself a magnet that attracted newcomers from abroad.

6 Michael Cockerell, *Live from Number 10: the Inside Story of Prime Ministers and Television*, London, Faber, 1988, p. 298.

More perilous than any foreign threat, for de Gaulle, was the menace to French unity posed by dissidents within France itself – "overmighty subjects" in the language of Tudor England. For de Gaulle, these included white settlers in Algeria, rebellious army officers, communist party chiefs, and their like. De Gaulle had never served in Africa; he did not share the African army's mystique, its love of panache, its spirit of independence. French military power would have to be re-established in Europe; only the metropolitan forces, fully mechanized, equipped with the most modern weapons, would restore France to her accustomed position as a great power.

De Gaulle looked askance, too, at political parties of the Establishment with a penchant for intrigue, subterfuge, and indiscipline. As far as de Gaulle was concerned, France had become *ingouvernable* as she had been in the days of the Fronde (a rebellious party of powerful nobles who opposed the royal court during the seventeenth century). In future, the General would not tolerate any "state within the state." French prestige abroad would be rebuilt. France would be governed under a republican constitution that would be democratic, effective, and respected. The *immobilisme* of the Fourth Republic would end for good.

The Fifth Republic was de Gaulle's personal handiwork; it proved sturdier than even his best friends could have anticipated. (By 1995, the Fifth Republic had lasted longer than each of the two Empires – under Napoleon and Napoleon III respectively – the July Monarchy, the Second and the Fourth Republics.) France made great economic progress. Something like a million and a half European settlers from North Africa (about a million from Algeria) returned to France. Most of them were now penniless, the victorious Algerians having seized their property. Nevertheless, the newcomers proved a major economic asset to France which profited from "their energy, organizational skill, and love of risk."[7] (The Algerian reflux also included many North African Jews who rejuvenated and massively augmented the Franco-Jewish community, turning it into Western Europe's largest.)

The French economy kept expanding. (In 1966, for the first time, it surpassed the British economy in its total output. Thereafter, the French economy remained the second within the European Community, following West Germany's.) The new constitution (adopted by a referendum in 1958) hinged on the presidency. In the olden days, the president had been a ceremonial head of state who received ambassadors in state, and pinned medals on the chests of the deserving. Under the Fifth Republic, the pomp became even more impressive. There were the great receptions at the Elysée, with the glitter of gold, diamonds, and candlelight. There would stand the dignitaries of the regime, men such as Georges Pompidou (de Gaulle's successor to the presidency in 1969), Michel Debré (de Gaulle's first prime minister, one of the architects of the constitution), and André Malraux (a distinguished writer, minister of state for cultural affairs), waiting in the first row like schoolboys for the president's ceremonial arrival. For ten years de Gaulle stole the limelight so effectively that none could compete. In addition to a gift for political showmanship, the General had great physical courage and an imposing personality; his retorts could crush like Queen Victoria's. Even his speeches to the public could display a mordancy that would have caused to blench almost any political consultant, ghost writer, or pollster in the US. His romanticism was tempered by realism. He possessed what counted perhaps even more in his country, a marvelous mastery of the French language: *il gouverna par le verbe* (he governed through the word).

7 William B. Cohen, "Legacy of Empire: the Algerian Connection," *Journal of Contemporary History*, vol. 15, 1980, pp. 97–123, esp. p. 100.

De Gaulle, moreover, possessed international stature to an extent that much exceeded France's position as a world power. His distrust for the US was widely shared alike by leftists and old-style patriots throughout Western Europe where American power was supreme. Eastern Europeans did not hold de Gaulle's anti-American sentiments, but they could identify with his patriotism. At the same time, de Gaulle – unlike Churchill – appealed to the Third World: a man who could rightfully claim to defend both the interests of his own country, and the ex-colonies' right to independence. If anything, de Gaulle's name was honored even more in francophone Africa and in Latin America than in France itself.

The Fifth Republic: Institutions and Politics

The new constitution was tailor-made for de Gaulle, the first president. He personally designated the prime minister. Subject to certain restrictions, the president could dissolve the Assembly at any time, and for any issue solely at his discretion. Far-reaching emergency powers were available to him when the independence of the nation or the integrity of its territory were threatened. He could bring major issues before a referendum; he had the nominating power for all civil and military offices. It was the president who was specifically charged by the constitution to guarantee the regular functioning of government. As the French say, *l'appétit vient en mangeant* (appetite grows by eating); hence presidential powers grew apace with their continued exercise. But "the steady violation of the spirit and the occasional infringement of the letter of the constitution in order to strengthen the presidency caused little stir among the French," a people not given to superstitious reverence toward the prevailing constitution.[8] It was an imperial presidency that gave to the *président de la république* even greater powers than those wielded by a British prime minister or a West German chancellor. At a time when the powers of the US president *vis à vis* Congress would contract, those of his French colleagues would expand. Nevertheless, French presidentialism developed serious weaknesses. The president held the power; his underlings took the blame. No scandal was ever allowed to touch the presidency, however embarrassing. But this came at a price. There was inadequate public discussion of nepotism and waste of public funds. All too often, the opposition therefore simply took to the streets. Ironically enough, the strong presidency envisaged by de Gaulle turned into what Jean-François Revel later described as *l'absolutisme inefficace* (incompetent absolutism).

The president was aided by the cabinet, headed by the prime minister. The prime minister directed the action of the government, bore responsibility for national defense, and assured the execution of the laws and exercised the rule-making power – but on condition that all decrees and ordinances were signed by the president. In addition to other functions, the prime minister defended the government's policy before parliament. As long as the president and the prime minister belonged to the same party and shared the same views, this duality of executive power did not matter seriously. Trouble would come later when a president and prime minister of differing parties were forced into a loveless cohabitation. (In 1986 President François Mitterrand, a socialist, called on Jacques Chirac, leader of the right, to form a government.)

8 Vincent Wright, *The Government and Politics of France*, New York, Holmes and Meier, 1989, p. 35.

The French parliament wielded much less power than it had done during the Third and Fourth Republics. It consisted of two Houses: the National Assembly and the Senate. Members of the government could neither hold parliamentary nor any other national office, an arrangement that pleased traditional spokesmen for the separation of powers as much as it would have upset a British parliamentarian at Westminister. Legislation could be initiated either by the government or by both Houses; finance bills, by contrast, had to originate in the Assembly. All laws had to be submitted to the president for promulgation. Parliament could legislate without restriction over matters such as civil rights, nationality, criminal law, and the parliamentary electoral system. Parliament also decided fundamental principles with regard to education, social security, and national defense. Wide scope, however, remained under this arrangement for legislation by executive orders issued by the government. (A complex arbitration procedure, operating through bodies such as the Constitutional Council, dealt with disputes that might arise when parliament invaded the residual powers of the government.) The constitution thus placed all manner of restrictions on the French parliament: the government had effective control of parliamentary agenda; the financial powers of parliament were severely curtailed; as was its power to force a government from office.

The president enjoyed many other advantages. There was no way in which he could control the press. But ORTF (French radio and television) functioned as a tool of government at a time when there were no competing commercial channels. As Sanche de Gramont (Ted Morgan), a French journalist and historian, put it, during the 1960s, eight million owners of French television sets were treated to a sunshine image of France as a world leader, without domestic problems, a land of bicycle-race champions and world-class surgeons. And the government never hesitated to introduce minor corrections into the news. "When George Bidault (a liberal Catholic, and a former Cabinet minister) returned from exile shortly before the June 1968 National Assembly elections, he said to a press conference 'don't vote Communist, don't vote Gaullist.' Only the first half of the sentence was reproduced in the evening news which reaches 12,000,000 persons; they have expert splicers at ORTF."[9] To do justice to the French, in the 1969 presidential elections, both Georges Pompidou and Alain Poher, the two chief candidates, pledged themselves to loosen government control over TV, and expressed support for independent commercials on the British model. Nevertheless, French presidents used official TV for all it was worth.

The first clash came in 1962. In October of that year, the National Assembly censured the manner in which de Gaulle proposed to amend the constitution by turning the presidency into an elective office. All political parties, with the exception of the Gaullists, voted for a motion censuring the government. In the subsequent referendum, the Communists, the Socialists, the moderate Catholics (united in the MRP), the Radicals (that is to say centrists), and even many right-wingers campaigned for a *non* vote. But nearly two-thirds of the voters (62 percent) supported de Gaulle as against 38 percent who opposed the General. Parliamentary elections followed. According to the final results, the UNR (Union for the New Republic, as the Gaullists were then named) gained an unprecedented 40.5 percent of the vote. The parties that had sustained the Fourth Republic all did poorly. (The Socialist Party, SFIO, or *Section française de l'Internationale ouvrière*, received 15.2 percent; the Radicals and their allies 7 percent; independents and moderates 7.4 percent, and MRP 5.3 percent.) Only the Communists held their own with 21.3 percent

9 Morgan, *The French: Portrait of a People*, p. 237.

Election day was indeed the Day of the General.[10] By contrast, the MRP, Radicals and Socialists went into a decline from which only the Socialists would recover.

French politics thereafter were marked by *bipolarization*. During the Fourth Republic politics had hinged on the centrist parties and their intricate parliamentary maneuvers that resulted in rapid changes of government. It was a stylized political ballet that came to bore the spectators. Under the Fifth Republic, by contrast, the strongest party in the country was the governing party. Bipolarization involved government by a well-organized right-wing coalition of a kind unknown under the Fourth Republic. It would rule for more than 20 years. Under the new system, the presidency became the supreme electoral prize – as was the case in the US. Moreover, the individual parties themselves became "presidentialized" in the sense of giving increased power to their respective leaders, a process accelerated by the impact of television which exalted the role of individual champions on the screen. At the same time, the political parties increasingly developed into "catch-all" organizations (*partis attrape tout*). In order to do so, they had to cultivate the art of political compromise and give up some of their former ideological quarrels. In a way never anticipated by de Gaulle, political parties remained crucial to the French political structure. (Ironically enough, the constitution of the Fifth Republic, as created by de Gaulle, was the first in French history actually to mention political parties.)

This political structure was remarkably solid. A romantic mythology notwithstanding, France by the 1960s was far less affected by challenges from the street than ever before in her history. In 1968 students and workers in Paris briefly joined for massive political demonstrations and strikes – the so-called Events of 1968. The students had come to hate overcrowding in dormitories, lecture rooms, and libraries; they were tired of antiquated plants and out-of-date curricula. The workers wanted higher pay. A minority of young rebels looked to a Messianic transformation of society, but there was never a chance for revolution. The "Events" turned into a festival and a public "happening" which left the traditional power structure almost unchanged.

From 1958 to 1974, the Gaullists, remarkably, ruled with an absolute majority in the National Assembly. The Gaullists formed the strongest political party, and the new parliamentary system provided them with a safe parliamentary base. De Gaulle firmly kept the key positions in the hands of his own faithful, men such as Michel Debré, Georges Pompidou, and Maurice Couve de Murville, who would usually do the General's bidding. Essentially, the Gaullists retained their identity, even though their party's nomenclature underwent a number of confusing changes. (It had been founded in 1947 as the Rally of the French People, RPF; it later became known as the Union for the New Republic, UNR; thereafter as Union of Democrats for the Republic, UDR.) The party was transformed into an effective mass organization with an estimated 500,000 members, and strong grass-roots organizations. The UDR was "ecumenical" in the sense that it enjoyed support from many different social groups. (It attracted votes, not merely from middle-class and lower middle-class people, but also had substantial support among workers, especially skilled people and supervisors.) The party was also a political supermarket as regards ideas. There was old-fashioned *Gaullisme gaullien*, defined by personal loyalty to the general; there was *Gaullisme droitier*, fired by hatred of communists; there was *Gaullisme présidentiel*, displayed by voters who simply backed the government

10 Roy C. Macridis, ed., *Modern Political Systems: Europe*. Englewood Cliffs, NJ, Prentice-Hall, 1963, p. 239; Paul Godt, ed., *Policy Making in France from de Gaulle to Mitterand*, London and New York, Pinter, 1989.

whatever it did; and there were others. The party provided home for all and sundry: economic liberals and *dirigistes*; protagonists of the welfare state and critics of the welfare state; pro-Europeans and anti-Europeans; supporters and opponents of conscription; there was something for almost every political taste.

The Gaullists likewise received support from the *Fédération nationale des républicains indépendants* (IR), founded by Giscard d'Estaing in 1965. (The various Giscardist parties later joined with a number of centrist groups to form the Union for French Democracy or UDF.) The IR was socially more conservative but politically more liberal than the Gaullist party. Giscard d'Estaing thus had much support from practicing Catholics, elderly middle-class people, and from women – a party of pious widows, sneered his critics. His backing also derived to a disproportionate degree from managerial, commercial, and professional occupations. His overall policy was even more "European" than Pompidou's. (Giscard had actually been born in Koblenz, in the German Rhineland, where his father had served as director of finance in the French occupation after World War I.)

Overall, the conservatives' coalition turned from national glory – the goal nearest to de Gaulle's heart – to the pursuit of economic efficiency and prosperity – the themes dearest to de Gaulle's successors. The leaders formed part of a genuine élite. De Gaulle liked men with a fine war record. (André Malraux, a leading Gaullist intellectual, later a minister of state, had done well in the Resistance during World War II, rising to be colonel-commandant of a brigade. Michel Debré, prime minister 1959–62, had won the coveted *Croix de guerre*; so had Jacques Chaban-Delmas, prime minister 1969–72, and Pierre Messmer, prime minister 1972–4.) Some of them had gained experience as mayors of large cities (Chaban-Delmas in Bordeaux, Jacques Chirac, who became prime minister in 1974, in Paris.) They comprised among their number numerous graduates from the *grandes écoles*, including the *Ecole normale supérieure* (Pompidou) and the *Ecole nationale d'administration* (ENA). (The so-called *énarques* included Chirac and Giscard d'Estaing as well as other politicians of later prominence such as Michel Rocard, Laurent Fabius and Alain Juppé. The *énarques* in particular filled top jobs in the administration, nationalized industries, and private enterprise. Chosen for their ability, they formed a freemasonry who considered themselves the *crème de la crème*, and regarded service to the state as the highest honor a Frenchman could achieve.) Many leading men had seen service in the financial administration, the élite of the French civil service. (Chirac had been a counsellor at the *Cour de comptes*; Giscard and Chaban-Delmas had been *Inspecteurs des finances*.)

They were men of culture. For instance, Georges Pompidou, a former professor of literature, had written on Taine, Malraux, and Racine. The French right was just like the French left in that intellectuals were taken seriously in a manner inconceivable either in English-speaking countries or West Germany. Frenchmen found nothing strange in the fact that Pompidou should correspond, say, with François Mauriac, a leading Catholic thinker, on the spiritual significance of Dostoevsky's *The Possessed*. De Gaulle's letter to Jean-Paul Sartre, disassociating himself from Bertrand Russell's Vietnam tribunal, an anti-American propaganda stunt, was a public event of a kind inconceivable in an English- or German-speaking country.

Gaullist Legacy

The Fifth Republic, under conservative governance, has been described by Stanley Hoffmann, a leading expert on France, as resting on a "state-led symbiosis between the

ruling élite, the national organization of businessmen (CNPF) and the largest organization of farmers (FNSEA)."[11] The civil service élite assured stability, continuity, and made
many of the key economic decisions. Hence the Fifth Republic might be described in
Hoffmann's words as *la république des fonctionnaires*. The picture may be somewhat overdrawn. There were dissensions both within and between the major lobbies. The *énarques*
had no agreed party line; indeed, quite a number of them were Socialists. Nevertheless,
the middle classes formed the most powerful group within the state, especially given the
weaknesses and divisions within the trade-union movement.

The opposition was even more divided than the Gaullists and their supporters. Apart
from the Communists, de Gaulle's main critics were the Socialists. Their party was in
severe trouble until rebuilt by François Mitterrand who, in 1971, took over the leadership
from Alain Savary. By this time traditional hostilities had softened. The anti-clerical
legacy (once represented in rural France by the conflict between the village schoolmaster
and the *curé*) went by the board; so did most of the party's Marxist inheritance. The
Socialists now looked to neo-Keynesian remedies for French economic ills. The party
became open to liberal ideas derived from members of the Club Jean Moulin and similar bodies whose members joined the Socialist Party. The party became interested in
novel ideas such as administrative decentralization – anathema to the old-style Jacobins.
Socialists also tended to be "European" in orientation. (Jean Monnet was a Socialist, so
was his disciple Jacques Delors, both leading figures in the history of the EC.) Not that
the Socialists were ideologically united – on the contrary, good socialists always liked
an argument. But they now pulled together where it counted – in practical politics.

Mitterrand's most important task was to enlarge the party's social base, for it could
not win as long as it remained identified mainly with school teachers, shopkeepers, civil
servants, clerks, and pensioners. The party also had some working-class support, about
25 percent of its membership during the early 1960s. But the party's appeal to the
workers did not rival the Communists' (who then claimed a working-class membership
of about 45 percent). Mitterrand also had to find a means of emphasizing the difference
between Gaullists and Socialists. After all, the Gaullists, between 1944 and 1945, had
been the first to institute national economic planning; in those early years, moreover,
the Gaullists had carried out more nationalizations than the Socialists had ever proposed
during the Third Republic. The Gaullists were as critical of the US as the Socialists.
Above all, Mitterrand had to appeal to an electorate whose majority feared the Communists, and would in the end vote for the powers that be.

Mitterrand thus called for a socialism that would entail not merely a change of *patrons*
but a change of life – a definition so all-embracing as to become acceptable to Marxists
and non-Marxists, Catholics and free-thinkers, feminists and traditionalists.[12] From being
a battle ground of different factions, the party became united, with a rejuvenated and
well-educated élite, an increased membership, a wider electoral appeal, willing and able

11 Stanley Hoffmann, "Year One," *New York Review of Books*, 12 August 1982, pp. 37–43 (a
major review article).
12 Frank L. Wilson, *The French Democratic Left, 1963–1969: toward a Modern Party System*, Stanford,
CA, Stanford University Press, 1971; Denis MacShane, *François Mitterrand: a Political Odyssey*,
London, Quartet, 1982; Daniel Singer, *Is Socialism Doomed? The Meaning of Mitterrand*, New York,
Oxford University Press, 1988; François Mitterrand, *The Wheat and the Chaff*, New York, Seaver
Books/Lattes, 1982; Sonia Mazey and Michael Newman, eds, *Mitterrand's France*, London and New
York, Croom Helm, 1987.

to make alliances with other parties on the Socialists' own terms. These partners included the Communists. In 1972, the Socialists and Communists went as far as to unite in the *Union de la gauche* for a single government program in the 1973 parliamentary elections. It was not an easy agreement to reach, given the long-standing tradition of mutual hostility between the two parties, worsened by more recent controversy over fundamental issues such as the Sino-Soviet split and the Soviet record in Eastern Europe. But Mitterrand was a brilliant tactician – one of those few democratic statesmen who, like de Gaulle, invariably out-foxed his Communist allies. In the 1973 parliamentary elections, the Socialists turned out to be the winners on the left; they attained 19 percent of the vote, and doubled the number of their deputies to 91. The Socialists gained a large infusion of new blood into what had long been an almost dormant party. In the long run, they would prevail over all their rivals on the left.

The French Communist Party (PCF), by contrast, never emerged from its traditional position as a militant ghetto. The party further eroded its image through a series of purges that faintly mirrored the bloody liquidation of dissidents periodically carried out in the Soviet Union. These purges included the so-called Servin–Casanova affair in the early 1960s when the PCF expelled from its leadership "Italians" (adherents of the "soft line" taken by the Italian Communist Party), Khrushchevites, and other miscreants who desired a premature *perestroika*. This is not to say that the PCF counted for nothing. On the contrary, the Communist Party's electoral strength remained impressive, despite other fluctuations in the national vote. (In the parliamentary elections held in 1973, the Communists gained 5,026,417 votes on the first ballot, almost as many votes as the party had gained in 1946 when the PCF stood at the height of its power in the immediate postwar years.) Despite internal dissensions, the Communist Party remained powerful and rigidly organized in a hierarchical fashion, according to the Leninist principle of "democratic centralism." It remained Muscovite in orientation. (The PCF thus strongly supported the Soviet invasion of Hungary in 1956. It was only in 1966 that the party's newspaper *L'Humanité* was willing to take an open stand against Moscow by criticizing a political trial in the Soviet Union.)[13]

The party was, at first, governed in the spirit of an absolute monarchy by Maurice Thorez, an arch-Stalinist who rejoiced in a Stalinist personality cult of his own. The PCF continued to be run on monarchical lines by Georges Marchais, after an uncharacteristically permissive interlude under Waldeck Rochet who served between the two afore-mentioned leaders (1964–8). Like other communist parties, the PCF was run by a nomenklatura whose members enjoyed all kinds of privileges, with their own automobiles, villas, chauffeurs, and bodyguards. The party's permanent cadres, a highly disciplined crew never numbering less than 10,000, tightly organized in "cells" and "sections", were supported by a dues-paying membership (estimated at about 225,000 to 275,000 during the 1960s). The party could draw on sympathizers in every walk of life, especially academia, the publishing industry, labor, journalism, the youth movements, even business. The party had built a economic empire with great investments, an impressive patronage machine, and mass organizations (especially among labor unions). The PCF commanded

13 For a general study of the French left as a whole, see Tony Judt, *Marxism and the French Left: Studies in Labour and Politics in France, 1830–1981*, Oxford, Clarendon Press, 1986; Irwin M. Wall, *French Communism in the Era of Stalin: the Quest for Unity and Integration, 1945–1962*, Westport, Conn., Greenwood Press, 1983; Ronald Tiersky, *French Communism 1920–1972*, New York, Columbia University Press, 1974.

its own intellectuals, lawyers, business experts, technicians, and strongmen. The party acted alike as a counter-church for the faithful, a political lobby, and a Mafia; it was more skilled in looking after its clients than any other oppositional group.

While the party could never claim to represent even a majority of the industrial working class, the PCF drew support from a substantial body of middle- and lower middle-class voters, making the PCF far more than a mere party of proletarians. In geographical terms, the PCF was strongest in the north-east (specially in the working-class districts of Paris, and in mining areas), in Mediterranean regions, and in the south-east where social and religious dissent had always been influential. The Catholic west (especially Brittany) and the Catholic east (Alsace, Lorraine, Savoy) proved almost inaccessible to the Communists. Nevertheless, the PCF remained formidable – all the more so because of its appeal to French intellectuals. The party claimed to be the legitimate heir of the Jacobins, of a great revolutionary tradition that France had given to mankind. Not even the Gaullists were as skilled in draping their party program with the tricolor as were the Communists. The French Communist Party was the most anti-German of French parties. The Communists never tired of denouncing West Germany for its alleged militarism and its Nazi past. The Communists were even more outspoken in their detestation of the US, in their estimation the world's chief warmonger. But as Tony Judt, an American expert on the French, points out, French Marxists, from Sartre and Merleau-Ponty to Althusser, had little to say to those who would understand the realities of French labor relations, politics, social and economic change. For all their pride in their assumed dialectical, critical, and investigative abilities, French Marxists proved even less competent in understanding the social realities of Eastern Europe and the Soviet Union, or the ongoing crisis that would beset all Marxist–Leninist systems throughout the globe. (In British historian Michael Howard's harsh phrase, intellectual Paris after World War II was a madhouse where Albert Camus and Raymond Aron provided almost the only sane voices.) It was only from the 1970s that the stranglehold of Marxism on the French intellectual imagination loosened, and finally broke.

For all its apparent strength, the PCF faced severe long-term problems that it would not solve. Over the long haul, its membership diminished and its discipline weakened. Traditionally, the PCF had been much more than a political party, a counter-society which provided for the party faithful all sorts of activities: from cycling, or chess, children's holiday camps to earnest self-improvement through study groups and lectures. The continuing rise in living standards, the growth of consumerism, tourism, and of a new youth culture weakened traditional bonds. Oddly enough, the PCF found itself out-flanked on the left by militant students of the New Left who rejectd the old-style party discipline in favor of a new utopian ideology that attempted to blend the thought of Karl Marx with the real or assumed insights of Sigmund Freud and Simone de Beauvoir.

Even the most blinkered of party hacks, moreover, could no longer ignore the work of giants such as Alexander Solzhenitsyn in uncovering Soviet realities. There were Communist attempts in France, as in other Catholic countries, to seek a new dialogue with the Catholic Church. The party, as always, also had to cope with heretics within the PCF's own ranks, disillusioned men and women, who tried to reform the party from within. From the mid-1960s, the PCF tried to liberalize its doctrines. But it did so by fits and starts; "de-Sovietization" thus turned out to be a long and painful process, while the party's electoral fortunes continued to decline.

Despite numerous forecasts to the contrary, it was de Gaulle, and his Fifth Republic that triumphed – not the Communists nor the right-wing militants. France continued to modernize her economy at an accelerating speed. The old France of small farms, corner shops, and village cafés increasingly retreated before urban industrial France – with plate glass, neon signs, tractors, trucks, and jet planes. The France of 1969, the year of de Gaulle's resignation from the presidency, was incredibly different from France at the time of liberation, 25 years earlier. De Gaulle presided over a country in the throes of immense change; according to René Remond, a distinguished French historian, the right, with its roots in the past, was even more innovative in this process than the left.[14] This transformation was not exactly the aim for which de Gaulle had fought. De Gaulle believed in the heroic virtues – not the institutions of capitalism as such. It was Pompidou rather than de Gaulle who changed Gaullism into a modern conservative movement that emphasized welfarism and private enterprise, rather than national glory. Nevertheless, it was de Gaulle who set the course, and restored to France her long-lost self-confidence.

De Gaulle, like Konrad Adenauer in West Germany, also built a new army. The French forces that came into being after the end of the Algerian War strikingly differed from their predecessors. During the Algerian War, the bulk of French forces had been deployed in Algeria – most of them conscripts, most of them footsoldiers fit only to fight guerrillas in the bush. De Gaulle, by contrast, wanted a mechanized army, equipped with the most powerful weapons money could buy, deployed in Europe, and trained to conduct a war of movement. This is what he got: a modern force, well equipped, far more formidable than any peacetime force that France had ever fielded since the end of World War I. The navy and the air force were likewise modernized, and France developed her own independent nuclear deterrent, however limited in size. French military modernization reflected the modernization of French industry during the 1950s and 1960s; French *Mirage* fighters and French tanks proved as good as any in the world.

There were, however, ironic inconsistencies in de Gaulle's attitude toward NATO and toward the US. The General never tired of criticizing the Americans' moralism and their inability to understand the harsh facts of *realpolitik*. But when de Gaulle condemned US policy in Vietnam (for instance, at a speech in Phnom Penh in Cambodia in 1966), his own moralizing would have done credit to a Yankee preacher. De Gaulle vaguely talked of a Europe from the Atlantic to the Urals – a Europe that would include Russia, but not the US. The vision was a fantasy. A moment's reflection should have persuaded the General that ties of history, culture, politics, and trade linked Western Europe to the US infinitely more closely than to Russia, no matter who ruled in Moscow. De Gaulle demanded that France should plan an independent role in the Western alliance, playing off her allies against one another and the US. Nevertheless, in the event of a war, France could not have stayed neutral. American support was essential – a fact perfectly clear to as competent a professional soldier as de Gaulle. (In fact, the General had good military reasons for resenting the deployment of massive US forces in South-East Asia. The Vietnam War diverted US resources, thereby paralleling – in de Gaulle's view – French errors in Algeria.) A practitioner of *realpolitik*, however, would not have denigrated France's chief ally; some of the most loyal Atlanticists were therefore found in the French ministry of defense.

On the other hand, the armed forces, as reorganized during the Gaullist years, were integrated into French society, a remarkable achievement in a country that had experienced both the Dreyfus case (a judicial scandal involving a Jewish officer wrongfully

14 René Remond and Jean-François Sirinelli, *Notre siècle, 1918–1988 (Histoire de France*, no. 6), Paris, Fayard, 1988.

convicted of treason in 1894, later rehabilitated) and the Algerian imbroglio. Hence-forth, the armed forces remained loyal to the government. (During the *événements* – the 1968 student riots in Paris and the widespread workers' strikes – the army remained firm.) Student demonstrations might frighten deans and provosts, but not generals, well aware that academic militants strove for a *coup de théâtre* rather than a *coup d'état*. By the same token, the army lost all praetorian ambitions. By the time de Gaulle left office, the notion of governing France through a military dictatorship would have seemed as outlandish to the mass of the French people as enthroning once more the Bourbon monarchy. Even nuclear weaponry was acceptable to the bulk of the electorate. France never developed a peace movement, or a movement for nuclear disarmament on the scale existing in Britain, the US, or West Germany. For even the most conservative of army officers, the Republic had ceased to be "the Slut."

Gaullist France proved equally successful in absorbing something like 1,500,000 refugees, Europeans who had left North Africa upon decolonization (the great majority from Algeria). The Algerian War had been fought with utter cruelty – Algerians against Algerians, Algerians against French, French against French. (Alistair Horne entitles his book about the Algerian War *A Savage War of Peace*.) The Algerian soldiers who had fought for France were abandoned with cynical indifference to rebel vengeance. The white Algerian refugees had lost all their possessions; many of them had been trauma-tized. They had also incurred widespread unpopularity in metropolitan France itself. To de Gaulle, they were a disloyal lot. According to the prevailing demonology of the left, the *pieds noirs* (white settlers in Algeria) were not only racists but also parasites whose prosperity had derived from the ruthless exploitation of native Algerian land and labor. Had this theory been true, Algeria should have benefited economically from the settlers' departure, whereas France should have suffered from their arrival. In fact, Algeria fared ill, whereas the returnees proved an asset to France.[15] France was certainly fortunate in that decolonization coincided with economic prosperity; the task of resettlement proved no more difficult in the case of the *pieds noirs* than of expatriate white Rhodesians, Kenyans, and their line. The Fifth Republic deserves credit for accomplishing the task with unforeseen ease.

The Fifth Republic likewise merits respect for the manner in which the remaining French colonies were peacefully emancipated in "Black Africa." Engaged in a bitter Alger-ian War, France could not at the same time hold on by force to the remainder of her African Empire. The French initially tried to associate the French African possessions with Paris through a "French Union" in which the member states enjoyed extensive powers of self-government. But in 1958 Guinea voted for immediate independence. In 1960 the remaining French African states followed suit. (The "French Union" was succeeded by the "French Community," a loose association. Senegal, Gabon, Chad, the Congo, the Central African Republic, and Madagascar stayed. Niger and the Ivory Coast relinquished formal membership, but continued their connection through special accords.)

Not that the militant right disappeared. The French security forces ruthlessly suppressed real or suspected assassins determined to kill the General. There was indeed no dearth of Frenchmen or Frenchwomen who still looked back nostalgically to *Algérie française* or to the Vichy regime, who disliked Jews, who hated immigrants – especially Arabs – or who simply felt – as French people had from times immemorial – that the state took too much in the way of taxes, and gave too little in return. But the Poujadists (followers

15 William B. Cohen, "Legacy of Empire: the Algerian Connection," p. 100.

of Pierre Poujade, leader of a French "tax revolt movement", and self-appointed spokesman for the small shopkeepers and artisans) could not turn their organization into a national movement. The militant right remained divided, and without true leadership.

In foreign policy, de Gaulle was in some respects uncannily far-sighted, in others surprisingly obtuse. A nationalist to the core, he came to understand the power of nationalism among Muslim Algerians as well as Eastern and Central Europeans. He felt certain that Soviet imperialism would not prevail in the long run over the national sentiments of Poles, Czechs, and East Germans. In trying to gain more political influence for France within the Western alliance, he moved closer to West Germany. Right from their first meeting at Colombey-les-deux-églises (1962), Adenauer and de Gaulle, two aging gentlemen, got on extremely well. West Germany and France cooperated both politically and economically. (The French succeeded in getting special protection for their large farming sector within the European Economic Community, while conceding comparable advantages to West German manufactured products in the French market.)

It was certainly unrealistic on de Gaulle's part to assume that – given a choice – West Germany would rely on France rather than the US. Yet, as we have pointed out before, the extent of de Gaulle's anti-Americanism can easily be over-estimated. Franco-American friction was real enough. (There was no French ethnic lobby in the US.) But American intellectuals tended to admire French culture. In the popular mind, France was associated with *haute cuisine*, high fashion, and *savoir faire*. No deep-seated conflicts divided the two countries. France thus stuck firmly to the West over issues such as Khrushchev's "ultimatum" over West Berlin, when Moscow demanded that West Berlin should be turned into a neutralized free city (November 1958). Guided by notions of prestige more than profit, de Gaulle and many of his supporters likewise attacked the "penetration" of Europe by US investors, managers, and technologists, an issue dramatized by Jean-Louis Schreiber's book *Le défi américain* (*The American Challenge*, 1968). But again, realism reasserted itself. US funds were obviously needed to promote French economic modernization. In 1966, following a reorganization of the government, Michel Debré became finance minister, and all but discarded the restrictive policies that had been previously followed.

How much then did de Gaulle achieve? Critics such as the French historian Serge Bernstein point out that much of de Gaulle's work had been initiated by the Fourth Republic which the General so much despised. The Fourth Republic had initiated decolonization by giving independence to Indonesia, Tunis, and Morocco. The Fourth Republic had begun to develop atomic weapons. The Fourth Republic had striven both for closer association and for French leadership in Western Europe. The Fourth Republic had successfully promoted economic expansion and economic modernization. (De Gaulle, in 1958, thus reluctantly appointed as his finance minister Antoine Pinay, a parliamentarian of the old school but, for businessmen, a representative of common sense.) De Gaulle was a leader who still believed in *grandeur* for France – at a time when most Frenchmen and Frenchwomen preferred *bonheur* (happiness). The means at the General's disposal were never equal to his ambitions. But for all his love of glory, de Gaulle "left a country closer to domestic appeasement than the one he had found."[16] By the very

16 Stanley Hoffmann, *Decline or Renewal? France since the 1930s*, New York, Viking Press, 1974, p. 433; Serge Bernstein, *The Republic of de Gaulle 1958–1969*, Cambridge, Cambridge University Press, 1993; Jack Hayward, ed., *De Gaulle to Mitterrand*, London, Hurst, 1993; Georgette Elgey, *Histoire de la Quatrième République*, 2 vols, Paris, Fayard, 1993.

manner in which the General stepped down from power, he peacefully consolidated the Republic. When he left office, France was infinitely better off economically than the most ardent optimist could have hoped for when de Gaulle took over the government in 1944. (He relinquished it in 1946, and returned in 1958.) Thereafter, de Gaulle created a new style of governance – later taken over by Mitterrand. De Gaulle conducted himself in a regal fashion, as did Mitterrand when he later gained the presidency. In a country whose citizens like to lambast authority, the presidency gained respect.

It was de Gaulle's tragedy that he clung to power too long. By the time of his resignation his grandeur was becoming tarnished. His anti-NATO line was widely criticized; so was the cost of France's independent nuclear deterrent; so was the showy regalism that increasingly irritated Frenchmen, especially those militant students and workers who had taken to the streets during the *événements* of 1968. It fell to Georges Pompidou, his successor, to rebuild Gaullism on new lines. Pompidou had started his career as a loyalist of loyalists. He had served as de Gaulle's prime minister for six years, longer than any prime minister in French Republican history. In 1968, de Gaulle replaced him, ostensibly at Pompidou's own request. According to one school of thought, de Gaulle wished to get rid of a potential *dauphin* (crown prince), a man grown too big for his boots. Another interpretation credits de Gaulle with an even more Machiavellian intent; de Gaulle wanted Pompidou as a successor, but ousted him so as to disassociate Pompidou from the government's own unpopularity after the 1968 riots. Whatever the rights and wrongs of this controversy, Pompidou was a Gaullist very different from de Gaulle and his original entourage. During the disastrous year 1939–40, Pompidou had honorably served as an infantry officer. But thereafter, he had neither rallied to the Free French forces nor to the armed Resistance. After the war he had briefly worked as a teacher and thereafter went into banking. He rose to be director-general of the Rothschild Bank in Paris where, in Vincent Wright's apt phrase, he had acquired a taste for the company of the well heeled, the well read, and the well bred. He was also a man of genuine culture and erudition whose views on art and literature made news in a way unimaginable for a British or American politician. He was well qualified for the presidency.

On taking over, Pompidou dispensed with some of de Gaulle's more costly extravaganzas. Some industrial prestige projects were abandoned. The franc was devalued so as to make French exports more competitive. In a more general sense, it was Pompidou who changed Gaullism from an old-style nationalist movement to a modern conservative body that emphasized wealth – not glory. It was Pompidou's supreme ambition to expand France's position as a great power. This object took priority over all other concerns. Pompidou thus clashed with his own prime minister, Jacques Chaban-Delmas, over the latter's proposal to restructure the French social security system, to introduce worker participation into the management of major enterprises. Pompidou himself had risen from obscurity by his own efforts. (He was born in the Massif Central, one of the poorest parts of France; he was the son of a primary school teacher in straitened circumstances.) No social guilt complex would ever trouble Pompidou. He saw French greatness in terms of the enterprise state.

Pompidou's foreign policy likewise diverged to some extent from his predecessor's. Relations with NATO improved. Pompidou personally represented France at crucial meetings of the EC. De Gaulle's opposition to the British entry into the EC was abandoned. (It was personal talks between Pompidou and Edward Heath, the British prime minister, that enabled Britain to enter in 1973.) In other respects, however, the Gaullist legacy continued. Pompidou maintained the trappings of an independent relationship with the

Soviet Union, embodied in presidential visits to Russia, and the conclusion of several economic and technical agreements. In the oil crisis of 1973, Pompidou ingloriously responded by courting the Arab states at Israel's expense, while seeking profitable armament and engineering contracts.

Toward the end of his career, tragedy struck the president. Pompidou sickened, and the strong-minded statesman turned into an invalid who feebly clung to office. At the same time, the Gaullist party weakened. The party suffered a severe electoral setback when the Gaullists lost their previous majority in the National Assembly. At the same time, they wielded diminishing influence within the presidential coalition that governed France. (It was, however, not until 1988 that the Gaullists for the first time became a minority within the right inside the National Assembly.) The Gaullists increasingly became the party of the elderly, the churchgoers, the country-bred, and the conservatively minded, especially conservatively minded women. When Pompidou died in 1974, his successor was Giscard d'Estaing, a liberal who had more in common with John F. Kennedy than Charles de Gaulle.

The Fifth Republic was not overly beloved by the public: it lacked the flamboyant inspiration of earlier French republics. In the olden days, the patriotic, anti-clerical primary school teacher *(instituteur)* had served as a moral role model for republicans. Under de Gaulle and thereafter, the primary school teacher became the archetypal social failure. To their number would later be added that host of once-famous French intellectuals who had once won fame by whitewashing the Soviet Union's and blackening the US's reputation. (Prominent intellectuals hostile to communism had included some French luminaries such as Raymond Aron, but the majority were foreigners such as Denis de Rougemont, a Swiss; Ignazio Silone, an Italian; Manus Sperber, an Austrian; Karl Jaspers, a German; Sidney Hook, an American; Stephen Spender, George Orwell, and Arthur Koestler, naturalized in Britain.) By contrast, practical politicians such as Pompidou and Giscard d'Estaing represented *la France qui gagne* (France which makes money) – not the disinherited. The new France was nevertheless immensely successful. During the 1960s and the 1970s France consistently outperformed the growth rates of Germany and the United States; French unemployment was among the word's lowest. Above all, the Fifth Republic attained what its predecessors had lacked – unchallenged political stability. It was a remarkable achievement.

5

Britain and the Smaller Northern Democracies, 1959–1974

Britain: Tories Take Charge

On Saturday, 30 June 1965, a funeral cortège made its way through a huge and silent London crowd. To the sound of slow music and muffled drums, a hundred sailors of the Royal Navy pulled a gun carriage bearing Sir Winston Churchill's last remains. The procession slowly went from Whitehall to St Paul's Cathedral where – in deliberate breach of court etiquette – the Queen sat waiting for the last arrival of her great subject. When the service was over, Churchill's body was buried in the family site close to Blenheim Palace, his birthplace. An estimated 350,000,000 people throughout the world watched on their TV screens. It was the end of an era.

Churchill (1874–1965) was the last survivor of the World War II triumvirate – Churchill, Roosevelt, and Stalin. (In Western Europe, only de Gaulle could remotely rival Churchill's fame.) No British prime minister thereafter could share in Churchill's national and international appeal. His demise also marked a historical break in a wider sense. When Churchill had moved into No. 10 Downing Street in 1940, Great Britain still ranked as one of the world's great powers, despite her evident or concealed weaknesses. The British Empire remained the greatest the world had ever seen. In terms of territories directly or indirectly under British control, the empire had reached its zenith by the end of World War II. In 1945 the British had reconquered the imperial territories briefly occupied by Japan; British troops policed the formerly Italian colonies, Ethiopia and Libya. Britain was supreme on the African continent; the Mediterranean seemed for a brief time a British lake. British troops were stationed far afield – in Germany, Austria, Greece, the Near East, the Indian sub-continent, the Far East. The British Empire seemed the world's greatest, and few Britons realized how far its might had come to depend on US aid. (Decolonization, it should be added, only began in 1947 when India and Pakistan achieved independence, followed in 1948 by Burma.) Even thereafter, enthusiasts would still place their hope in Britain's "Third Empire" in Africa which only began to dissolve in 1957 when Ghana peacefully assumed sovereign status. As regards Britain's status in Europe, Britain remained unquestionably the foremost European state – by no matter what criterion – military power, popular well-being, freedom from widespread crime (which actually dropped after the end of World War II), the purchase of consumer durables, or national production. (In 1951 even West Germany's gross domestic product amounted to only 56 percent of Great Britain's.)[1] Above all, Britain impressed visitors by its stability: a country where class struggles were contained, party strife remained in bounds, parliament was honored, kingship revered, and authority obeyed. (Rationing

1 Alfred F. Havighurst, *Britain in Transition: the Twentieth Century*, Chicago, University of Chicago Press, 1985, pp. 403–64; Martin Pugh, *State and Society: British Political and Social History, 1870–1992*, London, Edward Arnold, 1994.

continued after World War II, but the black market remained more restricted in Britain than in any other former belligerent country in Europe, while the British surely submitted the world's most honest tax returns.) A great deal of ink was spilled over upper-class British spies who furnished secrets to the Soviet Union and who supposedly typified patrician independence spiced with sodomy ("the homintern"). Less often mentioned was the fact that traitors such as Kim Philby were as little characteristic of the British upper class as Klaus Fuchs, another spy, was of German refugees in Britain, and that the Soviet and US secret services leaked no less than the British.

After the end of World War II, believers in democratic socialism all over the world looked to British experience under the Labour government (1945–51). Britain was the world's only major country where a social democratic government held sway. Labour had already occupied a powerful place in Churchill's wartime coalition when most ministries concerned with social and economic issues had been held by Labour men, while Churchill and Churchill's close allies ran military affairs and foreign policy. The British had performed well; for all the Nazis' Führer worship, British democracy had mobilized more effectively for total war than Germany. Rationing had been enforced more fairly than in Nazi-occupied Europe. Above all, Britain had won – and few Britons realized how dependent they had been on American economic and military aid in the pursuit of total victory, and how dependent they would remain in the aftermath of war. Overall, the British trusted their state and were willing to enlarge its powers.

The new Labour government was committed to extending the welfare state, managing the economy, and nationalizing key industries. Such a program alone would ensure "fair shares for all," a goal common to many Conservative and Liberal voters. The coal, iron, and steel industries were nationalized. The welfare state came to fruition with the creation of the National Health Service in 1948, a reform that no Conservative government thereafter dared to abandon. The Conservative Party, returned to office under Churchill's leadership in 1951, accepted the welfare state, Keynesian techniques of demand management, and also Labour's indifference toward creeping inflation. The Conservatives during the 1960s were fortunate in that world economic conditions improved; Britain's trade and industrial production continued to grow, albeit far more slowly than its main competitors'. By 1962 West Germany, for the first time, moved ahead. Thereafter the gap would continue to widen. Germany, France, and Italy all expanded economically at a faster rate than Britain.

When the war ended, Britain's political reputation likewise stood high abroad. Foreign well-wishers praised her stability. The French Fifth Republic, the Italian Republic, the German Federal Republic were all postwar creations. British political institutions, by contrast, seemed to be rooted in the distant past. Visitors might express their shock at, or admiration for, "Swinging London" of the 1960s; they might fret over student violence and rising crime rates; but overall Britain remained an extraordinarily stable country, despite student riots and miners' strikes. As Lord Annan put it in a brilliant study, the 1960s should not simply be remembered as an age of zaniness. British colleges and universities displayed great vitality; the theater and the arts flourished. British popular music swept the world. English soccer players regained their supremacy in the World Cup. Manual workers, for the first time, became habituated to taking holidays abroad. After the long deprivations in wartime and the postwar years, British people once more had a taste of honey.[2] British economic performance might leave much to be

2 Noel Annan, *Our Age. English Intellectuals between World Wars: a Group Portrait*, New York, Random House, 1990.

desired, but Britain was in no wise economically decadent. (Between 1938 and 1975, the British national income, in real terms, increased by 2.3 times.)[3]

Britain possessed another advantage, the so-called special relationship with the US. Not that all went well between the two countries. Britain and the US clashed over economic policies, and over the speed and direction of decolonization. From the 1960s onward, West Germany, not Britain, counted as the US's principal ally in Europe. There were also intangibles. The traditional British ruling class had widely disliked Yankees for their real or alleged vulgarity, materialism, and rootlessness. These prejudices, thereafter, were widely taken over by the left-wing intelligentsia.

As regards the US, the great majority of Americans could no longer trace their ancestry to the British Isles, as in the early days of the republic. War strengthened US nationalism, as the GIs returned, convinced that the US was best, and that no foreign country had anything to teach Americans. Once the war ended, the so-called GI Bill assured a college education to millions of veterans of the most diverse ethnic backgrounds. These men found new careers and their collective impact greatly weakened the power of the traditional East Coast Establishment, with its anglophile pretensions.

Nevertheless, relations between Britain and the US remained close. In wartime, some two million US servicemen had, for a time, been stationed in Britain. Better paid, better dressed, better equipped, they might arouse envy among British workers, but their country also gained respect. American jazz was admired and so was American wealth. More specifically, there had been no parallel in history for the close military integration achieved by the two countries in World War II. The Anglo-American alliance continued thereafter, fortified by a common language, and a common dedication to parliamentary rule. By and large, an American in Europe felt more at home in Britain than the US. By and large, Britons and Americans worked well together in those international bodies of which their respective countries formed part. The "special relationship" was more than just a rhetorical device for use in speeches on Empire Day.

For all Britain's physical and moral assets, there was, by the late 1950s and the early 1960s, a profound sense that something was wrong. The Victorian era had ended at last. Deference diminished; crime went up. The Labour planners who had so mightily expanded the welfare state had failed to reckon with the relative paucity of British resources, the perils of inflation, and the costs of empire. British textile producers, steel-makers, shipbuilders and their like had enjoyed freedom from foreign competition during World War II and its immediate aftermath, when foreigners eagerly bought all the merchandise that Britain could produce. In addition, the British maintained under arms large military forces, and developed nuclear weapons of their own, while financing expensive development schemes in Britain's African empire.

There were other problems: antiquated managerial methods in much (though not all) of British industry, inadequate training in much of the workforce, lagging industrial investment. While the British remained leaders in technology and science, modernization in much of British industry lagged behind. The trade unions developed into "the Fifth Estate of the Realm," immensely powerful but beset by demarcation disputes and sectional differences, with militant shop stewards convinced that the interests of capital and labor were incompatible and could be resolved only by strikes. (During former times, unions had popularly been regarded as spokesmen for the underdog, but by 1978

3 Roy C. Macridis, ed, *Modern Political Systems: Europe*, Englewood Cliffs, NJ, Prentice-Hall, 1978, p. 41.

an opinion poll showed that 82 percent of Britons considered unions too powerful.) This resultant unease found expression in a spate of books on the causes and cure of the "British disease," and in numerous television and radio programs filled with irreverent self-criticism. The old imperial greatness could no longer be maintained; nor could Britain act as a great power independent of the US, as demonstrated by the Suez fiasco of 1956. The British attitude towards the US was ambivalent. On the one hand, Britain was proud of its "special relationship" with the US; on the other hand, a resentful anti-Americanism was also common, not merely among left-wing intellectuals, but also within the so-called Establishment. To pessimists, the art of governance in Britain seemed to entail only the gradual management of decline.

No British leader, of course, would say such a thing in public – least of all a Conservative. The British Conservative Party could rightly claim to be the world's oldest – all others were upstarts by comparison. The Conservatives, moreover, regarded themselves as Britain's natural ruling party. (Between 1945 and 1990, Conservative governments held sway for 28 years, Labour for 17.) The Conservatives represented the bulk (but by no means the whole) of the British middle class and lower middle class. The elderly widely voted Tory; Anglicans were more likely to support the Conservatives than members of other Protestant denominations ("Nonconformists" in British parlance). Northern Irish Protestants of any class would almost invariably back the Tories – this to spite their Catholic compatriots. But, above all, the Conservatives also had substantial working-class support. Something like one-third of the skilled and unskilled working class would identify themselves as Conservatives; therefore, in terms of actual voting figures, the Conservative share was higher still.[4] In this sense, British Conservatives resembled new parties on the continent, such as the Christian Democrats in West Germany and Italy.

What exactly did the Conservatives represent? An answer is not easy to give, for there was no clear ideological line.[5] Instead, the Tories praised their traditional pragmatism and common sense – or what they took as such. Lack of consistency, moreover, did not worry the Tories. Tory speakers never tired of praising private enterprise, but it was Macmillan who in 1957 set up a Council on Productivity, Prices and Incomes, the first attempt to arrive at an agreement between government, unions, and industry. (Voluntary agreement did not work, hence both the subsequent Labour government under Harold Wilson and the Tory government under Edward Heath introduced legislation to control prices and wages. All these attempts failed.) Tory speakers lauded the empire, but men such as Iain Macleod believed in decolonization as much as any Labour intellectuals. Tories took pride in their reputed toughness, but they shied from fights. (Macmillan in particular insisted that no sensible government should ever quarrel with the National Union of Mineworkers, the Roman Catholic Church, and the Brigade of Guards.) Tories professed to stand for the traditional values of rural England: village church, manor, and timbered cottages, but they also valued the new consumerism. The Tories praised self-made men, but Tories also made a strong appeal to surviving traditions

4 D.E. Butler and Anthony King, *The British General Election of 1964*, London, Macmillan, 1965, p. 296. In 1964, according to a social survey, 74.7 percent of middle-class respondents favored the Conservatives; 60.7 percent of the lower middle class; 33.9 percent of the skilled working class; 30.9 percent of the unskilled. The respective figures for the Labour Party were 8.9, 24.8, 54.4, and 59.1 percent. Liberals 14.9, 13.7, 10.9, and 9.1 percent.
5 David Butler and Michael Pinto-Duschinsky, *The British General Election of 1970*, London, Macmillan, 1971, p. 66.

of social deference. Rising living standards, well-publicized scandals, rock music, consumerism, and the growing youth culture had all eroded inherited pieties, but islands of deference remained in Britain. Social deference went with respect for masculine ingroup loyalties – be it to a school, a trade union, or a regiment. As John Keegan, a British military historian, put it, Britain remained wedded to "a culture of ingroups each cherishing its own secrets, but conspiring automatically to defend the ethos of exclusivity."[6] To foreigners, this seemed a remarkably cohesive society, with a low crime rate, and little official corruption. But it was also a society that failed to promote rapid economic change and still displayed much class animosity.

The Conservatives wielded considerable electoral advantages. They were associated in the public mind with all of Britain's traditional institutions: the great country houses, the Anglican Church, the public schools, and the old universities (Oxford and Cambridge above all), and also the great London clubs (whose importance, however, began to diminish during the 1960s). This image was, of course, only partially correct. Labour cabinets would contain just as many graduates from Oxford and Cambridge as Tory cabinets. Labour intellectuals proved just as snobbish – or more so – than society hostesses. Nevertheless, the Conservatives had the prestige of being the aristocratic party in a country where knighthoods and peerages as yet counted for a great deal. David Cannadine, in a major work, has discussed the rise and fall of the British aristocracy.[7] He does so in terms of the nobility's and gentry's strikingly reduced share in income, landed wealth, political power, and social prestige over the last century. His book makes indispensable reading for any student of British society. Nevertheless, the aristocracy as yet exercised influence much beyond its numbers. (It was Mrs Thatcher, the daughter of a grocer, and prime minister from 1979 to 1991, who did more than any of her predecessors to deprive the noble-born and the "wet" of high office.) Even thereafter, the British titled classes continued to serve widely as an international role model. (Both British and foreign TV audiences still watched in the 1980s with fascination a television period drama series, *Upstairs, Downstairs*, with English lords, ladies, and their servants. By contrast, no viewer would possibly have wanted to see the East German *nomenklatura* at play in Pankow, or watch Mozambican party dignitaries enjoy "high life" in Maputo.)

While largely ceasing to rely on landed wealth, the aristocracy went on being reinforced by able newcomers from business, the professions, and politics. The Melchett clan may serve as an example. Ludwig Mond, the founder of the family's fortune, was a German Jew who came to England in the nineteenth century. He thereafter made his name as an industrial chemist, and as inventor of an important process for recovering nickel. His son, the first Lord Melchett, developed his father's business into a giant conglomerate, ICI (Imperial Chemical Industries). The third Lord Melchett became chairman of the nationalized British steel industry – the family having passed the entire gamut from private entrepreneurship to nationalized wealth, both embellished by a peerage. Even landed wealth did not disappear. The fragmentation of landed property, brought about by death duties and by economic factors, did not eliminate the aristocratic component, especially as divided parcels of formerly great estates might still be held by members of the same extended family. There remained intricate aristocratic

6 Cited in Barrie Penrose and Simon Freeman, *Conspiracy of Silence: the Secret Life of Anthony Blunt*, New York, Farrar, Straus and Giroux, 1987, p. 556.
7 David Cannadine, *The Decline and Fall of the British Aristocracy*, New Haven, CT, Yale University Press, 1990.

connections; and traditions of aristocratic service survived. There were still traditional magnates in Tory politics, represented by men such as Lord Home, the fourteenth earl in the line (briefly prime minister in 1964).

The Conservatives also appealed to farmers, businessmen, managers, and shop-keepers. The Conservative Party was indeed the businessmen's party *par excellence* – and yet the Tory party in no wise represented the free enterprise system pure and simple. The party had a long tradition of state interventionism, protectionism, and welfarism. Tory merchants and bankers might praise private enterprise in theory; but for most of them neither Friedrich von Hayek, Ludwig von Mises, nor Milton Friedman ranked as prophets. Free enterprise economists within the Conservative Party at the time were few and far between. To a Tory magnate they appeared decent chaps, no doubt, but without social cachet. (It was only under Margaret Thatcher that P.T. Bauer, a Hungarian-born economist, the British Milton Friedman, was raised to the peerage so that he might confound in the upper chamber Lord Balogh, a socialist, and another Hungarian-born economist.)

Above all, the Tories relied also on a substantial bloc of working-class voters. The share of Tory working-class voters thereafter continued to grow, especially among fore-men and the highly skilled. What made British workers vote Tory at a time when class consciousness in Britain as yet remained strong?[8] Political scientists for generations had characterized British political culture as consensual, gradualistic, pragmatic, incremental, and deferential. Why should this have been the case? Marxists used to argue that the imperialist countries, in particular Great Britain, managed to bribe the metropolitan "aristocracy of labor" by superprofits drawn from the colonies, thereby dividing the working class and avoiding revolution. But if this explanation were correct, the British workers should have become more, not less, radical during and after World War II when British capitalists were forced to sell a large share of their overseas investments to pay for the war and its aftermath. In any case, modern research has seriously questioned the extent of colonial superprofits.[9]

There are cruder explanations to account for the moderation of British working-class politics. During the "Red Scare" that followed World War I in Britain (as in the US), Sir Basil Thomson, then head of the CID (Criminal Investigation Department) dismissed fears of a British revolution on the grounds that sport and royalty would always provide a "steadying influence" among the lower orders.[10] But Sir Basil's views surely rested on an over-simplification. British workers did indeed like the monarchy – just as they liked soccer. But far more important was the unifying force of patriotism, a sense of national distinctiveness experienced in a tight little island whose people had always stressed their difference from foreigners. As the general secretary of Equity (the British actors' union, not an unsophisticated body) put it, "British Equity welcomes foreigners working in our country, even when they are recruited to play such an obviously British part as God."[11]

8 According to Gallup Polls, 56 percent of respondents in 1961 thought there was a class struggle in the country; by the summer of 1964 the proportion stood at 48 percent (Butler and King, *The British General Election of 1964*, p. 37).
9 L.H. Gann and Peter Duignan, *Burden of Empire: an Appraisal of Western Colonialism in Africa South of the Sahara*, Stanford, CA, Hoover Institution Press, 1971 edn.
10 Christopher Andrew, *Her Majesty's Secret Service: the Making of the British Intelligence Community*, New York, Viking, 1988, p. 239.
11 Reprinted from "This England," *New Statesman and Society*, 21 September 1991, p. 29.

Above all, British people rightly considered themselves to be living in a free and tolerant country, even though they tended to regard government as such with some cynicism (apparently, however, less so than Americans, and more so than West Germans).[12]

Given such advantages, the Conservative Party, at the end of the 1950s, seemed set for power. Indeed, a great many Conservatives at the time thought that they might go on ruling Britain for a generation. The party had an efficient central organization through its Central Office; yet there was no danger that the bureaucracy would become a power in its own right. As R.T. Mackenzie, a leading political scientist of the period, put it, "the Conservative Central Office has always been subservient to the parliamentary party [the Conservative caucus in parliament]; it has never developed the evils associated with the terms 'boss' and 'machine' in American politics."[13] The prime minister, formerly, was chosen by an inner ring of party leaders, widely known as the "Magic Circle." (It was not until 1965 that the introduction of voting by MPs made the process more formal and more seemly to a democratic electorate.) However chosen, the leader of the Tory party, as of other parties, had to be a member of parliament. Once chosen, the leader controlled the Central Office and appointed the party's leading officials. The leader, however, was no autocrat; he or she had to live with the party, and serve it well. If the leader failed, he or she might unceremoniously be forced to resign.

No such problems, however, seemed to plague the party during the late 1950s. Harold Macmillan (1894–1986) had taken over after the Suez crisis and Anthony Eden's subsequent resignation. Macmillan had all the right connections. He was an old Etonian and a Balliol man. He had served with courage in the Grenadier Guards in World War I. He belonged to that tightly knit intellectual aristocracy in which distinguished families, such as the Macmillans and the Butlers, held leading positions in academia and publishing. (R.A. "Rab" Butler, a former Indian civil servant with a social conscience, Macmillan's rival for the premiership in 1957, was born into the same set.) Macmillan was likewise a leading businessman, head of the Macmillan publishing firm. And he had married the daughter of a duke.

Macmillan, moreover, had panache, elegance, an air of social distinction, and a ready wit. He had held high ministerial office. Despite an affectation of polished frivolity, Macmillan also had a social conscience. As a biographer put it, "Macmillan sought consistently – as did Disraeli whom he so much admired – to identify the Conservative Party with the manual workers and their families. He had no sympathy with *laissez faire* liberalism. His purpose was to win working-class support for the Party and for the traditional social structure of Britain."[14] Macmillan (three times wounded in World War I) returned from the trenches with a patrician liking for the British working class whose sons he had commanded in battle. Macmillan's social conscience became even more troubled when he witnessed the impact of unemployment in his coal-exporting and shipbuilding constituency of Stockton. His response was shaped by the writing of

12 In 1963, 44 percent of British respondents in a poll regarded government with some distrust, as against 53 percent of Americans, but only 24 percent of West Germans.
13 R.T. Mackenzie, *British Political Parties: the Distribution of Power within the Conservative and Labour Parties*, London, Heinemann, 1963, p. 559.
14 Nigel Fisher, *Harold Macmillan: a Biography*, New York, St Martin's Press, 1982, p. 367; Alistair Horne, *Harold Macmillan*, 2 vols, New York, Viking Press, 1989; Anthony Sampson, *Macmillan: a Study in Ambiguity*, London, Allen Lane, 1967; Harold Macmillan, *Riding the Storm, 1956–1959*, London, Macmillan, 1971.

John Maynard Keynes with whose works Macmillan became familiar as his publisher. Macmillan, in this respect, was in no wise unusual among Tory magnates. His views were shared by men such as Iain Macleod, a much younger man, also a Guards officer, wounded in World War II, later Secretary of State for the Colonies, and a powerful proponent of decolonization in Africa. Macmillan's social conscience did not end with British people. His family opened their door to German Jewish refugee children (as did those of Margaret Thatcher and James Callaghan). In addition, Macmillan knew how to appeal to the new consumerism. A Tory election poster in the 1959 campaign showed a smiling, young, and fair-haired Mom cleaning the family car, helped by Dad and two young children, with the caption: 'Life's better with the Conservatives."

Macmillan, Butler, and their friends had much in common with moderate Labourites such as Hugh Gaitskell. Many years later, an anonymous reviewer in *The Economist* suggested that Macmillan should have tried to "Thatcherize" the British economy.[15] It was an anachronistic judgment. The Conservative Party always had a hankering for protectionism, state intervention, and patriarchal rhetoric. In this respect, Macmillan was far more typical of his party than the handful of committed free marketers found within the party's ranks. By the time Macmillan stepped into the premiership, he was 63 years old, shaped by the experiences of two world wars, the Great Depression, and disillusioned by what he regarded as the ills of unrestrained capitalism. The country as a whole shared this mood. Thatcher herself was no Thatcherite when first elected to the House of Commons in 1959. The bulk of the Tory leadership – indeed, the British Establishment as a whole – believed in compromise, in splitting the difference, in meeting the other chap halfway. There was dislike for confrontation, whether involving trade union bosses at home or "native" leaders in the empire overseas. It was the search for consensus that dominated boards, committees, and commissions. The ruthless pursuit of a policy once set was not somehow good form. An enlightened politician's first concern was to avoid unemployment. If the price was overmanning in industry, public subsidies to inefficient enterprises, high taxes, budgetary deficits, and inflation – so be it! The British, never having experienced runaway inflation like the Germans, did not regard inflation as a sovereign device robbing the public, but as a lesser evil compared to joblessness.

The British Establishment's sense of social commitment was apt to go with an odd blend of self-righteousness and snobbish disdain for mere hucksters. Not that Tory (or for that matter Labour) leaders objected to making money. British banking and British agriculture, for example, carried social prestige, and also remained highly efficient. Manufacturing, by contrast, never gained the same acceptability. Retail trade, similarly, was disdained – an occupation unbefitting a gentleman, and also one incapable of creating value – a prejudice shared by Tory squires and Labour dons alike. Conservative leaders joined with Labour leaders in supporting large economic units. Labour preferred state enterprises, Conservatives big private industry. Both showed little interest in the small businessman, offering little encouragement to private enterprise. Tory and Labour chiefs alike were apt to be paternalists, convinced that ordinary people needed guidance from their betters, lest workers be exploited, consumers cheated, and the poor left without support.

Whatever Thatcherite critics might say in later days, however, Macmillan got off on the right foot. His electoral campaign in 1959 was a model of its kind. He was a

15 "The Late Developer," *The Economist*, 1 July 1989, p. 73.

showman on TV (having studied American techniques). Ministers in his day actually looked forward to cabinet meetings brightened by the prime minister's theatrical touches. Macmillan conveyed an image of steadfast calm, avuncular poise, and diplomatic know-how. He knew how to turn state visits abroad to domestic advantage. (He arrived at a summit meeting in Moscow wearing a white fur hat which impressed British TV viewers even though – unbeknown to Macmillan – the white hat offended Russians who regarded it as the Finnish national headgear.) The Tories emphasized the extent of British prosperity, while censuring Labour for its alleged financial irresponsibility. The internal divisions that had plagued the Conservative Party after Suez disappeared from public consciousness. When the polls were announced, the Conservatives had gained additional votes and seats in every major region except Scotland and south-east Lancashire; they now emerged with an absolute majority in parliament. (The Conservatives won 356 seats, Labour 258, Liberals 6, Independents 1.) In terms of votes cast, the Conservative victory was, however, much less impressive. The Conservatives obtained 13,749,830 votes; 49.4 percent of the total. Labour secured 12,215,538 votes; 43.8 percent of the total. The Liberals received 1,638,571 votes; 5.9 percent of the total.[16] Labour had not been crushed; nevertheless, Labour was the first party in British electoral history to lose four successive general elections. Many conservatives – and not only Conservatives – imagined that the Tories were set to rule for the next generation.

The Tory government did not, however, meet such expectations. Indeed, the most striking changes made by the new government were of a kind not mentioned in Tory campaign literature. In theory, the Tory party was still the party of Kipling and Empire Day. In practice, the Tories and Labour developed what amounted to a bi-partisan policy with regard to decolonization. The Asian empire had been the first to go after World War II. (India and Pakistan both gained independence in 1947.) For a time thereafter, the British still wanted to maintain predominance in the Middle East and develop the African empire. But the Suez venture went awry, as the US joined the Soviet Union in opposing an Anglo-French assault on Egypt for the purpose of undoing Egypt's nationalization of the Suez Canal.

The Suez fiasco profoundly affected the Tory Establishment. Macmillan, in particular, felt convinced that the "special relationship" with the US, and Britain's links with Europe, were far more important than Britain's ties to the empire. The "winds of change" in Africa neither could nor should be resisted. Macmillan, or rather his Colonial Secretary Iain Macleod, turned out to be like de Gaulle – an outstanding decolonizer. It was under Tory governance that the bulk of Britain's African empire was dismantled – much to the disgust of men such as Sir Roy Welensky, last prime minister of the Federation of Rhodesia and Nyasaland (1953–63), and his friends and allies in the "Monday Club," a remaining holdout of Tory imperialists. Imperial loyalties now ceased to be respectable among those Britons who considered themselves well educated and well born. It was perhaps not mere chance that Welensky, one of the last believers in the imperial cause, should have been a "colonial" (in former British imperial parlance, a white person burdened by the social disability of having been born in a British imperial possession). (Welensky's father had been a Lithuanian Jew, his mother an Afrikaner. He was born in Rhodesia and spoke with a Rhodesian accent. Moreover, he had never enjoyed more than an elementary school education, and he had first made his name in Rhodesia as a trade-union organizer, and also as his country's heavy-weight boxing champion.)

16 Butler and King, *The British General Election of 1964*, p. 303.

The first African colony to achieve sovereign status was the Gold Coast (henceforth known as Ghana, 1957). Nigeria achieved independence in 1960, followed by Tanzania in 1961, Uganda in 1962, Kenya in 1963. In the same year, the Federation of Rhodesia and Nyasaland was dissolved, contrary to previous promises; Malawi and Zambia achieved independence thereafter in 1964. Macleod and his supporters defended the British retreat on the grounds that the newly independent countries would strengthen the Commonwealth by their freely chosen membership; the Commonwealth would continue to give influence to Britain in world affairs as a moral force, and as an international forum. The newly independent countries turned out not to be as peaceful, prosperous and democratic, nor as anglophile, as had been assumed by the British advocates and architects of their independence. Decolonization, moreover, went with increasing immigration from the Commonwealth into Britain, with the unanticipated consequence of turning Britain into a multiracial country. But neither decolonization nor immigration proved reversible.

This was hardly surprising. Anti-colonialism in the metropolitan countries had by now acquired both the optimism and the moral fervor once associated with the anti-slavery movement and other Victorian crusades. Anti-colonialism, indeed, had by now become part of an accepted orthodoxy in most of Western academia. (The very vocabulary of scholarship changed as terms drawn from the European experience with the Third Reich – "collaboration," "resistance" – became part of a new scholarly terminology.) Decolonization was marked by the unwillingness or inability of the various colonial powers to collaborate, or even effectively to plead their case to an ever-more skeptical public. Above all, colonialism was no longer acceptable to that new class of Asians and Africans who had acquired a Western education, who had once served their imperial masters in subordinate capacities, as teachers, clerks, interpreters, detectives, welfare officers, military officers, but now were determined to step into the erstwhile rulers' shoes. These men appealed to widespread and genuine popular grievances. To maintain colonial rule against their will would have entailed a permanent military deployment of a kind no Western power was willing to maintain. Colonialism henceforth was both dead and damned.

Macmillan, by contrast, attempted to strengthen the European connection. In 1959 Britain adhered to the Stockholm Convention which set up EFTA (European Free Trade Association comprising, in addition to Britain, Austria, Denmark, Norway, Portugal, Sweden, and Switzerland). In 1961 the Macmillan government also applied for admission to the EEC. It was a courageous decision, given the widespread disapproval within the ranks of the Conservatives, even more so of Labour. In 1963, however, de Gaulle vetoed the application – much to the relief of traditionalists within both the major British parties who stood determined not to surrender British sovereignty. Macmillan restored good relations with the US after the Suez fiasco; indeed, he exercised considerable influence on US policy by reason of the fatherly role that he successfully assumed toward President John F. Kennedy. Above all, Macmillan steadfastly supported NATO and the US connection, both during the crisis engendered by the construction of the Berlin Wall in 1961, and the potentially disastrous Cuban confrontation (1962).

In domestic affairs, however, the Macmillan government stumbled from crisis to crisis. The Conservatives tried to carry out their own version of an "incomes policy" – to no avail. The government set up a National Economic Development Council ("Neddy"), but it accomplished nothing. Inflation increased, leaving a major economic problem for Macmillan's successors. It was not that the British lacked scientific or technological imagination. Britain continued to rank immediately behind the US in the number of Nobel prizes won. The British had helped to pioneer modern technology – jet planes, penicillin, computers – but British industrialists seemed to lack the ability to turn pioneering ventures into commercial successes.

Britain also had to cope with social problems unfamiliar to Victorian reformers. Traditionally, Britain had been an avowedly Protestant country. The Church of England remained the Established Church. But fewer and fewer Anglicans would attend services; the time would come when practicing Catholics (many of them Irish immigrants and their assimilated descendants) would outnumber practicing Anglicans (Episcopalians in US usage). Britain as a whole became overwhelmingly secular in outlook; by the late 1960s, the Victorian legacy had been largely shed – except for the armed forces, the judicial system, and for the Queen – as distinct from her wayward relatives.

Britain insensibly also turned into a multiracial country. People of color had lived in Britain for centuries (black sailors had fought at Trafalgar). But mass immigration from the Commonwealth only began after World War II, when means of transport cheapened, when the US put new restrictions on the immigration of West Indian immigrants, and when postwar prosperity created new jobs. Initially, there were no restrictions on immigrants from the Commonwealth. The number of newcomers seemed manageable. (Until 1961 British emigration to the Commonwealth exceeded immigration from the Commonwealth to Britain.)

But the number of new citizens from the West Indies, India, and Pakistan kept multiplying. (In time there would be more practicing Muslims in Britain than practicing Anglicans.) But no consideration was given to the enormous changes entailed by the transformation of Britain into a multiracial society. (In this respect the British paralleled the French experience; France likewise acquired a large North African minority, so to speak, in an absent-minded fashion.) Throughout the 1950s, Britain's immigration laws remained far more liberal than those of any other Commonwealth country.)

Support for Commonwealth immigration derived from a strangely assorted lobby. Employers wanted labor at a time when Britain experienced full employment. Commonwealth loyalists insisted that Britain, the imperial motherland, could not justly exclude Commonwealth citizens. (West Indian immigrants, moreover, spoke English as their native tongue: why admit German-speaking Jews but keep out English-speaking Jamaicans?) Labour leaders called for workers' solidarity. Left-wing Christians, such as Father Trevor Huddleston, regarded colored immigration to Britain as a form of British reparation to exploited Africa. Lord Pakenham insisted that free immigration alone accorded with Christianity.

Unfortunately, from the pro-immigration lobby's standpoint, the overwhelming majority of the British electorate (some 80 percent according to opinion polls) disagreed. In 1962, therefore, the Macmillan government passed the Commonwealth Immigration Act which imposed various restrictions. By that time, however, the points had been set. Britain, irrevocably, had become a multi-ethnic, multicultural country. Britain would be enriched by West Indian music, Nigerian cuisine, Indian enterprise. But Britain would also face racial problems similar to those which troubled the US – racial discrimination, racial riots, and demands for racial reparation.

The process which, for good or ill, transformed large areas of urban Britain was begun without reference to the British people as a whole, let alone those living in the urban regions most affected. The new racial problems developed in places far from the manors of humanitarian Tory lords, the colleges of humanitarian Tory dons, the palaces of humanitarian Tory bishops.

In time, the Tory paternalists' lack of involvement with their voters' concerns helped to break the habit of social deference within the Conservative Party, and the long domination of the upper and upper-middle classes within its ranks. Recognizing that Tory grandees could no longer be relied upon to act in their own best interests, Conservative voters and constituency activists began to turn to people of their own background.[17]

There were other changes. The capital now claimed to be "Swinging London" (a title hardly justified by the realities of conventional life in Hampstead or Kensington). The government, moreover, had to cope with everlasting scandals. These culminated in the Profumo affair, a godsend to sensation-loving journalists. There were rumors of espionage. There were sexual scandals (the British secretary for war and the senior Soviet naval attaché in London sharing the affections of the same call girl: "Thank God it was a woman" supposedly went Macmillan's reply when the news was first brought to him). Macmillan, moreover, had personal problems; he would brook no rival; he had made plenty of enemies in his own party; he seemed out of touch. In the end he resigned (1963), ostensibly for reasons of health. The party's new leader, Sir Alec Douglas-Home, plucked from the House of Lords and transplanted to the Commons, did not come across as a good choice. ("Just Alec – not Smart Alec" commented a leading popular paper.) Instead of ruling for the next generation, the Tories suddenly faced the most formidable electoral challenge since 1945.

Labour Wavers

The British Labour Party, the Tories' chief challenger, was a remarkable body. Having won the 1945 election, Labour had emerged as one of the world's most prestigious social democratic parties. Unlike the socialist parties in France, Italy, or Spain, the British Labour Party faced no serious opposition on the left – the Communist Party of Great Britain, a clique of Soviet loyalists, counted for little. There was a handful of fellow travellers within the Labour Party, some in the unions, some in fashionable society. But they did not amount to much. There were *marxisant* intellectuals such as Christopher Hill, an outstanding historian. But Hill – like most of his friends – later deserted the cause. There were a few highly placed Soviet agents, the so-called "Cambridge Spies," recruited at Cambridge University during the 1930s. They have since become the subjects of an engrossing literature that weaves treason, snobbery, official cover-ups, and homosexuality into a tale of upper-class decadence. Sir Anthony Blunt, Knight Commander of the Victorian Order, Fellow of the British Academy, Surveyor of the King's Pictures, member of the Royal Household – a Soviet spy? In fact, the Cambridge spies were quite untypical of their class. Britain was no more vulnerable to espionage than any other major country; perhaps less so, given Britain's ability to keep the wartime "Government Code and Cipher School" at Bletchley Park a secret for so many years. Overall, the British communists wielded little influence – much less than their comrades in France, Italy, and West Germany. The Labour Party could indeed claim to be an anti-communist bastion, whatever over-zealous members of the British intelligence community might believe.

17 Andrew Roberts, *Eminent Churchillians*, London, Weidenfeld and Nicolson, 1994, pp. 238, 242.

Taken as a whole, the Labour Party was, in fact, an intensely British institution. The party was insular in outlook, convinced that a Labourite Britain would provide a moral inspiration for the world at large. (As Kenneth O. Morgan, a prominent Labour Party historian points out, a surprisingly large number of Labour leaders and Labour theoreticians had colonial connections. They shared the colonial civil servants' paternalism and their belief in the benevolence of the state.)[18] In some respects, the Labour Party was even more traditionalist than the Conservative Party. Whereas the Tories were unsentimental about their founding fathers, Labour liked to hearken back to its pioneers. The Labour Party – like the Anglican Church – moreover tried to be as comprehensive as possible, providing a home for several doctrines. There were Labourites of every kind: Marxists, Christian socialists, municipal socialists, guild socialists; there were Scottish and Welsh nationalists; there were Irish Catholics (important as a result of Irish working-class immigration to Britain); there were black immigrants from the Commonwealth; there were militant women, ecologists, and members of strange fringe groups. Above all, the party owed a great debt to trade unionists and party organizers trained in Baptist, Methodist, or Calvinist congregations. Though they had mostly lost their ancestors' faith, they kept their ancestors' earnestness.

The Labour Party was likewise a coalition in organizational terms. Individual members were organized in constituency Labour parties; more powerful still were the trade unions affiliated to the party. Both were represented at the Annual Conference, with a National Executive Committee in which the constituency parties after 1951 acquired an increasingly powerful position as against the parliamentary party. The constituency parties tended more to the left. In the early 1960s, for instance, the National Executive Committee and the Trades Union Congress (TUC) issued a joint statement on defense. In their view, Britain should unilaterally give up nuclear weapons, and leave NATO. Hugh Gaitskell (1906–63), then the party's leader, however, rejected this resolution for himself, and declared that neither would the parliamentary party be bound by it.

There were other problems. In theory, Labour was committed to the public ownership of the means of production, distribution, and exchange. In practice, the party was split between a majority who wanted only piecemeal change, and a minority who desired to restructure society. The militant left was strong among intellectuals, constituency workers and elected officials in big cities, shop stewards in the unions. Among them, utopian dreams remained at a premium. Admittedly, the Soviet Union had lost the romantic appeal that it had possessed during the 1930s and 1940s. Individual dons such as Balogh went on to praise the Soviet Union's assumed economic dynamism. But it was now Third World tyrants such as Mao Zedong, Ho Chi Minh, and Fidel Castro who appealed to self-described idealists who lauded revolutions in distant lands with an enthusiasm that they later tried to forget. Intellectuals there were aplenty in the Labour Party. But as regards intellectual originality, not much remained. The bulk of Labour's postwar heritage had derived, not from Labourites, but from Sir William Beveridge and Lord Keynes, both of them Liberals. What endured was an intense moral commitment to the welfare state, to public planning for full employment, and to the improvement of society in general. Particular emphasis was placed on education, as befitted a party in which – as in the French Socialist Party – teachers and professors were well represented. But there was all too little discussion on how British industry could be made more

18 Kenneth O. Morgan, *The People's Peace: British History, 1945–1989*, Oxford, Oxford University Press, 1990, p. 72.

competitive and more efficient. The main problems of society supposedly hinged on the just redistribution of the available wealth.

Labour's leadership in the main derived from the professional middle class. (Gaitskell, a spokesman for "sensible socialism," was the son of an Indian civil servant; he was educated at Winchester, a well-known public school, as were other prominent Labourites such as Douglas Jay and Richard Crossman. Gaitskell later studied at Oxford and became an economist. Harold Wilson, Gaitskell's successor to the Labour leadership in 1963, was the son of an industrial chemist; he likewise went to Oxford, and also began his career as an economist, assistant to Beveridge.) Yet the Labour Party could justly claim to represent the bulk of organized (as opposed to non-unionized) labor in Britain. With their huge membership, their financial clout, their moral appeal, and their legal privileges, the unions held a commanding position. No postwar British government seriously challenged the unions before 1968. The Labour Party thus could rely on massive working-class support not available to socialists in France or Italy. Moreover, a substantial (though a declining) number of genuine workers represented Labour in parliament: Labour was in no wise a party run by, and for, *apparatchiks*.[19]

The British working class – like the working classes in all industrialized countries – was immensely varied. There were farm laborers in remote hamlets. There were working-class people in small towns and in great metropolitan centers. Many still lived in decaying industrial neighborhoods, in back-to-back houses where life centered on the pub, the fish-and-chip shop, the cinema, the trade-union hall, or perhaps the chapel. But the character of the British working class was changing. Many had moved to "new towns" no longer reliant on declining industries such as shipbuilding, coal mining, steel, or textiles. The "new towns" looked neat and prosperous with gardens and parks. The people who lived in them commonly owned a car; they would spend their evenings in their own living room, watching the "telly" with their family rather than going to the pub. Labour had to fight for their votes with the Tories in a way that Labour would never have had to compete in a Welsh mining village. Nevertheless, by the late 1950s and the early 1960s, Britain in many respects still remained a traditionalist country in which social attitudes changed but slowly. Hence a comparatively small shift in voting could make a major electoral difference.

Such a shift occurred in 1964. Labour won at the general election, but the victory was not impressive. (The party gained 12,205,814 votes, 44.1 percent of the total, as against 12,001,396 votes, or 43.4 percent of the total, for the Conservatives. The Liberals did well with 3,092,876 votes, or 11.2 percent of the total, and regained credibility as a third party. In parliamentary terms, Labour ruled only by a small margin, with 317 seats in parliament, as against 304 for the Tories, and 9 for the Liberals.) Success at the polls at least prevented the Labour Party from disintegrating. Victory also proved that the party need not necessarily lose the votes of the newly affluent workers. A 1959 cartoon had shown a triumphant Macmillan giving a friendly address to a TV, a washing machine, a "fridge," and a Mini car. "Well, gentlemen, I think we all have fought a good fight." Douglas-Home could not make the same claim.

The Labour Party, for its part, gained new confidence. As late as 1959, Richard Crossman, one of its leading intellectuals, had still prophesied that competition from the

---

19 In 1959, members of parliament elected for Labour included 90 workers, 44 persons of a miscellaneous background, 26 businessmen, 98 people in the professions (D.E. Butler and Richard Rose, *The British General Election of 1959*, London, Macmillan, 1960, p. 129).

communist bloc would cause capitalism to founder worldwide. Labour could but hold itself in readiness to save Britain in the coming crash. This mood of doom contrasted with Labour's non-dogmatic approach embodied in its 1964 program, *Labour in the Sixties*. (It sold a million copies.) Harold Wilson (born 1916), the party's new leader, gave voice to this mood of cheerful moderation. He believed in the rationalization more than in the nationalization of industry. He looked toward a new Britain in which socialism would be harnessed to science. A Labour government would plan for increased efficiency in those industries in which Britain was clearly falling behind. Once the British economy had regained its dynamism, there would be money aplenty to pay for those increased social services that Britons now regarded as a birthright. Wilson, a professional economist and a former Oxford don, appeared a promising leader. He spoke with a homely Yorkshire accent; he had a ready wit and a gift for repartee – the very image of the solid, pipe-smoking Englishman. (The pipe was in fact a television gimmick. At home, Wilson smoked a cigar, an indulgence associated in British political folklore with pot-bellied capitalists, not – as in the US – gangsters or marines.)

Initially, things did not go badly for the new government. Living standards in Britain rose until the early 1970s. Technical and university education expanded, though perhaps not in the way that would have best suited the economy. Labour began to defer to new constituents – gays, feminists, black and Asian immigrants from the Commonwealth – to the displeasure of traditional white working-class constituents. The Wilson government continued to work well with the US, despite the anti-Americanism aroused by the Vietnam War. There was student unrest in Britain, but compared with the troubles experienced in the US, Japan, France, and West Germany, militancy in Britain did not amount to much. As regards the economy, traditional industries nationalized under Labour – coal, steel, the railways – ran at a loss. But there were other publicly owned enterprises that made a profit, including electricity, the airlines, the post office, and gas (the latter benefiting from great new supplies of oil and gas discovered under the North Sea).[20]

Problems, however, soon accumulated. Having been surpassed economically by Germany, Britain, in 1966, for the first time fell behind France; British economic leadership within Western Europe, taken for granted at the end of World War II, became a matter of memory. Wilson had little understanding of this process. He and his followers talked as if Britain still exercised political – or at least moral – primacy in Europe. Wilson had a penchant for highly personalized government; he suffered fools but not rivals. He was not excessively burdened by political scruple, but he intrigued without flair, and without lasting success.[21]

Above all, the Wilson government lacked a consistent policy concerning economic issues, such as the balance of payments, the exchange rate, the modernization of industries. Difficulties worsened as the pound was once again devalued. Wilson did not effectively control his cabinet; he surrounded himself with an oddly assorted group of dons and

20 Carl Tremont Brand, *The British Labour Party*, Stanford, CA, Stanford University Press, 1964, p. 336. For Wilson's own account of his government, see Sir Harold Wilson, *The Labour Government, 1964–1970: a Personal Record*, London, Weidenfeld and Nicolson, 1971; Ben Pimlott, *Harold Wilson*, London, HarperCollins, 1992.
21 For a fine portrait see Kenneth O. Morgan, *Labour People*, Oxford, Oxford University Press, 1987, pp. 246–64, and an annotated bibliography. For a harshly critical account of Wilson's first government, see Clive Ponting, *Breach of Promise: Labour in Power, 1964–1970*, London, Hamish Hamilton, 1988.

journalists without public standing. Taxation increased; social services deteriorated in quality. A new planning department, the Department for Economic Affairs, competed with the more traditionally minded Treasury, but made no difference to Britain's ability to compete in the world markets. The government stumbled from one disaster to the next: the devaluation of sterling in 1967 was only one of many. Militarily, the government tried to reduce Britain's commitments by ending conscription and relying solely on regular soldiers (a policy first announced in 1957). Britain likewise reduced the British Army of the Rhine (BAOR), and abandoned Britain's former position east of Suez. (In 1967 South Yemen achieved independence; Britain thereby lost the use of Aden, once a major imperial bastion.) The British likewise abandoned official (though not unofficial) commitments in the Persian Gulf, much to the disadvantage of the Western position worldwide. (The "Trucial Sheikhdoms" achieved independence from British supervision in 1971, becoming known as the United Arab Emirates.) Britain continued to produce its own nuclear weapons, but could not compete with either the Soviet Union or the US. (Britain's own rocket, Blue Streak, was abandoned in 1960, and Britain thereafter largely became dependent for its strategic defense on American-made rockets and submarines.) Not that British history at the time was simply a tale of disaster. Specific industries such as agriculture, services such as banking and insurance, continued to perform well, but these were privately owned; their success could hardly serve as an argument in favor of socialism.

Nor did the Wilson government have much success in Commonwealth or foreign affairs. Wilson initially predicted that the Unilateral Declaration of Independence (UDI), proclaimed by Ian Smith's white settler government in 1965, would last only a few weeks, at worst a few months. But Wilson turned out to be mistaken. His error reflected, not Rhodesian realities, but the arrogance of the new class of planners, welfare administrators, and educators who now dominated the Labour Party. Britain's physical power, they assumed, might diminish, but her moral authority would increase through the Commonwealth. It was incumbent therefore on Britain to take a strong line with settlers such as Ian Smith, unconsciously perhaps identified by Wilson with old-style bosses at home – hard-faced men without gentility or conscience. Moreover, to an academic such as Wilson, no less than to the British civil service élite, it seemed inconceivable that white backwoods men could for long survive against the moral disapproval of Britain and the world at large. How could an administration composed of provincial farmers, lawyers, and businessmen – besotted by racial prejudice, afflicted with a "colonial" accent, a tendency to pronounce "car" as "cor" – run Rhodesia against British, indeed, worldwide opposition? (In fact, UDI lasted for 14 years, from 1965 to 1980, and the Rhodesian gross national product nearly doubled during the first decade after UDI.) Wilson did no better in European affairs. A second, and indeed very courageous, attempt to enter the EEC met with yet another rebuff from de Gaulle (1967).

In electoral terms, Labour faced other long-term problems. Wilson turned a blind eye to what came to be called "entryism." For many years the Labour National Executive Committee had maintained a list of militant organizations whose members were denied entry into the party. Wilson abolished this provision, and thereby helped to strengthen the Trotskyites and other assorted Marxists (the Militant Tendency) within the Labour movement. Far from strengthening Labour, the doctrinaire weakened the party in electoral terms. Wilson's personal appeal wilted; there were all manner of scandals; to be known as a "Wilson knight" (a man raised to the knighthood under the Wilson government) became a term of reproach among London hostesses. From a wider perspective, Britain, like the rest of the Western world, witnessed a partial decline of the old labor-intensive industries; hence the traditional working class contracted in size. More and more voters changed their boiler-suits for jacket, collar, and tie; the cloth cap ceased to be regarded as the working man's chosen headgear. The new electorate, of course, did not necessarily vote Tory – but neither was it loyal to Labour. On the contrary, Labour's share of the total British vote began to erode.[22] This decline went with diminishing confidence in Labour's traditional program. In 1964, 57 percent of Labour "identifiers" had still put their trust in the nationalization of additional industries; by 1970, the percentage had fallen to 39. In 1964, 89 percent had called for more spending on social services; by 1970, the percentage had dropped to 60 – still a majority but no longer reflecting an almost universal consensus.[23] At a time when the French Socialist Party was being infused with new confidence and vitality under François Mitterand's leadership, Labour in Britain seemed set for permanent decline.

Above all, the trade unions widely lost the confidence that they had previously enjoyed in the country at large, and this distrust extended into the Labour movement itself. (In 1956, 59 percent of Labour identifiers had refused to believe that Labour held excessive power. By 1970, only 40 percent of Labour identifiers would oppose this proposition – a striking change within a party dependent on the trade-union connection.) The unions sponsored a majority of Labour members of parliament; the unions played a decisive role within the Labour executive; they called the tune at Labour's Annual Conference; they paid most of the Labour Party's expenses. Between them, they had become almost a separate estate of the realm, endowed with all manner of privileges. But for these advantages, the unions ultimately had to pay a heavy price: their membership would decline, their political power would erode, and union leaders would cease to be consulted as a matter of right on major government decisions. (A similar decline eroded labor's strength in the US.)

Trade unions were formerly immune from litigation for any of their activities which were not a conspiracy to commit an illegal act. Hence no one could sue a union for negligence, deceit, threats of injury, libel, or slander. Unions were not responsible for the actions of their own officials. Collective agreements could not be directly enforced. No worker had a legal right to join a trade union. Unions could make their own rules on whom to reject or accept. In practice, unions could become hiring and firing agencies. The minister of labor could appoint an arbitrator in an industrial dispute only if both parties agreed. Only by declaring a state of emergency could the government safeguard essential supplies; it could not order strikers back to work. Britain was the only industrialized nation without a comprehensive legal structure for industrial relations.

During the 1950s and 1960s, however, this future change was as yet far from apparent. Ever since World War II, the incumbent government had attempted to enlist union cooperation. Churchill had gladly collaborated with the unions in his great wartime administration, and deferred to them thereafter. Macmillan had feared the unions, and Wilson flattered them. But of the government's four attempts to enlist union cooperation,

22 The percentage of the Labour vote as a share of the total vote stood as follows: 47.8 in 1945; 46.1 in 1950; 46.4 in 1955; 43.8 in 1959; 44.1 in 1964; 47.9 in 1966; 42.9 in 1970; 37.1 in 1974 (Feb.); 39.2 in 1974 (Oct.); 36.9 in 1979; 27.6 in 1983. See Chris Cook and John Paxton, *European Political Facts: 1918–84*, New York, Facts on File Publications, 1986, p. 187. For a general interpretation, see Patrick Cosgrave, *The Strange Death of Socialist Britain: Post-war British Politics*, London, Constable, 1992.
23 See Ivor Crewe, "The Labour Party and the Electorate," in Dennis Kavanagh, ed., *The Politics of the Labour Party*. London, Allen and Unwin, 1982, p. 39.

made between 1945 and 1968, only one was successful, Clement Attlee's. The trade unions considered that wage restraints interfered unfairly with the workers' right to bargain freely for the terms of their employment. Critics of the unions considered that the unions' ability to paralyze economic policy was intolerable, especially in so far as wildcat strikes were concerned. The unions played a dangerous part in opposing the moderniza-tion and rationalization of industry, fearful that their members' livelihood might thereby be threatened. But there was also the wider issue of who should rule Britain. As Gerald A. Dorfman, an American political scientist, put it "the fundamental question at issue was how power in the modern British political system would be distributed."[24] Wilson, in 1968, for the first time attempted a counter-attack against union power, but he failed, as would his successor Edward Heath.

There was also bitter controversy over inflation, over the size and cost of an ever-expanding public service, the growing burden of taxation, the rapid growth of "quan-gos" (quasi non-governmental bodies) with huge but ill-defined powers – "a gigantic system of outdoor relief for party hacks."[25] (Quangos steadily expanded both in number and function. They comprised bodies such as the Manpower Services Commission, the Health and Safety Commission, the University Grants Committee, and so on. By 1979, they had a staff of 214,000 persons, and jointly spent some £5,800 million, about $8,700 million.) Constitutional lawyers took pride in the sovereignty of parliament; the British parliament was subject neither to a Supreme Court nor a Bill of Rights; in theory, parliament could do anything but make a man into a woman and a woman into a man. But, in practice, parliamentarians could do little to direct these enormous and expanding bureaucracies; they lacked the investigative mechanisms, even the staff, avail-able to their opposite numbers in the US Congress. High among other discontents were fears concerning black and Asian immigrants from the Commonwealth, especially West Indians, and Indians from East Africa. In 1951, people of color living in Britain had only numbered about 75,000; 15 years later the population had reached 929,000 of whom 213,000 had been born in Britain. Britain, complained opponents of immigration, was being turned into a multicultural and multi-ethnic society, a change never approved by the public at large, and one that benefited only employers of cheap labor. After bitter debate, a series of Immigration Acts set limits to immigration. (By the late 1970s, about 75,000 newcomers were being accepted each year, less than the number of emigrants from Britain.) Black voters overwhelmingly voted Labour, and thereby aroused the Tories' wrath. Black activists, moreover, stepped up their demands, calling – not only for formal equality – but for positive steps to redress past discrimination. The subject thereby remained intensely contentious, though citizens gradually came to accept that the island in future would contain black and Asian as well as white Britons.

In a more general sense, politics became more professionalized. Since 1945, govern-ment had grown enormously, and as it did, the politicians' profile changed. In prewar days, MPs had commonly been people of importance in their own right; their status had not depended on membership of the House of Commons. But, as the years went on, mem-bers became part of a political class – political researchers, ministerial aids, consultants.

24 Gerald A. Dorfman, *Government versus Trade Unionism in British Politics since 1968*, Stanford, CA, Hoover Institution Press, 1979, p. 8.
25 S.E. Finer, *The Changing British Party System, 1949–1979*, Washington, DC, The American Enterprise Institute, 1980, p. 158; Philip Norton, *The British Polity*, New York, Longman, 1991, pp. 193–6.

They had a good chance of gaining some kind of ministerial office as government expanded and the number of ministers and their parliamentary secretaries grew apace. (By the 1980s it had exceeded one hundred.)

Not that Britain lacked admirers in the US even at this period of evident social stress. In the olden days, US anglophiles had mainly derived from the Eastern Establishment; now Britain appealed to the liberal-left. According to American well-wishers such as Bernard D. Nossiter (author of *Britain: a Future that Works*, 1978), the British had developed a humane society that deserved praise more than censure. But Nossiter missed the discontent that was now found even among Labour supporters in Britain regarding the evident deficiencies in the public services – including health and education – the burden of taxation, and the shortcomings of British industry, and the intransigence of unions. Harold Wilson's jaunty good humor failed to retrieve the situation for Labour; neither did his evident opportunism, nor the quality of his political appointments. When Wilson left office in 1970, his party was in disarray. (A critic wrote about *The Rise of Harold Wilson and the Fall of the Labour Party*.)[26]

Not that the Tories were in a much more favorable position. They suffered from internal splits, particularly the cleavage between free marketers and interventionists. The former, represented by men such as Enoch Powell, a former Classics professor, rejected any kind of "indicative planning," or any sort of official incomes and pricing policy. Instead, he attributed the country's economic difficulties to the over-sized governmental sector and to governmental interference with market forces. Powell, however, wrecked his political career by intemperate remarks concerning Asian and African immigration, and was dismissed from the Tory "shadow cabinet."

Edward Heath, the Conservative Party's leader since 1965, by contrast, occupied a half-way position between the interventionists, on the one hand, and the free marketers, on the other. He looked to individual enterprise, but he did not regard a drastic reduction of government as the best way of assuring national prosperity.[27] It was Heath who guided the party through the general election of 1970, and the Tories won with a small majority. (The Conservatives gained 13,145,123 votes, 46.4 percent of the total; Labour won 12,178,295 votes, 43.0 percent of the total. In the House, the Conservatives had 330 seats, Labour 287, Liberals and others 13.) The Tories' success was not, however, an occasion for Tory self-congratulation. On retirement, Heath became an honored elder statesman, but in office he had few victories. If anything, Britain's economic troubles worsened. The electorate had become much more volatile than in the past; former party loyalties had diminished; the striking fluctuations in voting reflected "a desertion of Labour more than an access of strength to the Conservatives."[28]

26 Ken Coates, *The Crisis of British Socialism: Essays on the Rise of Harold Wilson and the Fall of the Labour Party*, London, Bertrand Russell Peace Foundation, 1971; Philip Ziegler, *Wilson: the Authorised Life of Lord Wilson of Rievaulx*, London, Weidenfeld and Nicolson, 1993. For other biographical works, see Austen Morgan, *Harold Wilson: a Life*, London, Pluto, 1992; Paul Foot, *The Politics of Harold Wilson*, Harmondsworth, Penguin, 1968; Pimlott, *Harold Wilson*; Dudley Gordon Smith, *Harold Wilson: a Critical Biography*, London, Hale, 1964.
27 Butler and Pinto-Duschinsky, *The British General Election of 1970*, pp. 69–77.
28 Ibid., p. 174. Bruce P. Lenman, *The Eclipse of Parliament: Appearance and Reality in British Politics since 1914*, London, Hodder and Stoughton, 1992, provides a critical reassessment. For works on Heath, see John Campbell, *Edward Heath: a Biography*, London, Cape, 1993; George Hutchinson, *Edward Heath: a Personal and Political Biography*, Harlow, Longman, 1970; Margaret Irene Laing, *Edward Heath: Prime Minister*, London, Sidgwick and Jackson, 1972.

British politics as a whole, moreover, continued to suffer from a lack of decisive leadership. According to a thesis put forward by Richard Crossman and others, British prime ministers were increasingly becoming like US presidents. Prime ministerial power and patronage supposedly was leading to a form of personal government in which the cabinet became a rubber stamp. At the same time, the power of parliament diminished, as party discipline tightened, the bureaucracy's size and functions kept growing, and major decisions were increasingly made beyond parliament's reach. (The later practice of televising parliamentary proceedings added to the viewers' perception of parliament as political theater.) But parliamentary majorities remained essential, and neither Wilson, nor James Callaghan (Labour prime minister from 1976 to 1979, and one of Labour's ablest leaders) wielded presidential authority. Nor did Heath. In many ways, Heath resembled Wilson more than Heath's predecessors. Churchill had descended on his father's side from a great ducal family. Douglas-Home had stepped down from a peerage; Macmillan had been among the grandest of the *grande bourgeoisie*. Heath, by contrast, was a builder's son; his mother had worked as a lady's maid. Heath made his way as a member of the new civil and military meritocracy; he had gone to Oxford on a competitive scholarship; during World War II he had served in the army, and left the service with the rank of lieutenant-colonel. Heath was anything but a Philistine: he was a fine yachtsman who once captained the British national sailing team, he was a connoisseur in art and music. (Having retired from politics, he taught for a time at Illinois Wesleyan University where he conducted the university orchestra, and lectured alike on Japanese art and on international statesmanship.) For all these accomplishments, he lacked the killer instinct – he was not the man to change a country.

Britain's economic difficulties remained unsolved, as the country had to cope alike with a worldwide slump, rising labor costs, strikes, and inflation. Secrecy in government militated against efficiency. Above all there were, in the language of Tudor kings, the "overmighty subjects" who dominated the labor union movement. The Heath government tried to control them but utterly failed. Heath especially had to accept defeat over a great miners' strike which shattered the government's income policy (1972). Heath differed from the Labourites in wanting to curb the power of the trade unions, to scale down (though not to eliminate) the welfare state, and to favor business. Like Harold Wilson, Heath was a technocrat who believed in the power and beneficence of the state.

The Heath government's single major achievement was Britain's adhesion to the EEC in 1973, by which time de Gaulle had died, and Heath had established excellent personal relations with the French president, Georges Pompidou. But the decision was far from popular. (In the House of Commons, Heath permitted a "free vote" by which members might vote according to their conscience rather than the party line. The decision was carried by 356 votes to 244: 69 Labourites supported the motion despite the party's decision to vote against it, but as many as 39 Conservatives voted "no".) A major part in this shift was played by Roy Jenkins, Labour's most outstanding performer in the House of Commons, without whose powerful advocacy parliament might never have voted in favor of joining the EEC in the first place.

Heath's expansionist budgets reduced unemployment, always his first priority, as it had been Macmillan's. But for all his personal integrity, Heath turned out to be one of the most unsuccessful prime ministers in British history. When he left office in 1974, inflation was rampant and on the rise. The money supply was out of control. (He mistakenly blamed inflation on the rise of oil prices since 1973.) Heath believed in compassionate Toryism, philanthropy *de haut en bas*, as befitted a former officer concerned above all with the welfare of his men. But he had little idea of how the country's troubled economy would pay for his vision. He treated his backbenchers like a high-minded headmaster would his Sixth Form (the equivalent of American Twelfth Graders in British schools); no wonder Heath had problems in parliament.

But, above all, Heath could do nothing to manage the labor unions, particularly the National Union of Mineworkers. The unions' power increased as the government's diminished. Determined to get the best possible terms for their members (and also to justify their own jobs), union activists kept pushing for higher wages without regard for productivity. Worse still, the unions continued to engage in bitter jurisdictional disputes with rival unions, and resisted labor-saving devices that might have endangered their members' jobs. The union movement itself changed as the General Secretary's power declined; the left increasingly won authority on the General Council and militant shop stewards in the workplace. The unions' conservatism was matched by enormous conservatism in most other professions.

There were other weaknesses. British management widely, though not inevitably, proved inferior to Germany's and Japan's. British trade unions not only remained powerful, but were also divided by quarrels over turf, and combative into the bargain, with a legacy of great class resentment. (In no other country could intellectuals in particular compete with their British brethren in the art of the social putdown.) The British educational system lacked that solid apprenticeship training that provided Germany with a great army of well-taught specialists and foremen, the non-coms of industry. Despite the rapid expansion of British universities, the British lagged behind in general as well as in technical education. The élites were well trained. But a much smaller proportion of British people attained a full course of secondary education than German and French people. Worse still, by 1993 it was estimated that 15 percent of British students aged 21 could not read and 20 percent could not add. (Educational levels are hard to compare internationally. Attendance rates are easier to establish. As regards the percentage of students enrolled at the age of 18, Britain in 1986 stood near the bottom of the scale with Spain, exceeded, in ascending order, by Australia, France and Sweden, the US, West Germany and Switzerland.)[29]

Another general election followed in 1974 – this at a time when the left had considerably increased its strength within the Labour Party, with leaders such as Michael Foot and Anthony Wedgwood Benn. This time Labour managed to win with a small majority (301 Labour seats in the House, as against 296 Conservative, and a much larger number of seats going to candidates belonging to neither of the great parties: 14 Liberals and 23 others). Wilson returned to No. 10 Downing Street. But while the electors had withdrawn their support from the Conservatives, they had failed to give their confidence to Labour. There was no mandate for decisive action over such contentious issues as wages, prices, the restructuring of the failing British economy, or the settlement of the Northern Irish issue. Wilson devalued the pound, froze prices and wages, and again placated the unions – all to no avail. Wilson by now was exhausted and bored with his work. The bounce had gone. His cabinet now contained several luminaries, known to the public in their own right. The prime minister's standing had declined, both within his own party and the country at large. Wilson was set on his last, and most unfortunate years in office. Consensual politics broke down; even a good many Labour voters became convinced that Britain could not forever put up with trade-union privilege, high spending, inflation, and the lordliness of Whitehall.

Scandinavia and the Low Countries

Social democracy, by contrast, seemed to work well in the Scandinavian states. The northern countries were ethnically homogeneous (at least until the 1980s, by which time immigration had created substantial minorities). The Nordic states had small populations and a large amount of land. They lacked class distinction (though Sweden especially evolved a new political class of men and women who had made their ways as functionaries in the Social Democratic Party, mostly worked in the public sector, and were linked by kinship and marriage). Lutheran in religion, the three kingdoms had increasingly turned toward secularism while retaining the Lutherans' moral earnestness. (There was little official corruption.) They were all constitutional monarchies, with a legacy of state interventionism bequeathed by the enlightened absolutism of olden days to the democratic polities of the present. In each of the three Nordic states, a large proportion of the population lived in the capital. Oslo, Copenhagen, and Stockholm, respectively, were centers of culture, learning, business and politics. (Stockholm and Oslo also served as foci of traditional liberalism, in contrast to Copenhagen, a major manufacturing center, and also a left-wing stronghold.)[30] As regards their respective economies, the Nordic states combined a most productive agriculture with efficient service industries (banking, insurance, and education). (Nordic schools, among other things, taught English to Scandinavians to such good effect that English became almost a second language to educated Scandinavians.) Scandinavians were equally good in high-precision engineering. (The Volvo car became an international symbol of high-quality engineering.) Scandinavians were also honest. (A global survey of corruption completed in 1995 put Denmark at the top of the scale as the least corrupt country in Europe, followed in descending order by Finland, Sweden, Switzerland, The Netherlands, Norway, and Ireland. Further down on the gauge of greased palms came Britain, Germany, the US, Austria, France, Belgium and Luxembourg, Portugal, Spain, and Hungary. Turkey and Greece brought up the rear.)[31]

In politics, the Scandinavians took a lead in issues such as ecology and the rights of women. The Scandinavians, especially the Swedes, rivaled the British and Americans in their pretension to occupy the high plateau of international morality. The Scandinavians took a particularly active part in international aid programs, in support of the UN and its various agencies, and in the then fashionable glorification of the Third World. But the Scandinavians differed in other aspects of foreign policy. Norway and Denmark were both members of NATO (albeit with Denmark as NATO's weakest link in the defense of North Western Europe.)[32] Denmark, in 1973, became a member of the EC, together with Great Britain and Ireland. (The Norwegians had rejected membership through a

30 David Gress, "The Nordic Countries," in Gerald A. Dorfman and Peter J. Duignan, eds, *Politics in Western Europe*, Stanford, CA, Hoover Institution Press, 1991, p. 130.
31 "A Global Gauge of Greased Palms," *The New York Times*, 20 August 1995, p. 3. Worldwide, the least corrupt country was New Zealand; the most corrupt countries, China and Indonesia.
32 Nigel de Lee, "The Danish and Norwegian Armed Forces," in L.H. Gann, ed., *The Defense of Western Europe*, London, Croom Helm, 1987, pp. 58–94.

referendum in which the opposing parties clashed with a degree of emotional fervor unexpected from the country's sober-minded citizens.)

The Swedes, by contrast, remained wedded to an uncompromising neutrality which they considered to be theirs almost by divine right. Unlike their Finnish neighbors, Sweden had never been attacked by the Soviet Union. Unlike Denmark and Norway, Sweden had not been occupied by the Germans in World War II, having been saved from German domination by the Allied victory. ("If the Western allies win, we shall be democrats, if the Nazis win, we shall be Aryans" was the guiding principle ascribed to Sweden by its critics.) Swedes, nevertheless, took professional pride in their neutrality as much as in their social institutions. Swedish politicians would lecture Americans in the best US pastoral style on real or alleged American misdeeds in Vietnam and elsewhere in the Third World. For a time Sweden also became a refuge for US draft evaders with sufficient means for a lengthy spell of overseas residence. But, to do them justice, the Swedes, like the Swiss, maintained a substantial armed force and an excellent arms industry. Theirs was not neutrality on the cheap. The Swedes had other reasons for complacency. From the 1930s onward, the Swedish Social Democratic Party had created a comprehensive welfare state; Sweden, like its Scandinavian neighbors, suffered little from poverty. Until the late 1970s, unemployment remained small and the per capita GDP stayed high.[33] Swedish socialism never attempted to operate in a closed economy; Sweden remained a low-tariff country (linked to EFTA). Sweden did not try to run a planned economy – the Swedes would not even adopt voluntary planning, French style. Farming remained in private ownership, and so – with minor exceptions – did industry. Swedish trade unions favored the efficient use of labor; Swedish trade unionism did not suffer much from demarcational or jurisdictional disputes, British fashion. Swedish social democracy, moreover, benefited from the leadership of Tage Erlander, a moderate and judicious man, who ran the Social Democratic Party from 1948 to 1968.

Not that all went well with Sweden. In 1968 Olof Palme assumed the prime ministership, determined to steer a more socialist, and also a more anti-American, course. In 1970 Sweden replaced its bicameral system with a unicameral system, thereby removing a brake, albeit a weak brake, on the popular chamber. Taxation kept rising; unemployment went up; the state expanded its holdings, and put a great deal of money into failing industries such as shipbuilding and steel-making. State-run social services squeezed out private social services. The government increasingly enforced equal work for equal pay, a principle fair in theory, but harmful in practice, as newcomers could no longer underbid established firms in paying lower wages. The wage differential diminished alike between skilled and unskilled labor, and between young and old. Hence the employers' incentive to hire young workers diminished; unemployment and hidden unemployment grew apace. The share of the state in the gross national income went up. (By 1991 the Swedish tax burden was the world's heaviest: 57 percent of the GDP, as against the EC's average of 41 percent).[34] The underground economy rose, as it did in countries such as

33 "Sweden and the Rest of the World: Sweden and its Economy Compared to Other Countries," *Bulletin*, Ekonomifakta Group, Stockholm, Sweden, 1991. For a detailed critique see Arthur Shenfield, *The Failure of Socialism: Learning from the Swedes and the English*, Washington, DC, Heritage Foundation, 1980. See also Dankwart A. Rustow, *The Politics of Compromise*, Princeton, NJ, Princeton University Press, 1955; Jonas Pontusson, *The Limits of Social Democracy*, Ithaca, Cornell University Press, 1992; Peter Swenson, *Fair Shares*, Ithaca, Cornell University Press, 1989.
34 "Sweat it out Sweden," *The Economist*, 28 November 1992, p. 22.

Italy. Sweden was plagued by a variety of social ills: a striking rise in the number of unmarried couples and unwed mothers, rising crime (including juvenile delinquency), alcoholism, and drug abuse. None of these afflictions were peculiar to Sweden which remained a stable and prosperous country. But, clearly, Sweden's reputed "Third Way" would not lead to a Nordic welfare utopia.

Belgium and Holland (The Netherlands) shared certain characteristics with the Nordic states. Both combined constitutional monarchy with rigid adherence to the rule of the law, respect for a powerful central bureaucracy, and a well-tried parliamentary system. (Belgium and Holland alike were governed by shifting coalitions of a centrist orientation.) Both enjoyed a high standard of living. Both depended heavily on foreign trade. Both were densely populated. (The conurbation linking Amsterdam and Rotterdam is one of the world's most thickly settled regions.) Both Belgium and Holland built massive welfare states. Both had to make major economic readjustments to preserve their prosperity. Belgium had been a pioneer in the first industrial revolution based on the production of coal, iron, steel, and textiles. Belgium developed into the world's largest per capita exporter. Many of its traditional industries could no longer compete on the world market, but the Belgians continued to sell abroad high-grade transport and tele-communications equipment, paper products, agricultural goods; they provided numerous services, including banking and construction. The Dutch proved equally inventive, with a productive agriculture, a broad range of services, a great transportation system, and new high-tech industries.

There were other similarities between Belgium and Holland. Before World War II, both countries had unavailingly sought security through neutrality. Both were overrun by the Nazis, and liberated by the allies. Chastened by German occupation, Belgium and Holland thereafter became founder members both of NATO and the EEC. (Benelux, a customs union consisting of Belgium, The Netherlands, and Luxembourg, ratified in 1947, had indeed been a pioneering venture and an inspiration to its neighbors.) The Benelux states, in particular Holland, turned into a reservoir of public servants – honest, competent, multilingual, experienced in transnational cooperation, who took a major part in staffing international bodies such as the EC, NATO, the World Bank, the IMF. (In the early 1970s Sicco Mansholt, a Dutchman, presided over the EC. Addeke Boerma, a second Dutchman, chaired the UN's Food and Agriculture Organization (FAO). Joseph Marie Luns, a third Dutchman, served as NATO's secretary general.)

Holland and Belgium each lost a great empire after World War II. (The Dutch East Indies achieved independence under the name of Indonesia in 1949. The Belgian Congo, later known as Zaïre, became a sovereign state in 1960.) In both countries, decoloniza-tion caused serious problems regarding relations with the US, as Washington favored decolonization, and thereby aroused the wrath of those Belgian and Dutch people who still believed in their own respective country's imperial mission. In both cases, moreover, the end of empire proved more traumatic to the former colonies than to the metropolitan countries. Numerous pessimistic forecasts notwithstanding, both the Belgian and Dutch economies adjusted rapidly. Few black Zaïreans were admitted to Belgium either before or after decolonization. Holland, by contrast, experienced a massive reflux, as some 250,000 repatriated Indonesian Dutch, as well as some 150,000 non-Europeans settled in the "mother country." The "belated discovery that the Netherlands had become a multi-racial society caused the country its first true imperial hangover."[35] But the ex-colonialists

35 H.L. Wesseling, "Post Imperial Holland," *Journal of Contemporary History*, no. 15, 1980, p. 138.

did very well upon their return; indeed, an Indonesian connection became essential to success in the bureaucracy and the army.

For all their resemblance and common historical traditions, Belgium and Holland also displayed striking differences. Historically, Belgium had been a Catholic country, Holland Protestant (with a steadily increasing Catholic component). Holland spoke Dutch; Belgium was divided between Flemish-speakers, French-speakers, and a small minority of German-speakers. Both Belgian and Dutch society had traditionally confronted the problem of *verzuiling* (pillarization) whereby several sociocultural groups existed in uneasy collaboration. But *verzuiling* worked differently in each country. The four pillars of Dutch society were Catholics, Protestants, socialists, and upper-class anti-clericals ("liberals", strong among urban professionals). From the end of the 1950s, the pillars began to crumble; decision-making shifted from the pillars to the central government which assumed enormous importance as a provider of social services of every kind.[36]

The Belgians were familiar with similar divisions, but Belgian politics was further complicated by the clash between French-speakers and Flemish-speakers (a conflict made worse by the economic decline of the French-speaking "rust-belts", and the rise of new, high-tech industries in the Flemish-speaking regions, formerly among the most backward parts of the kingdom). Traditional struggles between clericals and anti-clericals, workers and employers, were further complicated by linguistic conflicts which affected every aspect of politics. (The status of Brussels, a polylingual region set between Wallonia and Flanders, remained particularly contentious.) More and more power devolved to the regions. (By 1988, more than one-third of all taxes was levied by the regional authorities rather than the central government.) But for all their quarrels, petty and not so petty, Belgians managed to keep in existence a binational state, a feat that had proven equally impossible to attain for Greeks and Turks in Cyprus, Czechs and Slovaks in former Czechoslovakia, Jews and Arabs in Palestine. The Belgians' secret was decentralization: Belgium in practice divided between French-speaking Wallonia, Flemish-speaking Flanders, with Brussels as a third unit. Belgian politics remained among Western Europe's most complicated. (Not only was the country divided into Walloons and Flemings, but each of these two communities in turn were historically split between clericals and anti-clericals.) Nevertheless, Belgium held together and also provided a model for intra-European cooperation. (It was not for nothing that Brussels, capital of a multinational state, successfully served as center both of NATO and the EU.)

36 M.P.C.M. van Schendelen, "Politics and Political Science in the Netherlands," *Political Science and Politics*, summer 1987, p. 791; Gale Irwin, "Belgium and the Netherlands," in Dorfman and Duignan, eds, *Politics in Western Europe*, pp. 87–121.

6

Italy and the Iberian Peninsula, 1958–1978

Italy, the Iberian states, and Greece have certain features in common. In the past, they have suffered major failures in sustaining a democratic order. Italy, Spain, and Portugal all share agricultural sectors characterized by latifundia in the south, and smaller farms in the north, a division which has strongly affected both culture and politics. Italy and the Iberian states all avoided the Reformation upheaval and remained Catholic. Nevertheless, they all experienced bitter internal dissensions which divided Catholics from anti-clericals, centralizers from regionalists, monarchists from republicans, workers' parties from the bourgeoisie. All these countries were late in experiencing the industrial revolution. Yet, in the end, they all successfully transformed their respective economies, and escaped from the clutches of autocratic government.

Italy: Political Structure

No Western state had a worse press just after World War II than the Italian Republic. Italy had been disgraced by fascism and defeated in war. The Italian political system was said to be in a state of hopeless disrepair. "The socialization process in Italy is discontinuous and fails to inculcate a strong positive allegiance to the system. . . . In the area of party politics, the picture is one of unrivalled gloom."[1] Italian public life was described as being marked by "the paralysis of government, the rapid decay of public administration, the accumulation of unsolved problems, the spread of unrest."[2] (In Britain and the US there was also an undercurrent of anti-Catholic sentiment directed against a country in which the Church was particularly powerful.) Not surprisingly, a standard American textbook concluded that during the early 1960s, "impoverished Italians and those who smart under other forms of social oppression . . . would gladly exchange the freedom of elections and democratic constitutionalism for the tangible rewards of socialism: permanent employment, three meals a day . . . To the growing millions who want higher living standards, security, and social equality, communism is attractive."[3]

1 Raphael Zariski, *Italy: the Politics of Uneven Development*, Hinsdale, Ill., The Dryden Press, 1972, pp. 333, 334; Margaret Carlyle, *The Awakening of Southern Italy*, Westport, Conn., Greenwood Press, 1985 reprint; Vera Lutz, *Italy: a Study in Economic Development*, London and New York, Oxford University Press, 1962; Muriel Grindrod, *The Rebuilding of Italy: Politics and Economics, 1945–1955*, Westport, Conn., Greenwood Press, 1977; George H. Hildebrand, *Growth and Structure in the Economy of Modern Italy*, Cambridge, MA, Harvard University Press, 1977.
2 Luigi Barzini, "On the Locomotive," *Encounter*, vol. 33, no. 3, July 1969, p. 80.
3 Clifford A.L. Rich, "Politics and Government in Italy," in Clifford A.L. Rich, ed., *European Politics and Government: a Comparative Approach*, New York, Ronald Press, 1962, p. 299.

On the face of it, such pessimism concerning Italy's democratic future seemed well justified. Italy after World War II had produced one outstanding statesman, Alcide de Gasperi (1881–1954, prime minister from 1945 to 1953), head of eight successive coalitions, founding father of the Italian Republic. De Gasperi was Italy's greatest political leader since Cavour. But de Gasperi had no successor of his own stature. The Republic over which he had presided with such distinction had itself been born a frail child. In a referendum in 1946, the republican coalition defeated the monarchists by a narrow margin – and that partially through electoral fraud. Like the Weimar Republic, the Italian Republic had begun its career with widespread opposition among the citizenry, and, like the Weimar Republic, the Italian Republic had been born of defeat. Also, of all the major countries in Western Europe, Italy was by far the poorest. The new republic, moreover, was marked by remarkable instability. (Between 1945 and 1976, less than 30 years, Italy had 35 cabinets, with an average life of ten months. There were able men aplenty, but none stayed in office long.)[4]

Instability seemed built into the very constitution. This document had been drawn up by men determined that Italy should never again be ruled by a strong man such as Benito Mussolini, that never more should Italy succumb to slogans such as "*il Duce ha siempre ragione*" (The Leader is always right). The president of the republic was elected – not by a popular vote in the Gaullist fashion – but by a joint session of the two houses of parliament and regional representatives. Real power rested in the first place with the secretaries general of the major parties, and in the second place with their constituent organizations. Formal power was vested in parliament consisting of the Chamber of Deputies (*Camera dei deputati*) and the Senate (*Senato*). The former was elected for five years under a system of proportional representation that permitted the multiplication of lesser parties. The latter represented regions. The president appointed the prime minister and, on the prime minister's advice, the council of ministers (*Consiglio dei ministri*).

But the causes of instability were even more deeply seated. The Italian constitution gave special privileges to parties whose legitimacy, in the case of Communists, Socialists, and Christian Democrats, derived from the anti-Fascist struggle of the past. The electoral rules called for a rigid form of proportional representation, and thus enhanced the power of party bosses (*partocrazia*). Yet the parties themselves lacked stability. Except for the Italian Communist Party (*Partito comunista italiano*, PCI), all Italian parties were themselves coalitions. This was natural in a country as diverse in its composition as Italy, a country in which, for most citizens, regional sentiments outweighed national loyalties. (Emigration, oddly, heightened the sense of Italian nationality, as Sicilians, Calabrians, Sardinians in Chicago or New York would all be lumped together as Italians.)

There were countless other conflicts in Italy. Catholics clashed with anti-clericals (a breed hardly known in English-speaking countries). Anti-communists stood arrayed against communists, rich against poor. There were more subtle distinctions that separated, say, *garantiti* from *emarginati* (people with a guaranteed source of income from marginalized persons), insiders enjoying special protection or patronage from outsiders without access to the powerful. In Italy both the laws and their execution seemed unpredictable. As a British observer put it with some asperity,

---

4 Roy Macridis, Christophe S. Allen and Winston L. Anselm, "The Mediterranean: the Politics of Instability," in Roy C. Macridis, ed., *Modern Political Systems: Europe*, Englewood Cliffs, NJ, Prentice-Hall, 1978, p. 493.

many laws simply cannot be obeyed. Every other year some whole category of leading citizens is consequently arrested, with great show, and then usually released
again ... Often they deserve it; but it is impossible not to feel some sympathy
for the directors of opera houses who were led away handcuffed because they had
committed the grave offense of having hired singers through an agent.[5]

Italy also remained backward for long in the sense that a larger proportion of people
labored on the land than in any major Western European country except Spain. (In
1966, the percentage of people employed in agriculture stood at 32.6 in Spain, 24.9
in Italy, 17.6 in France, 10.8 in West Germany, 8.5 in Holland, 3.4 in Britain.)[6]
Admittedly, the flight from the land continued at a rapid rate in Italy. Nevertheless, for
the time being, a relatively large share of Italians lived in villages and small country
towns. Italy remained marked by striking divisions between the cities and the countryside, as well as by remarkable differences within the countryside: say, the fertile Po
valley against the arid hills of Calabria.

Italy's troubles were deeply rooted in history. Italy is a land of regions; its keynote is
diversity. The country's unity was achieved only recently, largely completed in 1861, and
– as we see it – under the auspices of Savoy, Italy's Prussia. The new rulers believed in
strict centralization exercised through prefects as agents of the central government in the
backwoods.[7] Theoreticians criticized this administrative uniformity, but politicians once
in power all upheld the central government's prerogatives. The Fascists were centralizers,
and so were their successors the Christian Democrats, despite the Catholic thinkers'
professed commitment to regional diversity. The Christian Democrats insisted that
centralized government was essential, lest specific regions should fall under the leftists'
sway. By contrast, Socialists and Communists who had favored centralization of the
Jacobin kind when they stood at the threshold of power in 1945, later became advocates
of regional autonomy. In most of Italy, they enjoyed little support, but had a great deal
of backing in particular provinces such as Tuscany. Centralization, however, did not
work well – no matter who ruled in Rome; indeed, there were remote areas in Sardinia,
Calabria, and Sicily where the central government could be largely ignored.

The North, the center, and the South in fact constituted almost separate Italies within
the boundaries of the same state. Guido Reni, president of ISTAT, the Italian Statistical
Office, likened Italy to a married couple that lives under the same roof but is actually
"separated" at home. The South was regarded by Northerners as a part of the Third World,
a great reservoir of troublesome people. Southern Italian migrants were derided as *mangia-
saponi* ("soap eaters," who supposedly used soap for filling their stomachs rather than washing their hands). At the same time guilt-ridden Northern intellectuals developed peculiar
views concerning Southern villagers supposedly wedded to magic concepts that juxtaposed
woman and cow, man and wolf, baron and lion, goat and devil – and other such fancies.

Generalizations are, of course, always dangerous. Legend notwithstanding, it was not
true that the entire South (*mezzogiorno*) was poverty-stricken, its people priest-ridden,

5 Brian Lyttleton, "Experts in Expedients," review of John Haycraft, *Italian Labyrinth: Italy in the
1980s*, in *The Times Literary Supplement*, 25 April 1986, p. 439.
6 Anthony Sampson, *Anatomy of Europe: a Guide to the Workings, Institutions, and Character of
Contemporary Western Europe*, New York, Harper and Row, 1968, p. 63.
7 Robert C. Fried, *The Italian Prefects; a Study in Administrative Politics*, New Haven, Yale University Press, 1963.

superstitious, and all involved with *mafiosi*. Such prejudices, popular in the North, and spread abroad by movies such as *The Godfather*, require a little correction. All the same, the South as a whole was much more backward than the North; disparities between the North and the South would continue, despite continuing economic development through-out Italy. To give just one example, the province of Milano, including the city and the surrounding communities in central Lombardy, still accounted in 1988 for 28 percent of Italy's national income, and less than 7 percent of its population. If Milan were still an independent city state, as in the olden days, it would be richer than the whole of Switzerland.[8]

Despite massive attempts to develop the South, and despite considerable progress made, the average Milanese in 1988 remained twice as wealthy as the average South-erner. Milan, once part of the Hapsburg empire, moreover, remained linked to central Europe, and stood a world apart from a port such as Naples. The overwhelming majority of Italians had only one thing in common: they were Catholics or former Catholics. (Italy was the only country in the world where 28 percent of Communist Party members admitted to attending Mass regularly.)[9] Otherwise, Italy was divided by striking dif-ferences in class, dialect, history, and lifestyle. These splits were worsened by official cor-ruption, and by scandals reaching the highest in the land; by huge entitlement programs that in turn placed a heavy burden on taxpayers. The state poured huge subsidies into state corporations which ran at a loss. Not surprisingly, successive Italian governments had to cope with huge budgetary deficits, and fitful inflation.[10] (And then, in the 1990s, the widespread Italian corruption scandal – *tangentopoli*, "Bribery City" – brought the old parties to their knees.)

This was not the end of Italy's troubles. The bureaucracy was huge in size, reviled for its real and alleged inefficiency, but above all for the way in which it was used for party patronage. The public sector and education employed an ever-growing proportion of the labor force (51.9 percent in 1961; 69.1 percent in 1983). Pensions consumed an ever-increasing share of the national budget. There was a great array of public corporations (*ènti pubblici*) known for their secrecy, their widespread links to political parties, their blatant enrichment of favorites, their waste of public money, and the extent to which their spoils helped to sustain the existing power structure. *L'ente crea l'esistente* (the public corporation creates that which exists) commented Italian Communist leader Palmiro Togliatti in an almost untranslatable Hegelian pun.[11] This public sector was so large and variegated that its overall performance could not be easily assessed. There were islands of efficiency such as the Bank of Italy, which did an excellent job. By and large, however, the public sector performed poorly compared to the private sector. Many a tourist, for example, had horror stories to tell about the failings of the Italian postal and telephone systems. (A study conducted in 1990 by *Confindustraria*, the association of Italian industrialists,

8 "Italy's Capitalist City", *The Economist*, 19 March 1988, p. 75.
9 Samuel H. Barnes, *Representation in Italy: Institutionalized Tradition and Electoral Choice*, Chicago, University of Chicago Press, 1977, table, p. 52.
10 For general histories, see Denis Mack Smith, *Italy and its Monarchy*, New Haven, Yale Univer-sity Press, 1989; Denis Mack Smith, *Italy: a Modern History*, Ann Arbor, University of Michigan Press, 1959; Norman Kogan, *A Political History of Italy: the Postwar Years*, New York, Praeger, 1983.
11 Cited by Giuseppe Di Palma, *Surviving without Governing: the Italian Parties in Parliament*, Berkeley, CA, University of California Press, 1977, p. 266.

found that out of 100 phone calls, 50 did not get through on the first try.) The Italian railways, another public enterprise, likewise remained backward in 1990; Italy by that time risked being isolated from countries such as France and Germany which were creating a European system of high-velocity trains. (On the other hand, Italian highways outshone the autobahns.)

There were complaints of equal severity concerning many other aspects of Italy – its university system and its law courts. According to its critics, Italy was a country run, not for the benefit of the ordinary citizen, but for the benefit of political parties, privileged entities each with their own clientele. Corruption kept growing as the state expanded. (Aid voted for the *mezzogiorno*, in particular, was destined for the pockets of political protégés, some of whose clients included gangsters.) Not that Italians were unduly squeamish. Not much blame, if any, attached to the politician who somehow "forgot" to register a donation to his party. But there was no excuse for the man who filled his bank account with millions earmarked for earthquake relief. All major parties, including the Communists but excluding the neo-Fascists, participated in this game, above all the regnant Christian Democrats. But for the Communist peril, they would sooner or later have been voted out of office. But as long as the Communists appeared a major threat, the Christian Democrats could hold on to office without embarking on major administrative and political reform.

Worse still was the crime problem. The founders of the Italian Republic, men such as de Gasperi, had been *galantuomini*, gentlemen who neither took nor proffered bribes. But their immediate successors deliberately chose to swell public enterprise and state power in order to feed the large and growing structure of their parties. This increased the stakes for which criminals might compete. Hence crime kept expanding in scale and sophistication. The old-fashioned criminal gang in the *mezzogiorno* might stage a coup by abducting a landowner for ransom. The new-style criminals wore white collars and carried briefcases. They bought their way into political parties, subsidized politicians, and penetrated public corporations – even the publishing world. They became brokers of government contracts and licenses. They came to dominate entire industries, such as trucking and construction. Conventional appraisals of international crime stress its involvement in the arms and drugs traffic. But more important still were the huge profits engendered for criminal syndicates by the huge payments made by the Italian government agencies to the impoverished South. Big-time crime took its cut from the government contracts, and from robbing health, welfare, and pension funds. Corruption, finally, operated on a scale that would have aroused alike both Al Capone's admiration and astonishment.

Given the size and exactions of the state machinery, Italy, moreover, developed a huge underground economy, designed to escape the attention of statisticians and tax gatherers. Its size was variously estimated at between 25 percent and 30 percent of the product; the underground economy helped to carry the burden of public enterprise. Pessimistic forecasts concerning Italy thus would fill a small library; they gained in persuasiveness, color, and entertainment value by a series of well-publicized scandals which gave the impression of a country perpetually on the brink of breakdown.

Nevertheless, the Italian Republic accomplished a near-miracle. Immediately after World War II, Italy profited from Marshall aid. More important still, Italy benefited from its links to the massive Italian-American community in the US. (Between 1820 and 1975, more than five million Italians had legally come to the US; 243,152 of them arrived between 1941 and 1960, and 214,111 more in the following decade.) Their letters and return visits to friends and relatives in Italy provided ordinary Italians with detailed information concerning wages, living conditions, and lifestyles in the US considerably more reliable than the counter-reality widely constructed in academic journals, seminars, and left-wing journals. Italian-American Catholics supported the Church in Italy, financially aided the CD, invested funds in the "Old Country," and sometimes returned to Italy as "Americans," often full of new ideas, with savings accumulated overseas. (The role of the returned immigrant as yet remains to be fully studied.)

Italy recovered from the effects of World War II with startling speed. The Italian economy, once thought to be immutably backward, expanded and diversified. Contrary to its reputation, the Italian Republic presided over the most successful period in modern Italian history. There was no effective Fascist revival. Unhampered by Fascist regulations or by colonial preoccupations, Italy modernized its economy. This included a flourishing tourist industry, new oil refineries, petrochemical complexes; Italy excelled in the production of cars, typewriters, specialized machinery, and in industrial design; the country underwent a new industrial revolution.

Not that everything went well. By the late 1950s, Italy was still stricken with Europe's greatest unemployment – two million people out of work. Prosperity had passed by most of the South, Sicily, and Sardinia. The slums of Naples had improved little over the past hundred years, with poor people still living in caves and underground cellars, or crowded into a single room with their children. But during the 1960s, the South saw startling overall improvements in wages and living standards. From a country that exported people abroad, Italy, by the early 1970s, had turned into a country that imported workers. The Italian Republic survived all challenges, despite the many pessimistic forecasts from its creation. Despite the strength of the monarchist vote in 1946, the restoration of the monarchy did not turn into a major political issue. (Italian Catholics, unlike so many *bien pensant* French Catholics at the end of the last century, did not think of their republic as a "Slut"; likewise, Italian Catholics did not necessarily admire the House of Savoy that had seized the Papal State from the Holy See.) Neither was there a military coup; when it came to the crunch, the men in resplendent uniforms bowed to those in sober business suits.

Italian respondents to public opinion polls would indeed describe their country's politics and politicians with a certain cynicism – more so than other Europeans. But Italian voter participation in national elections remained high. And when the Republic later met a genuine challenge from the Red Brigades, an ultra-revolutionary terror organization, Italians rallied to the Republic. In Norman Kogan's words concerning the Italians, "perhaps their sense of national political identity was not as weak as their responses to pollsters indicated. Perhaps there was more consensus and less fragmentation than they expressed."[12]

The achievement of this consensus was itself remarkable, for Italian unity in the nineteenth century had been established on slender foundations. The state had essentially been founded by a minority, a well-educated, secularized middle class which took little account of Italy's regional diversity, or of the Church, or of the poor. In the twentieth century, Fascism, with its boastfulness, brutality, and incompetence, had proved yet one more divisive force. After World War II, under the Republic, the country was once again unified in a national as well as a political sense, and the regnant system of government attained full legitimacy.

12 Kogan, *A Political History of Italy*, p. 342.

Italy: the Establishment Parties

After the political scandals (*tangentopoli*) of the early 1990s, only the bold will feel inclined to praise Italy's defunct party system. Television viewers in Italy and abroad then watched how councillors, cabinet officers, even former cabinet ministers appeared in court, having supported the Mafia and other crime syndicates. Nevertheless, much of the credit for Italy's postwar miracle must go to the former ruling party and its associates. Italy's political map was, of course, as complicated as Italian society, with four distinct segments. On the far right stood the Monarchists and the neo-Fascists (the latter known as the *Movimento sociale italiano*, MSI). Their adherents were political outcasts. (In 1960, when the MSI briefly formed part of a parliamentary majority, Communist-inspired riots led to the fall of the government.) On the left there was the PCI (*Partito comunista italiano*), complete with its solid establishment of functionaries, propagandists, intellectuals, and street fighters. Formally, the PCI was a perennial outsider in Italian politics. Informally, it became part of a counter-establishment with substantial "pull" and patronage. The ruling party, with the largest electoral support, was the Christian Democratic Party (*Democrazia Christiana*, CD). This unfailingly received a plurality from an electorate who consistently distrusted the Communists. (Between 1946 and 1976 the CD's share fluctuated between 35.2 percent and 38.8 percent; the highest percentage was attained in 1948 with 48.5 percent. Communists did only a little worse. During the same years their percentage of the vote went from 18.9 percent to 34.4 percent.)[13] This left several minor groups left and right of center, too small to form governments on their own, but desirable, sometimes essential, as coalition partners for the CD. These parties included the Liberal Party (*Partito liberale italiano*, PLI), founded during the nineteenth century in the classical tradition of free enterprise and "laicism." It was a party known for the financial rectitude of its leaders, and for the efficiency which distinguished Liberal "fiefs" such as the Bank of Italy. There was the Italian Republican Party (PRI) created in the tradition of Giuseppe Mazzini (1805–72), enlightened and populist. There was the Italian Social Democratic Party (*Partito socialista democratico italiano*, PSDI), and the Italian Socialist Party (*Partito socialista italiano*, PSI). Between 1946 and 1974 support for these smaller parties dropped as follows: PSI from 20.7 percent of the electorate to 9.6 percent; Liberals from 6.8 percent to 1.3 percent; PSDI from 7.1 percent in 1948 to 3.4 percent; PSI from 20.7 percent to 9.6 percent; Republicans from 4.8 percent to 3.1 percent. Only the MSI increased from 2.0 percent in 1948 to 6.1 percent.)

The ever-changing coalitions between these parties should have led to governance by inexperience. In practice, the same names and faces always returned. If an author were to create a senior Establishment figure for a political novel set in post-World War II Italy, the imagined VIP might be drawn as follows. He would be a man (never a woman), from a middle-class background, brought up in a small town. He would be well educated (even in the Italian Communist Party the number of university graduates from a bourgeois background continued to increase at the workers' expense). He would have obtained a degree from an Italian (not a foreign) university. He would probably have worked in the Resistance or gone into exile during the Fascist era, taken his seat in the Constituent Assembly after World War II, then in the Chamber of Deputies. He would thereafter have held a variety of ministerial offices, as well as party offices, or jobs in public corporations. (On a lower level, he might have been a mayor and head

13 See tables in Barnes, *Representation in Italy*, p. 40.

of a provincial party organization.) He would in all likelihood have ended his career with a life appointment in the senate – silver-haired, with a dignified style in oratory, worldly wise in the ways of patronage and in dealing with countless *raccomandazioni* on behalf of deserving clients. Once entrenched in the inner élite of his chosen party, he would have stayed in politics for a long, long time. Raphael Zariski, an expert in the field, confirms, "usually only death or senility removes an Italian politician from office."[14] Having been compelled by Mussolini to celebrate youth as the springtime of the fatherland (*giovinezza, giovinezza, primavera della patria* – youth, youth, springtime of the fatherland), Italians thereafter were quite willing to be ruled by elderly gentlemen.

A few brief case histories will illustrate the point. Amintore Fanfani (born 1908) began as an economics professor at the University of Milan. During World War II, he emigrated to Switzerland and on his return in 1945 became the CD's press secretary. Thereafter he sat in the Constituent Assembly, later in the Chamber of Deputies. He rose to ministerial office, variously in charge of labor, agriculture, internal affairs, and subsequently headed the government at various times as prime minister. Between 1954 and 1959 he served as general secretary of the CD where he represented the left-of-center faction known as the *Iniziativa democratica*. Fanfani diminished the influence of Catholic Action (a Christian organization), vastly extended the party's patronage system, and played a leading role in bringing about the "opening to the left" (1962) which brought the Socialists into the government under Pietro Nenni.

Nenni himself (born in 1891) belonged to an even earlier generation. He came from a peasant family in the Romagna, became a socialist before World War I, at a time when Mussolini was also a socialist, and spent some time in jail in Mussolini's company. Nenni fought in World War I as a volunteer, thereafter briefly supported Fascism – this during a brief period when celebrated Italians such as Arturo Toscanini and Giacomo Puccini did likewise. Nenni soon broke with Mussolini, edited the socialist paper – as Mussolini had done – and was arrested. Nenni fled abroad, spent 17 years in exile, and fought in Spain. He was arrested by the Nazis in occupied France during World War II and turned over to the Italians, but was liberated in 1943. Thereafter, he organized partisan fighting, later served as a deputy in the Constituent Assembly, and then as deputy prime minister. In 1947 the Socialist Party split over the question of whether or not to continue collaboration with the Communists. Nenni at first continued to defend the Communist connection, but from the mid-1950s took a more centrist position, and returned the Stalin Peace Prize when the Soviet Union invaded Hungary in 1956. He responded warmly to the CD's "opening to the left," contrived to extend his party's patronage (particularly in the electrical power industry), and between 1963 and 1968 again served as deputy prime minister. He pushed for yet greater resolution in "opening to the left," and ended his career as a life senator – a key figure in Italian political life, and a pillar of constitutional respectability.

His rival Giuseppe Saragat (born 1898) studied economics and at first went into banking. He turned to socialism, and – still a young man – went into extended exile, first in Austria, then in France. When the Duce's rule tottered, Saragat returned to Italy, held a ministerial post in the short-lived wartime government headed by Ivanoe Bonomi, then served as ambassador to France, and then as president of the Constituent Assembly. In 1947 Saragat attacked the "Popular Front" line taken by the Socialists; he broke with the PSI and formed a splinter party of his own which merged, in 1952, into the newly

14 Zariski, *Italy: the Politics of Uneven Development*, p. 184.

founded PSDI, headed by Saragat as general secretary. Saragat repeatedly served as deputy prime minister in coalition governments, as foreign minister, and finally as president of the republic (1964–71). He was pro-American, pro-Atlanticist, but he never succeeded in his object of building the PSDI into a social democratic party on a par with British Labour or the German SPD.

The parties led by these men shared certain organizational features: a large membership, and an extensive extra-parliamentary organization with considerable power in making political decisions. Each major party had a series of assemblies, arranged hierarchically on a sectional or communal, a provincial, and a national level (*partocrazia*). Corresponding to these assemblies, there were permanent party organizations on the sectional, provincial, and national planes. The leader of the party's extra-parliamentary organization was the party's general secretary. In the CD's case, general secretaries such as Aldo Moro and Fanfani also served as prime ministers. Similarly, deputies and senators widely held ranks in the party organization at a lower level. The larger parties also had extensive support organizations for women, youth, and particular occupations. But there was also a grimmer side to party politics. Parties operated as patronage machines, with jobs and contracts reserved for party favorites. Party organizations and party functions grew in size and complexity, and so did their need for money. Corruption during the de Gasperi years had been on a modest scale, conducted in a gentlemanly fashion; thereafter, malfeasance became ever more brazen; public money went into innumerable private pockets. There was a political underworld where party bosses mingled with crime bosses – not surprisingly, Italians widely despised their government.

The key to Italian politics were the Christian Democrats. Italians might dislike their ruling party – but anything was better than the Communists. Until recently, the CD dominated Italian party politics. Between 1945 and 1981 the CD provided every prime minister, and most prime ministers thereafter. (The main break came much later, in 1983 when Battino Craxi, a Socialist, became premier in a coalition government with the CD. He stayed in office until 1987, heading Italy's longest-lived government since de Gasperi's.)

To do justice to the CD is a hard task. By the early 1990s its historical role seemed to have disappeared. The communist threat had gone at home and abroad. The CD's reputation had slumped, as had the reputation of all old-established parties. Cabinet ministers, heads of departments, police chiefs, judges were discovered to have been in the *mafiosi*'s pay. Party barons such as Giulio Andreotti (seven times prime minister, and once a pillar of the Establishment) were under investigation for alleged links to the Mafia. The very term Christian Democrat had become discredited – so much so that the party's general secretary Mino Martinazzoli himself proposed, in 1993, that the party return to its prewar name: the Italian Popular Party.

But the CD's past role must be understood in context. The CD had presided over the Italian economic miracle and over the creation of a reasonably stable republic – stable compared with Italy's political past. The CD won legitimacy and acceptance for Italy in postwar Europe. Above all, the CD was a coalition to keep the Communists out of power. As such, the CD was a political supermarket: it contained something for almost every taste. Had it not been for the communist menace, the CD would surely have broken asunder, for it lacked a cohesive social program. There were within the CD advocates of private enterprise, but they formed a minority. (Nothing would be more mistaken than to look on the CD simply as the party of Italian big business which was itself politically split.) The CD only took a decisive stand where the Church was concerned.

In matters concerning the rights of parochial schools, religious classes in public schools, or the morality of abortion, the CD spoke in an unambiguous manner. "When religious considerations are at stake, the CD ceases to be a catch-all party and becomes a party of principle."[15] It was only for political reasons of great urgency that the CD sold out on these as well.

This generalization weakened as secularization advanced and traditional loyalties lessened. (To the forecasters' surprise, a referendum in 1973 decided in favor of legalizing divorce. Despite strenuous opposition from the Church, the CD put up only a pro forma fight.) All the same, the CD depended heavily on Catholic support groups such as the Civil Committees of Catholic Action, the *Coltivatori diretti* (a farmers' group), Catholic labor organizations, especially the Italian Confederation of Free Trade Unions (CISL), and also on the Church's network of parishes. When Fanfani became general secretary he tried to improve the party's grass roots organization by building party cells in factories. Under Fanfani, the party bureaucracy (*partocrazia*) increased in influence. But even Fanfani could not make his organization dominant; it became, as Norman Kogan explains, yet "one more faction in the shifting league of interests which composed the Christian Democratic Party."[16] Within the CD, as in all other parties, factional disputes were apt to be envenomed by personal vendettas. No CD leader could survive unless he was a master of compromise.

Overall, the various CD leaders proved surprisingly good at this task. Composed of many different groups, the CD could justly claim to be a *Volkspartei*, with some support from every social class, with strong regional backing, especially from the South and the north-east. (The South had for long chafed under the rule of a centralizing monarchy which had disdained the South, and had imposed conscription and heavy taxation; Southerners had looked to the Church to defend their liberties. In Lombardy and the Veneto, by contrast, the Church had appeared as the Italians' defender against the Austro-Hungarian monarchy which had once owned these provinces.) As regards the party's occupational makeup, industrial workers, in 1961, accounted for about 25 percent of the CD's membership. This was less than the Socialists' share of about 30 percent and the Communists' of 40 percent. Nevertheless, no politician could ignore the Catholic workers, both those within the CD, and within the socialist parties. The self-employed (as against the state-employed) lower middle classes were well represented within the CD; supporters included shopkeepers, artisans, and also married women and pensioners. Of course, none of these social groups could be taken for granted. The CD had in particular to compete with the Monarchists and neo-Fascists for the votes of lower middle-class people. The middle bourgeoisie – engineers, army officers, also school teachers and advocates, customarily addressed with respect as *dottore* – were apt to divide their votes between the CD and the Liberals; the same applied to bankers and industrialists. In addition, the CD had substantial support among farmers and peasants, though again, the rural vote was split, with substantial support going to the socialist parties and the PCI.

Within the CD, the welfare-oriented groups gained the upper hand against the advocates of private enterprise, so much so that the CD could, in some ways, be regarded as a social democratic party. The CD thus enacted programs for land reform, for low-cost housing, and for strengthening the public sector (for instance, through the nationalization of the electrical industries). The CD also endeavored to develop the South through public bodies such as the *Cassa per il mezzogiorno* (a major source of patronage), through the provision of an improved infrastructure, and through compelling state-owned firms to locate a specific share of their new enterprises in the South. The leftward tilt became more marked as the Catholic Church itself increasingly inclined toward the center-left. In 1958 Pope John XXIII succeeded Pius XII. (As Patriarch of Venice, John had already wished the Socialists a successful party congress.) In 1961 the new Pope issued his encyclical *Mater et magistra* (Mother and teacher) which endorsed a mixed economy, rejected the uncontrolled free market, and heartened those Catholics who looked for an accommodation with the PSI, the "opening to the left" (*appertura alla sinistra*).

The opening to the left met with considerable controversy where groups such as the *Coltivatori diretti* wanted nothing to do with it. But after the 1958 elections, politics moved leftward, and within the CD there were powerful factions that wished to profit from this trend. They included in particular the "Dorotei" (thus named after a convent where they had first met). They included men such as Emilio Colombo and Aldo Moro, the latter a law professor from Bari. Fanfani put together a compromise program which Nenni could accept (it included the nationalization of the electrical industry). A year later, Moro, who in 1959 had succeeded Fanfani as the CD's secretary general, formed a coalition with the PSI, with himself as prime minister and Nenni as a deputy. The Socialists also made some concessions. (For instance, they gave an assurance that they would not desert NATO as long as the alliance remained defensive in character, and as long as the alliance obligations stayed confined to Europe.) Government by left-of-center coalitions continued in one form or another until 1994.

Moro (1916–78) was a lawyer's lawyer, pedantic and dry as dust. But he held his coalition together. Indeed, the *appertura alla sinistra* enjoyed support from the most unexpected sources. The US State Department favored changing course; so did the bulk of US academics interested in Italy; so did the CIA; so did reformists within the Church; so did the international prestige journals such as the *New York Times*, *The Financial Times*, *The Economist*, *Il Giorno* (owned by ENI), and *La Stampa* (owned by Fiat). Indeed, Fiat, as well as other major Italian firms, pursued their own opening to the left. In 1966, for example, Vittorio Valletta, president of Fiat, concluded a deal to build 600,000 cars a year in the Soviet Union. Hard-line left-wingers exulted. Fiat had for long been an arch-villain in the eyes of Italian Marxists – a giant family firm which dominated the city of Turin much more thoroughly than the House of Savoy had ever done in the days of its glory. Suddenly, Fiat stood out as the Soviets' chosen friend; Fiat's new factory town in the Soviet Union was called Togliattigrad, an irony that would have assuredly pleased Palmiro Togliatti, the "Italian Stalin," had he still been alive.

The opening to the left had many other supporters. CD strategists hoped thereby to isolate the PCI. The Church welcomed the move at a time when the Papacy attempted both internal reforms within the Church, and endeavored to improve relations with the communist governments in Eastern Europe. Above all, the opening to the left benefited all those who looked to a further expansion of the Italian welfare state. Welfarism was deeply ingrained in the Italian tradition, both in private and in public enterprise. Italian workers received a higher proportion of their remuneration in kind and services than most other workers in Western Europe. Moreover, family firms continued to play a major role within Italian capitalism (i.e. Fiat for cars; Olivetti for typewriters; Pirelli for tires; Marzotto for textiles; Pesenti for cement). These family firms had developed a paternalistic style of their own, and the Italian welfare state in part built on these private traditions.

Above all, the expansion of public enterprise greatly increased the patronage at the politicians' disposal. Italian public enterprises such as ENI (National Hydrocarbon Agency) and IRI (Institute for Industrial Reconstruction, originally a Fascist creation) increased the scope of their operations, augmented their clientage, and turned into powerful political baronies in their own right. Naturally, ENI and IRI also came to be listed among the world's major money-losing enterprises. (Some critics, in fact, accused the CD of maintaining islands of backwardness for the sake of maintaining party patronage.)[17]

The *appertura alla sinistra* did not, however, isolate the PCI. On the contrary, the newly formed *Partito socialista di unità proletaria* became a valued ally for the PCI and "a handy receptacle for all kinds of left-wing deviationists" who might otherwise have disturbed the harmony and discipline that the PCI wished to maintain within its own ranks. As a result of its leftward lurch, Italy was prevented from putting through reforms such as the much-needed reconstruction of the public services. Far from diminishing in influence, the PCI actually gained electoral strength and patronage. (Its share of the popular vote went up from 22.7 percent in 1958 to 34.4 percent in 1976.) To be fair to the CD, however, the party did keep the Communists at bay – whatever the mistakes committed by CD strategists and their CIA advisers. (It was only in 1974 that CIA involvement ended in Italian politics.)[18] The CD could also take credit for liberalizing antiquated and oppressive laws inherited from the Fascists (such as legislation restricting the free migration of peasants into cities). Whatever Italian governments planned, none achieved truly effective control over the economy, given the weaknesses of the public services, the extent of the "Second Economy," and the average Italian's resolve not to submit to a pervasive bureaucracy.

On the other hand, the CD had an impressive record in foreign affairs. After World War II, the Italians had had their fill of imperial glory. Xenophobia was at a discount in a country heavily dependent, and increasingly so, on trade with its European neighbors, and on the migration of Italians to other European countries. (It was only during the early 1970s that Italians ceased to seek work abroad in large numbers.) In addition, Italy was linked to the US by many different bonds. Vast immigration had begun from the 1890s; US troops were stationed in Italy; Italo-American trade expanded after the war; Italian-Americans greatly improved their economic and social position. The PCI's most skillful ventures in anti-American propaganda could not counter the influence of American media and, even more importantly, of letters and monetary remittances sent home by Italians and Italian-Americans. US Catholics, including of course Italian-American Catholics, gave substantial support to the CD. Neutralism of the Swedish variety might appeal to left-wing intellectuals, but it was never a practical alternative for Italy.

In 1949, Italy joined NATO as a founder-member, and thereafter stood out as one of its most loyal supporters in spite of PCI opposition. (The movement for nuclear disarmament never attained as much visibility in Italy as it did in West Germany and Britain.) In relation to its gross national product, Italy had one of the smallest defense budgets in NATO; nevertheless, in terms of manpower and also in technological expertise, Italy's contribution was substantial. Italy was also important to NATO by reason of its strategic position in the Mediterranean, all the more so when NATO's defenses

17 See, for instance, Judith Chubb, *Patronage, Power and Poverty in Southern Italy: a Tale of Two Cities*, Cambridge, Cambridge University Press, 1982.
18 Angelo Codevilla, *Informing Statecraft: Intelligence for a New Century*, New York, Free Press, 1992, pp. 251–2.

in the eastern Mediterranean weakened through ongoing disputes between Turkey and Greece. Not that relations between Italy and the US were entirely smooth. Politicians such as Fanfani discovered for Italy a new "Mediterranean mission": Italy should serve as a bridge between the Arab world and the West, a task that supposedly suited Italy, in particular, by reason of the country's geographical location and historical experience. The doctrine in fact ignored the unfavorable legacy left by Italy's own imperial past; for critics, the "Mediterranean mission" was no more than an opportunistic device to favor the Arabs, with their oil riches and their market potential, at the expense of Israel, the US's ally. But overall, Italy's commitment to NATO as a whole never wavered.

In 1957 the Italian parliament also ratified the treaties providing for the European Economic Community (EEC). The cause of European unification had wide appeal, not merely among the CD, but also among a good many socialists. (For example, Nenni had been a member of Jean Monnet's Action Committee for a United States of Europe.) The main beneficiaries, however, were the Italian Christian Democrats who felt thoroughly at home in a European parliament where they formed part of the strongest political bloc. (By the late 1960s, Christian democrats held 44 percent of the seats, socialists of varying persuasions 25 percent, liberals of differing kinds 18 percent.)[19] For Italy, membership of the two powerful blocs had other political uses. South Tyrol contained a German-speaking minority which objected to Italian overlordship. Austria brought the matter to the UN (1960–61). In the end, in 1969, Austria and Italy signed an agreement which essentially favored Italy, a member of NATO and the EEC, as against Austria, a neutral country. The German-speaking Tyroleans, for their part, never managed to gain acceptance by the international community as an oppressed nationality on a par with Basques or Palestinians. German-speaking revisionists at the time were out of favor with the other European nationalities on both sides of the Iron Curtain.

Italy also gained in economic terms from the EC. Admittedly, there were problems, especially with regard to the EC's Common Agricultural Policy (CAP) which benefited French and German more than Italian farmers. But Italy profited a great deal in other ways, through transnational trade, investments, facilities for labor migrants, for techno-logical innovation, and so forth. During the 1960s, the Italian economy expanded in an impressive fashion – so much so that political opposition to the EC largely ended. The socialist parties might have been expected to benefit from these opportunities. They might also have learned to cooperate. (The three socialist parties, during the early 1970s, could mobilize about one-fifth of the vote between them.) The socialists, however, missed their chance, and Italy failed to develop a powerful moderate left, comparable to the SPD in Germany or the Labour Party in Britain.

Italy: Challenge from Left and Right

The main challenge to the Italian Establishment came from the PCI. The party com-manded a substantial and fairly steady share of the popular vote (26.9 percent in 1968; 26.6 percent in 1987). The party was well disciplined, well organized, and had the largest card-carrying membership of any party. (By the early 1970s something like four million Italians were members of political parties, the largest bloc in any Western country, despite customary allegations that Italians were prone to political apathy. Of

19 Sampson, *Anatomy of Europe*, p. 41.

these four million, 1.7 million were Communists, 1.6 million Christian Democrats, and about 750,000 belonged to the three socialist parties.)[20] The PCI considered itself to be the workers' party *par excellence*. (As indicated before, about 40 percent of its members were workers, the largest percentage for any party.) Communists ran many municipal governments such as "red" Bologna. In the South, where industrial progress lagged behind, Communist working-class membership was less: on the other hand, a great many share-croppers, poor peasants, and farm laborers opted for the Communists. The Communists also had regional strongholds in north-central Italy, including Emilia, Tuscany, Umbria, and the Marches, with a political tradition of their own — culturally and politically suspicious of Rome and all its works. These regions accounted for about half the PCI's membership, and here the Communists gained support, not merely from workers, who in other parts of Italy would have been far more likely to vote for the CD than for the PCI.[21]

The Communists were also powerful in the trade-union movement. They had a strong voice in the CGIL (*Confederazione generale italiana del lavoro*) where they provided senior officials such as Giuseppe De Vittorio and Luciano Lama. CGIL, however, was not simply a Communist preserve; the movement contained several competing factions. CGIL, moreover, had to compete with the Catholic CISL (*Confederazione italiana sindicati lavatori*). Nevertheless, the PCI was a great power as far as labor relations were concerned; the Communists had a striking capacity for organizing strikes, for utilizing industrial disputes in the PCI's political interest, for mobilizing a great reserve army in the streets, supported — when the need arose — by professional strongmen.

The PCI also did much to engage intellectuals in its work, much more so than the French Communist Party. Whereas the French Communist Party stressed its own proletarian character, the PCI allotted a substantial role to intellectuals in organization, political education, and public relations. Intellectuals, of course, had a disconcerting habit of arguing with their superiors and a penchant for washing the party's dirty linen in public. But intellectuals also provided the party with people skilled in dialogue and willing to indulge in self-criticism, thereby enhancing the party's credibility among outsiders.

The PCI also had substantial backing from middle-class people, particularly from those dependent directly or indirectly on the state or on public corporations. In a sense, the PCI was also an Establishment party in that the PCI provide extensive patronage. (By the early 1970s, more than 1,200 mayors were Communists, and Communists or Communist-led coalitions dominated six out of Italy's 15 regions.) Communist municipal administrations provided jobs, public housing, education, even municipal pharmacies. Communist administrators had a reputation for efficiency. It paid to be in the Communists' good graces. Communists could help a construction firm to get contracts, an industrialist to get orders, a merchant new markets (especially in Eastern Europe and the Soviet Union). Communist patronage was equally useful for a civil servant anxious for promotion, an academic looking for a professorship, a writer in search of a good

20 Zariski, *Italy: the Politics of Uneven Development*, pp. 180–1.
21 Sidney Tarrow, "Communism in Italy and France: Adaptation and Change," in Donald L.M. Blackmer and Sidney Tarrow, eds, *Communism in Italy and France*, Princeton, NJ, Princeton University Press, 1975, pp. 575–640. For a study of the PCI in local government, see Robert H. Evans, *Coexistence: Communism and its Practice in Bologna 1945–1965*, Notre Dame, University of Notre Dame Press, 1967. For the PCI's international position see Donald L.M. Blackmer, *Unity in Diversity: Italian Communism and the Communist World*, Cambridge, MA, MIT Press, 1968.

publisher. Communism also appealed to a good many rich young men, inspired by a sense of guilt, a sense of adventure, a longing to improve humanity, or to spite their parents. Such youngsters included, for example, Giangiacomo Feltrinelli, inheritor of a great publishing firm, recruited into a party well aware of the advantages that the young Milanese with his huge fortune and extensive social connections might provide for the party of the proletariat.

Among communist parties the world over, the PCI was unique in its flexibility. Palmiro Togliatti (1893–1964, general secretary until his death in 1964) had risen under Stalin; he was a hard-liner loyal to Moscow, hostile to NATO, hostile to the US, but he was also an *apparatchik* with a difference – intelligent, reasonable, with intellectual tastes. (Stalin called him "the Professor.") Ultra-militants within the PCI (and later within the "new left" outside the party) might talk about intensifying the contradictions of capitalism by engaging in the armed struggle. Togliatti knew better; instability in Italy after World War I had not led to the dictatorship of the proletariat, but to the dictatorship of Fascism. Togliatti instead believed in the tactics of the "United Front" which he had seen at work in the Spanish Civil War.

Under Togliatti, the PCI thus looked to alliances with other "progressive" groups, including small farmers, shopkeepers, managers of small firms, minor entrepreneurs. The PCI now looked to peaceful penetration into the power structure, and to peaceful expansion of its huge clientage network. The party's ultimate aim was defined as the hegemony rather than the dictatorship of the proletariat, a fine distinction which remained undefined. Togliatti put an end to anti-clerical propaganda, treated bishops with respect, and dropped the blood-curdling threats once made against the bourgeoisie. Togliatti even modified the party's views with regard to the EEC. By 1962 Italy had benefited so greatly from its European links that Togliatti speculated whether traditional doctrines concerning the international class struggle had ceased to apply to Western Europe. In 1963 the PCI dropped its opposition to the EEC; a few years later, Italian Communists were active members of the Italian parliamentary delegation in Strasbourg. As regards relations between the world's communist parties, Togliatti began to advocate a new doctrine of "polycentrism" which entailed a measure of independence for the world's communist parties from Moscow's control. Nevertheless, Togliatti remained a loyal defender of the Soviet Union. (He approved of the Soviet invasion of Hungary in 1956.) As regards Italy's military obligations, the PCI's slogan remained unambiguous: "Italy out of NATO – and NATO out of Italy."

Luigi Longo (general secretary 1964–72) adopted a similar approach. Longo, a co-founder of the PCI, was an elderly man by the time he reached power. Longo, like Togliatti, had risen under Stalin. (During the 1930s, Longo had represented the PCI within the Comintern; later, he had served as inspector-general of the International Brigades during the Spanish Civil War.) But Longo lacked Togliatti's personal ability and personal standing both within the PCI and the world communist movement at large. Moreover, no matter what the PCI might say, the majority of the Italian electorate remained fearful of the PCI; they did not want PCI participation in a coalition; they stayed convinced that the PCI only put up a show of moderation for the purpose of ultimately setting up its own dictatorship. Such, after all, had been the policy of "fraternal" parties in Central Europe. Why should the PCI prove different?

More fundamental changes began to occur under Enrico Berlinguer, Longo's successor. Berlinguer was younger than Longo, a better writer, better speaker, and better strategist. Italy, moreover, had changed in far-reaching fashion by the time Berlinguer stepped into the general secretary's office. Between 1963 and 1969 exports had doubled; Italy had built a super-highway system hardly inferior to West Germany's; Italian consumers bought an ever-increasing number of television sets, refrigerators, and cars. Old, established, working-class neighborhoods in the cities changed in character, as did traditional villages. The same social forces that changed the CD's character also operated with regard to the PCI. There was a new Italian youth culture – complete with motor bikes, jeans, and rock music. The proportion of white-collar workers expanded within the Italian workforce – as it did all over the Western world. The student population grew larger than ever in Italy's past, with a new jargon and new "lifestyles" heavily influenced by the American example. Among youthful militants there was a shift in revolutionary loyalties. Enthusiasm for the Soviet Union had become *passé*; instead, the radiant future supposedly beckoned from Cuba, the People's Republic of China, from North Vietnam, or even more exotic places such as Angola and/or Mozambique.

The PCI led the world's major communist parties in attempting an accommodation to these new forces. In 1973 Berlinguer made a major speech in which he called for a partnership in government between the CD and the PCI – communist hegemony by other means: "In Italy, to transform the society in a socialist sense it would not be enough for the Left to arrive at 51 percent of the vote. It would be a majority that would be far too weak. What would be necessary would also be the agreement of the masses represented by the DC [CD]."[22] This speech would later be called Berlinguer's "great historical compromise" address. When Longo re-baptized the "Historical compromise" into "historical bloc," a more traditional term in Communist Party directives, it became clear that conflict had been joined within the PCI. The traditionalists lost out, and the PCI's policy thereafter continued to moderate in a manner that would surely have horrified Togliatti. Under Berlinguer, the PCI accepted Italy's membership in NATO. (Berlinguer, in 1974, actually committed himself to saying that he felt safer on the Western side.) The PCI condemned the hard line taken by the Portuguese Communist Party during the Portuguese revolution of 1974.

The PCI also formally denounced ultra-left terror in Italy itself. Violence began to shake Italy from 1967 onward and reached its peak during the late 1970s. In a sense the Italian "68" began a year earlier than it did in France, and the impact of violence on Italian society was more profound. The disorders did not derive from deprivation. On the contrary, Italy, like France, did extremely well during the 1960s. (Between 1961 and 1970, the average growth rate of Italy and its major allies stood as follows: Spain 7.3 percent; Italy 5.7 percent; France 5.6 percent; West Germany 4.6 percent; US 3.8 percent; Britain 2.8 percent.)[23] Violence derived in the main from the well read and the well fed – from those who looked to a world of utopian equality, but not to a world without waiters. Terrorists included all manner of men and women, well read and well bred, proud of their alienation from Italian society – ex-members of Catholic Action, millenarian Marxists, and also neo-Fascists.

22 Cited by Tarrow, "Communism in Italy and France," pp. 634–5.
23 Directorate of Intelligence, *Handbook of Economic Statistics*, 1990, Washington, DC, US Government Printing Office, 1990, p. 9; Robert C. Meade, Jr, *Red Brigades: the Story of Italian Terrorism*, New York, St Martin's Press, 1990; Sidney Tarrow, *Democracy and Disorder; Protest and Politics in Italy, 1965–1975*, Oxford, Clarendon Press, New York, Oxford University Press, 1989. For the extreme right, see Geoffrey Harris, *The Dark Side of Europe: the Extreme Right Today*, Edinburgh, Edinburgh University Press, 1990.

The neo-Fascists were a mixed lot, without central direction, a common program, or a shared ideology – Bohemian anarchists rather than disciplined storm troopers. They had no Duce, no Führer to lead them. Nevertheless, they were dangerous enough. (Believers in spontaneous terror, terrorists on the extreme right actually killed more people than the extreme left.) The right-wing terrorists profited from links with the police and the security services, and from ties to what might be called the internationale of the ultra-right. Like the extreme left, the ultra-right despised the Italian Republic, the established parties and all conventional institutions. Terrorists of whatever ideology profited from the Italian people's progressive disillusionment with the "partocracy" which used public office for private gain, and from the *immobilisme* derived from the Christian Democrats' uninterrupted hold on power since the end of World War II. Right-wing terror, moreover, had a peculiarly disconcerting quality. Unlike left-wing terrorists, right-wing murderers did not accompany their assaults by specific political demands or by attempts at self-justification. Right-wing terror was destined simply to disorient the public. Fortunately for their country, the mass of Italians proved too tough.

The terrorists on the extreme left, by contrast, seemed more intelligible. Unlike the neo-Fascists, the ultra-leftists initially attacked only property. Later, the so-called Red Brigades began to murder political opponents, using methods elaborated by crime syndicates that killed for cash. By the mid-1970s, outspoken anti-communist politicians and intellectuals faced considerable personal danger; they were apt to be gunned down in the streets without much fear of retaliation. Terror culminated in the kidnapping and subsequent murder of Aldo Moro in 1978. (In true gangster style, the Red Brigades took his body in the boot of a car to the center of Rome and left it there to intimidate the kidnappers' enemies.) The PCI benefited from this disorder in an indirect fashion, by proclaiming itself the party of moderation, by condemning violence conducted by youngsters who claimed for themselves the status of a homicidal élite. Indeed, the PCI could justly claim to have become an unofficial member of the government. But Moro's murder was too much. Moro (secretary of the CD since 1959) was a devout Catholic, courteous, a born conciliator, and personally popular in the Chamber. His killing was an outrage, and the Red Brigades' strategy misfired; Italians rallied to the threatened Republic, and between 1978 and 1983 Italy saved herself from threatened chaos. At the same time, the PCI began a gradual electoral decline from which the party never recovered. (The decisive change came in 1990 when the PCI's party congress at Bologna changed the party's name and very nature.)

The Iberian Peninsula

The Iberian peninsula forms a geographical unit, but it is a region ethnically split. Basques, Gallegos, Catalans, and Castilians stand divided within Spain; Spain itself remains divided from Portugal (*de Portugal ni buen viento ni buen casamiento*, "from Portugal neither a good wind or a good marriage" asserts a Spanish proverb). Of all Western Europe, the Iberian peninsula constituted the most backward part, although there were islands of prosperity. (Catalonia, for example, was one of the first regions in the Mediterranean to industrialize.) But, overall, Spain and Portugal commonly used to remind travellers of Eastern Europe in their economic retardation. Moreover, both Spain and Portugal had suffered dictatorial rule for several decades. In Spain, General Francisco Franco (1939–75) had made himself *caudillo* as a result of the Spanish Civil War of the

1930s. In Portugal, António de Oliveira Salazar, an economics professor turned politician, ran the government for an even longer period (1928–68). Spain and Portugal were, over-all, the least industrialized countries of Western Europe – reservoirs of migrant laborers looking for employment in Northern Europe. Experts a generation ago ascribed the *immobilisme* of the Iberian states variously to the hegemony of a reactionary church, to the persistent power of aristocratic cliques, to geographical propinquity to the African continent, or to assumed deficiencies in the national character. Above all, it was widely supposed that backwardness was inherent in the repressive Iberian regimes.[24]

The critics had good reason for their disapproval. Both Spain and Portugal built a strong corporatist state in which the state owned or controlled numerous industries, while the workers' bargaining ability was restricted or eliminated. Nevertheless, the Salazar and Franco dictatorships at least prevented armed upheavals or endemic violence in the streets. There was not that mood of intense uncertainty and apprehension that had preceded, and partly caused, the Spanish Civil War. During the 1960s, economic development in fact greatly accelerated both in Portugal and Spain. (Between 1968 and 1973, the rate of growth of the gross domestic product per capita went up by 7.4 percent in Portugal, 5.8 percent in Spain.) Industrial production strikingly increased; imports and exports augmented substantially in relation to the gross domestic product.

Portugal

Portugal had for long enjoyed the reputation of being one of Europe's most back-ward countries. (During the 1960s and 1970s, Portuguese labor migrants traveled all the way to France and Germany in search of employment.) Nevertheless, from the 1950s onward, Portugal underwent rapid economic development. The country gained from a massive increase of foreign, especially of West German and British, investment. Portugal substantially expanded its fishing fleets, its hydroelectric facilities, its production of petrochemicals, cellulose, and chemical fertilizers. More and more people moved into the cities; hence many Portuguese farmers were compelled to improve their methods, and cut back on labor, with far-reaching consequences for their country's economic future.

Widespread misconceptions to the contrary notwithstanding, there was also impress-ive economic growth in the Portuguese empire.[25] Ironically, this was stimulated at least in part by the outbreak of guerrilla warfare, beginning in 1961 in Angola, followed by risings in Mozambique and Portuguese Guinea. Portugal vastly expanded her armed forces overseas; the requirements of the army in turn created a military market. The launching of partisan operations had the unintended effect of easing relations between the metropole and the white settlers in Angola who suddenly realized that they could not stand on their own; hence provincial *separatismo* ceased to be popular among the Portuguese colonists. The metropole was no longer hampered by fears, widely held in the days of Salazar, that white settlers might one day seek to set up an Angolan state on Rhodesian lines. The Portuguese began to open their doors to foreign lenders whom they had previously viewed with mistrust. Foreign investors, technicians and businessmen thereafter achieved more prominence than before in the Portuguese colonies. Angola,

24 Vitorino Magalhaes Godinho, *A Estrutura da Antiga Sociedade Portuguesa*, Lisbon, Arcadia, 1971.
25 L.H. Gann, "Portugal, Africa and the Future," *The Journal of Modern African Studies*, vol. 13, 1975, pp. 1–18.

especially, experienced an extraordinary boom. (Between 1963 and 1973 the colony's exports increased nearly fourfold in value; the index of industrial production more than doubled; new townships sprang up in the bush.) Seen merely from an economic viewpoint, the 1960s and early 1970s formed Angola's golden age in spite of a civil war started by African nationalists in 1962.

The Portuguese, however, encountered an insoluble military problem. They faced revolts in three widely dispersed territories: Angola, Mozambique, and Portuguese Guinea. The Portuguese army, small in numbers and wholly unprepared for guerrilla warfare, underwent expansion. The Portuguese in Africa – unlike the British in previous guerrilla wars in Malaya, Kenya, and Cyprus – faced the problem of fighting partisans operating from privileged sanctuaries outside Portuguese territory, a difficult military task. The Portuguese soon lost control over much of Portuguese Guinea, an inhospitable land largely covered with tropical rain forest, the most unpopular posting in the Portuguese empire, and the weakest link in the imperial chain. Guerrillas also secured substantial advances into parts of Mozambique, and threatened the border regions of Angola. Not that the Portuguese position was hopeless from the purely military standpoint. The Portuguese kept control over the bulk of their empire. Guerrillas could not prevent the construction of new enterprises such as the Cabora Bassa dam in Mozambique. Neither did the war prove a financial disaster. (Between 1958 and 1963, military expenditure rose enormously as a share of Portugal's total expenditure, from 22.4 percent to 42.4 percent. Thereafter the proportion declined to 27.6 percent by 1974.)[26] Casualties, moreover, remained low in a war of hit-and-run affairs; there was none of the bloodletting that had marked the French colonial war in Indo-China.

But the Portuguese lost the war on the political front. The various guerrilla movements secured substantial support from the Soviet Union; alternatively, from the People's Republic of China. World opinion, or what passed as such, universally condemned the Portuguese. War was unpopular among Portuguese conscripts except whites recruited in the colonies; many young Portuguese indeed escaped from the draft by seeking work abroad. War likewise struck at the officer's morale. Portugal formed part of NATO; ambitious Portuguese officers received training in the US and other NATO countries where they became peculiarly aware of their own army's backwardness, and also of the unpopularity of Portugal's colonial claims in the world at large. Ambitious Portuguese military leaders looked to the modernization of the Portuguese armed forces in Europe, not to a "dirty" war in the bush.

Combat officers in particular began to question the advisability, even the justice, of the war. The bulk of the actual fighting in the colonies was directed by ensigns or junior lieutenants – mostly conscripts, apt to draw invidious comparisons between their own hardships and the new professional opportunities enjoyed by those of their college classmates who had managed to stay out of uniform. There was little glory to be gained in petty incidents that might involve sabotage on a railway track or a jeep blown up by a mine; there was no popular support for the war, as the Portuguese military quickly lost the battle both for metropolitan and world opinion. There were jealousies between professional and conscript officers, between field and staff officers, between security service (DGS) and army officers, officers in élite units and those in run-of-the-mill formations, and between officers and senior non-coms (regular sergeants rarely achieved promotion

26 Rona M. Fields, *The Portuguese Revolution and the Armed Forces Movement*, New York, Praeger, 1976, p. 56.

into commissioned ranks). Above all, the captains, majors, and colonels of the regular army, the backbone of the armed forces, remained endlessly on active service; they were posted on long tours of duty from one territory to another; their family life was interrupted as the authorities refused to localize the various wars by permanently assigning specific units to each colony, and thereby once more evoking the specter of *separatismo*.

The Portuguese political system was ill designed to cope with these troubles. The authoritarian regime headed by António de Oliveira Salazar (1889–1970) had lasted from 1928 to 1968. Salazar's relatively moderate dictatorship gave to Portugal 40 years of stability after the turbulent years of the First Republic (1910–26). There was no civil war in Portugal – as there was in Spain – no executions, no militarism. Salazar's *Novo estado* nevertheless possessed serious weaknesses which worsened when Salazar was succeeded by Marcelo das Neves Caetano. Caetano intended to liberalize an authoritarian regime; he reconstituted the ruling *União nacional*; he permitted criticism, relaxed press censorship, softened existing press regulations, and expanded social welfare programs, all according to his slogan "evolution without revolution."[27] Salazar had been profoundly anti-American, fearful of alleged US designs to take over by indirect means the European empires in Africa. Caetano, by contrast, was more willing to open up Portuguese society, and to admit foreign (including US) investments, to Portugal and the colonies. Nevertheless, the Caetano regime failed. Like the Fourth Republic in France, the Portuguese *Novo estado* knew neither how to win nor how to end a colonial war that was steadily becoming more unpopular.

After the initial coup in 1974, the revolution lurched further to the left. This shift occurred not because most officers were enamored with Marxism–Leninism, but because they were politically unsophisticated, because the militant left offered unambiguous answers to Portugal's ills, and because the left regarded Portugal itself as a financial colony of the Anglo-Saxon powers, thereby putting the blame for Portugal's ills on foreigners. The revolution itself, however, helped to engender new troubles. Portugal's economic growth rate thereafter plummeted – more so than the EEC average. Revolution exacted an even higher price in the former colonies; their economies collapsed, as civil wars continued, and as somewhere between 600,000 and 800,000 Portuguese were stripped of their property and departed to start life anew in Portugal, South Africa, or Brazil.

Faced with ongoing crises, the MFA (Armed Forces Movement) split into several factions. General António de Spínola was the head of the first revolutionary government. A general popular with corporals and privates, a reformer who desired a kind of dominion status for the colonies, a traditionalist who sported a monocle, Spínola was one of those officers who could justly claim to be called an honorable and gallant gentleman. But he lacked political *savoir faire*, and was replaced as prime minister by a communist sympathizer. A counter-coup, launched by Spínola, failed; and for a moment it appeared that Portugal might turn into a Western European Cuba. Militant leftists expropriated great landed estates as well as small ones owned by migrant workers; mobs broke up meetings of moderates, and seized oppositional radio stations. The Portuguese Communist Party, while denouncing "infantile revolutionaries," had serious hopes of gaining power and remodeling Portugal on the lines of the "people's democracies" in Eastern Europe. Major industries were nationalized, and a good deal of land was expropriated, especially in the Alentejo.

27 Richard Gunther, "Spain and Portugal," in Gerald A. Dorfman and Peter J. Duignan, eds, *Politics in Western Europe*, Stanford, CA, Hoover Institution Press, 1991, pp. 186–236.

But there was also massive hostility to the militant left, especially from the peasants of northern Portugal (where smallholdings were the rule, rather than the large estates found in the South). Portuguese politics were further complicated by extensive ties between Portuguese and foreign parties. The Portuguese Communist Party (PCP, the oldest extant Portuguese party) received massive aid from "fraternal" parties in Eastern Europe. The Portuguese Socialist Party (PS, founded in 1973 in West Germany) was backed by the socialist international, especially by the West German SPD. The Center Democratic Party (CDS), a pro-Western free enterprise party, had connections to the German CDU and also to the wider Christian democratic movement in Western Europe. The CDS also received help from Portuguese immigrants in the US, as did the Popular Democratic Party (PSD, earlier known as PPD), a non-Marxist body that looked to the creation of a Portuguese welfare state.

Between them, the moderates outnumbered the communists and the ultra-left. There was, moreover, a decisive shift in the balance of power within the army, now beset by chronic indiscipline. In 1975 General Ramalho Eanes defeated an attempted left-wing coup, and restored authority to those who wanted a depoliticized army bound by traditional ties of military professionalism. (In 1976 Eanes was elected to the presidency.) By this time the bulk of the Portuguese electorate was tired of strikes, commotions, riots, and the general climate of uncertainty. Elections to the Constituent Assembly, held in 1975, produced a massive majority for the moderate parties. (The Socialists garnered 38 percent of the popular vote, with 115 out of 245 seats in parliament, the PPD got 26 percent of the vote with 80 seats; the CDS 8 percent with 16 seats. By contrast, the PCP only managed to gain 13 percent of the vote, and its allies 4 percent. Henceforth, the Communists were excluded from power in Portugal.) It was the first decisive defeat suffered by Marxist–Leninists during the 1970s worldwide.

This is not to say that the Portuguese revolution was simply undone. The preamble of the Portuguese constitution, alone in Western Europe, proclaimed as its aim the "transition toward socialism." The text of the constitution referred to the "collective appropriation of the means of production," and to the expropriation of large estates and major business firms. All nationalizations effected since 1974 formed, according to the constitution, an irreversible conquest of the working class. Portugal thus remained committed to a socialist program – this at a time when the socialist economies of Eastern European and the Soviet Union were already in serious trouble. The founding document of the Portuguese democracy stood out as a partisan document rather than a charter establishing a broad consensus concerning the rules of the parliamentary game; in this respect the Portuguese constitution resembled the constitution of the Second Spanish Republic which had gone down to defeat before World War II.

The revolution, with its massive nationalization program, seriously impeded Portugal's ability to compete in the world market. The government had to shoulder the expense incurred in massive subsidies paid to inefficient firms. Unlike Spain, Portugal shouldered a massive foreign debt; Portuguese workers acquired constitutional rights to job security which greatly interfered with employers' ability to discipline or discharge workers. It was only during the mid-1980s that Portugal reversed this course, making serious attempts to reduce inflation, diminish budget deficits, cut down foreign debts, and privatize a number of public sector corporations.

Nevertheless, parliamentary democracy was restored in Portugal. (The process was completed in 1982 when the non-democratic Council of the Revolution was abolished.) The soldiers henceforth remained where they belonged – in their barracks, not in the council chamber. The armed forces rapidly declined in size (from over 200,000 in 1974 to 63,500 in 1985). There was also a fundamental change in the composition of the political class. Under the new dispensation, Portuguese politicians were apt to be young, averaging 40–45 years, overwhelmingly middle class, with a strong representation of lawyers in parliament, engineers and economists in government. The *Novo estado* with its economic corporatism, and its political obscurantism thereafter, seemed light years away.

Spain

Spain during these years remained subject to the dictatorship of General Francisco Franco (born 1892). Franco had been carried to power during the Spanish Civil War (1936–9), a catastrophic conflict in which Spain was bled white. The Spanish clash of arms had engaged the world's attention to a greater extent than any other civil conflict in history. Both supporters and opponents of the doomed Spanish Republic believed that the battle between democracy and fascism would somehow be decided on the Spanish stage. This surmise turned out to be utterly mistaken.

General Franco was a perfect practitioner of power. His own father styled him *un cabrón y un chulo* (a swine and a pimp).[28] Some of his own generals called him worse. But criticism left the *caudillo* unfazed. He had deliberately avoided Blitzkrieg tactics in the Spanish Civil War so as to consolidate his own power, and grind down the enemy in a bloody war of attrition. A born actor, Franco thereafter cheated his German and Italian allies, cannily refusing to enter World War II on their side. Franco cheated his Spanish friends, the Falangists who had admired Mussolini, and the Carlists who looked to the restoration of the monarchy. Franco forced these diverse supporters to join a single party of his own creation, *Falange española y tradicionalista y de las juntas de ofensiva nacional sindicalista* (later known as the National Movement). But despite its sonorous title, the party lacked real influence, and merely acted as a patronage machine and a cheerleading team. All real power rested with Franco, "by the Grace of God, Chief of Staff, General-issimo of the Army and Caudillo of Spain and the Crusade." Franco even cheated the army which had borne him to power. He maintained a grossly swollen officer corps. Generals and admirals found well-paid jobs in the civil administration, parliament, major state enterprises, and the cabinet. Junior officers stayed impecunious, but received psychic rewards through flattery, social privileges, and pep talks. Neither was the army entrusted with real political power: senior officers were regularly posted from one military region to another so as to prevent ambitious men from building their own power base. Franco was a hard man indeed. (Even Hitler commented after a conference with the *caudillo* that he would rather have all his teeth pulled out than face yet another meeting with Franco.)

The Spanish conflict was quite exceptional in the history of revolutionary warfare and displayed Franco's peculiar political genius. The three "classical" revolutionary wars all had one feature in common. In the English Civil War of the seventeenth century, the war waged by the French Revolution against its domestic enemies, and the Russian civil war following the Bolshevik seizure of power in 1916, the revolutionaries had commanded the capital and the economically most developed parts of the country. The

28 Paul Preston, *Franco: a Biography*, New York, Basic Books, 1994, p. 456.

counter-revolutionaries had operated from the geographical periphery. To be precise, the west, the north of England, Wales, and Ireland had rallied for the English king; the Vendée and Brittany for the Bourbons; the South of Russia and Siberia for the "Whites." In the Spanish Civil War, the same generalization seemed to apply. Barcelona, Madrid, the Basque country stood for the Republic, and the most backward rural parts of Spain and North Africa for Franco. But Franco won. A mediocre soldier, he yet proved supremely good at grand politico-military strategy. Unlike the Republicans, he grasped the key positions of the Church and of the independent rural smallholders, neglected or despised by the Republic. Whereas the Republicans were divided, Franco united his faction, and crushed his enemies.

Having won the war, the army was showered with praise, but neglected as a military instrument. Its equipment remained obsolescent; modernization only came in a gingerly fashion after the US concluded an executive agreement with Spain, permitting the US to use Spanish bases (1953). (There was no formal pact. Many Congress members wished to ostracize Spain because of its fascist connection. Spanish conservatives, by contrast, feared contamination from American ideas of political freedom, democracy, and consumerism – not to mention Protestantism.)[29]

Spain had other problems. Spain was unpopular in the US. During the Spanish Civil War, American Catholics had widely sided with Franco, but they were a minority in a country where the majority had sympathized with the Republic. To them, Spain appeared a reactionary country, a last outpost of fascism. There was no pro-Spanish ethnic lobby. The great majority of emigrants from Spain had gone to Latin America where they could speak their own tongue. Those who did go to the US were mostly Catalans or Basques, or intellectuals of any ethnic background, out of sympathy with official Spain.

Spain, during the 1940s and 1950s, created numerous industrial enterprises wholly or partly owned by the state. These were protected from foreign competition by high tariffs; the parastatals received massive subsidies from the treasury when they failed to make profits. Wages were kept down artificially, but at the same time employers were restricted in their ability to dismiss workers. Not surprisingly, state-supported industries, such as steel and iron, were thoroughly inefficient. The *franquistas* looked alike to centralized government and centralized economic planning. They equally detested regional autonomy for ethnic minorities, and consumerism for the masses. In a sense, they were right-wing Jacobins who eulogized both "Spain one and indivisible" and the imagined virtues of the countryside.

During the 1950s, however, the hard-liners lost control. Terror diminished, as Franco increasingly posed as a friendly grandfather rather than a martial *caudillo*. Spain tightened its links with various Spanish-speaking countries in Latin America. In 1955 Spain joined the UN, and from 1970 onward received preferential treatment from the EC. Spanish workers migrated abroad in ever-increasing numbers. (By 1975, 250,000 Spaniards were working in France, 132,000 in West Germany, 50,000 in Britain and the Benelux countries.) Spain opened to tourists to such an extent that revenue from the tourist industries and remittances from labor migrants became important assets in the national economy. There was also massive migration within Spain; this in turn resulted in new social tensions, as Spanish-speaking workmen settled in Basque and Catalan-speaking districts, thereby giving a fillip to local nationalism. Young people (including

29 R. Richard Rubottom and J. Carter Murphy, *Spain and the United States: Since World War II*, New York, Praeger, 1984; Preston, *Franco: a Biography*.

the children of high-ranking soldiers and officials) looked to Western Europe (especially France) for cultural inspiration, and to the US for mass entertainment.

From 1957, Franco formally abandoned autarky. *Que se haga* (let it be done) said the old man, thereby changing from postwar Spain's Brezhnev to its Gorbachev, all in one lifetime. By now a new generation of highly trained technocrats had largely replaced those hard-liners who had gained high administrative positions during and after the Civil War. Under the new dispensation, scarce resources were no longer to be allocated by governmental planning, but by market mechanism. The elaborate structure of controls was partially dismantled. Spain, henceforth, adopted a tight money policy to counter inflation, and a uniform exchange rate to replace the multiple, and discriminatory, exchange rates of old. The new economic policy received strong support from international bodies such as the IMF and OECD which supplied the necessary loans. There was massive foreign investment, with startling results. Admittedly, the new medicine was at first bitter. As in East-Central Europe after the breakdown of communism, there was at first massive unemployment. But Spain thereafter achieved a belated economic miracle. (Between 1960 and 1972, the income of every Spaniard in employment increased on the average threefold.)[30]

Spain also changed in many other ways. In 1968, for instance, Franco formally abrogated the historic decree issued in 1492 by King Ferdinand and Queen Isabella to expel the Jews from Spain.[31] The old restrictions on free speech receded. Communists and socialists extended their influence among students and workers. More importantly, life profoundly altered through growing links with the EC and the US – through tourism, mass entertainment, commercial and military contacts. Spanish society altered beyond recognition. The proportion of Spaniards employed in agriculture continued to decline in a striking fashion (from 46 percent in 1930, to 41 percent in 1960, to 17 percent in 1980). Cities grew apace. Industrial production grew in an impressive manner, and so did the gross national product. (By 1977, Spain's per capita income was approaching Italy's, and exceeded Ireland's.) Consumerism came to Spain, as it did to the rest of Europe. During the mid-1960s, for example, there were relatively few automobiles on the roads; by the mid-1970s traffic jams had become common. Wages went up, including rural wages. The exodus from the countryside to the cities continued; the olden-day Spain idealized by Francists changed beyond recognition. As Stanley G. Payne, historian of the Franco regime put it, its last 25 years, from 1950 to 1975, was the time when Spain witnessed the greatest sustained economic development and general improvement in living standards in all Spanish history.[32] According to traditionalist critics, young Spaniards henceforth valued only the "three Cs": *coche*, (car), *casa* (house), *compañera* (girlfriend). It was an astonishing outcome for a regime of a *caudillo* wont to praise the heroic life and despise consumerism.[33] Spaniards could pride themselves on an economic achievement unparalleled in any other country except Japan.

30 Raymond Carr, *Spain: 1808–1975*, Oxford, Clarendon Press, 1982, p. 746.
31 Howard M. Sachar, *The Course of Modern Jewish History*, New York, Vintage Books, 1990, p. 646.
32 Stanley G. Payne, *The Franco Regime 1936–1975*, Madison, Wisconsin, University of Wisconsin Press, 1987, p. 463; Adrian Shubert, *A Social History of Modern Spain*, London, Unwin Hyman, 1990.
33 At the time of Franco's death, only 22 percent of the labor force were employed in agriculture, as against 40 percent in services, and 38 percent in industry.

Economic growth went with political transformation. True enough, Spain remained a conservative country, its bureaucratic élite dominated by the upper and upper middle classes. Nevertheless, there were striking changes. The Catholic Church, once a stronghold of conservatism, shifted toward the left under Pope John XXIII's leadership (1958–63); many young priests in Spain turned toward socialism, and identified their cause with that of militant university students and workers. This power shift within the Church created an entirely new phenomenon in Franco's Spain – anti-clericalism from the right rather than the left, as the Church became identified with social reform. Opus Dei, a reformist Catholic association, acquired increasing political influence; prominent members moved into key offices in economic affairs, the state administration, and the cabinet. Censorship weakened. The courts became more liberal than in the past. "Nonpolitical" strikes were legalized (1962), and during the 1960s and the early 1970s, the number of strikes rapidly increased. At the same time, Spain adopted a new, reformist Organic Law of the State (1966).

Franco also changed his line in foreign policy. In the past he had always opposed a united Europe and publicly attacked "Europeanism." During the 1960s, however, the General changed his tune, and, after lengthy delays, the European Community agreed to begin negotiations concerning Spain's future membership. (Spain, together with Portugal, was finally admitted to full membership of the EC in 1986.) Spain also adjusted in other ways, accepting at long last the international doctrine of decolonization. Whereas Portugal fought a long war to retain its empire, Spain surrendered Spanish Guinea without firing a shot (1968). Under its new name of Equatorial Guinea, the country thereafter passed under the bloody tyranny of Francisco Macías whose own form of "scientific socialism" proved infinitely more destructive than Spanish rule at its worst. Supposedly one-fifth of Equatorial Guinea's population perished; by contrast, the Franco era seemed in retrospect a golden age – a point studiously ignored by the General's critics both at home and abroad.

Spain also underwent a profound psychological change. By the early 1970s, the men who had risked their lives in the trenches during the Civil War had become old, their tales of war stale by dint of repetition. The fanatical loyalties and hatreds of the 1930s had come to seem incomprehensible to most of the men and women born after World War II; the tunes of the Beatles widely seemed more appealing than the strains of a regimental band. When Franco died in 1975, after having governed for nearly 40 years, Spaniards heaved an immense sigh of relief. There was a sudden end to officially sanctioned conformity, and all the taboos of yesterday – social, sexual, religious – suddenly turned fashionable.

There was a revival of regional independence movements. Catalonian nationalism was of old standing; Catalans had bravely fought for the Republic, and been brutally suppressed thereafter. But Catalonia was one of Spain's most advanced regions economically. Catalonia (*Catalunya*) with a population larger than Denmark's and an area bigger than Ireland's, an ancient history and culture, could not be suppressed as a nation. During the 1960s, Catalan self-confidence revived, supported by priests, as well as secular intellectuals, middle-class people, and workers. The execution of Salvador Puig Antich, a young Catalan anarchist guilty of having murdered a policeman, aroused widespread disturbances in Catalonia. There was likewise trouble in the Basque provinces. Whereas the Catalan language is related to Spanish, Basque is totally distinct. Basque nationalism in its early phase had expressed the Basque intelligentsia's nostalgia for an idealized rural past, based on equality, democracy, and Catholicism. The Basques, like the Catalans, had fought for the Republic and lost; it was in opposition to Franco that Basque nationalism took a socialist and secular turn,[34] accompanied by violence. (This centered on the main Basque resistance group known as ETA, *Euzkadi ta Azkatasuna*, and assorted Marxist–Leninists). Franco tried to keep the lid down, but the old ruthlessness had gone. The government proved quite unable to find a formula that would satisfy even moderate Basques. Even less capable of resolution were the deeper problems concerned with industrialization: prosperity occasioned massive immigration of non-Basques into Basque provinces; resultant Basque discontent could not be stilled.

By the 1960s, Franco's National Movement seemed antiquated, and the regime had obviously aged. Franco himself affected the image of a benevolent grandfather rather than a conquering general; to his opponents he seemed like a Spanish version of the emperor Franz Josef in his dotage. Moreover, Franco, unique among dictators, himself established a formal procedure for replacing his regime. King Juan Carlos, sworn to office in 1969, was expected to provide both continuity and change. Franco hoped that the king would perpetuate a reformed Franco regime after Franco had gone. Franco died in 1975 – the last of those European dictators who had seized power before World War II, and among them, the greatest survivor.

The new monarch, however, disappointed all Franco's hopes. Juan Carlos was a firm believer in parliamentary democracy and committed to change. Even the shrewder men within Franco's former entourage understood that change had become inevitable, and began to make deals with the opposition. Political repression had long been relegated to the police special services. The armed forces, by contrast, gladly held aloof from such rough work, and were no longer held responsible for its excesses. Having become more professional in its outlook, the army largely abandoned its olden-time praetorian ambitions.[35] Elections held in 1977 finally laid to rest the Franco regime. It was an unexpected achievement, for the transition to democracy – like the Spanish Civil War – occurred at a time of worldwide economic difficulties. Once a byword for political violence, Spain now astonished the world by its moderation.[36]

---

34 Marianne Heiberg, *The Making of the Basque Nation*, Cambridge, Cambridge University Press, 1989.
35 Julio Busquets, *El Militar de carrera en España*, Barcelona, Editorial Ariel, 1984.
36 See Paul Preston, *The Triumph of Democracy in Spain*, London, Methuen, 1986; Stanley G. Payne, *Politics and the Military in Modern Spain*, Stanford, CA, Stanford University Press, 1967; Raymond Carr and Juan Pablo Fusi Aizpurua, *Spain: Dictatorship to Democracy*, London, Allen and Unwin, 1979.

PART II

Transnational Cooperation and Conflict, 1958–1974

7

Keys to Western Security, 1958–1974

The EEC, 1958–1974

Philosophers and visionaries have discussed for centuries the desirability of uniting the various states of Europe into one commonwealth. Napoleon in part achieved this aim – but only by brute force and for a short time. Hitler employed unlimited terror, but his "new order" collapsed even more quickly than the Napoleonic Empire. When World War II ended, the prospects for a peaceful union seemed dim. War had left a legacy of hatred and suffering that is hard to comprehend in retrospect. Millions of Europeans had tales of horror to tell. Nearly all European countries had been at war with their neighbors, engaged in conflicts that might entail one or more changes of sides. Most European states had experienced defeat and foreign occupation; national hatreds could therefore reasonably be expected to intensify. Every occupied country had been divided by bitter internal struggles which pitted compatriots against compatriots. France, to give just one example, had been split between collaborators, *résistants*, and *attentistes* (those who hedged their bets). *La guerre franco-française*, the Franco-French war, was not just a war of words but virtual civil war in which *miliciens* had exchanged shots with partisans, and regular French soldiers had fired on one another in Syria and West Africa. Even the *résistants* had been disunited: there were rifts between communists and the rest, between those who had "rallied" to de Gaulle in 1940 and those who only joined the Resistance much later. The resisters themselves stood aloof from the million and a half French soldiers who had endured captivity in Germany; the prisoners of war, in turn, disdained French-men conscripted into the Reich as forced laborers. And few of those worried about the handful of *déportés* who had survived Nazi extermination camps, and returned to France with inconvenient stories of horror and betrayal. Things were no better in Italy, or in Germany where war had – if anything – intensified prewar hatred. (*Aber die eigenen Deutschen waren die Schlimmsten*, "But our own Germans were the worst," went an often-repeated phrase at the time.) Given this legacy of hatred and insecurity, it seemed unlikely that the former belligerents would recreate a peaceful democratic order – much less that they would successfully cooperate in a transnational Europe.

Yet Western Europe's success defied the pessimists' predictions. As we have seen in preceding chapters, Western Europeans successfully reconstructed a democratic order wherever democracy had earlier been overthrown. The communists on the extreme left, fascists and their ilk on the extreme right, remained permanent outsiders in the politics of Western Europe. It was the moderates who wielded power in every Western European country liberated by Anglo-American armies. The moderates included numerous outstanding politicians. The Western statesmen assembled at the Munich Conference in 1938 had been described by Hitler as a lot of little worms. Their most bitter opponents would not thus have described Charles de Gaulle, Konrad Adenauer, Alcide de Gasperi.

No matter whether they were Tories, Christian Democrats, Labourites, or Social Democrats, the leading statesmen understood that they had essential features in common. They spoke a common cultural language. It was a good omen for trans-European cooperation.

The religion of nationalism gradually weakened. Not that most Western Europeans had come to dislike the razzle dazzle of military splendor. But even in Britain, indisputably a victor country after World War II, most returning servicemen no longer claimed their campaign medals as they had done after World War I: countless medals lay unclaimed in storehouses. In Germany, military disillusionment had gone much further: after the end of World War II it was common to see hard-earned military decorations bartered on the black market for a few cigarettes. Despite wartime horrors, national antipathies thereafter seemed to decline, particularly among educated people on the European continent; such at least was the message of public opinion surveys; such also was the message conveyed by the balance sheets of travel bureaux and hotel chains – tourism became big business, and foreign travel became a popular pastime, instead of a privilege confined to the rich.

Politically, the hard-line right, xenophobic and anti-semitic, had largely been discredited by the war. The Catholic Church had severed former links with the hard right in every country but Spain; the Church's outlook was internationalist and conciliatory. The Church overwhelmingly backed moderate parties, in particular the Christian Democrats. (Leading architects of a united Europe, statesmen such as Konrad Adenauer, Charles de Gaulle, Alcide de Gasperi, and Robert Schuman were mostly practicing Catholics.) Unlike the British Labour Party, the social democratic parties on the Continent also had a strong international tradition. While the Christian democrats cooperated on a trans-European level through the Nouvelles Equipes Internationales (set up in 1947), the social democrats collaborated through the Socialist Internationale (reconstituted after World War II). Powerful also was the tradition of the Resistance which widely sympathized with the concept of a united Europe in every European country, including Germany.

Equally important was the American factor. The US did not merely assist Western Europe through the Marshall Plan, but also pushed Western European countries toward closer economic and military cooperation. (The Marshall Plan was itself administered in such a fashion as to make Europeans work together. Instead of handing out aid to individual countries, the Americans preferred to deal with the OEEC (Organization for European Economic Cooperation). The OEEC would prepare programs, and decide how to allocate aid between its various members. By doing so, the Europeans would be encouraged to cooperate and create a market of continental size. Such an association would be a boon to world (including US) trade, promote prosperity, weaken communism, reduce the chances of economic conflict among Western European nations (the Americans thought economic nationalism had caused World Wars I and II), and promote democracy.

It was a statesmanlike decision. From the standpoint of its immediate self-interest, the US might have been expected to prefer dealing with divided European governments at loggerheads with one another, and easy to play off one against another. But a more enlightened concept of self-interest prevailed, as it did with regard to tariffs. The US thus no more reverted to prewar protectionism than to prewar isolationism. The Bretton Woods Agreement (1944) sanctioned the convertibility of the Western currencies – at least in theory – while the dollar became the main reserve currency. GATT (General Agreement on Tariffs and Trade, 1947) obliged participants gradually to limit the various protectionist measures in force at the time. The US became the world's greatest export market: first for Western Europe in the immediate postwar period, for Japan in the 1960s and 1970s, for South Korea, Singapore, Taiwan in the 1980s, and then for the developing world as a whole.[1]

In a more intangible sense, the US stood out as an international demonstration model for the advantages of a federal union. Would the Americans ever have achieved global economic leadership, had New York, Texas, and California all developed as sovereign nations, each with their own currency and customs barriers? Surely Europeans should benefit from the US example. We have traced the history of Western European association in a preceding work.[2] Here we shall merely recapitulate the main points. The process began with the creation of the European Coal and Steel Community (ECSC), operational in 1953. Its first president was Jean Monnet, an outstanding French businessman and civil servant, and a moderate socialist by conviction. Monnet provided much of the personal push and enthusiasm to turn dreams into an organizational reality.

The ECSC represented in an institutional form a long-standing partnership between German coal and French iron producers, a connection which had survived world crises and wars. France would gain guaranteed supplies of Ruhr coal for her steel industries. An agreement would tie Germany before her full power had recovered, at a time when France still held the better cards. West Germany gained international respectability after the horrors of World War II; as a full member of the ECSC, West Germany would no longer rank as an occupied country, but as a European power. (In personal terms, moreover, Adenauer got on well with de Gaulle; the two elderly but tough-minded gentlemen understood one another.) Italy joined, in part, for the economic advantages, in part because the Christian Democrats generally saw eye to eye with Christian democratic policy-makers in France and West Germany. Belgium, Holland, and Luxembourg had already pioneered an economic association through the creation of Benelux (initiated as a customs union in 1944).

The British, by contrast, stood aloof, convinced that the ECSC had nothing to offer to their nationalized industries, suspicious of a Europe dominated by Christian democratic parties, and sure that their future rested with the Commonwealth and the US connection. The Labour government suspected French motives; they were upset at the tactless ways of ECSC negotiators; they looked down on the continental states as losers in World War II, losers supposedly beset by LMF ("lack of moral fiber"). Labourites as well as Conservatives wanted to maintain British sovereignty at all costs. But there was one more fear – never admitted in public, pervasive at the time, though destined to disappear in later generations – the traditional fear of Catholicism.

Catholic workers played an important part in the British trade-union movement and in the Labour Party. Nevertheless, there was prejudice against them, fully shared by Ernest Bevin and his wife. (According to Sir Gladwyn Jebb, a high official in the Foreign Office, Mr and Mrs Bevin would both become most uneasy whenever they saw a priest

1 Dario Vello, "Europe and the New Economic Order," *The Federalist: a Political Review*, 1992, no. 1, p. 44.
2 Peter Duignan and L.H. Gann, *The Rebirth of the West: the Americanization of the Democratic World, 1945–1958*, Oxford, Blackwell, 1992. See also Walter Laqueur, *Europe in our Time: a History, 1945–1992*, New York, Viking Press, 1992; Gerald A. Dorfman and Peter J. Duignan, eds, *Politics in Western Europe*, Stanford, CA, Hoover Institution Press, 1991, ch. 13; Sir Richard Mayne, ed., *Handbooks to the Modern World: Western Europe*, New York, Facts on File, 1986; Roger Morgan, *West European Politics Since 1945: the Shaping of the European Community*, London, Batsford, 1972.

in a *soutane*. Mr Bevin would mutter "Black crows," convinced that Catholic priests brought bad luck! No counter-argument would shake him.) In Britain, as in the US, however, anti-Catholic sentiment declined, as Irish immigrants and their children rose socially and economically, and as the Catholic vote became increasingly important.)

Despite initial difficulties, the ECSC proved a success, and in 1957 turned into the European Economic Community (EEC, operational in 1958, renamed in 1967 the European Community, EC). The EEC came into being a year after the Soviet invasion of Hungary had re-emphasized the Soviet threat (and had also occasioned a mass defection of leftist intellectuals from the communist parties in Western Europe). The EEC rested on a complex division of powers between national governments and the community, national agencies and community agencies. The Founding Fathers of the US had deeply thought about these problems and resolved them in an exemplary fashion. The Founding Fathers of the EEC, by contrast, fudged a great many inconvenient questions. They did so because they never resolved the struggle between advocates of a loosely constructed league, a confederation, and a more tightly constructed federal state. (Monnet described himself as a functionalist; by solving practical questions piecemeal, Monnet believed, Europe would unite in practice.)

Effective management of the EEC (based in Brussels) fell to a Commission with nine members chosen by the national governments but pledged to independence. The Commission formed the EEC's executive; its ethos was profoundly influenced by the centralizing notions of the French bureaucracy. Paralleling the Commission was the Council of Ministers, the organ of the national governments, responsible for coordinating Community and national policies. (In theory, the Council could decide by a majority vote. In practice, the French in particular refused to subordinate to a majority what they regarded as their vital national interests. The dispute was partially settled in 1966 through the so-called Luxembourg Compromise which permitted each member state to veto a decision that it held vital to its national interest.)

The third major body was the Parliamentary Assembly (renamed the European Parliament in 1962), with proportional representation chosen by national parliaments. The Assembly's powers were small, membership not very prestigious – hence complaints about the EEC's "democratic deficit." (Until the European Court of Justice gave its judgment in the so-called "isoglucose case" in 1979, there was no obligation on the Council even to obtain the Parliament's opinion before adopting a law.) Parliament suffered from rapidly changing membership, and also from the lack of a fixed abode. (The Permanent Secretariat was located in Luxembourg; plenary sessions alternated between Luxembourg and Strasbourg; committee meetings took place in Brussels so as to facilitate consultation with the Commission's staff.) No more disruptive routine could have been adopted for members – not to mention their respective partners.

Parliament's standing slowly improved. Under the so-called Luxembourg Treaty of 1970 the EC was empowered to raise its own revenue through customs duties, agricultural levies and VAT-based (value added taxes) contributions from member states. Parliament thereafter sought to extend its influence both over finance and legislation. Parliament developed transnational groupings. (By the early 1970s, these comprised 50 Christian Democratic members, 37 Socialists, 22 Liberals and their allies, 19 Gaullists, and 11 Independents.) In 1979 direct voting was introduced. But, overall, the European Parliament was too much insulated from national parliaments and national parties, too insulated also from popular opinion, to meet the expectations of genuinely ambitious Euro-parliamentarians.

In addition, there was a Court of Justice which, initially, served the EEC as well as the ECSC. The Court's legal principles were uneasily drawn from Roman law and, later, also British common law. (In 1967 the EEC and the ECSC were formally unified, with a single Council and a single Commission for all European "communities": the ECSC, EEC, and "Euratom," the European atomic agency.) In addition, a number of other technical bodies came into being such as ELDO (concerned with the development of space vehicles).

As a rough and ready generalization, France at first wielded the greatest political influence within the EEC, especially after the disastrous Algerian imbroglio had come to an end (1962). West Germany, by contrast, had the greatest economic say, corresponding to its position as Western Europe's greatest economic power, and its role as the EEC's chief paymaster. (The German tax-payer bore the heaviest burden.) Overall, the EEC did a remarkably good job. France, West Germany, Italy, and the Benelux countries, the founder members, cooperated effectively; customs barriers were gradually reduced, and disappeared altogether by 1968. Western Europe thereby adopted gradualism rather than shock treatment; sufficient time was given for economic readjustment in the various member countries; there was no attempt at a "Big Bang" of the kind later advocated widely for the East Central European states after the collapse of communism.

Obstacles to the free transfer of capital and the movement of labor likewise diminished. (EC workers were assured of equal treatment in all member countries as regards employment, wages, and other working conditions.) Labor unions as well as capitalists discovered the merits of transnational cooperation. (The major unions joined to form a European Trade Union Confederation, ETUC, with its headquarters in Brussels. By 1984, ETUC had 34 affiliates representing 43,000,000 workers.) The Community later tried to develop a comprehensive policy with regard to science, technology, nuclear power, and space research. Intra-European trade vastly expanded. Institutional support for the EEC grew apace. During the early 1950s, the EEC's main backers had been intellectuals, bureaucrats, politicians, and managers in certain major transnational corporations. By the late 1960s, the EEC (now the EC) could draw on much solid support from agricultural, financial and industrial lobbies throughout Western Europe. Living standards went up; production both increased and diversified. The EC flourished.

At the same time, the feelings of Western nations toward one another began to change. Memories of World War II dimmed; yesteryear's great war leaders died (de Gaulle in 1970, followed in the 1970s by Montgomery, Eisenhower, and Zhukov). To the generation born after 1945 these generals seemed men of another era. Selective oblivion went with improved sentiments held by Western European nations toward one another. The French, to give just one example, might have been expected to hate the Germans – after three German invasions in the space of 70 years. In fact, only 19 percent of respondents in a 1965 poll placed Germany at the top of the list enumerating the nation "disliked most." (Germany was followed by the Soviet Union with 15 percent; the US with 11 percent; Britain with 10 percent; Italy with 9 percent.) The person most likely to detest the Germans was an aging peasant woman who had only received an elementary education. By contrast, the college-educated French "opinion leaders" were pro-German; it was no longer chic to lambast the *boche*.[3] (The most popular countries were Belgium and Switzerland – 24 percent and 13 percent respectively – both of them in part French-speaking countries.) Hostility toward the US, Italy, and Britain was

3 Manfred Koch-Hillebrecht, *Das Deutschenbild: Gegenwart, Geschichte, Psychologie*, Munich, C.H. Beck, 1977, pp. 56–7.

balanced, however, by an almost equally great percentage of respondents who placed these countries at the top of the popularity stakes (11 percent for the US; 9 percent for Italy; 8 percent for Britain – albeit only 6 percent for Germany.) The fact remains that by 1960 a Franco-German war, or – for that matter – an Anglo-French war, would have appeared inconceivable to most Europeans – this within less than two decades of one of the most devastating conflicts in history.

In a more general sense, the past seemed increasingly irrelevant to the young, even in France where historical memories had always profoundly influenced politics. As Henry Rousso, a French historian, points out, educational specialists had been apprehensive about introducing contemporary history into the syllabus for advanced students. Examination answers might turn into bitter polemics concerning World War II. Not to worry! "This period of our history seems to have about as much personal meaning to many candidates as the Media Wars," concluded an official report in 1972. A year later there were complaints about howlers in the exam. (For the prestigious *agrégation*, the qualifying examination for secondary school teachers, the Maginot Line was mistaken for the demarcation line between unoccupied and occupied France in World War II; Marshall Pétain appeared as president of the Third Republic. Quarrels about the past, therefore, softened as memories began to dim.)[4]

Sectarian differences likewise diminished. The Catholics formed substantial minorities in the US and in The Netherlands; in West Germany and Switzerland, they had obtained near numerical parity with the Protestants. In all these countries, the social and economic position of Catholics substantially improved. (In 1961, the US elected John F. Kennedy to the presidency, the first Catholic to hold this office, a choice that Franklin D. Roosevelt had still regarded as politically out of the question during his own lifetime.) Anti-semitism likewise declined. US Jews in particular advanced to numerous positions in academia and corporate life which had hitherto been closed to them. Not that dislike disappeared. Pierre Mendés-France (a Jewish Frenchman, prime minister 1954–5) might have gone further in politics had his name been Dupont. But anti-semitism as a major political force had seen its day in the West, surviving only east of the Iron Curtain and in the Muslim world.

This process went with a slow and gradual decline in a condition known to Dutch sociologists as *verzuiling* (pillarization), a state in which society rests on pillars that separately support the roof. Belgium, to take an example, was divided into French-speaking, Flemish-speaking, and German-speaking segments. Few Walloons could talk passable Flemish, or had ever read a Flemish classic. But this was not all, there was also politico-cultural segmentation. Socialists and, to a lesser extent, Catholics were not merely united in a parliamentary organization. The respective parties had also provided to their followers cooperatives, cafés, meeting rooms, dance halls, libraries, and gymnasiums; the parties had furnished old-age pensions and assistance to the needy, clinics and educational work. Increasingly this ceased to be true as television, tourism, the new youth culture, and consumerism changed accustomed lifestyles and reduced visible class differences. Intra-European cooperation both reflected and accelerated these changes.

Not that all went well with the EEC. An association such as the EEC, built on innumerable compromises, could not escape constant conflict. Leaders such as de Gaulle (and later Mrs Thatcher) remained determined that the EEC should remain a loose

4 Henry Rousso, *The Vichy Syndrome: History and Memory of France since 1944*, Cambridge, MA, Harvard University Press, 1991, p. 267.

association of sovereign states; their vision of the future was very different from the "Europeanists" strongly entrenched within the EEC's growing bureaucracy. There were problems which derived from the economic disparity between the industrial core states and the backward agricultural periphery. This disparity led to massive labor migration from countries such as Portugal, Spain, South Italy, Yugoslavia, Turkey, to the industrialized North. To cure these problems, EEC planners attempted to subsidize industrial development in backward regions – with dubious results. There were unresolved party issues between Christian democrats and socialists. Moreover, from the very start of the EEC, the German reunification issue loomed in the background. (In endorsing the EEC treaties, the West German SPD insisted that it would only accept the agreements on the assumption that these would not make the unification of Germany more difficult.)

Agriculture proved a particularly difficult subject to resolve. During the three decades following World War II farming methods were revolutionized by land consolidation, the use of tractors, better seeds and fertilizers; output expanded; countless farmers and farm workers sold their land and moved to the cities. Nevertheless, farmers called for protective tariffs and subsidies, a particularly serious matter for the Christian democratic parties which relied heavily on rural votes. The EEC rested in part on a tacit compromise: free trade in industrial goods to please manufacturers (particularly those in West Germany) balanced by agricultural protection to satisfy farmers in France, and – to a lesser extent – in Italy and West Germany. In 1962, after the longest negotiating marathon in the EEC's history, the EEC adopted basic regulations for a common market in agriculture. But this new Common Agricultural Policy (CAP) continued to divide the European countries – not surprisingly so, given the great differences between highly urbanized countries such as Great Britain, endowed with an efficient, highly mechanized farming industry, and countries such as France, West Germany, Italy, and Spain where small farmers remained numerous and influential in politics.

Agricultural protection proved expensive, accounting for by far the greatest part of the EC's expenditure. Agricultural protection dominated the EC's external trade policy, interfering with the ability of poorer countries to export their own agricultural produce. Protection led to the accumulation of unsaleable surpluses – mountains of butter and lakes of wine. Protection contributed to ecological problems. (For instance, excessive production of pigs unexpectedly led to difficulties with pigs' excrement, an organic substance, yet a pollutant when produced to excess.) Agricultural protection led to serious quarrels both within the EC, and between the EC and the US. Agricultural protection injured even the French, the CAP's principal protagonists. (By the early 1990s, farming accounted for only 4 percent of the French GDP. French people employed in the rest of the economy would have gained from lower tariffs.) CAP also promoted bureaucratic growth: 96 percent of EC regulations dealt with agriculture.

Nevertheless, farmers continued to be thought worthy of special favors for reasons which cannot be quantified. Farmers maintained the beauty of the countryside merely by tending fields and keeping fences in repair. Abandoned farms, by contrast, turned into unsightly wilderness. During two world wars, many Europeans had gone hungry. Hunger left a psychological legacy which made the farming industry appear more important than any other. Farmers, moreover, supposedly stood for a particularly desirable way of life, embodying the nation's very soul. This consideration continued to play a part in politics, even though traditional peasant cultures disintegrated, while old-fashioned cultivators left the land, retired, or died. Successful farmers, by contrast, turned into businessmen, as skilled in accountancy as in agronomy.

The EC's difficulties worsened owing to its lack of broad popular support. The Eurocrats did not manage to create enough convincing symbols; official documents, written in bureaucratic Euro-speak, lacked mass appeal. The EEC met with opposition particularly from people who did not do well, or believed themselves to be badly off: small farmers, small businessmen, workers in antiquated industries, pensioners, and the unemployed. There was political opposition, especially from the extreme left and the extreme right, but also from many moderates. The EEC's bureaucracy – large, privileged, highly paid, and impersonal – was remote from ordinary Frenchmen, or Germans. Officials would usually serve in Brussels for many years. They went home on holidays, and mixed almost only among their own kind. Their Brussels became almost a separate city, with something of Washington's or Canberra's rarefied atmosphere. Their supra-nationalism failed to catch on among their respective compatriots; it lacked the color, the sense of devotion that only traditional nationalism seemed to evoke. Football crowds went on cheering (or at times committing mayhem) for their national teams. Only a small portion of Western Europeans thought of themselves as Europeans first, British, French, or German second. There was, indeed, widespread though unfocused dislike for the new denationalized Europe – with its plate glass and concrete buildings, Euro-speak, Eurocrats, and *Gastarbeiter*. Men and women might still be willing to die for Germany, for Britain, or for France, but none of them would risk his or her life for the EEC. Europe remained – as de Gaulle had both hoped and anticipated – *l'Europe des Etats*.

There was also the British question. The British at first stayed out. (Even after the Treaty of Rome had been signed in 1957, the Foreign Office regarded the Common Market issue largely as a trade question, to be left to the Treasury, and the treaty was not even properly translated into English.) In 1961, the British at last began negotiations for admission to the EEC. By this time, the British gross national product had fallen much behind West Germany's, and West Germany had replaced Britain as the US's main European partner in NATO. In 1967 the British withdrew from Aden (on the Red Sea) and, a year later, Britain announced that within three years it would evacuate all military and naval bases east of Suez. De Gaulle, who had vetoed the original British application to the EEC, died in 1970. In 1973 the British finally secured membership of the EC in a settlement achieved through personal talks between British premier Edward Heath, a conservative, and French President Georges Pompidou. The new British European Parliament members took an active part in improving the status of the European Parliament; they insisted on greater accountability for the Commission and the Council.

The British accession to the EC left EFTA (European Free Trade Association) as a rump, with Switzerland as its wealthiest member. (EFTA had been set up in 1960, with Austria, Britain, Denmark, Norway, Portugal, Sweden, and Switzerland as its founding states.) EFTA got little publicity. Yet its people had a much higher gross domestic product per head of population than those of the EC ($11,750 as against $7,575 in 1985). Whereas the EC required 17,000 civil servants at the time, EFTA only had 71 employees, nine of them part-timers. English was EFTA's working language – hence no need for the 5,000 translators and linguists employed by the EC. Unlike the EC, EFTA had no costly programs on farming, customs, transport, and so on. EFTA lacked a common foreign policy; EFTA members did not abandon one iota of their sovereignty; they were held together by free trade.

EFTA, however, heavily depended on the EC with which EFTA did more than half of its business. (EFTA became the EC's largest trading partner, outstripping the US and

Japan.) Free trade agreements were concluded between EFTA members and the EC, but covered only industrial goods, not agriculture or services. Even commerce in manufactured goods faced an array of technical barriers plaguing both EFTA and the EC's own members – restrictions linked to EC specifications on product size, composition, safety, and so forth. To guard against being side-tracked, the EFTA states thereby began to draw closer to the EC, with the ultimate object of obtaining full membership. (In 1973 Denmark and Ireland also joined the EC, whereas Norway stayed out.)

Contentious also was the question of who would run the EC. In a numerical sense Germany was under-represented within the Brussels bureaucracy and within the European Parliament. Germany also paid a disproportionately high share of the EC's "social" expenditure. (For instance, in 1975 the EC set up a Regional Development Fund to assist the EC's own "backward" areas.) Though superior in economic power, Bonn was content to cooperate with Paris in a partnership which informally dominated the EC. (This entente was solidified by close personal relations between French president Valéry Giscard d'Estaing, in office 1974–81, and German chancellor Helmut Schmidt, in power 1972–83.) German taxpayers objected that they in particular bore an excessive burden within the European context; by contrast, Frenchmen and Britons, particularly those on the extreme left and right of the political spectrum, complained that Germany was becoming too powerful, and that the Bonn Republic would conquer by the D-Mark what the Third Reich had failed to win by its panzers.

More immediate in its consequences were the "oil shocks" begun in 1973. Rising oil prices went with a worldwide economic downturn; "the thirty golden years" after World War II ended. (Nobel Laureate Milton Friedman points out, however, that in US economic history the postwar era merely saw normal economic growth, not exceptional prosperity.) There were far-reaching social changes in Western Europe and the US alike; more women entered the workplace; women diversified their skills, and began to rise in the managerial hierarchy. At the same time there was a striking increase in divorce and in the number of children born out of wedlock. For the first time in history, social scientists began to talk about the "feminization of poverty." The rise of mass unemployment led governments to give priority to national interests – this at the EC's expense. Traditional industries such as steel, textiles, and shipbuilding declined; yet Europeans discovered that they were being outdone in high technology by the US and Japan. Many restrictions remained within the EC. These comprised, among others, vexatious border inspections of goods in transit; restrictions on the movements of people, goods, services, and capital; differences in national product norms; problems connected with differential taxation; patents; standardization in service industries; complex issues connected with the standardization of computers, communications, and such like.

The EC likewise contended with a wider cleavage that divided the beneficiaries of public funds and public employment from those citizens who felt aggrieved as taxpayers. There was rivalry, not so much between socialism and capitalism, as between different schools of capitalism. The French would stress the role of the state in shaping economic policy. It was not for nothing that France had created the modern centralized state; the French example had helped to shape the public service and financial administration of the modern world. (*Dirigisme* was a French word. The modern *mandarins* in France were indeed the heirs of Jean-Baptiste Colbert, chief minister of King Louis XIV who had proclaimed *l'état c'est moi*.) Within the EC context it was, above all, the European Commission in Brussels that represented the French bureaucratic tradition which looked upon the great bureaucrats as agents of modernization and progress.

German capitalism likewise placed much reliance on public authority. A substantial part of German capital investment derived from public savings; the state favored specific enterprises by tax breaks and the provision of cheap loans. German capitalism – intimidated by a long history of class struggles – specially favored cooperation between workers and management (corporatism). German capitalism allocated a major role to the leading banks, whose representatives played a major part in the board rooms of major private enterprises. Having experienced the traumatic effects of runaway inflation in the wake of two world wars, German capitalism put special emphasis on sound money. This was the creed of the *Bundesbank* whose financial influence within the EC was hard to exaggerate. The Germans' commitment to hard money clashed with British convictions that unemployment was a greater threat to the commonweal than inflation.

And so dissensions continued. "Euro-pessimism" was in the air, derived in part from the rise of Japan to the status of an economic superpower, and the relatively slow pace of European progress in the new technologies that hinged on the computer, robots, and biochemical advances. Above all, there was the Americans' predominance. (During the late 1960s, Jean-Louis Schreiber's book *Le défi americain*, translated in 1986 as *The American Challenge*, turned into the Euro-pessimists' Bible.) Euro-pessimism seemed all the more justified in view of the oil shocks suffered by the world economy in 1973, a general slowdown in economic expansion, and widespread unemployment. There were problems with NATO. The Middle East was shaken by the Yom Kippur war in 1973. The US was bitterly divided by the Vietnam War, the Watergate Scandal in 1973, and President Nixon's resignation in 1974. In 1974 Turkey invaded Cyprus, thereby apparently making the Turko-Greek split unbridgeable. The EC seemed ill equipped to meet these predicaments.

NATO

When World War II ended, there was no commitment to a continued American military presence in Europe. President Roosevelt had expected to withdraw all American soldiers within two years; isolationism remained strong, especially in the Midwest. It was not merely left-wingers who wanted to "bring the boys home," but also conservatives with the most impeccable credentials, men such as ex-president Herbert Hoover. It was Stalinist intransigence which recreated the Western alliance. Contrary to Soviet and pro-Soviet propaganda, moreover, it was not bellicose Americans who had inveigled peace-loving Europeans into an aggressive pact. It was, above all, pressure from the British (and to a much lesser extent from the Canadian) government that had finally persuaded the US to join the accord and to return to Europe militarily. (The formation in 1949 of the North Atlantic Treaty Organization, NATO, had been preceded by the creation of the Cominform, in 1947, the Berlin blockade initiated in 1948, and the communist takeover in Prague in the same year.) In the words of Lord Ismay, a British general, and secretary-general of NATO, NATO was formed to keep the Russians out, the Germans down, and the Americans in! From the British standpoint, NATO was an extension of the wartime alliance which had given victory to the allied cause, and which had also enhanced British might by getting the US to underwrite British arms expenditure.

History and Functions

US support for NATO was at first only tentative. There was, indeed, European criticism of America's alleged resolve to fight "to the last European." The decisive shift came with North Korea's assault on South Korea in 1950. This act of aggression, openly supported by Stalin with propaganda and arms shipments, caused the US to embark on massive rearmament. The Korean War, moreover, confirmed Americans in their fear that the Soviet Union might try on a large scale in Western Europe what the North Koreans had attempted on a small scale in South Korea – the pursuit of revolution by military means. By dint of its sacrifices in the Korean War, the US had demonstrated its willingness to support a threatened ally. Henceforth, there would be no more talk about America's being willing to fight to the last allied soldier. It was the greatest shift ever in US foreign policy.

As far as West Germany was concerned, NATO membership likewise served both national and international interests. By joining NATO, Konrad Adenauer achieved for the Federal German Republic legitimacy, equality of status with the occupying powers and equality of esteem. Membership in NATO and the European Community would firmly anchor Germany in the West, silence the voice of neutralism, encourage the Americans to stay in Europe, and also encourage foreign investors. Rearmament (effective from 1955 onward) posed a number of problems. Anti-militarism had flourished in defeated Germany. Contrary to allied fears and expectations, the beaten *Wehrmacht* veterans mostly evinced little desire once more to put on uniform, especially at a time when jobs had become plentiful and living standards kept improving. *Ohne mich* – without me – was a widely heard response on the part of young Germans to demands for German rearmament. But Soviet pressure on Western Europe, and the steady increase in Soviet military might, between them led to German rearmament; the *Bundeswehr* became NATO's largest army component, an essential link in Western European defense. German rearmament occasioned bitter disagreement within Western Europe, and also within West Germany itself. (It was only from 1959 onward that the German Social Democratic Party fully accepted West Germany's role.) But, thereafter, Germany became America's main ally in Europe, and guaranteed the peace in Europe just as the US–Japan security treaty kept the peace in the Pacific.

France joined NATO in part for reassurance against the Soviet Union, and even more so for the sake of preventing a future German *revanche* by locking West Germany into a common security system. The Italians welcomed integration into the EC and NATO as a means of recovering their lost legitimacy and their former status as a major power. Italy in particular benefited from American fears that Italy might fall prey to communism, from the strength of the Italian lobby in the US, and from the tight links existing between Catholics in the US and the Papacy in Italy. In the post-Korean arms race, Italy obtained an end to the restrictions put on her by the postwar peace treaty. "There can be no doubt that Italy was a major beneficiary of the Cold War."[5] The Low Countries and Norway, for their part, remembered how neutrality before World War II had failed to serve their respective interests; all had endured the trauma of occupation; all were resolved to prevent such a disaster in future. Every NATO partner thus had a firm interest in making the alliance last.

5 A.J. Nichols, "European Integration and the Nation State: Some Thoughts on the 1950s," *Contemporary European History*, vol. 2, November 1993, p. 285.

To coordinate NATO was, nevertheless, a matter of considerable complexity. Though equal in theory, the partners were unequal in practice. The US provided the leadership, a substantial body of troops, the rearmament of Germany, the greater part of the naval and air forces, and the bulk of the nuclear weaponry available to the Western allies. (The British and French built their own nuclear deterrents, but these did not provide their respective owners with true strategic independence.) In order to run NATO, the allies set up a complex organization. The Council served as the supreme organ of the alliance, with permanent representation from each member government. The Council was responsible for implementing the provisions of the treaty; its work was organized by the secretary general who directed its secretariat and its five divisions: political affairs, defense planning and policy, defense support, infrastructure, logistics, scientific affairs. The Council's chief administrative officer was the secretary general. The Council was assisted by a host of specialized committees and agencies that dealt with matters as diverse as the press services and economics.

NATO's military direction lay with the military committee composed of the chief of staff of each member state. Subordinate to the military committee were the major commands and planning groups: Supreme Command Europe (SACEUR); Supreme Allied Commander Atlantic (SACLANT); Allied commander-in-chief Channel (CINCHAN); Canada–US Regional Planning Group (CUSRPG); and a number of other military agencies. Supreme headquarters were in Paris, and later shifted to Brussels. (Here NATO's impact, however, was much smaller than the EC's. By 1990 there were still fewer than 2,300 NATO officials in Brussels, as opposed to 14,000 EC Eurocrats.) Subordinate agencies were located in Paris, Bonn, and Rome.

NATO was, above all, more than a military alliance. It developed an extensive system of committees dealing with subjects as varied as political collaboration; the settlement of intra-alliance disputes; consultation on foreign policy; economic, scientific, technical, social, and cultural cooperation. The Secretary General of NATO, who headed its international staff, became almost as powerful a man as the SACEUR. The alliance united policy-makers and executives of many different nationalities in a common task. No other alliance in history had comprised such a diversity of partners or cooperated on such a broad range of subjects, nor lasted as long. (By the early 1980s, NATO comprised Belgium, Canada, Denmark, France, Greece, Iceland, Italy, Luxemburg, The Netherlands, Norway, Portugal, Spain, Turkey, the United Kingdom, the United States, and West Germany – enlarged in 1990 by the unification with East Germany, though with a special status within NATO.) No doubt NATO had its troubles. But these were kept in bound and NATO worked. Contrary to all previous predictions and previous precedents, German, French, British, Dutch, Italian, and American military men cooperated successfully. NATO remained an alliance whose members had joined freely; they were not simply satellites such as the Soviet Union's Warsaw Pact partners.

Not that NATO worked without a great deal of friction. Alliances are uneasy partnerships by their very nature. As Lord Macaulay wrote a century and a half ago, "Jealousies inevitably spring up. Disputes engender disputes. Every confederate is tempted to throw on others some part of the burden which he himself ought to bear. Scarcely one honestly furnishes the promised contingent. Scarcely one observes the appointed day."[6] NATO deserved these strictures. Unlike the members of the Warsaw Pact, each NATO member

6 Thomas Babington Macaulay, *The History of Engand from the Accession of James II*, Chicago, Belford, Clarke, 1867, vol. 4, p. 123.

remained a genuinely sovereign country; its members could leave the alliance as they pleased. (In 1966 France withdrew from NATO's military command, though France continued to cooperate with the alliance. NATO's headquarters had to move from Paris to Brussels.) Individual members remained free to decide the percentage of the GNP, the size and the composition of the forces which they would contribute. NATO's sphere of action remained confined to Western Europe and its strategic role remained defensive. Threats to the alliance that might emerge elsewhere, in Africa, the Middle East or the Caribbean, would still have to be dealt with by its individual members – an arrangement initially welcomed and later regretted by the Americans. NATO possessed no coordinated intelligence service; the intelligence services of the individual countries would continue to operate in an uneasy, and often mutually hostile, fraternity. NATO also lacked a propaganda organization capable of rivalling the Soviet propaganda machine in Western Europe. NATO likewise wanted for an agency for political warfare. In this regard, the allies differed among themselves and even individual member states, including the US, pursued no consistent policy. The absence of a coordinated political strategy became all the more obvious from the later 1950s onwards, when the Soviets became more skillful in their foreign policy, increasingly used "peace" slogans and anti-nuclear movements for their own purposes, and resolved to make their weight felt in the Third World.

NATO also had many technical problems. The alliance proved much less adept at standardizing its equipment than the Warsaw Pact. NATO's command structure was overly complex. Reliance on nuclear deterrents created difficult, probably insoluble, problems, as the Soviet Union perfected its own nuclear arsenal. The West consistently underestimated its own capacity for conventional defense. Benumbed by head counts, Western planners were apt to overrate the value of non-Soviet divisions within the Warsaw Pact, most of which might have proved unreliable in the event of a conflict. Hence, as William Park, a British student of strategy, put it, "NATO was born with an inferiority complex regarding its conventional force capabilities, unwarranted even in the early years."[7]

NATO's sense of inferiority *vis-à-vis* the Red Army was hardly justified. By the late 1950s, after West Germany had put in place a substantial new force, the *Bundeswehr*, the Western allies were already in fairly good shape, despite the Soviet Union's numerical superiority. The NATO forces, moreover, kept experimenting to improve their fighting capability. But, overall, NATO troops were better equipped and trained. They had stronger logistic support and a better backup structure. NATO aircraft maintained on the average much higher sortie rates than their Warsaw Pact opponents. The Western allies were superior at sea. They enjoyed the advantage of defensive lines. Nobody, of course, knows how the alliance would have worked in the event of a Soviet attack. (The traffic problems that would have arisen from the clash of huge mechanized armies in the great conurbations of Western Europe would, alone, have been logistical nightmares – not to speak of the chaos that would have arisen from the employment of "tac-nukes.")

---

7 William Park, *Defending the West: a History of NATO*, Boulder, Colo., Westview Press, 1986, pp. 21–6. See also Duignan and Gann, *The Rebirth of the West*, ch. 7 on NATO; L.H. Gann, ed., *The Defense of Western Europe*, London, Croom Helm, 1987; Sir Nicholas Henderson, *The Birth of NATO*, London, Weidenfeld and Nicolson, 1982; Lawrence S. Kaplan, ed., *NATO after Forty Years*, Wilmington, Del., SR Books, 1990; and *NATO and the United States: the Enduring Alliance*, Boston, Twayne, 1988; Alfred Grosser, *The Western Alliance*, New York, Continuum, 1980.

But given the over-centralization and inflexibility of the Soviet forces, their morale problems, and the unreliability of the Soviets' Warsaw Pact allies, NATO would certainly have given a good account of itself.[8]

Even more contentious was the proposed use of nuclear weapons both on the tactical and the strategic level. It was NATO's sense of numerical inferiority that had first impelled the Europeans in NATO to demand that the US defend them with tactical nuclear arms. (Eisenhower supported this policy which was, however, opposed by active duty generals such as James Gavin, one of the outstanding US air-borne commanders of World War II.) The reason for the numerical balance was in the main budgetary. None of the Western allies was willing to match the Warsaw Pact armies in terms of manpower, tanks, and guns; the Europeans proposed to spend more money on social welfare than on the military. Initially, NATO relied on its superiority in atomic weapons and on the qualitative superiority of its equipment. But these advantages evaporated as the Soviets improved their own armaments. During the 1950s, therefore, NATO began to deploy a great array of tactical nuclear weapons for direct battlefield support. (The French and British built their own nuclear deterrents – not so much to intimidate the Soviets as to assert French and British power within the Western councils. Existing treaty obligations forbade the Germans to do likewise.)

Of all the major Western powers, it was West Germany that relied most heavily on the US nuclear guarantee, and which housed the largest number of battlefield nuclear projectiles on its soil. This dependency created its own psychological problems and its own peculiar ambivalence. The Germans wanted the US to deploy tactical nuclear weapons on German soil so as to provide the maximum deterrent; the Germans looked to a "forward" defense entailing an allied stand on the Elbe rather than the Rhine. But at the same time German opinion, particularly left-wing opinion, dreaded the enormous concentration of atomic weapons on German soil which would turn Germany into a nuclear battlefield, and thereby spell *finis Germaniae*, an end to Germany.

Nuclear weapons, of course, could not be tested in maneuvers. In combat, they would have turned any battlefield into a desert. By about 1957, NATO had deployed about 7,000 tactical nuclear weapons in Europe.[9] They included land mines, mortar rounds, recoilless rifle charges, air-dropped bombs, and artillery shells. Later, intermediate range nuclear force missiles were added – at the Europeans' request, but nevertheless against bitter anti-US opposition, especially from German, British, and Dutch pacifists and ecologists. No strategist could work out a rational system of defense with doomsday

---

8 The Soviet Union, on paper, possessed 175 divisions, augmented by approximately 60 satellite divisions, by 1959. It was estimated that the Soviet Union could provide another 125 divisions within 30 days of mobilization. But, as regards actual frontline divisions, the Soviet force was less impressive; there were eight tank divisions stationed in East Germany, with another seven divisions in Hungary and Poland. By 1959, NATO's forces in Western Europe comprised just under 22 divisions in the Central Area, including three from Britain, five from the US, two from France, seven from West Germany, two from Belgium, two from The Netherlands, including some Canadian forces in addition. The northern flank comprised one Danish and one Norwegian division. The southern flank included 12 divisions from Turkey, five from Greece, and seven from Italy. NATO divisions were overall twice as large as Soviet divisions in terms of manpower. NATO had a decisive maritime superiority. For details, see the Institute for Strategic Studies, *The Soviet Union and the NATO Powers: the Military Balance*, London, The Institute, 1959.

9 Thomas Hirschfeld, "Tactical Nuclear Weapons in Europe," *Washington Quarterly*, Winter 1987, pp. 101–21.

weapons which threatened to destroy not merely most enemy forces, but the very theaters of operations in which these forces would operate. Initially, the allies relied on a doctrine of massive retaliation (proclaimed by the US in 1954, and officially adopted by NATO in 1957). Any Soviet assault would be met with the full might of the US nuclear arsenal. The Soviets, however, themselves built a powerful nuclear rocket force. Allied superiority vanished, as the allies would not use their economic predominance to outbuild the Soviets at every step. In 1967, the allies adopted a new doctrine of "flexible response," of measured retaliation. Missiles improved in quality and grew in quantity. No expert can be sure what actually would have happened had these weapons been used in combat – no doubt they would have occasioned nuclear Verduns and wiped out friends and foe alike.

Equally contentious were the problems concerned with strategic nuclear weapons, that is to say inter-continental ballistic missiles. Initially, only the US had the capacity to attack the Soviet Union with nuclear bombs and destroy its main cities. As the Soviets improved their own weaponry, US nuclear strategy was modified during the 1960s when Robert McNamara was secretary of defense. Deterrence of nuclear war rested on the country's assumed ability to absorb a nuclear strike and still destroy the Soviet Union. The Soviet Union, however, soon caught up with the US. By the late 1960s, US planners reconciled themselves to a doctrine aptly named MAD (for mutual assured destruction.) According to prevailing orthodoxy at the time, any effort to upset this balance was considered destabilizing. As Stanley Kober, an arms expert, put it, "it was this logic that impelled McNamara passionately to oppose the construction of antiballistic missiles (ABMs)."[10] The Americans thereafter tried to limit the construction of ABMs through accords such as the 1972 Strategic Arms Limitation Treaty (SALT I). But the Kremlin never accepted the US strategic assumptions; the Soviets continued to work on ABM technology on the grounds that every weapon in history had always produced a counter-weapon.

The MAD doctrine had far-reaching political consequences. The NATO allies all relied on the US deterrent; yet they also had understandable doubts whether the Americans were truly willing to sacrifice New York for London, Paris, or Hamburg. Would the Soviets and Americans not be tempted to abstain from using strategic nuclear weapons, preserving their respective homelands as nuclear sanctuaries, while destroying both Western and Eastern Europe with tactical nuclear weapons? Fortunately, the world never found out. One thing is clear, however, the US never attempted to use to the full its technical and scientific superiority in a race decisively to out-arm the Soviet Union. (In building intercontinental ballistic missiles (ICBMs) the US did not even aim at parity with the Soviet Union.) In our opinion, the US's failure to use to the full its capability was a grave mistake – not rectified until Ronald Reagan assumed the presidency, and reordered US priorities.

Alone among the powers, the US even set up an arms control lobby within its own bureaucracy, the Arms Control and Disarmament Agency (created in 1961). Dedicated to "balanced" arms reduction, the Agency formed a counter-weight to the armed services. The Agency even maintained its own program to support doctoral dissertations, and thereby linked itself to a burgeoning arms control lobby in academia. The arms controllers came to live in a world of their own, complete with a jargon quite incomprehensible

10 Stanley Kober, "Strategic Defense, Deterrence, and Arms Control," *Washington Quarterly*, Winter 1987, pp. 123–52.

to ordinary citizens. Unfortunately, arms control ran into numerous theoretical and practical difficulties. The arms controllers widely lacked a historical perspective. (For instance, the Washington Naval Treaty (1922) had set fixed limits on naval construction by the great powers. By accepting this self-denying ordinance, the US barred itself from building a decisive naval supremacy which would perhaps have deterred Japanese aggression in the Pacific 19 years later. Yet the Japanese were left dissatisfied by the Treaty. Even in open societies such as Weimar Germany, rearmament after World War I had been effectively concealed through clever subterfuges designed to circumvent the disarmament clauses of the Versailles Treaty. Intelligence proved even harder to obtain in closed societies such as East Germany (where the Soviets clandestinely set up intermediate range ballistic missiles (SS-20s), detected only after the reunification of the East and West German armies.) The Soviet Union was even harder to penetrate, for the Soviets falsified not merely statistics but even their cartography. They constructed, for example, an entire archipelago of secret cities (perhaps 100 in all). These were solely devoted to military research and arms production. These cities did not appear on any maps. Access to them was severely restricted; information on their work was unavailable. Their respective inhabitants lived privileged lives; largely worked with, socialized with, and even married only their own kind. The world was quite unaware of what went on in this clandestine universe, with its nuclear accidents, its secret work done on super-weapons (including a "super-plague", undertaken despite the declared ban on biological weapons production). Even after the Soviet Union had been dismantled, President Yeltsin himself claimed not to have known everything that went on in the military–industrial complex.[11]

US arms controllers obviously remained much more ignorant. They had indeed access to reports submitted by spies and to evidence provided by satellites. But the former were of necessity scanty and contradictory; the latter incomplete, because even the best images could provide little or no evidence of what went on inside the buildings photographed by satellites. More serious still was the disarmament lobby's mindset, their widespread failure to appreciate the ethnocentric nature of their own assumptions. The rest of the world, especially the communist and also the Islamic countries, did not share the legalistic and moralistic norms widely taken for granted by Washington policy-makers. The disarmament lobbies provided well-paid jobs for an army of consultants, counselors, and other real or assumed experts. But their success in enhancing the security of the US was more dubious indeed.

In addition, there were constant quarrels within NATO concerning the allies' respective contribution to the alliance. The Americans, especially, felt that the Europeans did not fully pull their weight. This assumption rested on comparative statistics for defense expenditure to which the US always contributed the most as a percentage of the gross national product. Nevertheless, such comparisons could be misleading. The definition of defense spending included the costs of US non-NATO defense commitments. Hence US spending totals were biased by including the cost of maintaining US forces in areas where the NATO allies had no treaty commitments. After all, the US saw itself as a global power with global responsibilities especially to contain communism. NATO had regional responsibilities only. Comparisons concerning costs were apt also to take inadequate account of differentials; it was more expensive to maintain an American volunteer than a *Bundeswehr* conscript. (Within Western Europe itself, the NATO allies always

11 See ch. 4 on the military–industrial complex in Richard F. Staar, *The New Military in Russia*, Annapolis, Md, Naval Institute Press, 1996.

supplied the bulk of the land forces – between 80 and 90 percent.) Disputes about burden-sharing did not end the list of troubles that beset NATO. There were serious divisions both within the ranks of NATO's European partners, and between Europeans and Americans. Two allies – Greece and Turkey – almost came to blows over Cyprus. (Even long-standing allies such as Britain and France at times addressed one another in terms more suited to enemies than allies.)

Nevertheless, NATO worked. The ties between North America and Western Europe tightened; no transatlantic endeavor in history achieved greater success. NATO worked effectively both as a military and a political alliance. In both capacities, NATO created a great array of new links between the US and Western Europe. English became NATO's military lingua franca just as English became the standard language of air and sea communications. The US furnished much of NATO's conventional, and most of its nuclear, weaponry; the US supplied NATO's supreme commanders; the US provided much of the military technology and equipment. Many European officers and technicians were trained by Americans.

NATO also served as a channel for new ideas, sometimes with unintended consequences. (For instance, the Portuguese army, which rose against the country's dictatorship in 1974, had been influenced by ties to NATO as well as by the experience of a lengthy and unpopular colonial war. General Francisco da Costa Gomes, one of the leaders of the revolution, had earlier served as a senior liaison officer with NATO.) NATO also influenced the US. A great American army was stationed in Europe. Larger still was the number of American dependents, the wives and children of servicemen and civilian officials who, between them, created permanent American enclaves and intensified reciprocal relations between Western Europe and North America.

In wider geo-strategic terms, NATO's full success will not become apparent until all military archives produced by the former Warsaw Pact states are open to inspection. However, a good deal of once-secret information has already been made available from the former German Democratic Republic. These records provide striking details concerning the aggressive nature of Warsaw Pact planning and, we should add, the mendacious character of communist propaganda. While claiming to face an aggressive enemy, the Warsaw Pact leadership planned not for a defensive war but for massive offensives, supported by the first use of nuclear weapons. (In case of war, Warsaw Pact forces would strike through West Germany, Austria, Denmark, and thereafter occupy France.[12] Given the excellence of Soviet and East German intelligence services, the purely defensive nature of NATO's military planning was, of course, well known to the Warsaw Pact's leadership. This did not prevent communist planners from consistently misrepresenting NATO's operational designs so as to conform to the aggressive image of the enemy created by communist political warfare experts.

Despite its numerous and well-publicized deficiencies, NATO did deter the Soviet Union from blackmailing the Western European countries. Deterrence worked because the US remained faithful to its commitments. Without US backing, the various continental states of Western Europe could hardly have stood up to Soviet pressure, particularly at a time when the communist parties were powerful in France and Italy. The Soviets, of course, tried to influence Western Europe through a variety of propagandist

12 Mark Kramer, "Warsaw Pact Military Planning in Central Europe: Revelations from the East German Archives," Cold War International History Project, Woodrow Wilson International Center for Scholars, *Bulletin*, Fall 1992, pp. 1, 13–14.

and diplomatic means. But, except for a brief moment in 1974 when the existing Portuguese dictatorship toppled, and the Portuguese Communist Party briefly hoped to gain power, Western Europe remained immune to communist takeovers, or to being "Finlandized".

Diverted from Western Europe, the Soviet Union thereafter intensified its endeavors along what might be called the outer periphery of the Western world. By the early 1970s, the Vietnam War and the domestic unrest of the 1960s had weakened American self-confidence. America's financial stability was threatened by inflation. By an act of deliberate abnegation, the US had conceded to the Soviet Union an apparent superiority in missiles as well as conventional arms. In addition, the Soviets during the 1960s and 1970s, built a great navy, the world's second largest fleet. From Moscow's standpoint, Soviet military might would aid alike diplomacy, Soviet scholarship, and revolutionary expertise in promoting Third World "national wars of liberation"; these in turn would form stepping stones on the road to worldwide victory for Marxism–Leninism. Soviet propagandists in the West might laud "peaceful coexistence." But peaceful coexistence, according to the official Marxist–Leninist theoreticians, could only exist between rival state systems. There could be no peaceful coexistence between opposing social systems; conflict was inevitable, and socialism Soviet-style was bound to win.

During the 1970s, the Soviets thus made substantial advances. Angola and Mozam-bique, formerly Portuguese colonies, emerged (1974) from colonial control as Marxist–Leninist republics, led by self-styled "vanguard parties." Indo-China (South Vietnam, Cambodia, and Laos) and Ethiopia likewise fell under Marxist–Leninist governance, as did South Yemen. The Marxist–Leninist cause was sustained by a large Cuban expedi-tionary force (mainly deployed in Angola), by a direct Soviet invasion of Afghanistan (1979), and the establishment of a Marxist–Leninist government in Nicaragua with Cuban support. This huge effort looked impressive enough on the map. But neither Angola nor Mozambique could be turned into effectively ruled dictatorships; on the contrary, armed oppositional groups continued to hold their own, massively sup-ported by South Africa. The US successfully backed anti-Soviet guerrillas in Afghanistan. Ethiopia, Moscow's ally, failed to maintain its imperial hegemony over Eritrea and other disputed provinces. The Sandinistas failed to hold their own in Nicaragua, despite massive Cuban and Soviet support. Israel successfully defended itself in the so-called Yom Kippur War of 1973, against the Soviet Union's Arab friends. Everywhere in the Third World, self-styled Marxist–Leninist movements met with defeats. Being limited in its operations to Western Europe, NATO had no direct part in this remarkable counter-revolution. The Soviet Union's main opponent throughout the world was the US. But the US effectively cooperated with individual NATO partners, such as Britain and France, and NATO provided a secure center in Europe.

Contrary to Soviet predictions, the Marxist–Leninist tide thus proved neither irresist-ible nor irreversible. NATO held firm; so did its individual components. Instead, it was the Soviet empire that began to falter, exhausted by the immense effort involved in holding and both exploiting and subsidizing its Eastern European dependencies, main-taining military primacy on the European continent, securing a naval presence on every ocean, and sustaining revolutionary commitment in the Third World.

In the long run the NATO allies were also surprisingly successful in keeping the military out of politics. West Germany's ability in creating the *Bundeswehr*, an army wholly loyal to the constitution, was one of the West's great success stories. The French army submitted to the Fourth Republic. The Spanish, Greek, and Portuguese armies, all heavily involved in politics, ultimately conformed to the constitutional pattern. In the US, fears of an impending *Seven Days in May* (a TV drama concerning a fictional US military coup) remained confined to the entertainment industry and liberal campuses. At the same time, the military gained or regained public trust. (In German as well as Russian and US public opinion polls, the military remained the public institution in which respondents had the greatest degree of confidence.)

Through political decisions at the highest levels, the armed forces of the former Eastern bloc were organized and constantly trained to carry out an offensive war. Only in the mid-1980s, with the advent of the Gorbachev era, was greater emphasis given to defensive tasks, though even this did not lead in any fundamental way to the abandonment of earlier plans. The decisive, decades-long role of the Western alliance and its armed forces in the maintenance of peace and freedom is obvious enough. NATO's determined stance, as well as the responsible policy that the Western democracies pursued when the leadership of the former Warsaw Pact finally decided on a course of dialogue and negotiation, was the most important factor in the collapse of the communist dictatorships and the emergence of a fundamentally new situation.

National Components

NATO operated as a transnational organization with a complex, indeed an overly complex, structure. But in the last instance, the alliance depended for its effectiveness on the strength of its individual national components. Armies by their very nature are among the most "national" of all institutions, and reflect alike the weakness and the strength of their respective national states. Armies, moreover, are apt to intervene in politics during major national crises when civilian authority has lost credibility. Several European armies did interfere, make the attempt, or were suspected of disloyalty. But in every case civilian rule prevailed; armies returned to the barracks. At the same time their technical efficiency and sophistication clearly increased. Relatively backward countries on Western Europe's rural periphery – Turkey, Greece, Spain, Portugal – continued to rely on relatively large conscript armies. But, as industrialization proceeded, the general trend was toward smaller forces with a growing percentage of highly trained regulars and soldiers on extended contracts (*Zeitsoldaten*) in *Bundeswehr* parlance. It was in France, as well as the aforesaid southern countries, that armies intervened, or had earlier intervened in politics. But in the end neither Greek colonels nor Spanish generals prevailed in politics. As John Keegan, a leading British military historian, put it, "looking back over forty years . . . the development of Western Europe's armies in that period constitutes a collection of episodes in which the citizens of the states involved may take a certain national and even collective pride."[13]

Most problematic of all was the French army. It had suffered a shattering defeat at German hands in 1940, but many more troubles would follow. The army was rebuilt, an uneasy amalgamation of Free French troops loyal to de Gaulle from the beginning, colonial forces which rallied to the General after the allied invasion of North Africa, elements of the French regular army, and partisans organized into the "French Forces of the Interior." This army gave a good account of itself at the end of World War II, but nevertheless suffered from a collective sense of inferiority. The French army

13 John Keegan, "Western Europe and its Armies, 1945–85," in Gann, *The Defense of Western Europe*, p. 23.

depended at first almost entirely on foreign (mainly US) equipment; the soldiers looked ragged and unfamiliar in their US and British-made uniforms; the officers were poor men within the world's military profession, for the planners of the Fourth Republic had little interest in military matters, and thought above all of modernizing the French economy. True enough, the army secured some excellent officers; Frenchmen bore the burden of conscription without much complaint. But morale was shattered by two successive defeats. The French lost the colonial war in Indo-China. Then came the Algerian débâcle, a traumatic event that led to de Gaulle's accession to the presidency and the formation of the Fifth Republic.

De Gaulle reformed the armed forces, just as he reformed the constitution. Not that the army lived up to its reputation of *la grande muette* (the great silent one); *la grande bavarde* (the great talker) would have been a more suitable description. But de Gaulle rid the army of the rightists. The army's loyalty to the Republic was assured; never again would dashing *paras* or dour Foreign Legionaries attempt to challenge civilian authority. The army remained a fairly popular institution; France never developed a peace movement comparable in scale and intensity to Holland's, Britain's, or West Germany's. (Overall, the peace movements and the protests against nuclear arms were more powerful in Protestant than Catholic countries.) At the same time, de Gaulle modernized the armed forces. De Gaulle was determined to end the Algerian War, in part because he wished to transform an army composed mainly of infantry, deployed in Algeria, to an army strong in armor, backed by nuclear weapons, an army fit to regain for France her accustomed position as a great military power. In large measure he succeeded. The quality of French armaments vastly increased; France developed into a nuclear power; the army became highly mobile (with eight armored divisions, two mechanized infantry divisions, three partly mechanized infantry divisions, and a parachute division by 1979). France acquired a leading position in certain military industries. (By 1991, for example, France occupied the first place in the world for military software.) Though not formally part of NATO's military command, these forces could not have avoided involvement had the Soviets ever launched an attack against Western Europe. A US military expert concluded: "with capabilities extending across the full range from a militia to a nuclear force, France possesses a flexibility of military options unmatched by any other Western European nation."[14]

Even more surprising was the success attained by the German *Bundeswehr*, under what appeared unfavorable auspices at the time. When World War II ended, the allies were determined to wipe out German military power for all time. Subconsciously perhaps, the war against Germany appeared to the Americans a replay of their own Civil War in which the South had been forced to surrender unconditionally, subjected to Reconstruction (spelled "Re-education" in postwar Germany).

"Re-education" in fact worked, though not in the sense anticipated by US advocates of re-education. World War II left Germans disillusioned with the military. German rearmament under Konrad Adenauer occurred – not in response to German popular

---

14 Colonel Wilfred L. Ebel, "The French Republic," *Military Review*, August 1979, p. 50. For the French army in general, see Paul-Marie de La Gorce, *The French Army: a Military–Political History*, trans. Kenneth Douglas, New York, George Braziller, 1963; George Armstrong Kelly, *Lost Soldiers: the French Army and Empire in Crisis, 1947–1962*, Cambridge, MA, MIT Press, 1965; Douglas Porch, "French Defense and the Gaullist Legacy," in Gann, *The Defense of Western Europe*, pp. 188–212.

agitation, but mainly in response to allied demands for a West German contribution to Western military defense after a series of major crises: the Berlin blockade in 1948, the detonation of the first Soviet atom bomb in 1949, the North Korean attack on South Korea in 1950, and the development of a military force in East Germany (the *Kasernierte Volkspolizei*, started in 1952, renamed *Nationale Volksarmee* in 1956).

When recruiting began for the *Bundeswehr*, the new army met with widespread opposition. Liberal and left-wing critics (especially the social democrats) feared that the army would become a school of militarism and a danger to West Germany's democratic institutions. The hard-line right, by contrast, was contemptuous of the new army on the grounds that it was soft, that the *Bundeswehr's* new doctrine of *Innere Führung* (discipline through self-discipline) would never work. The *Bundeswehr*, the charge sheet continued, was not a genuinely German institution, but an instrument of allied policy, more highly integrated into NATO than any other of its components, and lacking even its own General Staff. The *Bundeswehr* also faced far-reaching political and moral problems of a kind that sprang from Germany's troubled past. Should the *Bundeswehr* attempt to take over any military traditions derived from the Nazi *Wehrmacht* or the Imperial German Army? Was there, or was there not, a "usable past" for a democratic German army? Could a German soldier be expected to fight in a future conflict that would certainly pit *Bundeswehr* against the *Nationale Volksarmee* – German against German? None of Germany's allies confronted such moral predicaments.

Nevertheless, the *Bundeswehr* turned out to be one of West Germany's most outstanding achievements, paralleling in the military sphere West Germany's success in building an effective political democracy, and the strongest economy on European soil. From being treated with suspicion by a considerable segment of West Germany's population, the army gained popular acceptance. In words ascribed to Hitler, the Third Reich had relied on a Royal Prussian Army, an Imperial Germany Navy, and a National Socialist *Luftwaffe*. The new *Bundeswehr*, by contrast, was loyal to the democratic order. (To the surprise of anti-militarists, officers and enlisted men within the *Bundeswehr* were actually more sympathetic toward organized resistance against the Hitler regime, and also to the role of opposition parties, than the population at large.) The *Bundeswehr's* officer corps continued to contain a substantial number of noblemen, and also sons of former officers and civil servants. But the West German officer corps was nothing like as inward-looking as the French officer corps (with a large component of officers who were themselves sons of officers and non-commissioned officers). But there was none of the class sentiment that had characterized the *Reichswehr* (the army of the Weimar Republic) as much as the Imperial German Army. A worker's or an artisan's son was no longer barred from promotion to the highest rank.[15]

The British armed forces likewise occupied a key position in Western defense, though their composition strikingly changed. Before World War II the Royal Navy had been the world's first, Britain's "Senior Service." But as British imperial power declined world-wide, Britain's navy dropped to third place in terms of manpower deployed by the three

15 For statistics, see Eric Waldman, *The Goose Step is Verboten*, New York, Free Press of Glencoe, 1964, p. 210, 221, 238. For the *Bundeswehr* in general, see Wolfram von Raven, ed., *Armee gegen den Krieg: Wert und Wirkung der Bundeswehr*, Stuttgart, Seewald, 1966; Donald Abenheim, *Reforging the Iron Cross: the Search for Tradition in the West German Armed Forces*, Princeton, NJ, Princeton University Press, 1988; Dennis Showalter "The *Bundeswehr* of the Federal Republic of Germany," in Gann, *The Defense of Western Europe*, pp. 212–54.

British services (the Royal Air Force came second, the army first). Global strategy altered as the Suez Canal lost in importance, and the Cape route gained accordingly. (By the early 1960s, supertankers of over 100,000 tons were in operation; these could not be accommodated even after the Canal had been widened. Another break came with the Wilson government's decision to withdraw all British forces from east of Suez, 1967–8). The navy became primarily a small-ship fleet fit above all for anti-submarine warfare. Even so, the Royal Navy continued as the mainstay of NATO's European naval forces. The British likewise built their own nuclear deterrent, mainly developed, like its French equivalent, for the purpose of legitimating its owner in the desired status of a great power.

Henceforth Britain's main defensive role was on land, as it had been in the days of Henry V in the fifteenth century. During the immediate postwar period, the British army's role was particularly important; Britain at first supplied the bulk of the soldiers available to the Western allies in Europe. The British continued conscription, but in 1957, after the Suez débâcle, they reverted once more to an all-professional force. The new regular army was highly efficient, and much better paid than the prewar professional army. Recruits derived from the ranks of skilled workers and technicians, not from the farm and urban laborers who had once volunteered for Queen Victoria's army. The officer corps still retained some of the old class structure (with a substantial intake of public school boys and now also many graduates from Catholic boarding schools). But relations between officers and men were much easier than in the old conscript army; the road to promotion lay open to all qualified men.

The new army spent less time on the parade ground than the old conscript army, less time with the regimental barber; it was highly proficient in a technical sense. (Nine out of a hundred soldiers belonged to the once unfashionable REME (Royal Electrical and Mechanical Engineers), founded in World War II.)[16] Not that snobbery ceased to count. The Green Jackets (light infantry), cavalry, and Guards regiments, known as the "Black Mafia," tended to get most of the best jobs; they looked down on the infantry, who in turn looked down on the non-combatants. But, overall, it was a remarkable body, one of the most successful British institutions in postwar Britain. It was a model of a democratic force whose loyalty to the civilian government was never questioned. It also displayed great operational efficiency.

The army maintained a substantial commitment to NATO. (Between three and four divisions were deployed in Germany.) The army also became involved once more in the never-ending disputes of Northern Ireland. In 1969 almost an entire division departed to Northern Ireland where Catholics clashed with local security forces dominated by Protestants. Initially, most Catholics welcomed the British imperial troops, but the honeymoon soon ended, and the British found themselves equally disliked by both parties. But at least full-scale civil war was avoided. The army also remained capable of fighting a conventional war thousands of miles away from their home base – as the Argentinians found out in the Falkland War (1982).

16 Henry Stanhope, *The Soldiers: an Anatomy of the British Army*, London, Hamish Hamilton, 1979. Also see R.N. Rosecrance, *Defense of the Realm: British Strategy in the Nuclear Epoch*, New York, Columbia University Press, 1968; Anthony Verrier, *An Army for the Sixties: a Study in National Policy, Contract and Obligation*, London, Secker and Warburg, 1966; Dan Smith, *Defence of the Realm in the 1980s*, London, Croom Helm, 1980; Corelli Barnett, *Britain and her Army, 1509–1970*, London, Allan Lane, 1970; Roger Beaumont, "The British Armed Forces since 1945," in Gann, *The Defense of Western Europe*, pp. 24–57.

The British, like American intellectuals, were apt to shy away from triumphalism and nationalist conceit. The army in particular never got the credit it deserved. (The British capitulation at Singapore in 1942 became part of an anti-colonial morality tale in which "bring-the-whisky" sahibs were duly chastised by their Asian enemies. By contrast, the magnificent British victory at Imphal-Kohima, the greatest defeat hitherto suffered by Japanese forces on land, was duly forgotten by all but a few specialists; so was the equally brilliant reconquest of Burma by the British 14th Army.) In fact, the British army performed outstandingly well. It was also alone among Western armies in winning every post-World War II guerrilla campaign in the Third World: against the Mau Mau rebels in Kenya, the Chinese communists in Malaya, and Indonesians in North Borneo. (It was an unconscious tribute to British arms that most Western European forces adopted the British-style beret, just as in earlier days the French *képi*, later the German *Pickelhaube*, had dominated international styles in military headgear.)

It was, however, the US military which provided NATO's sheet anchor. The US military was unique; it was the only Western force with a worldwide commitment; it provided the world's largest navy, the main part of Western nuclear weaponry, the greatest air force, and a substantial land force. Without the presence of the 7th Army in southern Germany, Western Europe's defense would have lacked credibility. When the war ended the US army had been Europe's second largest. But, as after every great conflict in US history, the Americans rapidly permitted their army to decline in number and quality. By the time of the Berlin blockade, the US army could field only a single division and a few additional regiments in Germany – this at a time when Soviet propaganda was at its height in accusing Washington of planning aggression. Following North Korea's invasion of South Korea, the Americans, however, rapidly increased their forces (to a total of five divisions in the 1960s), with a powerful tactical air force as a complement to the US's army armored counter-attack capability.

Before World War II, the US had relied on an army of regulars; war occasioned reliance on the draft, continued after World War II through the Selective Service Act of 1948 (subsequently amended). In addition, the US relied on an age-old American tradition of part-time service, as represented by the army reserves and national guard. But in peacetime or war, it was the regulars who formed the cornerstone of the military edifice. The officers were mostly middle-class people, college educated, but in no wise part of a self-perpetuating élite. (US officers were less likely than their French or German colleagues to be the sons of military officers.) The officer corps was well integrated into civilian society, as witnessed by the ability of retired officers to do well in civilian occupations (especially in industrial corporations and government service). The enlisted men and non-commissioned officers traditionally derived from white-collar and blue-collar workers.[17]

17 Sue E. Berryman, *Who Serves? The Persistent Myth of the Underclass Army*, Boulder, Colo., Westview Press, 1988. For a sociological account, see Morris Janowitz, *The Professional Soldier: a Social and Political Portrait*, Glencoe, Ill., Free Press, 1960. For general accounts, see Allan R. Millett and Peter Maslowski, *For the Common Defense: a Military History of the United States of America*, New York, Free Press, 1984. Robert Leckie, *The Wars of America*, New York, Harper and Row, 1981. Russell F. Weigley, *The American Way of War: a History of United States Military Strategy and Policy*, New York, Macmillan, 1973. Colonel Harry G. Summers, *On Strategy: a Critical Analysis of the Vietnam War*, New York, Dell, 1984, and his "United States Armed Forces in Europe," in Gann, *The Defense of Western Europe*, pp. 286–309.

The American military met with a variety of woes which mirrored those of US society at large. The military suffered from inter-service rivalry among army, air force, navy, and marines. There was overlapping of functions, and duplication of services (especially with regard to logistics and maintenance.) The US military was highly bureaucratized – more so even than, say, the British defense establishment. Military, like civilian, society displayed the Americans' characteristic admiration for gadgetry, politicking, endless experimentation, and the self-proclaimed expertise of civilian consultants. More than any other, the US military was influenced by industrial and engineering models, with an emphasis on cramming facts.

These weaknesses were multiplied by the Vietnam War. The selective draft worked in an inequitable fashion; there was bitter political opposition. The 7th Army in West Germany was depleted of its best officers and non-commissioned officers. Morale slumped; drunkenness and drug addiction became common; there was pervasive disrespect for authority, and also mounting crime and racial friction. At the same time, inflation reduced soldiers' real pay; to foreigners, especially Germans, the US army suddenly appeared to be a host of drunken paupers, and the US army's prestige slumped accordingly.

Fortunately, the US military's weaknesses were balanced by great strengths. The US armed forces possessed an enormous capacity for rapid improvisation and for recuperation from disaster. In World War II an army composed mainly of civilians in uniform had learned from its mistakes, and defeated the magnificent *Wehrmacht* and the equally magnificent Japanese Imperial forces. The Americans had successfully defended South Korea against North Koreans and Chinese. In Vietnam, the Americans had defeated the communist forces in every major engagement. The Americans had been defeated politically; their military status would thereafter be raised by political means. President Nixon ended the draft (a process completed in 1973). The end of conscription was ambivalent in effect. The generation of John F. Kennedy, Jimmy Carter, and George Bush had served in uniform. They had not necessarily liked the military, but at least they understood how it worked. Thereafter, a new generation stepped into office, men such as Bill Clinton, who not only had never served as a soldier or sailor, but who had no close friends who had done so either.

The professionalization of the military created a psychological rift between professional middle-class people (who rarely served) and the military. The all-volunteer military opened many new opportunities to black Americans. It surpassed all other US institutions (save athletics) in its ability to overcome racial prejudice, and, from the late 1960s onward, create an integrated force in which poor people of any race could gain advancement. On demobilization, veterans of any color, moreover, transferred technical training, discipline, and self-confidence into productive civilian careers. The professional army thereby acted as an instrument for social advancement. (Contrary to a widespread misconception, the US army was never at any time an underclass army. This mistaken assumption derived from a blend of pacifism and social prejudice.) The appointment in 1977 of Clifford Alexander, a black, as the secretary for the army seemed to ratify what was occurring at all levels. Overall, the all-volunteer force regained its former efficiency. Re-equipment, begun in the 1970s, and completed during the Reagan presidency, vastly added to the army's fighting capacity. In a more general sense, the military in later years increasingly came to be commanded by men who had served as combat officers in the Vietnam War, men conversant with high-tech weaponry, determined to avoid past military mistakes, and reluctant also to fight abroad without solid political support at home.

In a wider sense, it was the Americans who played the decisive part in keeping NATO together. American senior officers proved adroit politicians, employing skills honed at home with much credit abroad. American officers persuaded their allies to cooperate in joint maneuvers, joint weapons projects, joint diplomatic initiatives. Having learned to cooperate effectively with the British in World War II, Americans now mastered the art of joint decision-making on innumerable sub-committees and committees, commissions and headquarters. Without this cement, NATO would have broken asunder.

There were also striking changes in weaponry as the high-tech revolution changed military procurement. By the late 1970s, the threat of massive nuclear exchanges between the superpowers had lost credibility, while the Soviets continued to outnumber NATO in conventional forces. But the NATO powers continued to outdo the Soviet Union and its allies in high tech, applied to the military through improvements in fields such as ECM (electronic counter-measures) and a series of technical innovations collectively known as "Stealth" (the name of a new bomber invisible to Soviet radar). Military reform started under Carter after 1978, was extended during the Reagan presidency, and applied by the US on the battlefield under Bush. As Harold Brown, Carter's former defense secretary put it, "we designed the high-tech weapons, the Reagan administration bought 'em and trained people to use 'em, and the Bush administration used 'em [in the Gulf War]".[18] Silicon Valley in California and, to a lesser extent, European equivalents such as "Silicon Glen" in Scotland, became powers in their own right.

Weapons on their own, of course, do not decide wars. (The best of French tanks in 1940 were superior to their opposite numbers in the *Wehrmacht*; yet the Germans overran France because they were superior in generalship, strategy, political determination, training, and tactics.) But the US also improved in general war-fighting capability (for instance, by developing the concept of an "airland battle" entailing deep penetration of the enemy's rear echelons) so as to shatter massive formations poised for assault. The Soviets apparently became convinced that they could not possibly win a land war in Western Europe. The Gulf War subsequently provided a devastating demonstration of US military superiority.

As the Cold War ended, the extent of NATO's success was all too easily overlooked. According to many Cold War theoreticians, including even former Secretary of Defense James Schlesinger, the bipolar world of the Cold War had imposed on the two superpowers a unique system of restraint in so far as each side recognized the constraints implicit in each other's capacity for massive retaliation. Supposedly, there was an unintended order in this bipolar system, a global equilibrium, ultimately thrown into disarray by the dissolution of the Soviet empire. Unfortunately, this analysis obscures reality. As Jonathan Clark, an American foreign policy expert, eloquently put it:

> the facts cannot be forgotten so readily. The Soviet Union really did try to blockade Berlin and draw Greece behind the Iron Curtain; children really did hide under their desks during the Cuban missile crisis; Soviet tanks really did roll into Prague, Budapest, and Kabul; on Soviet orders, refugees really were shot and allowed to bleed to death under the Berlin Wall; dictatorships in Cuba, Ethiopia, Angola, and Mozambique really did rise on the backs of Soviet-equipped and -trained security services; state sponsors to anti-American terrorism really were fêted in Moscow; the Soviet Union really did bankroll the Communist parties of

18 Cited in Charles Lane, "Perry's Parry," *The New Republic*, 27 June 1994, pp. 21–4.

Western Europe and Latin America. None of this was a dream. To combat all this, the West really did live on the nuclear high wire. And as for conventional war during the Cold War, the history books burgeon with the records of major conflagrations.[19]

Clark's list can easily be extended. Even Senator Joseph McCarthy, at the height of anti-communist hysteria, could never have imagined the so-called Cambridge spies, upper-class Englishmen, impious hedonists in the bargain, who from their undergraduate days were trained by Soviet spy masters to infiltrate the highest positions of government. Thriller writer John Le Carré, at his most imaginative, could not have come up with a character such as Aldrich Ames, an American CIA official in Soviet pay, or Markus Wolf, the East German espionage chief, whose agents penetrated West Germany at every level – right into the Chancellor's office. These were indeed dangerous years for the West. For all its errors, NATO played an essential part in reducing their perils.

19 Jonathan Clark, "The Conceptual Poverty of US Foreign Policy", *The Atlantic Monthly*, vol. 272, no. 3, September 1992, p. 57.

8

The Cold War, 1958–1974

Leninist Legacy

For 45 years after World War II the Soviet empire appeared the mightiest in history. Moscow's word was law from the Elbe to the Pacific. Supported by an immense array of military might and an all-powerful Communist Party (10 million members), the Soviet Union appeared invincible, and only a handful of hard-line anti-communists predicted its future demise. This empire was locked in a permanent struggle between socialism and capitalism, a confrontation between the Warsaw Pact countries and the Western powers, above all the US. The contending parties fought their battles in many different ways – through diplomacy, propaganda, scholarship, commerce, and sometimes through wars waged by proxies. For nearly half a century, the world faced the specter of World War III, entailing the possible annihilation of both contenders.

Who was responsible? The Soviets and their allies uniformly blamed Western monopoly capitalism: the West was always wrong. In the West, where scholars did not have to conform to a single propaganda line set by the ruling party, opinion swayed, influenced by changes in domestic politics as well as changes in academic fashion. Revisionism was the product of the Vietnam War and widespread academic disillusionment with "Amerika." Revisionists projected these sentiments on to the Cold War screen. The traditional school, represented by Robert Conquest, Richard Pipes, Merle Fainsod, and Leonard Schapiro, believed that the Soviet revolution had been flawed from the beginning; the Soviets thus bore responsibility for the Cold War. This view was abhorrent to revisionists such as William Appleman Williams. The revisionists censured US capitalism for its greed, and, above all, for its insatiable appetite for new markets both in the "Second" and the "Third World." It was this relentless search for new economic opportunities that set off the Cold War. President Truman, according to revisionist critics, should have trusted Stalin instead of blackmailing Moscow with nuclear weaponry. The Soviet Union's strategy, in this interpretation, was primarily defensive. The US should, therefore, have freed itself from misplaced anxieties concerning world communism, a monster of capitalist myth. The primary cause for the world's instability was the US empire, constructed both to keep Western Europe under US sway through NATO, and to extend US power into the Third World. To men such as Louis Beres, salvation for the world would only come if the US were to abandon a misplaced *realpolitik*, and instead undergo "a revolution of consciousness" resulting in "an expanded awareness of global interdependence."[1]

---

1 Louis René Beres, *Reason and Realpolitik: US Foreign Policy and World Order*, Lexington, MA, Lexington Books, 1984, p. 127. For a country-by-country survey, see David Reynolds, ed., *The Origin of the Cold War in Europe*, New Haven, Yale University Press, 1994. For a recent reappraisal, see Martin Walker, *The Cold War: a History*, New York, Henry Holt, 1994; for the wider diplomatic

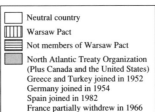

Map 1   Europe in the Cold War
Source: Peter Duignan and L.H. Gann, *The Rebirth of the West*,
Oxford, Blackwell, 1992, p. 718.

The revisionists, of course, were not all of one opinion. Some held that Bolshevism might have created a humane society had it not been corrupted by Stalin's malignancy and the evils inherited from Russia's autocratic past. Others, like Jerry Hough, argued

setting, see Peter G. Boyle, *American–Soviet Relations from the Russian Revolution to the Fall of Communism*, London, Routledge, 1993. Revisionist or semi-revisionist interpretations include Denna Frank Fleming, *The Cold War and its Origins, 1917–1960*, Garden City, NY, Doubleday, 1961, 2 vols.

that even Stalin had not been as bad as he had been painted. But all agreed in considering the US as the chief villain in the Cold War.

A second school of thought, popular among many European conservatives as well as progressives, envisaged the Soviet Union as just another great power, determined to hold on to its sphere of influence in Eastern Europe, resolved simply to maintain the status quo. Many scholars and policy-makers thus regarded the Cold War as no more than the normal rivalry between two great powers. As a seventeenth-century statesman had inelegantly put it regarding the rivalry between Protestant Sweden and Catholic Austria, "there is only room for one cock at the top of the dung heap." The Soviet Union, according to this school of thought, did not therefore deserve particular censure since its aims were limited and defensive.[2] Alternatively, the Cold War derived from "a mutual – or more precisely, reciprocal misunderstanding," a viewpoint expressed not only by liberal scholars such as John Gaddis, but also by John Lukacs, an arch-Tory. Not only was the Cold War unnecessary, but both contenders equally erred in taking excessive risks. Hence "We All Lost the Cold War."[3]

The Cold War sprang from Russian imperialism, according to another school of thought; the Soviet empire had merely been the Russian empire writ large. Whether ruled by Mongol chieftains, Russian Czars, or commissars, Russia had always been an aggressor state, and a danger to its neighbors. Habituated to the rule of tyrannical cliques, the Russian people had always served its rulers in expanding Moscow's power – an interpretation that appeals to Polish, Lithuanian, Georgian, and many other nationalists. This viewpoint, moreover, is hallowed by age. Already in the mid-nineteenth century, scholars as different as Karl Marx, the German revolutionary, and Constantin Frantz, a German reactionary, had agreed on one thing – Russia was a threat to Europe. Yet another interpretation, put forward by David Reynolds, regards the Cold War as an outcome of World War II. Hitler's unexpected victories left the *Führer* in control of Europe from the Bay of Biscay to the Black Sea. His defeat could be achieved only by the two extra-European superpowers whose disagreements resulted in the division of Europe into two militarized blocs. Thus the Cold War was "not so much the inevitable goal of history as one of Adolf Hitler's most durable legacies."[4]

Reynolds has a point. But alliances do not inevitably mutate into hostile confrontations after the destruction of a common enemy. In theory, the Soviet Union and the US could have reached accommodation in 1945 – as Roosevelt, Churchill, Truman and Attlee had all desired. For the wartime allies' failure to do so, we ourselves blame no individual statesman, but the Soviet system as a whole, a viewpoint shared by scholars such as Robert Conquest, Adam B. Ulam, Hugh Thomas, and other leading Sovietologists.[5] We reject explanations put forward by the "blame Russia" school: this ignores

2 Louis J. Halle, *The Cold War as History*, London, Chatto and Windus, 1967.
3 John Lukacs, *The End of the Twentieth Century and the End of the Modern Age*, New York, Ticknor and Fields, 1993, p. 14; John Lewis Gaddis, *The United States and the Origins of the Cold War, 1941–1947*, New York, Columbia University Press, 1972; Richard Ned Lebow and Janice Gross Stein, *We All Lost the Cold War*, Princeton, NJ, Princeton University Press, 1993.
4 David Reynolds, ed., *The Origins of the Cold War in Europe*, New Haven, CT, Yale University Press, 1994, p. 21.
5 See, for instance, Peter Duignan and L.H. Gann, *The Rebirth of the West: the Americanization of the Democratic World, 1945–1958*, Oxford, Blackwell, 1992; Adam B. Ulam, *The Communists: the Story of Power and Lost Illusions, 1948–1991*, New York, Charles Scribner, 1992; and *Dangerous Relations: the Soviet Union in World Politics, 1970–1982*, New York, Oxford University Press, 1983;

the anti-authoritarian and democratic legacies that Russia has inherited from the past. This interpretation also disregards the way in which the Russians (and also other nationalities) had widely resisted, by force or by stealth, the imposition of the Soviet regime, and the manner in which the Russians themselves had been victimized by the former Soviet dictatorship, together with all other national groups. The true beneficiaries of the Soviet empire were the Soviet *nomenklatura*. They gained advancement through their real or assumed loyalty to the ruling party, and through lack of scruples in furthering both their own respective careers and the party's interests. The *nomenklatura* dominated the key institutions of the Soviet state; the Soviet Union's foreign as well as domestic policy was designed, in the last instance, to serve the *nomenklatura's* collective self-interest.[6]

The *nomenklatura* was essentially supranational – as was the Soviet Union's very title. True enough, ethnic Russians held most of the leading jobs. But these men and women formed part of an international ruling class whose members had a great deal in common. Whether trained in Moscow, Prague, or East Berlin, a leading communist would feel at home in party offices everywhere, and – in public – speak the same party jargon with the same stilted terminology. There were bitter disagreements both within and between the various national parties. Nevertheless, all ruling communist parties shared similar characteristics – part brotherhood, part old boy's network, part Mafia, part club, and part counter-church. In more concrete terms, the party provided the senior cadres with an ideology and an organization, innumerable privileges, sustained by universal "double speak" and "double think."

Cynics, of course, there were in plenty among the communist cadres. The force of ideology weakened in every country where Marxism–Leninism held sway. But ideology – elaborated by a huge establishment of professionals – never ceased to count. It was the ideology itself which alone justified the *nomenklatura's* power. The Cold War did not derive from mistakes committed by any one particular politician, or from misunderstandings. The Cold War inhered in the very ideology of communism. The conflict began when Lenin forcibly seized power in 1917. In theory, at any rate, the communist cadres saw themselves embroiled in an international class war, unavoidable in its causation, predictable in its final outcome. In the course of this struggle, capitalism would ultimately perish from the earth; the proletariat would prevail – led, of course, by an enlightened vanguard, the Communist Party. Compromises would have to be made on the way, temporary alliances would have to be formed. Tactics varied, and so did strategy.

Stalin had believed that the two great world camps – the capitalist and the socialist systems – would ultimately come to blows. Stalin tried to weaken US strength by all means at his disposal. (Hence he sanctioned, for example, North Korea's attack on South Korea in 1950, an attack which would not have been made without Stalin's specific approval.) Stalin, as we have pointed out in our *Rebirth of the West*, was a man who had falsified historical accounts, statistics, treaties, even maps. He had betrayed, jailed, tortured, shot most of his revolutionary associates. Overall, Stalin had killed several times more people than Hitler. It seems ludicrous to see him described by revisionists as a man whom Western statesmen should have trusted. NATO and the Warsaw Pact were not

Robert Conquest, *Power and Policy in the USSR: the Study of Soviet Dynastics*, London, Macmillan and New York, St Martin's Press, 1961; and *Present Danger: Towards a Foreign Policy*, Stanford, CA, Hoover Institution Press, 1979.
6 Jiri Hochman, *The Soviet Union and the Failure of Collective Security, 1934–1938*, Ithaca, Cornell University Press, 1984, p. 172; Martin Malia, *The Soviet Tragedy*, New York, Free Press, 1994.

comparable: NATO was an alliance by voluntary agreement; the Warsaw Pact an empire by imposition. The Western European governments rested on consent; the Eastern European regimes on force. It was not only hard-line reactionaries who feared Soviet expansion. Clement Attlee, Ernest Bevin, Kurt Schumacher, Willy Brandt, Léon Blum – democratic socialists all of them – dreaded the Soviet Union as much as the most ⁃hidebound US reactionary. It seems ludicrous to cast these European socialists as witting or unwitting agents of US corporate profiteers.

Revisionists argue that the Soviet Union, after World War II, merely desired to assure its own security and, for that purpose, felt compelled to create an eastern European *glacis*. Moscow, according to this interpretation, would have been perfectly willing to confine its ambitions to its own sphere of influence. NATO, according to this school of thought, was created under US duress. But, in fact, the Soviet Union recognized no sphere of influence. The postwar crises included an attempted communist takeover in Greece (where, between 1946 and 1949, the Soviet Union and its allies supported communist insurgents); the Soviet blockade of West Berlin in 1948; the North Korean attack on South Korea in 1950 (approved by Stalin after much initial hesitation); the Cuban crisis of 1962, not to speak of the Soviet-supported activities of the French and Italian communist parties. These crises all shared one common feature: they entailed attempted communist expansion at Western expense – not the other way round. Stalin sought peaceful coexistence with another social system only once – with Nazi Germany (1939–41), from the Nazi–Soviet non-aggression pact to Hitler's invasion of the Soviet Union. This was well understood by Western Europeans, especially the British, and also the Canadians, who put pressure on the US to abandon isolationism and support Western Europe against the Soviet threat.

Stalin died in 1953, and his harsh doctrines were thereafter revised by Khrushchev (1956) and by Brezhnev. Henceforth pro-Moscow communists called for "peaceful coexistence" between capitalist and communist states. But such peaceful coexistence by no means entailed peaceful coexistence between competing social systems. As Erich Honecker, head of the former German Democratic Republic, explained in 1976 at the 11th Party Congress of the SED (Socialist Unity Party) "peaceful coexistence . . . never signifies peace between social classes, between exploiters and exploited." On the contrary, peaceful coexistence has itself served as an instrument for intensifying the international class struggle.[7]

Fortunately, according to Soviet theoreticians, the global "correlation of forces" kept changing in Moscow's favor. This was good news for the progressive forces of all mankind, for the Soviet Union, "objectively speaking," formed the center of the world's revolutionary forces, as against the United States, the leading imperialist power. Moscow therefore aimed at making this change "irreversible." Widely dismissed in the West as "rhetoric," these assumptions were real enough to Soviet power-holders. The class struggle would be waged in countless ways: through conventional diplomacy, cultural conventions, fronts, peace congresses, and trade; and also through less conventional means not excluding disinformation, blackmail, kidnapping, and murder. Above all, the communists placed their faith in "united front" tactics. Communist parties in the West were thus enjoined to form common fronts with any non-communist body which sought, for whatever reason, to reduce defence spending in the West, cut down on military research, prevent the deployment of cruise missiles and neutron bombs, weaken the ties of NATO,

7 Entry "Friedliche Koexistenz," *DDR Handbuch*, Cologne, Verlag Wissenschaft und Politik, 1985, vol. 1, p. 482.

or enhance Soviet industrial potential, whether through credit arrangements or by export of strategic goods. In short, the Soviets saw *détente* as part of a continuing struggle for world domination, a struggle that they meant to win.

In this respect the Soviet empire strikingly differed from its czarist predecessor. Czarist Russia had been a great power, ambitious, but willing enough to settle for defined spheres of influence in competition with other great powers. But, unlike St Petersburg, Moscow recognized no permanent Western spheres of influence. (Almost immediately after World War II ended, for instance, the Soviet Union went beyond wartime agreements regarding partition by seeking to participate in control of the industrial Ruhr region allocated to the British occupation zone – this without even a hint of corresponding concessions to the West in the Soviet sphere. Shortly thereafter, in 1946, communists, supported by Moscow, initiated a rising in Greece, a country clearly within the British sphere of influence according to an informal wartime agreement between Stalin and Churchill.)

Had the Soviet Union merely planned to safeguard its own security as a conventional great power, the Soviets could certainly have built round the Soviet borders a chain of neutral states modeled on Finland and Austria, both capitalist yet inoffensive. Alternatively, had the Soviets merely aimed at preserving communism within their "outer empires", within their European satellite states, Moscow need not have supported Marxist–Leninist revolutionaries as far afield as Cuba, Angola, Vietnam, and South Africa, thereby incurring great military, financial, and diplomatic risks for the empire as a whole. But Soviet policy had its inbuilt dynamic whereby the *nomenklatura*'s collective interest required success abroad as domestic reverses could be offset by foreign victories. Not surprisingly, therefore, all major crises in the Cold War derived from communist initiatives undertaken in the non-communist world; by contrast, not a single international crisis resulted from any Western incursion into the Soviet sphere of influence as established after World War II.

The communist system, of course, was neither uniform nor unchangeable. By the 1960s, communist governance in Hungary or in Poland strikingly differed from, say, communist rule in the Soviet Union, or in Albania, or in Cuba. Communism everywhere came to be modified by local factors that did not fit tidily into the framework of Marxist–Leninist philosophy. Kindness, compassion, moral integrity did not disappear in communist countries any more than sloth, pride, and disobedience. Even during the worst days of Stalin, the party bosses had not all been slave drivers, nor the ordinary people willing serfs. Communism did not create a society of robots. There were also great cleavages between countries where communism had been imposed by foreign conquest and countries where communist governance had derived from internal revolutions.

Not all communist countries, moreover, experienced terror to the same extent. Walter Ulbricht in East Germany, for example, had not been an exemplar of moral rectitude, but he did not use the axe as Stalin had done, or as did Stalin-like strong-men such as Ho Chi Minh, Kim Il Sung, Pol Pot, or Mao Zedong. Nevertheless, terror – open or covert – was inherent in all systems of government built on Leninist foundations. It is a mistake, therefore, to assume that the Cold War started at any particular date, or that the Cold War derived from Stalinist deformations, or from diplomatic misunderstandings, or from US aggression, or from Soviet fears, to be laid to rest by a wise and conciliatory diplomacy. The Cold War was implied by the very nature of the Soviet regime; the Cold War began when the Bolsheviks forcibly seized power in Russia in 1917; the Cold War ended when the Communist Party of the Soviet Union was banned in 1991.

This interpretation runs counter to revisionist orthodoxy. But the tide of new works produced by the partial opening of Russian archives and the availability of new documentation has shifted the debate to the right. Lenin emerges as a tyrant, like Stalin. The human losses inflicted by Bolshevism on the Soviet Union were staggering – no matter what yardsticks are used. (Even sturdy revisionists are now reduced to debating whether Stalin's victims should be accounted in seven or eight digits.) Stalin did not merely act for defensive motives, nor did his immediate successors. Altogether, the publication of new Soviet sources has not, "as a rule, been kind to the revisionist enterprise."[8]

Was the Soviet empire "totalitarian"? Historians such as Stephen Cohen have dismissed the very term "totalitarian" as a part of the Cold War vocabulary. The Soviet Union remained riddled by dissent. Indeed, it had only been Stalin's evil genius that had so grossly distorted Soviet history. As Cohen sees it, communism's corruption was not, however, inevitable. All roads need not have led to the Gulag Archipelago. There was no inner totalitarian logic that inevitably resulted in terror.[9] Had power fallen to a "right oppositionist" such as Nikolai Bukharin (liquidated during Stalin's "Great Purge") Soviet communists might have developed a humane and progressive society. Unfortunately, however, Cohen cannot find a single example of such a communist society; all have used terror to a greater or lesser extent. (Even Bukharin did not object to terror against the bourgeoisie.) The "Stalinist deformation" argument, moreover, is dangerous from a Marxist viewpoint. For if one wicked man, or even a clique of wicked men, can distort an entire social system, what becomes of Marxist–Leninists' materialist philosophy?

In pursuit of the Cold War, Moscow enjoyed numerous advantages, most of them destined, however, to diminish or evaporate as the global struggle dragged on. The Soviet Union possessed enormous human and natural resources; so did the Soviet Union's satellites. The Soviets enjoyed the prestige of victory in World War II. The Red Army had crushed the *Wehrmacht* in history's greatest land campaign. Once the war ended, the Soviet Union remained a warfare state, with 30 percent, or 40 percent, or perhaps even more, of the Soviet GNP devoted to armaments. Soviet military doctrine stressed the sustained offensive and surprise. Unwise therefore to rile the bear! Better red than dead! Better a live jackal than a dead lion, an admirable doctrine – for jackals, as the late Professor Sidney Hook used to say.

The Soviets also had ideological strengths. True enough, the communist movement suffered from nationalist schism. In 1948 Tito broke away. In the 1960s communist China declared itself the true center of the world revolution. Within the Soviet Union's own sphere of influence there was a measure of diversity. (In 1956 Khrushchev proclaimed that there were different roads to socialism.) But the Soviets always held the upper hand. Only the Soviets decided what deviations on the road to socialism might or might not be acceptable within their "outer empire." And the Soviets were not burdened by scruples in dealing with either friends or foes. As Alexander Dubcek (an advocate of humane socialism, and victim of the Soviet invasion of Czechoslovakia in 1968) explained many years later in an interview with the German journal *Der Spiegel* (1 March 1993, p. 174) "only after practical experiences . . . did we realize that we were dealing, not with socialists, but with criminals."

8 Steven Merrit Miner, "Revelations, Secrets, Gossip and Lies: Sifting Warily through the Soviet Archives," *New York Times Book Review*, 14 May 1995, pp. 19–21.
9 Stephen Cohen, *Rethinking the Soviet Experience: Politics and History Since 1917*, New York, Oxford University Press, 1985.

The Soviet cause had once been supported in the West by an army of leftist intellectuals: H.G. Wells, George Bernard Shaw, Leon Feuchtwanger, Bertold Brecht – the list of distinguished admirers would fill a *Who's Who*. By the 1970s, this army had been much diminished by desertion. Nevertheless, for most left-wingers, Soviet communism still seemed preferable to fascism or clerico-fascism. Unlike Nazis, communists, at least in theory, still looked toward a utopian future for working-class people of whatever race. And, unlike Christians, the communists rejected Original Sin. Within the Soviet Union and the "people's democracies," the communist system also provided material advantages to those who toed the line. A creative artist, at the zenith of his or her career, ranked high within the *nomenklatura*. (A leading ballet dancer, for example, during the 1970s, earned a monthly salary of between 900 and 1200 rubles, a well-known writer between 800 and 1,000 rubles, in addition to other perks. By contrast, the first secretary of a smaller Union Republic took home 810 rubles, the director of a large coal-mining enterprise 622, a colonel 500. The average worker's pay packet amounted to 130 rubles, including bonuses. The Soviet minimum wage stood at between 60 and 70 rubles.)[10] In practice, the Soviets and their allies had indulged in "ethnic purges" of the most brutal kind: millions of people – Germans, Ukrainians, Kulaks, Crimean Tatars, Poles, and many others – had been driven from their respective homes under the most terrible circumstances. But to bodies such as the US National Council of Churches, the World Council of Churches, or the General Assembly of the UN, communist misdeeds somehow seemed not so objectionable as the lesser offenses committed by white settlers in Africa or white southerners in the US.

The Soviet cause in foreign lands was, moreover, defended both within and outside the empire by a huge network of front organizations, espionage rings, and disinformation agencies. Their full extent will only become clear once the newly opened archives in the former Soviet bloc have been fully explored. Soviet diplomacy likewise relied on a network of "fraternal" communist parties in the world at large; provided these took a pro-Moscow stance, they were aided by Moscow in a variety of ways: through direct subsidies, diplomatic support, technical counselling, commercial contracts, and such like. Most of these parties were small in size and influence; but there were also some powerful bodies among them, especially the French and Italian communist parties whose fortunes we have outlined in chapters 4 and 6.

Soviet diplomatic and intelligence services had their weaknesses as well as their strengths. In the Soviet Union and its satellites, officials were apt to report to their superiors what superior officials, and their superiors, wanted to hear. This practice, of course, was also common in the West. But in the Soviet Union self-inflicted disinformation was not balanced by reports from an independent press, independent universities, independent banks and businesses. Soviet and eastern bloc diplomats in general mixed mainly with their own kind. Their performance was not improved by the communist practice of using postings or trips to the West as rewards for the party faithful. Evidently, the Soviet and satellite *nomenklaturas* to some extent believed their own propaganda: that communist victories were irreversible, that the toiling masses would never abandon socialism having once tasted its sweet fruits.

The Soviet rulers, moreover, misunderstood their own "objective" role in world affairs. The Soviet *nomenklatura* presided over the greatest empire in world history. It would

10 Mervyn Matthews, *Privilege in the Soviet Union: a Study of Elite Life Styles under Communism*, London, Allen and Unwin, 1978, pp. 23–7, 33.

have behoved Moscow to support, or at least not excessively to incommode, the world's other remaining empires, especially those maintained by France and Britain in Africa. By flattering Western imperialists, the Soviets might have weakened NATO (de Gaulle, especially, a man ever-thirsty for glory, might well have succumbed to Soviet bland-ishments). The Soviets, in our opinion, also made the wrong choice in the Middle East. Stalin, after World War II, had tried to force Turkey and Iran into a state of depend-ency. By doing so, he made sure that both would seek support from the US. Khrushchev and his successors sought to remedy this mistake by moving into the Arab world, and massively supporting Arab countries by arms and aid. Brezhnev, in particular, put his money on the Egyptian horse.[11] But successive Arab–Israeli wars glaringly revealed the weakness of the Soviet Union's Arab allies, their lack of cohesion, and the extent of their internal dissensions. Had the Soviets played the Israeli card, and supported Tel Aviv, they might have gained support among Zionists worldwide, and particularly in the US, at little cost. But the Soviets chose to act otherwise, without gaining gratitude from either their Arab or African clients. Worse still from the Soviet standpoint, the very arguments advanced by Soviet diplomacy and Soviet propaganda to injure the British and French empires would ultimately be used to destroy the Soviet Union itself.

Soviet diplomacy, however, also had many strengths; Soviet diplomacy was patient. With certain terrifying exceptions, Soviet diplomacy was averse to risk. (Moscow gambled over Cuba, but the Soviets permitted Yugoslavia, even Albania, to break away from the empire without firing a shot because Moscow feared unwarranted complications.) But Soviet diplomacy was always supported by skillful public relations campaigns. (Com-munist disinformation agencies managed to make fantastic figures, containing supposed Soviet increases in economic production, acceptable to experts in the West. Professional spies and professional statisticians in this respect proved as vulnerable to communist propaganda as professional academicians. Soviet agitprops and their allies in the West widely succeeded also in capturing words such as "peace" and "national liberation" for their own cause.)

Soviet diplomacy also made good use of liberal-left intellectuals – fellow travelers and dissidents within Western countries – and of men and women who did not fully sym-pathize with Moscow but who opposed anti-Soviet policies for a variety of other reasons: because they dreaded militarism, disliked capitalism, objected to Middle America, feared a Nazi revival in West Germany, detested Western colonialism, or hated the Jewish state created in former Palestine. There was a decline in the number of those "political pilgrims," castigated by historian Paul Hollander, distinguished foreigners such as George Bernard Shaw, Leon Feuchtwanger, and Beatrice Webb, who had ignorantly extolled the Soviet Union as the workers' land of hope and glory. (From the 1960s, "political pilgrims" were more apt to eulogize Red China, Cuba, and North Vietnam.) The communists, moreover, now met vigorous intellectual opposition from an international set of scholars and journalists, men such as Raymond Aron, Leo Labedz, Sidney Hook, Walter Laqueur, Melvin J. Lasky – many of them Jewish, most of them drawn from the anti-communist left, and expert at showing up communism's own internal contradictions. They contri-buted to influential journals such as *Commentary, Encounter, Survey, Der Monat*, and thereby gained the intellectual initiative once claimed by Marxist scholarship. Nevertheless, leftists in Western academia, the prestige media, and the mainline churches widely

11 Alexei Vassiliev, *Russian Policy in the Middle East: from Messianism to Pragmatism*, Reading, England, Ithaca Press, 1993.

continued to equate anti-communism with fascism, McCarthyism, or petty bourgeois nastiness in general. To be known as an impenitent "Cold Warrior" counted as a professional disadvantage, not only in major Western universities, but also within bodies such as the US Agency for International Development, and the Arms Control and Disarmament Agency.

US diplomacy was moralistic and legalistic in outlook; its US practitioners were subject to a multitude of internal lobbies and to public opinion; all too often diplomats believed an agreement between all parties to sign a document was itself a solution to whatever problem was in dispute. Soviet diplomatists, by contrast, were little affected until the 1980s by any influence emanating from outside the reigning Soviet Establishment. They were quite prepared to practice what Lenin had called "revolutionary deception." (Thus, at a conference held in Princeton in 1993 on the Cold War, former Soviet policy-makers, such as ex-Foreign Minister Alexander Bessmertnykh, admitted quite freely that the construction of a huge radar installation at Krasnoyarsk was in clear violation of existing treaty obligations.) Western intelligence services had a poor record in assessing Soviet capabilities or predicting Soviet intentions. As Thomas Power, a US expert, put it:

> The CIA's history . . . is rich with failures to predict major events, among them the first Soviet atomic bomb, the North Korean and Chinese invasions in [South] Korea, the Hungarian revolt, Fidel Castro's victory and Khrushchev's subsequent placement of missiles in Cuba, the invasion of Czechoslovakia, and the invasion of Afghanistan. Above all, the CIA failed to predict – even to imagine – the collapse of Soviet communism. . . .[12]

Not surprisingly, the Soviet challenge appeared indeed formidable both to the US and the world at large.

Germany: Pivot of a Continent

The key to Europe's future was Germany. Crushed in World War II, Germany, as it had existed in 1937, was stripped in 1945 of its eastern provinces, about one-third of prewar Germany's territory. The rest was divided into four occupation zones, to be administered as a single economic unit under an Allied Control Council in Berlin. The city of Berlin, divided into four sectors after World War II, likewise split into two halves: East Berlin became the capital of East Germany; West Berlin remained a Western-occupied enclave within East Germany, the Western allies having failed to insist on Western-controlled access routes to West Berlin when Germany had originally been partitioned. This was a dangerous omission because the Western allies could thereafter always be subjected to Soviet pressure on West Berlin. (In 1948, the Soviets thus instituted a full-scale blockade of West Berlin. This was rendered nugatory by the stout support given by West Berliners to the Western allies, and, above all, by the US and Britain's unique achievement in supplying the beleaguered city by air.)

12 Thomas Power, "The Truth about the CIA," in *The New York Review of Books*, vol. 40, no. 9, 13 May 1993, p. 55. For a detailed assessment, see Angelo Codevilla, *Informing Statecraft: Intelligence for a New Century*, New York, Free Press, 1992.

But even thereafter West Berlin remained a neuralgic point in East–West relations. West Berlin turned into a prosperous city (albeit heavily subsidized by West Germany). Berliners solidly supported the Western occupation. West Berlin's very existence as a bastion of freedom posed a threat to the communist dictatorship in East Germany: no matter what East German propaganda asserted, every truck driver and every housewife in East Berlin knew that things were better in the West. Even more annoying, from the communists' standpoint, was West Berlin's commitment to social democracy. The city was governed by a succession of outstanding Social Democratic mayors, including men such as Ernst Reuter and Willy Brandt; their party incurred even greater hostility than the so-called bourgeois parties on the grounds that Social Democrats successfully competed with the communists for the workers' loyalty.

Worse still, from the communists' viewpoint, uninterrupted traffic for the time being continued between East and West Berlin. Hence East Germans determined to emigrate to the West could easily slip across the frontier. Their ability to do so was a desperate matter for the East German authorities. Like all communist authorities the world over, the East Germans had invented a new crime *Republikflucht* ("flight from the Republic," actionable in various ways from 1950 onward). "Unauthorized emigration" from East Germany was severely punished. Nevertheless, an estimated 2,687,000 people fled from East to West Germany between 1949 and 1961. East Germany thereby lost about 15 percent of its population, including many of its best-educated and best-qualified people – an emigration rate unequalled by any country in modern times. In addition to these refugees, West Germany received another 12 million or so Germans expelled from Germany's former eastern provinces annexed to Poland, and from Czechoslovakia. By contrast, East Germany's very existence was endangered by the demographic hemorrhage.

More important even than West Berlin's future was Germany's. Germany was the key to Europe: by the early 1960s, the West German economy had grown to be the largest in Europe; the *Bundeswehr* had grown into a powerful force; the Federal German Republic had replaced Britain as the US's strongest ally in NATO. If West Germany could be neutralized, NATO could hardly survive; the US might be forced out of Europe and the global correlation of forces would decisively shift in Moscow's favor. Beginning with Stalin, the Soviets thus repeatedly dangled the carrot of reunification before the West German electors – to be achieved at the price of neutralization. According to Bonn's critics, Germany thereby lost a chance for peace; Germans should have opted for an "Austrian solution," entailing a united but neutralized Germany. (In 1956 the four allies had agreed to withdraw from Austria which remained a neutralized but democratically governed state.)

Such a settlement would not, however, have worked for Germany. In Austria, the Soviets had only occupied a small area; they had not set up a communist state of their own. Austria's neutralization, moreover, operated in the Soviets' strategic favor by creating a territorial barrier between NATO's position in Germany and Italy. In Germany, by contrast, the Soviets had created their own satellite state. "Unification in freedom" (Konrad Adenauer's slogan) would have entailed free elections in the GDR, the extension of the Western free-market economy to East Germany, the dismantling of the East German state, and the SED's demotion from a ruling party to a sect. Neither Stalin, Khrushchev, nor Brezhnev could have made such a sacrifice without endangering the very existence of every Soviet satellite in East Central Europe.

The SED's own policy-makers followed, if anything, an even harder line: after all, their own jobs were on the line had Moscow decided to permit German "reunification in freedom." During the 1950s, in fact, the SED had looked to German reunification under communist auspices, thereby ousting Western "monopoly capitalism." As Willy Stoph, the East German minister of defense put it in 1956 in a speech to the East German *Volkskammer* (parliament), the Bonn government merely formed an "Anglo-American protectorate administration." The *Bundeswehr* was a gang of German mercenaries in the US service. "Alien" and "cosmopolitan" elements threatened the very foundations of German *Kultur*. German honor and German culture alike required a national rebirth. The SED alone could serve as the firm bulwark for the German people's struggle for national liberation.[13] No quibbling here about peaceful coexistence – and this three years after Stalin had died, and Khrushchev had vowed to pursue a more conciliatory policy toward the West.

Not surprisingly, therefore, Soviet pressure continued on Berlin, the West's weakest position. In 1960, the Soviets (quite illegally) declared East Berlin to be an integral part of the German Democratic Republic (GDR). In 1961, the East German government built the Berlin Wall which physically separated West Berlin from its hinterland. The Berlin Wall in turn became part of a huge barrier, defended by mine fields, barbed wire, and watch-towers which separated East from West Germany and largely (though not entirely) stopped the continuing exodus from East Germany. East Germans could no longer "vote with their feet" to gain freedom in the West. East Germans had to make do with what they had; the East German labor force was stabilized; in a sense, the building of the Wall (known in communist jargon as the "anti-fascist protection wall") marked the second founding of the East German state.

The Wall cut off East Germany from West Berlin, but also separated West Germany from East Germany. The influx of East Germans with sorry tales to tell largely ceased; instead, West Berlin (a city exempt from German draft laws) became a haven for young West Germans unwilling to serve in the *Bundeswehr*. Many of them channeled their hopes into utopian forms of socialism that bore no reality to the world of "real existing socialism" beyond the Wall. West Berlin became a major center for dissidents of every description who parodied the city's leftist Weimar heritage, but without a spark of the old wit or creativity.

In East Germany, the ruling GDR party thereafter tried to persuade its own people that they formed a separate German nation, distinct from West Germany, by the GDR's socialist and anti-fascist credentials. The new socialist German nation supposedly had inherited all that was best in German history. But the would-be nation-builders totally failed in their endeavor. Marxist–Leninists could no more manufacture a national consciousness for the GDR than for the Soviet Union, Yugoslavia, Ethiopia, or Angola. In East Germany, as everywhere else, the "national question" foiled communism. Germany differed from all the eastern bloc countries in that it was divided. East Germans compared their own brand of socialism, not with socialism as practiced by the other members of the Warsaw Pact, but with free enterprise as it functioned in West Germany. No wonder that the bulk of East Germans regarded their own system as a failure. Communist propaganda was not remotely comparable in its impact on the East German population to what Nazi propaganda had been in its impact on the citizens of the Third Reich.

Nevertheless, the SED brilliantly succeeded in one specific respect – in widely manipulating intellectual opinion in the West. The ordinary German knew perfectly well that socialism did not work in East Germany, that East Germany's misfortune lay

13 Cited by Wolfgang-Uwe Friedrich, "Wir sind ein Volk: Die Deutschen und die deutsche Einheit, 1845–1990," *German Studies Review*, Winter 1992, p. 145.

in having been occupied at the end of World War II by the Soviets rather than by the Western allies. Intellectuals, by contrast, were widely persuaded otherwise. To give just one example, Ralf (later Sir Ralf) Dahrendorf, a leading German sociologist, a man who could not by any stretch of the imagination be accused of being a fellow traveler, nevertheless explained in 1965 that the GDR did not simply rest on Soviet bayonets; the GDR had created a comprehensive welfare state, established a new legitimacy, and indeed built "the first modern society on German soil." (Sir Ralf would later change his mind shortly before being raised to the peerage.)[14]

West Germany abandoned its former claim that only the democratically elected government of West Germany could rightfully speak for the German people. Though the preamble to the West German Basic Law had called on all Germans to work for national unity, this aim was given up as a national policy. Instead, Chancellor Brandt, his supporters, and also many conservatives, insisted on a new "realism." As he saw it, the logic of facts had to be accepted. The two Germanys would coexist for a long time – perhaps for ever. Instead, the new realists stressed the virtues of a German *Kulturnation* whose bonds derived from a common language and culture.

Brandt's policy of effecting a transformation through a *rapprochement* (*Wandel durch Annäherung*) was later also accepted by the CDU and its Bavarian sister party, the CSU. (Indeed, West German hard-liners such as Franz Josef Strauss, a Bavarian Catholic, one of the *Bundeswehr's* founding fathers, turned out to be one of *Ostpolitik's* most outstanding advocates.) *Ostpolitik*, discussed at length in Timothy Garton Ash's classic, *In Europe's Name*,[15] would lighten the lot of East Germans by easing travel restrictions and other forms of constraint. West Germany would recognize "existing realities" east of the Elbe; reunification would therefore be postponed to a distant, perhaps a mythical, future. But in the meantime, East Germany would be softened up through increased commercial and cultural contacts to the West. West German markets would expand. East Germany would be preserved from total economic collapse (a consideration important for those who planned to take over East Germany in the long run). The Soviet Union might ultimately be induced to make more political concessions. The danger of new confrontations (including East–West confrontations over Berlin) would diminish. Germany's reputation, besmirched by the Nazi past, would improve worldwide (considerations important for Brandt, who had left Nazi Germany as a political refugee, as they were for *Wehrmacht* veterans such as Helmut Schmidt).

The consequences of *Ostpolitik* are not easy to summarize. Clearly, the West German tax-payer thereafter massively subsidized the East German regime, both directly and indirectly, just as the Soviet bloc and the Soviet Union itself were subsidized by Western credits and trade advantages. East Germany's communist regime was further legitimized. (An agreement concluded between the two German states in 1972 gave full legal recognition to the GDR, a major victory for the communists who longed for acceptance by the Western Establishments. Much to the East German *nomenklatura's* disappointment, no East German head of state was ever invited to the White House, the ultimate test of social acceptability.) For these concessions, East Germany paid a price. Travel, trade, tourism,

14 Ralf Dahrendorf, *Society and Democracy in Germany*, Garden City, NY, Anchor Books, Doubleday, 1969, pp. 401, 406, 408, 410–11; *Reflections on the Revolution in Europe: in a Letter Intended to Have Been Sent to a Gentleman in Warsaw*, New York, New York Times Books, pp. 18, 53.
15 Timothy Garton Ash, *In Europe's Name: Germany and the Divided Continent*, New York, Random House, 1993.

even telephone calls, increased between East and West Germany. East German pensioners were allowed to settle in the West (where they would no longer form a charge on the GDR). The two Germanys developed a clandestine traffic in human beings, as political prisoners were released from East to West Germany for hard cash. These clandestine transactions had a corrupting effect both on East and on West Germany. Immense amounts of money changed hands, and enormous sums ended in the clandestine bank accounts of highly placed power-brokers, especially of the Communist Party in East Germany.

Ostpolitik fitted in with a shift in Soviet strategy. By the late 1960s, Leonid Brezhnev had become convinced that a *rapprochement* with Bonn was desirable. The Soviets felt that they were getting behind in the race for technological supremacy. (The US achievement in putting a man on the moon made a stunning impression.) The Soviet Union was facing tensions on the Soviet–Chinese border. The Soviet Union needed Western credits and Western technical know-how (for instance, expertise for the building of oil and gas pipe lines). The Soviets therefore favorably responded to Brandt's plea for a *détente*. In 1970, the Federal German Republic affirmed the existing boundaries in East Central Europe; the Moscow Treaty was followed by a German–Polish treaty signed in Warsaw next year. In 1972, the US and the Soviet Union initiated talks for the SALT II treaty, one of several arrangements that purported to limit nuclear arms. More important still, the Soviets and the Western powers in 1975 signed the Helsinki Conference Final Act. According to Moscow's interpretation, the Act entailed formal Western approval for the status quo in East Central Europe. But, at the same time, the Helsinki Act placed new emphasis on human rights, thereby placing a dangerous (and, from the Soviet viewpoint, an unexpected) weapon into the hands of dissidents, not only in Poland, but also in the Soviet Union itself.

Did *Ostpolitik* and *détente* help or hinder the communists? The available documentary evidence is contradictory. Clearly, the *détente* politicians acted for different motives. The Soviets wanted to formalize the status quo in East Central Europe, but not in the Third World where the revolutionary tide as yet seemed to be flowing their way. The Americans still had their hands full in Vietnam, and wished to reduce international tension. Brandt himself looked at *détente* from the viewpoint of a Berliner, more specifically a denizen of West Berlin. Soviet dissenters approved of any international arrangements that gave international recognition to human rights. Ukrainian and Belorussian nationalists relished the publicity given to international issues which gave publicity in any form to the separate representation of these two states in the UN, a favor foolishly conceded by Stalin for his own ends.

As regards *Ostpolitik's* effects on East Germany in particular, the jury once again is still out. GDR hard-liners greatly feared *Ostpolitik* as an instrument for "softening up" the GDR. (Contrary to his subsequent reputation, Erich Honecker, "Red Erich," had actually started as a reformer.) According to hard-liners, East Germany would end as an economic dependency of West Germany. This was a reasonable assumption as East Germany became steadily more indebted to the Federal German Republic, and more reliant on West German trade. Cooperation with West Germany also rendered impossible the cultural isolation of East Germany from the West. East German soft-liners, by contrast, argued that East Germany needed West German commerce, investment, and know-how if East Germany were to survive. In this respect, the soft-liners were equally correct. They overlooked, however, that the very structure of a centralized communist state, with its command economy, prevented East Germany from participating in the new industrial revolution, based on computers, on biochemical innovations, on hugely expanded services.

No matter whether East Germany chose cooperation with West German *Ostpolitik* or socialist isolation, "real existing socialism" would meet irresolvable contradictions.

Brandt's *Ostpolitik* did little to combat the disinformation campaign successfully promoted by the East German regime concerning the supposed social achievements of Germany's "first workers' and peasants' state." On the contrary, academic criticism of the East German dictatorship was muted in West Germany. Indeed, Professor Klaus Schroeder, head of the research center for GDR studies at the Free University of Berlin, speaks of tacit collusion between scholars in the former GDR and so many West German scholars concerned with the GDR. Both played down (and have a joint stake in continuing to play down) that odd mixture of brutality, autocracy, self-righteousness, and incompetence that had characterized governance in the former East German state.

Neither did *Ostpolitik* diminish East Germany's pervasive militarism. A much higher proportion of young East Germans served in military or paramilitary organizations than West Germans. Military might was glorified. (Indeed, elderly West Germans of a nostalgic temperament liked nothing better than to watch the changing of the guard in East Berlin, done in proper Germanic style (albeit with a Soviet rather than Prussian goose step.) Nor did *Ostpolitik* deter East Germans from actively supporting so-called wars of liberation in the Third World. In countries such as Angola, ex-patriate East Germans continued to make their name as professional instructors in military science and secret police procedures, subjects in which Germany had already long previously acquired an unfortunate proficiency.

Above all, East German military and political cadres continued to play with fire in the field of military planning. (When the two Germanys finally united, and their respective armies joined into one, *Bundeswehr* officers presiding over this fusion discovered to their surprise the most startling details concerning East German military designs. The East Germans, for instance, had made detailed plans for suddenly seizing West Berlin by a *coup de main*, an operation which would surely have set off World War III. The East Germans had likewise prepared for a *Blitzkrieg* in which West Germany would have been swiftly overrun by combined land–air operations in cooperation with East Germany's Warsaw Pact allies.[16] East Germany, in some respects, fully merited its reputation as a Red Prussia, albeit one that, unlike the old Prussia, oddly combined militarism with *Schlamperei* (muddle-headed incompetence). Not surprisingly, therefore, British historian Timothy Garton Ash, a leading expert, concluded that *Ostpolitik* merely achieved for the East German regime stabilization without liberalization.

Nevertheless, *Ostpolitik* also injured the East German dictatorship, albeit in an unexpected fashion. As economic contacts between the two German states tightened, West German marks began to circulate in East Germany in ever-increasing quantities. West German marks were used both on the black market, and also legally, in state-owned shops whose services had previously been reserved for members of the *nomenklatura*. The beneficiaries of this system were East Germans with friends and relatives in the West, or technicians with useful skills. By contrast, members of the *nomenklatura* (particularly those in lower or middle-ranking positions) lost out; discontent spread among the cadres on which the regime depended. (The Cuban communist regime would encounter similar difficulties when Fidel Castro, in 1993, permitted dollars freely to circulate in Cuba, in addition to Cuba's own worthless currency.) In this sense, *Ostpolitik* worked.

16 Jörg Schonbohm, *Zwei Armeen Und Ein Vaterland: Das Ende der Nationalen Volksarmee*, Berlin, Siedler Verlag, 1992.

Ostpolitik also went with a four-power arrangement on West Berlin (1971) which stabilized the Western position in West Berlin. This was followed in 1972 by a US– Soviet summit in Moscow, and the conclusion of a treaty limiting strategic nuclear weapons (SALT I). *Détente* in Europe culminated in the Final Act of the Conference on Security and Cooperation in Europe at Helsinki (1975) which, among other things, guaranteed (in Clause VII) respect for human rights, fundamental freedoms such as freedom of thought, conscience, religion, or belief.[17] For Soviet negotiators, this terminology appeared like the terminology of the Constitution granted to the Soviet Union by Stalin – a useful device to pacify inconvenient critics. But the Helsinki Act had the unintended consequence of strengthening political opposition at home, and therefore proved a serious mistake from the *nomenklatura*'s standpoint.

Cuban Crisis

Détente was real, but never fully applied to the Third World. After Stalin's demise, Khrushchev and his successors increasingly became convinced that the "global correlation of forces" could be shifted by strengthening socialism in the former Western colonies which had attained political independence. In the New World, Soviet influence became predominant in Cuba. The Cuban revolution during the 1960s became a revolutionary paradigm which deserves a short excursus of its own. Polemical studies concerning the Cuban revolution now fill many library shelves; overwhelmingly, they sided with the Cuban revolution, praised even by mainstream publications such as the *New York Times*, and the *Encyclopedia Britannica*. According to this orthodoxy, prerevolutionary Cuba was a prime example of a Third World country oppressed by Western, especially US, monopoly capitalism. Cuba's pre-revolutionary economy, the argument continues, was essentially agrarian, characterized by extensive farming (that is to say, the cultivation of large acreages with a minimal outlay of capital), by a monoculture (making Cuba heavily dependent on the production of a single crop – sugar), and by extreme dependency on the United States, which furnished Cuba with the bulk of its foreign capital and markets. Industrial production was limited to a few branches using domestically produced sugar, nickel, and tobacco. Stagnation and the "structural deformation" of the economy were made worse by profiteering in high places, by prostitution and gambling, and by pervasive inefficiency. Cuba, at the time of Fidel Castro's takeover, therefore remained in an "essentially underdeveloped condition."[18]

The facts show otherwise. From the outbreak of World War II to the end of the 1950s, Cuba in fact experienced striking economic expansion. Between 1941 and 1958, the national income tripled (from $689 million to $2.2 billion). Industrial wages compared favorably with average per capita wages in countries as varied as Austria, Mexico,

17 For the various treaties and their full text, see J.A.S. Grenville and Bernard Wasserstein, *The Major International Treaties since 1945: a History and Guide with Texts*, London and New York, Methuen, 1987.
18 *Encyclopedia Britannica*, "Macropaedia" series, 1975, vol. 5, p. 353. For our analysis of the Cuban situation with greater statistical detail see L.H. Gann and Peter J. Duignan, *The Hispanics in the United States*, Boulder, Colo., Westview Press, and Stanford, CA, Hoover Institution Press, 1986, pp. 94–104. For Cuban government versions, see "Cuba": *Dirección General de Estadística de Cuba*, La Habana, Editorial Nacional de Cuba, 1965; and Francisco Lopez Segrera, *Cuba: Capitalismo Dependiente y Subdesarrollo, 1510–1959*, La Habana, Casa de las Americas, 1972.

and Egypt. Judging by such indicators as per capita income, literacy, the availability of medical care, the proportion of persons employed in farming and manufacturing, and the extent of urbanization, Cuba ranked considerably higher than Mexico, a country widely praised at the time by Castro himself for the "progressive" nature of its economic institutions. There was certainly a great deal of discontent in Cuba, reflected by an increase in emigration to the United States after Fulgencio Batista's *coup d'état* in 1952. But there was no mass emigration comparable to that which took place later under Fidel Castro.

Widespread misconceptions notwithstanding, Cuban agriculture, for instance, was being progressively mechanized. Farm wages in Cuba substantially exceeded those in Austria or Portugal, not to mention Mexico. Land ownership was less highly concentrated in Cuba than in Mexico, Argentina, or the United States. Cuba, moreover, was not just one gigantic sugar-cane field. While sugar did dominate the agricultural economy, Cuba also produced substantial crops of rice, beans, bananas, and coffee. Between 1939 and 1958, the amount of land devoted to sugar decreased substantially; the sugar industry, including the industrial process and distribution of the crop, in 1954, amounted to only about one-quarter of the national income.

The US stake in Cuba's agricultural economy was diminishing. US control of the sugar industry declined from about 70 percent in 1928 to about 35 percent in 1958. Moreover, the sugar mills and other US-owned plants were apt to be the most modern and efficient in Cuba – those that paid the highest wages and that normally would make the best agreements with the Cuban trade unions. Cuba's problems thus derived not so much from poverty, but, at least in part, from an exceedingly uneven rate of development. Cuba had a growing urban sector but a backward hinterland that lagged far behind the cities, with a middle class too large for the economy to sustain. Social tensions increased. There were striking disparities of income between city and countryside; there were equally noticeable tensions within rural communities. The great mass of the agricultural population had no stake in the existing regime; nor did the soldiers, recruited from the villages and disgusted by their miserable pay, their lowly social status, and the manner in which their leaders enriched themselves.

Above all, there were serious tensions within the Cuban middle class. The white population of Cuba consisted, in descending order of social esteem, of *criollos* (old Spanish), *gallegos* (new Spanish immigrants, many of them from north-western Spain), and *polacos* (Eastern European immigrants, many of them Jewish). A substantial number of Cuba's shopkeepers, artisans, and petty entrepreneurs were Jewish, Spanish, or Chinese immigrants who had come to Cuba after the turn of the century and had helped expand the economy, but who were not native to the country. The United States poured investments into the sugar industry, railways, a variety of public utilities, and, above all, into the land. As Theodore Draper states: "The only business in which the Cubans had a monopoly was politics."[19] The Cuban bourgeoisie contained within its ranks a large body of men and women unhappy with the foreigners' apparently excessive stake in the economy and dissatisfied, above all, with their own scanty professional prospects. The revolution gained its leadership and its initial strength primarily from dissident middle-class people – from lawyers without briefs, physicians without patients, and professors

19 Theodore Draper, *Castroism: Theory and Practice*, New York, Praeger, 1965, p. 107; Cuban Economic Research project, *A Study on Cuba: the Colonial and Republican Periods*, Coral Gables, University of Miami Press, 1965, pp. 421, 429; Truth about Cuba Committee, *Facts, Data, and Statistics on Pre-Communist Cuba*, Miami, The Committee, 1956.

without students – all imbued with a naïve trust in the redeeming qualities of a popular revolution and in their own ability to master the forces they would unleash.

Castro achieved power on what might be called, broadly speaking, a "popular front" ticket designed to appeal to both liberals and radicals of many different stripes. Once in power, Castro rapidly moved to the left. In 1959, anti-communism officially became a state crime; in 1961, Castro issued a declaration stating that he was a Marxist–Leninist and that he would remain a Marxist–Leninist to his dying day. At the same time, Castro successively broke with his former allies. The middle class was excluded from political participation and its economic power was shattered. Dissident intellectuals suffered brutal persecution. There was a mass exodus of specialists, technicians, academic people, and skilled workers. The exiles took abroad much of the enterprise, technical knowledge, and skills that the revolution desperately required. The industrial workers lost the right to strike. Far from distributing the land to tillers, Castro collectivized most of Cuban agriculture, and industries were nationalized – with disastrous effects to the economy. Castro provoked a break with the United States by confiscating American investments, and Cuba became increasingly dependent on Soviet subsidies and Soviet trade. Backed by Soviet military might, the Cuban Communist Party claimed for itself not merely a monopoly of political power, but immunity from all criticism, and the right to control every aspect of national life. As in all communist countries, there was a mass exodus: something like one-tenth of the Cuban population emigrated, including entrepreneurs, managers, professional people, workers (over 50 percent of the migrants were working class), the country's economic élite; their departure enriched the countries of their adoption and impoverished the land of their birth. Castro also tried to export Castroism and to communize Latin America, but especially Central America.

The Soviet Union had not created the revolution. (Indeed, the pro-Moscow Cuban Communist Party had initially cooperated with Fulgencio Batista, the fallen dictator.)[20] But, once in power, Castro received full support from the Soviet Union, and Cuba increasingly became dependent on Soviet economic help – this at a time when the US had imposed an economic boycott on Cuba in retaliation for Castro's seizure of US property on the island. The Bay of Pigs fiasco (discussed in chapter 2) further worsened US–Cuban relations, as did Castro's commitment to exporting revolution to the Third World. Moscow increasingly supplied military, as well as economic and diplomatic, help to Cuba, and in the end resorted to an uncharacteristic gamble. In 1962 Khrushchev placed nuclear missiles on the island, thereby setting off the Cuban missile crisis and risking World War III.

The Cuban crisis remains subject to debate. This will not be resolved until all relevant Cuban and former Soviet archives have been opened. But some speculative conclusions seem in order. Khrushchev was more adventurist than Stalin; he was convinced that Soviet industrial might was increasing fast, and would match the US's by the early 1980s. He believed that the time had come for the Soviet Union to break out of the Eurasian containment fashioned by the West.[21] Khrushchev, moreover, thought that President Kennedy would not fight over the issue; in addition, the Western allies had by no means been united over the Berlin issue. (De Gaulle and Adenauer had stood firm; the British might have been willing to trade.) According to Adam Ulam, a leading

20 Theodore Draper, "The Communist Party of Cuba," in Witold S. Sworakowski, ed., *World Communism: a Handbook, 1918–1965*, Stanford, CA, Hoover Institution Press, 1973, pp. 98–105.
21 Zbigniew Brzezinski, "The Cold War and its Aftermath," *Foreign Affairs*, Fall 1992, pp. 31–49.

authority on communism, the Soviet intention was not to defend Cuba against a future US attack, nor to pacify Castro, nor to close the existing "missile gap" between the US and the Soviet Union by getting Soviet missiles into closer proximity to the US. Khrushchev's real intention was to use the missiles as bargaining counters for a German settlement, and at the same time achieve a propaganda victory over the West.[22] Such a stunning success would be all the more desirable at a time when Khrushchev wished to consolidate his position at home, and when the world communist movement was already bitterly divided, with Beijing and even Tirana challenging Moscow's revolutionary legitimacy.

In the short run, the Cuban missile crisis turned out to be a Western success. President Kennedy emerged with his reputation tremendously enhanced – a man of courage and yet of moderation. (The Americans dismantled their missiles in Turkey in return for the Soviets taking their missiles out of Cuba.) Immediately after the crisis, moreover, the US, Britain, and the Soviet Union signed a nuclear test ban agreement by which the participants agreed to abstain from all except underground tests. The Soviet Union had suffered a serious blow to its prestige; Khrushchev's game of *va banque* had apparently failed. Rivalry increased within the Soviet military establishment between the adherents of Khrushchev (who put his faith primarily in strategic missiles) and Khrushchev's critics (who placed more emphasis on conventional forces). Responsible senior commanders such as Marshall Matvei Zakharov bitterly condemned Khrushchev's willingness to take perilous risks, his "military dilettantism" and "lack of realism." As Zakharov put it, the emergence of nuclear missiles, cybernetics, electronics, and computers had completely changed the military balance. Hence, a "subjective approach" and "hare-brained schemes" would only lead to irreparable disaster. The Cuban crisis therefore weakened Khrushchev (displaced from power in 1964), and also promoted a more extensive US–Soviet dialogue on numerous issues, including strategic arms.[23]

On the other hand, the Soviet Union also achieved major gains. The withdrawal of Soviet missiles was purchased by the Kennedy administration with a blanket guarantee not to invade Cuba. Immunity was extorted for a major Soviet base in defiance of the once inviolable Monroe Doctrine. The crisis furthered Soviet interest in promoting revolutionary change in the Third World as a means of strategically outflanking the West.

Middle East and Third World

The Cuban crisis raised even wider issues. For one thing, Castro was a master of public relations techniques; for a time he became the hero of leftist intellectuals throughout the Western world. Castro beards came into fashion, berets became *de rigueur* (surprisingly so because berets had been the favorite headgear of Pétain adherents in France during World War II). Castro stood for the left-wing intellectuals' growing infatuation with the Third World, a new phenomenon. During the aftermath of World War II, committed leftists such as Christopher Hill (a British Marxist historian), Jean-Paul Sartre, Julien Benda, Maurice Merleau-Ponty (French leftist mandarins), even Emmanuel Mounier (a

22 Ulam, *The Communists*, pp. 228–36.
23 Richard Wolff, "Zakharov," in Harold Shukman, *Stalin's Generals*, New York, Grove Press, 1993, p. 338.

Catholic) had praised Soviet communism and all its works. Their enthusiasm success-ively diminished as a result of Khrushchev's "secret" speech concerning the crimes of Stalin, the Soviet invasion of Hungary (1956), and Czechoslovakia (1968). Each of these crises entailed an ever-increasing number of defections from the communist ranks.

Instead, leftists turned their attention to the so-called Third World, especially the newly independent states of Asia and Africa. These countries were pitied for their poverty, and praised for their courageous independence struggles. Much ink was spilled over the assumed virtues of Third World peasants rooted in the soil. "Third World" revolutionaries became the new culture heroes of self-styled progressives in the West, particularly so in France, where most intellectuals had sided with the Algerian insur-gents in the Franco-Algerian conflict. Neither the Old Left's nor the New Left's views of Western colonialism, of course, bore much relation to reality. The bulk of Western investments went to the "First," not the "Third World." Third World investments did not necessarily yield super-profits; on the contrary, a great deal of money was lost as well as gained. (Neither was there any truth in the unexamined assumption, current on leftist campuses, that Western capitalists made higher profits under right-wing dictators than under democratic regimes.) *Dependista* scholarship (which stressed the Third World's dependency on the First) had other weaknesses. *Dependistas* failed to understand the dominant role of the local bourgeoisie in the economic life of supposedly "dependent" countries such as the Argentine and South Africa. Neither could *dependistas* explain how certain countries managed to break the supposedly unbreakable manacles of poverty which supposedly shackled the Third World. Taiwan, South Korea, and Singapore each experienced an economic miracle which no left-wing economist had predicted.[24]

Tiers-mondisme remained for a time a powerful concept which profoundly affected *realpolitik* as well as academic fashions. To the Americans, the Third World appeared a crucial political arena. Freed from Western colonial rule, the Third World nations would hold a global casting vote in the East–West contest. Poverty was the nursemaid of communism. In its own interest, the West should therefore render economic aid to the Third World in order to promote global prosperity, enhance Western markets, and prevent the spread of communism. Bodies such as the Peace Corps (initiated in 1961 by President Kennedy) thus derived their impetus both from considerations of *realpolitik* and humanity.

In fact, however, events in the Third World nowhere shaped the superpowers' ulti-mate destiny. In this respect, Marxist–Leninist theoreticians erred even more than their colleagues in the Western world. Marxist–Leninists quite mistakenly imagined that super-profits derived from the Third World played a crucial role in Western capitalism's untoward survival. To adapt Winston Churchill's phraseology, the Third World sup-posedly formed Western capitalism's "soft underbelly." The struggle against the West should therefore be intensified by supporting "national liberation struggles" in colonies such as Angola, Mozambique, semi-colonies such as Rhodesia, and "nominally independ-ent countries of a colonial type" such as South Africa. (Soviet theoreticians considered,

---

24 See, for instance, L.H. Gann and Peter Duignan, *Burden of Empire: an Appraisal of Western Colonialism in Africa South of the Sahara*, New York, Praeger, 1967; L.H. Gann and Peter Duignan, eds, *Colonialism in Africa*, Cambridge, Cambridge University Press, 1969–1975, 5 vols; L.H. Gann, *Neocolonialism, Imperialism, and "New Class,"* Menlo Park, CA, Institute for Humane Studies, 1975. For opposing views see, for instance, Paul A. Baran, *The Political Economy of Growth*, New York, Monthly Review Press, 1957; Walter Rodney, *How Europe Underdeveloped Africa*, Washington, DC, Howard University Press, 1981.

quite erroneously, that South Africa was a Western financial dependency, even though the bulk of South Africa's capital was, by the 1960s, engendered domestically.) Liberation struggles should be carried out in collaboration with all "progressive forces," including "national bourgeoisie," of the colonial and ex-colonial countries.

Support for Third World "liberation struggles" went with the massive expansion of the Red Navy. At the time of the Cuban crisis, Khrushchev found that he was helpless against US maritime power. Never again, the communist leadership vowed. During the 1960s, and 1970s, the Soviet navy became a powerful force, designed not to protect the Soviet Union's coastline or scanty sea-borne trade, but to strike at US commerce. In addition, the Soviet Union built a strong airlift capability with an impressive range of action. To support this strategy, the Soviets stressed "proletarian internationalism," a prominent concept in Soviet thought since 1975. Proletarian internationalism required the solidarity of the world communist movement with the various "liberation" groups, the primacy of the USSR and the CPSU within this global movement, and cooperation between Third World communist parties and individual communist countries in the greater cause of world revolution. Thus, proletarian internationalism provided a rationale for direct military assistance to potential allies through Soviet proxies like Cuba and East Germany, and for a division of labor among communist regimes: Cuba provided the soldiers, East Germany the training cadre for secret police and palace guards. By advancing in the Third World, the Soviets meant to weaken the First World.

For similar reasons, the Soviets became actively involved in the Middle East. Here we shall limit ourselves to indicating that the Soviets initially backed the nascent Jewish state in order to incommode the British empire. Moscow soon changed course, and became one of Israel's sternest opponents. Within the Soviet Union, Zionists were treated as criminals. Outside the Soviet Union, Soviet propaganda classed Israel among the global villains. "Israeli–imperialist–Zionist aggression" supposedly constituted a major threat to world peace. Hence the Soviet Union supplied Israel's enemies, including Egypt and Syria, with arms, cash, and counsel. The PLO (Palestine Liberation Organization) became one of the Soviet Union's favored foreign protégés. Armed by the Soviet Union, Egypt and Syria in 1973 launched a full-scale attack against Israel (the so-called Yom Kippur war, the third in a series of bloody Arab–Israeli clashes). Taken by surprise, Israel for a moment seemed in grave danger, threatened by greatly superior forces. But the Israelis soon rallied. The US, under President Nixon, supplied massive aid to the Israelis (aided only in this endeavor by Portugal, alone among Washington's European allies). The Israelis massively counter-attacked. In the end, the bulk of Egypt's army was saved only by the threat of Soviet intervention, and by US pressure directing the Israelis to withdraw.

Israel had once more survived. It was a major defeat for the Soviet Union with its intense hostility to the Jewish state. But, in many other parts of the Third World, Soviet policy as yet seemed to work well. Soviet theoreticians as yet expected to build socialism among tribal communities, and achieve miracles of socialist production among subsistence cultivators and herdsmen. By the late 1970s, self-described Marxist–Leninist governments professed friendship to Moscow as far afield as Mozambique, Angola, Ethiopia, South Yemen. Indo-China (including North and South Vietnam, Cambodia, and Laos) had fallen under Marxist–Leninist governance. In practice, this revolutionary outlay profited the Soviet Union little, given the instability of their respective regimes, their economic mismanagement, and their bloody internal dissension. To them the Red Star as yet seemed ascendant.

9

The New Left and the Cultural Revolution

A quarter of a century has elapsed since the student revolution of the 1960s reached its apogee. Former participants include corporate executives, college presidents, and cabinet officers. Most have long since abandoned their youthful ideals; yet many remember the 1960s with nostalgia – a time when the world was young, hopes were high, and utopia stood round the corner. *Time* magazine, not exactly a mouthpiece of starry-eyed radicals, called them (in 1968) "the most conscience stricken, moralistic, and perhaps the most promising [generation] in American history."[1]

In the US the student revolution went with far-reaching demographic changes. The student revolution appealed above all to the post-World War II baby boomers who had now become old enough to go to college. (Working-class youths were much less affected.) Nowadays, US college administrators argue above all about declining college enrollments, budget cuts, and rising costs. In the 1960s such preoccupations would have appeared petty. Many colleges were in chaos; teaching had partially or wholly come to a standstill; militants hoped to change the world. Student riots had erupted in the US, Japan, Germany, France, and Italy. The demonstrators' message was similar. *Studium ist Opium* (studying is an opiate) roared the militants during the great demonstrations in West Berlin in 1968. *L'imagination au pouvoir* (let imagination rule) shouted their French colleagues during the massive riots in Paris during the same year. Drugs and four-letter words figured more prominently in the so-called Free Speech Movement in Berkeley. Huge crowds of students or would-be students took to the streets in the US and Western Europe. The demonstrators shared a love for participatory democracy and unconstrained sex, rock music, and drugs. Generalizations are hard to make; the student left and their non-academic supporters varied greatly – from dedicated activists to hangers-on, from non-political hippies looking for a good time to young men and women prepared for martyrdom. There were Marxists of every conceivable shade. There were liberals such as Allard Lowenstein, a pioneer of the US student and the anti-war movements, a crusader against apartheid in South Africa, and also a critic of Marxist–Leninists. (He called communists "Nazis with promises.")[2] There were religious activists such as Hugo Gollwitzer, a German Lutheran theologian who had successively criticized Hitler, and languished in a Soviet camp; he supported the New Left because he hoped for a neutral Germany. Robert McAfee Brown, an American theologian opposed the draft and the war in Vietnam because he considered US intervention unjust.

Despite differences, there were broad similarities in terminology, attitudes, and life-styles among the young radicals. All militants shared the same contempt for trade that

1 *Time*, 13 May 1968, pp. 22–38.
2 William H. Chafe, *Never Stop Running: Allard Lowenstein and the Struggle to Save American Liberalism*, New York, Basic Books, 1993.

had once characterized Jane Austen's minor gentry. Entrepreneurs of all kinds were beyond redemption; no value attached to risk-taking or managerial ability. But worst was surely the petty bourgeoisie – better a wicked poet than a virtuous grocer! The revolutionaries, however, possessed an instinct for publicity worthy of big-time advertising, and thereby helped to change the language of public discourse. They looked to "sexual" as well as political liberation and empowerment. Oddly combining hedonism with puritanism, they envisaged the pursuit of sexual pleasure as a moral duty. They created new rituals of counter-politics, with sit-ins, teach-ins, and ceremonial burning of flags, bras, and draft cards. The cultural revolution speeded existing trends. Student activists did not create feminism, but the revolution popularized the feminists' aims. The student revolution did not set off black militance, but gave increased resonance to black demands. The cultural revolution did not bring about drug usage which had long predated the 1960s, but the revolution did expand drug use among US students who made addiction seem "cool." (Drugs were much less popular among German students who, on the whole, were less political and more concerned with university governance than their confrères in the US.) Homosexuality had been practiced since time immemorial, but activists now elevated the practice from a vice to a virtue.

By the 1960s, gender politics acquired increasing resonance. More women entered the labor force; women began to move into managerial and technical jobs hitherto closed to them; contraceptive devices became available to all who wanted them and were publicized in the most respectable of ladies' journals. One of the major developments in the cultural revolution in the late 1960s, according to political scientist John H. Bunzel, was the changing role of women in virtually every part of society. This entailed the extensive use of the pill and a more "permissive" code of sexual conduct. But women also pushed for "empowerment," equality, entitlement and unrestricted advancement in business, the professions, the academic world, and in the political arena. Advocates of women's rights thereafter joined the advocates of other constituencies – homosexuals, lesbians, racial and ethnic minorities – who claimed for their members equal, and later, often both preferential and deferential treatment.

The year 1968 saw the emergence of militant feminism and the assertive and acerbic feminist voice. Feminism in the US was, of course, much older; US women had been the first to go to college in considerable numbers. The US had helped to pioneer the feminist movement (which came to Germany much later than to the US). But revolutionary activism on US campuses gave a fillip to militant feminism. Betty Friedan's *The Feminine Mystique* (1963) provided the inspiration for setting up NOW (National Organization of Women) in 1969. NOW owed much to black militancy; even the term "liberation movement" was borrowed from the blacks. Men – not only capitalism, imperialism, or racism – now seemed enemies to ultra-militants. As with gays, one specific act defined the movement and brought militant feminists to national prominence: the disruption of the Miss America contest at Atlantic City in September 1968. The New York Radical Women group inspired similar protest groups around the country; these opposed men, marriage, and patriarchy, and glorified bra-burning, lesbian rights, and abortion.[3]

The gay liberation movement was part of the general social protest of the 1960s. The riots at Stonewall Inn, a New York Greenwich Village gay bar in June 1969, brought the gays into the limelight, much as the 1968 Chicago riots had publicized the New Left.

3 Irwin Unger and Debi Unger, *Turning Point. 1968*, New York, Charles Scribner's, 1988, p. 5.

Men dominated the homosexual movement at that time;[4] but Stonewall was one of the first coming-out "happenings" which marked gay and lesbian rights advocacy in the US. Gays joined with peace demonstrators, feminists, black militants, Chicano militants, and a host of others in a great army, different in aims, but sharing common lifestyles. The homosexual movement gained strength in the early 1970s by using New Left tactics.

The campuses played a major part in many of the new movements. Radical students used campuses as privileged sanctuaries; and, owing to the administration's widespread permissiveness, militants were allowed to disrupt campus operations and to violate their opponents' constitutional rights. Bomb threats and anonymous telephone calls were the order of the day – a subject obscured in academic memory. (In 1987, Sidney Hook, a leading American philosopher, discovered to his surprise that no major foundation had as yet made a single grant of any significance for a scholarly study concerning the violent disruption of US academic life during the period, though millions of dollars had been awarded for liberal-left projects.)[5]

Members of the New Left were mostly young (in their late teens and early twenties), mostly born after World War II, the baby boom generation. The New Left initially appealed only to students, but soon recruited radical clergy, and faculty, especially in the humanities and social sciences. The New Left was primarily concerned with the civil rights, anti-nuclear, and anti-war movements. The civil rights crusade began with the Montgomery bus boycott (1955–6) and expanded to student sit-ins and freedom rides (1960–1). Early apostles of the New Left commonly came from communist families and the rest were reared in left-liberal households. New Left students, however, looked askance at the Old Left because of Stalinism and communism's "democratic centralism." Liberals were widely distrusted, usually because of their support of capitalism or the Cold War.

Many militants professed to despise their parents and to seek total autonomy over their lives. Yet students, far more than working-class youngsters, relied heavily on their families for funds and, often, for housing. The New Left widely castigated "formal democracy" as a mask for privilege, but they took for granted their own democratic liberties, and extensively used the courts to defend their own civil rights. American radicals in particular condemned "Amerika" for its hegemonic pretensions, but few US militants ever changed their nationality. (When caught in trouble while traveling abroad, they were among the first to wave their US passports.) Leftist students detested the police, yet they expected to be protected against hard-hats and criminals. (In West Berlin, students occupied houses supposedly left vacant by their owners, and suitable therefore for "societal expropriation." These houses, however, belonged to pimps and other ruffians who proceeded to beat up the student squatters. What did the students do? Good Germans – they rang for the police!)

In every Western country radicals complained of being silenced by a ruthless Establishment. This did not prevent would-be revolutionaries from making appearances on television, and from publishing with prestigious as well as "underground" presses. In a more general sense, militants accepted as given Western security from Soviet domination. (Even in isolated West Berlin, surrounded by a Wall, the 1948 blockade of West Berlin by the Soviets, and West Berlin's rescue by an Anglo-American airbridge had

4 Martin Duberman, *Stonewall*, New York, Dutton, 1993.
5 Sidney Hook, "A Curious Phenomenon: a Report," *Measure* (New York), no. 69, June 1987, pp. 6–7.

been consigned to total oblivion by the radicals.) Not for student revolutionaries any apprehensions that their own respective countries might succumb to Soviet aggression, as the Soviet satellites of East Central Europe had done. Student dissidents likewise regarded Western postwar prosperity as part of the natural order. Most students were by that time unacquainted with that gnawing fear of unemployment that had tortured their elders. Militants instead resented consumerism. They detested a prosperous industrial society in which ordinary people enjoyed the advantages available in the olden days only to noblemen and patricians: personal credit (through a credit card); a carriage (the automobile); fine clothes and jewelry (available now to all but the very poor); access to theater and opera (made possible by radio and television), and recreational travel. The new consumer society first developed in the US; hence it was the US that was demonized with the greatest fervor. Yet foreign radicals also looked to the US as an example; for the first time in history, US radicals had more influence on their European counterparts than Europeans did on Americans.[6] American slang and American street talk could be heard around the world. Fashion-conscious Frenchwomen began to shop around for *les jeans;* and *die Szene* (the "scene," the left-wing milieu) became part of the new German vocabulary.

General Characteristics

The New Left in the US had turned into a worldwide movement of radical students during the 1960s. The movement spread throughout Western Europe, especially through university campuses. European students opposed the Vietnam War and nuclear weapons. Demonstrators throughout the Western world were apt to share similar sartorial tastes and hair styles. The old-style proletarian cap became *vieux jeux*, as did the jacket, and the tie (except for a small Maoist cadre who preferred to wear Mao grey jackets or conventional dress). Traditional academic and clerical attire went by the board (except for leftist German parsons who wore clerical gowns during demonstrations, while holding church services in blue jeans). Snap-brim hats ceased to be worn (a fashion initiated to the hatters' distress by John F. Kennedy). Jeans, sandals, bandanas, and ponchos were in – the more bizarre the better. Beards and long hair once more became popular among young men as they had been in Victorian times. Young women no longer shaved their legs or used lipstick; by contrast, a face painted in glowing colors and abstract design was *à la mode*. Henceforth, a student was as easily recognized by his or her dress or hair style as a British Guards officer by his red tunic and bearskin cap. The same uniformity extended to choice of vehicle. Four-door sedans with fins in the 'fifties fashion were "out"; a Volkswagen bus adorned with psychedelic design was "in."

Outlandish ways of talking and dressing went with a remarkable demographic shift which affected every Western country. World War II and its aftermath had seen striking

6 Maurice Isserman, "The Not-so-dark and Bloody Ground: New Works on the 1960s," *American History Review*, vol. 94, no. 4, October 1989, p. 991. Major works on the movement include Edward J. Bacciocco, *The New Left in America: Reform to Revolution, 1956–1970*, Stanford, CA, Hoover Institution Press, 1974; Unger and Unger, *Turning Point, 1968*; Todd Gitlin, *The Sixties: Years of Hope. Days of Rage*, New York, Bantam Books, 1987; Ronald Fraser et al., *1968: a Student Generation in Revolt*, New York, Pantheon, 1988; Peter Collier and David Horowitz, *Destructive Generation: Second Thoughts about the Sixties*, New York, Summit, 1989; David Caute, *The Year of the Barricades: a Journey through 1968*, New York, Harper and Row, 1988.

demographic growth, a dramatic rejuvenation that no demographer had been able to predict. Instead of declining, the birthrate had suddenly gone up – the "baby boom." By the 1960s, the US contained a much higher percentage of men and women in their early twenties than ever before or thereafter: 76 million Americans were born between 1946 and 1964, the largest cohort in the history of demography. (The baby boomers were also called the New Generation, the Spock Generation, the Woodstock Generation.) They were better educated than their parents, going to college at the highest rate ever. A minority within this cohort sought to recreate the world or to escape from it by prolonged adolescence. They challenged American–European political, Christian, and cultural values, transformed the war movement, influenced American and European lifestyles, music, and the sexual revolution (the pill also helped).

Europe had experienced youth movements before: the *Sturm und Drang* period of the late eighteenth century, the Romantic revival of the nineteenth century, the *Jugendbewegung* that preceded World War I, and the *Wandervogel* enthusiasts thereafter. But all of these had affected only a small portion of the élite. The new youth movement affected a great mass of youngsters – this at a time when university places kept expanding at a prodigious rate in every Western country, above all in the US. (In 1940, 15.6 percent of 18–21-year-olds went to college, by 1970, the percentage had risen to 51.4.) As John B. Judis put it:

> This diffusion of education was only tangentially related to adult work requirements or social responsibilities. Quite the contrary, the new period of education created an extended transition between childhood and work and between puberty and adulthood. The new group of 14- to 22-year-old Americans, called "adolescents" by psychologists, sought to fill it with sexual experimentation, new forms of cultural expression, drugs, delinquency and finally new politics.[7]

What of their social status? Their leaders overwhelmingly derived from the middle and upper class – as Marx, Engels, Lenin, and Castro had done before. The new generation of students had missed the hardships of World War II and its aftermath; they were used to an age of affluence. Living standards kept going up; young men and women had more money to spend on average than their forebears. The youth market became a major concern to merchandisers, and advertisers, and to music- and movie-makers.

Indeed, the movement depended heavily on universities and colleges. Institutions of higher learning greatly expanded during the 1960s all over the Western world; yet universities remained unable to meet the rising demand for more university places. The sheer number of students overwhelmed college administrators, and sometimes the police. (For example, more than half a million students participated in the demonstrations and strikes held in Italy in March 1968.) The language of political discourse coarsened at the universities; civil discourse between the generations became impossible. Nevertheless, US universities at the same time increasingly turned into miniature welfare states, with a rapid growth of campus agencies designed to provide career counseling, psychological treatment, and other services unknown to the students' parents and grandparents – this while the students also insisted on ending the university's role *in loco parentis*.

On US campuses especially, the students of the 1960s and the 1970s were among "the freest – and at the same time, most carefully nurtured and cherished – beings

7 John B. Judis, "The Activist as Hero," *The New Republic*, 25 October 1993, p. 42.

in Western history."[8] Yet many militants displayed a surprising element of self-pity: radicals were apt to regard themselves as white "niggers" or – to put the matter into traditional religious terminology – as persecuted saints sent to preach truth to unbelievers. Student militants likewise inherited from more traditional sectarians that peculiar mixture of moral indignation and self-righteousness, that intense conviction that they alone occupied the commanding heights of morality.

Since World War II, intellectual alienation in the United States had produced an adversarial culture that condemned American society root and branch. Its adherents saw America as flawed and corrupt, imperialist and capitalist. Psychiatrist Bruno Bettelheim found many of the New Left psychologically disturbed, estranged from the world they lived in and angry at themselves, their parents, and their society. Their alienation was projected on to the screen of American life in general. Radicals believed naïvely in the perfectibility of man and society. Since they set unrealistically high standards for the US (but not for communist states such as China or Cuba), it was easy to attack "Amerika."

In their own way, the men and women of the American New Left were, however, as Amero-centric as the most chauvinist of bar-room patriots. The New Left, and not only the New Left, regarded "Amerika" as a new House of Bondage (an interpretation that went counter to the real immigrant's experience); the US became the world's new villain, and center of all evil. Whereas the Old Left had encouraged industrialization, the New Left extolled those rural pursuits of which the militant campus youth had no firsthand experience. Blue jeans worldwide replaced the proletarian cloth cap; rock and roll took the place of old-fashioned marching songs; the unstructured "demo" replaced the disciplined rallies of old. Whereas popular artists such as Fred Astaire in his musicals had idealized the upper class, rock and rap glorified the underclass.

The politics of youth (that is, mainly white, middle-class youth) mingled with the black struggle for equality. During the 1950s and 1960s the legal barriers to black advancement in the US shattered – this against bitter Southern resistance, broken by civil disobedience and the force employed by federal courts, administrators, and troops. The migration of black Southerners, mainly rural, to the Northern cities accelerated, at a time when Northern industries still provided substantial employment for semi-skilled labor. The black middle class expanded, and its voice in US politics grew more influential. But, at the same time, the problems of big city slums worsened; crime grew and – contrary to the white liberals' optimistic hopes – white and black Americans failed to integrate. The politics of youth, however, were associated with the romantic idealization of the underclass. At the same time, drugs were widely glamorized by middle-class intellectuals, pop singers, and trendy psychologists such as Timothy Leary who called on the public to "tune in, turn on, drop out." Above all, politicians of every stripe, left or right, increasingly catered to the young.

During the 1960s and early 1970s, "the illegal use of drugs spread to every segment of society."[9] College students were the first to expand drug use, calling them recreational drugs, that is, marijuana and psychedelic substances like LSD; then the counter-culture took the mind-altering drugs and usage spread throughout the country as adults imitated

8 Rober Nisbet, "Who Killed the Student Revolution?," *Commentary*, January 1970, vol. 34, no. 2, p. 12.
9 See Edwin Meese III, "Criminal Justice: a Public Policy Imperative," in Annelise Anderson and Dennis L. Bark, eds, *Thinking about America: the United States in the 1990s*, Stanford, CA, Hoover Institution Press, 1988, p. 450.

students and young people. The peak year for the "druggies" of the counter-culture was 1967. The Haight Ashbury in San Francisco and the East Village in New York were the drug Meccas of the young and liberated. The Summer of Love (1967) led to murder, rape, "bad trips," and flight from hippie ghettos to create rural communes or "tribes."

Militants regarded themselves as outcasts persecuted by the academic establishment. But, in fact, presidents, deans, and professors of élite universities usually sought to conciliate rather than confront the militants. Indeed, a substantial proportion of professors (especially the younger teachers) sympathized with the students. Many professors themselves disapproved of the Cold War; they felt out of touch with a capitalist, consumer society and a proliferating college bureaucracy; they abhorred the war in Vietnam, and US global imperialism as they saw it.

The student revolts also depended heavily on the free publicity provided by newspapers and television – whether during the violent commotions over the People's Park in Berkeley or riots staged to disrupt the Democratic Party's National Convention in Chicago in 1968. Without the silver screen, student protests and riots would not have had much of a public impact; selective television reporting gave disproportionate attention to the student movement and earned them both popularity and confidence. The "movement" equally profited from grants made by progressive foundations to radical bodies, and from the willingness of major publishers to put out radical books in inexpensive paperback editions. Unlike industrial workers or clerks, moreover, campus militants did not depend for their living on eight-to-five jobs. College students, teachers, and campus hangers-on could dispose of their time much more freely than ordinary folk. The militants had adequate leisure to participate in "demos" and those endless discussions on strategy and tactics thought to embody "participatory democracy."

A part of the movement was infused by a millenarian element. The militants looked to a sudden transformation of the world, but only after an interminable amount of discussion and "consensus-building." Then the trumpets would sound and the walls of Jericho would collapse. The great majority of militants were not therefore genuine insurrectionists – not for them the dull work of arms drill, checking arms caches, or drawing up hit lists. The student revolutionaries, however, displayed much imagination in creating new rituals: candlelight processions, fasts, teach-ins, love-ins. So-called public debates with conservatives inevitably turned into mock show trials designed to inflict ritual humiliation on the "class enemy." "Sit-ins" and "teach-ins" were used with similar skill to coerce or intimidate the "backward" or unwilling.

Much has been written about the ravages occasioned in US academia by Senator Joseph McCarthy and his allies in the "witch hunts" of the early 1950s. But the damage done to universities by the intimidation of radicals and by the persecution of conservative professors during the 1960s was, in our view, more violent, and affected more people, and has, by contrast, remained an almost taboo subject. The center and the right were intimidated; many institutions suffered great loss. To give just one example, the once-famed Faculty of Germanic Studies at the Free University of West Berlin was decimated. Outstanding scholars such as Momme Mommsen and Katharina Mommsen, Eberhard Lämmert, Peter Wapnewski, Rainer Gruenter, and Eckehard Catholy left. Their departure reduced the faculty to a state of regrettable obscurity. In Berlin, Berkeley, Birmingham, Stanford or wherever, for all the militants' verbal commitment to free speech, they stood resolved to deny free speech to their critics. And faculty hiring practices favored the left and people of color. Black activists insisted only blacks could teach black history. (Chicano militants later claimed, in a similar fashion, that only they were fit to teach Latino studies.) Conservatives were out, and New Left adherents soon rose to prominence, as shown by Roger Kimball's *Tenured Radicals*.[10]

For a time there was a "Fifth Internationale," an informal network of radical activists which extended all over the world, with rapid communication from capital to capital. In Europe, the "Prague Spring" and the "Polish October" made a considerable impact, much more so than in the US. But, in addition, Europeans also looked to the US. Thus revolutionaries in Paris, in the "events" of May 1968, took heart from the previous April occupation of Columbia University by American students; these in turn had been inspired by the earlier student riots in Berkeley and Tokyo. Whatever their national affiliation, the activists uniformly detested capitalism. They were, however, ambivalent with regard to "real existing socialism." No matter how hard the Communist Party of the United States of America (CPUSA) tried, communists could evoke no interest among US voters. (Some New Leftists in the US thus identified with Czech students braving Soviet tanks in Prague in 1968. "Welcome to Czechago" proclaimed some placards worn by protesters to the Democratic Convention in Chicago.) By and large, however, US militants paid little attention to dissidents within the Warsaw Pact countries. Instead, the militants lionized Third World tyrants such as Castro, Che Guevara, Mao Zedong, and Ho Chi Minh – a dark chapter in the history of the Western left.

The Beat writers (Jack Kerouac and Allen Ginsberg), the Frankfurt School of Sociology (Herbert Marcuse), the Italian dissident communist Antonio Gramsci, and French radical thinkers such as Michel Foucault and Jacques Derrida assumed academic prominence. The New Left claimed to represent the poor, the disinherited, and the alienated against American bourgeois society. At first the New Left was not Marxist but espoused "a radical alternative to what they saw as staid or deadlocked party politics."[11] The Port Huron Statement of Students for a Democratic Society (SDS) in 1962 laid down the New Left's principles. These were: abolish poverty, eliminate racial segregation, end the Cold War, assure nuclear disarmament, reform the universities, and, most importantly, practice democracy from the bottom up. The Port Huron statement denounced communist rule in East Central Europe – the New Left was never Stalinist. The SDS, however, blamed both East and West for the Cold War. The SDS's parent organization, the League for Industrial Democracy, considered this stand as "soft on communism." In 1965, the SDS thus broke away from the League, and thereafter considered the US as the main menace to world peace.

The New Left also rebelled against science and technology. This revolt was not, of course, new. American, like European, conservatism had always comprised a pessimistic streak, hostile to industry. But such views had been confined to a small minority. The Old Left had cherished inventors, scientists, and engineers; in this sense, Marx and Lenin had differed in no wise from Ford and Carnegie. The New Left seemed blind to the enormous improvements made in living standards all over the world by the industrial revolution. Children of affluence, student militants were estranged from industrial pursuits; some indulged in an idyllic nature worship quite removed from the realities of industrialized states; others preferred to riot and demonstrate, and scorn the American way.

The new intelligentsia unwittingly shared certain values of old aristocrats. Olden-day counts and countesses had despised "trade"; so did the new militants (as did the urban

10 See Roger Kimball, *Tenured Radicals*, New York, Harper and Row, 1990.
11 See the entry by Todd Gitlin in the *Oxford Companion to Politics of the World*, Oxford, Oxford University Press, 1993, p. 629.

underclass). Not for them the search for profits or the virtues of thrift, punctuality, and plodding labor. "Turn on, tune in, drop out" was the now fashionable injunction. But campus militants did not expect that this counsel should be followed by those bank clerks, hospital nurses, car mechanics, and other dull persons on whose services militants had to rely for their everyday convenience. The class struggle took other, and unexpected, forms, as upper-class students, male and female, fought pitched battles against young police officers drawn from the lower middle and working classes – "pigs" (in America), *Bullen* (in Germany), *barbouzes* in French – all terms of derision. For the first time since World War II, it became chic to jeer at workers (provided that they were white), and Jews (provided that they were Zionist).

The emergence of the New Left further splintered progressives in the Western world. In the US, the Old Left, represented by bodies such as the CPUSA, (orthodox pro-Moscow communists), the Young Socialist Alliance (Trotskyists), and the Progressive Labor Council (Maoists) tried to use the student movement for their own ends. But the gap between Old and New Left proved too hard to surmount. Traditional Marxists had blamed capitalism for keeping the workers poor; the New Left denounced capitalism for making Western workers rich, slaves of consumerism, while impoverishing Third World people. The Old Left had extolled the Soviet Union as the workers' fatherland; the New Left derided the Soviet example. The Old Left had believed in discipline; the New Left cherished spontaneity.

The Old Left had put its trust in the "scientific" analysis of society; the New Left believed in intuition. The Old Left had read the Marxist classics; the New Left read little and surprised their elders by their ignorance. It was now fashionable to reject Soviet communism, but extol Maoism or Castroism. The Old Left had been led by middle-aged people; the New Left was guided by the young. The Old Left had believed in tight organization; New Left organizations, such as the SDS and SNCC (Student Non-violent Coordinating Committee), were decentralized in the extreme. The Old Left had eulogized the Western proletariat (cloth cap and all); the New Left professed to speak for outsiders of a different kind – blacks, gays and lesbians (all despised in the Soviet Union), and the underclass of the big city slums (reviled by Karl Marx). Above all, militant students sympathized with black South Africans and with Third World peasants without, however, in the least understanding African conditions or peasant values. (Genuinely traditional cultivators in African villages had no time for youngsters who defied their elders, or for women who disobeyed their men.)

Ideology and National Differences

For all their similarities, the militants widely differed over tactics, strategy, and political aims. A small minority believed in violence. The violent-prone were most numerous in Japan, Germany, and Italy – the losers of World War II. (The worldwide student riots of 1968 actually started in Japan, and Japanese students had led the world in the tactics of mass confrontation and disruption, with thorough preparation: sharp-edged sticks, bags of stones, motor-cycle helmets, gas masks, and young women organized in first-aid squads, with precise directions for the television teams.)[12] But it was only in Italy that bodies such as the Red Brigades posed even a temporary danger to the country's democratic institutions. Extremist German groups such as the Red Army Faction were

12 Caute, *The Year of the Barricades*, p. 28.

less effective, though brutal enough. (The Red Army Faction incongruously shared its acronym RAF, smeared all over German cities, with the Royal Air Force which had devastated German cities in World War II.) The Vietnam War made Europeans suspicious of America's political judgment. The peace movement argued against the US nuclear umbrella and accused the US of brinksmanship. Violent organizations in the US included the Black Panthers, the Weathermen, the 1970s Symbionese Liberation Army, and militant (as opposed to peaceful) advocates of Puerto Rican independence, and the Venceremos Brigade. These groups shared a common delight in oratorical excess, a taste for sectarian infighting, a liking for radical chic, and striking military incompetence in street fighting or bombing.

The New Left in the US began to fall apart under the assault of radicals such as the Weathermen and the Red Chinese Progressive Labor Party. Che Guevara and Frantz Fanon became the relevant progressive authors, and the anti-war movement turned to attacks on capitalism and imperialism. The Weathermen went under ground in 1968 and launched its bombing campaign. (The term "Weathermen" came from a Bob Dylan song: "You don't need a weatherman to know which way the wind is blowing.")

The militants worldwide were split in other ways, according to the cultural traditions of their respective homelands. US radicals drew heavily on American traditions. For instance, they owed a great deal to nineteenth-century populists, anarcho-syndicalists, pacifists, and the religious millenarian inheritance; to a legacy of Hot Gospelling and Revival meetings which now found a counterpart in secular student politics. The American dissenters' cult of the poor and the outlaw was deeply rooted in US culture, where the hard luck story had always counter-balanced folk eulogies of the red-blooded, can-do hero. Also peculiar to America was the black civil rights struggle. Both black and white students, mostly city bred, volunteered for work in the Deep South as members of SNCC (founded 1960). The Deep South was no place for *poseurs*. Backed though they were by the federal courts and the US army, student organizers risked life and limb; thereafter, they brought back to the student movements in the North a sense of moral commitment, as well as a taste for the back-country look of Georgia and Mississippi – denim jackets, blue work shirts – and for rural Southern speech.[13]

The civil rights movement, however, soon divided. Martin Luther King, Jr had stood for legality, equal rights, and the politics of integration; he was also prepared peacefully to break the law and go to jail for doing so. He did what his conscience told him. From the 1960s, there was a striking shift. SNCC turned militant, and displaced Martin Luther King's Southern Christian Leadership Conference as the center of the civil rights movement in the South. The Black Power movement split from white civil rights groups and pursued a more raucous agenda. The Black Panther Party (first organized in 1966) called for black separatism instead of integration, confrontation in place of moderation. The Panthers abhorred capitalism, white or black, and instead called for revolution "blind to the fact that you can't make a revolution in a country where most people support the government."[14]

13 Isserman, "The Not-so-dark and Bloody Ground" pp. 990–1010.
14 William L. O'Neill, *Coming Apart: an Informal History of America in the 1960s*, Chicago, Quadrangle, 1971, p. 189. For the black struggle in particular, see Clayborne Carson, *The Movement, 1964–1970*, Westport, Conn., Greenwood Press, 1993; Richard King, *Civil Rights and the Idea of Freedom*, New York, Oxford University Press, 1992; Nicolaus Mills, *Like a Holy Crusade. Mississippi 1964: the Turning of the Civil Rights Movement in America*, Chicago, Ivan R. Dee, 1992.

Black power split the liberal coalition within the Democratic Party and turned Jews against black separatists. Eldridge Cleaver predicted that dead white bodies would litter the streets. Liberal-left calls for revolutionary change were met by conservative resistance and the reform movement ground to a halt. Nevertheless, black militance had a powerful echo. For the first time in history, riots and demonstrations were seen by millions of television viewers. (By 1964, 93 percent of all American families possessed a television set. Even the poor could mostly afford to own one.) For the first time in history, blacks were presented in a favorable manner to millions of Americans who preferred black demonstrators to white Southern sheriffs and snarling German shepherds. During the 1960s, moreover, white-inspired race riots largely ended; black inspired inner-city riots absorbed public attention instead. The campus left managed to transform these com-motions into archetypal expressions of racial rage, or even harbingers of apocalypse. (The damage done to law-abiding shopkeepers and their customers was conveniently ignored.) But would-be revolutionaries such as the Black Panthers and the Weathermen lacked alike moral integrity, the discipline, the organization, and the know-how to plan genuine insurrections. The revolutionaries failed to heed Marx's warning that the lumpenproletariat was too divided and too anarchic to be trained into a revolutionary army.

The Panthers and their friends did, however, manage to legitimize the phraseology of revolution. The campus left shared the underclass's dislike for the boring virtues of punctuality, austerity, courtesy, and obedience to constituted authority. The campus left lionized the underclass and popularized the argot of the street corner. (Well-bred young ladies at Ivy League colleges came to consider as "cool" the copious use of the word "motherfucker.") Black militants and their white friends also shared the misconception that black inner-city bandits and black campus revolutionaries with Jomo Kenyatta beards were somehow more "authentic" than black merchants or Marine Corps captains. Black militants were, however, as divided as their white colleagues. Black separatists despised those blacks who sought integration into US society, the aim of earlier radical leaders. "Third Worlders" considered themselves at war both with US "imperialism" and its Zionist "allies." In the US, as in Europe, anti-Zionism merged with old-fashioned anti-semitism, thereby further damaging the traditional Roosevelt coalition that had included both Jews and blacks.

The summer of 1974 was disastrous for Huey P. Newton. Reports had appeared in the press locating him at the scene of a drive-by shooting at an "after hours" club. He was indicted for pistol-whipping a middle-aged black tailor named Preston Callins with a .357 magnum, for brawling with two police officers in an Oakland bar, and for murdering a 17-year-old prostitute named Kathleen Smith. When the day arrived for his arraignment in this last matter, Huey failed to show. Assisted by the Panthers' Hollywood supporters, he had fled to Cuba.[15]

The New Left's participation in the black struggle was at best only marginal. White students overwhelmingly supported the black people's battle, but were not directly involved in its outcome. The Vietnam War, by contrast, immediately affected all young Americans of draft age, thereby providing the New Left with mass support. The war's direct impact on the students was small. (Most college students escaped the draft; most draftees escaped service in Vietnam; most of those sent to Vietnam escaped fighting.) Nevertheless, the draft weighed heavily on the consciousness of students and their parents; resistance to the draft also merged with a long-standing pacifist tradition in the

15 David Horowitz, "Black Murder Inc.," *Heterodoxy*, vol. 1, no. 10, p. 1.

US. With the exception of World War II, every major conflict fought by the US abroad had led to bitter opposition at home.

From 1945 onward, the peace movement had one primary objective: nuclear disarmament. In the US, anti-nuclear movements (SANE founded in 1961) also came to oppose the Vietnam War. (The term New Left, however, derived from British intellectuals who had broken with the Communist Party and cooperated to form the Campaign for Nuclear Disarmament, 1957.) There was no one anti-war movement; there were scores operating at all levels of society. Some only opposed wars waged by the capitalist West, but backed wars of liberation: recall the chant "one, two, many Vietnams." These movements were not coordinated, but many were captured by New Left students for use against the war in Vietnam. It was students who provided the bodies for many anti-war demonstrations and marches. The American peace movements were reorganized between 1955 and 1963 to protest, at first, against nuclear weapons. During the 1960s, they joined into a coalition of anti-war groups and became the center of opposition to the Vietnam War. Opponents of the war included not just draft-dodging students but priests and pastors such as William Sloan Coffin, Robert McAfee Brown, and the priest-brothers, the Berrigans (Daniel and Philip). By 1967, the leader of the civil rights movement, Martin Luther King, had joined the anti-war movement and added his group to the coalition.

Confrontation became the war resisters' favorite tactic: at demonstrations outside military bases or draft board offices, at sit-ins in colleges or outside the Pentagon, at marches through New York City or Washington, DC. Draft resisters attacked ROTC units on campuses, they seized draft files, burned draft cards or poured blood on them (as did the Berrigans and some radical nuns). Many draft resisters fled to Canada – surprisingly so, given Canada's own conservative orientation. The anti-war movement was dominated by the New Left from the 1960s until 1975. The movement, for a time, was highly effective. It played a major part in driving Lyndon Johnson from the presidential race, and in getting Robert Drinan as well as Bella Abzug elected to Congress in 1970. The movement likewise helped George McGovern win the Democratic nomination for the presidency in 1972. For a time, liberal-left elements captured the Democratic Party, and caused many conservative, working-class people to defect to the Republicans. (This trend was only reversed during Jimmy Carter's presidency, and again during Bill Clinton's.)

American society was polarized by the Vietnam experience. One of the most divisive and subversive slogans of the period was "Say yes to the boys who say no." The tactics of confrontation were later adapted by other dissident groups who learned from the students about sit-ins, "demos," and picketing. (The spilling of blood became a tactic of the Right-to-Life movement and of animal rights fanatics. "Going limp" when arrested became a rule for most demonstrators, just as it had been for student resistance groups.) The fragmentation of America intensified during the 1960s, and confrontational tactics became *de rigueur* for feminists, militant gays, radical blacks, American Indians, and other advocacy groups.

The war in Vietnam also wiped out the foreign policy consensus that had bound the US since 1941. Critics of the conflict came in many varieties: those, the great majority, who felt the war should not be waged because it could not be won; those who felt the costs of winning the battle were too high; and those who felt the struggle was wrong because it was a capitalistic, imperialistic attempt by the US to dominate the Third World. College students, especially the New Left, liberal academics and revisionist historians also opposed US intervention anywhere to defend so-called reactionary regimes or to suppress liberation movements.

The New Left believed that the American empire provided resources for domestic tyranny to exploit the workers and the poor. If the empire fell, so would domestic tyranny and capitalist exploitation, and then, the New Lift movement believed, it could recast "Amerika." The radical students and liberal professors therefore concentrated on criticizing, free-enterprise America, and, in particular, its Cold War diplomacy. According to the radical linguist, Noam Chomsky, "the United States has become the most aggressive power in the world, the greatest threat to world peace, to rational self-determination and to international cooperation."[16] Revisionist historians such as William A. Williams and Gabriel Kolko believed that American expansionism derived from American capitalism; the New Left reiterated the charge. Staughton Lynd became a prophet to the New Left when he called on its votaries to shatter capitalism, the source of America's aggressive foreign policy. Despite the blood-curdling horrors committed before, during, and after the Chinese Cultural Revolution of 1966–8, it became the "in thing" to cite Mao Zedong's *Little Red Book*, and to repeat the most extraordinary fairy tales about China's progress. (Stanford English Professor Bruce Franklin, a Maoist, insisted on reading from the *Red Book*, no matter what the course listing was; John Gurley, a Stanford economist, in effect became an apologist for Maoism, and praised China's econimic planning and state monopoly over all the modes of production.)

Cultural rebellion went with the worship of youth, and nowhere more so than in the US. (Only in America did the militants themselves take pride in being "kids.") Special to America was also the movement's initial hostility to communism. The Port Huron Statement, first published by the SDS in 1962, harshly condemned Stalinism. Thereafter, the movement underwent a striking transformation. Two years later (1964) Tom Hayden, a leading SDS activist and a SNCC veteran, bitterly reviled "the unions, the mainstream civil rights groups, and the liberal organizations as 'hollow shells.' "[17] As "united front" tactics became acceptable to the SDS, the movement was taken over by hard-line Marxist–Leninists. Henceforth, the New Left abandoned non-violence, and traded reform for the rhetoric of revolution.

More effective were those former militants who decided to make use of democratic institutions. Radicals, for a time, made their mark on the local politics of university towns; for instance, in Berkeley, where the radicals gained control of the city council. In state and national politics students and former students made a profound impact on the Democratic Party. University people supplied much of the drive and idealism that animated the campaigns of candidates such as George McGovern and Eugene McCarthy. Henceforth, the Democratic Party became the home team for cultural dissenters as well as for most ethnic minorities; it was the intellectuals' party *par excellence*. The electoral effects, however, were ambivalent. The electorate widely (and inaccurately) came to identify the Democratic Party with left-wing students. (Eugene McCarthy, for instance, was regarded by the conservatives as the candidate of lesbians, long-hairs, "commies," and other undesirables. In fact, he was a Catholic, traditionally schooled at St John's College. He had first been elected to the House of Representatives as part of Hubert Humphrey's staunchly anti-communist, Democratic Farmer–Labor Party in 1948.)

Militant US students also did their best to propagate the faith abroad. In Britain especially, US students helped to spread new lifestyles – from Maoism to Flower Power.

16 Quoted in Robert W. Tucker, *The Radical Left and American Foreign Policy*, Baltimore, The Johns Hopkins University Press, 1971, p. 10.
17 Bacciocco, *The New Left in America*, p. 239.

In Britain, the student revolution centered on institutions such as the LSE (London School of Economics), and also on the new universities built in the 1960s ("plate glass," as opposed to the "red brick" of older provincial universities). Oxford and Cambridge proved more resistant – their collegiate tradition with close personal links between teachers and students established through the tutorial system acted as powerful defenses. So did Oxbridge's avowedly élitist values, as dons (senior faculty) unself-consciously continued to congregate in Senior Common Rooms and to dine at "high table," looking down from above on the dining space in college halls for students. British universities were relatively small and well managed. Hence, the British student revolts (like those in Holland and Belgium) were altogether milder and better mannered than those in France, Germany, Italy, or the US.

The youth culture of the United States rapidly also transformed Britain when American hippies and Flower Power invaded, according to Noel Annan in his classic, *Our Age*. The counter-culture was about sex, fun and rebellion, but above all cannabis and LSD. Annan observed that some of his peers "enjoyed a second adolescence, began to smoke pot on weekends, got rid of their wives and married their secretaries or their student pupils. They began to grow their hair long and took to beards."[18] An important import was the women's liberation movement; another was gay liberation. British activists in the women's liberation movement were more genteel, better tempered, and less keen on bra-burning than their American sisters. The militant wing of English feminists, led by Germaine Greer (of *The Female Eunuch*, 1970, fame), complained above all at male dominance and men's odious ways. Most feminists in Britain (and also in America) were more concerned with equal rights and equal pay than with lesbianism or hostility to the masculine gender. British feminists had less success than their American sisters; for example, there were no laws or regulations requiring affirmative action, no quotas.

The other American import – gay liberation – shook up Britons more. Although the English had long had an active homosexual culture, it was also very private; to be caught brought jail and public shame. The gay liberation of the 1970s was different for it was public. Homosexual language, dress and behavior came from America. Homosexuality was no longer seen as "a tragic handicap," but rather became a glorious alternative. As homosexuality became politicized, public contempt and hatred reawakened. The Greater London Council (and others) began actively to promote the teaching of homosexuality in school, and the government cracked down. The 1960s and 1970s, nevertheless, Annan believes, saw a remarkable change in sexual attitudes and practices throughout society. Homosexuality became tolerated and the status of women improved.

Many in Britain thought the 1960s were full of "folly and futility" signifying decline and decay, but not Noel Annan. For him it was a time of great vitality in the arts and higher education. The country really acted as if it were liberated. British music (opera, ballet, and pop) were all at their height. New composers and new writers made the British theater burst into life and creativity. British TV and plays became the best in the world, and more and more books were published every year. In a final praise song Annan sums up the "sixties":

British designers became masters of zany, fetching, seductive fashion: the cooky look made life more gay. People began to dine out in the restaurants where the

18 Noel Annan, *Our Age. English Intellectuals between the World Wars: a Group Portrait*, New York, Random House, 1990, p. 240.

boys and girls who waited wore jeans . . . New magazines caught on, newspapers woke up and produced colour supplements and features, the arts became a feature and not a pimple on society's face. London became one of the world's musical centres in more ways than one. British pop music swept the world and English footballers regained their supremacy in the World Cup. It was a time when the manual worker began to take holidays abroad. Whatever the disappointments in politics, it was a time of great happiness. People felt it was good to be alive and at the same time learned concern for the unfortunate and dispossessed. They had had a taste of honey.[19]

France and Italy faced much bigger issues, including those derived from the sheer size of the new student bodies. Postwar demands for more "democratic" universities led to massive university expansion. But existing residential facilities, libraries, lecture rooms, and laboratories could not cope with the resultant huge student influx – not surprisingly there was trouble, trouble also among the rich. As Anthony Sampson, a British journalist put it: "When I taught for two years at a French university just after the revolt I came up against the full romanticism and double lives of the rebels: after ferocious demonstrations and strikes, many of the most radical students drove home to their parents in Neuilly or Passy."[20]

There were other differences between student activism in the US and in Western Europe respectively. In the US, the student movement, as we have seen, appealed to the post-World War II baby-boomers. In Germany, by contrast, the baby boom came ten years later than in the US – between 1955 and 1965. The German student movement owed nothing therefore to the baby boom. In Germany (and also in Italy), students in particular complained about aging professors (*Ordinarien*) whose reading was behind the times, whose lecture notes had become stale through repetition, and who yet ruled their respective departments with a rod of iron.

But academia's problems went much deeper. They included profound concern with the unmastered past: wartime collaboration in France, Fascist corruption in Italy, Nazism and genocide in Germany. In the immediate postwar years, these issues did not seem all that troubling to students. Having taken off their uniforms, most former soldiers put all their energy into rebuilding their respective countries (indeed, former officers often did remarkably well in switching from military to civilian skills). Except for a handful of intellectuals (including first-rate historians associated with bodies such as the Institute for Contemporary History in Munich), there had been little inclination to dwell on the horrors of the past. In Germany, by contrast, the 1960s generation widely questioned Germany's entire history – for German radicals mistakenly assumed that all roads in German history had led to the Third Reich.

Nevertheless, German radicals in particular drew on certain intellectual assumptions in the Nazi tradition. The Nazis had loathed political parties, detested the parliamentary *System*, and exalted their own *Bewegung* (movement). The new radicals did likewise. The Nazis had idealized the peasantry in Germany; the Radicals romanticized the cultivators of the Third World. The Nazis had loathed "International Jewry"; the radicals cursed "International Zionism." The Nazis had despised the US as a land of soul-less materialism;

19 Ibid., p. 156.
20 Anthony Sampson, *The Essential Anatomy of Britain: Democracy in Crisis*, London, Hodder and Stoughton, 1992, p. 71.

the radicals followed suit. The Nazis had condemned big cities; the radicals expressed contempt for suburbia. Both shared the same *Kulturunbehagen* (civilizational discontent) which German intellectuals had derived from the Romantic movement.

The German political scene had other exceptional features. Germany was a divided country. However successful politically and economically, the German Federal Republic did not as yet enjoy full sovereignty. The German Democratic Republic (East Germany) skillfully played on West German grievances, and spent a great deal of energy on pro-communist propaganda and infiltration in West Germany. West German student protesters were more apt to be pessimistic than their US confrères. (The "No Future" posters were everywhere.) The Germans were more inclined than the Americans to study the Marxist classics (especially the works of the young Marx), and also modern scholars such as Max Weber, Herbert Marcuse, and Jürgen Habermas. Feminist issues played a much smaller role in German universities at the time than in US institutions of higher learning. (The massive advancement of women into German universities came only after the student violence had subsided, and proceeded through quiet infiltration, not revolutionary agitation.) Unlike US students, German students drew on a great romantic heritage which, earlier in German history, had found expression in movements such as *Sturm und Drang* and the *Jugendbewegung*. Above all, German students were concerned more with university governance and *Chancengleichheit* (equal opportunity for all, a demand actually enshrined in the constitution of several German *Länder*).

The impact of the New Left in Germany, the US, or anywhere else should not, however, be exaggerated. In the US, party organizations were weaker, and student influence on politics was stronger than in Western Europe. But even among young people in the US, only about 15 percent supported the student left during the 1970s. Striking workers in the US, far from welcoming SDS support, jeered at leftist students wanting to join the picket line; such was the experience of SDS students from Columbia attempting to support a New York postal workers' strike. German militant Petra Kelly was horrified when she visited Moscow where freed political prisoners asked her to thank President Reagan for their release, and where ordinary workers raved about hamburgers and Coca-Cola as symbols of freedom.[21]

Leftists in general were no great threat to political establishments when they called for withdrawal from regular political parties and therefore reduced their own political influence. The great majority of young Germans went to school, did their stint in the *Bundeswehr*, trained for jobs – without the slightest desire to overthrow society. In Germany, as elsewhere, the left's impact was selective also in a geographical sense; many universities remained little affected. Nevertheless, radicals for a time dominated certain schools such as the Free University of Berlin. (There was no draft in Berlin; hence Berlin attracted draft evaders from all over West Germany.) Oppositional groups such as the *Notgemeinschaft für eine freie Universität* in West Berlin worked in semi-secrecy – in a city mainly protected by American arms. Militant students drew heavily on the US experience, as depicted by television, or by visiting lecturers from the US, such as Jacob Taubes. (Taubes preached with equal passion hatred of America, and also what are now called alternate lifestyles.) There was always a particular undertone of intolerance. German militants in theory might exalt the *Lustprinzip* over the *Leistungsprinzip* (joy over achievement),

21 Arnold Beichman, "Petra Kelly's Revealing Encounter," *New Perspectives Quarterly*, Winter 1988, p. 9. See also his most perceptive *Anti-American Myths: their Causes and Consequences*, New Brunswick, Transaction, 1993.

but there was covert approval for violence – not merely among murderous extremists such as the Baader–Meinhof gang, but also among the militant rank and file.

Italy in the 1960s faced a new generation, many of whose members failed to understand either the Cold War or the rationale for the creation of the European Economic Community (1958). Italian youngsters grew up in a time of rising living standards and economic growth, with higher expectations and sharper criticism of the political system than their parents. They were disgusted by "partocracy" and political corruption with its linkage to organized crime; they sought to use politics for the purpose of changing society. Near chaos and anarchy resulted in the larger cities through political violence when the Red Brigades copied Mafia methods of kidnapping and murder. The Red Brigades were anti-capitalist, anti-bourgeois, and anti-parliamentarian; they envisaged the US as the center of imperialism. University teachers extolled the merits of revolutionary radicalism and Leninism. The papers on the extreme left – *Lotta Continua* (continuous struggle), *Avanguardia Operaia* (workers vanguard) – daily called for violence, sabotage, and resistance to public authorities.

In public, the Communists would have nothing to do with Red Brigade tactics, though in private Communists welcomed the weakening of the bourgeois state. (It was socialist intellectuals who were more apt to make overt excuses for errant anarchists.) The Red Brigades, however, destroyed themselves. The kidnapping and murder of Aldo Moro, the Christian Democratic leader, in 1978, decisively turned public opinion against the terrorists. Many youngsters thereafter lost interest in politics and unions; they felt that politics went in hand with crime syndicates, and that elections were useless. Disillusioned young men and women then became concerned mainly with finding a job, courting a lover, succeeding in their studies, and enjoying friends and family.

Student unrest on a large scale broke out in Paris in 1968. Trouble began in Nanterre over minor issues such as student housing and student representation on university councils. But discord grew as *lycéens* (secondary school students) joined university students, and as students combined with striking industrial workers. The New Left in France drew on a multiplicity of Marxists (including Maoist and Trotskyite) traditions within the French *avant garde*. French radicals took their revolution seriously; the "events" of May 1968 were bloody, with barricades in the streets and fierce fights between police and demonstrators.[22] But appearances were deceptive. The Fifth Republic lacked a French equivalent of Italy's Red Brigades. The French public at large overwhelmingly backed the Fifth Republic, including de Gaulle's support for nuclear weaponry (1968, the year of the Paris *événements*, was also the year in which France exploded its first hydrogen bomb – with little public opposition). De Gaulle called elections and he was returned by the voters with an overwhelming vote of confidence. (A good many adherents of the New Left later became disenchanted and in the late 1970s turned to the New Right.)

From the mid-1970s, revolutionary ardor subsided both in the US and in Western Europe. The US left Vietnam, universities reformed themselves or seemed to do so; the young became older though not necessarily wiser. US activists increasingly turned to

---

22 For an idealized account see Hervé Hamon and Patrick Rotman's massive book *Génération*, Paris, Seuil, 1987. A major work is Raymond Aron, *The Elusive Revolution*, trans. Gordon Clough, New York, Praeger, 1969. Also see Sunil Khilnani, *Arguing Revolution: The Intellectual Left in Postwar France*, New Haven, Yale University Press, 1993. A brilliant exposé of the wider intellectual background is Tony Judt, *Past Imperfect: French Intellectuals 1944–1956*, Berkeley, CA, University of California Press, 1992.

feminist, gay, lesbian, and environmentalist causes; ethnic studies and multiculturalism played an increasing role in US secondary schools and universities. In Western Europe militance likewise declined. Activists turned to ecological issues (for instance, the Greens in West Germany). The rank and file widely became disillusioned with politics and parties; instead, there was a retreat into personal fulfillment summarized in the Spanish as the "three Cs": *casa, coche, compañera* (house, car, girlfriend).[23]

The New Left also affected religious life in the West. The Protestant mainline churches turned to the left; the World Council of Churches identified itself with the Third World as against the West. The peace movements in Britain and Germany owed a major debt to religious pacifists drawn from, or influenced by, Protestant churches. The Catholic Church also modified its former anti-communist militance partially in response to the new course set by Pope John XXIII and the Second Vatican Council (1962–3). The Vatican, in papal encyclicals and official newspaper editorials, several times in the postwar world, claimed communism was closer to Christianity than was capitalism! Liberation theology affected young Catholic priests and nuns who became soldiers in the anti-war, anti-capitalist and anti-American empire movements of the late 1960s and 1970s. While they condemned "cut-throat capitalism," they seldom criticized "cut-throat socialism."

Above all, the churches took an important part in the so-called peace movement in Western Europe. From the 1960s onward, there were some of the greatest peace demonstrations ever seen in Europe; churchmen, students, activists joined with housewives and workers to protest the Western military buildup. (No demonstrations of a similar size were ever launched against, say, the Soviet invasion of Afghanistan or the horrors of the Gulag archipelago.) Not that Western Europeans as a whole had become disenchanted with NATO. (On the contrary, public opinion polls indicated that German confidence in the alliance and in the *Bundeswehr* continued to rise during the 1970s.) But the peace cause continued to captivate, above all, the young and the well educated. Their hostility to what they regarded as US monopoly capitalism and US war-mongering was a legacy of the New Left. Neutralism, of course, came in many different guises; so did hostility to nuclear armaments (strongest in mainly Protestant countries such as Britain, Germany, Holland, weakest in France). But secular and religious pacifists in alliance did mange to mobilize substantial forces which – briefly and deceptively – may have benefited Soviet foreign policy.[24]

How Much Did the New Left Achieve?

In the short run, student revolutionaries disrupted campuses, and, for a spell, radicalized hosts of students. Soon the resistance to the Vietnam War took up most of the New Left's concern. The SDS increased from 600 members in 1963 to over 100,000 members in 1969. US participants in demonstrations against the war grew in numbers: from an estimated 25,000 to 500,000 in 1969. The movement not only got bigger, it also became more militant and more concerned radically to transform society. Late in the 1960s the New Left tried to organize the poor, directing student-centered education and radicalizing workshops, especially on university campuses and in factories. Some

23 See Walter Laqueur "Youth and Politics," *The Washington Quarterly*, Summer 1985, pp. 5–11.
24 L.H. Gann, "Reflections on the Western European Peace Movement," in Dennis L. Bark, ed., *To Promote Peace: US Foreign Policy in the mid-1980s*, Stanford, CA, Hoover Institution Press, 1984, pp. 97–114.

college campuses, perceived as supportive, safe havens or staffed with a radical faculty, were overwhelmed by the movement. Conservatives and others who disagreed with the radicals or supported the war were harassed and intimidated by class disruptions, sit-ins, threatening telephone calls, or worse.

Some campuses were more combustible than others: Stanford and Berkeley were more radical than the University of Chicago, for example. San Francisco State, an urban school with a liberal-left profile, was far more apt to riot than San Jose State. New York University collapsed into near anarchy, as did Columbia University, but Fordham University and St John's did not. Private schools, where the students paid for their tuition, were usually less prone to strike or occupy buildings than state-run schools. (Columbia, Stanford, and Yale were major exceptions to this generalization.) Parents and policemen turned into universal scapegoats – until such times as rebels in turn formed their own families. The US military, capitalism, and US imperialism were the principal enemies of radical students. Criminals, by contrast, were relegated to the ranks of society's victims, together with blacks, gays, Chicanos, Chicanas, and North American Indians – an incongruous medley.

The New Left collapsed with startling rapidity. (In 1968, the SDS in the US may have numbered 100,000 members; a year later, it had already been reduced to a handful of Maoists.) Few activists stuck with the revolutionary movements. The activists had overwhelmingly derived from privileged families with supportive parents; the activists usually did well at school and mostly found their way into well-paid jobs (especially those connected with the so-called helping professions, the law, college teaching, welfare services), and into more conventional politics (as did former activists such as Tom Hayden and Mario Savio). Even at the height of its influence, moreover, the "movement" had only captured a relatively small proportion of Americans – a fact obscured by television imagery. Most students simply wanted to go to class, do their work, and graduate. According to a Gallup poll investigation into the attitude of persons aged between 30 and 49 in 1993, only 16 percent had been involved in any organized protests or other social causes during the 1960s and the 1970s in the US; 15 percent had experimented with psychedelic drugs or regularly smoked marijuana; 27 percent had dressed as a hippie. Of the respondents, 83 percent thought that, in retrospect, the changes brought about in the 1960s had been deleterious by promoting more liberal attitudes to drugs; 61 percent thought that the changes had been bad by diffusing greater tolerance of homosexuality; 54 percent considered the changes bad by furthering the acceptance of premarital sex. On the other hand, 84 percent welcomed greater willingness to question government, and 82 percent applauded changes in the role of women.[25]

A united "Woodstock Generation," a uniform "Vietnam Generation," was a figment of journalistic imagination because the media gave disproportionate attention to the small number of student leftists. Instead, a fragmented mass of single-issue groups evolved from the New Left, and multiplied: deconstructionists, critics of "dead white European males" (DWEMs) and Western culture; multiculturalists; advocates of ethnic studies; gay and lesbian supporters; feminists. The "politically correct" movement was fathered by the New Left. Even though a majority of Americans opposed New Left ideas, these nevertheless dominated the élite culture and universities.

25   Reported in *San Francisco Chronicle*, 7 August 1989, p. 4. Also see Philip Abrams, "Rites de Passage: the Conflict of Generations in Industrial Society," *Journal of Contemporary History*, vol. 5, no. 1, 1970, pp. 175–90.

The New Left's impact on practical affairs was ambiguous. In foreign affairs, the New Left had little impact on transnational organizations such as the European Community (EC). The European peace movement interfered with, but did not disrupt, NATO. Indirectly, however, the student radicals left their mark on foreign policy. Student militance, as noted earlier, played its part in getting the US out of Vietnam. The Vietnam débâcle in turn made US presidents more cautious in foreign policy, more inclined also to consult with Congress than presidents had been wont to do in the olden days of the "imperial presidency." The New Left therefore had a role in shrinking America's role in the world – at least until the Reagan presidency. (Even President Bush had to build a coalition within the UN so as to intervene in Kuwait and Somalia.) The New Left and libertarians helped cause the end of the draft and largely exempted from military service the upper half of American society.

The student militants and their allies likewise had a profound effect on political styles. Olden-day establishments had been able to laugh at their own foibles in brilliant operettas such as *HMS Pinafore. Die Fledermaus*, or *Call Me Madam*. There was not much humor within the American New Left, or among its cultural heirs in departments of women's studies, gay and lesbian, and African-American studies. The new disciplines took over the New Left's cultural self-righteousness and anger. Politics, especially academic politics, received a new infusion of intolerance through the "politically correct" movement. At the same time, militants acted as if the American people had become a nation of victims, and as if victimhood were a guarantee of virtue.[26] In a more diffuse manner, the cultural revolution promoted a host of morally approved causes; organic foods, spiritual self-enhancement, multiculturalism (though not the serious study of foreign languages), pop psychology, gay and lesbian rights, rock, Chicano activism, Native American activism, and hosts of others. All displayed the same fervor: "Repent ye! Repent ye!," the talking heads seemed to say from the box. "The last day is at hand."[27]

The most fervent were the US women's movements. Their style owed a great debt to the black example. Activist women – like blacks – were divided into moderates who simply wanted equality of opportunity, and militants who stressed the superior moral worth allegedly inherent in femininity or blackness, as the case might be. Feminists, like black militants, regarded themselves as national role models. Radical feminists also spoke and acted as if they were a minority. They did so, partly because they were hypnotized by the black example, partly because "authentic" women, those who shared the militants' goal, were indeed a minority. (They were mainly professional women – teachers, lawyers, professors, physicians – mostly out of sympathy with those working-class wives who stayed at home and "baked cookies.") The US women's movement had long pre-dated the 1960s. US women had learned self-reliance on the turbulent frontier and in equally turbulent slums occupied by immigrants. By the end of the nineteenth century, European women activists had already been struck by the special spirit of independence displayed by their American sisters. The 1960s gave a great additional impact to militant feminism – this at a time when women were entering the labor force and universities in unparalleled numbers, and when more and more specialized jobs became available to the well educated. Hence, the very language of American politics

26 Charles J. Sykes, *A Nation of Victims: the Decay of the American Character*, New York, St Martin's Press, 1992.
27 Godfrey Hodgson, *America in our Time: from World War II to Nixon: What Happened and Why*, New York, Vintage Books, 1978, p. 88.

changed, as even tycoons appointed "diversity consultants" to improve corporate sensitivity. The New Left, then, was one of several important agents in expanding equality in America and in "raising consciousness" among women.

The New Left was therefore of importance, not so much for creating new issues, but for speeding existing trends. In the US and abroad, students greatly strengthened the anti-war movement, but opposition to the war was rife not only on the campuses. In the end, even conservatively minded Americans increasingly lost confidence, once the Vietnam conflict appeared to them, under the existing rules of engagement, as a "no-win war." Overall, however, campus pacifism did not prevail. Opinion polls after Vietnam repeatedly ranked the US military as the national institution most respected by the public. (Surveys in Britain, post-communist Russia, and Germany largely paralleled US findings in their respective countries.)

Student activists similarly took an impressive part in the US civil rights struggle. Nevertheless, the black American's battle for equality had likewise long preceded the students' intervention; the struggle was not decided on the campuses, but by the courts, backed by the might of the federal government. In opposing discrimination, black Americans owed infinitely more to their own efforts than to those of student activists; still the New Left helped expand equality in the US. Affirmative action programs also owed much to the student radicals; sit-ins and demonstrations pressured college administrations to hire more women, blacks, gays and lesbians, and to establish ethnic studies programs.

The same generalization applies to growing public interest in ecology. Student militants helped to promote the cause, but they had in no wise initiated ecological concerns in the Western world. Regards for ecological issues are of an older vintage, and were originally associated with the right rather than the left. (In Germany, the movement for *Naturschutz* (protection of nature) had dated from the Wilhelminian era. In Britain, the first demands for safeguarding the countryside derived from the "huntin', shootin' and fishin' set.") But the left changed the meaning of environmentalism; hunters and boy scouts became the enemy, as did industrialists. Rachel Carson's *The Silent Spring* (1962) had a profound impact in the US and on the birth of the environmental movement.

The student left likewise contributed to a political mind-set in which welfare programs became accepted as political entitlements. But again the growth of the welfare state was a universal Western phenomenon. The creation of the welfare state had long preceded the New Left; the New Left merely furthered the cause. (The welfare state's early architects had been conservatives such as Bismarck in Germany and Disraeli in Britain.) All over the Western world the welfare state continued to grow until the 1980s, quite irrespective of student activism. The most outstanding examples in the Western world were Sweden and Holland. In Sweden, the Uppsala School of Economics, with its socialist commitment, had for many years prevailed in politics – without benefit of student militance. In Holland, the student movement had likewise been restrained – "cheeky more than angry."[28] Yet nowhere in Europe did the welfare state make greater progress than in Holland.

In so far as the Cold War was concerned, the New Left was ambivalent in its effects. The Old Left of the 1930s had produced a handful of men willing to spy against their own countries on behalf of the Soviet Union. Many more had been willing to wear a

28 Flora Lewis, *Europe: Road to Unity*, New York, Simon and Schuster, 1992, p. 258.

foreign uniform to fight against fascism in Spain. Adherents of the New Left neither spied nor fought abroad, but indirectly the New Left weakened the West ideologically by attributing most of the world's evil to the capitalists, especially to US capitalists. The radical student movement was anti-military and anti-CIA; recruiting for both institutions became difficult on American campuses. Extremists identified CIA agents in US embassies overseas; by doing so they blew the cover of some of these agents and caused them to be killed. On the other hand, radicals may also have unwittingly harmed the Soviets by depicting the West as weaker and more divided than it was, thereby misleading Moscow about its real and assumed enemies.

According to Myron Magnet in *The Dream and the Nightmare: the Sixties Legacy to the Underclass* (1992), the counter-culture may also have contributed to urban poverty. The counter-culture trashed Western civilization in general, but especially American virtues of hard work. Personal responsibility was rejected; honesty, thrift, and sexual morality were derided. Society supposedly owed citizens entitlements: welfare benefits; inexpensive public housing; affirmative action to undo centuries of "white male oppression"; job training; special education; multicultural education; courses in ethnic cheerleading; sensitivity training. All this came to be known as PC, the "political correctness" movement. The new order, therefore, aided the growth of the underclass as the new counter-ethic discouraged people from taking responsibility for their lives. Senator Daniel Moynihan blames the "moral deregulation" of the 1960s for an explosion of deviancy, a growth of single-parent households and of illegitimacy, of increased drug use and crime.

The cultural revolution did particular harm by attempting to assure the sons and daughters of blacks and Hispanics (including Third World immigrants) that there was no point in striving and straining for advancement, that militants should drop out, rather than permit themselves to be co-opted by the "system." (A rich man's son or daughter could easily abandon the revolution, clean up, dress in conventional attire, and go to graduate school or into father's business. By contrast, a poor drop-out, having left college, found the road to prosperity infinitely harder.)

The linkage between the cultural revolution and the decline of the black family in the US remains to be investigated. According to scholars such as Andrew Billingsgate, the breakup of so many black families in the US was caused by unemployment and welfare payments tied to an absent husband. Black men who lost their jobs often walked out of their marriages. A more general explanation blames white racism, or simply poverty. But the black two-parent family had not been seriously disrupted during the Great Depression. Black marriage rates only fell, and illegitimacy only increased, during the 1960s when the country prospered, jobs were plentiful, and black as well as white incomes increased.[29] Racism had certainly been stronger in the US during the 1930s than during the 1960s, yet drug consumption thereafter went up. By contrast, persecuted Jews in the Nazi era did not take to drugs, even though the technology of producing drugs was known. Neither do poverty and physical deprivation alone explain the blacks' predicament. Londoners just after World War II lived in a city where many houses were destroyed; they received little or no coal in winter; they drew weekly rations whose inadequacy would have triggered a prison riot 30 years later; but there was almost no drug addiction and little serious crime at that time. Rather, it was the cultural revolution of the 1960s, with its lionization of drugs, its well-publicized contempt for traditional values, its

29 See Thomas Sowell's classics on the subject, including *Markets and Minorities*, New York, Basic Books, 1981; and *The Economics and Politics of Race*, New York, Morrow, 1983.

eulogies for radical chic, and its libertinism which bore most heavily on the weakest members of society, especially the black poor.

The cultural revolution had other unintended consequences. The revolution enriched fashion designers as even conventional fashions became lighter and brighter. The cultural revolution created a new demand for drug paraphernalia, coffee bars, boutiques, craft stores specializing in leather work, silver, pottery, and other hand-made goods. There were new markets for specialists in finger painting; for purveyors of cymbals and cymbalos, dashikis and saris; for "underground" publishers; for distributors of pornographic literature; for impresarios of "underground" dance companies; and for a host of other entrepreneurs. There was a new tolerance for homosexuals. The gay liberation movement was part of the general social protest revolution of the 1960s generation.[30]

The youth culture's new sensitivity went with avowed hatred for fathers, headmasters, police officers, soldiers, civil servants, and other persons supposedly imbued with repressive personality patterns. In fact, the politics of resentment were subsidized by the Establishment; in the US, for instance, through the National Endowments for Art and the Humanities. (Without money from the tax-supported Arts Council in Britain, and other official subsidies, the little presses and little magazines could hardly have stayed in business. Similarly, the Nuffield Foundation put money into the "underground" press.)[31] Above all, the New Left and the cultural revolution profoundly affected the universities, particularly in the US. A much larger proportion of the population attended college in the US than anywhere else in the world, yet the college population kept growing. In its quest for social equality, the US became a credentializing society. Colleges became for the US what the Church had been to olden-time Spain, and the army to olden-time Prussia: the country's defining institution. The road to success almost universally led through college. Americans boasted that Jack was as good as his master.

The campus became the revolution's home ground, and in turn was profoundly affected by student turmoil. Militants attempted to change the rules of the academic game by giving more power to students. German universities, for instance, widely introduced *Drittelparität* or *Viertelparität*, according to which one-third or one-quarter of the representation on governing boards was allocated respectively to professors and lecturers, students, and university employees. But such constitutional devices did not avail students in the long run. Students came and students went; students, moreover, easily got bored with governance. Administrators, by contrast, stayed; and continued to gain in power, prestige, and remuneration. By contrast, student activists failed to make permanent even quite minor reforms. (In France, for instance, militants could not abolish *bizutage*, the disgusting and often cruel rites of initiation imposed on freshmen entering the *grandes écoles*.) Universities became more bureaucratic as contending academic lobbies multiplied and universities developed into miniature welfare states. But the radical movement did succeed in introducing multiculturalism and other PC movements into the university. "Western Civ" courses, DWEMs ("dead white European males") were trashed; speech codes and re-education courses attempted to re-educate white male "chauvinists" and the politically insensitive of both sexes.

US student activists believed that universities existed to improve mankind. This assumption was deeply rooted in the American past. (As early as the 1860s, Sir Charles Dilke, an English traveler, had considered the "chiefest care" of American universities

30 See Martin Duberman, *Stonewall*, New York, Dutton, 1993.
31 Peter Fryer, "A Map of the Underground," *Encounter*, vol. 29, no. 4, October 1967, pp. 6–20.

"the war with crime, the war with sin, the war with death.")[32] Modern militants followed in this tradition. In their estimation, women's studies would promote gender equality; African-American studies would assist in black liberation; Chicano studies would rehabilitate oppressed Mexicans; gay studies would make homosexuality acceptable to the bigoted majority. Freed of Puritan bonds, artists would rejoice in producing new masterpieces that would delight the people and elevate their consciousness. But achievement in these disciplines failed to meet expectations. Ethnic cheerleading courses did not attract many whites; feminist and lesbian courses failed to convert *hoi polloi*.

The universities had other problems. Until the 1970s, jobs in universities and associated institutions expanded. So did posts for graduates in the public sectors. (Indeed, radicals in Germany talked of "the long march through the institutions" whereby radicals would ascend, by a Fabian strategy, into leading positions in the welfare services, the media, the universities, and thereby ultimately control society.) In Europe and the US, former radicals advanced into important jobs, especially in university teaching and administration. Some of these turned out to be excellent scholars, such as Nobel Prize laureate D.C. North. But in Europe, at any rate, their political impact was limited: strong among the Greens and peace movements, but weak elsewhere. In East Germany, "real existing socialism" failed in the very sight of West German "Sixty-Eighters" (participants in the massive demonstrations of 1968). The German Democratic Republic's moral bankruptcy was a fact that the Sixty-Eighters could not help but confront. In the US, Marxism remained more theoretical, and therefore retained greater attraction for leftist intellectuals. Moreover, the US had a much stronger millenarian tradition than Europe; hope for a radical reformation of society thereafter burned more brightly in the US than in Europe. Only in the US did Marxism retain a hold on the academic imagination.

New disciplines, such as gender studies, created a new vocabulary, new academic lobbies, and a new orthodoxy. In the US the new disciplines in practice excluded conservatives from teaching posts in women's studies, gay studies, ethnic studies, and similar courses. Conservatives were also unwelcome in area studies, particularly in the Latin American and African fields. (According to a survey completed in 1991, only 2 percent of professors engaged in area studies described themselves as "conservative" in a country where over half of the public did so.)[33] The new courses rejoiced in the injunction of olden-day Bohemians *épatez les bourgeois* (shock the Philistine). To give just one example, Stanford University in 1992 offered a course known as "Feminist Studies 138A," otherwise known as "Lesbian/Gay Identities and Representations," designed to address topics such as medical models of homosexuality, geographics of desire, lesbian histories and identities, drag and transgender, media appropriations and cultural politics.[34] Student demand for such courses was, in fact, small. But activists strove mightily to expand their own power by making ethnic and gender studies into academic requirements – reminiscent of *Diamat* (dialectical materialism) once taught with much acclaim and negligible effect at East German universities.

32 Charles Wentworth Dilke, *Greater Britain: a Record of Travel in English-speaking Countries during 1866 and 1867*, Philadelphia, J.B. Lippincott, 1869, vol. 1, p. 72.
33 "Politics of the Professoriate," *The American Enterprise*, July to August 1991, pp. 86–7; L.H. Gann, "African Studies: a Dissident View," *Academic Questions*, Spring 1989, vol. 2, no. 2, pp. 80–90.
34 *The Stanford Review*, 5 October 1993, p. 3.

For all their commitment to creativity, the New Left produced no literary nor socio-logical nor historical masterpieces. The giants of Western thought at the time – scholars such as Raymond Aron, Sir Isaiah Berlin, Sidney Hook, Sir Karl Popper – opposed communism and sided with the moderates. The New Left in the US and Germany alike professed to admire Germany's Weimar culture. But the New Left intellectuals could not replicate its achievements. There was among the militants too much drug abuse, too much anger, too much contempt for civic virtue, too much self-pity. Above all, they lacked two indispensable qualifications for literary achievement: *Sitzfleisch* (perseverance, self-discipline, literally a well-padded behind), and a sense of tragedy. Votaries of the "hip" lifestyle had taken pride in radically differing from the common herd. But the hip lifestyle was itself spread by mass marketing, and thereby negated its own principles.

As noted earlier, students played a part in ending the draft, and in forcing the US to withdraw from Vietnam. University-trained politicians, influenced directly or indirectly by the student left, later helped to reshape the Democratic Party where old-fashioned bosses and trade-union leaders were reduced to obscurity and a university-trained élite became dominant. (College-trained people with a social conscience would later serve Presidents Carter and Clinton in the cabinet and senior executive posts, especially those connected with social welfare. But whereas both Eisenhower and Nixon had appointed trade unionists to high office, not a single unionist served in the Carter or Clinton cabinets.)

Ironically enough, the leftists' performance was least effective in those political and economic studies in which leftists claimed special expertise. They saw themselves – so to speak – as the cartographers of a new world. But they drew the wrong maps. Contrary to the leftists' predictions, socialist countries such as Vietnam, Guinea, and Cuba remained poverty-stricken and corrupt. "Real existing socialism" proved a universal failure. West Germany was freer and more prosperous than East Germany, Austria than Czechoslovakia, South Korea than North Korea, Taiwan than China, Puerto Rico than Cuba. There was no understanding within the New Left of the profound crises that would destroy the socialist system. This purblindness extended to West German "Establishment" research concerning East Germany right next door. As an expert at the Free University of Berlin put it succinctly,

> The [East German] dictatorship relied on covert force; arbitrary arrests; closing of the borders, prohibitions of travel; aggression against the Czechoslovak Peoples' Republic; persecution of political opponents; extension of the espionage system and the security apparatus; and incitement to crimes against humanity. But these themes were not considered fit for research; their investigation largely remained an academic taboo until such time as the GDR had collapsed.[35]

The "sixties" culture had tried to reinterpret history in terms of race, class, and gender. In fact, these categories played little part in the collapse of communism in the Soviet Union and its satellites. The revolution against communism hinged on nationalism, religion, and the struggle for freedom and democracy through a free-market economy – categories which the New Left had ignored, or derided.

35 Forschungsverband "SED Staat," Freie Universität Berlin. Project Description by Klaus Schroeder, 1993.

The militants' political cartography proved no more applicable to the US. The US was seen as an interlocking mosaic of "differing communities" – blacks, women, homosexuals, Latinos, and others – to be led by "community leaders" or "opinion leaders" whose cross-cultural bargaining would equitably allocate power and wealth. (Lacking traditional European class divisions, Americans put more emphasis on race and ethnicity. Even the most chauvinist Russian never regarded Pushkin, greatest of Russian poets, as a black man. But Pushkin had an African grandfather and would have been classed as black by African-American studies or a US affirmative action board.) The model, however, was flawed because it did not make adequate allowance for those multiple loyalties that transcended those of mere race and ethnicity. Most Americans did not look on themselves as "hyphenated" citizens, as their grandfathers and grandmothers had done. The ordinary American could not easily be cast into the simple categories devised by academic activists. Most families were multi-ethnic. Americans of whatever color or national origin, moreover, did not share their "opinion leaders' " opinions. Many older African-Americans do not consider themselves as African: they prefer to call themselves blacks, colored, or Negroes. Mexicans oppose abortion in far higher percentages than most Americans, but Mexican-American politicians and academics are mostly pro-choice. On affirmative action, Mexicans are split about 50–50, but only 2 percent of the Mexican-American opinion-makers oppose affirmative action.[36]

Clearly, the New Left helped to change US political style and popular culture in a variety of ways. Two decades later, even conservative, God-fearing Americans thought nothing of going to an espresso bar (unknown in the 1950s) where customers might be served by young women wearing granny dresses, adorned with silver bangles, and perhaps silver nose rings. In provincial towns, as well as metropolitan centers, shoppers could find organic supermarkets where bookshelves exhibited journals with titles such as *Sufism, Mother Earth News, Vegetarian, Self,* or *Buzzworm,* and environmentalists and conservationists worked to save the spotted owl, the whale or old forests. Nevertheless, these changes were limited: according to public opinion polls, the institutions most respected remained the armed forces, the local church, and the local police force.

The New Left took pride in its commitment to artistic creativity. Legatees of the New Left later made successful careers as practicing artists, art consultants, directors of art galleries, artists-in-residence at major universities, and art bureaucrats – a mighty host. But, despite great expenditure of public and private funds, their collective effort produced no great art. To put the matter cautiously, the National Endowment for the Arts did not equal as a patron the Medici, or even those minor German princes whose courts had once made Germany famous for artistic endeavor.

The New Left wished to fight for liberty. Militants (and even many moderates) therefore derided commitment to "law and order" as fascism in disguise. But none of these critics realized that criminals were the poor people's worst enemies, and that sustained political terrorism formed the greatest conceivable threat to any country's prosperity. The revolutionaries desired to smash the shackles of traditional sexual morality. But for all the revolutionaries' propaganda, the majority of Americans stuck to the sexual values of their forebears. (The US Census Survey 1992–3 found, to almost everyone's surprise, that about 94 percent of all American couples living together were married;

---

36 Peter Skerry, *Mexican Americans: the Ambivalent Minority*, New York, Free Press, 1993; L.H. Gann and Peter Duignan, *The Hispanics in the United States: a History*, Boulder, Colo., Westview Press, 1986.

extra-marital affairs were rare. And only 2.2 percent of men stated that they had had sex with another man during the preceding year.)[37] Anti-militarists to the core, the revolutionaries failed to realize that in the US the military remained the most respected of public institutions. Committed secularists, the revolutionaries did not realize that – despite the sociologists' talk about modernization and secularization – the mass of Americans remained committed to the belief in religion and a divinely ordered world.

The revolutionary leftists wished to liberate youth from their elders. Yet it was from the 1960s onward that extended adolescence became a problem for American society, as young men and women increasingly called on their parents for financial help, residential facilities, and aid in child-rearing. The revolutionaries had wished to defend the poor and downtrodden, but the militants did not understand how they inadvertently praised the worst enemies of the poor – drugs, lawlessness, sexual libertinism, and the breakup of families. Particularly reprehensible was the romanticization of drugs. Drugs had long been known, but were not in wide use during the 1930s and the 1940s even though poverty and racism were much more prevalent than a generation ago. It was from the 1960s that crime rapidly expanded, and that drug usage in the US was applauded by a great army of pop singers, pop poets, pop professors, and pop psychologists. Anarchist Abbie Hoffman's "Revolution for the hell of it" turned into a cult of personal irresponsibility.

The militant left remained unable to read those danger signals for socialism that came alike from the Soviet Union, the Warsaw Pact satellites, and the People's Republic of China. The left remained intellectually divided, isolated, unable and unwilling to establish a dialogue with their critics. The left's attack on traditional values provoked a powerful counter-movement, the New Right, as Fundamentalists rallied in defense of religion, supported by many unbelievers. Revolutionary leftists could not cope intellectually with obvious truths about society: capitalism in Western Europe had been a success; socialism in Eastern Europe a failure. Campus activists derided the US, but it was the US that proved the world's most stable multiracial society: more civic minded, more creative, more stable than the former Soviet Union, former Yugoslavia, India, Sri Lanka, Nigeria, or any other multi-ethnic country anywhere. In North America and Europe alike, the ordinary citizen disliked revolutionary socialism in any shape or form. Nowhere on the globe did ordinary people accept the leftist intelligentsia's tacit claim to act as a moral role model and moral reference group for the nation at large. In the public mind, the New Left rather remained associated with drugs, family disruption, and civic irresponsibility. In the academic sphere, the New Left's very dogmatism helped to set off an anti-Marxist reaction – even in France where Marxists had dominated intellectual life. (The new philosophers included thinkers such as Alain Finkielkraut who returned to humanist values, and also put his message in lucid French.)

The New Left offered a deliberate challenge to the religious and social values held by the vast majority of Americans. The New Left thereby helped to set off a massive

---

37 "Sex, Lies, and Statistics," *The Economist,* 23 October 1992, p. 32. Nevertheless, sexually transmitted diseases increased, especially AIDS, and illegitimate births went from about 10 percent in 1960 to 25 percent in 1993. As regards religious beliefs, almost half the Americans believed that human beings were created by God – without descending from lower life forms – just 10,000 years ago. Only 11 percent of Americans opted for a pure evolution perspective, holding that God had no part in the process. See Frank Newport, "Half of Americans Believe in Creationist Origins of Man," *Gallup Poll Monthly,* no. 336, September 1993, pp. 24–6.

reaction on the right. Like the New Left, the New Right had two separate wings: the *engagés* committed to violence, and the constitutionalists who put their faith in legal means. Right-wing extremists attributed the world's ills to the Jews, blacks, Mexicans, IRS agents, lesbians, FBI investigators, homosexuals, and the Queen of England. The militants on the right shared with those on the left the same addiction to conspiratorial theories of history, the same brutality in dealing with their enemies, and the same self-pity with regard to their own pretended sufferings. But the militants on the right packed far more guns than the New Left had ever done. (In the US, right-wing thugs practiced mass murder by explosives; they also targeted abortion clinics. European skinheads, by contrast, more often beat up or killed immigrants, especially foreigners of the Muslim faith (Turks in Germany, Pakistanis in Britain, Algerians in France).

Immensely more powerful than the violent right was the new Religious Right. This drew its strength from Evangelical and Pentecostal Protestants, conservative Catholics, and Orthodox Jews. Its supporters were respectable citizens – the sort who directed Little Leagues, participated in parent–teacher associations, ran for school boards, and supported local charities. Like the activists on the left, the Religious Right sued for their causes in courts, put up candidates in local elections, and sought office in existing political organizations (especially the Republican Party). Between them, they formed a far more influential lobby than any grouping on the left. Henceforth, they stood resolved to win those culture wars which, in their view, the New Left had initiated.

PART III

Politics in the Atlantic Community,
from the mid-1970s to the 1990s

10

US Politics: Ford to Reagan

The Ford–Carter Interregnum, 1974–1981

Richard Nixon's resignation left the supreme executive office to his vice-president, Gerald Ford. Nixon had selected Ford as his running mate in 1973, a safe man, all-American in manner, speech, and appearance. Ford was an ex-athlete, a team player, loyal, solid, reliable.[1] An ex-football player, he had suffered injuries which occasionally caused him to stumble. His best friends would not have called him brilliant – "a Ford, not a Lincoln!" His opponents called him worse. ("Too dumb to walk and chew gum at the same time," according to Lyndon Johnson.) An Eisenhower Republican, he was associated with the East Coast Establishment. (His first decision on assuming office was to pick Nelson Rockefeller as his vice-president.) After many years of passionate controversy, Ford's presidency would once more represent the cause of moderation.

Ford had some attractive qualities. He spoke well to small audiences, albeit not to large assemblies – and not on television. Like Reagan, Ford was a great deal brighter than the media élites assumed. Above all, he had raised a large family; he lived modestly; there was not the faintest whiff of financial corruption in his life. These were important qualifications at a time when distrust of politics was in the air. The 1960s had seen bitter unrest over the Vietnam War, campus protests, and racial violence. The 1970s witnessed successive oil shocks, rising interest rates, surging inflation, the Watergate scandal, and also malfeasance on many levels of government. Americans have always expressed disdain for politicians as a group. (Most US citizens would have been surprised to hear the truth: that US Congress people were usually well qualified, that US presidents were men of far above average ability, and that official corruption in the US was small compared with other countries of sub-continental size such as India, the Soviet Union, or Brazil.) The Americans' sense of unease was heightened by investigative journalists and adversarial newscasters on television. But the most relentless bloodhound could not have found much wrong with Ford. He lived modestly; he had never set aside much money. By common consent, he was a man to be trusted.

1 For Ford, see W.S. Baroody, Sr, ed., *A Discussion with Gerald R. Ford: the American Presidency*, Washington, DC, The Institute, 1977; Richard Reeves, *A Ford, Not a Lincoln*, New York, Harcourt Brace, 1975; and Hugh Sidney, *Portrait of a President*, New York, Harper and Row, 1975. For excerpts of significant speeches and memoranda from Ford and other presidents, see Louis Filler, ed., *The President in the Twentieth Century: the Presidency in Crisis: From Lyndon B. Johnson to Ronald W. Reagan*, Englewood, NJ, Jerome S. Ozer, 1990; Gerald R. Ford, *A Time to Heal*, New York, Harper and Row, 1979. For an excellent general work, see Michael Barone, *Our Country: the Shaping of America from Roosevelt to Reagan*, New York, Free Press, 1990.

Table 10.1 Percentage of persons considering themselves middle class

	White	Black
1949	34	12
1975–88	47	24
1988–91	51	30

Source: The American Enterprise, *Public Opinion and Demographic Report*, May–June 1993, p. 82

In a more general sense, Ford was middle class to the core, a decent fellow from suburbia, and everybody's good neighbor. This was a splendid qualification for the presidency in a country where the middle class kept gaining in number and influence (see table 10.1). In the US, the great majority considered themselves to be "haves" rather than "have-nots," unlike Britain where self-described "have-nots" outnumbered the "haves." Campus radicals in the 1970s still dreamt of a second American revolution where the poor, ethnic minorities, the alienated, and progressive intellectuals would seize power from a declining bourgeoisie. Such aspirations, however, were irrelevant in a country where the middle class would inexorably increase in voting power (all the more so since middle-class people voted with greater frequency, organized more efficiently, and were better informed on public affairs than the poor).

But Ford soon ran into trouble, left as he was with the Nixon legacy. In 1973, Congress had passed the War Powers Act over Nixon's veto; the Act greatly strengthened the role of Congress in foreign policy and restricted the president's power to act on his own. In 1975 Ford, with surprising eloquence, asked Congress to provide aid to beleaguered South Vietnam. From the moment they had signed the Paris accords, the North Vietnamese had violated every provision of that agreement. They had illegally introduced 350,000 men into the South. The US proved unable to respond, reduced its economic and arms aid, and thereby encouraged the Vietnamese to send virtually their entire army to South Vietnam. "We cannot . . . abandon our friends while our adversaries support and encourage theirs. We cannot dismantle our defenses, our diplomacy or our intelligence capability while others increase theirs."[2] But Congress solidly opposed any further US involvement and South Vietnam fell to the enemy.

Ford nevertheless kept on Henry Kissinger as secretary of state, and continued Kissinger's policy of *détente*. In July 1975, Ford signed the Helsinki accords which resulted in strengthening civic liberties within the Soviet empire. This was an agreement fraught with serious long-term consequences for the Soviet Union, but its import as a weapon in the Cold War was lost on the president. (Ford refused to meet in the White House Alexander Solzhenitsyn, the greatest Russian writer of his time and an exile from the Soviet Union, even though Solzhenitsyn's artistry and moral courage had played an immense role in delegitimizing the communist cause both within his own country and abroad.) It was not a time for glory.

Ford's domestic policy was not conspicuously more successful. Ford had the misfortune of assuming the presidency at a time when inflation and unemployment stood at a higher level than at any time since 1947. Ford was a centrist; he vetoed numerous bills designed to expand public expenditure on housing, education, and school lunches. On

2 Cited in Filler, *The President in the Twentieth Century*, p. 145.

the other hand, he supported a public works program to help the unemployed, and, at long last, supported legislation to bail New York City out of bankruptcy. His most controversial act was to grant a full pardon to Richard Nixon. In granting the pardon, Ford hoped to spare the nation the spectacle of a former president in dock, a sight which many Americans, however, would surely have enjoyed. Ford's decision proved extraordinarily unpopular for him in public opinion polls; Nixon by contrast, emerged in a few years as an elder statesman, and an international celebrity. (In a public opinion poll in 1975 Britons improbably chose Nixon as their preferred president.) Increasing inflation and unemployment further added to Ford's troubles, as did constant clashes with a Congress dominated by Democrats.

Ford nevertheless performed well at the polls. In the presidential elections of 1976 Ford gained nearly as many votes as his opponent Jimmy Carter. (Ford won 39.2 million votes, 48 percent of the total, as against Carter's 40.8 million votes, 51 percent of the total.) But Carter won against an opponent who, in many ways, curiously resembled Carter. Both had more intelligence than they were given credit for by society hostesses. Both came across as honorable men, Carter as well as Ford. (Even Margaret Thatcher, a lady not inclined toward excessive charity in politics, insisted that "it was impossible not to like Jimmy Carter. He was a deeply committed Christian and a man of obvious sincerity. He was also a man of marked intellectual ability, with a grasp, rare among politicians, of science and scientific method."[3] Carter also had an unusual background. A farmer's son, he had graduated from the US Naval Academy, an élite school, and thereafter served for a time as an officer in Admiral Hyman Rickover's nuclear submarine service, the élite of the US navy. Carter was a Southerner, like Johnson. But whereas Johnson was a vulgarian and a bully who gloried in his bad manners, Carter was a gentleman. He was very religious, much concerned with sin and grace. He was likewise well read in philosophy, with a penchant for Schopenhauer's pessimism. Yet he was far from unworldly. He had done well as a peanut grower and a warehouse owner. He subsequently made his way in Georgia politics, and rose to gubernatorial office. To military men, Carter could thus convincingly talk as a former officer, to engineers as an engineer, to blacks as an advocate of civil rights, to workers as a spokesman for welfare reform, to churchgoers as a Christian, to politicians as a politician (as Governor, he had made a special effort to get to know the city mayors in Georgia).

But, above all, it was his regional affiliation that enabled him to win, despite his relatively liberal convictions. The South was the most conservative part of the US, yet Southerners voted for Carter because he was one of them. Kennedy's election had proved that a Catholic could attain the presidency. Carter's election established the same principle for Southerners. Carter's election also pleased those countless Americans, Southerners or Northerners, who had tired of the Democratic Party's lurch to the left. He was what he seemed, a moral man, a business man, a man transparently honest ("I would never lie to you"), an outsider far removed from Washington's professional cynicism, sound, solid, safe – not to be taken in by kooks or crooks.

This combination put Carter over the top – barely. The traditional Democrats supported Carter, including the labor unions (which provided financial support) and the public service lobbies (prominent among them the teachers). Above all, those white Southerners who had deserted the party for Nixon, once more returned to the fold. (In the 1972 elections, only 28.9 percent of Southern voters had gone to the Democratic

3 Margaret Thatcher, *The Downing Street Years*, London, HarperCollins, 1993, p. 68.

Party. By 1976 the Southern vote for the Democrats once more amounted to 54.1 percent, a remarkable achievement, given Southern criticism of affirmative action, school bussing, as well as rising taxes and inflation.)[4]

Carter, therefore, had a magnificent opportunity for rebuilding the Democratic Party as the natural party of government. He was not a radical. He understood that fear of crime was genuine and widespread in the cities, that the cry for "law and order" was not just covert racism. The Republicans' prestige had suffered severely by Watergate, a scandal neither forgotten nor forgiven by the electorate. But Carter failed. The party reforms of the 1960s and 1970s had been intended to turn the Democratic Party into a national mass organization that would represent the minorities, as well as adherents of unorthodox lifestyles. The old-fashioned city bosses were largely eliminated; and more power passed to liberals and new special interest groups: pro-choice feminists, multiculturalists, gays, ecologists, most of them college graduates, visible, audible, and widely contemptuous of the Democratic Party's traditional electorate. Party cohesion, therefore, weakened; hence House and Senate leaders thereafter increasingly resisted the endeavors of the Democratic National Committee to shape an agreed party policy. As Caroline Arden, herself a supporter of party reform, put it, the reform movement was well intentioned, "but like so many other progressive movements they just did not know where to quit"[5] (in making so many concessions to minorities).

Carter faced other difficulties. Television was not his best medium – at a time when the silver screen had come to dominate politics. It was certainly untrue that television caused American politics to degenerate into an exchange of soundbites. There was nothing in post-World War II politics to equal the sloganeering of the nineteenth century, such as "Fifty-Four Forty or Fight" (in relation to a US–British boundary dispute), or "Tippecanoe and Tyler Too" (referring to the presidential election campaign of Benjamin Harrison). But no politician could succeed who did not master the new techniques. Carter's provincial biases, moreover, did not help. He surrounded himself with local politicians, the "Georgia Mafia," whose honesty and competence proved no greater than the much-derided Washington élite's. By contrast, Carter failed to recruit policy intellectuals whose drive and ability might have reshaped the Democratic Party's ideology. (To be fair to Carter, he also appointed as his national security adviser Zbigniew Brzezinski, a former Columbia University professor, the Democrats' Kissinger, and one of the ablest men in the administration.)

Like Queen Victoria, Carter meant to be good and do good. His administration, he hoped, would break with the secrecy and corruption of the Nixon years. The president would side with the common people. (At airports Carter always carried his own bags.) At the same time he would institute tax reform, build a national system of health insurance, strengthen environmental protection, assure civil rights for women and minorities,

4 Richard M. Scammon and Ben J. Wattenberg, "Jimmy Carter's Problem," *Public Opinion*, March–April 1978, pp. 3–8; Herbert D. Rosenbaum and Alexej Ugrinsky, eds, *The Presidency and Domestic Policies of Jimmy Carter*, Westport, Conn., Greenwood Press, 1994; and *Jimmy Carter: Foreign Policy and Post-Presidential Years*, Westport, Conn., Greenwood Press, 1994; Garland A. Haas, *Jimmy Carter and the Politics of Frustration*, Jefferson, NC, McFarland, 1992; Erwin C. Hargrove, *Jimmy Carter as President*, Baton Rouge, Louisiana State University Press, 1988; Donald S. Spencer, *The Carter Implosion: Jimmy Carter and the Amateur Style of Diplomacy*, New York, Praeger, 1988; Joshua Muravchik, *The Uncertain Crusade*, Lanham, Md, Hamilton Press, 1986.
5 Caroline Arden, *Getting the Donkey out of the Ditch: the Democratic Party in Search of Itself*, New York, Greenwood Press, 1988, p. 13.

elaborate a national energy policy, formulate an urban policy, and effect comprehensive welfare reform. Certainly there was no shilly-shallying at the White House concerning government's assumed problem-solving ability. Carter would not serve hard liquor in the White House and was a man who preached and agonized – but this did no harm in a country which had always respected sobriety and preachers. He wrote well. On the face of it, he should have succeeded.

But, unfortunately for Carter, the political tide was running the other way. In the US as well as in Western Europe, welfarism entailed a growing tax burden which now bore on the workers as well as the wealthy. Unemployment went up. Moreover, the US suffered from inflation, and – rightly or wrongly – the lower socioeconomic groups in particular felt that they had been victimized by the declining value of money. So, suddenly, did the property-owning middle class. Symptomatic in this regard was California's Proposition 13 (designed to reduce home-owners' property taxes, approved by the California electorate as a popular initiative in 1978). By that time inflation (worsened, though not occasioned, by successive oil shocks) had caused the price of houses and real estate to rise. Americans therefore had to dig deeper into their pockets to buy housing, with less opportunity for young couples to buy a home, and with less money to spare for investment in industry. At the same time, the California property tax kept going up, since the tax was based on the price of housing. Even liberal veterans on a fixed income abandoned time-honored political preferences when mounting taxes threatened them with the loss of their homes. Proposition 13, or similar initiatives, generally proved a winning cause in California, and every other state. Moreover, for the first time in US politics, middle-class people began to speak the language of the oppressed – a remarkable change in national psychology.

Speaking in even more general terms, the size and functions alike of government still continued to go up in most of the Western world. Citizens came to expect more from governments than governments could provide with a balanced budget. Politics required more decisions on arcane subjects than governments could furnish with confidence. (Bismarck, Disraeli, and Lincoln were never expected to hold opinions on global warming, nuclear winters, the extinction of tropical forests and such like.) Not surprisingly, therefore, confidence in government widely diminished in the Western world. There was widespread loss of accountability. (For instance, by 1975, New York City, a Democratic bastion, and the world's greatest municipal welfare state, faced bankruptcy.)

By 1979, Carter's domestic policies were in disarray. The president's prospects failed to improve when, in a fit of panic, he removed from his cabinet his ablest officers, including Treasury Secretary Michael Blumenthal and Energy Secretary James Schlesinger. (According to Congressman Charles Wilson "he cut down the tall trees and left the monkeys.") A year earlier Congressional leaders had informed the president that his welfare reform plans would never pass. Carter's failure was hardly surprising. His plan would have increased the number of claimants to public financial aid by almost 22 million; in the end, some 66 million Americans would have received some kind of welfare – just about one-third of the nation! Moreover, the vast majority of persons obtaining welfare checks for the first time would have been in the middle-income group, some even in the upper-income group. Carter's additional welfare programs would have cost something like 20 billion dollars, a staggering sum nearly equal to all US agricultural exports in one year. Yet those who needed welfare the least would, overall, have gained the most. Those who would have needed welfare the most would have gained the least. An effective welfare state, moreover, presupposed a prosperous economy. But prosperity proved elusive. (By 1980, GNP growth was negative at 0.2 percent; the unemployment rate stood at 7.1 percent; the prime interest rate amounted to 20.5 percent.) Not surprisingly, the Carter administration appeared a mediocre, if not a failed presidency.

The Carter presidency was no more successful in foreign policy, partly because the administration was itself bitterly divided. Zbigniew Brzezinski took a tough stand against the Soviet Union, insisting that *détente* with the Soviet Union could be achieved by strengthening containment. (By contrast, Cyrus Vance, the secretary of state, believed that *détente* and arms control should take precedence over all other considerations; *realpolitik* should give way to *moralpolitik*, the politics of higher morality.) And Carter himself in the earlier part of his presidency pushed for a kind of "disarmed diplomacy," denying efforts to build up the military or to give arms aid to Third World nations.

There was one exception: the Arab–Israeli issue. Carter had an instinct for dealing with this problem, for it was deeply suffused by religion, and Carter himself was a religious man, presiding over a religious nation. In US politics Israel played a larger role than any other foreign state of comparable size. America's commitment to Israel is not explicable only in terms of the Jewish vote. (Only about 2 percent of Americans describe themselves as Jewish by religion.) But the Zionist cause enjoyed traditional support from humanitarian opinion, labor unions, and civil rights lobbies. (It was only from the 1960s that campus militants began to denounce Zionism as a capitalist plot.) In addition, Zionism also appealed to millions of Protestant sectaries who believed that the Second Coming of Jesus would not occur until the Children of Israel had returned to the Promised Land. Such convictions appeared strange to Europeans, but played a major part in the politics of the US. The strength of Christian fundamentalism probably rivalled the power of Muslim fundamentalism in the Near East. (Despite the secular trend of US state education and most of the US media, nearly half of the American population in 1993 believed in the literal truth of the Bible, and totally rejected the theory of evolution.)[6]

Appearances notwithstanding, religion also dominated the political cultures of the Middle East. Of course, Zionism was not born of the synagogue; it was a secular socialist movement. (Theodor Herzl, the movement's modern founder, had been almost ignorant of the Jewish religion. A small minority of ultra-orthodox Jews indeed rejected Zionism altogether as an impious attempt to pre-empt the Messiah.) Nevertheless, even secularist Zionists insisted that Palestine was the land chosen by Providence for the redemption of the Jewish people; no substitute would suffice. (Herzl would have been satisfied with a part of the Kenya Highlands, offered to the Zionists by the British government before World War I, the so-called "Uganda project." But the mass of committed Jews would accept none but the Holy Land.)

Zionism initially had largely met with rejection from the Jewish upper class in the West, and from the Jewish working class in Eastern Europe. But World War II, the Holocaust, and the near-destruction suffered by European Jewry brought about a decisive change. The majority of Jews thereafter backed Zionism – "never again!" As a result

6 Frank Newport, "Half of Americans Believe in Creationist Origins of Man," *Gallup Poll Monthly*, no. 336, September 1993, pp. 24–8. In 1993, 47 percent believed that God had created the Earth within the last 10,000 years; 37 percent believed in a God-guided evolution; 11 percent believed that the world evolved without God. Between 1939 and 1993 average church attendance went up from 41 percent to 45 percent among respondents.

of World War II, moreover, the Jewish American community became the world's largest, wealthiest, and most influential Jewry.

For the Arabs, religious issues likewise played a crucial part in the Palestine tragedy. A separate Arab state had never existed in Palestine. Palestinian consciousness is of recent origin. Palestine, like the Arab world as a whole, had for centuries formed part of the Ottoman Empire (shattered by World War I). But under the Turks, Palestine – with its sacred sites and sacred memories – had at least been ruled by fellow Muslims. The British conquest in 1917 was bad enough, but worse than infidel government at the hands of the British was infidel settlement by the Jews (authorized by the Balfour Declaration in 1917 of a Jewish homeland in Palestine). To the Arabs, Zionist settlement constituted a new Crusade, a new form of aggression by the West. Arab secularists hoped to annihilate the "Zionist entity" and create instead a secular Arab state. But territorial nationalism in the Middle East was weak compared with its European equivalent; the new Arab states set up after World War I were artificial creations commanding but limited loyalty.[7] The masses continued to identify themselves more in terms of their religion than their country, and widely rejected the modernizers' attempt to divide life into separate religious and secular spheres. Western might, and reputed Western insolence, further embittered Arab–Jewish relations, as many Arab militants took over the Nazis' anti-semitic legacy. Zionism was widely equated with a mythical World Jewry, mysteriously able to pull the strings alike in London, Paris, and Washington. The Jews, for their part, feared a new Holocaust. (Israel contained more concentration camp survivors than any other country on earth.) This was not a world in which compromisers gained honor.

As regards the Soviets, they might have done well, in terms of sheer *realpolitik*, to have backed the Jews rather than the Arabs. Indeed, the Soviet Union had been among the first countries to recognize the State of Israel. Czechoslovakia had initially sent arms to Israel during the country's war of independence. By further supporting the State of Israel, Soviet policy-makers might have tried to court Jewish voters in the US (and, to a lesser extent, in Britain and France). The Soviets would thus have furthered their professed aim of rallying on their side all "progressive elements" in Western society. The Soviets, however, chose to play the Arab card, partly because Soviet policy was designed to make friends in the Third World, partly because of the Soviet Union's pervasive distrust of Jews with their reputed cosmopolitan connections; Zionism was defamed in the Soviet Union and its satellites with greater vindictiveness than any other form of "bourgeois nationalism." But the Arab card turned out a loser.

Carter did not thereafter initiate the peace talks between Egypt and Israel. Indeed, the initiative of President Anwar al-Sadat in 1977 came as a somewhat unwelcome surprise, as Carter and the State Department had originally looked to a comprehensive Middle Eastern peace settlement in cooperation with the Soviet Union. But Carter saw himself as a global peace-maker, a role which suited both his domestic political interests and his moral convictions. Once Sadat had broken the ice, Carter did his best to facilitate further negotiations. Both combatants now stood to gain. Egypt had born the brunt of the Arabs' armed confrontation with Israel, and looked askance at its allies. There were also more tenuous psychological factors which favored Sadat's initiative. The Yom Kippur war had brought defeat to Egypt, but also battle honors – no more jokes about cowardly "Gyppos" whose tanks were only programmed to roll backward. With its ancient history,

7 David Fromkin, *A Peace to End All Peace*, New York, Henry Holt, 1989.

Egypt, moreover, had a greater sense of territorial – as opposed to Arab – nationalism than the other Arab states; Egypt also possessed a more varied sense of identity, Muslim and Arab, but also African, Mediterranean, and Nilotic. The Israelis, for their part, also needed peace. Their economy was in no better shape than Egypt's. Israel had also become dependent on a foreign power, the US, in a way that would have shocked Zionism's Founding Fathers. Israel, moreover, was now run by a right-wing government headed by Menachim Begin, a man whom – like de Gaulle – none could reasonably accuse of being a namby-pamby or a sell-out.

Carter, Begin, and Sadat formed perhaps the strangest triumvirate in history, but their agreement at Camp David formed Carter's one and only notable foreign policy success. Admittedly, the Egyptian–Israeli peace treaty did not fully satisfy either side. Israel evacuated the Sinai Peninsula, which, with its military bases and oil wells, was a strategic buffer. In return, Israel gained formal recognition and acceptance of legitimacy from the most powerful Arab state. Egypt, of course, was henceforth shunned by its former allies, but secured time and aid from the US to cope with its desperate internal problems, and pursued an "Egypt first" policy. (Syria took over the role of Israel's principal enemy.) Continued disagreement over the Gaza strip and the West Bank remained masked, with Israeli opinion itself bitterly divided whether to keep or to abandon the disputed regions. Despite widespread skepticism, however, Israel and Egypt thereafter stayed at peace, and no Arab coalition without Egypt could defeat Israel.

Carter's involvement in the Arab–Israeli issue was part of a wider design to retreat from the *realpolitik* of the Nixon–Kissinger era, to bring back higher morality to foreign politics, to defend human rights, and to reduce the burden of armaments. But foreigners have traditionally distrusted American (and also British) moralism as a cloak for self-interest. (Helmut Schmidt was particularly scathing with regard to Carter.) At a minimum, the Americans were thought naïve. As Margaret Thatcher put it, Carter's presidency showed that "in leading a great nation, decency and assiduousness are not enough." Above all, "he violated Napoleon's rule that generals should be lucky. His presidency was dogged with bad luck from OPEC to Afghanistan."[8]

To start with, Carter, from the end of 1978, sought agreement with the People's Republic of China (PRC), not in and of itself an inadvisable policy. But in seeking an accord, Carter weakened US commitments to Taiwan, a loyal ally, and a bastion of relative prosperity in Asia. Reassured by US goodwill, the PRC attacked Vietnam "to teach a lesson" to China's ungrateful ally. The Soviet Union thereby profited mightily. Moscow improved its strategic position by moving into the former air bases at Danang, and into the US's former naval facilities at Cam Ranh Bay – this at a time when the Soviet navy had become the world's second most powerful fleet.

Convinced that, in the last resort, the Soviets also sought peace, Carter sought a *rapprochement* with Moscow. In 1979, for instance, he signed the SALT II agreement. Carter and his entourage shared initially the disarmament lobby's guiding assumption, an assumption shared by the bulk of liberal academics in the US. The mere accumulation of arms formed in and of itself a threat to world peace; sooner or later, the guns would go off by themselves, as they had done in 1914. The arms race was a major cause of wars. This generalization has not the slightest basis in history. On the contrary, the US had in the past endangered itself by failing to arm to full capacity and placing its trust in arms limitations. (The Washington Treaty of 1922, for example, had prevented

8 Thatcher, *The Downing Street Years*, p. 69.

the US from decisively outbuilding the Japanese fleet, and thereby creating a true "Two Ocean Navy" which might have deterred the Japanese from attacking the US at Pearl Harbor in the first place.)

But Carter thereafter made the same mistake in the arms race against the Soviets. Though superior in wealth, productivity, and technological resources, the US accepted a position of *de facto* inferiority toward the Soviet Union. The US unilaterally scrapped several weapon systems. New disputes arose between the US and its NATO allies, as Helmut Schmidt in particular disapproved of Carter's Wilsonian moralism. Carter also sought a *rapprochement* with Cuba, ended reconnaissance flights over the island, lifted travel restrictions, and removed the ban on sending US currency there. Nevertheless, Cuba consolidated its alliance with Moscow. Cuba in turn strove to create a new revolutionary triangle in Latin America, with Panama as a conduit for trade in drugs and arms, and Nicaragua as a military base for the export of revolution. (In 1979 the Sandinistas took power in Nicaragua; thereafter, they built Nicaragua into the most heavily militarized state in Central America, while supplying advisers and weapons to leftist guerrillas in Guatemala and San Salvador.)

As indicated earlier, the Soviet Union and its Cuban ally likewise expanded their influence in Africa. In Angola, Cuban troops supplied massive assistance to the governing MPLA, a self-styled Marxist–Leninist party whose attempts to impose socialism on Angola wrecked the country. In the Horn of Africa, between 1977 and 1978, the Soviets and Cubans switched support from Somalia to a new revolutionary government in Ethiopia; for a time the Ethiopian empire seemed to prevail in bitter warfare both against Somalia and against rebels in Eritrea. Thus encouraged, the Soviets in 1979 invaded Afghanistan – a move which left Carter stunned and disillusioned – he announced his shock by admitting Brezhnev had lied to him.

Carter fared no better in Iran. The country fell victim to an Islamic revolution (1979) which replaced a corrupt but reasonably efficient modernizing monarchy with an infinitely more corrupt and inefficient republic. Tied to his American alliance, impeded by Washington's commitment to human rights, the Shah Mohammed Reza Pahlevi failed to put down the revolutionaries at a time when force might still have succeeded. (Subsequently, the governments of Syria, Algeria, and Egypt respectively showed good sense in avoiding such squeamishness in suppressing militant Muslims – no matter what the cost.) The Shah in the end was abandoned by his US ally. The US for its part went through the trauma of the Iranian hostage crisis, with the US media magnifying the US humiliation on television. An armed attempt to release the hostages failed, and added to the administration's embarrassment.[9] The Iranian crisis also weakened US relations with its Western European allies. (The French had acted quite irresponsibly in facilitating the movements of Ayatollah Khomeini while he was exiled in France. Thereafter, the French press widely showed a peculiar *schadenfreude*, not realizing that the US's predicament was also France's.) Carter made no attempt to treat Iranian action against US diplomatists as an act of war, as he might have done under international law. Carter's humanitarian sentiments (and also the noisy insistence of the media) forbade him simply to proclaim that he would not negotiate with gangsters, and that diplomatists – like soldiers – must risk their lives in their country's service. US humiliation seemed complete – worsened, if anything, by the president's lugubrious reflections in public concerning America's presumed national malaise.

9 Paul B. Ryan, *The Iranian Rescue Mission*, Annapolis, Md, Naval Institute, 1985.

And yet, overall, Carter achieved more for his country than his critics understood at the time. Inflation by the end of 1979 was at full blast. (The consumer price index rose by 14.4 percent between May 1979 and May 1980.) But it was Carter, not Reagan, who gave the chairmanship of the Federal Bank to Paul Volcker, a man willing to enforce price stability at the risk of a temporary recession. It was Carter's insistence on human rights – scoffed at by defenders of *realpolitik* – that placed into US hands a powerful propaganda weapon that also benefited Soviet dissidents. Shocked and disappointed by the Soviet incursion into Afghanistan (1979), the US began to rearm. (Massive increase in arms expenditure began at the end of Carter's presidency, not, as widely assumed, at the beginning of President Reagan's.) From the Soviet standpoint, the successive offensives in Africa and Afghanistan turned into long-term defeats. For all his failures, Carter had succeeded better than he knew.

The Reagan Years

Sea Change in Politics

Carter by 1980 still enjoyed wide respect. Ronald W. Reagan, the presidential challenger, by contrast, lacked any practical experience in foreign policy. Worse still, to some he was not presidential. "Ronnie Reagan – the B-movie actor," went the society hostess's and political science professor's assessment. Who could take seriously the hero of films with such titles as *Brother Rat* or *Bedtime for Bonzo*, all unsuitable for a prize at the Cannes Film Festival? Who would be impressed by a man who had served as a popular television show host and as a touring spokesman for General Electric products?

Admittedly, Reagan had twice served as Governor of California (1966–74), the most populous and richest state in the Union. But political experts did not regard California as a state typical of the US. California was known as a bastion for right-wing eccentrics in Orange County and left-wing eccentrics in Berkeley, a home for gurus and psycho-babblers – nothing solid about California! The liberal consensus was contemptuous of Reagan's domestic policies. Reagan had first put forward his message in 1964 in a nationally televised address "A Time for Choosing" (later known to Reagan admirers as "the Speech"). In this, Reagan had called for individual competence, initiative, responsibility, and freedom from government intervention – not a popular stand at a time when the welfare state kept expanding with massive popular approval.

Reagan's views on foreign policy seemed even more menacing at a time when the gains made by communists were generally supposed to be irreversible, and when peaceful accommodation with Moscow seemed only reasonable. Reagan's straightforward hostility to communism, by contrast, was considered by the enlightened as simplistic at best, perilous at worst – a throwback to the bad old days of McCarthyism. Reagan, moreover, bore a burden of political failure. (He had twice lost the Republican nomination: first in 1968, when he would surely have made a better president than Nixon, and again in 1976 when Reagan narrowly lost to Ford.)[10]

10 The literature on Reagan is immense. Particularly noteworthy are Lou Cannon, *President Reagan: the Role of a Lifetime*, New York, Simon and Schuster, 1991; Martin Anderson, *Revolution*, Stanford, CA, Hoover Institution Press, 1990; Robert L. Bartley, *The Seven Fat Years: and How to do it Again*, New York, Free Press, 1992; David Mervin, *Ronald Reagan and the American Presidency*, London, Longman, 1990; and Robert E. Denton, *The Primetime Presidency of Ronald Reagan*, New York, Praeger, 1988.

Reagan had other weaknesses. In 1976, he had chosen as his prospective running mate Senator Richard S. Schweiker of Pennsylvania, a committed liberal whose selection not only angered Republic conservatives, but also burdened Reagan with the charge of opportunism. By contrast, George Bush, Reagan's selection for vice-president in the 1980 election, was highly experienced in many political offices. Bush also had a distinguished war record as a flier in World War II, having faced real danger in real combat, not simulated peril on a movie set. But Bush was obviously an Eastern Establishment man – this at a time when even the most established of Establishment men claimed to be populists. The 1980 election should therefore have been a photo-finish.

But the results defied all estimates. Reagan won a smashing majority: 51 percent of the vote, as opposed to 41 percent for Jimmy Carter, and 7 percent for John Anderson, a moderate Republican. (Supposedly, the preliminary polls had in part been falsified by timid respondents who, under pressure of public opinion, had in public promised to vote for Anderson, but selected Reagan in the privacy of the polling booth.) Even more stunning was Reagan's electoral college vote: 489 as against 49. (Carter only won Minnesota, Rhode Island, West Virginia, Hawaii, the District of Columbia, and his own Georgia.) Millions of traditional Democrats had abandoned their party – white "ethnics," Southerners, even a good many Mexicans and Jews. The Christian Right largely abandoned Carter. So did labor unionists who refused to abide by their officials' directives, and heavily backed Reagan (except for those employed in the public sector). No US president had suffered a similar defeat since Herbert Hoover's loss in 1932. Carter's defeat was worsened by the Republicans' gain of 13 Senate seats. For the first time since 1952, Republicans obtained control over the Senate. The Republicans even had some gains in the House of Representatives, enough to hold the balance of power whenever Republicans managed to cooperate with conservative Democrats.

According to the defeated, the election result was a freak. Reagan had won because of his pleasant manner, friendly smile, and born actor's command over television as a political medium. Reagan had played the role of a lifetime, having credibly switched from Cowboy to King. Such an abnormality would not happen twice, for Reagan's presidential record was supposedly dubious. The budget deficit (operative since 1969) rapidly rose from the time Reagan assumed office (from $56 billion in 1980 to $111 billion in 1981–2, with rapid annual increases thereafter). Reagan offended environmentalists by weakening the regulatory powers of the Environmental Protection Agency (EPA); he upset civil libertarians by opposing affirmative action programs, by reducing the budgets of the Equal Employment Opportunity Commission (EEOC) and the Office of Federal Contract Compliance Programs (OFCCP); feminists suffered a severe defeat when the Equal Rights Amendment (ERA) was rejected in 1982, much to the president's unalloyed pleasure.

Worse still, in the opposition's opinion, was Reagan's foreign policy, a subject to which we shall return. He supported the *Contras* against Sandinista rule in Nicaragua. He began the largest peacetime military buildup in US history; he imposed harsh sanctions on Poland (which had cracked down on the internal opposition to communism), and on the Soviet Union. (Sanctions included an unsuccessful effort to prevent Western Europeans from building natural gas pipelines from the Soviet Union). In a frequently quoted statement to the National Association of Evangelicals in 1983, Reagan described the Soviet Union as an "evil empire," a characterization regarded as "simplistic" by the campus left, though not by the average Pole, Czech, or East German. A US attempt to intervene in the Lebanese civil war ended in disastrous casualties to US marines, and their withdrawal (1984).

In the presidential race of 1984, Reagan, moreover, faced a good team led by Walter Mondale. Mondale was an old-fashioned liberal, the kind who commanded respect among Shriners, Lions, or Rotarians – the last man on earth to be castigated as leftist. He shared his ticket with Geraldine Ferraro, a New Yorker, the first woman in US history to be chosen for a presidential ticket. But once again, the "Teflon President" seemed invulnerable. Reagan won by an even greater majority: 59 percent of the vote. (For good measure, he also gained every state, except Mondale's home base in Minnesota, and the District of Columbia, with its civil service vote. Only the blacks remained overwhelmingly loyal to the Democratic Party, irrespective of income or class affiliation.) More serious still for the Democrats was a nationwide swing toward the Republican Party, a shift which affected almost every major group, irrespective of gender, geography, ideology, age, or education.

The shift in US voting patterns reflected a wider change which affected every Western country. (Conservative politicians gained power in Britain, where Margaret Thatcher became prime minister in 1979, and in Germany, where Helmut Kohl stepped into the chancellor's office in 1982.) As we have pointed out before, improved communications (including tourism), popular entertainment (especially television), standardized music, and standardized dress changed traditional working-class culture and political allegiances. Henceforth, a politician could no longer assume that a Pennsylvania miner would necessarily vote Democrat, a Welsh miner Labour, or a West German *Kumpel* (mineworker) SPD. This transformation went with a wider restructuring of industry. The giants of old – coal mining, steel-making, shipbuilding – had depended on huge, complex hierarchies. But all these enterprises lost in relative importance to high-tech enterprises, built on a much smaller scale. Contrary to countless predictions, it was these smaller firms that pioneered the bulk of the new science-based and computer-based industries. At the same time, the power of labor unions diminished in every major Western country; hence union officials could no longer deliver their members' votes.

Equally significant was the impact of the welfare state. From the end of World War II, every Western country had seen a rapid expansion of social services. Social services entailed heavy costs; thus the burden of taxation kept becoming heavier for employers and workers as well as for rich people. (In the US, the federal tax burden on the average family with children went up from 12 percent of a household's income in 1960 to 24 percent in 1980, and thereafter remained stable.[11] In addition, of course, tax-payers had to meet tax bills from the states and local authorities.) Not surprisingly, popular enthusiasm for welfarism began to diminish, especially among those tax-payers who objected to helping the assumedly undeserving – alcoholics, drug addicts, drifters, thugs, and foreigners.

In a more intangible sense, there was throughout the Western world a new mood of what the Germans called *Staatsverdrossenheit* (disillusionment with the state as an institution). In the US, as elsewhere, the power of the state, especially of the federal government, had risen vastly as a result of World War I, the New Deal, World War II, and the subsequent "War on Poverty." As a result, federal taxation in particular greatly increased, and also came heavily to outweigh taxation raised by the states and local authorities. The federal government, in particular, expanded welfare services of many kinds. This process was ambivalent in its political effects.

11 William J. Bennett, *The Index of Leading Cultural Indicators*, Washington, DC, Empower America, Heritage Foundation, Free Congress Foundation, vol. 1, March 1993, p. 22.

Welfarism at first contributed to regard for the federal authority, a respect particularly noticeable among ethnic minorities. Roosevelt, in fact, had not done much for blacks, Mexicans, or Asians. But at least the institutions created by the New Deal did not discriminate against people of color. Hence blacks in particular switched allegiance from the GOP, Lincoln's party, to the Democrats, Roosevelt's party. Blacks, moreover, had traditionally looked to federal power. It was Washington that had emancipated the slaves, created the Freedmen's Bureau, the first major federal welfare agency. Later on, the growing black middle class looked for employment in federal agencies such as the Post Office. Not surprisingly, blacks remained the most loyal constituency within the Democratic Party. The Jewish experience was similar in certain respects. Jews had traditionally been excluded from, or restricted in, state employment in their former homelands in East Central Europe. By contrast, the New Dealers and their successors vastly expanded state employment. Jewish people found numerous new jobs in teaching, welfare, the law; hence Jews in particular developed a special regard for the federal power, and also for Roosevelt personally. (*Diese velt, jene velt, und Roosevelt* – this world, the next world, and Roosevelt – went a Yiddish pun.)

But, as the state expanded and its functions diversified, services failed to keep up with expectations. All over the Western world, but particularly in the US, angry citizens pointed to rising crime rates. (During the 1960s and 1970s, the robbery rate in the US increased sixfold, and the murder rate doubled.) Citizens railed at declining standards in public schools, rising drug consumption, at a time when welfare expenditure kept expanding. Not that Westerners had become free marketeers. No government in the Atlantic community would have dared to liquidate official entitlements, or reduce state power to what it had been at the end of World War II. Nevertheless, *Staatsverdrossenheit* affected every Western country, and Reagan became its chief beneficiary. Yet Americans remained a patriotic people – more so than any other in the Western world. Intellectuals might censure the US. So did Carter who mistakenly attributed to the US public his own sense of cultural malaise. But the overwhelming majority of Americans remained convinced that the US was the land of opportunity, assured that the US was the best place in the world, certain that America's best years still lay ahead.[12] Again the Republicans gained, and the Democrats lost, from Carter's inability to size up US popular psychology.

Reagan also enjoyed massive support from conservative intellectuals who became a power in US politics. They were a diverse lot who often quarrelled among themselves. Widespread liberal assumptions to the contrary, conservative intellectuals were not peculiarly well paid; on the contrary, US business overall proved somewhat parsimonious in supporting its self-proclaimed defenders. But other generalizations are in order. Conservative intellectuals were now full of confidence. They had, moreover, broken all connections with the racist right. Racism, whether associated with anti-semitism or negrophobia,

---

12 According to "The Gross National Spirit Index," *Public Opinion*, June–July 1981, p. 23 ff, 80 percent of all respondents (and 65 percent of all black respondents) were "extremely proud to be an American"; 84 percent of all respondents (and 80 percent of black respondents) considered that the US had a special role to play in the world; 92 percent of all respondents (and 86 percent of black respondents) considered that the US was the very best place in the world in which to live. According to "Americans Assess Opportunity," *Public Opinion*, June–July 1982, p. 21 ff, the great majority (69 percent) still believed that hard work could lead a person from rags to riches. More specifically, 77 percent of white respondents (and 69 percent of black respondents) thought that they had "a very good" or a "fairly good" chance of achieving the good (by which they meant a prosperous) life.

had become associated with the gutter. Avowed class prejudice had likewise disappeared – no more complaints among conservatives concerning "the great unwashed." Equally out of fashion was the traditional Southern romanticism which had equated slave-owners with Old World aristocrats.

The most influential of the new conservatives were old-fashioned liberals, heirs of Adam Smith, the kind who, a hundred years ago, would have voted for Ludwig Bamberger, a free-trading German Progressive, in the Imperial *Reichstag*, or William Ewart Gladstone in the British House of Commons. (Long before the term "supply-side economics" had been invented, Gladstone had delighted Victorian tax-payers in the 1860s by steadily reducing their tax burden while massively increasing tax revenue, a feat likewise accomplished by John F. Kennedy.) The American free-traders were secularists; they were optimists. Left to itself, they argued, the free market would guarantee alike prosperity, and personal and political freedom.

The free-marketeers by now had regained that intellectual respectability that they had lost from the 1930s onward. They had also become well organized throughout the English-speaking world, with constant intellectual interchange between the US and Britain. A major event in the intellectual history of the English-speaking world was the creation of the Mount Pelerin Society (1947). This was started by Friedrich von Hayek, an ex-patriate economist of Austrian origin, a Nobel Prize laureate, and author of *The Road to Serfdom* (which asserted that central economic planning would ultimately lead to the end of a liberal society). Hayek had a host of distinguished disciples, including Sir Keith Joseph (Thatcher's intellectual mentor) in Britain, and Milton Friedman and George Stigler, later Nobel laureates, at the University of Chicago, then the Hoover Institution. There was now a transatlantic network of conservative institutions. This included, among others, the Hoover Institution in California, the Heritage Foundation, and the American Enterprise Institute in Washington, DC, the Economics Faculty at Chicago University, the Institute of Economic Affairs, the Adam Smith Institute, and the Centre for Policy Studies in London.

Between them they provided an intellectual rationale for popular *Staatsverdrossenheit*. No more nonsense about those personages ironically styled in Britain "the Great, the Wise, and the Good," those supposedly impartial, incorruptible, all-seeing public servants who knew how to fine-tune an economy, and plan the way to prosperity! For the first time since World War II, the intellectual initiative in the English-speaking world passed from the moderate left to the moderate right. The left (styled liberals in the US) was now on the intellectual defensive. The free-market intellectuals, so to speak, had changed the intellectual terms of trade.

The extent of their direct political influence is much harder to measure. Mikhail Gorbachev may have exaggerated when he described a major work produced by Hoover scholars, *The United States in the 1980s* (edited by Peter Duignan and Alvin Rabushka), as the key to Reagan's political agenda. But Reagan warmly sympathized with free-market intellectuals, including scholars such as Martin Anderson, Annelise G. Anderson, John Raisian, Thomas Moore, Thomas Sowell, William Simons, Michael J. Boskin, and many others. (Reagan himself had majored in economics at a minor college where he had still been taught economics of the pre-Keynesian kind.) Free-marketeers received leading political appointments. Keynes henceforth seemed *passé*, and Friedman the height of intellectual fashion.

US conservatism's second major intellectual contingent derived from the anti-communist left. They had originally identified themselves as social democrats or liberals; it was Michael Harrington, a socialist, who had coined the word "neo-conservative" as a term of derision for those leftists who considered the communist system a tyranny, and backed the Vietnam War. In time, the neo-conservatives accepted this appellation as a badge of honor. They drew recruits from many quarters, including ex-radicals from the 1960s, disillusioned with the promises of Marxism. The neo-conservatives did not share the traditional conservatives' dislike for cities and industry – not for neo-conservatives T.S. Eliot's contempt for business. Neo-conservatives had no patience with isolationists, racists, or anti-semites. (A substantial proportion were Jewish, disgusted with Third World and militant black American support for the enemies of Israel.) The neo-conservatives were vocal, and now communicated their views to the public through a variety of élite publications (including Norman Podhoretz's *Commentary*, Irving Kristol's, *The Public Interest*, Adam Meyerson's *Policy Review*, and William Buckley's *National Review*). Neo-conservatives soon found that they had more in common with Republicans, and with Old Guard anti-communists, than with the left, "soft" or "hard." Reagan, with his polit-ical flair, deliberately courted neo-conservatives, and appointed some of them to major positions in the State Department, Defense, and other agencies. (They included Jeane Kirkpatrick, Elliott Abrams, Carl Gershman, Richard Pipes, Norman Podhoretz, Ben Wattenberg, Michael Novak, William Bennett, William Kristol, and Gertrude Himmelfarb.) Old-fashioned conservatives might grumble, but could no longer do without their new recruits. In addition, there were also traditionalists, such as Russell Kirk, determined to uphold what they regarded as traditional values. (They found support from publications such as *Intercollegiate Review*, a literary journal, and *The American Scholar*, which aimed at freeing academia from the shackles of "political correctness.")

Above all, there was the Religious Right (itself a coalition whose members were far from united either on theology or politics). This was a new departure. In the old days, competing denominations had fought one another. But yesterday's cleavages were increasingly replaced by a new split between liberals and conservatives which cut across all denominations, Jewish as well as Christian. Right-wing Protestants dropped those prejudices which had once led fanatics to identify the Church of Rome with the Scarlet Woman, the Great Whore of Babylon. Henceforth, Protestant fundamentalists, practicing Catholics, and Hasidic Jews widely, though not universally, joined in a new alliance which primarily, though not universally, benefited Republicans. Orthodox Christians and orthodox Jews were shocked at the new tolerance toward homosexuals, and also the *Roe* v. *Wade* decision (1973) which established a pregnant woman's right to abortion. Fundamentalists abandoned the political quietism of olden days and joined the political fray, as left-wing Christians had done during the 1960s. Religious conservatives of what-ever persuasion agreed that homosexual intercourse was the sin of Sodom, and abortion infanticide. Religious conservatives also called for state support, direct or indirect, for parochial schools, convinced mostly that public schools had turned into purveyors of academic failure and religious unbelief. The Christian Right created its own network of radio and television stations, and new political organizations. (These comprised the so-called Moral Majority, set up in 1978 by Protestant fundamentalists at the suggestion of Howard Philip, a Jew.[13] The Moral Majority (headed by Jerry Falwell) failed to meet its founders' expectations. It was replaced by Ralph Reed's Christian Coalition, an umbrella organization for conservative Christians, much better organized than the Moral Majority, and particularly active in local politics.)[14]

13 John B. Judis, "The End of Conservatism," *The New Republic*, 31 August 1992, pp. 29–32.
14 Stephen L. Carter, *The Culture of Disbelief*, New York, Basic Books, 1993, pp. 19–20.

The Christian Right aroused bitter hostility from the liberal left who overestimated the Christian Right's ideological and political cohesion. Liberals, in particular, objected to what they called the intrusion of religion into politics – forgetting that they themselves had earlier welcomed Christians such as the Rev. Martin Luther King and the Jesuits, the Berrigan brothers and Protestant theologians who had supported the civil rights campaign in the US, opposed the war in Vietnam, striven for decolonization in the Third World, and nuclear disarmament in the First World. It was Reagan's supreme political achievement to unify the new "triple alliance" between free-traders, neo-conservatives, and conservative Christians. This feat was all the more remarkable because Reagan himself was not part of the Religious Right. An ex-actor, wise in the ways of Hollywood, independently wealthy, skilled in the arts of legal tax avoidance, and a divorcé to boot, Reagan did not fit into the world of Sunday sermons and Sunday schools. But Reagan understood its values, spoke its language, and gained its confidence. The Religious Right, however, was not a disciplined army whose loyalty could be taken for granted by either party. Its relations with free-marketeers and neo-conservatives was ambivalent. But for a time the "triple alliance" held together, and admirably worked for the Reagan presidency; it failed twice, however, against Clinton.

Domestic Politics

Reagan was one of the most controversial presidents in modern US history. In this respect he resembled not merely Nixon but also Franklin D. Roosevelt, a politician whom Reagan much admired. On both sides of the Atlantic, the polemics against Reagan were numerous and bitter. Reagan, critics argued, was driven by an exaggerated fear of the Soviets' "evil empire" which, during the Reagan period, was already in a terminal crisis. Reagan thus embarked on a massive but largely unnecessary arms program, and thereby indulged in his own form of "military Keynesianism." Huge public expenditure did indeed give a fillip to the economy, but the gains were superficial and the price was immense. The defense buildup of the 1980s was not paid for by corresponding taxes. Hence the defense budget rapidly enlarged the public debt. The resultant deficits combined with unsound monetary policies and negative trade balances to turn the US into the world's biggest debtor nation. The US saved too little and spent too much. The US thereby became irrevocably dependent on the willingness of foreign creditors, including in particular Germany and Japan, to keep the economy afloat. Foreigners began to buy up US treasury bonds, US land, US factories, and other national assets. The defense effort, moreover, created a Frankenstein monster, the military industrial complex, which impoverished the country and gave the US a wrong sense of priorities.[15] Reagan's economic policies supposedly speeded industrial decline in the US as the US increasingly became incapable of competing with countries such as Germany and Japan.

This was not all. The new burdens were unequally shared. Reagan's tax policies and his opposition to welfare allowed the rich to get richer and the poor to get poorer. Trade unionism weakened; social services declined. The resultant inequities in turn worsened the US's color problem. As the British *Economist*, a conservatively minded weekly, put it, "the gap [in the US] between rich and poor is not just a matter of economic stratification.

15 For the anti-Reagan case, see Anthony S. Campagna, *The Economy in the Reagan Years: the Economic Consequences of the Reagan Administration*, Westport, Conn., Greenwood Press, 1994.

It is poisoned by racial differences."[16] Employment admittedly increased during the Reagan years. But some industries declined; some of the new jobs in the American economy earned little money, as well-remunerated workers in management were matched by poorly paid service personnel, mere "hamburger flippers" in fast food chains. The country suffered in many other ways. The infrastructure was allowed to decay. An excessively large portion of the GNP went into defense research, thereby siphoning many of the best US scientists and engineers into wasteful arms production – this at a time when the US's main allies concentrated on commercial enterprise.

There was worse to come, said critics. Justice was supposedly perverted by promoting the appointment of right-wing judges with a reactionary agenda, many of them with inadequate qualifications. The Reagan administration thereby "raised serious doubts among many citizens about the government's adherence to that rule [of law]."[17] The condition of women, ethnic minorities, and practitioners of unconventional lifestyles all deteriorated because of institutionalized bigotry. The environment suffered because of the administration's refusal to make a stand against entrepreneurial avarice, and because of Reaganite opposition to responsible funding for family-planning services both in the US and the world at large.

In a more general sense, according to social critic Sidney Blumenthal, the Reagan presidency equalled a "celebration of wealth, by the wealthy."[18] The Reaganite rich imposed on the US a "neokitsch aesthetic" where show business glitz ruled supreme. The Evangelical Christians, with their television shows, cable network sermons, radio schmaltz, "Christian" pop singers and "Christian" talk shows added to cultural degradation. The Reagan years, the literati concluded, were scoundrel time when self-interest prevailed over the commonweal. Greed supposedly went with "imperial overstretch." US imperial power overseas became too costly to maintain; hence, the US suffered political, as well as economic, decline. As in a Victorian morality tale, pride and selfishness, however, earned their just punishment. It was not for nothing that during the Reagan years Paul Kennedy, a distinguished Yale historian, suddenly achieved unanticipated and unwanted celebrity status by the publication of his book *The Rise and Fall of the Great Powers* (1987).

Crucial to the case against Reagan was the charge of "military Keynesianism," that Reagan had bought an illusory prosperity at the price of a huge and parasitic arms program. The Vietnam War had produced too many careerists who knew how to punch the right tickets, produce the right statistics, write the right reports, and think in terms of "containing" rather than crushing the enemy. Drug use had gone up; morale had gone down. All this changed under the Reagan presidency. The armed services improved in size, sophistication, fighting capability, and the will to win. In a certain sense, it was during the Reagan years that the US ensured it could win the Gulf War by massive modernization, and also by improving the logistic capabilities of the armed forces. The military had a better record in integrating white, brown, and black people than any other public or private institution in the US. Personnel increased in number and quality.

16 "American Survey," *The Economist*, 26 October 1991, p. 23. For a more general indictment, see Benjamin Friedman, *A Day of Reckoning: the Consequences of American Economic Policy under Reagan and After*, New York, Random House, 1988.
17 Lincoln Caplan, "The Reagan Challenge to the Rule of Law," in Charles O. Jones, ed., *The Reagan Legacy*, Chatham, NJ, Chatham House, 1988, p. 249.
18 Sidney Blumenthal, "Reaganism and the Neokitsch Aesthetic," in Jones, ed., *The Reagan Legacy*, p. 251.

This was a major achievement, especially for the army which, during the late 1970s, had faced a serious recruitment problem. Thereafter, deficiencies disappeared. (To give just one example, by the end of the 1970s, the army had suffered a shortage of over 10,000 NCOs, key personnel whose crucial importance is often forgotten. By 1984, the army actually had a surplus of non-comms.) There was a significant improvement in the educational standards of recruits, in morale, and discipline. Desertions declined in a stunning fashion (from 19.6 soldiers per 1,000 in 1980 to 7.1 per 1,000 in 1983).[19] Professional and media prejudice notwithstanding, the weight of military service did not in particular fall on the very poor. As Sue E. Berryman points out in a pioneer study, the US army was never an underclass army. Even in 1979, at a time of bitter debate about the supposed decline in the quality of recruits, the military was drawing from families of higher socioeconomic status than were full-time civilian employers. For black and Hispanic recruits the military was drawing from the same socioeconomic pools as were colleges.[20] The renaissance of the US's conventional forces alone was a major achievement of the Reagan administration.

Equally controversial was the Strategic Defense Initiative (SDI) begun during the Reagan presidency in 1983. Impressed by the US's inability to defend its cities against a missile attack, disillusioned by the MAD doctrine (mutual assured destruction through missile deterrence), Reagan resolved to reorient US nuclear strategy from offense to defense. Brilliant scientists such as Edward Teller were convinced that the job could be done by utilizing sophisticated computer and weapons technology. The project aroused bitter and prolonged controversy which, in the end, killed the enterprise. (In 1991, the Bush administration put forward a more limited goal: Global Protection against Limited Strikes (GPALS) which would safeguard the US against a few rockets set off perhaps by accident or discharged against the US by some fanatic dictator in charge of a smaller power. In 1993, the then defense secretary Les Aspin cancelled the program.)[21]

We are not qualified to pontificate regarding SDI's feasibility, but we are impressed by the ability of technology to achieve aims that orthodox opinion had previously considered chimeras. (Fifty years ago, tales concerning journeys to the moon rated as science fiction.) We are struck, moreover, by the obvious contradictions in the case against SDI. SDI will *not* work, and therefore occasions a disastrous waste of resources. SDI *will* work and thereby destabilizes the balance of power which alone maintains peace between the US and its Soviet (later its Russian) competitor. Whatever the truth, the Soviets, however, did believe apparently that SDI was workable. It was an opinion shared by Alexander Solzhenitsyn, an intellectual giant, who stated that the Cold War was won once Reagan had embarked on the so-called "Star Wars" program, and the Soviets understood that they could not follow suit. If Solzhenitsyn was correct, this alone would have justified SDI many times over.

Speaking of defense in general, the US spent a considerably larger proportion of its GNP on defense under John F. Kennedy than it did under Reagan. Yet, in terms of

19 David H. Petraeus, "The New Army," *Military Affairs*, January 1985, p. 17.
20 Sue E. Berryman, *Who Serves? The Persistent Myth of the Underclass Army*, Boulder, Colo., Westview Press, 1988.
21 Donald R. Baucom, *The Origins of SDI, 1944–1983*, Lawrence, University Press of Kansas, 1992; William J. Broad, *Teller's War: the Top Secret Story behind the Star Wars Deception*, New York, Simon and Schuster, 1992; Sanford Lakoff and Herbert F. York, *A Shield in Space?: Technology, Politics, and the Strategic Defense Initiative*, Berkeley, CA, University of California Press, 1989.

crisis indicators such as inflation, budgetary deficits, international trade imbalances, the US was better off under Kennedy than under Reagan. In any case, the hostility to President Reagan's assumedly excessive rate of defense spending derived from political rather than economic considerations. In 1988, for example, the US under Reagan devoted the same proportion of its GNP to defense as did Zimbabwe under Robert Mugabe – 6.3 percent to be exact. Yet no American critic ever attributed Zimbabwe's serious economic problems to military over-spending, or censured Mugabe, a left-winger, for devoting too many scarce resources to the Zimbabwean military. As we see it, military spending should be regarded as a national insurance premium well within the US's capacity to pay. This expenditure strikes us as particularly needful at a time when the Soviet Union's factories were pouring out military hardware on a scale not apparently known even to the Soviet leadership itself. To paraphrase economist Murray Weidenbaum, both critics and supporters of defense programs have overstated their case about the impact – positive or negative – of military spending on the US economy. The US economy is both complex and massive. It is not readily propelled or retarded by the relatively small share of the GNP devoted to military outlays.

Reagan's critics accused the president of initiating a decade of greed when compassion was at a discount. In fact, US charitable contributions increased, both in absolute terms and as a percentage of the GNP. The Reagan administration allegedly set out to benefit the rich and harm the poor. Admittedly, according to US statistics, the truly wealthy gained during the Reagan years a somewhat larger share of the GNP than they had held before, while the share of the poor somewhat diminished.[22] On the other hand, all classes benefited: the rich got richer, but so did the middle class and even the poor. At the same time, the rich, during the Reagan era, paid a higher portion of federal income tax than they had done before. (Between 1989 and 1990 the share paid by the highest 5 percent went up from 36.4 percent to 42.9 percent. The proportion contributed by the highest 10 percent rose to more than one-half, from 48.6 to 53.9 percent.)[23] Inequality between the rich and the poor somewhat increased, but this same trend appeared in many other industrialized countries, including Germany, Canada, Sweden, no matter who ran the government. The US, moreover, faced special problems. The US accepted massive numbers of immigrants, both legal and illegal. The US frontiers are much more porous than those of any European country; no one knows for sure how many undocumented aliens are living in the US at any one time. Moreover, the composition of the US population has continued to change. (Between 1980 and 1990, the proportion of Hispanic peoples went up by 53 percent; the share of Asians increased by 107.8 percent.) Some are highly skilled; many others, however, lack any formal education, industrial training, or knowledge of English needed for well-paid employment. As long as poor, young people keep coming to the US, the proportion of poor will necessarily go up – no matter what governments choose to do.

This immigration, moreover, occurs at a time when the gap between unskilled and highly skilled workers widens all over the industrial world. The ill educated get the rough end of the stick, now that computer literacy has become an indispensable qualification for many jobs. (The average male college graduate was paid 45 percent more

22 US Department of Commerce, Bureau of the Census, *Money Income of Households, Families and Persons in the United States*, Washington DC, August 1991, Table B.5. David R. Francis, "Economist Says 1980s Weren't So Terrible," *Christian Science Monitor*, 21 August 1992.
23 "Rich Pay More," *Executive Alert*, January–February 1993, p. 2.

than a high school graduate in 1980, but about 70 percent more in 1990.) The high school drop-out, by contrast, has a tough life (unless he succeeds, as did John Major, in becoming a British prime minister.) Robotization and computerization created many new jobs, but also eliminated existing jobs in industry and middle management. Overall, well-trained people with the right skills did well, despite complaints that the new service industries created only employment for ticket sellers, hamburger flippers, and housemaids. But no industrialized country of whatever political persuasion has yet found a way of adequately helping people with inadequate or outmoded qualifications, except by more training and education.

Disparities in family incomes also increased for other reasons which had nothing to do with whoever occupied the White House. Technological change rendering heavy physical labor unnecessary, the growth of service industries, and women's liberation joined to create the two-income family, with husband and wife both gainfully employed. Two-income families, on the average, made far more money than single-parent families whose head struggled to make ends meet. Finally, US poverty should also be judged in relative, as well as absolute, terms. Calculations concerning the income of the poor commonly exclude welfare and other transfer payments. Most US poor, moreover, are not poor by global standards. (An estimated 38 percent of the US poor are home-owners; 62 percent own at least one car.) "On a world scale that amounts to substantial prosperity."[24] Reagan's critics were apt to ignore these wider issues. They were also mistaken when they asserted that Reagan (and later Bush) permitted the US welfare system to be eviscerated. On the contrary, in 1990 dollars, overall expenditure on all "safety net programs" continued to rise.

What of the charge that an irresponsible Reagan administration enormously expanded the US deficit? The deficit did greatly grow, as a Republican presidency and a Democratic Congress cooperated in spending more on all manner of projects. But this problem also needs to be seen in perspective. In 1992, the US deficit amounted to 3.6 percent of GDP, less, in that order, than that of Australia, Sweden, Britain, Canada, and Belgium, not to speak of Italy and Greece, the latter with a hefty 14.5 percent of GDP.[25] Yet economists and politicians who predict disaster for the US on account of its spendthrift habits never make equally gloomy forecasts about Sweden or Canada, which indeed are often described as possible role models for the US. Reagan's critics also overlooked the effect on federal revenue receipts of declining inflation. When the dollar falls in value, salaries rise to keep abreast of rising prices. Hence, more salary earners are pushed into higher tax brackets. Under Reagan, however, inflation came to an end. As a result, estimates of future revenue turned out to be unrealistically high – to the budget planners' distress and the tax-payers' advantage.

Equally problematic is the charge that Reagan's policies caused foreign money to pour into the US so as to finance over-consumption occasioned by Reagan's tax reductions. Foreign investments in the US strike us as a boon rather than an evil. (During the nineteenth century, US economic expansion had owed a heavy debt to foreign, especially

24 Peter Gillies, "Rich Man, Poor Man: Putting Poverty in Perspective," *The German Tribune*, 17 January 1992, no. 11400, p. 8; Paul Craig Roberts, "What Everyone Knows about Reagonomics," *Commentary*, February 1991, pp. 25–30. For our own assessment, see our chapter, "The US: a Hopeful Future," in Peter Duignan and L.H. Gann, *The United States and the New Europe, 1945– 1993*, Oxford, Blackwell, 1994, pp. 276–306.
25 "Economic and Financial Indicators," *The Economist*, 15 August 1992, p. 90.

British, investments.) During the 1980s, moreover, the export of US capital to foreign countries greatly diminished, giving a $100 billion surplus to the US capital account. Why should foreign and US investors alike have wished to risk their money in the US? Why should they have picked a country then supposedly subject to a reckless policy of inflationary debt accumulation? The answer is simple, explains economist Craig Roberts.[26] The 1981 business tax cut, and the reductions in personal income tax effected in 1982 and 1983, raised the after-tax earnings on real investment in the US relative to the rest of the world. Many foreign investors during the Reagan years found the US a more promising place in which to invest than their own countries. This perspective points to the US's success – not its failure. In any case, the pessimists were mistaken in their gloomy prognostications concerning the future. By the early 1990s domestic savings had risen; borrowing by government, companies, and consumers had declined; hence the US no longer relied on foreigners to balance its debts.[27] Investments require savings. Reagan's critics represented the US during his presidency as the spendthrift in a Victorian morality tale who frittered away his inheritance. US profligacy was contrasted with the frugality of foreigners, particularly the Japanese. But as economists such as Fumio Hayashi, Robert E. Lipsey, and Irving B. Kravis point out, Japanese and US savings rates are hard to compare. Japanese accounting understates the value of assets used in production and makes Japanese investment look higher than it is. American experts count all government expenditure – including roads, bridges, schools, warships – as consumption, while Japan counts them as investments. When US savings and investments are broadened to include education, military capital, consumer durables (for instance, computers owned by firms and individuals), research and development, the US rate of capital formation looks distinctly favorable.

Hence the gloomy prognostications of Reagan's critics were not borne out by the facts. The US economy remained the world's most productive economy; the US worker stayed the world's most productive worker. (Per capita output in 1990 compared as follows: US 100; Canada 93; Switzerland 87; Japan 80; Sweden 79; West Germany 75; France 72; Britain 70; Italy 69.)[28] Industries such as steel-making and car manufacture made an astonishing recovery; American industry overall improved its product and performance. Sorrowful forecasts concerning the threatened "de-industrialization" of the US proved totally mistaken. In terms of GNP annual growth rates, the US during the Reagan years compared well with major competitors such as Japan and West Germany.[29]

Economic expansion on this scale, of course, also occasioned some disruption. In the US, as in all other industrialized countries, the proportion of persons engaged in manufacturing declined; the proportion of workers in the service industries expanded, so much so that the advanced manufacturing countries should really be known as service industry states. Reagan's personal role in these societal shifts was small; presidents play an infinitely smaller part in the economic fortunes of their country than legend asserts. But Reagan could at least take credit for lowering taxes, slowing the rate of growth of government,

26 Craig Roberts, "What Everyone Knows about Reagonomics," pp. 125–30.
27 "Debunking the Yellow Peril," *The Economist*, 26 February 1994, p. 74.
28 Herbert Stein, "A Guide to the American Economy," *The American Enterprise*, November–December 1991, p. 6; Michael Boskin, *Reagan and the Economy*, San Francisco, Institute for Contemporary Studies, 1987.
29 Martin Anderson, "When the Losers Write the History," *National Review*, 31 August 1992, p. 10.

rearming, and for assembling a distinguished group of advisers, including Martin Anderson, Arthur F. Burns, Milton Friedman, Alan Greenspan, Michael T. Halbouty, Jack Kemp, James T. Lynn, Paul McCracken, George P. Shultz, William E. Simon, Charles E. Walker, Murray L. Weidenbaum, Caspar Weinberger, and Walter B. Wriston. Reagan also made an unprecedented number of new judicial and legal appointments (including able men such as Edwin Meese). Even Reagan's most bitter opponents could no longer afford to look at the Republican Party as the assembly of the stupid, greedy, and reactionary.

In the 1980s there was a widespread consensus among members of the national media: Ronald Reagan was going to fail and would bring on economic disaster. But the economy soared to unprecedented levels. The media, however, widely refused to admit that "Reaganomics" was responsible. The drum-beat of negative opposition to the president's policies continued through the 1980s. According to one of the most common allegations, the poor got poorer under Ronald Reagan. In actual fact, the number of poor somewhat diminished from 14 to 13 percent during his administration, and the average income for the lowest one-fifth of Americans rose from $7,008 to $9,431. Inflation diminished from 8.9 to 4.6 percent – a reduction of 48 percent. Unemployment declined from 7.5 to 5.2 percent – a reduction of 45 percent. Interest rates went down from 21 to 5.9 percent – a reduction of 71.9 percent. Twenty-one million new jobs were created. The so-called "greedy eighties" witnessed the largest peacetime economic expansion in US history.[30]

At the same time, the Reagan years saw the completion of a major political realignment in which party identification was increasingly determined by income and, to a lesser extent, by color. In the olden days, the majority of Republicans were Northern white Anglo-Saxon Protestants. By 1984, however, their share had declined to one-third, while an equal proportion consisted of white Southerners, once the most loyal of Democrats. Republicans now drew their main support from citizens who made more than the average national income, while Democrats were primarily supported by voters who made less. As a result, the terms of political debate shifted to the right; only US academia remained a major exception to this general rule.

Reagan had an instinctive understanding of resultant political realities. In a conscience-stricken country benumbed by political preachers, Reagan never felt guilty, never pointed a finger, never raised his voice. He was, in fact, curiously detached alike from friends and foes. He did not try very hard to reward loyal support. He expected inconvenient or unsuccessful adherents to fall on their swords in the manner of Old Testament heroes, rather than to incommode their king. However, this genius for detachment also enabled Reagan effectively to delegate authority, and avoid being consumed by detail, as Carter had been. Reagan's supposed absent-mindedness – like Eisenhower's reputed obtuseness – was in fact a political asset exploited to the full by the president. Reagan's appointees were expected to give their chief that most precious prize – deniability at all times. Far from being dominated by his advisers, Reagan always got his way whenever he felt strongly on any subject. More than any other postwar president, Reagan set his own agenda both in domestic and foreign policy. Reagan thereby both strengthened the presidency and restored public confidence in a tarnished institution. Reagan, in fact, became the only postwar president able to fashion both his domestic and foreign policy entirely in the manner he pleased. It was indeed the role of a lifetime.

30 L. Brent Bozell, Chairman, Media Research Center, "A Case Study in Media Bias: Reaganomics vs. Clintonomics," in *Imprimis*, November 1994, vol. 23, no. 11, p. 4.

Foreign Policy

Reaganite diplomacy was, if anything, even more suspect to its critics than "Reaganomics." We have dealt with US–Soviet relations in detail in chapter 8 on the Cold War. Here we shall emphasize Reagan's personal role in this encounter. David Ignatius, a distinguished journalist, was not unusual among Reagan's censors when he accused the president of favoring "a hawkish rhetoric," and "military posturing," while lacking any kind of "flexibility and subtlety." Reagan stood for "fantasies of rolling back Soviet power," but in fact Moscow's foreign policy was far more creative than Washington's. "Reagan's first time tirade against the Soviet Union made him appear both a warmonger and a hypocrite." Not surprisingly, therefore, "by the end of Reagan's presidency, the United States appeared in some ways weaker, relative to the Soviet Union, than when Reagan took office."[31] And this was written in 1988 by which time the Soviet empire was tottering.

Not that there was anything peculiar about such views. They derived in part from a scholarly reappraisal concerning the very character of the Soviet Union itself. By the 1970s, the so-called revisionists had become a powerful force in US academia. As they saw it, the communist revolution had begun as a noble venture. The revolution thereafter suffered blemishes as a result of Russian backwardness, Stalinist excesses, and Western provocations; it was the West that bore the primary responsibility for the Cold War. But left to its own devices, Soviet communists would naturally evolve toward a more humane order. Above all, socialism was irreversible, and the West should therefore come to terms with a system that could not be subverted.

Since the breakdown of the Soviet empire, all this has been shown to be nonsense. The Soviet order had been unstable, communism corrupt; some of the most bitter charges indeed derive from former communist office-holders. Nevertheless, revisionists in the West for a time influenced even some opinion leaders who had not the slightest sympathy for communism. Typical among the media and academic élites were the views of Strobe Talbott (a former Rhodes Scholar, influential as a *Time* editor, and later President Clinton's chief adviser on foreign policy). Talbott's comments on Reagan's foreign policy were as scathing as the revisionists'. While he never denied the barbarity of the Soviet regime, he felt convinced that Reagan's approach was indefensible. According to Talbott, some truths about the Soviet Union should better have remained unsaid; nothing could have been more dangerous than to indulge in Reagan's favorite sport of bear-baiting.

Talbott, in particular, criticized with disdain the two great speeches made by Reagan respectively to the British Houses of Parliament (8 July 1983) and to the National Association of Evangelicals (8 March 1993), which Talbott reprinted as proof of Reagan's incompetence. What could be worse than to offend the Soviets by claiming that "the march of freedom and democracy . . . will leave Marxism on the ash heap of history"? How ill advised to eulogize those "who strive and suffer for freedom within the confines of the Soviet Union." How irresponsible to speechify about "the decay of the Soviet experiment," "the great revolutionary crisis" within the Soviet bloc, the Western countries' obligation "to assist the campaign for democracy," and the instability of a system

31 David Ignatius, "Reagan's Foreign Policy and the Rejection of Diplomacy," in Blumenthal and Edsall, eds, *The Reagan Legacy*, pp. 173–6. Also see Strobe Talbott, *The Master of the Game: Paul Nitze and the Nuclear Peace*, New York, Alfred Knopf, 1988. For Reagan's own views, see Ronald Reagan, *An American Life: the Autobiography*, New York, Simon and Schuster, 1990.

which lacks "peaceful means to legitimize its leaders."[32] Reagan's clairvoyant speeches were taken as proof of his assumed folly. Talbott at least accepted the reality of the Cold War. Others went even further and insisted that there had never, in fact, been a Cold War, that US policy-makers should have dismissed Soviet statements hostile to the US as rhetoric, and that in the US "orthodox conservatism was displaced by an obsession with unreal dangers."[33]

Again, not that there was anything unusual about such views. Prevailing opinion at official bodies such as the State Department or private associations such as the Council of Foreign Relations sympathized with Talbott more than Reagan. The US was supposedly disabled by the Vietnam War. The gains made by socialism might be regrettable, but were irreversible. However oppressive, the Soviet system had to be accepted as permanent; there was only one way to deal with Moscow – by dialogue, conciliation, and judicious Western concessions. A minority of scholars disagreed. (They included the contributors to major policy studies, issued by the Hoover Institution, and consulted by highly placed Reaganites, *The United States in the 1980s*, *To Promote Peace: US Foreign Policy in the mid-1980s*, and the *Yearbook on International Communist Affairs*.[34] But these scholars and others, such as Richard Pipes, Richard Staar and Edward Teller, were untypical of academia at large. To believe that communism should be resisted at all costs, or to strive for its destruction, was not acceptable in academia, even less so in Western Europe than in the US. (For instance when, in 1985, a conference convened at Geneva to deal with the possible collapse of communism, its participants were widely accused of being Cold War provocateurs, and its findings relegated to obscurity.)[35]

Reagan, however, understood perfectly that opinion in Senior Common Rooms, or even student dormitories at prestigious universities, was not the same as public opinion at large. He grasped that US patriotism remained a powerful force, that religion was a major factor in US politics, that anti-communism was a popular movement in the US which had given a new home to millions who had fled communist tyranny from as far afield as Poland, Cuba, China, and Vietnam. Nevertheless, speaking in general, Reagan preferred conciliation to conflict. (He tried to strengthen GATT and the Bretton Woods system; he tempered the anti-Japanese sentiments expressed by Senators and Congressmen.) But he would not budge on communism, having gained (like Ernest Bevin in Britain) personal experience of communist tactics in a labor union (in Reagan's case, the Screen Actors' Guild). To Reagan, the Soviet Union represented the "evil empire," to be resisted at all costs. Reagan, unlike so many other Western statesmen, was thus totally impervious to Soviet threats.

At home, Reagan picked a tough bunch of advisers, prominent among them two "Californians": Meese and Michael Deaver. Others included George Shultz (in the second term), James Baker, and Caspar Weinberger. Reagan worked well with Helmut Kohl.

32 Strobe Talbott, *The Russians and Reagan*, New York, Random House, Vintage Books, 1984, p. 70.

33 Godfrey Hodgson, *America in our Time*, New York, Random House, Vintage Books, 1976, p. 18.

34 Peter Duignan and Alvin Rabushka, eds, *The United States in the 1980s*, Stanford, CA, Hoover Institution Press, 1980; Dennis L. Bark, ed., *To Promote Peace: US Foreign Policy in the mid-1980s*, Stanford, CA, Hoover Institution Press, 1984.

35 The proceedings were published after a lengthy delay but only by the "Moonies'" publishing house. See Alexander Shtromas and Morton A. Kaplan, eds, *The Soviet Union and the Challenge of the Future*, 4 vols, New York, Paragon House, 1988–9.

Reagan, moreover, mightily appealed to the German public as distinct from German leftist opinion, by clearly and unambiguously calling for the opening of the Berlin Wall. Abroad, Reagan's closest associate was Margaret Thatcher. Britain had been the US's steadiest ally in World War II, and thereafter remained the US's most trusted friend within NATO. Nowhere else did an anglophone American feel more at home overseas than in the British Isles. (In US public opinion polls, Britain, together with Canada, consistently obtained the highest popularity ratings.) In addition, there were strong personal ties between Reagan and Thatcher. Both saw themselves as outsiders. Both were lampooned by the literati: Reagan as a cowboy, Thatcher as a *petite bourgeoise* of Victorian vintage, the kind who would tell a blushing bride on her wedding night to grit her teeth and think of England! Both believed in personal enterprise, hard work, free markets, and free trade. Both disliked bureaucrats, left-leaning professors, and TV anchormen. (Thatcher also lambasted lawyers, mayors, and bishops whom Reagan left unscathed.) Both were unashamedly patriotic at a time when flag-waving occasioned disdain alike in the London *Times* and the *New York Times*. The Reagan–Thatcher partnership was even closer than the association between Roosevelt and Churchill, or Kennedy and Macmillan, with Reagan very much the senior partner, whose support gave to Thatcher an international status higher than she could have expected otherwise.

Not that all went smoothly. Thatcher and Reagan, for example, disagreed on economic relations with the Soviet Union. (Reagan bitterly criticized Western European pipeline deals with the Soviet Union, while unashamedly dropping the grain embargo which Carter had imposed on the Soviet Union after the invasion of Afghanistan.) Thatcher likewise had misgivings concerning US interference in Grenada where, in 1983, the US smashed a Cuban-supported dictatorship, much to the islanders' relief. (Grenada was a member of the Commonwealth.) But Thatcher fully supported Reagan on matters considered essential by Reagan, for instance the bombing in 1986 of Libya in retaliation for terrorist attacks. (International terrorism thereafter diminished.)[36]

Reagan, in turn, backed Thatcher over the Falklands War. After a lengthy dispute, Argentinian forces in 1982 occupied the disputed islands (known to Argentinians as the Malvinas). Enlightened opinion, or what passed as such, universally expected Thatcher to accept the inevitable. But Thatcher rallied the British public, and British forces gained a brilliant victory. The conflict for a time occasioned a rift within the US administration. Latin Americanists, such as Jeane Kirkpatrick, sided with the Argentinians on the grounds that the US could not afford to endanger its Latin American links. Thatcher, however, enjoyed support from the bulk of US public opinion, and from "Europeanists" within the administration, such as Caspar Weinberger. (In 1988 Weinberger received an honorary knighthood from the Queen as a reward for what the Foreign Office described as his "unfailing support and assistance.") But, ultimately, the decision was not Sir Caspar's but Ronald Reagan's. Once again, the president had shown the right instinct. The Falklands War did not seriously damage relations between the US and Latin America. The British victory unexpectedly proved that a Western power could defeat a "Third World" country without becoming a moral outcast within the UN. The

36 For a discussion, see Coral Bell, *The Reagan Paradox: US Foreign Policy in the 1980s*, New Brunswick, NJ, Rutgers University Press, 1989. The pro-Reagan view is put forward in Peter Schweizer, *Victory: the Reagan Administration's Secret Strategy that Hastened the Collapse of the Soviet Union*, New York, Atlantic Monthly Press, 1994; and George Pratt Shultz, *Turmoil and Triumph: My Years as Secretary of State*, New York, Macmillan, 1993.

British triumph, moreover, accomplished what Argentinians had been unable to achieve on their own – the fall of the Argentinian military dictatorship.

Thatcher reciprocated Reagan's favors in 1986 when Britain, alone among US allies, supported attacks by US planes on Libyan installations in retaliation for Libyan support to Muslim terrorists. Above all, the Reagan–Thatcher relationship also assumed importance in the US's dealings with the Soviet Union. (Thatcher was the first Western leader who, immediately after Gorbachev's accession, decided, in 1984, that Gorbachev was indeed different from all his predecessors, and that the West could certainly do business with the Soviet Union's new head. And no one called Thatcher an appeaser!)

The US likewise maintained a special relationship with Israel whose importance in US politics vastly exceeded that of any other country of similar size. Israel occupied a peculiar place in US affection, not just because of the Jewish vote, but for more general reasons. The Israeli case appealed to the leftist conscience vote, those who sympathized with Jewry because of past persecution. The Israeli cause was equally favored by fundamentalist Christians who regarded Palestine as the land promised by God to the Children of Israel, or insisted that the Second Coming of Christ would not take place until the Jews had returned to the Holy Land.

There was no doubt in Reagan's mind where the US should stand, but his policy in the Middle East was marked by amateurish execution. The US was drawn into the affairs of the Lebanon. That country was divided into a multitude of Christian and Muslim communities which, for a time, had managed to coexist through a system of complex political compromise. This balance was destroyed by a massive influx of Palestinian refugees who attempted to do in Lebanon what they had previously failed to accomplish in Jordan. The Palestinians set up their own counter-state within Lebanon, intervened in Lebanese politics, and used their Lebanese strongholds as bases for guerrilla operations against Israel. Civil war broke out in Lebanon which wrecked a formally prosperous country; both Israeli and Syrian forces intruded into the country, and the PLO was compelled to leave. In 1982, Reagan ordered marines into Lebanon to oversee the PLO's departure, but the US forces thereafter came themselves under attack. Having suffered severe casualties, the marines withdrew in 1984. It was a severe blow to the US military which – as so often before and after – had received neither clear political directives nor a properly defined combat mission, and, most importantly, had ignored a basic rule of geopolitics – don't get involved in civil wars.

Worse was to follow. Reagan, on taking office, resolved to assist the *Contras* in Nicaragua who battled against the Sandinista government installed there in 1979. The Sandinistas were professed Marxists who were clients of Cuba, detested the US, and looked to a revolutionary future which would engulf, first, Central and, ultimately, the whole of Latin America. For that purpose the Sandinistas created what was, at the time, the most powerful military force in Central America, and actively supported guerrillas in neighboring states. The US Congress, however, looked askance at US intervention, and in 1984 adopted the Boland Amendment. Its legality was disputed by constitutional lawyers. But its purpose was clear. No official US agency was allowed to support directly or indirectly any military or paramilitary forces in Nicaragua.

The administration resolved to circumvent Congress by unofficial go-betweens and by using funds not formally granted by the legislature. US arms were sold to Iran in exchange for US hostages taken in Lebanon (1986). Arms strengthened Iran as against Iraq; the deal therefore pleased Israelis who preferred the distant devil in Teheran to the nearby Satan in Baghdad. Above all, profits from the arms deal went to the *Contras*, but also to private individuals who filled their own pockets. It was a dubious matter for the Reagan administration to campaign against international terrorism, but at the same time to deal with Iran. Reagan would have done better had he openly challenged the Boland Amendment, taken his case to the US public, and openly intervened in Nicaragua. As it was, the Iran–*Contra* deal remained the biggest blotch on the presidential escutcheon.

The US's third special relationship linked Washington to Bonn. The Federal German Republic was the US's most powerful economic partner in Europe; the *Bundeswehr* was NATO's strongest military component in Europe. Reagan got on well with Helmut Kohl, like Reagan a conservative who had won his spurs as governor *(Ministerpräsident)* of a German state *(Land)*. According to all public opinion polls, Germans were well liked in the US, and Americans well regarded in Germany. (The main exception comprised left-wing intellectuals. To express anti-German sentiments was perfectly in order among US literati who would not have dreamt of insulting Russians, Indians, or Nigerians. In Germany, anti-Americanism similarly remained *de rigueur* among the so-called *Schickeria* (the chic and politically correct), even at a time when anti-Americanism had come to be regarded as *passé* among intellectuals in France.) Alone among NATO allies, the US had no fear of German reunification.

Reagan's German visit was inauspicious. In 1985 Reagan joined Kohl in a wreath-laying ceremony at a military cemetery in Germany where some 49 members of the *Waffen SS* lay buried among 2,000 other soldiers. "Bitburg" thereafter became synonymous among Reagan's critics with the president's insensitivity toward the victims of Nazism. In fact, Reagan was not indifferent to the Holocaust. (He spoke the same day at Bergen-Belsen, a former Nazi concentration camp where 60,000 people had died.) Bitburg to Reagan meant German-American cooperation and a ceremonial affirmation that World War II had become history – this at a time when two-thirds of all Germans alive had been born after the end of World War II. (Purists could also have argued that the *Waffen SS*, though a bloody-minded lot, were not all war criminals, unlike the so-called *Totenkopf* ("Death's Head," or concentration camp guard units in the SS). From 1943, the ranks of the *Waffen SS* were filled by conscription.) At least those Germans who later made habitual excuses for ex-communists in the former German Democratic Republic should have accepted Reagan's explanation for the Bitburg fiasco.

Reagan's true moment of glory in Germany came three years later, by which time Soviet–US relations had begun to change in a startling fashion. Looking straight at the Brandenburg Gate in Berlin, as yet the symbol of German division, Reagan made one of his more prophetic speeches. "General Secretary Gorbachev, if you seek peace, if you seek prosperity for the Soviet Union and Eastern Europe, if you seek liberalization: Come here to this gate! Mr Gorbachev, open this gate! Mr Gorbachev, tear down this wall!"[37] It was a splendid performance. Did Reagan thereafter win the Cold War? According to a distinguished liberal historian, Fritz Stern, Reagan accomplished nothing of the kind. The collapse of the Soviet Union and the communist system – unlike the defeat of Nazism – was brought about by indigenous forces. Others, such as Wade Huntley, an American political scientist, went even further and insisted that the US actually lost the Cold War. Their case is contradicted, however, by native Russians such as Alexander Solzhenitsyn, greatest of living Russian novelists; Arkady Murashev, one-time Moscow police chief and later leader of democratic Russia; Sergei Khrushchev, son of Nikita S.

37 Cited in Cannon, *President Reagan: the Role of a Lifetime*, p. 774.

Khrushchev; Andrei Kozyrev, later Russian foreign minister – all of whom insist that the US did indeed win the Cold War, and that Reagan was the architect of victory.

Reagan, of course, was not responsible for the Soviets' own mistakes. Left-wing intellectuals in Germany might not understand the realities of Soviet domination in East Germany, but the mass of West Germans did, and they cheered Reagan for speaking the truth. Armed resistance against the Soviet invasion of Afghanistan did not depend on US encouragement, but it was the Reagan administration that supplied Afghan guerrillas with weapons. It was US diplomatic support that enabled Pakistan to function as a privileged sanctuary and supply base for Afghan partisans. The communists' own "liberation" strategy was now turned against them.

Reagan also encouraged anti-communist resistance in many other parts of the globe. In Africa, the Soviets had made great temporary gains when Angola achieved independence from Portugal (1974). Immediately thereafter, the MPLA (Movement for the Liberation of Angola), a Marxist–Leninist-inspired body, had attempted to institute a dictatorship. In due course the MPLA turned from being a "united front" into a dominant "vanguard party". About 400,000 Portuguese and persons of mixed origin fled the country, and their property was confiscated. The MPLA at first imposed a rigidly Marxist–Leninist program – with disastrous effects.[38] The Angolan economy faltered – so much so that in retrospect the Portuguese colonial era appeared almost as a golden age. Marxism–Leninism in Angola proved no more capable of homogenizing different ethnic communities into one "Angolan" nationality than Marxist–Leninists in the Soviet Union had been able to create a homogenized "Soviet man." Civil war broke out, with UNITA (based mainly on the Ovimbundu people in the south) the government's principal opponent. From the start, the Angolan War was internationalized. The Soviet Union and its European satellites backed MPLA; so did Cuba, which sent a massive expeditionary force to Angola. UNITA, for its part, relied on South Africa, which furnished troops, supplies, and cash. The South Africans, in turn, were resolved to prevent guerrilla infiltration from Angola to South-West Africa (Namibia), a formerly German colony under South African control since World War I. South African intervention met with widespread opposition in the West on the grounds that the South Africans were exporting apartheid. (In fact, the interventionists among the Afrikaners were liberals by the standards then prevailing in the ruling Nationalist Party in South Africa. The isolationists were conservatives who felt that South African soldiers should not risk their lives for one lot of blacks against another.) In addition, South Africa was also under worldwide censure for attempting to hold on to Namibia. South Africa was subjected to international sanctions in which the US participated, despite Reagan's initial attempt at "constructive engagement" with Pretoria. While boycotting South Africa, the US nevertheless used the presence of the South African army in Angola as its principal bargaining chip. In 1988, George Shultz, the new secretary of state and a scholar–statesman of great ability, successfully negotiated an agreement with the Soviet Union, South Africa, and Cuba whereby the Cubans would leave Angola, and the South Africans depart from Namibia.[39]

Pro-Soviet movements also began to lose out in other parts of the world. On attaining independence from Britain in 1967, South Yemen had turned into a Marxist state,

38 See Thomas H. Henriksen, "Lusophone Africa, Angola, Mozambique, and Guinea-Bissau," in Peter Duignan and Robert H. Jackson, eds, *Politics and Government in African States, 1960–1985*, London, Croom Helm, and Stanford, CA, Hoover Institution Press, 1986, pp. 377–407.
39 See Shultz, *Turmoil and Triumph*.

signed a friendship treaty with the Soviet Union, and permitted the presence of Soviet troops on its soil. In the end, however, the Marxist regime faltered, and in 1990 South Yemen was formally reunified with North Yemen, its former enemy. Marxism fared no better in Mozambique. Having shaken off Portuguese colonial rule in 1974, FRELIMO (Front for the Liberation of Mozambique), the ruling party, likewise attempted at first to set up a Marxist–Leninist dictatorship. But Mozambique's economy also collapsed; Mozambique was shaken by a civil war. FRELIMO's enemies were armed by South Africa; FRELIMO's hopes for a socialist war of liberation against South Africa faltered, and, acting in part under persuasion from Washington, South Africa and Mozambique in 1984 concluded the so-called Nkomati agreement in which the two countries agreed to peaceful coexistence and mutual non-interference.

Worse still was the blow suffered by Soviet prestige in Ethiopia. In 1974 the Ethiopian monarchy had fallen. Ethiopia thereafter was attacked by Somalia, formerly a Soviet ally. The Soviets then switched alliances and in 1978 Soviet advisers and Cuban troops helped to defeat the Somali invaders. Haile Mariam Mengistu established a blood-stained Marxist–Leninist dictatorship, but again Marxism–Leninism proved a failure. The Ethiopian economy crumbled. There was widespread civil war, and in 1991 a widespread guerrilla alliance finally forced Mengistu to retire from the presidency, and flee to Zimbabwe.

Whether in Nicaragua, Afghanistan, Angola, South Yemen, or Ethiopia, the Soviet cause had met with bitter resistance. The Soviet Union therefore could no longer compensate for failures at home with victories abroad. Reagan did not create the anti-Soviet opposition, but Reagan had a global vision. Unlike so many area specialists, Reagan felt convinced that the various struggles against Marxist–Leninism all over the world were, in some measure, interconnected. The Soviet rulers should, at the same time, be resisted politically and delegitimized ideologically. It was, in large measure, under Reagan's inspiration that the US now gave steady support to the anti-Soviet forces. The Soviet leadership was stricken by foreign defeats and by domestic failures, which in turn weakened the Soviet Union's position abroad. (For instance, East Germany, the most trusted of Soviet allies, was denied customary assistance through subsidized Soviet oil at a time when the Soviets desperately needed to sell their oil for hard currency.) No one knows whether SDI would have worked; but the mere possibility of its success occasioned the most severe apprehensions in the Soviet leadership. Soviet leadership in the Third World likewise proved ever more expensive to maintain. In the end, the Marxist–Leninist structure weakened, and was engulfed by the anti-communist tide.

In retrospect, Reagan appears a curious mixture, hard to fathom. The intellectuals despised him as a B-movie actor and a Philistine, yet Reagan had actually read widely in military history and strategy. He was censured as a man of make-believe, yet he showed great personal courage (for instance, during an assassination attempt). Reagan was in many ways a loner, a man aloof, yet he was also the great communicator. His gift for spontaneous repartee, for story-telling, and for electioneering was legendary. Criticized by a senior aide for his habit of taking naps, he told the man: "Hard work never killed anyone yet – but why take a chance?" During a formal dinner at the Hoover Institution (known for its commitment to budgetary economy), he told an after-dinner story:

A rich man settled in a small town in the Middle West. A skinflint, he never gave anything to charity. A deputation of dignitaries then called on him. "We have made enquiries about you," said their spokesman, "and we believe you could well afford a donation of $10,000 to the local hospital." "So you have made enquiries," growled the rich man, "but did you know that my poor old father suffers from tuberculosis and is confined to an expensive Swiss sanatorium? And did you know that my poor cousin is an alcoholic who must stay at an expensive rehabilitation clinic?" "No, we did not know," replied the spokesman, crestfallen. But the rich man was not finished yet. Pounding the table, he stormed, "and if I don't give a penny to my own kith and kin, why the hell should I give any to you?"

Reagan had a peculiar ability for sizing up people and gaining their trust. Gorbachev clearly liked the US president, and believed him. He did so in particular when Reagan insisted that the Soviet Union could not win the arms race against the US, that SDI was non-negotiable, and that SDI would provide its possessor with an effective anti-missile defense (a view rejected by many experts). Reagan thereby helped to change the world by changing Gorbachev's views about the Cold War. Reagan spoke the truth about the "evil empire." He put the Soviets under political, as well as financial, pressure by rearming and projecting US power, thereby vastly raising for Moscow the price of military competition. Like Thatcher, Reagan realized that Gorbachev truly differed from his predecessors, that the US might actually take up the challenge of disarmament, and cooperate with Moscow's new team. Reagan was unusual among US politicians in that he believed throughout that the Soviet Union was vulnerable. Above all, he firmly considered that foreigners all over the world preferred US democracy to communist dictatorship. "Unfashionable, misunderstood or held in contempt by political élites of all stripes," according to one of his campaign advisers, "never respected by the press, patronized privately by most of his own aides, Mr Reagan soldiered on with his populist vision and unexpected moves, essentially alone at the top. For eight of the most pivotal years of world history, this was more than enough."[40]

40 Jeffrey Bell, "Man of the Decade? Man of the Century?", *Wall Street Journal*, 27 December 1989.

11

US Politics: Bush to Clinton

Moderation Prevails: Bush in Power

In 1988 Reagan left office, one of the most popular presidents in US history. He was succeeded in the White House by George Bush, his vice-president, from a political selection board's viewpoint the ideal candidate. Bush came to the presidency "with a better political résumé and more senior government experience at the national level than any other president of this century."[1] He derived from a distinguished Eastern family (his father had served as a senator from Connecticut). He did splendidly as a naval pilot in World War II; he had gone to Yale, made the right kind of friends, joined the right kind of clubs, and married the right kind of wife. Bush did not merely preach but practiced family values – a model husband, model father, model grandfather. He was well mannered and well spoken. He had wide experience, having helped to found an oil company, having served in Congress, having represented the US at Beijing and at the UN, having run the CIA as director, and having served Reagan as vice-president. When he could muster sufficient energy, Bush was also a good organizer who built a superb campaign organization and raised money at a record rate.

These qualifications proved massive advantages in the presidential elections of 1988. As Reagan's former vice-president, Bush apparently stood for the Reaganite legacy; hence the elections in many ways turned into a vote of confidence in the Reagan record. The economy as yet did well. The Democrats made a poor choice in selecting for their candidate Michael Dukakis, a Massachusetts governor, a mild liberal who insisted on running his campaign on the slogan "competence, not ideology" against a man who could not be censured for lacking competence. Dukakis played on his background as the descendant of a Greek immigrant, but having gone to Swarthmore College and Harvard Law School, Dukakis hardly came across as a horny-handed toiler. Worse still, Dukakis seemed somewhat inept as he posed for a television camera riding a tank, and wearing a foolish-looking helmet. Bush, by contrast, spoke the language of ordinary Americans much better than his opponent (a quality that Bush shared with Franklin D. Roosevelt, another president of patrician background). Bush's campaign stressed family values and

---

1 Thomas E. Cronin, "The George Bush Presidency: an Appraisal," in Leo E. Heagerty, ed., *Eyes on the President: George Bush: History in Essays and Cartoons*, Occidental, CA, Chronos, 1993, p. 1. No authoritative biography as yet exists. Relevant works include Ryan J. Barilleaux and Mary E. Stuckey, eds, *Leadership and the Bush Presidency: Prudence or Drift in an Era of Change?* Westport, Conn., Praeger, 1992; Colin Campbell and Bert A. Rockman, eds, *The Bush Presidency: First Appraisals*, Chatham, NJ, Chatham House, 1991. See also Michael Duffy and Dan Goodgame, *Marching in Place: the Status quo Presidency of George Bush*, New York, Simon and Schuster, 1992; Bob Woodward, *The Commanders*, New York, Simon and Schuster, 1991.

a war on crime, both popular issues. Bush's campaign thus gave much prominence to one Willie Horton, a felon who, having been placed on furlough, committed as yet more felonies. (Contrary to widespread misconceptions, Bush did not run a racist campaign, however. "The Bush campaign was careful never to point out that Horton was black, and the issue would have cut as deep if he had been white.")[2] Bush won by a comfortable margin (53 percent of the vote as against 46 percent), and thereafter seemed firmly entrenched in power. Prognosticators felt certain that the presidency would remain unattainable for Democrats for many years to come – just as FDR had initiated a lengthy period during which no Republican was ever elected to the presidency. (As historian–journalist Michael Barone points out, Bush's electoral success in 1988 oddly resembled Roosevelt's in the 1940s: both presidents carried the big industrial states of the East and the Middle West, as well as the West; both their respective parties, however, failed to gain control over most big state governorships and legislatures.)

Once installed in the White House, Bush determined to be his own man – not Reagan's successor. To have been a Reaganite was henceforth a disqualification in the White House – no more talk of continuity! Bush represented old wealth; Reagan new money. Bush was reserved; Reagan cheerful. Bush was tongue-tied in public; Reagan never missed a chance of giving a good performance on TV or in the open air. Bush was a tactician; Reagan a strategist in politics. Bush was a pragmatist who unblushingly changed his mind when necessity commanded; Reagan believed that democracy was best.

Foreign Policy

Bush at once reordered priorities within the Atlantic alliance. Reagan's closest foreign associate had been Britain, led by Mrs Thatcher: indeed, Reagan's presidency had begun with a visit from the "Iron Lady." Bush's presidency started with a call from Helmut Kohl. Bush rightly saw Germany as the main European power, to be assiduously courted. Bush therefore backed Germany over issues such as the introduction of short-range missiles on to German soil. (Thatcher had previously pressed for the deployment in West Germany of a successor to the aging Lance missile. However defensible in military terms, Kohl considered such a step to be political suicide; the proposed new short-range missiles would only hit East Germans – "the shorter the missiles' range, the deader the Germans!") Bush instead proposed that in future conventional forces should be cut to an equal level between East and West. (Once the imbalance in conventional forces vanished, Bush argued, so would the need for nuclear weapons on the ground.) Bush made his position even clearer when, in 1989, he made a major speech at Mainz, Germany, where he described the Germans – not the British or the French – as partners in leadership.[3] For Bush, the German card was trumps – an assumption shared by US public opinion which had far more confidence in Germany than Britain, or even Japan.[4]

---

2 Michael Barone, *Our Country: the Shaping of America from Roosevelt to Reagan*, New York, Free Press, 1990, p. 667.

3 Geoffrey Smith, *Reagan and Thatcher*, London, The Bodley Head, 1990, p. 254.

4 According to a public opinion survey, published in *Der Spiegel*, 14/1994, pp. 79–81, 64 percent of American respondents expressed "much trust" or "some trust" in Germany; 57 percent of Japanese respondents did so, but only 47 percent of British respondents. By contrast, 71 percent of German respondents expressed "some" or "much" trust in the US, 67 percent in Japan, 47 percent in Britain.

Bush's realism also prevailed in his dealings with the communist world. No more talk of "evil empires." In his dealings with the People's Republic of China, Bush continued in the Nixon–Kissinger tradition. Just as Nixon had not allowed the horrors of Mao's Cultural Revolution to deter him from opening relations with Beijing, Bush would not permit the massacre of dissidents in Tiananmen Square to endanger Sino-American relations. In the olden days, Bush's tough-mindedness would have gained him applause from liberals resolved to improve Sino-American relations, anxious also to prevent US interference in China's internal affairs. By the late 1980s, however, the political climate had changed; liberals and conservatives frequently switched accustomed roles, as liberals began to call once more for US intervention abroad on moral grounds, while many conservatives started to look on US interference with greater skepticism. Hence a committed liberal, John B. Judis, now unfavorably compared Bush's China policy to Nixon's. Nixon in 1971 had needed Chinese support to balance the power of the Soviet Union. By 1989, however, the Soviet threat had vastly lessened. Therefore "the United States had little to lose by (at least) mildly rebuking China's brutal gerontocracy."[5]

More important still were relations between the US and the Soviet Union. The Bush presidency was implicated in an unforeseen cataclysm: the breakdown of Soviet communism, the fall of the Soviet empire, and the end of the Cold War. We shall deal with these events in chapter 17. At this point we shall only mention Bush's own role. Making fun of Bush's claim to have ended the Cold war, Bill Clinton later compared Bush to a crowing rooster claiming credit for the dawn. But Clinton erred; Bush, indeed, had done nothing to deepen that profound internal crisis that had stricken the Soviet Union from at least the 1970s. By far the most important role played by any individual was Mikhail Gorbachev's; for all his faults, he truly turned out to be one of history's heroes. Bush's role was more modest. He had never called for the dissolution of the Soviet Union, but would have preferred its peaceful transformation into a federal union in which all nationalities would pacifically coexist. (It was not for nothing that Bush, on a visit to Kiev in 1991, warned Ukrainians from indulging in "suicidal nationalism." His speech was lampooned in the US as "chicken Kiev," but Bush, a confirmed adherent of *realpolitik*, disliked the selfishness of imperial successor states as much as the egotism of preceding empires.) However, Bush helped to prevent violence at the Soviet Union's demise, and assisted in giving it a decent burial. With his moderation, good manners, and common sense, Bush was the right man, at the right time, at the right place. As Michael R. Beschloss and Strobe Talbott put it in their account,

> Bush made an indispensable contribution to the Cold War's end. From January 1989 [when Bush had acceded to the US presidency, and called on Gorbachev to improve US–Soviet relations] to December 1991 [when Gorbachev resigned and the Soviet Union ceased to exist], he [Bush] coaxed the Soviet Union toward worldwide surrender. He did so largely by exercising restraint and refraining from pushing the Soviet government too hard, thus never giving Moscow a pretext to reverse course.[6]

5 John B. Judis, "Foreign Policy: New World, Old Vision," in Leo E. Heagerty, ed., *Eyes on the President: George Bush: History in Essays and Cartoons*, Occidental, CA, Chronos, 1993, p. 47.
6 Michael R. Beschloss and Strobe Talbott, *At the Highest Level: the Inside Story of the End of the Cold War*, Boston, Little, Brown, 1993, pp. 468–9.

Bush, like Reagan, clearly understood that Gorbachev was indeed different from his predecessors, and that the "correlation of forces" had indeed decisively changed. In May 1989 Bush gave his first presidential speech on the Soviet Union, at Texas A. and M. (Kingsville, Texas), assuring his audience that his administration would now move "beyond containment." On 2–3 December, Gorbachev and Bush got together at a summit in Malta. Bush assured Gorbachev that, if Soviet society were reformed, and the satellites allowed to go their own way, the US would not regard such a course as weakness, and would not seek any special advantage. Less than a week later, the Berlin Wall opened, sealing the fate of the German Democratic Republic, the Soviet Union's most loyal ally. Bush refused to capitalize on the unexpected news by indulging in oratory; he thereby incurred censure from Democratic critics such as the majority leader in the House of Representatives Richard Gephardt, who made fun at the president's lack of overt enthusiasm at a time when the walls of modern Jericho came tumbling down. But from Bush's point of view, it made sense not to humiliate Gorbachev at a critical time when he remained the key figure in Soviet politics.

There was a price to be paid for restraint. Bush's circumspection during the "Bloody Sundays" at Vilnius and Riga in the Baltic angered both Baltic nationalists and their supporters in the US. To please Gorbachev, Bush had also refused (in September 1989) to meet Boris Yeltsin in the Oval Office, thereby deeply offending a touchy man who would soon play a crucial part in his country's history. It was the hard-liners' coup in August 1991 that convinced Bush that Gorbachev was yesterday's man; that the future lay with Yeltsin; that the Soviet Union had seen its day; and that the US must henceforth concentrate on good relations with successor republics. On 2 December 1991, Bush therefore recognized the independence of the Baltic states – this after considerable delay. (As he put it, "When history is written, nobody will remember that we took forty-eight hours more than Iceland or whoever else it is.") Consideration for Gorbachev did not, however, cause Bush to offer large-scale economic aid either to the Soviet Union or to the successor states. Given the ineffectiveness of foreign aid previously proffered by the US to the Third World, and given the unintended consequences of past generosity, Bush surely deserved commendation for his restraint. As Georgii Shakhnazarov, Gorbachev's adviser on Eastern Europe, put it, "even if he [Bush] is not a terribly bold leader or a great orator, we can trust him as a partner."[7]

Bush showed equal mastery in the German reunification issue. Whatever politicians might say in public, none of Germany's neighbors wanted Germany to be reunited again – not Britain, nor France, nor Poland, nor Holland. Even in Western Germany itself, few citizens expected the two Germanys to be unified in their own lifetime. But, as we shall stress again in chapter 12, the German Democratic Republic was nothing but a Soviet satellite. Once Moscow ceased to back the East German satrapy, its days were numbered; indeed, the ramshackle structure collapsed with a speed that no one – college professor, diplomat, or spy – had anticipated. (In 1989, Bush had even balked at the apparently bold forecast made by Vernon Walters, the US ambassador in Bonn, that Germany would be reunited within five years.)

Unlike Thatcher, or even François Mitterrand, the French president, Bush was not in the least frightened of a united Germany, and nor was the bulk of US public opinion. (In this respect, Jewish Americans, Polish Americans, and liberal voters in general were more apprehensive than the rest.) Once German unification appeared inevitable, Bush

7 Beschloss and Talbott, *At the Highest Level*, p. 482.

was determined to profit politically. He would be the first Western leader to support the winning cause; Kohl and his successors in reunited Germany would remember in future who their truest friend had been among the world's leaders.

A prudent man, Bush no more wished to rush unification than Kohl. But the very rapidity of East Germany's collapse forced diplomatic acquiescence. Bush agreed with Kohl that united Germany should remain part of NATO, an enormous concession from Gorbachev's viewpoint. In 1990, the Soviets essentially conceded all Western demands, with only minor reservations. (These included limits on the future size of the *Bundeswehr* and the stationing of non-German NATO forces in East Germany.) A few years earlier, such an arrangement would have appeared chimerical, but by now the Soviet Union's own existence was at stake, and the two Germanys formally fused on 3 October 1990. By now, Moscow wanted the US to serve as the European balance wheel. As Eduard Shevardnaze, Gorbachev's foreign minister, put it to Secretary of State Baker, "we want to see your troops remain in Germany." It was the end of an era.

Bush had handled the German problem with tact and ability. He had taken account of the Soviets' intense preoccupation with prestige, as well as German, British, and French sensibilities. He had not hesitated to diverge from Baker (who would have preferred a four-power conference). But a price was paid for helping Germany. Almost immediately, united Germany asserted her new-found strength in Yugoslavia where the breakup of the communist system had enormously worsened existing ethnic tensions. In 1991, Croatia seceded, and Slovenia soon followed suit. Bush had not favored a Yugoslav breakup, and neither had the State Department. But Germany quickly recognized the independence of Croatia and Slovenia. Both had belonged to the Austro-Hungarian empire; both looked toward central Europe; both were Catholic (a matter of particular importance to the Bavarian members of Germany's ruling CDU/CSU coalition). Having fought for their own right of self-determination east of the Elbe, Germans now saw no reason why Croats and Slovenes should not be entitled to the same privilege.

None can tell whether the breakup might have been effected peacefully by an international conference in which boundary revisions and minority rights were assured by agreement. Germany's own fate had, after all, been pacifically settled, at a US initiative, by the so-called Two Plus Four formula (entailing the participation of both Germanys and the four former victors – the US, the Soviet Union, Britain, and France). Germany's risky intervention in Yugoslavia, however, helped to prevent a similar settlement in the Balkans. The Serbs (who had been put at a grave disadvantage by the boundary settlements effected during the Tito era) determined to prevent secession, and at first the Yugoslav army unsuccessfully intervened. The Serbs thereby incurred widespread condemnation – surprisingly so, as international opinion had not earlier objected to Nigeria's suppression of Ibo secession, or Sudan's intervention against a threatened Southern breakaway. Whatever the rights and wrongs of the dispute, the Yugoslav state collapsed; neither Bush's diplomacy nor anyone else's thereafter could assure a lasting peace among Yugoslavia's successor states.

Bush, on the other hand, achieved partial success in the Middle East. The area was vital to the US as a principal source of oil, and, during the Cold War years, as a defensive bastion against Soviet expansion into the Indian Ocean and the Mediterranean. Iraq became one of the Soviet Union's main recipients of military aid. Favored with fertile lands, a relatively productive agriculture, and great oil resources, Iraq built a huge military establishment. (On paper, Iraq, by 1989, maintained 1,000,000 under arms. Its armored forces alone comprised, on paper, 4,500 main battle tanks, nearly as many as the US.)[8] Saddam Hussein, Iraq's dictator, had previously failed to defeat Iran in a long drawn-out war (1980–88). But his ambition remained unassuaged. He hoped ultimately to build a new Babylonian empire, centering on the ancient Mesopotamia, but including also the oil-rich Gulf states and Saudi Arabia. Backed by huge resources in oil, Iraq would develop a mighty arsenal of atomic, bacteriological, and chemical weapons, to become the policeman of the Persian Gulf and thereafter destroy the Jewish state.

As a first step toward the grand design, Iraq, in 1990, forcibly occupied Kuwait. Having already gained practice in committing all manner of atrocities against Iraq's Shiite and Kurdish minorities, the Iraqi forces ruled in Kuwait by blood and iron. The invasion earned condemnation from the UN, more particularly from the Bush administration. But the Iraqi dictator discounted such opposition. His own army was numerous and battle hardened. The US, in Saddam's view, remained paralyzed by the Vietnam syndrome. Internationally, the US could surely be isolated, the US domestic opposition would prevent the US forces from fighting an extended war and incurring extensive casualties.

None of these calculations worked. Bush's diplomacy created a massive coalition, which included Arabs as well as British and French participants. Militarily, only the British contingent was of real account. (According to US service men, the Arabs' battle hymn was "Onward Christian Soldiers.") But, diplomatically, Bush was able to turn an essentially American campaign into an international peace-keeping operation. The Gulf War strikingly differed from the Vietnam War in that few Americans of any political persuasion sympathized with the US's enemy. Most importantly, the Soviet Union now cooperated with the US. "In order to keep Gorbachev on board the anti-Iraqi coalition, Bush was reversing America's forty-five year-old policy of trying to keep the Soviets out of the Middle East."[9]

After the expiration of a UN Security Council resolution calling on Iraq to withdraw from Kuwait, the allied forces struck. The Iraqi forces soon collapsed, and Kuwait was liberated. According to Bush's critics, it was a "hollow victory." The allies had expelled the Iraqis from Kuwait, but had failed to overthrow Saddam Hussein (who remained in power after Bush had left office). Bush's action, said his censors, merely encouraged international savagery; the US should instead have aimed at freeing Kuwait through an entirely Arab coalition, led by an Arab general. Instead, the US shed blood and gained international discredit merely to repair Bush's domestic image as a wimp. Others complained that little was done for the Kurds, among the chief victims of Iraqi oppression, or that Israeli interests had been neglected. (When Iraq bombarded Israel with missiles, Israel was persuaded not to retaliate, lest the Arab members of the coalition be offended.)

The Kurds in Iraq indeed achieved only a tenuous measure of UN protection; Kurds – unlike Palestinians – were unable to gain international support for a state of their own, an ambition unacceptable alike to Iraq, Turkey, Syria, and Iran. Bush and Baker were not as friendly toward Israel as Reagan and Shultz had been. Nevertheless, the US victory was a victory also for Israel; the Iraq defeat a defeat of the PLO. The PLO's tradition of backing a loser cost the PLO dearly; it lost financial support from the Saudis and from Kuwait. The PLO thereafter reverted to the "two-state" solution, officially adopted in

8 See The Institute for Strategic Studies, *The Military Balance, 1988–1989*, London, The Institute, 1988.
9 Beschloss and Talbott, *At the Highest Level*, p. 262.

1988, but forgotten during the Gulf War, when the PLO had supported Iraq, and had once again sworn to "liberate Palestine inch by inch from the sea to the river."[10]

From the US's standpoint, Bush's diplomacy had worked well. Only US intervention could have brought victory. Given Iraq's military strength at the start of the Gulf War, no Arab country, and no coalition of Arab states, could have defeated Iraq on its own. The result would only have been more carnage, in all probability; an all intra-Arab conflict would have led to a war of attrition resulting in even more dead Arabs, while Kuwait would have remained Iraq's nineteenth province. In a serious error of judgment, the US forces were not allowed to follow up their victory. (The White House wanted to end the war in 100 hours.) Saddam was permitted to stay in power; his army Red Guard had not been destroyed, and this enabled him to threaten Kuwait once again in 1994. However, it was not in the US interest completely to annihilate Iraq as a state, and thereby leave Iran in unchallenged supremacy in the Persian Gulf, the State Department argued. Better wait until the mullahs had destroyed themselves by dint of corruption, hypocrisy, and incompetence. The State Department had always supported Iraq against Iran, fearing Iran more. But supporting Kurds and Shiites within a federal system would have kept Iraq whole and restrained Iran. Overall, the US had performed well both on the diplomatic and the military plane. The proficiency of US military forces impressed not only Arabs, but also the Soviet military leadership. The "Vietnam syndrome" weakened in US politics. Bush even spoke, somewhat ill advisedly, of a New World Order. Both internationally and nationally, Bush's position as a leader seemed unchallengeable.

Domestic Policy

"It's the economy, stupid," was one of the Democrats' most effective electioneering slogans in the campaign that terminated the Bush presidency. Having proclaimed his desire alike to be the "education president," the "environment president," and the architect of a new prosperity, Bush failed in all three endeavors. He did so, said his critics, because his original strictures on Reagan's "voodoo economics" proved all too well founded. However, Bush continued in Reagan's footsteps, and thereby incurred all the critiques occasioned by his predecessor. Supply-side economics, said the critics, led to financial profligacy which in turn left the US with an unmanageable burden of debt. Instead of saving money, Americans spent it. Manufacturing enterprises in the US increasingly became unable to compete with their opposite numbers in Germany, in Japan, and other advanced East Asian countries. (Books about the real or assumed economic virtues of the "Four Little Tigers" came to fill many library shelves.) Overall productivity slowed down; America's standard of living stopped rising during the Bush presidency. Caught in the vice of Reaganomics, Bush could no longer use deficit finance as a fiscal stimulus; the gap between haves and have-nots increased – the "Bush recession" became inevitable.

Bush, however, was no Reaganite. The commitment to supply-side economics, already weakened during Reagan's second tour of office, further diminished under Bush (who throughout his term of office had to deal with a Democratic Congress). Bush was working under other serious constraints. No matter what was said either by Reagan's admirers

10 Efraim Karsh, "Peace Not Love: Toward a Comprehensive Arab–Israeli Settlement," *The Washington Quarterly*, Spring 1984, p. 151.

or his critics, Reagan had never managed to achieve his fundamental goal: the reduction of the size and scope of government. Reagan had slowed the rate of growth only. No president thereafter succeeded in reducing welfare expenditure or pruning the welfare state. Not that Bush did not try. He used his veto 46 times. He appointed scores of conservatively minded judges (including Clarence Thomas to the Supreme Court). The budgetary picture would probably have been even more somber had Michael Dukakis been elected president, and "gridlock" between the White House and a spendthrift Congress thereby lessened. The fact remains that the deficit doubled, and the national debt went up from about $2.6 trillion to over $4.4 trillion during Bush's watch. Neither Reagan nor Bush could stem the tide of entitlements. Government remained committed to huge subsidies, grants, loans, and other favors designed to help special interests, such as the old and the poor, farming, banking, and other forms of manufacturing.

Bush offended conservatives in many different ways. He signed into law an increase in the minimum wage, thus raising the cost of doing business in the US. (Poorly skilled people henceforth would be less, not more, likely to be hired than before.) Bush helped to win approval for a landmark extension of the Clean Air Act of 1990, which imposed new charges on industry. Bush supported many other measures which might have been expected to increase his popularity among liberals but not conservatives. He helped to win approval for the Americans with Disability Act; he appointed William Reilly, a keen environmentalist, to head the Environmental Protection Agency (EPA). After a long fight with Congress, Bush accepted the Civil Rights Act of 1991. (This made it easier for workers to prove job discrimination and, for the first time, gave women the right to win damages in such cases. At Bush's insistence, the law was not, however, made retroactive, a position upheld by the Supreme Court in 1994.) Bush also signed into law a major tax increase (through his Budget Agreement with Congress in 1990), and thereby broke his elections promise ("read my lips") not to increase taxes. Last but not least, during the Reagan–Bush years "various forms of protectionism reappeared on the political scene under the name of 'competitiveness' and gained support not only among the anti-Reaganites."[11]

On the other hand, the Bush administration had considerable achievements to its credit. Inflation dropped during Bush's term of office (from about 5 percent to 3 percent per annum). Interest rates came down (from almost 9 percent to about 7.5 percent). The stock market registered impressive gains. In cooperation with Congress, the president put together a reasonable bail-out for bankrupt or floundering savings and loans associations – responding to a crisis derived from the early 1980s, an emergency not tackled in time in Congress. The US did experience a recession, but this was part of a worldwide slump which hit the other major industrial nations with greater severity than the US.

Bush's censors stressed the sufferings imposed on the poor by a continuing recession. But by the standard of previous slumps, the Bush recession was by no means severe. Recovery, moreover, began in the Bush era. Private consumption rose. Public investment boomed. (According to Clinton, the US infrastructure had crumbled owing to inadequate spending on public works. In fact, total investment in streets, highways, water and sewerage systems, mass transport, and airports amounted to $43.66 billion, a figure 41 percent higher in real terms than the amount spent in 1982.)[12] Far from declining

11 Nicolas Spulber, *Managing the American Economy, from Roosevelt to Reagan*, Bloomington, IN, Bloomington University Press, 1989, p. 124.
12 "The Infrastructure Myth," *Executive Alert*, May–June 1993, p. 1.

into economic decadence, the US in 1993 was listed as the world's most competitive country (ahead, in that order, of Singapore, Japan, Hong Kong, Germany, and Switzerland.)[13] But the Bush campaign unaccountably failed to trumpet the good news, and Bill Clinton naturally took credit thereafter for the return of prosperity.

Bush's administration also did well in international trade. In 1992, Bush negotiated the North American Free Trade Agreement (NAFTA) which would expand US markets, and benefit alike consumers in the US, Canada, and Mexico. Bush was a competent administrator who picked competent people (particularly in foreign and national security affairs – men such as Dick Cheney, James Baker, and Brent Scowcroft). What is more, Bush understood the art of delegating responsibility; he resisted the temptation of micro-managing the Gulf War from the White House, as Johnson had attempted for the Vietnam War. In a more general sense, the Reagan–Bush years had shifted the terms of political debate from left-of-center to right-of-center. (According to Gallup polls, more than one-third of respondents described themselves as conservative, nearly one-half as middle-of-the-road. The liberal remnant comprised no more than about one-seventh of the total.)[14]

Bush therefore seemed likely to win. Bill (William Jefferson) Clinton, Bush's opponent, by contrast, was little known nationally, the governor of a minor Southern state who had avoided the draft during the Vietnam conflict. Republican strategists, moreover, took comfort from Britain's experience. In Britain, Prime Minister John Major had won a spectacular victory in April 1992. Contrary to the polls (which were going as badly for Major as they were by that time for Bush), the British electorate decided at the last minute, and mostly in the voting booth, that they would rather live with a Conservative government than risk a return to Labour. Major's victory greatly cheered Bush, and British conservative experts crossed the Atlantic for the purpose of advising the Republican Party on how to replicate Major's triumph in America.

The British and the US elections, however, turned out to be very different. The majority of the British electorate as yet feared Labour, still associated with the wild men of the 1970s. The Democratic Party, by contrast, was no longer identified in the public mind with unkempt militants. On the contrary, reformers within the Democratic Leadership Council (DLC) had done their level best to return to the politics of the center. Even one-time activists such as Hillary Rodham Clinton, Bill Clinton's wife, took good care to appear safe, solid, and conventional, with a frock and hairdo fit for a PTA meeting in a staid suburb.

In the US, the position was complicated by the emergence of Ross Perot as a third party candidate. Perot was a wealthy businessman who beat the populist drum. He affected disdain for Washington's assumed blend of inefficiency, profligacy, and contempt for ordinary people. He appealed to those who had become disillusioned with US party politics. (In this respect Perot represented a much wider trend that affected every major Western country where the old-established parties all weakened at the end of the Cold War.) Both Clinton and Perot relentlessly hammered the president for his failure to provide leadership on economic matters, and for being out of touch and tired. Major, on the other hand, had appeared to British electors as a fresh face, untouched by the scandals of

13 IMD–World Economic Forum, cited by *The Economist*, 10 September 1994, p. 7.
14 According to *The Gallup Poll Monthly*, February 1993, p. 11, 4 percent of respondents said that they were "very conservative," 30 percent "conservative," 44 percent "moderate," 14 percent "liberal," and 5 percent "very liberal." The rest had no opinion.

the past. British electors had mostly blamed Mrs Thatcher and her long-standing chancellor of the exchequer, Nigel Lawson, for the country's economic problems. Bush, on the other hand, had been elected in his own right; he had served as president for four years, and as vice-president for eight years. Hence Bush took the blame for all shortcomings.

The 1992 presidential election thus turned into a referendum on domestic affairs in which Bush's achievements in foreign policy proved no help. The "evil empire" had vanished; the Gulf War had been won. Americans now felt entitled to a "peace dividend." According to voters' statements, the most important issues now were the economy, unemployment, the deficit, and health care – issues which Bush had failed to air adequately during his term of office. By accepting higher taxes, Bush had given away his best electoral slogan: "read my lips." Bush, moreover, was much less successful than Reagan in holding together the existing coalition between moderate Republicans, the Religious Right (embodied by the Christian Coalition under Pat Robertson), and the far right (represented by Pat Buchanan whose speech at the Republican Convention was given prominence by the national press). Dan Quayle, an able young senator, and Bush's running mate, was exposed to similar treatment on the part of journalists who depicted him as an unsophisticated backwoodsman. ("I wish I had studied Latin in high school – then I could have talked to ordinary folk when I visited Latin America.")

Above all, Bush and his leading officials seemed pure pragmatists, managers without ideological commitment. Men such as White House Chief-of-Staff John Sununu and budget director Richard Darman did not particularly care one way or another over issues such as the Clean Air Act, or the Americans with Disability Act, or the Civil Rights Act, or even the violation of Bush's 1988 pledge not to raise taxes. They were technocrats to whom the "vision thing" was an electoral handicap. Faced by Bill Clinton, young, keen, and active, Bush seemed tired: too proud, or too bored, or too exhausted to fight; incapable even of running an efficient campaign.

The presidential election of 1992 was a decisive defeat for Bush. (Clinton won 32 states, as against Bush's 18, and 43 percent of the electoral vote, as against Bush's 38 percent and Perot's 19 percent.) The Democrats made a clean sweep of the New England states (the first time since 1964), and major inroads into the Southern states which previously had voted solidly Republican. Although seven of the 11 states comprised within the old Confederacy remained loyal to Bush, Clinton secured victory in Arkansas (his home state), Tennessee, Georgia, and Louisiana. Clinton also gained the key Midwestern states, and the Western states (including the largest prize of all, California). The Republicans somewhat managed to improve their position in the House. But these modest successes in no wise made up for one of the major political upsets in US history.

Once more, a Democrat occupied the White House. Clinton henceforth would have to meet four great challenges. The first post-Cold War president, he would have to conduct US foreign policy when traditional objectives had shifted. Henceforth, the demand for interventionist policies overseas would come from the liberal-left rather than the right. Clinton would have to deal with the welfare state and its discontents; in his own words, he would have to reinvent government – this at a time when confidence in officialdom and official experts was waning all over the Western world. The new president would have to cope with intellectual challenges to liberalism put forward by bodies such as the Hoover Institution, the American Enterprise Institute (AEI), the Cato Institute, and the Progress and Freedom Foundation, as well as journals including *Policy Review*, *Standard*, and *National Interest*. The president would also have to counter the Christian Coalition (now led by Paul Reed, supported by personages such as Pat Robertson, founder of the

Christian Broadcasting Network). Contrary to the liberal image, the Coalition's members, overall, were well educated with good incomes. They stood determined to wage cultural war against abortionists, homosexuals, lesbians, and liberal professors. In doing so, they claimed the commanding heights of morality so long occupied by the left.

Above all, Clinton would have to hold together an ever more disparate coalition: traditionally minded white voters (unionists, housewives, pensioners); ethnic minorities (Latinos, especially blacks, the most loyal component of the Democratic Party); and social activists. White workers (and a minority of black and Hispanic voters) opposed affirmative action, a policy to which social activists were deeply committed. To the social activists, abortion was a legitimate medical procedure; to the traditionalists, abortion was murder. Even the activists increasingly quarrelled among themselves. The traditional Jewish–black alliance threatened to disintegrate, as black militants denounced Jewish (and also Korean, Chinese, and Armenian) shopkeepers in black ghettoes, censured Jewish leadership in the civil rights movement, and condemned Israel as a servant of Western imperialism. (However, no black activist called for an alliance between African- and Arab-Americans.) Blacks, Hispanics, and feminists disagreed over the apportionment of affirmative action benefits. The president would have to balance such conflicting claims – this at a time when blue-collar and white-collar workers of whatever ethnic descent or political affiliation faced a decline in median family incomes. In the US, moreover, as in the entire Western world, officialdom and official expertise were waning. (Between 1960 and 1988 social welfare expenditure had enormously increased as a share of the GNP and as a percentage of total government outlay. But so had crime, illegitimacy, drug use, and other ills.)

Clinton suffered from other disabilities. Whereas Bush and Dole had both served with distinction in World War II, Clinton had evaded military service during the Vietnam conflict. Whereas his father's generation mostly had worn uniform at one time in their lives, the Clintons probably had no close friend who had ever served in the military. The Clintons were liberals by conviction – bright, articulate, committed to social justice as they saw it, educated at top-level institutions, and conscious of their assumed status of an intellectual and moral élite. (Bill Clinton had gone to Georgetown, Yale, and Oxford; his wife, Hillary Rodham, to Wellesley and Yale.) The Clintons were perfectly attuned to that cohort of "boomer liberals" who, by that time, had risen to commanding positions within the prestige universities, the prestige media, and the Democratic Party. For a large segment of the electorate, however, this élite no longer commanded respect.

Yet there was also something reassuringly Establishment about Clinton. He was a Southerner, born in Hope, a small town in Arkansas. He had made his career as Governor of Arkansas, a Southern state. (It was not for nothing that Clinton, in the 1992 elections, had once more made inroads into the South which, in recent years, had turned solidly Republican.) He spoke with a Southern accent; he went to Church. He had indeed erred from the straight and narrow path of marital virtue. But so had millions of other Americans. Moreover, public standards had greatly changed from the days of Jack Kennedy and his predecessors, when the press had assiduously shielded incumbent presidents from any breath of sexual scandal. There were charges and counter-charges concerning crooked business deals in Little Rock. But by the standards of Rome, Paris, or Washington, the amounts involved were minuscule. Before taking office, moreover, Clinton had served as chairman of the DLC (Democratic Leadership Council), specifically formed to appeal to centrist voters. (The DLC was created in 1985. Derided by the left within the Democratic Party as the "Democratic Leisure Class," the DLC appealed to business interests and to middle-of-the-roaders. The DLC created its own think-tank, the Progressive Policy Institute, which became an intellectual force in its own right.)

In theory, therefore, Clinton should have done superbly well. Having begun to recover at the end of Bush's term, the economy kept expanding. Unemployment dropped to a level envied by Europeans (from 7.8 percent in 1992 to 5.59 percent in 1995). Clinton's program – a middle-class tax cut, more efficient government and less of it – seemed eminently acceptable to the suburbs which now determined US politics. But Clinton initially had much difficulty in asserting himself. The First Lady seemed snobbish, interfering, and dogmatic. The White House staff was full of young people, inexperienced, yet quarrelsome and arrogant. Attempting to hold a balance between social activists and social conservatives within his party, the president came across as indecisive, anxious to please everybody all of the time.[15] The White House staff was poorly organized. More dubious still seemed the Clintons' addiction to "new age" gurus.

Clinton, accordingly, made a poor start. His largest project sought to create a national health program. The project was initiated by a panel directed by Hillary Clinton. The program sought to cover all citizens and legal residents, providing them with an irreducible minimum in the way of benefits which would continue despite prolonged illness or changes in employment. (Illegal immigrants would be eligible for emergency and certain other services.) There would be a wide range of available services. There would be a choice between traditional fee-for-service and other plans. All Americans would get a national health identification card. A National Health Board would oversee the system and set up a national health budget.

During the 1960s, the plan would have had a wide appeal. In the 1990s, however, the plan faltered. The Clintons had made serious tactical mistakes by not including Republicans in the original planning. The Clintons faced widespread opposition from special interests, including the physicians. But, in a wider sense, the climate of opinion had changed. All too many ordinary citizens now distrusted the federal government, official experts, and official expertise. Supporters of the plan claimed that there was a national health crisis, leaving millions of Americans without insurance. Were they to be believed? Were officials to be trusted when they assured the public that the plan would not engender new taxes, more bureaucracy, more administrative foul-ups? The plan failed and was forgotten.

Divisive also were the "culture wars," symbolized by the controversy over admitting homosexuals to the military. In his 1992 campaign Clinton had promised that he would lift the ban on gays in the defense services immediately after his election. But Clinton met with unexpected opposition from the Congress, from the Joint Chiefs of Staffs, and from cultural conservatives who regarded homosexual conduct not as an acceptable form of sexual expression but as an abomination before the Lord. Clinton arrived at a compromise based on the principle "Don't ask, don't tell, don't pursue." But inevitably the compromise aroused resentment from every quarter. Conservatives denounced what they called "special treatment" for homosexuals, while liberals complained that the president had reneged on his campaign promise. Like the abortion issue, the homosexuality issue was one on which no politician could win.

15 See Elizabeth Drew, *On the Edge: the Clinton Presidency*, New York, Simon and Schuster, 1994; Bob Woodward, *The Agenda*, New York, Simon and Schuster, 1994; David Maraniss, *First in his Class*, New York, Simon and Schuster, 1995; and John Hohenberg, *The Bill Clinton Story*, Syracuse, Syracuse University Press, 1994.

The Democratic Party suffered further splits, as suburban ecologists and suburban animal rights advocates clashed with backwoods farmers and backwoods loggers, men and women who traditionally had voted for the Democratic Party. Controversy raged with equal bitterness over immigration (especially in border states such as Texas and California). Working-class "exclusionists" within the Democratic Party argued that immigrants unfairly competed for jobs with the native-born (especially unskilled people). Humanitarians within the Democratic Party, by contrast, rejected such arguments both on economic and humanitarian grounds. (In fact, a substantial proportion of legal immigrants were by now highly skilled or college trained.) Tax-payer lobbies, now influential in US politics, pleaded that immigrants, especially illegal immigrants, put an extra burden on social services. (There was, in fact, a sociological shift in the population of illegal immigrants to the US. In the olden days, illegal immigrants had mostly been single young men. But, increasingly, illegal as well as legal immigrants brought in their families – children and old people who naturally made greater demands on social services than unwed bachelors.) Liberal Democrats widely rejected such arguments as a form of "immigrant bashing." But the anti-immigrant lobby now also found support from other traditional liberals committed to protection of the environment and zero population growth. More fundamental still were disagreements over the general tax-payer's obligation to help the poor by funding social services. What were the limits of the welfare state? This was an issue which divided the Democratic much more than the Republican Party.

Equally important in American politics was the "gender gap." Women had traditionally voted for concerns of domesticity. (More women than men, on the average, had supported Prohibition.) Now the gender gap widened for wider socioeconomic reasons. Family ties weakened; divorce figures rose. (Their number doubled in the US between 1965 and 1979.) Hence families no longer voted as a unit, as they had tended to do in the olden days. But women, on the average, earned less than men; women, on the average, were more dependent on welfare. (By the time Clinton took office, about two-thirds of families in federally supported housing schemes were headed by women.) A disproportionately high proportion of women worked in the public services. Women benefited from affirmative action programs. Hence a higher proportion of women voted for the Democratic than for the Republican Party. By the same token, however, a higher proportion of white men voted for the Republicans, so that the Democrats may actually have lost in the bargain.[16]

Foreign affairs also entailed trouble for the president. Admittedly, US–EU relations went well, as the leftist intellectuals' anti-Americanism ceased to be fashionable. The EU had clearly failed to enunciate a policy of its own in Bosnia. Few Europeans, by the mid-1990s, wanted the US to leave NATO. (On the contrary, the French in 1995 reintegrated their military into NATO, thereby reversing de Gaulle's decision to withdraw, taken in 1966.) Clinton proved astonishingly successful at public appearances (above all during a visit in 1995 to Northern Ireland where Clinton's own staff was flabbergasted by the enthusiasm of the crowds).

The Clinton administration could likewise take credit for ratifying the North American Free Trade Agreement (NAFTA). This established free trade between the US, Canada, and Mexico. To back the treaty was a courageous decision for a president whose working-class supporters widely opposed the treaty for facilitating foreign competition against

16 Steven Sark, "Gap Politics," *The Atlantic Monthly*, July 1996, pp. 71–80.

US-manufactured products. In 1995 the US and the EU agreed on the new Transatlantic Agenda and thereby extended international cooperation.

The Clinton administration did equally well as a broker in the Middle East. In 1993 Israel and the PLO (Palestine Liberation Organization) ended nearly half a century of hostilities by signing a peace treaty. Jordan and Israel followed suit the next year. All combatants had by now arrived at the conviction that neither side could wipe out the other militarily, a conviction that formed a true guarantee for peace. (Whites and blacks in South Africa had come to a similar conclusion. To the delight of US policy-makers, and contrary to the forecasts of most professional Africanists, the Afrikaners and Africans negotiated a peaceful transfer of power entailing Nelson Mandela's advance from jail to the South African presidential office (1994), and the end of US sanctions on South Africa.)

But neither the Middle Eastern nor the South African solution had entailed direct US military intervention. Matters stood very differently in countries such as Somalia, Haiti, and Bosnia, all of which witnessed the deployment of US troops. In the Cold War days, military intervention in troubled countries abroad had been regarded as a right-wing cause; isolationism had been associated with the left in US politics. Once the Cold War ended, the ideological balance shifted. The most prominent isolationists were now Republicans such as Pat Buchanan, a cultural conservative, a protectionist, and a declared opponent of US entanglements in foreign parts. By contrast, it was now the liberals who called for US humanitarian intervention in foreign countries stricken by famine or civil strife. US military action, once denounced by progressives as an exercise in US hegemonism, turned into a moral duty, as in President Wilson's day. (US intervention in Bosnia enjoyed its greatest support among non-white people in the US who, presumably, were more likely to identify with Bosnian Muslims as a disfavored minority.)[17] For Clinton, intervention in Bosnia was a moral issue, not a venture motivated by electoral considerations.

Intervention abroad was not a Democratic preserve. In 1983, Reagan had sent US marines to strife-torn Lebanon – to no avail. In 1992, President Bush had despatched troops to Somalia from where they ingloriously withdrew in 1993. But Clinton was undeterred by these experiences. In 1994, US troops landed in Haiti for the sake of restoring democracy in that island. (US intervention had met with special support from the Black Caucus in Congress and from black activists, a constituency which Clinton could not ignore.) But neither democracy nor free enterprise flourished thereafter in Haiti, in Bosnia, or in Rwanda and Zaire (where US troops landed in 1996). Armies are not designed to act as a police force, least of all in a foreign country. To use armies in such a capacity is apt to weaken alike military morale and military efficiency. Success in such ventures, in our opinion, must always seem unlikely.

Given widespread disillusionment with an interventionist federal government, the mid-term elections of 1994 thus turned into a shattering defeat for the Democrats. The Republicans gained control of the Senate for the first time since 1986 (with 53 seats to the Democrats' seven). The Republicans won 36 out of 50 state governorships, as well as numerous seats in state legislatures and other civic posts. More surprisingly still, the Republicans secured a majority in the House of Representatives for the first time since

17 According to a 1995 Gallup Poll, 50 percent of non-white respondents considered intervention in Bosnia needful to protect US interests, only 27 percent of white respondents felt so. See *The Gallup Monthly*, no. 357, June 1995, p. 18.

1954. The Democrats, moreover, had again done badly in the South, formerly the Democratic Party's heartland. Nevertheless, almost half of America's voters did not vote and had little confidence in the government's ability to improve their lives, no matter which party was in control. Voter dissatisfaction was paralleled by a high rate of resignation from politics on the part of veteran campaigners who complained of mean-spirited campaign rhetoric and ever-rising electoral expense.

The Republicans put forward a new legislative program, known as the "Contract with America," organized by Newt Gingrich, House minority whip, subsequently Speaker. Gingrich had drive, energy, and organizing ability; he was alike tutor and drill sergeant to the great cohort of newly elected Republican House members on an anti-Washington program. By profession a college professor, Gingrich had taught at West Georgia College, a small Southern school. His subject was African history, a discipline which conservatives were *de facto* considered unfit to teach at US prestige universities – a disability which may have heightened Gingrich's visceral hostility to liberal orthodoxies. The "Contract with America" included a constitutional amendment requiring a balanced budget, a line-item veto enabling the president to eliminate specific items from the budget, cuts in income tax and capital gains tax, a reduction in welfare payments, and the imposition of term limits on incumbent legislators in the Congress. The Contract exalted the "family values" advocated by the New Right (and also by many Democrats); but as a gesture toward party unity the contract said nothing about the divisive issue of abortion. The contract underlined the dominance within the Republican Party of populists from the South and West, as against the more liberal and patrician Republicanism once dominant in the north-east. At the same time, the US – like Western European countries – experienced a new demand for decentralized government. The "new federalism" would diminish the power of Washington and enhance the power of the States.

President Clinton went with the tide. Bowing to growing popular hostility against mass immigration, he signed, in 1996, the Immigration Control and Financial Responsibility Act. (Of all countries in the world, the US accepted by far the largest number of legal immigrants: about a million a year, in addition to many illegal immigrants, estimated to number some 4,000,000 people. The new immigrants mainly came from Latin America and Asia rather than Europe. Whereas in the olden days, immigrants had mainly included young people of working age, the new immigrants contained a steadily growing number of aged people and children who made new demands on US social services. So did a growing number of political refugees, admitted on socially favorable conditions.) The new laws disappointed those who wanted great cuts in legal immigration, but the act took a hard line against illegal immigrants, and also restricted welfare benefits for legal immigrants. Even more controversial, for liberal Democrats, was the Personal Responsibility and Work Opportunity Reconciliation Act, 1996. The Act reduced federal welfare benefits for poor people, while giving new powers to the States for alleviating poverty. Liberal academics were disgusted. As Berkeley sociologists put it, Clinton had succumbed to an ignorant public which held the poor responsible for their own poverty. For the first time since the New Deal, a part of the Social Security Act, 1935, had been repealed in a manner conforming to the worst aspects of the US's "individualistic culture."[18]

The American electorate as a whole, however, approved of Clinton's shift. The elections of 1996 therefore ended, so to speak, in a draw. Clinton's opponent in the fight

18 Letter by Berkeley sociologists, headed by Robert N. Bellah, in *New York Review of Books*, 28 November 1996, p. 65.

for the presidency was Robert Dole, an experienced legislator and a genuine war hero. But Dole was old and looked old; a pragmatist to the core, he had changed his views all too often and thereby failed to inspire even his own Republicans. Clinton, by contrast, shared Nixon's vulnerability to scandals; he also had what was politely known as a credibility problem. ("Not a Lincoln, not a Ford, but a Dodge Convertible.") But Clinton played to Republican concerns: safe streets, law and order, a balanced budget, education, and family values. Mrs Clinton, a tough and ambitious lawyer, went one better by assuming the mien of a harried housewife. Above all, Clinton could take credit for a sound economy, a low rate of inflation, and low unemployment. He won with a substantial majority (49 percent of the popular vote, as against 41 percent for Dole, the rest for lesser contenders). The Republicans, by contrast, maintained control over both Houses of Congress. The US henceforth seemed set on a centrist course.[19]

19 In the House, Republicans thereafter had 221 seats, Democrats 197. In the Senate, Republicans held 55 seats, Democrats 45. Dole himself only did well in the Southern and Mid-Western states.

12

Germany: Divided and United

Deutsche, wir können stolz sein auf unser Land (Germans, we can be proud of our country) proclaimed a 1972 election poster – not for a right-winger's cause, but for Willy Brandt. Germany had once again become Europe's economic power house. The Germans were doing supremely well in commerce, industry, and even world soccer. Whereas US forces had fought in two major conflicts after World War II, and whereas US society was bitterly rent by racial divisions and by dissensions over the Vietnam War, West Germany had been at peace ever since 1945. West Germany had built an efficient welfare state. Trade unionists had become respected and respectable, partners with industrialists on directoral boards. The West German élites had become "open" to an extent unimaginable in the Weimar Republic, not to speak of the Wilhelminian Empire. Not that West Germany had become an egalitarian country. But patents of nobility or membership of prestigious student fraternities had ceased to be passports to success. West Germany's established rich had joined the international jet set. Vulgarity might go uncensored, but blatant nationalism had ceased to be chic. Germany was fortunate in other ways. Olden-time poverty had disappeared in West Germany, the grim deprivation of postwar years had become a matter of memory. West Germany's income structure no longer resembled a triangle, but an onion, with a huge bulge of middle-income people.[1] In this, as in every other respect, the Federal German Republic had become the US's star pupil, the very model of a modern Western democratic state.

The Social Liberal Coalition

Unlike political parties in the US, the three major German parties remained tightly organized, served by highly qualified research institutes and by disciplined bureaucrats. The major parties received massive funding from the federal government. (Contrary to the SPD's image, it was actually the wealthiest of all).[2] By the 1970s, the SPD had long ceased to be the party of the poor; in composition and ideology, it had come to resemble more the Democratic Party of the US than the party of Karl Liebknecht, Rosa Luxemburg, or Kurt Schumacher. In 1977, Egon Bahr, the SPD's chief executive officer, submitted a fascinating sociological study to the Federal Party Congress. The SPD had turned from a workers' party into a national party, a *Volkspartei*. Clerks, supervisors, teachers, and

1 Henry Pachter, *Modern Germany: a Social, Cultural, and Political History*, Boulder, Colo., Westview Press, 1978, pp. 326–9.
2 In 1992, the total revenue of the main parties was as follows (in DM): SPD 343,705,394; CDU 339,661,132; CSU 91,212,020; FDP: 88,563,747; Greens 59,693,294. See *The Week in Germany*, 17 April 1992, p. 2.

academics between them now outnumbered the workers. The average SPD member's income equalled the average income of the nation at large. Over-represented in the party were public service employees and, above all, men (only 20 percent of the SPD'S members were women.)[3]

The new cleavage within the SPD was of a cultural kind; it split apart traditionally minded Germans of whatever social background from the "other Germany" whose members read the novels of Heinrich Böll and Günter Grass, who prized their own conscience, their aesthetic sensibility, and their moral commitment. This new élite drew its strength from the young, but from university students rather than from industrial apprentices. They dominated the *Jusos* (the party's youth wing), and also the Greens. They were pacifist in inclination, and anti-American in outlook. They differed from corresponding age cohorts in the English-speaking countries in that they censured their elders, not merely for bourgeois conformity, but also for having given aid and comfort to the defunct Nazi regime. German youth, moreover, objected, often quite rightly, to the rule of elderly professors out of touch with present-day problems. The youthful left was environmentally conscious – again with good reason. (Before World War II, children born in Rhineland cities had swum in the Rhine as a matter of course; 40 years later, swimmers would have risked their lives in what had become an utterly polluted river.)

There were also generational problems of a more subtle kind. German students were apt to stay on at college longer than their opposite numbers in Britain or France. Advancement for the young was also apt to be slower. To give a specific example, young German officials still served as *Referendare* (on the lowest rung of the civil service élite) at a time when a graduate from the *Ecole nationale d'administration* already held an important position in a ministry or a ministerial cabinet. Educated young Germans willing to enter conventional or semi-conventional politics widely supported the Greens (whose nucleus was formed in 1972), or they supported the SPD. They had formed one of Brandt's main constituencies. Unfortunately for the SPD, the idealistic youngsters, however, offended the average German voter.

It was Helmut Schmidt (federal chancellor, 1974–82) who made sure that the left-wingers were kept in their place. Schmidt, a Hamburger by birth, had served in the *Wehrmacht* as a lieutenant and obtained his first grounding in politics as a member of the German Socialist Student Union. He later rose in the SPD's official hierarchy, made his name in the local politics of Hamburg, and later in the *Bundestag*. He gained wide ministerial experience (as federal minister of defense, and later of finance). He was tough. (As a parliamentarian he became known as *Schmidt Schnauze* – big mouth Schmidt. In time his manners improved, but his toughness stayed the same.) Schmidt was attractive to voters in other ways. (He was handsome in a Nordic way; in later years he appeared on TV the very image of an elder statesman as picked by an impresario in Hollywood.) He spoke well. He could win over even a hostile audience. (Speaking in excellent English, Schmidt thus addressed a British trade-union audience on the touchy subject of British membership of the EC. Affecting an air of courteous reserve, he explained that talking

3 Alfred Grosser, *Deutschlandbilanz: Geschichte Deutschlands seit 1945* (trans. from the French by Roberta Hall and Margaret Carroux), Munich, C. Hanser, 1970, p. 495. Above all, see the standard work on the subject, Dennis L. Bark and David R. Gress, *A History of West Germany*; vol. 1: *From Shadow to Substance,1945–1963*; vol. 2: *Democracy and its Discontents, 1963–1988*, Oxford, Blackwell, 1989; and David F. Conradt, Gerald R. Kleinfeld, George K. Romoser and Christian Søe, eds, *Germany's New Politics*, Tempe, Arizona, German Studies Review, 1995.

to a British Labour audience on the merits of European union was like expounding the merits of drink to a temperance meeting. He thereby broke the ice.) Schmidt possessed in full measure those amiable eccentricities beloved by cartoonists: he liked sailing; he played the organ; he enjoyed snuff; he wore a dashing cap (*Prinz-Heinrich Mütze*). He was married to a nice woman, a former botany teacher. Above all, Schmidt had personal dignity – this at a time when parties and politicians increasingly seemed to lose this particular quality, appearing powerful, but unloved. He was one of Germany's most outstanding politicians – but in the end became isolated within his own party.

Schmidt's coalition partner, the FDP (the Free Democrats), continued to play a crucial role in German politics. The party was small numerically, but it counted many supporters among small and medium businessmen, an important group in the German economy. In addition, the FDP represented the professions. (It was sometimes referred to as the party of the "three As": *Ärzte* (physicians), *Anwälte* (lawyers), and *Apotheker* (pharmacists).) Whereas the CDU and SPD shared a common commitment to state intervention, the FDP was a liberal party, keen on free trade and small government. The FDP thus played an essential role in restraining the powers of the state and pulling West German politics toward the center – no matter who governed. (Between 1949, when the Federal German Republic was founded, and reunification in 1990, West Germany had 28 years of Christian Democratic and 13 years of Social Democratic government. In all but eight of these years, the FDP formed part of the ruling coalition.) Political scientists rightly spoke of "the FDP's almost institutionalized role in coalition government,"[4] for neither of the two major contenders could do without the FDP's essential support. (It was only after reunification that the political spectrum began to widen.)

As a reward for cooperation, the FDP received the Foreign Ministry, headed by Hans-Dietrich Genscher (foreign minister, 1974–92). A lawyer by training, Genscher had worked his way up in the FDP's hierarchy, where he coped as well as he might with the numerous internal dissensions which in particular plagued the FDP. As minister for foreign affairs, he proved a fixture alike in German, European, and Atlantic politics. No other minister enjoyed equal tenure. (He continued in office, first under the Social Democrats, later under the Christian Democrats, and only resigned in 1992.) Genscher also held a variety of international key offices. (At various times he headed the European Council of Ministers and the NATO Council.) Above all, Genscher ran the Foreign Ministry as his own fief. As a German critic put it, "whoever had served Genscher from the beginning as a personal assistant or as a spokesperson for the Foreign Ministry today serves as an ambassador or departmental head."[5] West Germany's foreign policy thereby acquired a degree of continuity which Germany's neighbors might envy. Its principles were simple. Germany would tie its fate to France, and the Franco-German duo's to Europe. Germany would thereby at the same time restrain a potentially aggressive German nationalism at home, resist possible Soviet ambitions in Europe, conciliate the US, and maintain an agreeable status quo. German reunification was desired in theory, but in practice consigned to a remote future. Better to concentrate on the immediate object of improving the lot of East Germans by tourism, trade, and other overt or covert contacts.

4 Stephen Padgett, "Party Democracy in the New German Polity," *German Politics and Society*, no. 28, Spring 1993, p. 28; Conradt et al., *Germany's New Politics*.
5 Jochen Thies, "Bonn, Berlin und die politische Klasse Deutschlands," *Europäische Rundschau*, vol. 22, no. 1, Winter 1994, pp. 13–22.

In domestic politics, Schmidt faced a difficult task: to hold together an increasingly heterogeneous party, dependent no longer on the blue-collar workers, but on a multitude of industrial workers, employees (especially functionaries in public services), women, and professional people.[6] Schmidt took a hard line against youthful leftists. He took a harder line still against terrorist organizations such as the RAF (Red Army Faction). But though left-wing terrorists received an extraordinary amount of publicity, they were quite insignificant when compared to the paramilitary forces which had once been maintained alike by the extreme right and extreme left during the Weimar Republic. The SPD–FDP coalition expanded the rights of women, but in a manner guaranteed to offend practicing Catholics. In 1977, West Germany passed a new law which made divorces easier to obtain, and for all practical purposes accepted the "no fault" principle. The age of majority was reduced to 18. Abortion was made easier to obtain than hitherto. In addition, workers received extended rights of "co-determination" in industrial enterprises – this despite bitter opposition from employers who argued that their property rights were being infringed. Whereas the French role of *comités d'entreprises* remained purely consultative, the right of *Mitbestimmung* gave workers wider representation on company boards.

At the same time, however, the coalition faced serious economic challenges. The "German miracle" came to an end. True enough, Germany's democratic institutions functioned effectively; the public services worked; so did West Germany's federal system with its division of powers as between the *Bund* (federal government), the *Länder* (states), and local governments. Interest groups – labor unions, employer associations, agricultural leagues and what not – all played an effective part in maintaining West Germany's accustomed stability. But the oil shocks of the 1970s slowed down the era of experimentation in social and economic reform.[7]

Schmidt responded to the economic crisis in a way that pleased the liberals more than the socialists within his coalition. He worked for what would probably turn out an unachievable aim, the gradual unification of the West European currencies. Between them, Schmidt and the French president, Valéry Giscard d'Estaing, Schmidt's preferred partner in Europe, set up the European Monetary System (EMS) in 1979. The system was designed to achieve exchange rate stability, but in the long run did not meet the makers' expectations. Secondly, as Bark and Gress point out, Schmidt's strategy aimed at securing access to raw materials and energy.[8] There was, of course, nothing Schmidt could do to reverse OPEC's decision to raise oil prices. (Partly in response to this crisis, West Germany, like its EC allies, leaned to the Arab side in the continuing conflict between Jews and Muslims in the Middle East.) But, despite numerous expert predictions made at the time, there was no permanent oil shortage. OPEC failed to maintain its long-term cohesion. Oil prices rose but did not go through the roof, and ultimately dropped, as oil production kept expanding world wide, and as the industrialized states began to use energy more efficiently than hitherto.

Schmidt did, however, endeavor to strengthen international bodies such as the IMF (International Monetary Fund) and the World Bank in their dealings with the Third World, while resisting all suggestions that raw material prices should be set by international agreement. In a similar vein, Schmidt opposed protectionism at home and

---

6 For social change within the SPD see, for instance, Karlheinz Blessing, ed., *SPD 2000: Die Modernisierung der SPD*, Marburg-Berlin, Schüren Presse Verlag, 1993.
7 Bark and Gress, *A History of West Germany*, vol. 2, p. 279.
8 Ibid., pp. 280–1.

abroad, convinced that tariff wars would preclude economic recovery. Schmidt attempted to resist inflation, convinced that Germany could more easily cope with a limited amount of unemployment than even a limited degree of inflation – a conclusion deeply rooted in German history, but one which strikingly set German policy-makers against their British and US counterparts.

Schmidt clashed with the US in other ways. During the crisis-ridden 1970s, Schmidt was faced with constant demands both from the US and associated Western European powers for West Germany to stimulate its economy. The US also took a harder line against Moscow, especially after the Soviet invasion of Afghanistan. While condemning the military regime set up in Poland, Schmidt was willing to continue limited economic cooperation with Poland – Washington disagreed. There were harsh words between Schmidt and Carter on nuclear disarmament, and also on human rights issues. Above all, there were bitter personal clashes. Schmidt got on well with Republicans such as Ford and George Shultz. But Schmidt could not abide Carter. Patronizing in his manner and prone to lecture, the German chancellor distrusted Carter's neglect of Western European interests over issues such as the US Nuclear Nonproliferation Act, 1978, and, more importantly, the US's wavering response to the Soviet deployment of medium-range nuclear missiles aimed at the NATO countries of Western Europe in 1979. (NATO responded with the conditional deployment of Pershing II and cruise missiles.) Speaking in more general terms, Schmidt would not listen to sermons from Carter whom Schmidt regarded as a preachy amateur. (Carter's lust for moralizing in public did not prevent him from praising every communist tyrant whom he met: Tito, Ceauşescu, Kim Il Sung.) Not surprisingly, the dislike between Schmidt and Carter was mutual!

Nevertheless, Schmidt remained a firm Atlanticist. As we have pointed out previously, the SPD gave massive support to moderate socialists in Lisbon at the time of the Portuguese revolution (1974) when, for a short time, there seemed a chance that the communists might take over and turn Portugal into a "European Cuba." As Schmidt put it, "the Atlantic alliance remains the elementary foundation for our safety, and the necessary framework for our efforts at achieving global *détente*."[9]

Americans reciprocated such sentiments. Germans remained popular in the US, despite two world wars. (US public opinion polls placed Germans near the top of the list of preferred foreigners, headed by Canadians, British, and French.) Something like one-fifth of Americans claimed to be wholly or partially of German descent. Germans were fully integrated: German-Americans were not *Volksdeutsche* (ethnic Germans resolved to hold on to their ethnic heritage in Eastern Europe). As far as the average American was concerned, the Holocaust was history. Germans in the US were associated with precision engineering and hard work. War movies forever cast German soldiers in the role of mechanized Indians – ever brave and forever beaten in the end. The US–German alliance was never questioned.

Kohl in Power

Despite his tough demeanor, Schmidt was never – as the Germans say – lord and master in his own house. The ruling coalition became increasingly divided, specially over finance.

9 Grosser, *Deutschlandbilanz*, p. 523. For a detailed examination of the Atlantic partnership under Schmidt, see Barbara D. Heep, *Helmut Schmidt und Amerika: Eine schwierige Partnerschaft*, Bonn, Bouvier Verlag, 1990.

(Generous social welfare provisions, in particular, contributed to the rapid growth of a budgetary deficit, at a time when unemployment was increasing, and jobless workers required more and generous benefits.) In 1982, the FDP withdrew from the governing coalition, and joined the CDU in a new government headed by Helmut Kohl (formerly minister-president of the *Land* Rhineland-Palatinate, destined to be the longest-serving chancellor in modern Germany). It is tempting to see Kohl's victory as part of a great conservative movement affecting all the major Western states, including West Germany, Britain, and the US. The prestige of statism had indeed declined; intellectually, academic advocates of free enterprise were making their influence felt in universities across the Atlantic all the way from Chicago to Kiel. Still, Kohl's conservatism was quite distinct from either Reagan's or Thatcher's. Kohl was a Catholic committed to "social Catholicism"; Reagan and Thatcher were Protestants. Reagan and Thatcher were personally well acquainted; they shared a common philosophy and, of course, a common language. Kohl, by contrast, was a continental European who saw nothing wrong in picking as his closest foreign ally François Mitterrand, a socialist and a Frenchman.

In West Germany itself, committed conservatives were by no means happy at Kohl's cooperation with the FDP as a coalition partner. CDU right-wingers would have preferred to go it alone, convinced that the CDU on its own could win an absolute majority in the forthcoming elections. But middle-of-the-roaders thought otherwise, represented by men such as finance minister Gerhard Stoltenberg, the party's general secretary, Heiner Geissler, and Kurt Biedenkopf, an outstanding academic (later *Ministerpräsident* of Saxony after the completion of German unification, and one of the most gifted men in European politics). Genscher remained foreign minister. (At his insistence, Franz Josef Strauss, head of the right-wing CSU, and *Ministerpräsident* of Bavaria, was excluded from ministerial level.)

In 1983, West Germany went to the polls, and Kohl gained a stunning victory. The CDU won its greatest success since the 1957 glory days of Konrad Adenauer. The SPD (led at the time by Hans-Jochen Vogel) managed to obtain 38.2 percent of the votes and 193 seats in a *Bundestag* of 498 members. The CDU/CSU, by contrast, won 48.8 percent of the vote, good for 244 seats. Even so, the CDU/CSU lacked an absolute majority in the *Bundestag*, and continued to rely on the FDP (with 6.9 percent of the votes and 34 seats).[10] The Greens, committed to an environmentalist and anti-nuclear policy, secured 5.6 percent of the vote and 27 out of 498 seats in the *Bundestag*, and entered the national parliament for the first time. Though no political commentator understood it at the time, the 1983 election turned out to be one of the most important in modern German history – the election decided that a centrist rather than a left-of-center government would effect German unification. The only alternative would have been what Germans later called a "traffic light coalition" – green for the Greens, yellow for the FDP, red for the SPD. Such a coalition was not impossible to achieve, and existed, for instance, in the city state of Bremen.

Confirmed in his office as chancellor, Kohl was jokingly referred to as Adenauer's grandson, a chip off the old block. Kohl's political longevity exceeded even Adenauer's. (By 1996, Kohl's tenure as chancellor exceeded in length the Weimar Republic's entire life span.) Yet Kohl was in other ways quite different from the Federal Republic's founding father. He was a partocrat who had made his career in party politics. He was also a relatively young man, a member of a generation that could remember, at their most

10 *Facts on File*, vol. 43, no. 2208, 11 March 1983, p. 157.

impressionable age, the disgrace and defeat suffered by the Third Reich – not its initial years of meretricious splendor. (Kohl was born in 1930 and Genscher in 1927; when Hitler came to power Kohl was three years old, Genscher six.) It was Kohl who used Grass's phrase *die Gnade der späten Geburt* (the grace of being born late). (Kohl did not employ the phrase to exculpate either his own age cohort or himself from the Nazi legacy. Instead, he insisted that even Germans who, like himself, had been too young to be involved in Nazi crimes, still had to bear the consequences of German history.)

In fact, Kohl had come from a pious Catholic home; his parents had been anti-Nazis; at the tail end of World War II he had just been old enough to be drafted as a youthful *Flakhelfer* (an assistant in an anti-aircraft battery). (Youngsters like him were later referred to widely as *die Flakhelfergeneration.*) He entered politics through the ranks of the CDU's youth league (*Junge Union*) and made his way in the *Land* Rhineland-Palatinate, a stronghold of the CDU. (He also managed to get a doctoral dissertation at the University of Heidelberg, one of the earliest to be written on postwar German history.) In 1960, he was elected to the *Landtag* (the Land parliament) in Mainz, capital of the Rhineland-Palatinate, a Catholic city with a bishopric of ancient fame. Kohl was perhaps Germany's most underestimated politician. Big, powerful, a bear of a man, he would have done well in college football had he been born in the US. He was calm of demeanor, not easily put out. He spoke as a provincial, with a Palatine accent, and was, in appearance, a bit slow on the uptake. Yet Kohl always seemed to get the better of his opponents, especially those within the CDU.

Between 1969 and 1974, Kohl served as *Ministerpräsident* of the *Land* Rhineland-Palatinate, one of those powerful *Landesfürsten* who dominated German politics. He was a federalist by conviction, always keen to preserve the power of the *Länder* at a time when the expansion of the public sector gave an ever-increasing number of functions to Bonn. Kohl thereafter switched to federal politics, becoming chairman of the CDU/CSU's parliamentary group and, in 1976, the CDU's chairman.

Kohl's parliamentary career defied all prognostications, and his chancellorship (1982–   ) turned out to be the most extended in German history. (By 1994 he had won three general elections, albeit with declining majorities, and then was re-elected, albeit by only a narrow margin.)[11] Kohl's political longevity is all the more surprising given the extent of the problems that assailed him. Kohl had stepped into the chancellor's office promising to reduce budgetary deficits. Easier said than done. Political loyalties were weakening in Germany. The confessional element had declined in political importance; even churchgoing Catholics could no longer be relied upon to vote for the CDU. All the same, the CDU was in no wise a free-enterprise party pure and simple. Nothing would be more mistaken than to "view the Kohl government as a West German version of the Reagan government in the US."[12] The welfare state was deeply rooted in German history.

---

11 In the general election of 1994, the CDU gained 41.5 percent of the popular vote against the SPD's 36.4 percent. According to early returns, the CDU/CSU and its ally the FDP won 341 seats in a 672-seat chamber, a ten-seat edge over the 331 seats held by the combined opposition of SPD, Greens, and PDS. The SPD had increased its share of *Bundestag* seats by 16 seats, totalling 253 seats. The Greens won 7.3 percent of the vote (48 seats), the PDS only 4.4 percent (17 seats), and the extreme right, less than 2 percent.
12 Richard C. Eichenberg, "The Federal Republic of Germany (1945–1988)," in Gerald A. Dorfman and Peter J. Duignan, eds, *Politics in Western Europe*, Stanford, CA, Hoover Institution Press, 1991, p. 180.

Guild masters, mayors, bishops, princes had all contributed to its creation; so had politicians in the Bismarckian empire and the Weimar Republic. The welfare state was considered an instrument for maintaining social peace, and thus for maintaining national efficiency. More specifically, the CDU continued to appeal to farmers (many of them practicing Catholics) who insisted on being subsidized. The party also had a strong Catholic working-class component; the Catholic workers' expectations regarding social services differed little from those of their Social Democratic colleagues. Above all, the CDU had a long tradition of "social Catholicism." (The great cathedral at Mainz has on top a fine statue of St Martin, the patron saint, a mounted warrior who charitably cuts in half his cloak to give it to a beggar.) Kohl did effect some spending cuts by lowering certain social benefits and by freezing civil service pay, but Germany's budgetary problems remained an ever-lasting affliction.

Kohl also faced other difficulties. CDU as well as SPD loyalists were shocked when the *Republikaner*, led by Franz Schönhuber, a former *Waffen SS* volunteer, gained parliamentary representation. West Germany's good name was besmirched when it was discovered that West German firms were exporting military know-how and military hardware to Libya, an outlaw state. ("Has Bonn become a liars' republic?" asked the influential *Frankfurter Allgemeine Zeitung*.)[13] Fortunately, however, the radical right failed to extend its base, and, for all the *Jusos* and Green complaints concerning the re-emergence of German fascism, West Germany remained the most "European" of the EC's members.

Kohl meant to keep it that way. Kohl was firmly resolved to anchor Germany both in the EC and NATO; he was a firm advocate of a "European Germany," as opposed to a neutralist state uneasily veering between East and West, distrusted by both. Kohl, like Adenauer, considered that the EC, in turn, must depend on a close partnership between Bonn and Paris. (He got on surprisingly well with François Mitterrand, the French president, and a socialist of the kind Kohl denounced in domestic German politics.) Between them, they engineered Jacques Delors's elevation to the presidency of the European Commission (1985).[14]

We shall refer to the EC's development in chapter 16. Suffice it to say that Delors turned his office into a key institution. His cabinet (meaning high-level advisers) consisted of able people, forceful, well trained, who helped him to concentrate a great deal of power in the Commission's presidency. Urged on by Kohl and Mitterrand, the EC in 1986 passed the ambitiously named Single European Act. In 1990, at a meeting of the European Council in Dublin, Kohl and Mitterrand presented the other EC leaders with new proposals designed to speed up monetary union and bring about political unity. Political union in turn raised the issue of parliamentary control and the future powers to be conceded to the European Parliament. According to Kohl, the EC suffered from a "democratic deficit" which could only be liquidated by greatly extending the power

13 "Ist Bonn eine Lügenrepublik?" *Frankfurter Allgemeine Zeitung*, 28 January 1989.
14 For Kohl, see Peter Hinze and Gerd Langguth, eds, *Helmut Kohl, Der Kurs der CDU: Reden und Beiträge des Bundesvorsitzenden, 1973–1993*, Stuttgart, Deutsche Verlags-Anstalt, 1993; Hans-Otto Kleinmann, *Geschichte der CDU: 1945–1982*, Stuttgart, Deutsche Verlags-Anstalt, 1993; Werner Maser, *Helmut Kohl*, Frankfurt am Main, Ullstein Verlag, 1990; Klaus Hofman, *Helmut Kohl: Eine Biographie*, Melle, E. Knoth, 1990; Reinhard Appel, *Helmut Kohl im Spiegel seiner Macht*, Bonn, Bouvier Forum, 1990; Norman M. Naimark, "To Know Everything and to Report Everything: Building the East German Police State, 1945–1949," Stanford, CA, Cold War International History Project, no. 10, 1994.

of the European Parliament. Despite opposition from advocates of national sovereignty, the federalists moved ahead, their efforts resulting in the bitterly controverted Maastricht Treaty (1991) to which we shall refer again in chapter 16.

To sum up, the Federal German Republic had been supremely successful, and was once more a great power in Europe, with a prosperous economy and a stable currency, the strongest conventional military force in Europe outside the Soviet Union, and political, parliamentary, and societal institutions as solid as any in the world. Public opinion polls on controversial subjects must admittedly be treated with caution. (A cruel German cartoon shows a middle-aged householder being interviewed by a pollster. "Let me fill in your questionnaire first," says the householder, "and then I will tell you what I think about the Jews.") Nevertheless, polls do provide illustrative evidence of the way politics work. And, no matter what the literati said, West Germans were overwhelmingly satisfied with the country's democratic system, its rule of the *Rechtsstaat* (rule of law) and West Germany's West European and transatlantic bonds. It was an outcome that few would have predicted at the time of the Federal Republic's foundation (1949).

East German Failure

While the Federal German Republic went from strength to strength, the "other Germany" moved from weakness to weakness. Despite its founders' high hopes, the German Democratic Republic (*Deutsche Demokratische Republik*, DDR) failed to deliver on the magnificent promises made by socialism. There was single-party rule exercised by the SED (*Sozialistische Einheitspartei*), aided and abetted by several satellite parties (*Blockparteien*) which operated in close contact with the SED. The system was supported by a gigantic network of informers run by the *Stasi* (*Staatssicherheitsdienst,* state security service). Supposedly, one-fifth of the population served as informers at one time or another. (According to dissenters, the acronym DDR stood for *Deutsche Duckmäuser Republik* (German Toadies' Republic) or *Deutsche Denunziantenrepublik* (German Informers' Republic).) Students informed on their professors, pastors on their congregations, workers on their foremen, husbands on their wives, children on their parents. Indeed, the material in the *Stasi's* possession grew so huge as to be unmanageable. Overall, the socialist vanguard consisted not only of boorish and unpleasant but also incompetent people – a fact known not only to the population but also to senior functionaries such as Günter Schabowski and Carl-Heinz Janson.[15]

While the German Democratic Republic (GDR) remained in existence, and even after its collapse, a great deal was made by propagandists of the GDR's assumed social achievements (*soziale Errungenschaften*). Not all of its work was worthless. There were capable and well-intentioned people east of the Elbe, as there were to the west. But those who criticized the Federal Republic for its supposed lack of social concern were commonly unaware of the extent and cost of the West German welfare system; in effect, it was much more efficient than East Germany's. Nor did West Germany create "an infallible police state" with its nosey officialdom and that universal sense of dependency that

15 Carl-Heinz Janson, *Totengräber der DDR: Wie Günter Mittag den SED-Staat Ruinierte*, New York, Econ. Verlag, 1991; Günter Schabowski, *Der Absturz*, Berlin, Rowohlt, 1991; and *Das Politbureau*, Reinbek bei Hamburg, Rowohlt, 1990.

characterized East Germany (and which appealed to some East German intellectuals). Above all, the East German *nomenklatura* itself gave a vote of "no confidence" to its own welfare state by claiming special services, and by not sending their own children to those day-care centers and other facilities that they praised in public.

It was the failure of the GDR's welfare state to honor its promises which, in part, occasioned the GDR's lack of popular legitimacy. Before the GDR had walled itself off from the West in 1961, something like 3,000,000 people had voted with their feet to get out: it was as if 40,000,000 Americans had left the United States. Thereafter, it was laws against *Republikflucht* that kept the populace in line. However, in a publicity campaign that would have shamed Madison Avenue, East German propaganda persuaded much of foreign (albeit not its own domestic) opinion that "real existing socialism" had a genuine basis in the population, that socialism was irreversible, and that Germany's partition should be accepted as permanent. The bulk of West German intellectuals shared this viewpoint; so did many West German politicians. But Germans were not alone in this respect. In the opinion of Philip Windsor, contributing to an excellent standard work on Western Europe, published in 1986, there would be no German reunification in the foreseeable future. F. Stephen Larrabee, an American writing in 1989, the year in which the GDR collapsed, argued that reunification had ceased to be a real issue.[16] Statisticians and intelligence agents could be fooled even more easily than professors. In 1989, just before the GDR's demise, the *Statistical Abstract of the United States* asserted that between 1975 and 1985 East Germany's per capita income had actually been higher than West Germany's, thereby accepting fabricated East German statistics at their face value.[17] In fact, the GDR's economy turned out to be a disaster.

In some ways, East Germany was worse off at the end of the communist era than Germany had been after the collapse of the Third Reich. The Third Reich had sustained tremendous physical damage from bombing. Hitler and his fellow fanatics had degraded the public services and corrupted society. But the basic institutions had remained in being – public services and private organizations. The bourgeoisie had essentially survived, save for the Jews. The bulk of manufacturing industries had survived, and remained competitive on the international market. By contrast, the communists had inflicted much greater damage than the Nazis. Not that the GDR's story was one of complete disaster. Certain traditional industries (such as the manufacture of musical instruments, high-grade optical equipment etc.) still produced merchandise of high quality, but did so at excessive cost. Worst of all, the communists largely eliminated the private entrepreneur; the bourgeoisie disappeared; the country suffered from an enormous brain drain, as the emigrants to the West included most of the best-qualified and enterprising citizens. Instead, the communists installed a new élite which despised money-making and prized obedience, but lived like kings.

16 Philip Windsor, "German Disunity," in Sir Richard Mayne, ed., *Handbooks to the Modern World: Western Europe,* New York, Facts on File, 1986, p. 313; F. Stephen Larrabee, "From Reunification to Reassociation: New Dimensions of the German Question," in F. Stephen Larrabee, ed., *The Two German States and European Security*, New York, St Martin's Press in association with the Institute for East–West Security Studies, 1989, esp. p. 29.

17 *Statistical Abstract of the United States*, Washington, DC, US Department of Commerce and Bureau of the Census, 1989, p. 822, table no. 1411. The gross national product in current and constant (1984) dollars per capita was indicated as follows: East Germany, $8,309 in 1975; $10,330 in 1985. The corresponding West German figures were $8,115 and $10,320. More recent estimates put the GDR's real per capita income at something like one-third of West Germany's.

Central planning worked no better in East Germany than elsewhere in the Soviet bloc. Investments were widely misplaced, and East Germany was saddled with a great range of obsolescent industries. Wherever they seized power, communist planners failed to plan adequately for capital maintenance: roofs leaked; drains smelled; wall paint peeled; highways filled with potholes; trains clattered over ill-repaired tracks; machinery went without adequate maintenance. Work morale declined as employees took time off from their regular duties to stand in line for food or other essential supplies – all with the foreman's permission. Problems of pollution became almost insoluble, especially as East Germany depended heavily on brown coal. East Germany's nuclear reactors turned into potential time bombs. (Operations at major installations such as the nuclear power works at Greifswald had to be closed down after unification; they seemed beyond rescue.) While the propaganda machine kept blaring, the GDR's real per capita income fell to perhaps one-third of West Germany's. (Before 1945, the communist takeover, they had been comparable.)

The GDR also confronted desperate political problems – chief among them the GDR's inability to create a genuine identity for itself. Originally, the GDR had seen itself as the nucleus of a united socialist Germany. The GDR's national anthem, written by Johannes Becher, a Weimar veteran, proclaimed the glory of a united Fatherland, risen from the ruins, destined for peace and prosperity. But unification was later dropped as an issue; Johannes Becher's text might no longer be sung. The GDR's national anthem thereafter was the world's only anthem whose words were banned by its own government – a surrealist touch which Kafka could not have bettered. The GDR's *nomenklatura* thereafter tried to persuade both its own citizens and the world at large that East Germany, the world's "first German Workers' and Peasants' State," had become a new nation, defined by its socialist achievements. But as dissidents used to whisper, "Poland without socialism is still Poland. The German Democratic Republic without socialism is – the Federal German Republic."

There were other weaknesses to the former GDR's intellectual establishment. Given the gargantuan size of the GDR's academic establishment, and given the vast claims made for its creativity by Marxist–Leninist advocates, the quality of the work produced was poor. The profession of pseudo-sciences went with a curious mixture of *Besserwisserei* (know-it-all) and condescension toward those very "toilers" whom the *nomenklatura* romanticized. The GDR's "culture bearers" lived on a Magic Mountain. They pretended to speak for the workers, but did not realize that it was the workers who disliked them most. The GDR's cultural establishment praised ordinary folk, but in fact looked down on those popular dialects that were actually spoken by the common people. The GDR's cultural establishment claimed to represent youth, but the Party intellectuals' own perception of youth culture was based on the Soviets', and only faintly resembled the Germans' own traditional *Jugendbewegung*, with its banners and campfires. Neither had the SED any comprehension of the new youth culture, with its jeans and rock, that linked East and West Germany long before the Berlin Wall would fall. The SED tried to protect its fief from Western influence by a rigid censorship – but in vain. No barriers could stop West German television. Increasingly, the senior cadres lived in a world of their own, with their special shops, special restaurants, special sports clubs where like met only like, and married only like. (The top functionaries' gilded ghetto at Wandlitz became known to the populace as Volvograd because of the Volvos which supposedly stood outside each functionary's own villa.) By a curious twist of dialectic, Germany's finest espionage service came to serve the most ill-informed élite in German history.

German Unification

"Unity and right and freedom for the German fatherland" (*Einigkeit und Recht und Freiheit für das deutsche Vaterland*) run the opening lines of the Federal German Republic's national anthem. West Germany's Basic Law provided for ultimate unification. Even East Germany had likewise been originally committed to unification, albeit under socialist auspices. Only a united, centralized Germany could effectively compete on the world markets – no wonder that the British and Americans stood resolved to leave their German competitor weak and divided – thus Stalin in 1947.[18] In 1950 Walter Ulbricht, the GDR's founding father, had gone even further and threatened that, after West Germany's liberation, Adenauer and his henchmen would be tried by a People's Court, unless they managed to find refuge in Latin America.[19] (Ironically, it was not a West German statesman but Erich Honecker, the last head of the GDR, who had to find refuge in old age in South America.)

After Ulbricht's departure from office (1971), the SED changed its line. According to the SED's revised doctrine, East Germany had taken over the best of Germany's past, but would now develop into a new and separate nation, its identity defined by socialist institutions, and socialist dedication to a radiant future under socialism. Germany's division increasingly seemed permanent. In 1989, the two German states celebrated their respective fortieth birthdays; both had endured considerably longer than the Weimar Republic and Hitler's Thousand Year Reich put together. On both sides of the border there was now a new generation – men and women in their forties – who had never known a united Germany in their lifetime. East Germans had experienced 40 years of communist indoctrination at school, in the youth movement, in the army, at the workplace; their very language had been modified by communist terminology.

As time went on, East German society became more accommodating toward those of its citizens who simply desired to retreat into private life – into the new *Nischengesellschaft* (recess society) where silent dissenters might find their own little niche. Overt dissenters were jailed or forced to emigrate to West Germany. (Unlike the other Warsaw Pact states, East Germany alone was therefore stuck with a largely communist intelligentsia; overt critics were pushed out into the "other Germany.") The communist system, moreover, had a substantial number of beneficiaries: professional party cadres, Lutheran pastors, soldiers, spies, and also leftist intellectuals, such as the writer Christa Wolf, who derived fame by homeopathic deviations from the party line. (A stern critic of the capitalist West, in particular of the US, Wolf had no difficulty in accepting a fellowship from a capitalist foundation in California, once communism had broken down, and Wolf's former links to the *Stasi* had become a matter of public knowledge.) The idealism that had once animated communist resistance against Hitler had evaporated – replaced by force of habit and routine, hypocrisy and corruption.

West Germans likewise became increasingly used to the GDR. *Ostpolitik* rested on the assumption that Germany's division would last for a long time to come. West German trade with East Germany, and West German tourism to East Germany kept growing.

18 Bernd Bonwetsch and Gennadij Bordjugow, *"Stalin und die SBZ,"* in *Vierteljahrsheft für Zeitgeschichte*, vol. 42, no. 2, April 1994, pp. 279–303.
19 Cited in L.H. Gann, "East Germany from Partition to Reunification (1945–1990)," in Dorfman and Duignan, eds, *Politics in Western Europe*, p. 203.

(Between 1969, when Brandt became chancellor, and 1982, when Kohl assumed office, West German exports to East Germany more than trebled, and West German imports from East Germany more than quadrupled.)

Particularly curious was the intelligentsia's position. During the nineteenth century, German intellectuals had been among the foremost advocates of German unification; poets such as August Hoffmann von Fallersleben had apostrophized "German women, German trust, German wine, and German song", calling on Germans to stand united, and prize, above all, *"Deutschland, Deutschland über alles."* After the horrors of the Third Reich, such sentiments had lost their force. Some scholars cooperated with bodies such as the *Kuratorium Unteilbares Deutschland* designed to keep alive the ideal of ultimate unification. But many rejected unification altogether. The GDR had supposedly become a viable state, a point of view widely accepted among learned men such as Theo Sommer and Ralf Dahrendorf (later Sir Ralf Dahrendorf), a leading German sociologist, and Günter Grass, one of West Germany's most prominent novelists. A united Germany would threaten its neighbors. A partitioned Germany was the just price to be paid for Auschwitz. German unification would kill all chances of turning East Germany into a genuinely socialist state. A Reich restored would be run by West German philistines. In any case, Dahrendorf claimed, the GDR had become a viable state which had created a new legitimacy for itself, and had built "the first modern society on German soil."[20] (By the time this nonsense was written, about 16 percent of East Germany's population had fled to the West.)

Misconceptions about East Germany derived in part from what might be called West Germany's research deficit regarding the GDR. Foreigners might be pardoned for accepting the GDR's propaganda, including its falsified statistics. But what about West German scholars well acquainted with Germany's eastern provinces, linked moreover to East Germany by ties of family or friendship? Their record was disappointing. *GDR-Forschung,* research concerning the GDR in West Germany, had widely underplayed the inefficiency and brutality of the East German regime, underestimated the extent of East Germany's civil rights violations, while exaggerating East Germany's achievements. Once the GDR collapsed, West German politicians, businessmen, and academics were therefore quite unprepared for the real state of affairs in East Germany. West German scholars' attempts to analyze the East German predicament in terms of "value-free science" all too often led to disastrous errors; by attempting to recognize to the full East Germany's "immutable realities," GDR research in West Germany widely departed from reality altogether. Unwittingly, analysts had turned into praise-singers of a bankrupt regime.[21] (By an odd twist of intellectual history, it was the Free University of Berlin, founded as an anti-communist bastion, now placed in a walled-off city, that proved particularly prone to producing such dubious scholarship.) Not that politicians and journalists were any better than the scholars in understanding East German realities. The West German SPD (whose sister party was banned in East Germany) actually joined with the SED in a "Joint Commission on Fundamental Values" (1982). Brandt subsequently insisted that German reunification was "the living lie of the second German

20 Ralf Dahrendorf, *Society and Democracy in Germany*, Garden City, NY, Doubleday, 1969, pp. 397–411.
21 For a detailed analysis, see Klaus Schroeder and Jochen Stadt, "Der Diskrete Charme des Status quo: DDR-Forschung in der Aera der Entspannungspolitik," *Leviathan: Zeitschrift für Sozialwissenschaft, special issue*, vol. 21, no. 1, 1993, pp. 24–63.

Republic." Brandt's long-term ally, disarmament expert Egon Bahr, characterized any discussion of German unity as "pollution of the political environment." Theo Sommer (Germany's pre-eminent liberal columnist in *Die Zeit*) returned in 1986 from a visit to the GDR full of praise for its government, and its record of reconstruction, modernization, and restoration.[22] Not to be outdone, Helmut Kohl in 1987 hosted an official visit by Erich Honecker, "Red Erich," who received red carpet treatment as the first East German head of state to make such a call in the West.

All forecasts concerning the GDR's stability rested on certain assumptions. The Soviet Union would always be willing to defend its satellites within the Warsaw Pact against subversion as Moscow had done in East Berlin in 1953, in Budapest in 1956, and in Prague in 1968. The organs of the East German state, including the army, would prove reliable. The East German economy and East German welfare services would perform with reasonable efficiency. The East German population could somehow be shielded from Western influence, despite West German television programs, the growth of trade and tourism, and, above all, the ties of culture and kinship that continued to unite Germans on both sides of the border.

By 1989, however, all these conditions suddenly ceased to apply. We deal with the collapse of the Soviet empire in chapter 17. Suffice it to say here that by the 1980s the GDR was heavily indebted to the West, the GDR had become desperate for hard currency, and faced major problems in paying for Soviet oil and other essential imports. Worst of all, from East Berlin's viewpoint, Mikhail Gorbachev himself lost faith in his East German allies, and the system collapsed with startling rapidity. The breakdown started when Hungary opened its borders to the West in May 1989, thereby permitting both its own citizens and East German travelers to depart freely for the West. In 1990, the Central Committee of the Communist Party of the Soviet Union, incredibly, surrendered its constitutionally guaranteed monopoly of power.

In East Germany there was widespread agitation and huge demonstrations. The greatest center was Leipzig in Saxony, a traditional center of working-class militance, and home town of Walter Ulbricht, the SED's first secretary general. (When, in 1971, Ulbricht was replaced by Erich Honecker, it was East Berlin that became East Germany's most favored city, amply subsidized so as to impress foreigners as well as native Berliners.) The demonstrations were at first led by dissident leftists who desired "socialism with a human face," intellectuals (including leftist Lutheran clergymen) united in such bodies as the "New Forum." These reformers, however, were soon left far behind by popular opinion. By now the *nomenklatura* and its allies were discredited by East Germany's economic failure, by the privileges enjoyed by the self-styled "vanguard of the proletariat," and by the evident mendacity of government propaganda. Few Germans accepted the regime's never-ending self-praise, and its ever-lasting laments concerning spies, wreckers, and running dogs.

The *nomenklatura* itself lost heart, with many of its own members suffering from bitter disillusionment. Indeed, some highly placed former dignitaries, such as Günter Schabowski, a member of the East German Politburo in 1989, went further in their denunciation of communism than many a hard-line anti-communist. According to Schabowski, the entire system had been irredeemably perverted from the start since Marxism–Leninism itself rested on mistaken premises. In the end only the *Stasi* would

22 Jeffrey Gedmin, *The Hidden Hand: Gorbachev and the Collapse of East Germany*, Washington, AEI, 1992, p. 9.

have been willing to fight. In 1946, just before decolonization, British staff officers in India had made two parallel plans, "Madhouse" if the Indian army were to become unreliable, "Bedlam" if it should turn hostile.[23] In 1989, the GDR government would have faced Madhouse and Bedlam at the same time had it attempted to hold on to power. Deprived of Soviet support, even the GDR generals were now reluctant to start shooting, and thereby take personal responsibility for a hopeless cause. A system built on rigid hierarchy and strict obedience to orders would no longer operate when the established chain of command had broken down. In October 1989, Honecker fell from power. He was succeeded by Egon Krenz who, in turn, was replaced by Hans Modrow, both of them "reform communists" and believed to be personally untainted. By now, however, communists of any stripe could no longer master the situation. On 9 November 1989 (the very day the Kaiser's government had fallen at the end of World War I) the East German communist government capitulated to its people by opening the Berlin Wall. The East German state disintegrated with a speed that surprised, and indeed distressed, West German politicians and bureaucrats who would have preferred a more slowly paced handover.

On 18 March 1990, East Germans held free elections – the first since Hitler's takeover in 1933. The elections bitterly disappointed left-wingers who had hoped that East Germany would remain socialist, albeit free from the "deformations" of the past. Disappointed also were the hopes of those academicians who considered that the youth revolutions of 1968 had formed "the great rehearsal" for subsequent risings against the status quo both east and west of the former Iron Curtain. Race, class, and gender – the issues most stressed by the heirs of 1968 – played no appreciable part in the Central European revolutions of 1989 and 1990. Instead, the citizens' main concerns were national identity, freedom of speech and of religion, and a free-market economy. After 40 years of socialism in East Germany, 48.1 percent of East German voters opted for the Conservative Alliance for Germany, led by the Christian Democrats. The Social Democrats got 21.8 percent of the votes on an ultra-moderate program that accepted a free-market economy. The party of socialism, the PDS (the refurbished SED under new management and a new name), obtained only 16.3 percent of the vote, despite the party's newly found commitment to democracy and a mixed economy.

Worse still, from the left's standpoint, were the East German workers who deserted socialism, even in areas such as Saxony, once a center of proletarian militance. (Of the workers, 55.4 percent voted for the Alliance, 22.2 percent for the Social Democrats, only 11.9 percent for the PDS, allegedly their very own party.) The most loyal supporters of socialism were now the intellectuals. (The PDS received 31.0 percent of the intellectuals' vote, the highest of all occupational groups.)[24]

East Germany briefly installed thereafter a CDU government which negotiated with West Germany a monetary, economic, and social union (1 July 1990). It was not a pact between equals but nor was it an act of unconditional surrender, as had been the capitulation of the Third Reich in 1945. (Former communists complained bitterly of Western *Siegerjustiz* (victor's justice). But, in fact, the unification agreement amounted to a partial amnesty for crimes committed under "real existing socialism." A handful of petty

23 Byron Farwell, *Armies of the Raj: from the Mutiny to Independence, 1858–1947*, New York, Norton, 1989, p. 348.
24 Wolfgang C. Bibowski, "Demokratischer (Neu) Beginn in der DDR: Dokumentation und Analyse der Wahl vom 18 März 1990," *Zeitschrift für Parlamentsfragen*, 1990, pp. 1–18.

offenders were punished. But the bulk of communist functionaries, civil and military, peacefully drew their pensions.) Nevertheless, Germany was reunited as a capitalist state. The *Bundesbank* became the central bank for all Germany, the Deutschmark the currency for all Germany; the armed forces were merged under West German auspices. The reunification treaty (900 pages long) guaranteed security for foreign investors, unified the legal system, went some way toward solving the difficult problems of private property rights, unified working conditions, and unified social services. On 3 October 1990, "Unification Day," Germany's new national day, the GDR disappeared into the dustbin of history. In its stead five reconstituted additional *Länder* became part of the Federal German Republic.

Under the new dispensation, the East German and the West German parliaments merged. With the addition of 144 new deputies from the former East German *Volkskammer,* the total number of deputies in the *Bundestag* (the West German Lower House) rose from 519 to 663. The CDU and its allies increased their seats from 234 to 305, the SPD from 193 to 226, the Free Democrats from 48 to 57, the Greens and their associates from 42 to 59. The PDS joined with 24 members. The *Bundesrat* (the Upper House) was enlarged through the accession of the five new *Länder,* represented in proportion to their population. United Germany did not even adopt a new name but remained the Federal Republic of Germany. Whereas Bismarckian Germany had represented Prussian – that is, East German – predominance over West Germany, the balance of power in the new Germany had now swung decisively to the West. Incongruous as it seemed to his detractors, Kohl had emerged as united Germany's new Bismarck.

Kohl's handiwork therefore met with much criticism from the left. A new *Anschluss,* complained Kohl's censors. German unification should have been achieved by a constituent assembly which ought to have negotiated a new constitution for a new state. Unification, moreover, should have been achieved at a slower pace, with an extended period of readjustment. As it was, by simply letting individual East German *Länder* join the Federal Republic, West Germany brutally used its superior strength, and did so in a "triumphalist" spirit. West Germans, in fact, behaved as if they had won a war. West German corporations "colonized" the East's economy. West German consumer culture cheapened East Germany's more truly "German" culture. East German workers were seduced by Western consumerism and Western propaganda. Kohl, in particular, the charge sheet continues, had secured reunification by dishonest promises. Nobody, according to Kohl, would be worse off in a united Germany; sooner or later all Germans would be more prosperous than before.

As we see it, these objections carry no weight. West Germany quite properly dealt with East Germany on the basis of inequality – because the two countries were indeed unequal. Even from a purely demographic viewpoint, there was a great disparity. (West Germany in 1989 numbered an estimated 60,162,000; East Germany 16,763,000, the size of North-Rhine Westphalia, a single West German *Land*). More importantly, West Germany was successful whereas East Germany was bankrupt. The West German state was legitimate in the eyes of its citizens. The East German state was illegitimate for all but its former beneficiaries – party functionaries, agitprops, informers, and pastors and poets. After the Wall had broken in 1989, the East German state could no longer function, as emigration of East Germans to West Germany could no longer be stopped. The collapse of the East German state was a boon for all of Europe. With its military plans for sudden military strikes (one of them, for example, providing for a speedy seizure of West Berlin), with its huge espionage network directed against "the international class enemy," the GDR constituted a danger to international peace, and also to internal reform in formerly communist Czechoslovakia and Poland. The GDR's extinction contributed greatly to European pacification. An extended transition period to achieve unity in a gradual way would not have worked because the DDR no longer commanded obedience from its citizens. How many East Germans, by 1990, would have continued to obey the orders of communist officials? Even the local policeman was suspect. Having opened its borders, moreover, East Germany, under whatever government, was threatened by a massive exodus. "If the D-Mark does not come to us, we shall go to the D-Mark," as a popular East German slogan put it at the time.

Contrary to his critics on the left, and contrary also to his own party's subsequent propaganda line, Kohl did not by any means rush into unification. Even after the fall of the Berlin Wall, Kohl for a time remained reluctant to press for immediate unification, and would have preferred a confederal arrangement, with massive West German aid for the GDR. Kohl only changed course after he had visited Dresden in December 1989, and there had witnessed mammoth demonstrations calling for a united Germany. Kohl was by then also under diplomatic pressure to act speedily. Who could predict whether the Gorbachev government would survive? A right-wing coup was in fact attempted in Moscow a year later, in 1991. Its perpetrators were "serious men with ruthless intentions," bedeviled only by bad luck.[25] Had the plotters succeeded, a new, hard-line administration in Moscow would surely not have accepted agreements whereby the Soviet forces would leave East Germany within a specified period; Germany would hardly have been permitted to unite; a united Germany would not have been allowed to join NATO. Kohl's apprehensions, then, were quite comprehensible, his commitment to unity that of a statesman.

Kohl, moreover, had to act at a time when even Germany's European allies were far from enthusiastic about German unification. The French were initially hostile. (François Mitterrand in 1989 traveled to East Germany exhorting East Germans to reject unification.) Margaret Thatcher, the British prime minister, likewise would have preferred Germany to remain divided, provided East Germany were freed from communist dictatorship.[26] The Poles were mindful of historic threats from Germany, but border guarantees (and also the Helsinki Final Act, 1975, safeguarding existing frontiers) allayed Polish fears. Germany's smaller neighbors (Austria, Czechoslovakia, Belgium, Holland) were uneasy. Only the US, under the Bush administration, unswervingly supported German unity – not surprisingly so since the US felt no fear of a united Germany, and as Bush's personal ties to Thatcher were nothing like as close as Reagan's had been.

Kohl did, indeed, make quite unrealistic promises concerning the costs of unification. He underestimated the enormous difficulties faced by the former GDR, but so unfortunately did almost everybody else. Western intellectuals had filled many shelves with books showing how to change capitalist into socialist systems. But few had pondered the question of how to transform a socialist into a capitalist country. Kohl and his friends had no academic guidance in this respect. As we have pointed out before, academic research, and also intelligence agencies, had failed to analyze correctly the full extent of East Germany's economic disaster.

25 John B. Dunlop, *The Rise of Russia and the Fall of the Soviet Empire,* Princeton, NJ, Princeton University Press, 1993, p. 253. For the shift in Kohl's policy, see "Wahlkampf" in *Der Spiegel,* no. 38, 19 September 1994, pp. 18–22.
26 Margaret Thatcher, *The Downing Street Years,* New York, HarperCollins, 1993, p. 792ff.

GDR nostalgics (*Ostalgie*) went wrong in other respects. West German corporations did indeed come to control much of East Germany's economy. But the fault had been the communists'. They had destroyed the East German bourgeoisie. Not surprisingly, East Germany henceforth had to draw heavily on West German capital and managerial skills. Defenders of the GDR were correct in pointing to the drop in attendance at classical theater performances and church services under the new dispensation. But during the socialist era East Germans had gone to see Schiller plays for political as well as aesthetic reasons: they wanted to hear Schiller's great lines in defense of liberty. East Germans had filled the churches, not necessarily because they were good Lutherans, but because they wanted to hear the scriptural message that there was a Higher Power on earth than the Central Committee of the SED. Henceforth, East German citizens no longer had to hide their politics behind a show of aesthetic sensibility or religious commitment.

We likewise have no sympathy with scholars, such as Wolfgang Emmerich, who now stress what they describe as the GDR's originally humanitarian and idealistic inspiration, and its "anti-fascist" heritage. Right from the beginning, Lenin had preached and practiced what he called "revolutionary terrorism." Obsessed with the need for terror, Lenin had called for war to the knife against the proletariat's assorted class enemies. For Lenin and all his successors, revolution entailed the liquidation of the bourgeoisie. The class enemies would be exiled, jailed, or executed – at the very least they would be expropriated and reduced to silence. Marxist–Leninists ought not therefore to twist the past in order to secure present benefits.

We also disagree with those GDR sympathizers who hold that "real existing socialism" would have worked had it not been distorted by "Stalinist deformations." This is a perilous argument, particularly from a Marxist perspective. For if an entire social system can be distorted by one wicked man, even a clique of wicked men, what becomes of dialectical materialism with its elaborate speculations concerning "base" and "superstructure"? The same objection applies to those who complain that East German workers were seduced by a "false consciousness" created by Western propaganda and Western consumerism. For if one class can impose a false consciousness on another class, what becomes of "scientific socialism's" theoretical foundation? And why should East German workers be censured for desiring those privileges which had been freely available to the *nomenklatura*? In any case, a large mass of East German citizens had not merely opted in 1990 for better fridges and better television sets. They had voted against 45 years of *Stasi* supervision, of lying and spying, of *Parteichinesisch* (party jargon, literally "party Chinese"), against the party's ever-lasting mendacity and incompetence. Above all, the East Germans had rejected the *nomenklatura*'s claim to lead "the backward masses" into a happier world. For all the GDR nostalgia of later years – *schön wars doch* (it was great, all the same) – the GDR's demise was one of the happiest events in German history.[27]

27 See, for instance, Alison Lewis, "The Writers, their Socialism, the People and their Bad Table Manners: 1989 and the Crisis of East German Writers and Intellectuals," *German Studies Review*, vol. 15, no. 2, May 1992, pp. 243–66; L.H. Gann, "German Unification and the Left-wing Intelligentsia: a Response," *German Studies Review*, vol. 15, no. 1, February 1992, pp. 100–109, as opposed to Wolfgang Emmerich, "Affirmation – Utopie – Melancholie. Versuch einer Bilanz von vierzig Jahren GDR – Literatur," *German Studies Review*, vol. 14, no. 2, May 1991, pp. 325–44. General works include Hermann Weber, *DDR: Grundriss der Geschichte: 1945–1990*, Hanover, Fackelträger, 1991; Harold James and Marla Stone, eds, *When the Wall Came Down: Reactions to German Unification*, New York and London, Routledge, 1992; Timothy Garton Ash, *In Europe's Name: Germany and the Divided Continent*, New York, Random House, 1993; Gert-Joachim Glaessner

Divided We Stand, United We Fall?

Post victoriam omnes cives tristes sunt (after the victory all citizens are sad) said the Romans. German reunification had come about peacefully; the Soviet armies retreated without firing a shot. Yet much of German public opinion, at least published opinion, treated these momentous events as if Germany had suffered defeat. The problems facing united Germany were indeed stupendous, obscured by past propaganda and falsified DDR statistics, accepted in the West at their face value.[28]

United Germany's greatest problems were psychological and environmental. East Germany, like other formerly communist countries, experienced for a time a shattering decline in birth and marriage rates, symptomatic of profound fears concerning the future. Germans east of the Elbe would have to make a tremendous readjustment – hopes disappointed, credos betrayed. For the second time in German history an army of men and women claimed that they had known nothing of atrocities, that they had only obeyed lawful orders issued by a lawfully constituted state enjoying international recognition. Who in fact had been responsible for the failures of the past? What should happen to those who had gunned down refugees trying to cross the border, or to those who had ordered such shootings? Should all former communist officials be banned from positions of authority? Should allowance be made for those who had changed their political affiliation, or those who possessed indispensable skills? What of genuine idealists who had truly believed in Marxism?

These were difficult moral problems. True enough, the GDR had never practiced terror remotely on the scale perpetrated by Hitler, Stalin, or Mao Zedong. Nevertheless, the GDR's civil rights record had been bad enough. During its entire existence, the GDR had disclaimed all responsibility for the legacy of the Holocaust and other Nazi crimes. Like Austria, East Germany left this inconvenient inheritance at West Germany's door. In the land of "real existing socialism," nothing was quite real – not even the much-touted anti-fascist heritage. This generalization also applies to German–Jewish relations. The GDR took pride in its anti-fascist heritage, but its regnant ideology derided the Jewish faith, as it derided every religion. The GDR's government sided with the UN majority which for long stigmatized Zionism as a form of racism; the GDR therefore consistently supported Israel's enemies. It was only in West Germany that a viable Jewish community was rebuilt after the horrors of the Holocaust.

---

and Ian Wallace, eds, *The German Revolution of 1989, Causes and Consequences*, Oxford, Providence, Berg, 1992; A. James McAdams, *Germany Divided: from the Wall to Reunification*, Princeton, NJ, Princeton University Press, 1993; Philip Zelikow and Condoleeza Rice, *Germany Unified and Europe Transformed: a Study in Statecraft*, Cambridge, MA, Harvard University Press, 1995; Dirk Philipsen, *We Were the People: Voices from East Germany's Revolutionary Autumn of 1989*, Durham, NC, Duke University Press, 1992; Mary Fulbrook, "Popular Discontent and Political Activism in the GDR," *Contemporary European History*, vol. 2, no. 3, 1993, pp. 265–82; Peter Duignan and L.H. Gann, *The United States and the New Europe, 1945–1993*, Oxford, Blackwell, 1994, pp. 90–127. The indispensable general work of reference for the former GDR is *DDR Handbuch*, Cologne, Verlag Wissenschaft und Politik, 1984; see also Werner Weidenfeld and Karl-Rudolf Korte, eds, *Handbuch zur deutschen Einheit*, Frankfurt, Campus, 1993.

28 *Statistical Abstract of the United States*, 109th edn, p. 822. For a critique of academic research concerning the GDR in the US, see Norman Naimark, "Is it True What They Are Saying about East Germany?" *Orbis*, Fall, 1979, pp. 549–77.

Map 2   United Germany
Source: Peter Duignan and L.H. Gann, *The United States and the New Europe, 1945–1993*, Oxford, Blackwell, 1994, p. 111

Unlike East Germany, West Germany paid substantial reparations to Israel. German–Israeli relations improved. A number of Jews once more rose to high office.[29] Decimated by Nazi persecution, German-speaking Jewry of course no longer had the slightest hope of reclaiming that cultural predominance within the Jewish world which, since 1933, had irretrievably passed to the US. Nevertheless, German–Jewish history did not come to an end, as predicted in 1933. Sixty years later, Germany once more contained a Jewish community with three-generational families – grandparents, parents, and children.

29 These included Herbert Weichmann, a one-time mayor of Hamburg and later president of the *Bundesrat*, and Erich Kaufmann, Adenauer's legal adviser. See Howard M. Sachar, *The Course of Modern Jewish History*, New York, Vintage Books, 1990, p. 632. By 1995, Germany's estimated Jewish population was 60,000, many of them immigrants from Russia. The largest Jewish population in Europe resided in France, with an estimated 700,000, many of them immigrants, or descendants of immigrants from North Africa. The US, by contrast, had an estimated Jewish population of 5,000,000, though statisticians differed in their definition.

What of the crimes committed by communism? East Germans, after unification, had to make painful psychological adjustments, having been treated for 45 years by the former ruling party as minors (*Unmündige* in German, literally "unmouthed"). East Germans felt ill at ease as West Germans came to occupy many leading positions in East German corporate enterprise, academia, the public services and politics (*Besser-Wessies*, "know-better Westerners" or carpet-baggers). (In fact, these Westerners included remarkable people such as Biedenkopf, the new *Ministerpräsident* of Saxony.) In the ensuing wider political debates, many East Germans complained that they had been left to carry an unfairly heavy burden bequeathed to them by German history. Prosperous West Germans should show more generosity and sensitivity toward their ill-used compatriots (an unexpected argument from the mouths of former Prussians). West Germans retorted that they had worked for what they owned, and that they needed no civic lessons from idlers and turncoats. According to the media at least, united Germany was divided by new and ugly stereotypes: *Wessies* (West Germans) loudmouthed, pushful know-it-alls (the ugly American in new dress); *Ossies* (East Germans) lazy, ungrateful, stick-in-the-muds. (A German television program thus created a new character, one Motzki, a West German whose prejudices concerning *Ossies* far outdid Archie Bunker's concerning blacks.)

Allowing for exaggeration and propaganda, there were indeed enormous obstacles to Germany's psychological reunification. United Germany, went a favorite saying, was bigger than the old Federal Republic, more eastern, and more Protestant. The first two generalizations hold true, but not the third. The new *Länder* were not more Protestant but more secularist than the old *Länder*, less inclined to go to church, more inclined to vote for traditionally secularist parties such as the PDS (the reformed successor party of the SED), the Greens, and the FDP (heir to the German liberal tradition).[30] What will Germany's ultimate destiny be? Such theoretical concerns affected a great many practical issues such as the choice of a capital. Opinion on this subject was almost equally divided. Bonn appealed to those who wished to emphasize Germany's western connection, and who took pride in Bonn's lack of ostentation (the *Bundesdorf*, the federal village). Berlin, they argued, had been the capital of three bankrupt regimes: the Kaiser's empire, the Weimar Republic, and the Third Reich – not a reassuring record for the future. For all of its many cultural facilities, Berlin had ceased to be what it had been in Weimar Germany – the country's main cultural center. Even in a purely geographical sense, Berlin was no longer a centrally placed city; after the territorial losses suffered by Germany as a result of World War II, Berlin was about as near to the Polish border as Bonn was to the Belgian frontier.

By contrast, Berlin's defenders stressed that Berlin remained not only Germany's largest metropolitan area, but also its greatest manufacturing region. To choose Berlin as the capital would reassure East Germans. Both East and West Berlin desperately needed a new function as both had in the past been artificially subsidized to serve as showcases respectively for East and West Germany. Private investment in West Berlin

30 By 1994, there were 60.4 million voters in Germany, 79.8% in the West, 20.2% in the East. Corresponding figures for party membership were as follows. CDU/CSU: 895,000, 89.1% West, 10.9% East. SPD: 902,000, 97.3% West, 2.7% East. FDP: 110,000, 54.6% West, 45.4% East. Alliance 90/Greens: 38,000, 90.3% West, 9.7% East. PDS: 146,000, 0.5% West, 99.5% East. Republicans: 20,000, 75.0% West, 25.0% East (cited in Stephan Eisel, "The Politics of a United Germany," *Daedalus*, Winter 1994, vol. 123, no. 1, p. 165).

had been scanty, and almost non-existent in East Berlin. Much of the ordinary housing stock had run down. The removal of the Wall likewise entailed an enormous amount of physical reconstruction, with bold plans for a new Berlin. Berlin would master these problems more easily both as a national capital and as the capital to be of the *Land* Brandenburg.

The controversy ended in a characteristic compromise. In 1991, the *Bundestag*, by a narrow majority, voted that Berlin should once more become the official capital. But many ministries remained in Bonn, while the transfer of the remaining agencies proceeded at a snail's pace. (The total cost of the move was estimated at some 60 billion DM or 40 billion dollars.) United Berlin recovered its old dynamism – a multilingual city, destined to become the economic capital of central Europe. But even a united Germany remained far more decentralized than Britain, France, Italy, Portugal, or Sweden, whose respective capitals dominated almost every aspect of national life. (Munich in Germany remained the main center for high-tech industry and the arts; Hamburg, of course, served as the main port. Frankfurt housed the *Bundesbank*, and Karlsruhe the Supreme Court.)

The greatest step toward reunification was, however, dismantling the communist state, not an easy task, and one for which the West German public services seemed ill prepared. (The main exceptions were the *Bundeswehr* and the Ministry of Foreign Affairs, both of which contained a disproportionate number of former East Germans, and both of which had remained more prone to think in all-German terms than West Germany's other official agencies.) Contrary to widespread misconceptions, the communist state machinery had been extremely inefficient; only the *Stasi*, the SED, and the propaganda services had been well run. The local authorities had been ineffective; the *Länder* had been scrapped and needed to be effectively reconstituted. The law courts were distrusted. The financial system was in disarray. Private property in the means of production had been largely confiscated. Free enterprise could not be restored without completely restructuring the state, its agencies, and the laws which governed their operations.

This task was accomplished with remarkable speed and efficiency, despite a great many errors committed during the transition period. Restructuring began with the armed forces. (In modern German history all constitutional changes had gone hand in hand with military changes.) The NVA's personnel was greatly reduced in size, purged of its most senior officers, and absorbed into the *Bundeswehr*. No military "islands" would be allowed to exist where communist sympathizers would seek sanctuary through "inner emigration." A similar fate befell the civilian public services, including its senior functionaries, especially judges and police officers. (Saxony's minister of justice thus estimated in 1991 that more than one-third of the *Land's* current judges and district attorneys would not pass scrutiny.)[31] Also eliminated, at least in part, was East Germany's huge academic establishment replete with lecturers trained in Marxism–Leninism, fit only to teach *Diamat* (dialectical materialism), *Polök* (political economy), and other pseudo-sciences. The bulk of officials in the East German foreign service had to go, for only loyal communists had been appointed to such key posts, as also for propaganda and espionage organizations. The future appeared brighter only for technical employees such as railway and post office functionaries.

Despite its tribulations, East Germany, in an economic sense, was more fortunate than any of the other former members of the Warsaw Pact. East Germany alone had a "rich

31 Cited in Duignan and Gann, *The United States and the New Europe*, p. 100.

uncle," West Germany, able to provide a faltering economy with massive amounts of capital, technical expertise, and a potentially great market comprising the EC as a whole. East Germany's absorption into the German Federal Republic entailed huge capital transfers whose total size proved almost impossible to calculate, perhaps 4 percent of West Germany's GDP. (In 1991 the British journal, *The Economist,* tried to measure the total amount of money that would ultimately have to be disbursed; the "shopping list" was enormous. It included transfers for social security payments, the renewal of the infrastructure, the costs of privatization and continued subsidies to failed state education and collective farms. Huge amounts of money would be swallowed by projects designed to renew the telecommunication system, repair roads and railway tracks, improve housing (much of it run down), and what not. In addition, Germany had massive commitments to the former Soviet Union in connection with reunification: there were huge debts run up by East German firms, compensation to be paid to former owners, and the costs of undoing pollution damage.)[32]

Particularly complicated was the task of privatizing the *Kombinate,* the huge, vertically integrated, state corporations which had dominated East German industry. These had been heavily subsidized, heavily indebted, and heavily dependent on the Soviet trading network in East Central Europe which had collapsed with the downfall of the Soviet empire. A public trust agency, the *Treuhandanstalt* (abbreviated commonly to *Treuhand*) was charged with the task of selling these monsters. Its guidelines gave priority to the claims of new investors over those of former owners. It was a hard task and, in its critics' eyes, the *Treuhand* could do nothing right. On the one hand, the agency encountered condemnation from Western economists and investors for not proceeding fast enough with privatization and for subsidizing companies that should have gone out of business. On the other hand, the *Treuhand* was accused of a lack of social sensitivity in its rush to privatization; censors included trade unionists, SPD politicians, and CDU politicians concerned with the political consequences of widespread unemployment. These critics insisted that the *Treuhand* should do more to preserve East German jobs. In addition, the *Treuhand* was expected by many officials to help pay the costs of German unification, an impossible assignment.

And so it went on. East German agriculture had largely collapsed. There was massive unemployment as poorly run, and over-manned, state industries closed down. While East German critics complained about Western "colonization," West German cynics began to refer to East Germany as "f.o.b.", *Fass ohne Boden* (bottomless barrel). True enough, West Germany's economy remained the strongest in Europe. West Germany's gross domestic product was the highest ($1,208 billion in 1990, compared with $950 billion for France, $829 billion for Italy, $826 billion for Britain. East Germany's estimated GDP was only $88 billion.) West Germany was superbly good at manufacturing high-quality industrial products. West Germany was supposedly the engine that would pull from misery to prosperity all the formerly communist countries of East Central Europe. But West Germany's economy had troubles of its own. German labor costs were the world's highest. (For political reasons, they were steadily equalized between West and East Germany, despite the striking lack of productivity of East German workers. East Germany was therefore deprived of one of its few assets, relatively cheap

---

32 "Germany Recounts the Cost," *The Economist,* 29 June 1991, p. 43. By 1992, the total net transfer from West to East Germany was estimated at 180 billion DM: *The Economist,* 23 May 1992, "A Survey of Germany," p. 5.

labor, and unemployment worsened.) West Germany as well as East Germany lagged behind the US and Japan in high-tech industries. German service industries, in particular, suffered from a bureaucratic tradition in German culture which caused all too many employees in service industries to treat the customer not as a king, but as a subject, and a querulous subject at that.[33]

The German *Wirtschaftswunder* had become a memory of the past. (West Germany's average growth rate had declined from 4.5 percent in the 1960s to only 1.9 percent in the 1980s. In 1993 the growth rate actually diminished.) Unemployment went up in West Germany as well as East Germany. Employers complained of an economy excessively regulated and excessively taxed. German workers had obtained the best wages in Europe, together with excellent conditions for sick pay, vacations, and security of employment. German labor costs were the highest in Europe. Not surprisingly, employers shifted industries abroad (including the US). As Peter Trapp, a German economist, put it, Germany's social welfare economy was transformed into a "social partnership," with untoward consequences. The market counted for less and politics for more. Economic decision-making increasingly passed into the hands of trade unions, employers' associations, political action groups representing the handicapped, retirees, farmers, and politicians, who tried to replace economic competition with political compromise.[34] The welfare state, essential to the smooth functioning of Germany's consensus democracy, became overloaded, just as it did in countries such as Sweden and Holland.

Economic difficulties went with broader sociological challenges. Germany was an aging country, especially East Germany where for a time the marriage and birth rates dropped catastrophically after unification. West Germany's economic miracle had depended on huge waves of immigrants: first of all millions of Germans displaced from Silesia, East Prussia, and the Sudetenland; then refugees from East Germany; finally *Gastarbeiter* from southern Europe. But the bulk of Europeans, unlike the majority of Americans, did not look on newcomers as potential citizens. (In Germany, naturalization was particularly difficult, and dual citizenship hard to establish, lest the new citizen should face divided loyalties.) Far from wanting to assimilate foreigners, immigration was unpopular. Right-wing extremism was on the rise. There were murderous attacks on foreigners – assaults of a kind almost unknown before the two Germanys had united.

At the same time confidence declined in the major political parties. With its complex system of checks and balances, German – like US – politics appeared increasingly gridlocked. Like the US, Germany also had to cope with the "judicialization" of politics, as the courts, especially the Constitutional Court, were increasingly asked to solve political problems; hence the latter's composition likewise became a matter of political rivalry. There was no compensatory glory in Germany's foreign politics, which seemed ill advised or ineffective in trouble spots such as Bosnia and Somalia. There was pessimism in the air. Would Germany's Second Republic falter like the Weimar Republic or France's Third Republic?

33 For a detailed enquiry, see the article, *"Maul halten, zahlen,"* in *Der Spiegel*, no. 26, 27 June 1994, pp. 68–77. Germany also lagged behind in terms of employment in the service industries. By 1994, 72 percent of all persons in US employment worked in the service industries, 70 percent in Britain, 69.9 percent in Holland, but only 58 percent in Germany.

34 Peter Trapp, "What Happened to the German Economic Miracle," Stanford, CA, Hoover Institution, Working Papers in International Studies, 1–90–2, 1994.

Fortunately, the Federal German Republic's foundations were sounder than the pessimists assumed. At the end of the Weimar Republic, the constitutionalist parties had been outnumbered by extremists both on the right and the left – a republic with all too few republicans. The major parties of the Federal Republic, by contrast, remained solidly committed to democracy, and between them formed a substantial majority of the electorate. These parties were all led by moderates: Kohl in command of the CDU, Klaus Kinkel in charge of the FDP (as Genscher's successor at the ministry of foreign affairs), and Rudolf Scharping (chairman of the SPD since 1993). The Liberal Democrats, the smallest of the "classic" parties, would weaken for a time, their place being taken in part by the growing Green Party (with the possibility of "red–green" coalitions both on the federal and the *Länder* level). (Scharping, a pleasant-looking man, bearded and bespectacled, with a soft Mainz accent, had advanced in politics by the same route as Kohl, as *Ministerpräsident* of Rhineland-Palatinate, a conservative *Land* with a strong rural component.) German skinheads were as vicious as their confrères in Britain, France, Poland, and Russia. But unlike the Nazi storm-troopers or the communist *Rotfrontkämpferbund* in Weimar Germany, the skinheads were neither organized nor disciplined. The last thing they wished for was to put on uniform, go to war, and bleed to death in some Ukrainian foxhole. They threatened individual foreigners, but not German democracy as such.

Ex-communists in East Germany found a new home in the PDS. But even in Brandenburg, an East German *Land* badly hit by the unification economic slump, the PDS attained no more than 21 percent in the 1993 *Land* election. The PDS, moreover, was no longer a hard-line party such as the SED had been: no more clarion calls to class war; instead socialism would be introduced through the backdoor. In a more general sense, Marxism–Leninism had become dated even on its own terms. Marxism–Leninism had derived from an era dominated by coal, iron, and steel, by great enterprises based on steam power. Progress had been envisaged in terms of quantitative, not of qualitative, changes in industry. No Marxist theoretician had anticipated the new industrial revolutions founded on computerization and other forms of high-tech. Equally discredited was Marxism–Leninism as a moral force. The volunteers who had fought in the International Brigades during the Spanish Civil War had been idealists willing to die for socialism. Not so the aging partocrats who now sued in court for their pension rights. An anti-climactic ending for a party that had likened itself to Prometheus willing to steal fire from the gods! Not surprisingly, the PDS as a whole thereafter came to resemble more the reformed communist parties of Poland and Hungary than the communist parties, old style.

The SPD turned to the left as in 1995 Oskar Lafontaine replaced Rudolf Scharping as the party's leader. Lafontaine's accession marked the dominant position now assumed within the SPD by the once rebellious generation of the 1960s. Lafontaine, however, was in no wise a communist sympathizer – in fact, he knew little about communists. (In an entertaining gaffe he claimed that the famous line, *alle Menschen werden Brüder* (all men become brothers), derived from Schiller's "Ode to Joy," a poem once known to every educated German, was contained in The Internationale).[35] No matter what its opponents might say, the SPD remained a moderate, constitutional party. The Greens likewise claimed to challenge the Establishment. The Greens, though disunited, particularly appealed to the young and expensively educated. But, however critical of the *Bundeswehr*

35 *Der Spiegel*, 20 November 1995, no. 47, p. 29.

and NATO, the Greens in no wise formed a peril to German democracy. The German Federal Republic would not go the way of Weimar.

Despite its numerous problems, Germany's future looked good, even if the next few years promised to be troubled.[36] The face of East Germany in particular kept changing, as private enterprise re-emerged, as once grey cityscapes were enlivened by new shops and new department stores. Unification produced an army of losers, party secretaries without jobs, military officers without appointments. But East Germans, on the average, found themselves better off than in the olden days. Between 1991 and 1992 the investment rate (the ratio of investment to gross domestic product, GDP) rose from 42 to 46 percent, an unprecedented figure in German economic history. In the early 1990s, the money annually transferred from West to East Germany exceeded the total aid distributed by the Marshall Plan to all recipients. (To be exact, between 1990 and 1994 some $224 billion were transferred to East Germany.) Despite all public grumbling, only 9 percent of East German respondents to a 1994 public opinion poll considered their personal position bad or very bad; 54 percent considered their personal position good or very good. Many East Germans might continue to look on the market economy with measured skepticism. But in 20 years' time or less, East Germany's factories and infrastructure will be renovated as radically as they were in West Germany after the destruction of World War II. Despite the huge costs of unification, Germany prevented double-digit inflation. Public spending, by 1994, amounted to about 52 percent of GDP, but the government planned to cut it down to the level which it had reached before unification (about 33 percent).[37]

Germany was equally well placed in international affairs. The last Russian troops left the country in August 1994. (In a ceremony which ten years earlier would have been imagined only in Absurdistan, a *Bundeswehr* band played *Alte Kameraden* ("Old Comrades," a rousing German marching tune) to speed the Russian-Berlin brigade on its way.) For the first time in its history, Germany was surrounded only by friendly states. The Soviet Union had disintegrated (as had Czechoslovakia). The East Central European countries no longer looked on Germany as a threat, but saw her now as a market, a reservoir of capital and managerial skill.

Pessimists therefore regretted that the Federal Republic would henceforth constitute "the dominant nation-state in an enlarged Europe."[38] Germany's population and domestic product, they pointed out, were the largest in Europe. Germany enjoyed a special relationship with Russia. The smaller countries of East Central Europe, at the same time, looked to Germany for help against Russia's possible ambitions in the future. Germany backed the admission of Poland, Hungary, Slovakia, and the Czech Republic to the EU where the newcomers would surely support Germany. Germany also led the move to expand the EU by taking in Sweden, Finland, Norway, and Austria, which likewise would look to Germany. Germany's traditional partners, by contrast, would be politically weakened in an enlarged Europe – France in particular. Spain, Portugal, Greece, and Ireland would lose in economic terms. If the East Central European countries were to join the EU, they would wish to benefit from the subsidies paid by the wealthy members of the EU to their poorer partners. There were other grounds for

36 W.R. Smyser, "The Global Economic Effects of German Unification," in Gary L. Geipel, ed., *Germany in a New Era*, Indianapolis, IN, Hudson Institute, 1993, p. 267.
37 "Germany: Half-Hidden Agenda," *The Economist*, 21 May 1994, pp. 1–5.
38 Jacob Heilbrunn, "Tomorrow's Germany," *The National Interest*, no. 36, Summer 1994, p. 52.

pessimism. Since reunification, united Germany had become far more nationalistic and self-assertive than the old Federal Republic. Germany now had many more options for asserting European primacy than she had possessed in the past.[39]

Nevertheless, Germany's apparent strength within the EU should not be exaggerated. As regards population and GDP alike, France, Britain, Italy, and Spain rank next to Germany in that order. Any two of these countries combined outnumber Germany in both population and economic production. Far from seeking to enhance its military might, Germany in fact reduced its armaments. Far from wishing to exclude its EU partners from East Central Europe, Germany encouraged their involvement. Taken as a whole, Kohl's Germany, by the mid-1990s, was more peaceful, prosperous, and democratic than ever before in its history.

This transformation invites a comparison between Prince Otto von Bismarck (1815–98), founder of united Germany (1871), and Kohl, architect of German reunification more than a century later. At first sight, the two had nothing in common. Bismarck answered to a hereditary monarch; Kohl to a democratic electorate. Bismarck was a Prussian; Kohl a Rhinelander. No one ever underestimated Bismarck; whereas Kohl was for long Germany's most underrated politician. Bismarck was a Lutheran; Kohl a Catholic. Bismarck always wore a military uniform; Kohl was a civilian of civilians. Bismarck was an aristocrat; Kohl a commoner. Bismarck was a man of wealth, with landed property and judicious investments at the stock exchange; Kohl derived from modest circumstances, having started as an office manager, and ended as one of those professional politicians who by no means dominated German parliamentary life.

But there were also unexpected parallels. Both enjoyed striking political longevity. Both were able and ruthless men, prepared to put down friends as well as enemies. Both were personally honest, but willing enough to deal with corrupt people. (Bismarck, with his scathing wit, described one of them "corruptible for so little as to be practically incorruptible.") Bismarck laid the foundations of the German welfare state so as to buy off the Social Democratic workers. Kohl and CDU politicians of his kind extended the welfare state to the extent of having "social democratized" the CDU. Most important of all, both Bismarck and Kohl regarded themselves as good Europeans and good Germans. Having unified Germany by war, Bismarck thereafter worked for peace, convinced that the newly built Reich was "saturated," and must cooperate in the Concert of Europe. Kohl went much further, resolved to encase Germany in a European Union, solidified by a common currency. We ourselves, personally, do not share Kohl's vision of a European superstate. But as regards Germany proper, Kohl's handiwork will surely last longer than Bismarck's.

39 Timothy Garton Ash, "Germany's Choice," *Foreign Affairs*, July/August 1994, pp. 65–81.

13

France: 1974 to the Present

De Gaulle died in 1970. But his Fifth Republic remained firmly in place, its legitimacy soundly established. France, by the end of the 1970s, had an annual gross domestic product per capita larger than the US, Canada, Japan, Great Britain, notwithstanding numerous stereotypes to the contrary.[1] From the middle of World War II, moreover, France had experienced a startling demographic recuperation. (Over the long run, from the mid-1920s to 1990, the year of Germany's reunification, France had actually improved its relative demographic position *vis-à-vis* Germany.)[2] From the end of World War II, French productivity had increased at a startling rate, and by the late 1960s France had surpassed its old rival Great Britain in the size of its GNP, a change that would have astonished Victorians. Overall, the development of the Fourth and Fifth Republics alike had been an unforeseen success story.

The Political and Economic Stage

Despite all progress, France remained a land of contrasts. The olden-day France, famed for its châteaux, its picturesque little towns with their small farms, little boutiques and cafés, did not disappear. But, overall, France had become a global power whose exports exceeded in value those of Japan. The merchandise sent abroad no longer consisted primarily of high fashion, perfumes and other high-quality luxuries, but of high-precision machines, plastics, transport equipment, armaments, and tractors. A prewar economy – based to a considerable extent on antiquated forms of farming, restrictive family enterprises, and highly protective, often inefficient manufactures – turned into one of the world's most advanced economies. Many structural weaknesses, of course, remained. In France, as elsewhere in Western Europe, traditional industries, such as shipbuilding, coal mining, steel-making, and textiles, had trouble in holding their own against Third World competitors. There were complaints concerning lack of vigor in the banking world, an out-of-date fiscal system, clumsy distribution networks, poor liaison between pure and applied research, and deficiencies in the new high-tech industries.[3] Nevertheless, progress was immense. By the late 1980s, for example, the biggest French money-earners in the US were not Cardin suits, Saint-Laurent dresses, Bordeaux wines, or cognacs, but CFM 56 aircraft engines, co-manufactured on a 50–50 basis by the French

---

1 John Ardagh, *France in the 1980s: the Definitive Book*, Harmondsworth, Penguin, 1982, p. 382; François Crouzet, ed., *The Economic Development of France since 1870*, Aldershot, Edward Elgar, 1993.
2 France in 1924 had a population of about 40,000,000 and in 1990 55,900,000. During the same period united Germany's population went up from 64,000,000 to 77,900,000.
3 Ardagh, *France in the 1980s*, p. 29.

and General Electric. A subway commuter in New York, by this time, was probably riding in a French-made car (manufactured by *Ateliers du Nord*). On entering Manhattan by way of the triborough bridge, a motorist would throw his quarters into machines made by CSEE (*Compagnie des signeaux et entreprises electriques*).[4] French public relations firms widely continued to publicize abroad the image of France as the land of high fashion and leisurely refinement: indeed, the French garment industry remained successful on the world markets – but its one billion dollar sales to the US in 1985 was dwarfed by the six billion dollars worth of airplanes and helicopters imported into the US in the same year.[5]

By the early 1990s, France's production per worker outstripped Germany's, Japan's, and Britain's. A new France had come into existence centering, in part, on cities such as Toulouse, which had broken free of the traditional constraints besetting a French provincial town, and had become a major center for high-tech industries. From being a backwater, Toulouse had turned into a city with well over half a million people. The traditional élite of lawyers, physicians, and landowners had been overtaken by a new élite of scientists, managers, professors, and venture capitalists. Nostalgic memories of olden-day France notwithstanding, urban centers such as Toulouse had gained from the transformation. As Sir John Ardagh puts it, they had "secured not only more wealth and industry, but also far more cultural activity than before, and a more open social life."[6] What a change from the tight-lipped, tight-knit society described by Balzac!

France again counted on the international stage – a far cry from the humiliating days of Marshall Pétain's *Etat français*. Firmly integrated into the European Union and closely allied to Germany, France ranked as its second-most powerful member. France had also regained its position as a military power. Critics used to joke that French generals desired a German army bigger than the Russian army, and a French army bigger than the German army. By the early 1990s, the generals had their wish – at least in part. The French armed forces indeed outnumbered those of all France's European allies. (By 1994, France's defense forces comprised 409,000, Germany's 367,000, Italy's 322,000, the United Kingdom's 254,000.)[7] The armed forces enjoyed considerable prestige; the peace and anti-nuclear movements in France were much less powerful than they were in Germany or Britain. The once-famed Foreign Legion reverted to insignificance. Yet the French army no longer formed a threat to the democratic order; not even the pacifists feared that the army would ever leave its barracks to push a candidate of its own choice into presidential office. Unfortunately, the extent of France's economic and political strength went inadequately noticed – most of all by the bulk of French intellectuals.

In France, as in the rest of Europe, there were, of course, losers as well as winners. The losers included unemployed workers in decaying industries, particularly in the north and east of France. Family farms were beset by countless troubles; their owners' discontent

4 "It's High Time for a High-Tech Image," *France Magazine*, no. 7, Winter 1986–7, pp. 16–20. The products with the largest production increases (1984–5) were airplanes and helicopters, fissile products, uranium, controlling and checking equipment, refined petroleum products, public works equipment, aircraft engines, women's wear, and plastics.

5 Ibid., pp. 16–21.

6 John Ardagh, *A Tale of Five Cities*, London, Secker and Warburg, 1979, p. 288.

7 International Institute for Strategic Studies, *The Military Balance, 1994–1995*, London, The Institute, 1994.

appeared particularly stark in areas with strong regional traditions such as Brittany, Corsica, and the Languedoc. Generalizations with regard to the farming industry are, of course, particularly difficult, as conditions varied enormously. Successful farmers in part mechanized their operations, and accounted for an ever-increasing share of national production. By contrast, traditional family farms gradually disappeared. (Between 1956 and 1976 alone, something like half the farming population left the land.)

The psychological impact of this migration cannot be quantified, but it was enormous. The first to leave were usually the nobility and local bourgeoisie. The shutters of once elegant homes closed. Once-famous châteaux were sold for holiday homes. Thereafter, the more lowly placed people departed to seek work in town; shops, cafés, rural shoe-makers, harness-makers, tailors lost their customers, and closed their shops. At last, only the elderly stayed behind. But in the end, they also moved to town to live with their children or in-laws, and whole villages were abandoned. A stranger, say, in the Massif Central, might wander through the hushed streets of an empty village without meeting a soul. Silence! Not a horse neighed; not a cow mooed; not a dog barked. The village church might still stand, picturesque, but empty. The tourist could eat his or her fill from untended fruit trees in the orchards of untended farms. Then nature would regain her own as the decaying ruins were overgrown.

French novelists in the past had produced a great literature which depicted peasants as deeply rooted in the soil, instinctively attached to the land. Such stereotypes, however, bore little relation to reality. According to public opinion surveys, the majority of people in rural France wanted to get away from the villages, and get work in cities where life was easier, employment more regular than in the countryside, wages higher, medical and educational facilities were more easily available, entertainment and social contacts more varied.[8] Small farmers, moreover, had accumulated heavy debts. (Loans from the Credit Agricole multiplied by eight between 1960 and 1974.) Not surprisingly, hard-pressed cultivators were apt to develop a siege mentality, and France experienced a series of violent rural outbursts; those of the winter of 1980–81 were particularly bitter and became known as *la révolte des paysans*.[9]

France was also riven by other divisions; for instance, the split between centralizers and devolutionists who wished to give more power to the regions. The French state traditionally centered on Paris which occupied within France a position even more prominent than London held in Britain. Whether in politics, the arts, the theater, academia, or finance, Paris offered the most glittering prizes, as evidenced by that succession of great French novels in which ambitious provincials depart for Paris to make their name or seek a fortune. (François Mitterrand, the socialist leader, was belittled by his opponents during presidential campaigns as a "Rastignac" – an aristocratic but provincial parvenu in Balzac's novels – because Mitterrand had come from Bordeaux.)

Centralization was promoted also by the *grandes écoles* (professional schools of high standing which trained military officers, engineers, teachers, civil servants, archivists, and other specialists). The *grandes écoles* produced mandarins with the highest academic

8 Colin Dyer, *Population and Society in Twentieth Century France*, Seven Oaks, Hodder and Stoughton, 1978, pp. 200–202.
9 Vincent Wright, *The Government and Politics of France*, New York, Holmes and Meier, 1989, p. 265. Also see our general chapter on farming in Peter Duignan and L.H. Gann, *The Rebirth of the West: the Americanization of the Democratic World, 1945–1958*, Oxford, and Cambridge, Mass., Blackwell, 1992, pp. 519–28.

qualifications. The French Revolution had proclaimed liberty, equality, and fraternity. Nevertheless, French society remained highly stratified, comparable in certain respects to a meritocratic army. Its Guards Regiments were the *grands corps* constituting the higher civil service (just under 6,000 people, divided into some 30 corps). The higher civil servants were drawn largely, though not wholly, from the middle and upper-middle class. They were recruited almost exclusively from the *grandes écoles*, with the best students opting for the most prestigious corps. In the olden days the *Ecole normale supérieure* (which trained teachers and academics) had occupied the place of honor. But as academia lost influence and prestige, so did the *Ecole normale*. Instead, the *Ecole national d'administration* (ENA, set up in 1945) advanced to the top of the pyramid, as its technocratic approach seemed more attuned to the values of the Fifth Republic. ENA even challenged the *Polytechnique* (dominating the Corps of Mines and Civil Engineers) for its traditional and bureaucratic strongholds. *Enarques* (graduates of the ENA) also advanced into banks and corporations (which by 1994 gave employment to about one-fifth of all ENA graduates). The *grandes écoles* provided France with highly trained, highly motivated, and extremely able men and women who served French interests well, whether as planners in the domestic economy, or as international civil servants in the European Union and other transnational bodies. In an indirect sense, the *grandes écoles* also wielded enormous political influence. (Between the founding of the Fifth Republic in 1958 and 1995, 13 out of 14 French prime ministers, three out of four French presidents, and over 60 percent of cabinet ministers came from the *grandes écoles*, as did the majority of CEOs and leaders in the 50 largest corporations and banks.) Not that graduates were in agreement on political and economic questions. There were striking disagreements. Nevertheless, the *grandes écoles* created their own culture, their own loyalties, a peculiar self-confidence, and a pervasive sense of superiority. Not a shadow of scandal attached to French examinations which could not be swayed by political patronage or party connections.[10] The civil service operated by a system of institutionalized distrust through the *inspecteurs d'état*, an administrative élite which reported on every major matter of administrative concern. Central power reached into the provinces through the prefects, resplendent in their power, prestige, and – on gala occasions – in their dress uniforms of blue and gold. Far from diminishing, the power of the state and the bureaucracy greatly expanded after liberation. Gaullists, socialists, communists, even Christian Democrats called for a managed economy in which the state would hold the levers of command, and operate key enterprises such as the Bank of France. The centralizers of whatever persuasion drew on an age-old tradition dating back at least to Louis XIV and (Jean-Baptiste) Colbert (1619–83), a great Bourbon minister who had mightily labored to expand the power of the king. The centralizers met opposition from moderates, especially socialists, who criticized the way in which Paris stifled local vigor and local initiative, but these moderates ultimately failed to change in essentials France's long-established political culture.

In France, as in the rest of Europe, there was likewise a cleavage between "Europeanists" and advocates of national sovereignty. Broadly speaking, the former included economic winners – transnational corporations, professional people with international contacts, banks – while the losers backed the cause of French nationalism. Not that these divisions were hard and fast. Farmers, for example, were ready enough to condemn

10 Patrick Chamorel, "Elites Enjoy Life in France's Fast Lane," Institute of Governmental Studies, *Public Affairs Report*, vol. 36, no. 1, January 1995, pp. 1, 8–9.

Euro-bureaucracy and Euro-speak, while pleased to accept European subsidies paid to agriculture. But internal French disagreements now also merged with Euro-quarrels. Other disputes centered on immigration, the claims of a growing Islamic community in France, the advance of *franglais,* and the real or assumed threat to French culture posed by English, Donald Duck, Disneyland, and McDonald's hamburgers.

Above all, French people remained divided over the legacy of the French Revolution. The revolutionary mystique envisaged France as the motherland of liberty, equality, and fraternity. But the Revolution had also called for the "career open to talent," and France was in effect ruled by a meritocratic army recruited from the upper strata of the liberal professions, the leading cadres in private and nationalized industries, and above all, from the *grandes écoles.* Particularly powerful were the *énarques,* whose members supposedly ruled the land merely by ringing the right person in the right office, and starting the conversation *écoute cher camarade* (listen old buddy). The administrative élite was linked to business, as retired civil servants would take senior jobs in corporations. Equally strong were the ties between the administration and politics. Political favoritism influenced high-level appointments, as neither de Gaulle, Pompidou, nor Giscard scrupled to reward their friends. At the same time, civil servants were heavily represented in the legislature. (Ironically enough, after interminable criticism from the left concerning the interlocking nature of politics and administration, nearly three-fifths of the newly elected National Assembly in 1981 were officials, in part because of socialist strength among teachers who rank as civil servants.)[11]

But the greatest split of all was racial–religious. The loss of Algeria had led to a reflux, not merely of white *colons,* but also of Muslims who had fought on the French side, had fallen foul of the new authorities for other reasons, or were fleeing Muslim fundamentalist terrorism. More North Africans came in search of jobs. Some climbed the ladder of success – respectable shopkeepers, professions, a sprinkling of millionaires – but all too many remained at the bottom. In theory, a naturalized foreigner of any nationality was French. France would thus have no truck with the American concepts of multiculturalism. Citizens of whatever origin were expected to be French in language, customs, and behavior. (Algerian Muslim schoolgirls who turned up at school with their faces veiled would be promptly sent home.) But whereas assimilation had worked with French-speaking Algerians, Spaniards, and Basques, Muslim Arabs in practice remained largely excluded from French society. *Banlieux* such as Vaulx-en-Velin on the outskirts of Lyon turned into slums, disfigured by high-rise public housing units, stricken by unemployment, breeding grounds for crime and violence.

France, like Britain, had turned into a multi-ethnic and multicultural society. But in France, as in Britain, this transformation had come about without public debate, in the face of strong public disapproval. There was no agreement even on statistics. (Officially, there were less than 1,000,000 Algerians in France, but many had come illegally. Many more had become naturalized, and no longer were listed as aliens. Academic studies suggested that the number of ethnic Algerians in France might be closer to 3,000,000, by far the largest bloc in an estimated Franco-Arab population of 5,000,000.) Assimilation had largely failed. For all its egalitarian pretensions, French society thus stood out as "one of the most unequal of Western societies."[12]

11 Douglas E. Ashford, *Policy and Politics in France: Living with Uncertainty*, Philadelphia, Temple University Press, 1982, p. 79.
12 Ardagh, *France in the 1980s*, p. 381.

Center–Left–Right: Giscard d'Estaing to Mitterrand

Among the French élites, the very model of a modern mandarin was Giscard d'Estaing (president 1974–81). He came from an old and distinguished family of provincial notables who had served their country in official positions since the days of Louis XV, and had made their name in industry, banking, and the higher levels of the civil service. (The *Who's Who in France*, 1988, lists six Giscards d'Estaing, each with a distinguished career.) Giscard had participated in the Resistance. But even more remarkable was his ascent through the *grandes écoles*. In a land which prizes examinations, Giscard was one of the few graduates entitled to wear – not one – but three of the proudest badges conferred by the system: X, ENA, and IF, having passed alike the *Ecole polytechnique*, the *Ecole nationale d'administration*, and then having joined the *inspection des finances*, most exclusive of the *grands corps*. Though denigrated as a Philistine, Giscard was a man of culture who had published on history, politics, and also on his own life experience. (His heroes were an assorted crew which included Guy de Maupassant, Louis XV, and Louis XI, respectively story-teller, lecher, and saint.) For his opponents, however, Giscard's elevation to the presidency seemed the final triumph of the diploma-bearing meritocracy.

Such was not Giscard's self-image. Giscard had first made his name in politics as a youthful minister of finance in one of General de Gaulle's cabinets. He fell out of favor when he committed *lèse-majesté* by criticizing the great man ("Judas Giscariot" was one of the Gaullists' kindlier sneers). Giscard, however, had plenty of ability; he also commanded a political base as deputy and mayor of Chamalières (a wealthy suburb of Clermont-Ferrant). In 1974, Giscard managed to win the presidency, trouncing Jacques Chaban-Delmas, his Gaullist rival, at the first ballot, and then beating François Mitterrand, his left-wing opponent, by a slight majority in the second ballot.

Giscard was a moderate conservative, heir to the "Orleanist," as opposed to the Gaullists' "Bonapartist," tradition which continued to divide the right. (The Orleanists had been named after the Duke of Orleans, younger brother of Louis XVI, who accepted the French Revolution but was beheaded for his pains. The Bonapartists, by contrast, admired Napoleon's rule, with its rigid centralization and thirst for gore and glory.) Giscard's aim was to rally the center, liberalize the Gaullist state, free the economy from outdated restraints, and resist a left-wing takeover while, at the same time, fostering a more pluralist and more permissive society. The new president did choose for his prime minister Jacques Chirac, a Gaullist and a fellow *énarque*, but otherwise drastically reduced the number of Gaullist ministers. Having been forced to relinquish the presidency in 1974, the Gaullists suffered another blow in 1976. Chirac and Giscard had never managed to get on. (Chirac used to dread private meetings with the president who would drink his tea alone and never even offer an ash-tray to the chain-smoking Chirac.) Chirac resigned, replaced by Raymond Barre, a brilliant academic, and also a Giscard loyalist without a strong power base of his own.

The president and his cabinet then embarked on a number of reforms: the government liberalized divorce procedures; the voting age was reduced to eighteen; life became a little easier for prison inmates; women advanced to cabinet positions. (For instance, Simone Veil, a former resistance fighter, feminist, and a brilliant lawyer, became minister of health, and turned out to be the most popular member in the ministry.) There were cautious attempts at administrative decentralization. In particular, Giscard put an end to the anomaly of Paris having no mayor. (Ironically, the newly created job first went to Chirac, by now Giscard's most bitter rival in the ongoing *querelle des chefs*.) Giscard showed more sympathy than any of his predecessors for the growing ecology movement. A man of taste, he disliked the monstrous slabs of concrete and plate glass that had disfigured so many European towns during the 1960s. Giscard therefore used his influence to clamp down on the construction of skyscrapers in Paris which might have turned the capital into a Euro-Manhattan. (For instance, he scrapped plans for an International Commercial Center in Paris, a trendy monstrosity. He likewise prevented the extension of a Left Bank motorway by withdrawing official funds for the project.) Against bitter opposition from within his own supporters, Giscard liberalized existing abortion laws. (There was bitter hostility from the "right to life" lobby, *"Laissez les vivre"* (let them live), whose supporters objected to the changes either on religious grounds or because they feared a new threat to France's falling birth rate.) The bill only passed (1974) with the support of the Socialists and Communists.

Giscard, by contrast, lacked the traditional Gaullists' bitter suspicion of *les anglo-saxons*. Relations with the US improved, and US investment in France, like other foreign investments, now met with encouragement. When Britain renegotiated the terms of its entry into the European Economic Community, in Dublin, in 1976, the French president made concessions – without even informing his own ministers.

Giscard likewise favored reducing what Kohl later called the "democratic deficit" in the European Community's affairs, and backed direct elections to the European Parliament. (Chirac, less than lukewarm about the president's pro-European stance, later revealed that neither he nor the other ministers had been informed about this crucial decision, much less asked for their opinion.) Above all, the French continued to look for close relations with Germany, France's closest ally within the European Community, and also France's largest trading partner. (Helmut Schmidt and Giscard got on well, even though they could not speak each other's language, and instead conversed in English when they met.)

In economic affairs, Giscard tended to back small and medium-sized against big business. He preferred smaller projects to those huge prestige enterprises which had delighted de Gaulle and Pompidou. (Giscard thus axed several extremely expensive undertakings, including an aerotrain. Giscard likewise decided to dismantle the *Compagnie international pour l'information* (CII), started by de Gaulle as an exclusively French computer complex, and supported by state funds so as to outdo US competition.) In general, Giscard came to oppose the long-standing French tradition of *dirigisme*. In this endeavor, he was aided by the "new economists" who favored private enterprise, and who dominated institutions such as the *Fondation pour la nouvelle economie politique*.

Giscard's most important decision, perhaps, came in 1978, when the government announced the end of all price controls in industry. This was a true revolution. Price controls had been in operation since the beginning of World War II, and had been imposed on industry with varying degrees of severity ever since. (In specific trades, price regulation had been in force even longer. Bread prices, for example, had generally been regulated ever since 1791, and even before under the Bourbon monarchy.) In theory, French industrialists detested price controls; in practice, they happily adjusted whenever they were compensated by state subsidies (as in the case of the steel industry).

The new policy turned out to be a success. True enough, prices rose for certain commodities such as bread, and specific services such as transportation. But overall "the dramatic government move had little impact on the overall cost of living index."[13] At

13 Henri Le Page, "Paris," *Policy Review*, Spring 1980, no. 12, p. 71.

the same time, the government cut down on official subventions to nationalized indus-try, and stopped pumping money into ailing firms. This was a risky decision. The steel industry had long ailed in France, as well as in Britain, Belgium, and Germany's Ruhr region. EC policy-makers came to similar conclusions. For the first time, political leaders (including a substantial number of leftists) became convinced that unprofitable indus-tries should close, and that giving even one franc to an ailing firm entailed taking that franc away from a healthy firm. In a like manner, Barre, from 1976 onward, placed a maximum annual ceiling on the growth of monetary aggregates, the first time in French history that a monetary target was officially announced. Barre was the first leader of the Fifth Republic to break a long tradition of Keynesian monetary management.

Giscard, unlike the first president of the Fifth Republic, and unlike his successor, was "by all accounts, an immensely nice man."[14] But he was caught between the right and the left, and forced to veer between them. He thus came to seem inconsistent, even in his personal image. There was Giscard the glad-hander, photographed while shaking hands with the inmates of a prison; there was Giscard the sophisticated *énarque*; there was Giscard dining with garage hands and firemen; there was Giscard shining in high society; there was Giscard the dynamic, youthful Kennedy figure; there was Giscard the regal president; there was Giscard the honest man denouncing alike the timidity of conservatism and revolutionary confrontations; there was Giscard the opportunist who unwisely accepted presents from thugs such as the self-styled emperor Bokassa, one of France's African clients. Even the Gaullists found cause to criticize the "new monarchy," as Giscard's rule turned more and more personal, and as "the public grew tired of arbitrary decision making in [the] guise of reform."[15] The 1981 election turned out to be a defeat for Giscard. The Socialists (with Communist support) gained an absolute majority in the Assembly, and thereby initiated the "era Mitterrand."

Mitterrand (1916–95), likewise came from a *bien pensant* Catholic family, provincial but well connected. (His father Joseph had been a manufacturer, his brother Jacques a general.) François Mitterrand's academic qualifications included a diploma from the *Ecole libre des sciences politiques*, one of the most prestigious schools in France. When World War II came, Mitterrand joined the army, was wounded, taken prisoner in 1940, but later escaped, and returned to France. A committed right-winger, Mitterrand thereafter served the Vichy regime as a civil servant, and received for his loyalty the then much-coveted *Francisque* medal. Mitterrand then praised Pétain, and mixed on friendly terms with characters such as René Bosquet, head of the Vichy police who, among his other assignments, oversaw the deportation of tens of thousands of Jews to German concen-tration camps.

Displaying convenient flexibility, Mitterrand, in 1943, joined the Resistance, and later the Gaullist administration. (After liberation he insisted that "heads must roll.") Then came a distinguished ministerial career during the course of which Mitterrand consigned to oblivion his Vichy past, as indeed did so many of his compatriots. Under the Fourth Republic, Mitterrand served for a time as minister of the interior under Pierre Mendès-France (a Socialist of outstanding ability and a genuine war hero with a fine record as a flier). In those distant days, Mitterrand stood out as a spokesman of empire, acceptable to the toughest of *pieds noirs* in the toughest bar in Algiers. Algeria was part of France, Mitterrand proclaimed at the outbreak of the Algerian War (1954).

14 Wright, *The Government and Politics of France*, p. 45.
15 Ashford, *Policy and Politics in France*, p. 25.

From Flanders to the Congo there was room only for "one law, one nation, one parliament."[16] But times change, and Mitterrand emerged in due course as a leading light of *Tiers-mondisme* within the French Socialist Party, the *beau idéal* of conscience and virtue. *"Mais, monsieur Mitterrand, vous n'avez pas le monopole du coeur"* (but Mr Mitterrand, you don't have a monopoly of goodness) Giscard grumbled – but to no avail.[17]

In 1971 Mitterrand advanced to be the first secretary of the Socialist Party, which he refashioned and led to victory in the 1981 general election. Accepting several Communist ministers into a coalition cabinet, Mitterrand then embarked on a new attempt to turn the French Republic into a socialist state. Under the premiership of Pierre Mauroy (1981–84) the state again intervened on a large scale in the economy. Whereas by now most major industrial countries responded to continuing economic crises by deregulating their economies and denationalizing major public companies, France went the opposite way. Mitterrand returned to a massive nationalization program, particularly in banking. (By 1985, companies in the public sector represented 21 percent of sales and 23 percent of employment, 30 percent of exports, and 53 percent of the fixed assets of all French companies.) According to its advocates, nationalization would see the beginning of new times (Mauroy), continue a French tradition (Jacques Delors), promote salubrity (Michel Charzat, chairman of the Assembly's special commission on nationalization), expropriate the expropriators (Pierre Joxe, chairman of the Socialist group in the Assembly), save the country's future economic management (Mitterrand), and – oddly enough – end *bureaucratisation* and *étatisation* of the economy (Jacques Attali, special consultant to the president).[18]

Despite such encomiums, nationalization did not work. Losses suffered by nationalized companies increased (in real terms from $5.3 billion in 1981 to $8.3 billion in 1983); subsidies to publicly owned enterprises kept rising, as did salaries, wages, and public debts. Worse still, concluded Jean Gandois, chairman of the leading French chemical company and a Socialist appointee, nationalized companies are not able to exercise in the economic field the leading role that was the principal justification of their nationalization. Nationalization has failed everywhere essentially for two reasons: the government won't let them fail and political reasoning, not economic logic, rules, and so voter-workers are not fired from state-owned businesses.

Hence Mitterrand once more changed course. The alliance with the Communists broke down (1984). As we explained in chapter 4, the French Communist Party had steadily weakened; the party's sense of certainty faltered, and the members' commitment to quasi-military obedience vanished. Many party cells disappeared; activists ceased to participate regularly in meetings and marches, and membership kept declining. The traditional working-class bastions eroded in the industrial "red belt" around Paris, and in the decaying steel-making and coal-mining centers of the north-east. While the

16 Richard Brace and Joan Brace, *Ordeal in Algeria*, Princeton, NJ, van Nostrand, 1960, p. 115.
17 Valéry Giscard d'Estaing, *Le Pouvoir et la Vie*, Paris, Cie 12, 1988, p. 330. A sensation was caused by the investigative journalism of Pierre Péan, *Une jeunesse française: François Mitterrand 1934–1947*," Paris, Fayard, 1994; see also the major review essay by Tony Judt, "Truth and Consequences," *The New York Review of Books*, 3 November 1994, pp. 8–12.
18 Bertrand Jacquillat, *Nationalization and Privatization in Contemporary France*, Stanford, CA, Hoover Institution Press, 1988, pp. 6–8; William James Adams, *Restructuring the French Economy: Government and the Rise of Market Competition since World War II*, Washington, DC, The Brookings Institution, 1989.

Communists desperately tried to keep to their accustomed clientele, it was the Socialists who had gathered the votes of the newly discontented: militant students, immigrants, feminists, and the like. Slogans concerning "Socialism with a human face" lacked mass appeal. Above all, the French Communist Party suffered from its inability to break the umbilical cord with Moscow whose image was now tarnished beyond redemption.

As regards foreign policy, Mitterrand had no patience with anti-Germanism, traditional both among the extreme left and the extreme right.[19] Mitterrand likewise lacked the visceral anti-Americanism that had distinguished so many right-wing as well as left-wing intellectuals. His regime, moreover, rejected any return to France's traditional protectionism, and instead opted for a more liberalized international economy. As regards foreign policy, French troops participated in the Gulf War, and also in the ill-fated UN peace-keeping operation in Bosnia (1994). Relations between Mitterrand and Kohl over German and European affairs were nothing like as close as had been the links between Giscard and Helmut Schmidt. (Mitterrand was displeased by the pace of German unification, by Kohl's failure adequately to consult Mitterrand over German plans, by lack of German participation in the Gulf War, and by disagreements over the Yugoslav issue.) Nevertheless, Kohl liked Mitterrand as a person. Germany remained France's most important trade partner and chief European ally. Germany and France continued to cooperate closely in military matters (by expanding mixed Franco-German units), and issues such as ecological collaboration (for example, in cleaning up the Rhine). The Franco-German partnership continued to dominate the EU. France went on closely to cooperate with Germany on key issues such as EMU (European Monetary Union, discussed at greater length in chapter 16).

The French political scene changed in a wider sense. Marxism–Leninism by this time had ceased to be chic. The legacy of the 1968 revolution now widely appeared tawdry. Moreover, the French intellectuals' love affair with Moscow had ended. No Marxist intellectual could compete with giants such as Alexander Solzhenitsyn and Raymond Aron, or even lesser lights such as Alain Finkielkraut, a spokesman of the emergent "new right." The Sartrean infatuation with socialism, the contempt for capitalism, the studied disdain for the US increasingly became *ringard* (fusty, dated) in the eyes of the young. Intellectuals began to speak without blushing of *la France qui gagne* (France which makes money). Leisure played an increasing part in the average citizen's life. (The French even appointed an under secretary of state for leisure, irreverently referred to by the public as *le ministre de la paresse* – the minister for idleness). In such circumstances, the French Communist Party's Twenty-Fifth Congress, held in 1985, was a dispiriting affair – no longer celebrated as a "high mass" for the edification of the faithful, but a "troubled and turbulent gathering" in which the defeated quarreled over the past.[20] By contrast,

19 Sunil Khilnani, *Arguing Revolution: the Intellectual Left in Postwar France*, New Haven, Yale University Press, 1993; Tony Judt, *Past Imperfect: French Intellectuals 1944–1956*, Berkeley, CA, University of California Press, 1992. Changes in philosophical thought are discussed in Mark Lilla, ed., *New French Thought: Political Philosophy*, Princeton, Princeton University Press, 1994.

20 John Eisenhammer, "Communists Lose their Base," *New Statesman*, 8 February 1985, pp. 11–12. For a history of the PCF, see D.S. Bell and Byron Criddle, *The French Communist Party in the Fifth Republic*, Oxford, Clarendon Press, 1994; Ronald Tiersky, *French Communism, 1920–1972*, New York, Columbia University Press, 1974. As regards the French left in general and French leftist intellectuals, the indispensable author is Tony Judt who wrote, among other works, *Marxism and the French Left: Studies on Labour and Politics in France, 1830–1981*, Oxford, Clarendon Press, 1986; *Past Imperfect: French Intellectuals, 1944–1956*, Berkeley, CA, University of California Press, 1992.

American influence remained strong – not on French "high" culture, but all the more so on popular culture. France remained France, but visitors flocked to Euro-Disneyland, and even Mickey Mouse learned how to speak French.[21]

French politics accordingly swung rightwards. Mitterrand now had to cooperate with conservative prime ministers such as Jacques Chirac (who had reorganized the Gaullists in the RPR (Rally for the Republic), and who served as prime minister from 1986 to 1988), and Edouard Balladur (appointed prime minister in 1993). Mitterrand himself proved a survivor, securing in 1988 re-election to the presidential office against a divided right. But the Socialist Party fell on evil days, struck by the crisis which beset European social democratic parties as far afield as Italy, Germany, and Spain. The 1993 elections for the French legislature turned into a Socialist catastrophe. The party halved its share of the vote and lost all but 54 of the 252 seats that it had held in the outgoing National Assembly. The right, by contrast, gained a decisive victory, with 247 seats as against the 126 seats held previously. (The UDF turned into the second-strongest party with 213 seats, as against the 131 gained before. As a result, the RPR and UDF between them controlled more than three-quarters of the 577 seats in the National Assembly.)[22]

On the face of it, the Socialists' decline is not easy to explain. Mitterrand was a supremely capable politician, having undergone numerous political metamorphoses. (Catherine May, a Mitterrand biographer, counted seven in all.) The French Socialists now concentrated on newly popular issues, such as civil rights and concern for immigrants (*touche pas à mon pote* (don't touch my pal) went the slogan). The Socialists also stressed ecology and the defense of women's rights. (The first French woman prime minister was Edith Cresson, 1991–2, a Socialist, albeit not a lady troubled by extensive sensitivity: she censured the Japanese for being greedy and British men for being gay.) The Socialists also endeavored to give more power to the regions. They supported the cause of united Europe, with Delors as their most outstanding office-holder and spokesman. The Socialists had criticized the privatization program begun by Chirac from 1986 but, far from reversing the campaign, they extended it after Mitterrand's second victory in 1988. As communism declined, moreover, the Socialists no longer needed to "conceal their pragmatic reformism behind a rhetorical Marxism for fear of being outflanked on the Left."[23] The leftist intellectuals had lost their former confidence, and their sting no longer hurt, as it had done in the past. The olden-day Socialist verities all went over board, even the Socialists' residual anti-clericalism. (Mitterrand thus abandoned the Socialists' historical commitment to extend state control over professional schools.)

Worse still was France's persistent Algerian problem. In 1994 the continuing civil war between the secularist military regime in Algeria and Islamic fundamentalist insurgents spilled into France, as Algerian terrorists hijacked an Air France passenger plane. Taking no chances, the government severed air and sea links with Algeria, and cracked down on militants within France's Muslim community (now estimated at between four and five million). The Algerian civil war presented France with a dilemma. What would happen if the fundamentalists were to win, and if several million refugees from Algeria were to seek refuge in France? The Algerian civil war also embittered cultural conflicts within the French public school system where Islam contended with the French secularist

21   Richard F. Kuisel, *Seducing the French: the Dilemma of Americanization*, Berkeley, CA, University of California Press, 1993.
22   *Keesing's Record of World Events*, London, Longman, 1993, p. 39788.
23   Peter Morris, *French Politics Today*, Manchester, Manchester University Press, 1994, pp. 138–9.

tradition. In a more general sense, the war in Algeria envenomed ethnic strife in France between North African immigrants and French nativists represented in particular by the National Front. Even the French government itself split over the Algerian war. (Charles Pasqua, the interior minister, sided with Algerian hard-liners who wished to smash the rebellion with a mailed fist. By contrast, Alain Juppé, the foreign minister, called for a dialogue, as did Henri Emmanuelli, secretary of the French Socialist Party, and also the Clinton administration in the US.) Decolonization, after all, had not freed France from the Algerian cancer.

Equally novel in French politics was the anti-abortion movement which, like the Islamic fundamentalist movement, drew on religious inspiration. In 1993 the National Assembly had outlawed interference with abortion clinics, but militants remained undeterred. The French anti-abortion movement did not resort to the "armed struggle" as did fanatics in the US. But militants such as Gerard Calvet, a Benedictine monk, and Claire Fontana, a practicing Catholic and a mother of eight, likened abortion doctors to those Nazi doctors who had performed experiments on concentration camp victims. The Truce of God, a powerful anti-abortion movement, maintained links with like-minded bodies in the US and promised to create a civil disobedience movement, based on US experience, that would put an end to a new holocaust. The Truce of God likewise collaborated with anti-abortion movements in Europe, including "Scream for Life" in Holland which held US-style prayer meetings and vigils outside abortion clinics.

What had gone wrong in French politics? Mitterrand increasingly came to resemble de Gaulle – regal bearing, autocratic demeanor, and all. Like a Bourbon monarch, Mitterrand also patronized a huge construction program in Paris. Unfortunately, he lacked the good taste and sense of balance once associated with French kings. (For instance, the new National Library, designed by architect Dominique Perrault, was of "mastodonic" proportions, and rose from an urban wasteland.)[24]

Much more serious was the controversy concerning Mitterrand's wartime record. Unlike de Gaulle's, Mitterrand's had been tarnished, and as the facts became known, the left, especially the young left, was profoundly shocked. The Socialist Party fared no better than its leader. A party that had promised a better life for the people seemed increasingly reduced to merely "managing" an economy beset by heavy unemployment. Having proclaimed its own moral purity, the Socialist Party (like so many other governing parties in Europe at large) became enmeshed in corruption scandals. Party membership dropped, as the party divided into factions whose members insisted on washing their dirty linen in public. Having been in power for many years, the party had run out of ideas and support from the electorate.

The right, by contrast, consolidated. True enough, the conservatives – the RPR and UDF – failed to put an end to those rivalries that had occasioned defeat in 1981. (The UDF, for example, favored the Maastricht Treaty, whereas a majority of the RPR opposed it.) The rise of the racist *Front National* (FN), moreover, cost the established right the monopoly on the vote of the non-left electorate. But, despite gloomy forecasts, the FN failed to extend its power; its leader Jean-Marie Le Pen did not secure election to the Assembly in 1993, and remained head of a faction.

The presidential elections of 1995 turned into yet another Socialist defeat. In France, as in Italy and Spain, the Socialists' reputation had been besmirched by a variety of

24 Olivia Snaije, "The French President's Cultural Legacy," *Christian Science Monitor*, 9 May 1995, p. 10.

scandals of the kind apt to hit parties overly long in office. Mitterrand, by now an aging and a sick man, would not run for office. (Neither would Jacques Delors, the Socialists' most powerful personality after Mitterrand.) Led by Jacques Chirac, the conservatives won on a promise of reducing unemployment and putting France's financial house in order. The moderate right's victory was all the more remarkable as Chirac had refused to have anything to do with Le Pen, no matter what political advantages such cooperation might entail. The conservatives, moreover, had again been divided. (In the first ballot, Chirac had secured only about 21 percent of the vote, his rival Edouard Balladur 18 percent. Jospin had obtained 23 percent, more than any other candidate.) Nevertheless, the 1995 elections marked a watershed. Chirac and the right as a whole henceforth controlled alike the presidency, about two-thirds of the Senate, more than 80 percent of the Assembly, 20 of 22 regional councils, four-fifths of the departmental councils, and most of the big cities. Never before had a ruling party gained such a concentration of power in the Fifth Republic.[25]

On taking office, Chirac reintegrated France into NATO. Otherwise, his foreign policy was marked by ill-will toward Israel, and carping against the US. (He assailed the US's role toward Cuba, Iran, Iraq, and the Israeli–Palestinian conflict.) At home, Chirac had to cope with an overgrown public service resistant to reform. Above all, France suffered from high unemployment (12 percent in 1995); moreover, about one-third of all unemployed had been without work for over a year, and were thus particularly hard to place. In France, as everywhere else in the Western world, the voters made contradictory demands: they wanted lower taxes but massive social expenditure, particularly so in France where trade unionists and *fonctionnaires* alike remained well entrenched and determined to maintain their privileges even at the cost of lengthy strikes. In a more general sense, intellectuals, parties, churches, and the political élites of whatever persuasion had lost much of the respect they had previously enjoyed. Within NATO and with the EU, Paris would have to arrive at new compromises (a subject discussed at greater length in chapter 16). France, a country traditionally open to immigrants, now had to contend with an anti-immigrant backlash, powerful in every major European country. Criticism of immigrants went with a more general sense that the country was out of control, and that the élites had lost touch with ordinary people. (ENA graduates were themselves among the harshest critics of "enarchy.")

Nevertheless, France, overall, had been fairly successful. The Fifth Republic stayed securely in place, its legitimacy by now established more firmly than that of its predecessors. In France, as elsewhere in Europe, a great deal of ink was spilled over the rise of the regions and the decline of the nation-state. But, in truth, Burgundy or Brittany or the Languedoc were no more likely to achieve independence than Wales or Bavaria. France would remain united and, overall, prosperous beyond the imagination of French people in any previous age. France, moreover, no longer had any enemies on its borders. The country was at peace with all its neighbors, surrounded only by friendly powers – a state of affairs that would have astounded past French rulers from Louis XIV to Clemenceau. Despite its manifold troubles, France had good reason for confidence in the future.

25 "The Judgment of Paris," *The Economist*, 13 May 1995, pp. 49–50.

14

Britain: 1974 to the Present

Every European country, at some time or another, has been stalked by the fear of decline. But in no European state, during the 1970s, was this feeling as pervasive as in Britain. (Even the former term "Great" had by then gone out of usage.) British academics and journalists produced by the dozen books with titles such as *The British Disease*, *The Stagnant Society*, *The Suicide of a Nation*.[1] A profound sense of disquiet likewise percolated into British politics. Was Britain becoming an ungovernable country?

Island in Decline?

On the face of it, these terrors seemed ill founded. By 1979 the United Kingdom's output in goods and services had more than doubled over the preceding 30 years. The average growth rate of 2.5 percent of the GNP during that period compared favorably with the performance of the economy during all peacetime periods in the twentieth century.[2] No matter what the "declinists" said, life in Britain, by the late 1970s, had become a great deal easier than ever in the island's history. The British armed services performed well whenever they were called on to fight: no matter whether in Kenya, Malaya, or the Falkland Islands. The British had retained their traditional penchant for the hard sciences (as demonstrated by the number of Nobel Prize laureates born or naturalized in Britain). There was technological inventiveness aplenty: the *Concorde* (passenger jet plane), the great Humber Bridge, the Channel Tunnel (linking Britain and France, completed for traffic in 1994) displayed British engineering at its best. Britain did well in the "Third Industrial Revolution," gaining the lead in Europe in telecommunications and the manufacture of computers and semi-conductors. "More is happening in the electronics industry in Britain than anywhere else in Europe – both in production and application," as Kenneth Baker, formerly a minister for information technology, put it in a published statement.[3]

---

1 G.C. Allen, *The British Disease*, London, Institute of Economic Affairs, 1976; Michael Shanks, *The Stagnant Society*, Harmondsworth, Penguin, 1972; Arthur Koestler, ed., *Suicide of a Nation? An Enquiry into the State of Britain Today*, New York, Macmillan, 1964. Others comprised W. Beckerman, ed., *Slow Growth in Britain: Causes and Consequences*, Oxford, Clarendon Press, 1979; Alan Sked, *Britain's Decline: Problems and Perspectives*, Oxford and New York, Blackwell, 1987.
2 "The British Economy since 1945," *Economic Progress Report*, London, The Treasury, no. 100, 1978, p. 1.
3 Cited in Roger Woolsnough, "Britain Leads Europe in Electronics Industry," *Europe*, January/February 1985, p. 38.

There were other bright spots in the tapestry. British academia was highly respected, so was the business of British art enterprise: the Beatles and other pop groups were known the world over, marvelously combining protest with profits. "Serious" theater flourished, as did classical music, opera, the ballet, and other arts. British banking and other financial services held their own throughout the globe. Britain, during the 1970s, became a major producer of oil and natural gas, while continuing to hold large reserves. Blessed with great natural coal resources, a pioneer, moreover, in the development of nuclear power, Britain was in a uniquely strong position in Western Europe with regard to energy supply. Despite deficiencies in the British cuisine, the British tourist industry had become a major enterprise. British agriculture was one of the world's most efficient. The British also held other trump cards. They had a low (though a rising) crime rate. They had a remarkably "clean" public service. (Characteristically, a brilliant British TV series *Yes, Minister* parodied senior British civil servants as hide-bound élitists, preoccupied with titles, honors, and promotion, but never as financially corrupt. Indeed, what could Sir Humphrey, head of the mythical Department of Administrative Affairs, have done, had he been caught stealing? He would have been cut by his friends, divorced from his wife, and expelled by his club. Nothing left for him but to emigrate to one of Britain's former colonies, not excluding the US.)

True enough, Britain had serious labor troubles. Britain was steadily falling behind or losing out altogether in those traditional industries that had made her great in the eighteenth and nineteenth centuries: textiles, shipbuilding, coal mining, iron and steel. But these industries were encountering serious trouble in every European country. It is easy to forget, moreover, that British economic greatness had never rested on the manufacturing industries alone. Even at the height of Britain's imperial glory, the service industries and agriculture had always played a vital part in assuring British power and prosperity.

Nevertheless, Britain had suffered a profound decline in relative terms. At the end of World War II, Britain stood out as the most powerful and productive state in Western Europe, and mistress of a great empire to boot. The British labour movement enjoyed unchallenged primacy among the world's democratic socialist movements. British Tories were widely admired abroad for their flexibility in combining patriotism and social reform. By the early 1970s, however, West Germany had already overtaken Britain's economic lead; thereafter, France displaced Britain from the second place. During the first 60 years of the twentieth century, Britain had remained ahead of nearly all European countries; the low growth rate "was a matter of concern only to sophists, calculators and economists."[4] Thereafter, the gap widened and, by whatever measurement used, Britain fell behind its main European competitors, especially West Germany. The empire had gone, and with it the old imperial confidence. Victorious in World War II, Britain was now being outdone in every respect by the vanquished.[5]

Britain suffered from steady inflation, attributed by the injudicious to greedy British workers ready to strike at the drop of a hat, or to greedy oil sheikhs raising the price of fuel. Inflation went with unemployment. (By 1980, the number of jobless people had risen to 2,000,000, a total unknown since the Great Slump.) Admittedly, unemployed

4 Samuel Brittan, "How English is the English Sickness?" *Washington Quarterly*, vol. 3, no. 4, Autumn 1980, p. 151.
5 By 1970, Britain's per capita income ranged, in order, behind Sweden's, Denmark's, West Germany's, France's, Norway's, Belgium's, and Holland's. For details, see *The Economist Book of Vital World Statistics*, New York, Times Books/Random House, 1990, p. 34.

people now enjoyed social benefits unknown in the olden days. In Britain, as elsewhere, unemployment was softened by an extensive underground economy. But, psychologically, "stagflation" (combining an economic recession with high inflation) produced a pervasive sense of cynicism and despair.

What accounted for this remarkable shift in the condition of Britain? The literature on the subject is so extensive that we can only summarize it in brief. Britain, critics argued, had declined in a relative sense for an entire century. According to free-enterprise advocates, the country had increasingly been hamstrung by excessive regulation, swollen entitlement programs, and inefficient public enterprise. Private industry was excessively protected and excessively subsidized. British trade unions were old-fashioned, short-sighted, mired in an antiquated class-war ideology, beset by jurisdictional disputes, hostile to the modernization of industry, and ever suspicious of employers. Cultural critics blamed the pervasive impact of British aristocrats and British gentlefolk with their anti-commercial and anti-entrepreneurial bias. These people not only despised trade; they had weakened the entrepreneurial ethos by co-opting middle-class business people into their ranks, and infusing them with upper-class prejudice.

We ourselves do not regard the cultural arguments as convincing. Trade-union militancy had not in the past interfered with industrial progress. Neither had advancement to the peerage stopped men such as Lord Marks (of Marks and Spencer, the British equivalent of Macy's or the Emporium) from making a great deal of money. By contrast, Yorkshire iron masters and Lancashire cotton spinners had traditionally kept aloof from the gentry. Yet in the post-World War II era, they had done much worse than the Marks. According to Corelli Barnett, a leading British historian, British upper-class culture, with its snobbish disdain for technology, had already promoted British economic decadence before World War II. This argument does not explain, however, why the British at that time should still have developed such engineering wonders as the PV Merlin engine (the best aero-engine at the time) or "Colossus" (an ancestor of the modern computer), or "Hobart's Funnies" (an array of specialized tanks that helped to clear the beaches at the invasion of Normandy in 1944). Britain, moreover, remained efficient in non-industrial enterprises such as farming, and in services such as banking, insurance, and retailing, pursuits of crucial importance to industrial as well as pre-industrial Britain. As regards the much-maligned governing classes, they had ruled with a modicum of corruption, copiously shed their own blood in Britain's defense, effectively maintained democracy, and yet mobilized Britain more effectively in World War II than any other country.

Another assumed culprit for Britain's troubles was the monarchy. British kingship, went the argument, differed strikingly from Scandinavian or Dutch royalty by dint of Britain's pageantry, rivaled only by the Papacy's. Unfortunately, "the royal family has thrived in recent years as the all-purpose antidote to international decline, economic decay, and social unrest."[6] Royalty embalmed anti-industrial values as amber embalmed a fly. Yet this theory fails to explain why it was monarchical Britain which pioneered the Industrial Revolution. Neither does the argument account for the way in which the pomp of British monarchy equally appeals to republican audiences in the New World, even though the stylish pageantry of British royalty openly defies those values most prized by egalitarian and secular-minded intellectuals in America. Other critics of Britain's economic performance blamed the public schools and Oxbridge with their emphasis on humane rather than technological studies. However, the bulk of the French leadership,

6 David Cannadine, *The Pleasures of the Past*, London, Collins, 1989, p. 9.

trained in the *grandes écoles*, likewise lacked technological expertise (except for graduates of the *Polytechnique*). Yet France performed well under its *énarques* (graduates of the *Ecole nationale d'administration*), as did Germany under civil servants trained in law.

We ourselves prefer the explanation given by Ludwig Erhard, a leading free-enterprise economist, an architect of the postwar German *Wirtschaftswunder*. According to Erhard, Britain's troubles were severe, but fundamentally they were everybody's problems. The difficulties that face all the major industrial countries in the West cannot be explained in terms of national character, or even particular national institutions. They spring from economic misconceptions, for "a policy based on unsound regulative standards is doomed to failure in its design and impact."[7] The expansion of state machinery, state controls, and state-run entitlement programs in turn forever tempts governments to expand the money supply and thereby promotes inflation. No wonder that Britain by the 1970s was in disarray.

Labour's Loss

Labour was ill fitted to cope with accumulating reverses. In 1976, Wilson resigned, to be replaced by James Callaghan, a sexagenarian of wide ministerial experience. Callaghan had begun to reap the advantage of standing in his party as "the man with the fewest enemies."[8] He was "the reluctant choice" of the center and right who considered Callaghan the only politician capable of stopping Michael Foot, candidate of Labour's left. Callaghan was a professional politician, tough and capable, with wide support in the parliamentary Labour Party and among the more moderate labor unions. Son of a widowed mother who brought him up in a strict Baptist home, he had worked his way up in the world from modest circumstances. He was a fine orator and a man of obvious integrity. He disliked the "trendy left," and his distaste for the permissive society was politically prudent.[9]

But Callaghan faced an impossible situation. His party was divided both at the top and at the bottom. Callaghan faced steady opposition even within his own cabinet, especially from Tony Benn, one of the party's principal left-wingers. Ironically enough, Benn was of impeccably patrician origin. The son of Lord Stansgate, he had changed his name to Tony Benn in place of the Rt Hon. Anthony Wedgwood Benn. Displaying the zeal of the convert, Benn, a born aristocrat, came to idealize the British worker. From being a centrist, he moved steadily toward the extreme left – to uncritical support for a centralized economy and union militancy in domestic policy, and to determined backing for neutralism and unilateral disarmament in foreign relations. His opponents called him a "holy fool." But Benn was neither. He wrote well; he spoke well; he was a master of parliamentary procedure. He was also a formidable figure in Labour's internal quarrels. (It was Benn who created for Labour a new "electoral college" system for choosing the leader.)[10] With such friends Callaghan needed no enemies.

7 Ludwig Erhard, "We Have these Problems, too", in Patrick Hutber, ed., *What's Wrong with Britain*, London, Sphere Books, 1978.
8 Peter Kellner and Christopher Hitchens, *Callaghan: the Road to Number Ten*, London, Cassell, 1976, p. 172.
9 Kenneth O. Morgan, *Labour People: Leaders and Lieutenants. Hardie to Kinnock*, Oxford, Oxford University Press, 1987, p. 270.
10 Morgan, *Labour People*, p. 306; Jad Adams, *Tony Benn: a Biography*, London, Macmillan, 1992; Gerald A. Dorfman, *Government versus Trade Unionism in British Politics Since 1968*, London, Macmillan, 1977.

More serious still were dissensions within constituency parties. Militants, some of them Trotskyites, gained increasing power in district Labour parties, where the militants' discipline, cohesion, and willingness to sit through endless meetings gave them influence far beyond their numerical strength. In municipalities run by militants, councillors engaged in high spending, careless borrowing, and selling vast tracts of municipal lands. (Some of these transactions later became the subject of a major enquiry by the Fraud Squad.) Great Britain seemed increasingly to become ungovernable. Deep-seated animosity between Catholics and Protestants in Northern Ireland erupted into violence (from 1969 onward). There was trouble in the black ghettos of large British cities, such as the Notting Hill district in London. During and after World War II, Labour and Conservatives alike had come to consider the unions as the "Fourth Estate of the Realm," to be courted and consulted on all major questions of domestic policy. Unions had enjoyed wide popular support, going far beyond the working class. (Sir David Low, a distinguished cartoonist, habitually represented the Trade Union Congress as a great, friendly, lumbering white horse.) There was not much friendliness left by the late 1970s when workers in declining industries such as mining fought, not merely for bigger wage packets, but in defense of an accustomed way of life. The intimidation exerted by flying pickets, raucous demonstrations at sites such as the Grunwick works in North London, the almost kamikaze-like fervor displayed by militant leaders, occasioned a radical shift in public opinion. (According to a 1980 poll, 75 percent of respondents considered that unions hindered industrial productivity. By contrast, 71 percent sided with the police.)[11]

The Labour Party and the unions, moreover, faced an even profounder challenge. In Britain, as in every other major industrial country, the traditional working class kept diminishing as a proportion of the labor force. By contrast, the Tories gained ever more adherents among skilled workers, craftsmen, foremen, supervisors, self-employed people, non-union workers, specialists in high-tech industries. They, in particular, were "Thatcher's people." They looked askance at rising taxation, at race riots, at liberated lifestyles among their supposed betters, and at rising inflation. There was also widespread discontent at unemployment, and at constantly rising wage claims on the part of teachers, miners, civil servants, and local government officials. In human terms, a large portion of the electorate had had enough of scruffy subway trains, rubbish left uncollected in the streets of big cities, crippled hospital services, interruptions in electricity supply and sewage disposal.[12]

Labour thus suffered a shattering defeat in the 1979 general election. The Tories gained an absolute majority in the House of Commons, and secured power for one of

---

11 *Christian Science Monitor*, 12 September 1980. The same poll also indicated that 85 percent of respondents were loyal to the monarchy; only 10 percent wanted the monarchy to be replaced by a republic.

12 Kenneth Watkins, "The British Election of 1979 and its Aftermath," *Policy Review*, summer 1979, p. 103. The literature on the Thatcher revolution is extensive. See her own account, Margaret Thatcher, *The Downing Street Years*, New York, HarperCollins, 1993; *The Path to Power*, London, HarperCollins, 1995; Peter Riddell, *The Thatcher Decade: How Britain Has Changed During the 1980s*, Oxford, Blackwell, 1989; Shirley Robin Letwin, *The Anatomy of Thatcherism*, London, Fontana, 1992; Geoffrey Smith, *Reagan and Thatcher*, New York, Norton, 1991; Andrew Adonis and Tim Hames, eds, *A Conservative Revolution?: The Thatcher–Reagan Decade in Perspective*, Manchester, Manchester University Press, 1994; Hugo Young, *The Iron Lady: a Biography of Margaret Thatcher*, New York, Farrar, Strauss, Giroux, 1989; Dennis Kavanagh, *Thatcherism and British Politics: the End of Consensus?*, Oxford, Oxford University Press, 1987.

the longest electoral spells in modern British history.[13] Margaret Thatcher assumed the premiership, which she would hold longer than any other British prime minister in the twentieth century.

The Thatcher Decade

Thatcher was the only British prime minister to turn her name into a concept – Thatcherism. No pundit, however, predicted any such thing at the time. Thatcher had not been a Thatcherite when she first went into politics. Her ministerial career (as secretary for education and science, 1970–4) had been neither particularly distinguished nor particularly right-wing. On the contrary, it was bodies such as the Bow Group (co-founded and chaired from 1955 by Geoffrey Howe, a foreign secretary under Thatcher, and one of her most unhappy cabinet ministers) that helped to pioneer the new conservatism with its emphasis on personal choice, private enterprise, and lessened state power. When Thatcher took office, political experts did not expect her to resist the trade unions more effectively than her predecessors had done.

Her start in Commonwealth affairs was likewise conventional. On the face of it, Thatcher should have sided with the Rhodesian white settlers. Racially prejudiced the colonists might be, but otherwise their values were Thatcher's. Rhodesia was a country where white men might get drunk, but not drugged. The settlers ran a government reasonably free from corruption and reasonably efficient. The settlers differed from many other ruling classes in that they paid the bulk of the country's taxes and (with some exceptions) conscripted their own sons. They provided much of the country's entrepreneurial, managerial, and technological skills. The senior civil servants, parliamentarians, and cabinet ministers who served the ruling Rhodesian Front came from a background similar to Thatcher's. (They were mostly born in small towns; they were well educated, and a high proportion of them had held commissions of field rank in World War II.)[14] Initially, Thatcher thus shocked anti-colonialists by expressing sympathy for the "Internal Settlement" devised in Rhodesia by Ian Smith and Bishop Abel Muzorewa, designed to turn white-ruled Rhodesia into Rhodesia/Zimbabwe under a new arrangement where blacks would hold office and whites hold power. The Foreign Office, however, strongly opposed this settlement. As Lord Carrington, the foreign secretary, pointed out to Thatcher, such a settlement excluded the two main guerrilla factions (ZANU and ZAPU); hence the Rhodesian civil war would continue. To recognize Muzorewa would alienate the Carter administration in the US and, above all, disrupt the Commonwealth. Thatcher gave way, and in 1980 Rhodesia achieved independence as Zimbabwe, run by a Marxist government formed by ZANU.

13 The Tories obtained 14,697,753 votes, that is 43.9 percent of the total, as against Labour's 11,406,768, or 39.1 percent. The Liberals managed to win 4,313,931 votes, that is 13.8 percent. All other parties did badly, including the semi-fascist National Front. The Conservatives secured some 3,000,000 votes more than they had won in the 1974 election, and commanded an absolute majority in the new House of Commons (with 339 seats for the Tories, and 10 for the allied Ulster Unionists, 268 seats for Labour, and 11 for the Liberals; see *Keesing's Contemporary Archives*, 8 June 1979, p. 29645).

14 For a detailed analysis, see L.H. Gann and Thomas H. Henriksen, *The Struggle for Zimbabwe: Battle in the Bush*, New York, Praeger Special Studies, 1981, esp. p. 38, n. 15.

The decisive change for Thatcher came with the Falklands War. In 1982, Argentinian forces invaded the islands (known to the Argentinians as the Malvinas). From the Argentinian dictatorship's viewpoint, seizure of the Falklands was the one issue on which the Argentinian people would unite under the military regime of general Leopoldo Galtieri. The Argentinian military, like the Italian Fascists pre-World War II, envisaged a confrontation as an easy game in which Britain, a decadent pluto-democracy, would inevitably yield to a healthy, young, warlike people, with its face to the sun. In Britain, enlightened opinion, or what passed as such, insisted for different reasons that Britain neither would, could, nor should resist. The islands had been left practically undefended and were in truth indefensible. What was the point of attempting to fight a campaign 8,000 miles away from the British homeland? (The convenient naval base of Simonstown in South Africa had long been relinquished.) What chance did the British have against an enemy greatly superior in numbers, operating within the range of shore-based aircraft? The islands were too remote, too unimportant to warrant bloodshed. The entire Third World would back the Argentine. In any case, patriotism, even more so pride of empire, were outmoded sentiments to which no British government should pander. Let the Foreign Office find some face-saving formula, and forget the incident.

But the British response was totally unexpected. There was public outrage. Few British people might be able to identify the islands on an unmarked map, but somehow their seizure by Galtieri seemed the final mark of British decline. Even a petty tyrant now dared to insult Britain, and impose his rule on a distant British community. Thatcher shared these sentiments. She had, moreover, good personal relations with President Reagan (a point discussed in chapter 10); there would be no second Suez this time. The British rapidly mounted an expeditionary force, and recaptured the Falklands. Had the campaign failed, Thatcher's career would have ended then and there. But the British performance was outstanding. To take a large naval force at short notice across half the world, to land in the face of heavy air attacks carried out by well-trained pilots, to defeat an enemy who outnumbered the British by four to one in the air, and by two to one on land, was a remarkable achievement.[15]

The Falklands War also recapitulated several lessons not often taught in political science seminars. A peaceful demeanor and a willingness to negotiate do not offer assured freedom from aggression. (At the time of the Argentinian invasion, the islands were defended only by a handful of British marines.) Even possession of nuclear weapons does not assure immunity from assault on the part of even a non-nuclear power. (The British nuclear arsenal proved irrelevant during the conflict.) The greatest threat to a military tyranny does not derive from domestic opposition but from military defeat. (It was the British victory which toppled the Argentinian generals – an uncovenanted benefit for Argentina.) The British armed forces deserved the public confidence accorded to them above all other institutions. Patriotic sentiments had not vanished in Western industrial nations. Above all, the Falklands War also turned into a personal victory for Thatcher. She had understood the national mood; she had taken the political risks; she had won the glory. In 1983, she thus again confounded the pundits by winning a decisive majority in the general election. (The Conservatives won an overall majority of 144 seats in the Commons, a feat replicated in 1987, albeit with a majority reduced to 102.) Henceforth

15 See, for instance, Peter Calvert, *The Falklands Crisis: the Rights and the Wrongs*, New York, St Martin's Press, 1982; Antony Preston, *Sea Combat off the Falklands*, London, Willow Books, Collins, 1982; Sir John Woodward, *One Hundred Days*, London, HarperCollins, 1992.

Thatcher's position seemed unassailable: "The Lady Not for Turning," "The Iron Lady," "The only Man in the Cabinet."

Thatcher's foreign policy gave absolute priority to the US over the EC connection. The United Kingdom had cooperated with the United States in a great variety of defense projects; they were close partners in NATO; they shared many military secrets – this despite periodic spy scandals. The "special relationship" was strengthened by the close personal bond which linked Thatcher and Reagan (he thought she was "great"), and also by ties between lesser officials on both sides of the Atlantic. (For instance, George Shultz, US secretary of state, 1982–9, got on extremely well with Sir Geoffrey Howe, British foreign secretary, 1983–9). The US, as we have seen, supported Britain in the Falklands campaign. Of all the US allies, only Britain thereafter backed the US when US planes bombed Libya to avenge Libyan acts of terrorism. Again, of all the US allies, only Britain made a serious contribution to the Gulf War. Nevertheless, the "special relationship" proved a wasting asset. After Reagan left office, the Bush presidency's links with London were nothing like as close as they had been before. In a more general sense, Britain's trade proportionately increased with the EC, and diminished with the US. (In 1970, before Britain had joined the EC, 31 percent of her trade was with the 11 other countries now in the EC; 18 percent was with North America. By 1992, the proportions had respectively shifted to 54 percent and 13 percent.)[16] The "special relationship" disappeared under President Clinton, a Rhodes Scholar, who nevertheless resented British conservatives, and, like Bush, regarded Germany as the US's principal European partner.

By contrast, Thatcher always remained critical of the EC. Completion of the Channel Tunnel (1994), the greatest engineering achievement of the twentieth century, would demolish Britain's position as an island. Nevertheless, Thatcher remained an islander at heart. In Thatcher's, as in Churchill's worldview, Western Europe should always play the second fiddle to North America's first. Whereas Sir Edward Heath, her predecessor in office and former boss, had been an enthusiastic "European," Thatcher looked at the EC connection with cautious disapproval. She disliked subsidies to European farmers; she resented British deference to Euro-judges and Eurocrats; she sniffed at directives from Brussels; she detested any real or supposed interference with British sovereignty through the operation of a European social charter. She detested Jacques Delors' design for building a European superstate. Thatcher got on quite well with Helmut Schmidt (not with Giscard d'Estaing). But she dreaded a united Germany. Thatcher was a British Gaullist. But, like de Gaulle, Thatcher never had the slightest intention of withdrawing from the EC. Her very toughness increased British influence in Brussels. Oddly enough, it was during her premiership that the very question of whether Britain should withdraw from the EC disappeared from the domestic political agenda after the 1983 general election. (Her successor, John Major, once more allocated a central place in British foreign policy to the EC. So did the Labour Party which in practice abandoned its former anti-EC stance, and came to favor cooperation in particular with the EC's other socialist parties.)

As regards the People's Republic of China, Thatcher's policy was grimly realistic. To her government fell the unpleasant task of negotiating, in 1984, the future retrocession of Hong Kong to China (scheduled for 1997). Hong Kong had been created by British colonialism, sustained by British colonialism, and led to prosperity by British colonialism. The six million citizens of Hong Kong desperately desired to remain under the Union Jack, and mistrusted the special conditions promised by Beijing for the future. But the

16 "Time to Choose," *The Economist*, 26 September 1992, p. 59.

British position was untenable alike in a legal, economic, military, and diplomatic sense. The British lease from China for the so-called New Territories was due to expire in 1997. Hong Kong depended on China for trade, even for water. Militarily, there was no way in which the colony could have been held against a hostile China, and no country in the world would have supported Britain in the event of a showdown. The British authorities thus probably got the best deal they could, given the British negotiators' poor hand in completing the last chapter in the history of Western decolonization.

As far as the Soviet Union was concerned, the story was happier, and Thatcher's foresight indeed striking. An unflinching anti-communist, she was the first Western leader to understand that Gorbachev was truly different from the other Soviet leaders. Gorbachev first visited London early in 1985; he made a lasting impression on Thatcher, who thereafter understood that Gorbachev was indeed a man with whom the West might do business, and she strongly supported Reagan in this sense.[17]

Thatcher's foreign policy was controversial in the British context – but not unduly so; there were plenty of Britons of whatever party who agreed with her. It was Thatcher's domestic policy that made her the most admired and the most detested personage in British public life. She was an outsider. Not that Tories had ever excluded outsiders from supreme office; Benjamin Disraeli (Lord Beaconsfield) had been a Jew, Sir Robert Peel a cotton spinner. But Thatcher was a woman – this in a land where, until recently, power lay with exclusively male fraternities such as regiments, clubs, and senior common rooms. She was small-town, lower-middle class ("the grocer's daughter from Grantham") – worse, she was not in the least ashamed of her origins. In different circumstances, she would have made a formidable headmistress in a girls' reformatory school, sternly resolved to guide her charges to the path of virtue. She discarded unsuitable, or seemingly unsuitable, ministers with the same unconcern as a Victorian principal would have sacked an assistant teacher. She was also well educated (with an Oxford chemistry degree), intelligent, and – like Reagan – utterly fearless in the face either of political opposition or assassination attempts. She was also a dogmatist and an autocrat, and gleefully bullied the highest in the land, including her own cabinet ministers whom she changed with bewildering rapidity.

In the meantime, her own Tory party itself was undergoing profound change. The Guards officers, the landed gentry, the "huntin', fishin' and shootin'" set largely disappeared from the House of Commons. Queen Elizabeth II maintained monarchical prestige in her own person. (At a state visit to Moscow in 1994, she got an enthusiastic reception, and Russian ladies in formal presentations took pride in curtsying to Her Majesty – this after 75 years of communism.) But all too many "royals" unwisely mixed adultery with publicity, and thereby further weakened the reputation of the traditional upper class. Thatcher despised them all. Instead of consensus, Thatcher looked to confrontation; instead of accommodation, she yearned for victory. She preferred professionals to amateurs, players to gentlemen. If anything, she disliked old-fashioned Tories even more than "lefties". As a former cabinet minister of aristocratic antecedents put it with some bitterness, "Margaret looks down on people like me. Because she and the others like her rose by their own merits, they dislike those born above them."[18] Thatcher instead

17 David Remnick, *Lenin's Tomb: the Last Days of the Soviet Empire*, New York, Random House, 1993, p. 192.
18 Cited by Jeremy Paxman, *Friends in High Places: Who Runs Britain?*, London, Michael Joseph, 1990, p. 80.

favored self-made people, especially those who had started the climb to the top with the aid of competitive university scholarships.

In particular, Thatcher liked Jews. (Anglo-Jewry, overall, was more conservative politically than American Jewry, even though their respective ethnic make-up was similar. Finchley, Thatcher's parliamentary constituency, had a not inconsiderable Jewish vote.) Sir Keith (later Lord) Joseph was Jewish. So were several of her cabinet ministers, including Nigel Lawson, a chancellor of the exchequer, David (later Lord) Young, Leon (later Sir Leon) Brittan, and Malcolm Rifkind, the latter a Jewish Scotsman. It was with glee that she raised to the peerage German-born Chief Rabbi Immanuel Jacobovits so that he might expound to the House of Peers those old-fashioned virtues that the Church of England now supposedly neglected, and which their Lordships allegedly despised. ("Out go the Etonians. In come the Estonians," Harold Macmillan supposedly said after one of Thatcher's early cabinet reshuffles.)

Equally important to Thatcher were those right-wing think tanks that advocated the merits of a free-market economy and an "enterprise society." Foremost among them was the Institute of Economic Affairs (founded 1957, run by (Lord) Ralph Harris and Arthur Seldon), and the Centre for Policy Studies (initiated by Joseph and Thatcher herself after the Conservatives' electoral defeat in 1974). The Adam Smith Institute was established in 1977 by three men working in the US at the time, with close links to US academia. Finally, there was the old-established Mount Pelerin Society, with its transatlantic links. Between them, the intellectuals employed in these and other institutes provided alike for Thatcher and Reagan a group of policy advisers equally at home at the LSE, the University of Chicago, or at the Hoover Institution in Stanford. At the same time, conservative intellectuals greatly rose in status within the Tory party whose magnates had once regarded such people as socially on a par with book-keepers, village chemists, and Methodist parsons.

The Tories, old-style, had taken good care to compromise with the trade unions. They had done so partly from conviction, partly from fear. The NUM (National Union of Mineworkers), led by Arthur Scargill, had inflicted two devastating defeats on the Heath government, in 1972 and 1974. Under Thatcher, the NUM meant to teach yet another lesson to the Tories – but this time they dealt with Margaret Thatcher. Having called a strike without a ballot, the miners lacked support from the union movement as a whole. The miners were divided. The government was resolute, having accumulated ample stocks of coal in advance. The miners chose mass picketing as their main weapon, but the resulting violence alienated the British public. After a long and bitter struggle (1984–5), the miners lost. Their defeat marked the decline in traditional industries and traditional working-class loyalties. (Had they but known it, the miners and Thatcher also shared most traditional values.) The government's victory also marked a triumph over organized labor as a whole. Union membership continued to decline in Britain. Worse still from the union leaders' standpoint, their old position in government had gone. They would never again be deferred to, or at least consulted, as a matter of course.

Thatcher also made an equally striking departure in economic policy. Neither she nor her advisers were orthodox monetarists. But, unlike its predecessors during the 1960s and the 1970s, the new administration considered persistent devaluation of the currency as a greater peril than unemployment. Thatcher attempted to bring inflation under control – but not wholly with success. The Thatcher government dropped a formal incomes policy, and all pretense at a full employment target. Subsidies to favored industries were reduced. Above all, Thatcher promoted privatization, and thereby introduced into politics a new concept which thereafter came to be admired worldwide. Major industries were transferred to private ownership, especially when Lawson became chancellor (1983). Privatized industries included British Gas, British Airways, British Telecom, Enterprise Oil, Sealink, Jaguar, Rolls Royce, British Aerospace, and many others.

Thatcherism and its Aftermath

How much did the Thatcher revolution achieve in the end? Not much, according to her critics. Inflation continued to pose problems to the British economy. Unemployment rose (reaching more than 2,000,000 in 1991.) During the early 1980s, North Sea oil revenue had provided a series of surpluses in the current account of the balance of payments. But from 1985 to 1986, Britain once more experienced deficits. Public spending continued to rise. Thatcher's fight against leftist-controlled local governments only accelerated the continuing power shift to central government. Many of her educational cuts were ill considered. Yet welfare spending actually increased as even Conservative voters wanted to retain the benefits of the welfare state. During the Thatcher era, private household debts went up; so did the country's total indebtedness as a share of the national income. More damning still from the Thatcherite viewpoint, the total tax burden rose (between 1980 and 1989 from 35 to 37 percent). There were tax riots; beggars and homeless people once more appeared in the streets. No matter what economists told them, Britons continued to believe, in common with other Europeans, that taxation should be used as an instrument to redistribute income, and to provide all citizens with a basic income. (In this respect a striking difference remained between Europe, on the one hand, and the US and Australia, on the other, both the latter countries having been created by immigrants.)[19] No matter what Tories said about the need to go "Back to Basics," traditional values continued to weaken; crime continued to increase (although not significantly so by US standards). The proportion of babies born outside marriage went up to over a quarter of all recorded births. Libertinage remained in fashion with some of the juiciest scandals provided by Tory MPs and royal personages.

Privatization, on the other hand, proved a success. The list of publicly owned companies transferred to private ownership was huge. Socialists might complain about the disadvantages of "selling the family silver," but productivity rose in publicly owned industries as well as industries transferred to private ownership; overmanning declined. Privatization was blamed by Thatcher's critics for promoting the "deindustrialization" of Britain, and widening the gap between the North, with its rustbelts, and the South with its service industries. But in the end Britain gained, as inefficient industries closed or were sold off, and replaced by more efficient enterprises.

Privatization, moreover, proved tremendously popular with renters of municipally owned houses and apartments who were now allowed to purchase these properties.

19 According to Tom Smith, a public opinion researcher, 81% of Italian respondents believed that taxation should be used to redistribute income, 77% of Hungarians, 64% of Dutch, 63% of British, 56% of West Germans, 42% of Australians, 28% of Americans. The percentage of those who believed that the state should provide a minimum income to each citizen was 79% for Hungarians, 76% for Italians, 64% for Germans, 63% for Britons, 60% for the Dutch, 42% for the Australians, 38% for Americans. Jolyon Jenkins, "Shocking Pink," *New States and Society*, 10 November 1989.

(The percentage of owner-occupiers rose from about 53 percent of all households to 66 percent.) There was likewise a striking increase in the number of individual share-holders (from 7 percent to over 21 percent of the adult population.) Overall the Gross Domestic Product (GDP) rose by 27 percent over the Thatcher years, even though rich people gained proportionately more than poor people. More importantly, Britain began a worldwide trend. A policy which, in 1980, had appeared adventurous to some and unworkable to most, thereafter found imitators all over the world. Rich countries, poor countries, capitalist countries, socialist countries, all turned to selling state-owned enter-prises. Thatcher could reasonably claim that her government had initiated an ownership transfer amounting to "a global revolution."[20]

There was also a shift in British social values. Britain had traditionally been a deferen-tial country. Britons – the English at least – had loved lords and ladies; the British aris-tocratic and gentry values had been widely diffused as prominent people in every walk of life – bankers, mine-owners, trade-union leaders, grocers, pianists – could acquire splendid titles. The men (more rarely the women) heading Britain's major universities, government departments, commissions of enquiry, public corporations, major private enterprises, even galleries and museums, generally seemed cut of the same cloth, no matter what their social origins. They spoke English with the same accent, or learned how to do so. They wished to make Britain a better country. They possessed, or at least professed to possess, a sense of *bourgeoisie oblige*. No matter what their party allegiance, they put their trust in the welfare state. Liberals such as Lord Beveridge, Labourites such as Aneurin Bevan, Tories such as "Rab" Butler, all had a part in its making. In their own eyes they formed a moral and aesthetic as well as an intellectual élite. They were "the Great, the Wise, and the Good," whose names filled the *Who's Who* and the *Dictionary of National Biography*. At their best, they were public spirited and fair, believers in consensus rather than confrontation; they believed in the power of the state to do good – by sustaining the poor, enlightening the ignorant, uplifting the Philistines. At their worst, they were snobs, practitioners of the putdown, an art in which Whitehall and Oxbridge stood unequalled.

Thatcher was the first prime minister in British history to challenge them all – lords, high commissioners, town councillors, dons, barristers, archbishops – worthies whom even Reagan had left unscathed. Not surprisingly, Thatcher endured more personal vili-fication than any modern prime minister since Chamberlain. Playwright Dennis Potter called her "the most obviously repellent manifestation of the most obviously arrogant, dishonest, divisive, and dangerous British government since the war." Lady Warnock, a philosopher, head of Girton College, Cambridge, was more forthright still. Thatcher was lower-middle class, her clothes and hair were insufferable, "packaged together in a way that's not exactly vulgar, just *low*."[21] Producer Jonathan Miller deplored her "odious suburban gentility and sentimental saccharine patriotism, catering for the worst elements of commuter idiocy."[22] Oxford, Thatcher's own university, refused to grant her an hon-orary degree – the only prime minister in the twentieth century so slighted. Society hostesses groused (albeit not to her face) that she spoke English with the improved accent of a British nanny, and that she bought her clothes at Marks and Spencer's. Not that knighthoods and peerages ceased to be valued even by professed advocates of social

20 "The Greatest Asset ever Sold," *The Economist*, 21 August 1993, pp. 13, 17–20.
21 Cited in "That Woman and the Chattering Classes," *The Atlantic*, December 1981, pp. 26–39.
22 Cited by Riddell, *The Thatcher Decade*, p. 3.

equality. But there was a discernible change in British attitudes. "The Great, the Wise, and the Good" had indulged in the snobbery once displayed by Jane Austen's minor gentry, and the moralism inherited from the English parsonage. After Thatcher they never recovered their accustomed supremacy. Britain, in some respects, became a more egalitarian country – more like Britain's north-western European neighbors. In this respect, Thatcher had unwittingly strengthened the European connection.

Having dominated British politics for more than a decade, Thatcher, in 1990, fell to a series of high-level intrigues within her own cabinet and parliamentary party. Thatcher called it "treachery with a smile." (A contemporary British cartoon showed a tiny man, wearing striped pants and a top hat, marked "Tory." Awkwardly, the little man tries to step into a giant pair of lady's shoes, and pick up a huge handbag.) Thatcher's achievements were considerable. Britain's economic importance improved. The Labour Party was forced to the center, while the Conservative Party enjoyed, and continued to enjoy, one of the longest periods in office.

Nevertheless, Thatcher's impact was less than expected by her friends or feared by her enemies. Ironically it was Thatcher, a committed Tory, who completed British decolonization in Africa by overseeing the end of settler rule in Rhodesia. (In this respect, her role paralleled de Gaulle's in Algeria.) In Britain, public expenditure rose rather than diminished. A tireless propagandist, she yet failed to bring about that cultural transformation which she sought; she was better at discrediting socialism than at legitimizing capitalism. Economies in higher education, while injurious to universities, failed to promote an "enterprise society." Privatization did not prove an automatic success, even though many privatized enterprises did well, and privatization stayed an international buzz word.

The British trade unions ceased to be the "Fourth Estate of the Realm." As in most industrialized states, the proportion of unionized labor diminished in the British workforce. In Britain, as elsewhere, an ever-growing number of unionists made their living in white-collar occupations (including the information and entertainment industries). In Britain, as everywhere else, more women filled jobs formerly reserved to men. British labor unions by no means ceased to be important. (A higher proportion of British than of German, US, and French workers stayed union members. However, a smaller percentage of British workers were covered by collective bargaining agreements than in Germany or France.) Overall, British unionists increasingly resembled German and US union members in becoming less ideological, more flexible, more willing to modernize than in the olden days.

Thatcher, however, did her country a disservice by further promoting centralization, this despite her commitment to democracy and the free market. In this respect, Britain differed from her main European partners. In France, communes and their mayors had acquired wide discretion in planning; the prefects' vaunted power had greatly diminished. The German *Länder* enjoyed far-reaching powers. Regionalism had advanced in Italy, Spain, and Portugal. In Britain, by contrast, the powers of central government mightily expanded at the expense of those local governments that a Tory should have supported.

Thatcher's successor was John Major, a compromise candidate. In the US, he would have been stigmatized as a high school drop-out, unfit for higher political office. (He had left school at the age of sixteen.) In Britain, by contrast, he made his way, first in banking, then as a Tory politician. His opponents called him a wimp. But his performance provided no evidence for this particular charge. Major purported to represent a new classless Britain where a working-class boy from Brixton could rise to the highest office in the land. At the same time he was more conciliatory than his predecessor. He made far fewer personal enemies than Thatcher. In foreign policy he got on well with Helmut Kohl, and often followed the German's lead. Major diverged, however, from the Franco-German duo over the Maastricht Treaty (1992), over projects for a common foreign and security policy, a common monetary and a common social policy. At the end of 1991 he put the case against a social charter to the House of Commons, enlivened, as usual, by those boos, cheers, and catcalls beloved by parliamentarians in Westminster. The British government, he said, had broken the ability of trade unions to disorganize the British economy; he would not allow Britain to return to the bad old days.

Under Major the British economy did reasonably well, profiting from a modest recovery affecting all Western countries.[23] Major also played a major part in recasting higher education in Britain, and thereby subtly reducing class differences. Under his premiership, the number of university students rose rapidly (from 261,900 in 1988 to 436,200 in 1993). The former polytechnics escaped from their former dependency on local governments and assumed the new dignity of universities. Universities in general became more businesslike in their operations; some even assumed the unfamiliar role of entrepreneur. Critics, of course, were many. Some complained of Americanization, that quantity was bought at the expense of quality, that reform promoted government intervention and government intervention diffused philistinism. Others censured higher education in Britain for precisely the opposite reasons. Despite recent growth, Britain still provided a university education for a much smaller proportion of its youthful population than competitors such as Germany, not to speak of the US. On the other hand, public spending per student, as a percentage of the GDP, was higher in Britain than in any other European country. (Britain was followed in descending order by Holland, Ireland, Denmark, Germany, France, Spain, and Belgium.)[24] Whatever its failings, Britain's tertiary education remained one of its most successful industries, and Major had a good claim to be known as "the education prime minister."

Nevertheless, Major faced troublesome challenges. The Tories were divided on many issues, especially on British commitments to the EU and EMU (European Monetary Union). As Malcolm Rifkind, Britain's foreign secretary, pointed out in 1996, EMU, once operational, would have untoward consequences. No matter what Britain did, the EU would be split. Half of the existing EU members might be full members; the remainder, and also the new applicants, would be unable to meet the requisite criteria for many years.[25]

At the same time, the British monarchy was beset by scandals. "In 50 years time," King Faroukh supposedly predicted during World War II, "only five kings will be left in the world – the four kings in a pack of cards, and the king of England." Immediate postwar developments seemed to bear out the king's prediction. Monarchy crumbled in Italy, Greece, Iraq, and also Faroukh's Egypt. Kingship, on the other hand, remained respected in the Low Countries and Scandinavia. Kingship returned to Spain as a guarantor of democracy and constitutional government. In Great Britain, above all, Queen

---

23 Between 1993 and 1994, the British GDP went up by 3.3 percent, a modest increase, but second in the EC only to Denmark. Industrial production went up by 6 percent, again only exceeded by Denmark. *The Economist*, 20 August 1994, p. 80.
24 "Universities Challenged," *The Economist*, 24 September 1994, pp. 55–6.
25 "Britain Squashed by Europe," *The Economist*, 21 September 1996, p. 55.

Elizabeth II (crowned 1953) appeared the very model of a modern monarch – always courteous, stately, and commonly better informed than her ministers who, of necessity, possessed only a fraction of the political experience acquired by the Queen during her lifetime appointment. The monarchy represented the "dignified" part of Great Britain's unwritten constitution. Unwittingly, the monarchy also symbolized those traditional family virtues now widely assailed by professors and entertainers as stuffy, patriarchal, or sexist. It was not for nothing that millions of television viewers all over the world watched the fairy-tale wedding between Prince Charles and Lady Diana Spencer (1981); they enjoyed royal magnificence and also a celebration of idealized matrimony.

The British monarchy in fact proved astonishingly good at manipulating the media. But a heavy price was paid for courting publicity. British "royals" turned into global celebrities – endlessly watched, interviewed, filmed, and photographed – with all sexual adventures displayed for a global audience. By 1994, even as staid a journal as *The Economist* (22 October 1994, p. 15) proclaimed its opposition to monarchy. Academicians and journalists alike widely entered a guessing game to predict how long the monarchy would last. But the majority of Britons would continue to prefer the monarchy with its accustomed splendor to a presidency. (Foreigners widely shared this preference. According to the *Gallup Poll Monthly*, December 1995, both Queen Elizabeth II and Diana, Princess of Wales, held their place among the ten women most admired by Americans.)

More seriously, Major could no more solve the Northern Irish question than could his predecessors. Ireland, having joined the EC in 1973, enjoyed a modest prosperity, aided by substantial transfers from the EC. Ireland, a neutral country like Switzerland, benefited from its EC and UN connections by garnering a substantial number of important posts in international organizations. While remaining a Catholic country, Ireland increasingly opened to secularist lifestyles and outside influences, derived in part from the huge Irish diaspora in the US, Britain, and Australia. British imperialists had once forecast that "Home Rule" meant "Rome rule," but Irish history in no wise bore out this prediction.

By contrast, Northern Ireland (known as Ulster to British loyalists) remained a divided country, split between a Protestant majority and a Catholic minority (about 42 percent of the population, but with a growth rate higher than the Protestants'). In 1969, the IRA (Irish Republican Army) began a campaign of terrorism for the purpose of uniting Northern Ireland with the South. The Protestants fiercely resisted, and Protestants formed terrorist groups of their own, resolved to maintain the British connection. Both the IRA and the Protestant gunmen represented minorities within their respective communities. (Sinn Fein, the political arm of the IRA, only won about one-third of the Catholic vote in Northern Ireland.) Both parties, however, proved good at back-alley killings. (Between 1969 and 1994, some 3,168 persons were murdered, including 648 members of the British security forces. Both Thatcher and Major were also intended victims.) The British army stood between the two sides, without, however, being able to stamp out terror. Britain did away with the Protestants' former supremacy; the British authorities stripped the local government of Northern Ireland of most powers, enforced direct rule, enforced fair employment laws, and other civil rights legislation.

Subsequent talks between London and Dublin gave to the Republic of Ireland some official standing in the dispute. Protestants, especially militant Protestants, therefore felt increasingly alienated, and Unionism as a monolithic movement splintered into rival parties. (Northern Ireland, or Ulster, was unusual in Europe at the time in that the terrorists on both sides mainly derived from the working class rather than the intellectuals. Middle-class Protestants felt more inclined towards compromise.) Britain became increasingly reluctant to maintain a permanent stake in Northern Ireland, and keep on paying huge subsidies to Northern Ireland. Public opinion in Ireland was likewise increasingly repelled by Northern Irish violence, and increasingly reluctant to take over the disputed province. IRA violence also alienated even radical Irish-American nationalists who had supplied substantial financial support for the cause. The IRA thus agreed to a ceasefire (proclaimed in 1994 by Gerry Adams, head of Sinn Fein). But the truce would apparently not hold.

The Labour Party, by contrast, represented a much less formidable challenge to the Tory government. In response to the electoral defeat of 1979, Labour had retreated from the reformism of Wilson and Callaghan, becoming the party of unilateral disarmament, and of full-blown socialism. Displaying an apparent death wish, the party briefly selected for its head Michael Foot, "a decent leftist litterateur, and the weakest leader the party ever had."[26] Foot (1913–) was a popular novelist's dream of a leftist British intellectual. He was well born (his father was a privy councillor), but heir to the British dissenting tradition. He studied at Oxford where he turned into a Popular Front supporter and a Labourite. He also rose to be president of the Oxford Union (a grand debating society), thereby attaining a position which, in the olden days, assured its holder of political advancement. He later made his mark in the Labour Party, not just as a politician, but also as a gifted polemicist. (His many books included *Guilty Men*, published in 1940 with Frank Owen and Peter Howard, perhaps one of the most influential political philippics published in the twentieth century.) He reached ministerial office in 1974 (as secretary of state for employment), advanced to be Lord President and Leader of the House of Commons (1980–83). Foot led Labour into the 1983 general election, the greatest disaster sustained by his party since 1918. Dreamy and dishevelled in appearance, with his hair untidy and collar askew, Foot appeared to his critics as an honest man, no doubt, gifted, no doubt, learned, no doubt – but the very paradigm of an innocent abroad.

The party thereafter split, and a number of highly placed dissidents created a new party, the Social Democrats. Labour, accordingly, suffered total disaster in the 1983 elections. (Labour gained less than 28 percent of the vote, the party's worst performance since 1918.) Labour's future seemed all the more in doubt as inner cities crumbled, traditional staple industries disappeared, and as traditional Labour strongholds continued to lose population. Labour began to rebuild its strength under Neil Kinnock (elected leader in 1983 in succession to Foot). Kinnock had been born in South Wales, one of Labour's traditional bastions. He began his career as an adult education lecturer, and thereafter made his way in the Labour Party. Kinnock was a man of resolution, and a fluent orator to boot. Under Kinnock's guidance, the Labour Party returned to moderation. Unlike the olden-day Labour stalwarts, Kinnock had no wish to socialize key industries, or to equalize property by imposing a wealth tax. He firmly supported NATO against the Labour Party's pacifists; he equally favored the EC. (He was indeed on terms of close personal friendship with European socialists such as Felipe Gonzales in Spain.) No serious Labour politician thereafter would question Britain's adherence to the EC. Under Kinnock, Labour even accepted Thatcher's privatization of public housing, a striking shift in Labour orthodoxy.

26 Hugo Young, "The Rewards of Labour," *The New Republic*, 27 May 1991, p. 23.

Labour, however, had to compete with the Liberal Democratic Party (founded in 1988 as a merger between the old liberal Party and the Social Democrats, now Britain's third-strongest party). The Liberal Democrats strongly supported the European Union, though they strove to reduce the powers of its Commission, and desired a clear division of functions between the various branches of Euro-government. The Liberal Democrats, heirs to the old Liberal tradition, stressed the "green imperative," emphasized education, lauded the free market, and eulogized ethnic diversity in a new Britain. Led by Paddy Ashdown, a former Royal Marine captain, and an ex-diplomatist, the Liberal Democrats represented a challenge in that they vied, in particular, for the votes of those progress-ively minded professionals who had contributed so much to Labour in the past. Above all, Labour as yet failed to shed its reputation as a left-wingers' haunt. To the surprise of the pollsters, the Tories under Major once more won a smashing victory in the 1992 election. (The Conservatives gained 41.93 percent of the vote, and 336 seats out of 651 seats in the Commons. Labour won only 34.39 percent of the vote, and 271 seats, des-pite continuing recession.)[27] The Labour Party (like the Tory Party) kept losing members, as single-issue pressure groups became increasingly powerful.[28] Their members tended to be young, highly educated and highly motivated. They were familiar with the machinery of law and government. They knew how to conduct academic research. They were good at putting their case to journalists, TV anchormen, civil servants, and parliamentarians. A parliamentarian anxious to be re-elected, a civil servant keen on promotion, would be ill advised to be rude to one of their delegations. Their members represented all kinds of good causes, environmental protection, wildlife preservation, humane treatment of orphans, criminals, and madmen. But while they mainly looked to the left, they did not necessarily support Labour; a great many preferred the Liberal Democrats.

Kinnock's successors continued to steer a reformist course, but nevertheless seemed unable to break the Tory Party's dominance in British politics. ("We are like Japan," com-plained a journalist, "but without the money.") Change, however, apparently came with the election to the labour leadership of Tony Blair (1994). Blair was young and handsome. He had charm and charisma. He was squeaky clean (nicknamed "Bambi" in politics). He looked like Clinton – but without the scandals. Blair thus managed to attract a wide fol-lowing among an electorate which increasingly had become both bored with, and tired of, Tory dominance. (By 1994, 60 percent of a public opinion poll hoped that Blair would succeed as prime minister.)[29] He castigated the ills occasioned by social atomization.

Blair personally admired Clinton whom he resembled in his ability to project a "nice guy" image. (Like Clinton, Blair is married to a successful woman lawyer.) Blair insisted that Britain's future was with Europe, but that Europe's future would depend on cooperation between sovereign states. Whereas the Conservative Party was riddled by scandal and internal discord, Labour substantially extended its membership. Even tough-minded German industrialists woefully complained that the German SPD contained no leader of Blair's stature and common sense.

---

27 Anthony King, ed., *Britain at the Polls, 1992*, Chatham, NJ, Chatham House, 1993; Richard Heffernan and Mike Marqusee, *Defeat from the Jaws of Victory: Inside Kinnock's Labour Party*, London, Verso, 1992; David Butler and Dennis Kavanagh, *The British General Election of 1992*, New York, St Martin's Press, 1992.
28 "A Nation of Groupies," *The Economist*, 13 August 1994, pp. 49–51. Between 1965 and 1985 the Labour Party declined from 800,000 to 300,000 members.
29 Jürgen Kröning, "Ein Mann mit Charme und Charisma," *Die Zeit*, 5 August 1994, p. 818.

Blair's message now made a wide appeal. He stressed the need to come to terms with the age of software and the information revolution. He took a tough line on crime, and favored free trade – much as President Clinton. As far as Blair was concerned, Labour should be a "catch-all" – not a class – party, able to attract voters from every part of British society. (In 1995, the Labour Party's leadership voted to drop the party's 77-year-old commitment to the "common ownership of the means of production, distribution and exchange," the British socialists' shibboleth.) Blair and Gordon Brown, Blair's choice for chancellor of the exchequer, moreover, committed the party to free trade, accepted a free market, and – in theory at any rate – called for a balanced budget. The Labour Party, justly, criticized the Tories' penchant for centralization. The Labour Party also promised to consider far-reaching constitutional reforms, including elected assemblies for Scotland and Wales, devolution of power to England's regions, more freedom for local governments, a referendum on changing the British electoral system, and a bill of rights. At a time when American voters expressed increasing dissatisfaction with their own political institutions, the British looked across the Atlantic for models of reform. But the Labour Party also advocated a national minimum wage, and – like the Clintons in the US – thought that the "undeserving rich" should be made to pay for their sins. Despite this ambivalence about the role of money-making – possibly because of it – Labour continued to make new converts. By 1994, two-thirds of respondents in a major poll thought that Labour had changed for the better; a four-to-one majority favored a minimum wage; three out of four supported Maastricht's social charter from which Major's government had opted out. A substantial majority (52 percent) stated that they would vote Labour in the next election.[30] At a time when the Tories steadily lost votes, a "Clintonized" Labour Party once more claimed the ability to govern.

30 "Striding Clear," *The Economist*, 1 October 1994, pp. 71–3.

15

Italy and the Iberian Peninsula:
1979 to the Present

Italy is a land where disaster seems to lurk around the corner. Who has not heard of the Mafia? But even sober-minded journals like to paint the Italian picture in the darkest colors. "Italy's Pension Paradise Faces Fund Shortage," insists the *Christian Science Monitor*. "Italy: Nail-Biting Stuff," "Italy: Can Pay, Won't" proclaims *The Economist*.[1] In truth, of course, Italy's development represents one of the most remarkable success stories in Europe. To be more specific, economic growth between 1950 and 1963 was so remarkable as to be appropriately called a miracle. The country's serious troubles began in 1973 when the rapid rise in international oil prices gravely hit Italy, dependent on foreign sources for 85 percent of its energy. There were other difficulties: high unemployment, high labor costs, vast public expenditure, a staggering public deficit, and vast entitlement programs (including a most generous system of state pensions.)[2]

Generalizations, of course, are difficult, for there is not one, but many Italies. As we pointed out in chapter 6, there is a striking division between the North and the South: the former prosperous, linked to Central Europe; the South, more poverty-stricken, and "Mediterranean." Salaries, work habits, consumption, kinship patterns – everything divides by invisible bars. A second split divides private from public enterprise. The former is generally efficient, the latter much less so. Overall, the public sector remains large and ungainly and, by the early 1990s, accounted for a larger share of the GDP than in any other major country in Western Europe. (In 1992 Italy's proportion stood at the top and was followed, in order, by France, Germany, Belgium, Spain, Holland, with post-Thatcher Britain at the bottom.) The public sector contains islands of efficiency, but remains known for corrupt links to political parties and organized crime, and for a propensity for running at a loss. (In particular, Italy lags behind in communications, a key to the economy. The social services have become politicized; sickness and disability pensions, for example, are used on a large scale to reward political supporters.)

---

1 Headings respectively from the *Christian Science Monitor*, 16 February 1994, p. 9; *The Economist*, 1 August 1992, p. 40, 9 October 1994, p. 58.
2 Frederick Spotts and Theodor Wieser, *Italy: a Difficult Democracy. A Survey of Italian Politics*, London and New York, Cambridge University Press, 1986, p. 300. Other works include George H. Hildebrand, *Growth and Structure in the Economy of Modern Italy*, Cambridge, MA, Harvard University Press, 1965; Paul Ginsborg, *A History of Contemporary Italy: Society and Politics, 1943–1988*, London, Penguin, 1990; John Haycraft, *Italian Labyrinth: Italy in the 1980s*, London, Secker and Warburg, 1985; Paul Furlong, *Modern Italy: Representation and Reform*, London, Routledge, 1994. For an excellent brief survey, see Norman Kogan, "Italy," in Gerald A. Dorfman and Peter J. Duignan, eds, *Politics in Western Europe*, Stanford, CA, Hoover Institution Press, 1991, pp. 265–96.

Nevertheless, the Italian achievement remains astonishing. At the end of World War II, Italy was a divided country, stricken by war, beset by deprivation. The social deprivations of the period were wonderfully recorded in film classics such as *Bicycle Thief*. By the early 1990s such movies looked dated; poverty had largely disappeared. Italy had become the world's fourth or fifth economic power, both an exporter of capital and a magnet for foreign investments. (By 1990, more than $20 billion had been placed in Italy by financiers from abroad, attracted by Italy's high interest rates and the lira's relative stability). Italians were renowned as savers; Italian industrialists were known for their inventiveness and the quality of their designs. Italy's economic growth rate was one of the highest in Western Europe.[3]

Statisticians, in fact, may have underestimated the full extent of Italy's industrial growth. The "official" economy was paralleled by the *industria sommersa*, the underground economy, an intricate network of small firms and cottage industries which operated so as to escape the scrutiny of tax inspectors, trade-union officials, licensing board, and such like. (The underground economy supposedly accounted for 20–30 percent of Italy's true GNP.[4] The best guesses derive from studies of bank deposits, for even black marketeers trust the banks.) It was small business, in particular, that changed the economic map of Italy. In a country where kinship ties and kinship loyalties remain strong, the family firm functions with particular efficiency. The new firms changed the industrial map of Italy, operating, above all, in provincial towns in areas hitherto largely dependent on agriculture. They spread from Emilia-Romagna, the Veneto, and Tuscany into Umbria, Abruzzi, Puglia, and the region below Rome. They turn out clothing, leather products, shoes, furniture, textiles, toys, jewelry, machine tools, and what not. The low price and high quality of their products make these firms remarkably resistant to the ups and downs of the international economy. (Some of the most profitable, in fact, operate in the communist Tuscan countryside, and produce an oddly successful form of "communist capitalism.")

Italy: the Old Order Weakens

Italy's economic dynamism in turn produced far-reaching social change – both positive and negative. The influence of the Catholic Church declined. (To the Italian bishops' displeasure, the Italian electorate in 1974 approved of a law legalizing divorce. The voting was 59.1 percent in favor, 40.9 percent against, though this still represented substantial conservative strength.) Instead of being an exporter of labor, Italy turned into an importer as Croats, Albanians, and North Africans, in particular, sought jobs in Italy. By contrast, the number of Italians looking for work in Northern Europe decreased strikingly; the birth rate lessened, and so did the size of the Italian family.

Direct US influence on Italy, strong after World War II, diminished. So did the US's direct influence on Italy as a whole. After World War II, the US had re-equipped the Italian army, provided Marshall aid, and fought communist influence in every shape or form, whether in politics or trade-union matters. But as time went on, the Italian Establishment became too confident to be directly manipulated. The influence of the

3 The GDP growth, annual average, 1960–90, exceeded alike, in descending order, that of the US, Germany, and Britain, amounting to just under 4 percent. *The National Times*, November 1994, table "superstars," p. 17.
4 Spotts and Wieser, *Italy: a Difficult Democracy*, p. 216.

Italian-American community on the motherland, strong immediately after World War II, likewise diminished; henceforth, the US touched on Italy in a more indirect fashion, through popular culture, entertainment, academic contacts, student exchanges, investment, and trade. By contrast, Italy was firmly integrated into the European Community. (It was not for nothing that the treaties establishing the European Economic Community, (later European Community, later European Union) had been signed in Rome, 1957.) Throughout most of Italy living standards went up; Northern Italy, in particular, now stood out as one of the most prosperous parts of Europe; life changed even in the remoter parts of the *mezzogiorno*. Illiteracy, still widespread after World War II, practically disappeared.[5]

Italy's political institutions, unfortunately, did not match the vigor of Italian society. Given the Italian peninsula's vast social and cultural disparities, the architects of Italian unity in the nineteenth century would have done better to unify the country on a confederal basis. Instead, Italy had been united by Royal Savoyard Jacobins who strove to build a centralized state, one and indivisible. This state was ruled by centralized political parties whose dominance was strengthened by a complex system of proportional representation. Whatever the constitution-makers' intention, the system functioned for the benefit of parties and party bigwigs, the partocracy. The party magnates, not local electors, chose the candidates for each constituency; once elected, deputies owed their primary allegiance to party bosses, not the people. Hence, the party overlords between them shared out rewards, while taking turns in shuffling portfolios.

There was, indeed, a strong and well-organized opposition, the Italian Communist Party. But the Communists remained distrusted by the majority. Try as they might to soften their line, they failed to enter the government. The bulk of Italian voters remained convinced that, at heart, the Communists meant by a democratic coalition two wolves and a lamb deciding by a two-thirds majority what should be served for dinner. Equally taboo to the governing coalitions was an electoral alliance with the neo-Fascist MSI (*Movimento sociale italiano*). The Christian Democrats, however divided, appeared the lesser evil, and kept in power through shifting electoral pacts with various smaller parties. (From 1963 onward, the principal partner was the Socialists.)

The Duke of Newcastle, a corrupt British eighteenth-century prime minister, had once complained that his main task in politics was to find pastures on which his sheep might graze. Every Italian prime minister would have echoed the Duke's lament with even greater fervor because twentieth-century Italian patronage had turned from an aristocratic to a democratic entitlement. Places, emoluments, and contracts had to be found for an ever-growing army of citizens. The resultant system weakened the public services, corrupted nationalized enterprise, and spread political cynicism. There was widespread fraud and widespread tax evasion. In 1994, for example, the glitz and glamor of Italy's fashion industry was dimmed by a scandal involving huge bribes paid to tax officials. But the world of fashion was no more prone to tax evasion than any other major industry. (According to modest government estimates, seven out of ten Italian companies fiddled their tax returns, supposedly costing the country $64 billion a year.) The humble were as likely to cheat as the rich, as contracts went to crooks, and pensions to phony invalids. Nevertheless, the Italian economy progressed, Italian society functioned effectively, and the Republic continued to operate, despite threats from the extreme left and the extreme right. This, in truth, was the Italian miracle.

5 Ibid., p. 300. Angelo Codevilla, "A Second Italian Republic," *Foreign Affairs*, Summer 1992, pp. 146–64.

Italian reformers suggested numerous ways of mending the system. Advocates of decentralization called for the diminution of the power exercised by the prefects whose influence rivalled that of their French colleagues. Power instead should devolve to the regions.[6] Alternatively, the power of parties might be diminished by creating a strong presidency, with a president directly elected in Gaullist style. The change was favored by a number of prominent politicians, including Socialist leader Bettino Craxi; but such plans were anathema to the leading party directorates, and with good reason. As Angelo Codevilla, a political scientist, has put it, "the principle of direct contested election of government officials, whom the voters can turn out of office, was the very negation of Italian political oligopoly."[7] A third way of reforming the state would have entailed a legislative branch elected – French or British style – in single-member districts. But again the Italian political establishment successfully resisted such plans.

In theory, the Communists should have benefited from the weakness of Italy's "political class." Enrico Berlinguer was an outstanding leader. (He directed the party from 1976 to his death in 1984. His office passed to Alessandro Natta, succeeded in 1988 by Achille Occhetto.) The party enjoyed wide support, particularly among workers and intellectuals. (At the height of its power, in 1976, the PCI scored 34.4 percent of the vote.) The PCI followed a conciliatory course in advocating a "historic compromise" with the CD. The party broadened its power by gaining control over numerous local authorities, ranging from cities such as Bologna to assorted rural communes. Above all, Berlinguer led the party on its long march out of the Soviet camp.

The Communist Party built a clientage system almost as extensive as, and much better disciplined than, the Christian Democrats'. Nevertheless, the Communist Party, from the late 1970s, began to decline. During the 1980s, the intellectual prestige of Marxism diminished in Italy, as in the rest of Europe. Between 1978 and 1985, the number of new recruits nearly halved (from 100,483 to 60,293).[8] The newcomers, admittedly, were better educated in a formal sense than their predecessors, but they lacked the old faith and the old dedication to the party as a counter-church. The youth culture, the new consumerism, the disruption of traditional working-class loyalties, profoundly affected party discipline and party cohesion. Well established in local governments, former militants turned into city hall bigwigs. Berlinguer's battle for a "historic compromise" took for granted that politics would continue to revolve around the traditional parties, but this assumption was itself flawed. On the contrary, the Communists became associated with the "partocracy." (The Berlinguers themselves derived from the Sardinian nobility. Enrico's wife was a practicing Catholic, and he himself was related to two Christian Democratic presidents of Italy, Antonio Segni and Francesco Cossiga.) Disastrous for the Communists also was the terrorism exercised by the Red Brigades (see chapter 6). Revolutionary socialism stood discredited (especially as the Red Brigades also attacked orthodox communists). Moro's murder also removed from Italian politics a man who had sincerely believed that the CD could compromise with the Communists. His murder

6 Robert C. Fried, *The Italian Prefects: a Study in Administrative Politics*, New Haven, Conn., Yale University Press, 1963; Norman Kogan, *The Government of Italy*, New York, Thomas Y. Crowell, 1962; and *The Political History of Post-War Italy*, London, Pall Mall Press, 1962.
7 Codevilla, "A Second Italian Republic," p. 153.
8 Statistics cited by Stephen Hellman, "Strategy and Organization in the Crisis of the Italian Communist Party," paper presented at the Seventh International Conference of Europeanists, Washington DC, 23–25 March 1990.

demonstrated that willingness to cooperate with the left did not assure anyone's physical safety – not even the most highly placed, Communist-approved politician.

As regards labor relations, the workforce shrank in Italian factories, and the PCI seemed increasingly unable to protect its clientele. (In 1980, an all-out strike collapsed in the Fiat works despite the PCI's vigorous support for the strikers.) Try as it might, moreover, the PCI could not dissociate itself from the obvious and increasing weakness of the ruling communist parties east of the Elbe. The Communists increasingly lost votes (particularly to the Italian Socialist Party); dissension within Communist ranks grew ever more. In 1989 "democratic centralism" (the keystone in the Leninist ideology, long since under attack within the PCI) was formally abandoned. In 1990 the PCI was refounded as the Party of Democratic Socialism (PDS), which thereafter claimed to form part of the constitutional left. Toggliatti's ghost was laid at last. Italy's internal Cold War was over.

The Christian Democrats (CD) did no better than the communists. The CD was a loose coalition held together by the fear of communism and the desire for patronage. Above all, the CD appealed to practicing Catholics. (In 1985, 36.8 percent of Christian Democrats attended mass regularly, 13.9 percent of Socialists and 5.6 percent of Communists, but only 1.8 percent of neo-Fascists.)[9] But the fear of communism weakened, and so did religious loyalties. (Despite the Church's opposition to the use of contraceptives, for instance, Italian Catholics practiced birth control to such effect that the Italian birth rate dropped to one of the lowest in Europe.) Scandals went on unceasingly, amply reported, and even magnified by the media. The collapse of the Banco Ambrosiano (1981) besmirched the reputation, not merely of Establishment politicians, but of the Vatican itself. All parties declined in public estimation – but most of all the CD which had held power ever since the Republic's inception and which therefore earned more censure than any other political group. Excluded since the mid-1970s from the great northern urban centers, and even from Naples, the CD held on in the South where organized crime was strongest, and the patronage system was at its most pervasive. *Miseria e malgoverno* (poverty and bad government) reached scandalous proportions; so did the power of criminal syndicates.[10] The CD suffered further as its great postwar achievements for Italy – a democratic order, economic prosperity, a respected international status within the EC and NATO – had come to be taken for granted. At the same time, the CD lost much of its former patronage, and much of its influence at the regional and local level. The management of pensions and other welfare programs was increasingly controlled by regions and trade unions. In 1983, the CD, for the first time, ceded the premiership which went to a Socialist, Bettino Craxi. Craxi, a former journalist and writer, became Italy's longest-serving prime minister (1983–7). But the Socialists no more stood aloof from *tangentopoli* (graft city) than their allies and opponents.

Italy: the Old Order Breaks

Testing time for the old system came with a series of referendums asking the electorate to decide on the country's constitutional future. Reformers called for the abolition of a

---

9 Spotts and Wieser, *Italy: a Difficult Democracy*, p. 302.
10 Judith Chubb, *Patronage, Power and Poverty in Southern Italy*, Cambridge, Cambridge University Press, 1982; *The Mafia and Politics*, Ithaca, NY, Center for International Studies, Cornell University Press, 1989.

system that encouraged electoral fraud. A complex system of preferences made for an easily identifiable voter bloc that could be manipulated by the Mafia and other such groups in the South. Craxi's Socialist Party opposed the change. So did the CD leader Giulio Andreotti, who ridiculed the referendum as petty politics, of interest only to "four cats." Andreotti, however, proved mistaken. A "yes" vote found support from a broad coalition which strangely united the PDS, prominent Italian bishops, and *Confindustria* (the Italian employers' federation). The results were unprecedented. Northerners and Southerners, rich and poor, Catholics and atheists, town folk and country folk, united to reject the regnant political system. As a result, electoral legislation in 1993 created a new order in which three-quarters of the seats both in the Senate and the Chamber of Deputies were directly elected by a simple majority (the system favored by public opinion), the remainder by proportional representation (the system principally preferred by party bigwigs).

The most decisive blows against the old system were struck, however, by the judicature, which unexpectedly turned into a revolutionary force. The Italian judicature need not be idealized. Italy suffers from all the problems which affect the US: overcrowded courtroom calendars, over-full jails, over-complex technicalities, overly numerous laws. As laws kept proliferating, their enforcement became ever more arbitrary. In Italy, moreover, the burden of proof rests on the accused. Years ago, an eminent jurist had complained that, if he were accused of stealing the Leaning Tower of Pisa, he would go into hiding, until the courts had established that the tower was still in place. More recently, Ferdinando Imposimato, a magistrate famed for his fearless investigation of the Mafia, stigmatized with much eloquence a system which made a judicial defense easier for a guilty than an innocent person. The magistracy, moreover, was widely politicized, and magistrates could use their extraordinary powers of arrest to follow a political agenda. As Joseph LaPalombara, a political scientist, put it, "It is unclear whether this power is more pernicious when exercised at the behest of political parties or when the judges take it into their own hands."[11] Yet it was the magistracy, with its sense of civic duty, that disrupted the *ancien régime*.[12]

The *mani pulite* (clean hands) campaign, begun by Italian magistrates from the early 1990s, shook every pillar of the Italian Establishment. Trials became televised spectacles watched with fascination by a huge public. Antonio Di Pietro, the Milan magistrate who began the "clean hands" prosecution, became a national hero. The traditional system of protection no longer worked, as even magnates such as Sergio Cusani, manager of the great Ferruzzi business group, found himself in the dock for allegedly distributing over $100 million to various political parties. Politician after politician squirmed in the witness stand – to the Italian public's astonishment and delight. Not even former premiers were spared – men such as Craxi and Andreotti (seven times Christian Democrat prime minister) turned out to be giants with feet of clay who earned vocal public derision, together with the entire "political class" which they represented. The traditional wall of silence collapsed as prosecutors attacked big business. (According to one specific estimate, the cost of systematic kickbacks linked to big public works contracts had amounted to some $4 billion during the years 1982–92.)[13] As investigations proceeded, the list of accused began to read like a *Who's Who* of Italian business, with magnates

11 Joseph LaPalombara, *Democracy, Italian Style*, New Haven, Yale University Press, 1987, p. 251.
12 For a general survey, see Mino Lorusso, *L'era di Achille: occhetto e la politica italiana da Togliatti a Berlusconi*, Florence, Polte alle Grazie, 1994.
13 "The Purging of Italy Inc.," *The Economist*, 20 March 1994, p. 69.

from every major industry under investigation. The *mani pulite* campaign had a disruptive effect at first, as public confidence declined, and as even honest officials became
reluctant to sign public contracts, lest they become innocently involved in new scandals.
Nevertheless, the *mani pulite* campaign would have the long-term effect of disrupting
traditional restraints on trade and, in effect, freeing Italian markets. The anti-corruption
campaign, linked to pressure from the EU, also encouraged designs for privatizing huge
and inefficient state conglomerates. (The biggest fish among them was IRI, short for
Instituto per la ricostruzione industriale which, by 1994, reported a $6.2 billion loss.)
Privatization proceeded all too slowly. Nevertheless, a start had been made by 1993 as
the government offered for sale numerous companies such as *Credito italiano* (banking)
and *Nuovo rignone* (engineering).

Finally, there was an assault on organized crime. Organizations such as the Mafia,
the Camorra, and 'Ndrangheta had long functioned not merely as criminal syndicates,
but virtually as mini-states, with their own territories, laws, population, intelligence
services, and armed forces. The new Mafia penetrated local government, established close
ties with parties and politicians, worked their way into banks and industries. Above all,
the Mafia established an awesome record of killing investigators attempting to prise open
its business secrets. (The Mafia's victims included prominent people such as General
Carlo Alberto Dalla Chiesa, official investigator; Boris Giuliano, police chief in Palermo;
Michele Reina, a CD politician; Mario Francese, investigative journalist; Cesare Terra
Nova, left-wing politician and anti-Mafia expert; Piersanti Mattarella, president of the
Sicilian Regional Council; Emanuele Basile, officer in the Carabinieri; Gaetano Costa,
judge; Giovanni Falcone, chief prosecutor in Palermo, and his friend Paolo Borsellino,
judge, the very embodiment of Italy's civic spirit, slain by a car bomb in Palermo.)

For a change, the government responded with vigor. The authorities assumed broad
police powers, reminiscent of those special anti-terrorist laws that had been used to
suppress urban guerrillas such as the Red Brigades after the kidnapping and murder of
Aldo Moro in 1978. The authorities at last committed themselves to creating a national
investigative force on the lines of the FBI. The courts received added assistance to secure
convictions. (For instance, evidence given during preliminary hearings was henceforth
treated as valid, even if later withdrawn under threats. Witnesses henceforth might be
questioned at long distance, thanks to video recordings and satellite links.) Italian judges
could henceforth avoid absurd proceedings such as the transfer of an entire Palermo
court, including lawyers and defendants, to the US so as to hear secure evidence. Above
all, the public was now thoroughly aroused against crime. Instead of being romanticized
in meretricious US movies such as *The Godfather* and *Once Upon a Time in America*,
gangsters in Italy were recognized for what they were – murderous scum. Conventional
politicians were despised more than ever. (In 1992, prime minister Giuliano Amato and
president Oscar Luigi had to be hustled out through a side entrance lest they be beaten
up by enraged spectators during a state funeral for murdered police officers.)[14] Three
years later, Italy witnessed a court-room drama beyond any screen-writer's imagination.
Giulio Andreotti, seven times prime minister, the most powerful of Christian Democrat
politicians, went on trial facing charges that he had served as the Mafia's political
godfather. An entire system seemed under indictment.

The 1994 elections gave the death blow to the old system. Admittedly, the old
"political class" was by no means eliminated, as numerous new parties were constituted

14 "A Message from Sicily," *The Economist*, 25 July 1992, pp. 47–8.

from fragments of the old. Profiteering did not disappear; nor were traditional loyalties forgotten. Nevertheless, there was a shift in power. The new elections were fought between three main electoral alliances. The right-wing Freedom Alliance was composed of Forza Italia (founded only in 1994, the year of the election); the Northern League (LN), a regional group; and the National Alliance (AN, neo-Fascists, formerly MSI). The centrist Pact for Italy contained the remnants of the CD, including the Italian Popular Party (PPI). The left-wing Progressive Alliance embraced the PDS, the Greens, the Democratic Alliance (AD), the Socialists, and various minor groups. Pollsters favored the Progressive Alliance, but the right won a stunning victory. (The Freedom Alliance gained 42.9 percent of the proportional representation vote and 366 seats in the Chamber. The Progressive Alliance received 34.4 percent of the proportional representation vote, and 213 seats; the Pact for Italy got 15.7 percent of the proportional representation vote and 46 seats. More specifically, the PDS managed to secure only 20.4 percent of the vote, and the PPI (the CD's heir) just 11.1 percent.) Yesterday's kings and captains had departed.

In 1994 a new right-wing coalition came into power, headed by Silvio Berlusconi, founder and head of *Forza Italia*. Berlusconi was a billionaire who had started modestly as a real-estate developer in Milan, and then built a great media empire, allegedly with corrupt help from old-style politicians such as Craxi (who had served as best man at Berlusconi's wedding but escaped to Tunisia when the old order collapsed). Berlusconi's personal wealth and influence was enormous. A *US News and World Report* essay likened Berlusconi to some imaginary US president who also happened to own CBS, NBC, CNN, HBO, the *Los Angeles Times*, Columbia Pictures, *US News*, KMart, Random House, huge amounts of real estate, and the Dallas Cowboys.[15] (*Forza Italia* (go for it Italy) was the Italian soccer supporters' battle cry.) In many ways, Berlusconi also invited comparison with Ross Perot, an American financial magnate who, in 1992, had gained substantial support as presidential candidate by his ability to manipulate the media, his readiness to condemn Washington and all its works, his boasts of being a self-made businessman, and his declared willingness to introduce economy into government. Berlusconi stood for a new electorate of television viewers, sports fans, and sports enthusiasts; *Forza Italia* turned into the leader's fan club.

Berlusconi's least attractive ally was the *Alleanza nazionale* (AN). Gianfranco Fini, their leader, did not bear the slightest resemblance to Mussolini. Fini, an ex-journalist, never threatened, never screamed. He was courteous and elegant. He insisted that his party had foresworn the olden-day fascists' taste for a state-controlled economy. (Contrary to its reputation, Fascism had been a movement of the left, and Mussolini had begun as a socialist.) Fini likewise distanced himself from the Fascists' militarism, and with good reason (no AN supporter had the slightest wish to put on uniform and dive for cover in some Ukrainian foxhole, as their grandfathers had done). The party, moreover, could claim with perfect justice that the AN was unique among Italian parties in that the AN had never participated in the old political system. *Dio, patria, familigia* (God, fatherland, family) was a slogan which appealed to conservatives all over Europe. But the AN's core consisted of olden-day *missini* (MSI sympathizers). Fini's critics styled him an old-style absolutist who would lead the country to ruin (*l'état c'est fini*). The AN for its part insisted that Italy should return to the olden-day virtues, that immigration

15 "Insider Trading in Italy: Conflicts of Interest are Hurting a Popular Prime Minister," *US News and World Report*, 17 October 1994, p. 59.

should end, that Italy should be reserved for Italians. Above all, the AN stood for a centralized Italy; AN's remedy for Italy's political ills seemed poison for all those who wished to upgrade the regions.

Regionalism found expression in the Northern League. The League's supporters felt convinced that Northerners were exploited alike by Rome and by the South. Northerners, urged the League, paid taxes so that Roman politicos might buy votes in the South, pay off the Mafia, maintain costly public corporations, extend an already swollen bureaucracy, and provide development aid to undeserving Calabrians, Apulians, Sicilians, Sardinians, and their like. The League detested immigrants – not just newcomers from North Africa, but also from Southern Italy. Not surprisingly, Umberto Bossi, the League's leader, was denounced by conventional politicians as a provincial bigot, his movement denigrated as a strawfire which would soon burn out. But the League also stood for the devolution of power to three major regions. Above all, the League formed the only major party in Europe unreservedly committed to free enterprise.[16] (The others were smaller groups such as the *Freisinnige Partei* in Switzerland and the *Liberale Forum* in Austria.) But regionalism and a free-market commitment formed a formidable combination that might strongly affect the rest of Europe in future.

Italy's political turmoil weakened the country's international position, particularly the inclusion of neo-Fascists in the Cabinet. (The AN, among other demands, called for the consideration of ancient Italian claims on the territory of former Yugoslavia.) Italy's EU partners thus refused Italy's demands to join a European "Contact Group" to negotiate a ceasefire in the war in Bosnia (1994). Similarly, the Italian foreign minister, Antonio Martino, received a cool reception when, on a visit to Washington, he advocated Italian claims for inclusion into an enlarged UN Security Council. Anxious to legitimize his government, Berlusconi thus gave public assurances on Italy's existing foreign commitments. He also declared support for an enlarged European Union which, in future, should turn toward Eastern Europe. His own reservations concerning the Maastricht Treaty should not slow progress toward European convergence. Italy's troubles, in the end, did not weaken her European commitments.

The Berlusconi government, however, failed to re-establish stability. (Berlusconi himself met with massive criticism on the grounds that he was soft on crime, and engaged in dealings as dubious as those of his predecessors.) New elections thus took place in 1996. The center–right coalition *Polo per le libertá* ("Freedom Pole," comprising *Forza Italia*, *Alleanza nazionale*, and a Catholic moderate group) stood arrayed against an alliance led by the PDS, with the Olive Tree as its symbol. Contrary to what the world press widely reported, the Freedom Pole actually increased its share of the vote (6 percent over 1994), and obtained more votes than the Olive Tree grouping. However, the Northern League ran on its own, thereby depriving the center–right of a substantial share of the anti-left vote. In various constituencies, the unreconstructed Fascists likewise managed to gain enough votes to prevent center–right candidates from beating its left-wing opponents.

The PDS, the reformed Communists, now led the government. As Luigi Berlinguer, president of the PDS deputies, incautiously put it, "we have waited 40 years for this to happen." (Forty years earlier, Berlinguer's party had extolled Stalin as humanity's "immortal benefactor.") But now, the PDS did everything to make Italians forget the

16 Umberto Bossi (with Daniele Vimercati), *Vento dal Nord: la mia lega, la mia vita*, Torino, Sperling and Kupfer, 1992; Giulio Savelli, *Che cosa vuole la Lega*, Milan, Longanesi, 1992.

communist past. Though by far the largest party in the new governing coalition, the PDS appointed as candidate for the prime minister's office, Romano Prodi, a leftist Catholic with a blameless career. The hammer and sickle, as a party symbol, was consigned to the bottom of the olive tree. Moderation was the watchword for the future.

In all probability, the PDS would indeed have to tread carefully – for financial reasons alone. (In 1950, the public sector debt had amounted to 52 percent of the national debt; by 1993 it had risen to 120 percent. The burden of taxation had vastly increased, and so had the benefits and burdens of the welfare state.) Two out of every five Italians by now received some form of government largesse. Italy had indeed benefited greatly from her membership of the EU. (Her compliance with Euro-trade regulations had also improved; in 1995, Italy received fewer complaints for flouting Euro-trade rules than either Germany or France.) But the size of Italy's budgetary problem would make it difficult for Italy to satisfy existing requirements for joining EMU. As Martino, himself a distinguished economist, put it, Italy had become "a truly international country," with Swedish taxation, South American finance, and Angolan public services."[17]

For all its political instability and governmental corruption, Italy's general progress had nevertheless been remarkable.[18] From being a poverty-stricken country, Italy had become one of the world's major industrial states; Italians had gained fame in every cultural pursuit known to the Western world. The communist specter had disappeared. The power of the party bosses had diminished; that of the citizen-voters had grown. Italy, moreover, continued to show political vigor in local government. In certain respects, the city of Naples, for instance, proved a model. Naples had long been castigated for urban decay and pervasive civic corruption – a town where nothing worked well except the Camorra (the Neapolitan mafia). But during the mid-1990s, Naples revived under one of Italy's great reforming mayors, Antonio Bassolino (a former Communist who had switched to left-of-center). Public buildings were restored and newly painted. Parks reopened. Police protection improved. Garbage disposal once more functioned. Tourists came in ever-increasing numbers. The principal Camorra chiefs went to jail. More astonishing still, Neapolitan drivers stopped at the red light; even pedestrians began to obey traffic rules. An entire city apparently had begun to acquire civic responsibility. Italy would continue to astonish foreigners and natives alike.

Spain and Portugal: Democracy Consolidates

Spain in olden days was regarded as a land of bitter passions whose people rejoiced either in building or burning churches. The Spanish Civil War seemed to bear out these stereotypes. But all expectations to the contrary, post-Franco Spain turned out the very model

17 Antonio Martino, "Limping Forward," *National Review*, 20 May 1996, p. 27.
18 See Mark Gilbert, *The Italian Revolution: the End of Politics, Italian Style?* Boulder, Colo., Westview Press, 1994. Gianfranco Pasquino and Patrick McCarthy, eds, *The End of Post-war Politics in Italy*, Boulder, Colo., Westview Press, 1993; Matt Frei, *Getting the Boot: Italy's Unfinished Revolution*, New York, Times Books, 1995; Patrick McCarthy, *The Crisis of the Italian State: from the Origins of the Cold War to the Fall of Berlusconi*, New York, St Martin's Press, 1995; Robert Putnam, *Institutional Performance and Political Culture in Italy*, Cambridge, MA, Harvard University Press, 1988.

of judicious moderation. Given the extent of Spain's difficulties, this was a striking achievement. Not that all went well. By the mid-1990s, Spain suffered from extensive political corruption (though not on the Italian scale), from high labor costs, from a succession of strikes, and from high unemployment. Nevertheless, Spain was by past standards a prosperous country. Felipe Gonzales (head of the ruling Spanish Socialist Workers' Party, prime minister since 1982) commanded international respect. Spain was firmly linked to the EU. Spain gave extensive rights to its various regions, while preserving the unity of the Spanish state. The old quarrels between Church and anti-clericals ended. The army left politics and returned to the barracks. Right-wing authoritarianism and left-wing revolutionary socialism alike disappeared from the political arena. Spanish economic development accelerated, and for a time became the fastest in Europe. A highly *dirigiste* economy was liberalized — and this largely under Socialist auspices. Isolation ended as Spain — once known to its critics as a North African outcrop in Europe — became an active member of NATO (1981) and of the EU (1986). Whereas Italy remained preoccupied with the memories of Fascism, and Germany had to contend both with a Nazi and an East German communist past, Spain deliberately consigned to political oblivion both the Civil War and its bloodstained aftermath.[19] Spain emerged as a successful democracy, with a legitimate political order, and a vigorous civil society — all this with little bloodshed. Spain replicated success at home by success abroad. Spain assumed a place of some importance within the EU. Spain increased her economic influence in Spanish-speaking America where Spanish merchants, manufacturers, and investors found new markets. Spain's transformation from a military dictatorship to a constitutional state provided inspiration for Latin America where democracy henceforth made substantial progress. Spain also benefited indirectly from the expansion of Spanish in the US where, by dint of Hispanic immigration and expanding commerce with Latin America, Spanish became the most widely spoken and most widely studied foreign tongue.[20]

The premier architect of Spain's recovery was King Carlos whom we have discussed in chapter 6. Almost equally significant was Adolfo Suárez (in office as prime minister 1969–81). Suárez's name is not a household word among political scientists. It should be, for he played as important a role in Spain as Mikhail Gorbachev would later do in the Soviet Union, and F.W. de Klerk in South Africa. Suárez, a former Franco bureaucrat, relied on the UCD (Union of the Democratic Center), a middle-of-the-road party containing many former Franco supporters ("old dogs in new collars," as they were jokingly called). The Suárez government put into force a new constitution (ratified 1978) which provided

19 Stanley G. Payne, *The Franco Regime, 1936–1975*, Madison, Wisconsin, University of Wisconsin Press, 1987; *Politics and the Military in Modern Spain*, Stanford, CA, Stanford University Press, 1967; *Spain's First Democracy*, Madison, Wisconsin, University of Wisconsin Press, 1993; Raymond Carr and Juan Pablo Fusi Aizpurua, *Spain: Dictatorship to Democracy*, London, Allen and Unwin, 1979; Richard Gunther, Giacomo Sani and Goldie Shabad, *Spain after Franco: the Making of a Competitive Party System*, Berkeley, CA, University of California Press, 1988; Richard Gunther, "Spain and Portugal," in Dorfman and Duignan, eds, *Politics in Western Europe*, pp. 214–64; Victor M. Pérez-Díaz, *The Return of Civil Society: the Emergence of Democratic Spain*, Cambridge, MA, Harvard University Press, 1993; Paul Preston, *The Triumph of Democracy in Spain*, New York, Methuen, 1986.
20 By 1990 Spanish accounted for about 60 percent of all US high school instruction in foreign languages, as opposed to about 33 percent in 1968, and almost 0 percent in 1900. See "Auguries," *Orbis*, vol. 39, no. 2, Spring, 1995, pp. 313–14. Spanish advanced at the expense, in descending order, of Latin, French, and German.

for a constitutional monarchy, a bicameral legislature, and provincial rights. (Subsequent arrangements made Spain one of the most decentralized countries in Europe. The Basque country, *Catalunya*, and 15 additional regions received far-reaching concessions.) Spain, moreover, avoided imposing a uniform model across the country. Each region negotiated its own terms; Basques, Catalans, and Andalusians got more powers than the remainder. These compromises satisfied all provincial autonomists with the exception of Basque militants. It was a compromise which strikingly differentiated Spain from Italy.

Governmental moderation was replicated both on the right and on the left. The Church dropped out of politics. (Spain therefore never developed a Christian Democratic party of the German or Italian kind.) Manuel Fraga, formerly a Franquist minister, later leader of the conservative Alianza Popular, turned into a model of parliamentary propriety. So did Santiago Carrillo, the Communist leader, who turned his party from clandestine conspiracy to constitutional moderation and "Euro-communism." The Spanish Communist Party (PCE), which had once terrified the Spanish bourgeoisie, henceforth rejected Leninist doctrine concerning the "dictatorship of the proletariat" and "proletarian international-ism," while condemning the Soviet Union for invading Czechoslovakia and Afghanistan. Nevertheless, its electoral support kept declining, reducing a once powerful party to political insignificance.

Having refashioned Spain, the UCD likewise collapsed with startling rapidity. The 1982 elections gave an absolute majority to the Spanish Socialist Workers' Party (PSOE), led by Felipe Marquez Gonzalez (born 1942), a lawyer who had specialized in labor law, and set up a labor law office to help workers in his native Seville. From 1982 onward, Gonzalez established a personal regime that would rival or exceed in longevity Mitterrand's in France, Thatcher's in Britain, and Kohl's in Germany. (In 1993, Gonzalez was re-elected to his fourth term of office.)

The prime minister's achievements would have delighted an old-style monarch governing according to the rules of enlightened absolutism. Spain, one of Europe's most mountainous countries, had traditionally been divided by great geographical obstacles which had promoted provincial isolation. No more! The government invested great sums in highways, airports, and high-speed rail-lines. (During the early 1980s, something like 5 percent of the GDP was spent on public works.) Once-isolated parts of Spain became easily accessible; internal migration accelerated, with the result that Castilian was spoken more widely than before in regions such as the Basque country and Catalunya. Regional autonomists deplored the effect of such cultural shifts, but could not prevent them. (According to expert calculations, 60.8 percent of Barcelona's population by 1993 spoke Castilian as their first language. Only 34.2 percent of the city's people habitually used Catalan. The majority of Catalonian library users likewise preferred Castilian.)[21]

In a political sense, the Spanish socialists in effect dropped socialism for welfare capitalism. ("Radishes" went the all-European jokes concerning such compromisers, "Red outside, white inside.") Spain built its own kind of welfare state; nevertheless, tax expenditure in Spain remained less as a proportion of the GDP than in Canada, Germany, Austria, France, Belgium, Holland, Luxemburg, Sweden, and Denmark (in ascending order).[22] Industrialization proceeded apace. (Spain, for instance, became a substantial manufacturer of cars.) More impressive still was the expansion of the service industries which became Spain's greatest money-earner. By 1982, Spain's economic

21 Juan Gomez, "Parlem Catala," in *Cambios*, 16 August 1993, pp. 36–8.
22 "Economic Indicators," *The Economist*, 24 September 1994, p. 112.

structure essentially resembled France's – a far cry from Franquista eulogies to rural Spain. Spaniards thus ceased to migrate to north-western Europe in search of jobs. Instead, Spain herself attracted newcomers.

Spain's foreign policy was consistently pro-European. Spain, like Portugal, Italy, and Ireland, received EC subsidies to develop backward regions. The European Union placed several of its offices in Spain (including the Agency for Health and Safety at Work, and the European patent office). But Spain's Europhile commitment was based on more than financial advantages. After a lengthy period of isolation, Spaniards longed for their country to rejoin Western Europe, and they fully succeeded. Spain's attitude toward the US was more complex. Franco's generation had been traumatized by Spain's defeat in the Spanish–American War of 1898 and the loss of Cuba, Puerto Rico, and the Philippines. Spanish right-wingers thereafter detested the US with even greater venom than Britain (which continued to cling to Gibraltar, much to the Spanish military's disgust). But after Franco's death, these ancient quarrels were forgotten.

A number of new controversies took their place. The rise of militant Hispanic movements might have been expected to create a new interest in Spain's cultural legacy, in *hispanidad*. But Hispanic activists centered their attention on the US. To them, the Spanish *conquistadores* had been oppressors who had robbed the Indians of their land, their culture, their dignity. In a manner incomprehensible to Spain's tradition of *caballerosidad* (chivalry) Hispanic activists in the US claimed victim status from which European Spaniards ought properly to be excluded.

Within Spain, the US was at first censured by young Spaniards for having strengthened the Franco regime through defensive agreements with the Spanish dictatorship. (In fact, these military ties promoted "Americanization" within the armed forces, first of all within the navy and air force, later also the land army.) As we have seen before, Spain differed from Italy and resembled France in that few people had left the motherland to emigrate to the US – few letters, few visitors from friends and relatives in the US, few personal bonds. No wonder that Spanish capitalists as well as intellectuals widely enjoyed tweaking Uncle Sam's beard by supporting Fidel Castro (whose own family had descended from Spain). (In this respect Spain found support both from the Papacy and from the French government. Both opposed the US's continuing boycott of Cuba. Both hoped to transform Cuba through trade and investment rather than confrontation.) Nevertheless, Spain was willing enough to join NATO, and a majority of the electorate approved this choice in a referendum (1982).

Not that all went well thereafter. Spain suffered from a high rate of unemployment, numerous strikes, and relatively high inflation. In Spain, as in Italy, the birth rate dropped below replacement rate, and Spanish life became increasingly secularized. The ruling party, moreover, began to be afflicted by those symptoms which trouble any party overly long in power – complacency and a penchant for clientism. State-owned bodies such as INI (Instituto Nacional de Industria) accumulated heavy debts. Official malfeasance increased, even though corruption in Spain never reached Italian levels. Gonzalez depended on the Catalan National Party as a coalition partner, but the Catalan Party also became involved in corruption scandals. Violence continued in the Basque country where ETA (*Euskadi ta Askatasuna*, "Basque Homeland and Liberty") divided into ETA–Político-militar, and the more extremist ETA–Militar, considered itself at war with Madrid. As always, urban guerrilla warfare evoked counter-terrorism, as a shadowy state police organization, the Anti-Terrorist Liberation Groups (GAL), in turn committed murders of their own.

There was also a great deal of labor unrest. In 1994 alone, Spaniards endured more than a thousand strikes. Stoppages which would probably have paralyzed a major city in the US were regarded as not much more than an inconvenience in the Spanish capital whose citizens had to put up with slow-downs or interruptions in metro, train, and bus services. Spain lost more working hours through strikes than any other European country (estimated losses amounted to 600 work days per annum in Spain, 200 in Italy, and 90 in France). Under Franco, strikes had been prohibited. After Franco's demise, the Spanish workers regained the right to strike, and relished the new freedom which many of them equated with democracy. Spain was once again assailed by official scandals and corruption. Hence, in the 1996 elections, the conservatives gained a narrow victory. (The conservative People's Party, led by Jose Maria Aznar, gained 38.9 percent of the votes and 159 seats. Felipe Gonzalez and his Socialists won 37.5 percent of the votes and 141 seats.) However, even critics of malfeasance and of the new "strike culture" preferred shady dealings and labor unrest to the olden-day class struggles: better to stop work than burn convents! For aging Spaniards, who still remembered the Civil War, Spain's transformation was indeed miraculous.

Portugal in many ways differs from its Spanish neighbor. Portugal is a much smaller country, and does not have to contend with the same regional divisions which divide Spain. On the other hand, the Portuguese revolution (1974) had been more dramatic than Spain's peaceful transition from the Franco dictatorship. Decolonization proved a shattering experience for Portugal, perhaps even more severe than Spain's loss of Cuba (1899). Portuguese decolonization broke the dictatorship and, in a wider sense, changed the country's age-old trans-oceanic posture to engagement with Europe (and, coincidentally, Spain). Portugal, a founder member of EFTA (set up 1959), first applied to join the EC in 1977, and became a full member in 1986. (Portugal's trade with Spain in particular had previously been small, but thereafter rose rapidly.) In 1991, Portugal (and also Spain) ratified the Maastricht Treaty. Portuguese, like Spaniards, henceforth grumbled at bureaucratic and judicial interference from Brussels, but at the same time benefited from European aid (paid in the name of "cohesion" by the richer to the poorer EC countries).

Not that Portugal's overseas interests ended. Portuguese is spoken by an estimated 150,000,000 people throughout the world, by more persons than use German. Only about 10,000,000 Portuguese speakers are citizens of Portugal. The great majority of Lusophones live in Brazil. Much to the horror of linguistic purists in Portugal, a Portuguese Brazilian convention called for official recognition of the Portuguese phraseology evolved in Brazil, and other former Portuguese possessions. But Spain has more influence in Spanish-speaking America and more capital to export than Portugal has in Brazil. (The Portuguese in Brazil are subject to the same crude bar-room jokes told at the expense of Poles in the US, Irish in Britain, Belgians in Holland, and Frisians in Germany.) The Portuguese revolution and its aftermath confirmed that Portugal's future would be in Europe.

At the same time, Portuguese politics continued to move right. The Portuguese Socialist Party (PSP), led by Mario Lopes Soares, had formed its first government in 1976, and regained a majority in the 1983 elections. The Socialists, however, could never gain an absolute majority. Hence they depended on coalitions with more conservatively minded groups, including the Social Democratic Party, led by Anibal Cavaco Silva, prime minister from 1985. (He held a doctorate from York University, England, had a distinguished career both in academia and banking, and had widely published on economics, including budgetary policy and the public debt.) In the 1987 election, the PSD gained just over 50 percent of the votes, thereby providing Portugal with the first government since the 1974 revolution which held an overall majority. This success was repeated in the general election of 1991,[23] Soares having exchanged power for presidential dignity (1986). The heady days of the revolution now seemed light years away, and Portugal's – like Spain's – democratic future appeared unchallengeable.[24]

23 The PSD won 50.4 percent of the votes, and 135 seats. The PSP, led by Jorge Sampaio, won 30 percent and 72 seats. The Communists gained 8.8 percent and 17 seats on a joint platform with smaller parties. *Keesing's Record of World Events*, London, Longman, 1991, pp. 38545–6.
24 Richard A.H. Robinson, *Contemporary Portugal: a History*, London, Unwin, 1979; Walter C. Opello, Jr, *Portugal's Political Development: a Comparative Approach*, Boulder, Colo., Westview Press, 1985. *Portugal*, Boulder, Colo., Westview Press, 1991; Thomas C. Bruneau and Alex Macleod, *Politics in Contemporary Portugal: Parties and the Consolidation of Democracy*, Boulder, Colo., Westview Press, 1986.

PART IV

Transnational Cooperation and Conflict,
1975 to the Present

16

Keys to Western Security, 1975 to the Present

European Union

Overall, the EEC had proved a stunning success after 1958. Trade barriers diminished between EEC members (custom barriers finally ended in 1968). The EEC (later known as the EC, European Community, 1965, then the EU, European Union, 1992) went a long way in assuring the free movement of workers within its boundaries. Labor unions as well as capitalists discovered the merits of transnational cooperation. Existing obstacles to the free transfer of capital diminished. The EEC set up a variety of transnational agencies. There was a striking expansion of commerce between the EEC's members, and also between the EEC as a whole, EFTA, and foreign countries, including the US. Living standards improved. The EEC states (with West Germany, France, Italy, and the three Benelux states as founder members) cooperated politically as well as economically. The idea of a new war between France and Germany, or France and Britain, or Britain and Germany thereafter seemed inconceivable, a subject either for jokes or nightmares. It was an astonishing story, and the US could take some credit for having helped to turn the dream into a reality.[1]

An association such as the EEC, built on innumerable compromises, could not escape constant conflict. Leaders such as de Gaulle and, later, Mrs Thatcher, remained determined that the EEC should remain a loose association of sovereign states; their vision of the future was very different from the "Europeanists" or federalists strongly entrenched within the EEC's growing bureaucracy. There were innumerable problems which derived from the economic disparity between the industrial core states and the backward agricultural periphery. This disparity led to massive labor migration from countries such as Portugal, Spain, South Italy, Yugoslavia, Turkey, to the industrialized north. To cure these problems, EEC planners attempted to subsidize industrial development in backward regions – with dubious results. There were unresolved party issues between Christian democrats and socialists. Moreover, from the very start of the EEC, the German reunification issue loomed in the background. (In endorsing the EEC treaties, the West

---

1 The literature on European unification is immense. See, for instance, Peter Duignan and L.H. Gann, *The Rebirth of the West: the Americanization of the Democratic World 1945–1958*, Oxford, Blackwell, 1991; Gerald Dorfman and Peter Duignan, *Politics in Western Europe*, Stanford, CA, Hoover Institution Press, 1991, esp. ch. 13; Ian Thomson, *The Documentation of the European Communities: a Guide*, London, Mansell, 1989; Stanley A. Budd and Alun Jones, *The European Community: a Guide to the Maze*, London, Kogan Page, 1987; Richard Mayne, ed., *Handbooks to the Modern World: Western Europe*, New York, Facts on File, 1986, p. 643; Also see, by the same author, *The Recovery of Europe*, London, Harper and Row, 1970; and Stanley Hoffmann, "The European Community and 1992," *Foreign Affairs*, Fall 1989, pp. 27–47.

Map 3   The European Free Trade Association (EFTA) and the European Union
Source: Modified from Peter Duignan and L.H., Gann,
The Rebirth of the West, Oxford, Blackwell, 1992, p. 719

German SPD insisted that they would only accept the agreements on the assumption that these would not make more difficult the unification of Germany.) Above all, agricultural politics in Western Europe remained nationalistic and protectionist after 1957.

The EEC did not solve all these difficulties. Whereas some countries (The Netherlands and Denmark) were aggressively for free trade, others (Germany and France) were protectionist in agriculture and high-tech industries. The Common Agricultural Policy (CAP) (financed by the EC from 1969 onward) aimed at rationalizing agricultural policies. This proved a hard assignment, given the profound sociological differences between highly urbanized countries such as Great Britain, endowed with an efficient, highly mechanized farming industry, and countries such as France, West Germany, Italy, and Spain where small farmers remained numerous and influential in politics (especially in the Christian Democratic parties). Helped by protection, or by guaranteed prices much higher than those prevailing on the world markets, European farmers produced mountains of surplus grain, grapes, butter, and beef. Hence tension increased among the states of the EC, and also with the US. CAP promoted bureaucratic growth: 96 percent of EC regulations came to deal with agriculture. The key weakness of the EC's agricultural system was its price policy and subsidies which encouraged a massive rise in the production of unnecessary farm products. These problems of over-production became even more acute after the 1960s. So did trade difficulties derived from the association of the "overseas territories" of EEC members with the Treaty of Rome – tackled only in part by the Treaty of Jaunde in 1962.

Contentious also was the British question. EC policy was in the main determined by a Franco-German *entente*, solidified by close personal relations between German chancellor Helmut Schmidt (in office 1972–82), and French president Valéry Giscard d'Estaing (in power 1974–81). The British felt themselves particularly aggrieved in the field of agriculture where the British were among the most efficient producers, and resented having to pay excessively high prices for food so as to subsidize continental, especially French and German, farmers. Americans likewise criticized EC farm policies, which discriminated against US agricultural exports. During the Falklands War, US public opinion and the US government staunchly backed Britain – much more so than any European country.

The EC had other problems. There was the oil shock of 1973, and experts suddenly forecast an everlasting shortage of energy. The economics of Western Europe experienced a downturn; the "30 golden years" after World War II ended. The rise of mass unemployment led governments to give priority to national interests at the EC's expense. Traditional industries such as steel, textiles, and shipbuilding declined; yet Europeans discovered that they were being outdone in high technology by the US and Japan. "Euro-pessimism" was in the air. Europe seemed to fall behind.

The 1970s, however, were not simply a barren epoch. In 1973, Denmark and Ireland as well as Britain joined the EC. (Only Norway kept aloof, after a bitterly fought referendum in 1972, the second instance, with Britain, where EC membership turned into a passionate political issue.) Parliamentary governance returned to Portugal and Spain after a long-lasting era of authoritarian rule. (This peaceful changeover facilitated the admission of these two countries to the EC in 1986, following Greece's adherence in 1981.) In 1975, the EC set up a Regional Development Fund and a Regional Development Committee to give assistance to the EC's own "backward areas." More importantly, perhaps, in 1978 Helmut Schmidt and Giscard d'Estaing created as their joint brainchild the European Monetary System (EMS), with its own currency, the ECU (both an acronym and the name of an ancient French gold coin). The EMS was designed in part to deal with the problems arising from the US decision to scrap the postwar system of fixed exchange rates and to replace it with floating rates. The EMS aimed at a tighter system, but in practice became "a Deutschmark zone." In 1979, as we have seen, the EC was further strengthened by the first direct election to the European Parliament.

In a more general sense, the late 1970s witnessed a general disenchantment with Keynesian policies, increasing distrust toward the regulatory state, state direction, and the real or assumed imperfections of the welfare state. (Even in Sweden, the very homeland of welfarism, the 44-year rule of the Social Democrats was temporarily broken in 1976 by a "bourgeois" coalition.) Free-enterprise economics became intellectually respectable. In 1977, Milton Friedman received the Nobel Prize and, in 1979, Margaret Thatcher became Prime Minister of Britain, determined to turn her country into an enterprise state. (She was re-elected in 1983 and 1987.) In the US Ronald Reagan moved into the White House (1981) replacing a Democrat, Jimmy Carter, and stayed for two terms, thereby continuing a period of Republican domination over the US executive branch of government. In West Germany, Helmut Kohl stepped into the chancellor's office in 1982, heading a CDU–FDP coalition. In the same year, François Mitterrand assumed the presidency of France. Mitterrand was a socialist who had invigorated the Socialist Party. Nevertheless, his election also signified a shift away from the extreme left, as the Socialists in 1978, for the first time since 1936, had garnered more votes than the Communists.

The Atlantic economies (especially the US economy) began to recover from the oil shock of 1973; oil became less expensive and plentiful. The winds of change were now blowing from the right. Even Communist leaders (such as Santiago Carrillo in Spain, and Enrico Berlinguer in Italy) were calling for ideological revision of their respective parties' doctrine – a remarkable reassessment that paralleled far-reaching shifts in the Soviet Union itself. The European economies did relatively well, despite widespread unemployment. The EMS performed more effectively than its critics had imagined. Even the British cooperated with the EMS, even though they did not, for the time being, join the system. Moreover, in 1984, the Europeans reformed CAP to make it less expensive (CAP had absorbed about 70 percent of the Community's budget), and to render CAP more acceptable to the British, and less wasteful. Priority was given to the reduction of those "lakes of wine" and "mountains of butter" whose existence consumers in socialist countries would have envied. In addition, the EC, in 1985, set up an Integrated Mediterranean Program to help its backward southern periphery, and Italy, in particular, stressed its "Mediterranean vocation."

The extension of the EC went with a new challenge that none had considered at the time the Community had been formed. Europe bought from Japan the most advanced industrial products available: cars, computers, videocassette recorders and their like. As Chalmers Johnson, an American scholar, put it, the movement toward unity in Europe entailed a clear-cut trade strategy aimed at recapturing competitive ability from Japan, and the United States.[2]

There was likewise political rivalry between the EC and the US, rivalry even between the US and Germany, the latter Washington's main ally. (The US and Germany, for instance, differed in their attitude toward the Iranian dictatorship. Washington tried to isolate Iran. Bonn, by contrast, applied to Iran the equivalent of their former *Ostpolitik* toward East Germany, seeking to "soften" the enemy by trade and investment.)

Nevertheless, the EC and the US agreed on the major policy objectives, and the EC turned out to be a stunning success. By 1984, 40 years after the Normandy invasion (and before Spain and Portugal joined) the EC's gross domestic product amounted to about two-thirds of the US's ($2,400.4 billion as against $3,627.9 billion). Its population was larger than the US's (272 million as against 232 million.) The EC's exports were larger than the US's ($227.2 billion as against $217.88 billion.) The EC's members between them maintained more men under arms than the US (2,109,000 as against 2,350,000).

2 This chapter draws heavily on Peter Duignan and L.H. Gann, *The United States and the New Europe, 1945–1993*, Oxford, Blackwell, 1994, pp. 53–9.

Indisputably, moreover, the Western European states became more firmly integrated into a wider Atlantic community, and at the same time drew more closely together and lived peacefully. Led by statesmen such as Helmut Kohl, Germany's new Bismarck, the EC became a permanent fixture, in which was firmly embedded as its greatest constituent first West Germany, then reunited Germany. Henceforth, a Franco-German war, or an Anglo-French war, conflicts of a kind familiar to earlier generations, had become inconceivable. West Germany remained firmly cemented into the European community, linked to its Western neighbors by NATO, trade, tourism and by a great variety of ties through civil servants, trade unionists, academics, and businessmen from different countries. The EC likewise created new bonds between politicians faced with new tasks that often transcended traditional divisions within their own countries. As a Belgian parliamentarian put it, "in all our countries religion is terribly important. It binds together every Catholic party in Europe, both leftists and conservatives, simply because they are Catholics ... In Europe people can sort themselves out on different lines."[3]

Europeans thereafter improved the machinery of economic cooperation. In 1968, the last customs barriers had come down within the EC. The EC went a long way in assuring the free movement of workers within its boundaries. The treaties guaranteed Community workers equality of treatment in terms of employment, wages, and other working conditions. The movement of capital was liberalized. The Community developed a comprehensive policy regarding research and technology. Moreover, the EC also profited again from strong leadership in the late 1980s. Jacques Delors, president of the EC Commission from 1985 on, was a man cast in the Monnet mold. (Delors had started life as a banker, later rose to be chief of social affairs in the Plan Monnet, a Socialist cabinet minister, wedded to that blend of Christian democracy and social reformism that had provided the Community's original inspiration.) Delors stood resolved both to improve the EC and extend its scope. From June to December 1985, the Intergovernmental Conference (IGC) met to work out reforms of the EC treaties for the Luxembourg meeting of the European Council. The European Council thus has led the drive for a unified internal market. In 1985 it asked the Commission to put forward a proposal for achieving a unified internal market by 1992. A few months later the Commission published a 93-page report with almost 300 specific suggestions to remove restrictions with dates for council approval before December 1992. In 1986 the EC promulgated the Single European Act (entering into force on 1 July 1987, a date that future generations of European school children will probably have to memorize for their history examinations).

The Single European Act (SEA) made many changes in legislative procedures, brought better political cooperation in foreign policy matters (European Political Cooperation, EPC) within the framework of the European communities. Most importantly, the SEA worked for further economic and monetary union, and extended policy areas of concern beyond the legal framework of the 1957 treaty. The SEA, for instance, introduced a new system of voting whereby most EC decisions could henceforth be made by a qualified majority, whereas previously most had been made under a unanimity rule. The switch to a qualified majority was intended to strengthen Brussels as against the governments of member states. But there were unintended consequences. The unanimity rule had imposed a specific discipline on member states. Issues likely to fail were rarely brought

3 See Daniel J. Nelson, *Defenders or Intruders? The Dilemmas of US Forces in Germany*, Boulder, Colo., Westview Press, 1987.

up before the Council of Ministers in the first place. This was true because a single dissenting vote would not only defeat the issue in question, but also weaken confidence in the working of the EC as a whole. Under the qualified majority rule, by contrast, member states could afford divisive issues to be brought before the Council of Ministers with much less concern than previously. Hence there was more bickering than before, and more opportunity for posturing to impress nationalists at home.

Nevertheless, public opinion as yet wisely favored a European superstate. Whereas the Treaty of Rome in 1957 had drawn its main inspiration from bureaucrats, intellectuals, politicians, and magnates of heavy industry, the program for EC "1992," the new target date, by contrast received support from corporate capitalists engaged in a broad range of enterprises which had already extended the scale of their operations through massive trans-frontier mergers. EC "1992" was backed likewise by professionals with transnational outlets for their respective skills, and by those who wanted a united Europe for its own sake; they were generally a confident lot. The EC had succeeded beyond its makers' most cheerful dreams.

Maastricht and Beyond

The 1970s had seen some economic dislocation and "Euro-pessimism." During the 1980s, however, there was economic recovery through most of the Western world. The EC continued to do well; not surprisingly, there were applications from new members which hoped that their adhesion to the EC would strengthen their democratic institutions, aid economic development, and provide them with largesse from the EC's richer states. The first of the new applicants was Greece (1981). Its accession marked a new chapter in the EC's history as the EC now extended to the eastern Mediterranean, and as Greece constituted the first Orthodox state within a union hitherto dominated by Catholics and Protestants. But Greece also brought into the EC its long-standing conflict with Turkey, while involving the EC directly in the affairs of the Balkans with their enormous potential for future ethnic strife. Even more important was the admission of Spain and Portugal (1986). With the accession of the two Iberian states, the EC's population grew from some 272,000,000 to over 320,000,000, thereby considerably enlarging the EC's internal market. The new arrangements enhanced the influence of the southern, less industrialized, and more "peripheral" countries within the EC at the expense of the more prosperous states. (Spain's estimated GDP per head of the population in 1984 was 73 percent of the EC's average; Portugal's only 46 percent.)

Despite these successes, a genuinely free-trade zone proved hard to achieve. For one thing, compliance with the great volume of EC regulations varied (with Britain's record the best, Italy's and Greece's the worst). Aggrieved firms might complain to national judges or to the European Court. But the Court worked at a snail's speed. (By the end of 1990, EC governments had failed to carry out 51 of its rulings; Italy alone had ignored 22 rulings.) The French government was another offender as Paris feared far more the wrath of French farmers blocking highways than polite recriminations on the part of France's EC partners.

Beset by many restrictions, the EC continued to lag behind Japan and the US in many high-tech industries, including bio-technical industries and computers. Trade within the EC was obstructed by restrictive regulations imposed by member governments under all sorts of pretexts: industrial safety, health, quality control. These barriers, in particular, impeded those small innovative companies that had played such a major part in the US in pioneering new industries and creating new jobs. (Firms doing business in other EC countries had to cope, among other impediments, with vexatious border inspection of goods in transit, differential taxation, differential forms of quality control, differential patent law.) Effective unification entailed the creation of a common market for technical skills – hard to achieve in a continent where inherited guild traditions remained strong in some member states (particularly Germany), and where qualifications for professional people varied widely from country to country. Standardization was equally difficult to achieve in the realm of technical specifications for products such as telephones, telex, electronic equipment. Standardization was equally needful in transnational financial services concerned with insurance policies, mortgages, consumer credit, and such like. Freedom, argued the interventionists, paradoxically required an interventionist superstate.

The most outstanding among the new interventionists was Jacques Delors (President of the European Commission from 1985). As head of the European Commission, he could rely on a small but effective corps of advisers, and thereby managed to concentrate power in his own office. Delors was French to the core. He mainly drew on French advisers; he used a Frenchified administration; he desired a new Europe resembling the French Fifth Republic. The European Council would serve as a collective head of state, resembling the French presidency. The Commission would serve as the executive, responsible both to the European Council and the European Parliament. The new Europe would pursue a common foreign policy; hence rules regarding unanimity among participating governments would have to be modified in certain respects. Delors also wished to endow a European Union with a social purpose. As he saw it, competition between great capitalist conglomerates must be balanced by joint action for social justice. Delors' grand design found support among the Euro-bureaucracy, among great corporations with transnational ties, among a growing number of socialists (including British Labourites who had in the past looked askance at the European idea), and among enthusiasts for a European superpower able to outface the US and Japan.

According to Delors, the EC also faced serious structural problems which only closer union would solve. All advanced nations were beset by unemployment. But Europe's were especially severe. (Between 1970 and 1990, the US and Japan had created 29,000,000 and 12,000,000 new jobs respectively. The EC had added 9,000,000 jobs, but an unduly high proportion were in the public sector.) Free marketeers blamed excessive state intervention, excessive labor regulation, and excessive labor costs for these problems. But Delors and his followers believed that these ills could at least in part be cured by European unification. Delors was backed by Kohl and Mitterrand whose political longevity matched their respective personal ability. For Kohl, an effective European union would banish the ghosts of Germany's past. For Mitterrand, European union would still assure France a glorious future. From a cautious functionalism, EC policy-makers turned to building a European superstate.

As noted earlier, the cause of European unity scored the first major success through the Single European Act (SEA) in 1987. At first sight the provisions of the Act looked modest enough. (The London *Economist* called it "a smiling mouse.")[4] But the Act had far-reaching consequences. It aimed at turning into a reality the EC's original goal of making Europe a single market, a "Europe without frontiers," where people, goods, services, and capital could move freely. The EC's political institutions and bureaucracy would gain additional power – to the intense disapproval of critics such as Margaret

4 *The Economist*, 30 November 1991, p. 47.

Thatcher. The jurisdiction of the European Court would extend; regional aid, research, environmental safeguards would be strengthened. So would the powers of the European Parliament, thereby lessening what Kohl called the EC's "democratic deficit."

The federalists' greatest concern was to establish EMU (European Monetary Union). The first stone was laid in this structure with the creation of the EMS (European Monetary System) in 1979. This began as a device to manage exchange rates at a time when most EC currencies were apt to depreciate against the then all-mighty D-Mark. During the 1980s, the EC countries collaborated most effectively in reducing inflation (down from 21.2 to 5 percent in Italy; from 13.6 to 2.7 percent in France; from 5.5 to 1.2 percent in Germany between 1980 and 1988). Following this striking success, a committee was set up in 1988 under Delors' chairmanship. This produced the "Report on Economic and Monetary Union in the European Community" known as the Delors Report which set out a three-stage process. A summit in Madrid in June 1989 agreed that the first stage toward EMU should start in 1990, and that an intergovernmental conference should work out the later stages. The next summit, held at Strasbourg in December of the same year, decided that the crucial conference would be held at the end of 1991, at Maastricht, eastern Holland. What was at stake, as Stanley Hoffman put it in a masterly survey, was "the future of the nation-state in Western Europe. Delors's logic is ultimately the construction of a federal state . . . legitimacy would be provided by universal suffrage, expressed in the election of the European Parliament."[5]

By the time the Maastricht conference assembled, communism had collapsed in East Central Europe; when the conference ended in 1992 the Soviet Union had itself disintegrated. The resultant euphoria did not prevent hard bargaining. The final agreement embodied a transnational compromise. Generally speaking, German views prevailed regarding the future of EMU; the French, in the main, had their way over political union; Britain insisted on its continued right to opt out of specific arrangements such as the EU's new social charter; Portugal, Spain, Greece, and Ireland received concessions with regard to subsidies paid by the "rich" to the "poor" states within the EU. The new arrangement defined its aim as "an ever closer union of the nations of Europe," in the 1957 Treaty of Rome. The new agreement extended the EU's powers in environment, education, consumer protection, health, and an all-European infrastructure, and also set up a schedule for EMU. There was equal concern for a common foreign and security policy, to be achieved by voluntary cooperation. Defense was to be coordinated with NATO, and the WEU (Western European Union) was to serve as the EU's military arm. (Nine out of the 12 EU members were members of the WEU.) Members, moreover, would work together on immigration and political asylum, on organized crime and the narcotics trade. A Europol was to be set up to become a European CID or FBI.

The Treaty on Monetary and Political Union extended for Brussels far-reaching new powers over the nation-states in the EU. The treaty would create a single European currency by 1 January 1999, with a common monetary policy and an independent central bank. States would have to meet strict economic standards (on inflation, cutting subsidies,

5 Stanley Hoffman, "The European Community and 1992," *Foreign Affairs*, Fall 1989, p. 41. See also Derek W. Urwin, *The Community of Europe: a History of European Integration since 1945*, London, Longman, 1991, esp. pp. 234–7; Michael Burgess, *Federalism and European Union: Political Ideas, Influences and Strategies in the European Community, 1972–1987*, London, Routledge, 1989; Roger Morgan, *West European Politics since 1945: the Shaping of the European Community*, London, Batsford, 1972.

and attaining a balanced budget) before they could substitute their respective national currencies for the ECU. According to advocates of the Maastricht Treaty, all members would benefit. A genuine single market, with common standards, a single customs system, and a single currency would help to create a new prosperity. The European Parliament would gain new powers, including the right to ratify treaties, block or amend EU laws by a majority vote, and the right to be consulted on the appointment of new Euro-commissioners. European Monetary Union would facilitate the free movement of capital within Europe – as yet divided into separate financial markets with different rules.

Euro-wins and Euro-failures

From its beginning, however, the EU suffered from an identity crisis. Was it an association of sovereign states (de Gaulle's and Mrs Thatcher's concept)? Or was it to be a superstate in which members would surrender their sovereignty? From the beginnings of the EEC, the Eurocrats had fudged the issue through Monnet's functional approach. The Maastricht Treaty's diction only reflected these fundamental inconsistencies. The accords were poorly drafted, cast in Euro-legalese hardly intelligible even to experts. With its opaque language and ambiguities, the Maastricht document constituted neither an ordinary treaty nor a constitution comparable to the US constitution, with its internal logic and clear separation of powers.

The architects of Maastricht held certain fundamental assumptions. The formation of a European superstate had become a historical necessity. Existing European nation-states had become obsolete in their present form; only great transnational units would guarantee future prosperity. Nation-states would therefore have to devolve some of their existing authority. Power would flow upwards to new supranational authorities, and downwards to regional bodies at the base of the pyramid.

These assumptions, however, did not work. True enough, the constant growth of the power of central governments had indeed made desirable greater autonomy for regional or local authorities. (Federalism, indeed, worked well alike in Germany, Switzerland, Austria, and the US.) Nevertheless, the nation-state remained economically viable. (The world's most successful countries, the US and Japan, were nation-states. In East Germany, 40 years of communist indoctrination had failed to create a separate East German nation.) More importantly, the existing nation-states of Western Europe retained an emotional appeal which no supranational authority could match. In this respect, they were quite different from the defunct Yugoslavia and the defunct Soviet Union whose authority symbols had long been hated by the disaffected. No Euro-celebration could match the dignity and splendor embodied in such national events as a royal wedding in Britain. Nor did administrative devolution from the center to the regions necessarily entail the emergence of new states. During the 1970s, in particular, enthusiasts had predicted the emergence of new states – an independent Flanders, Wallonia, Wales, Scotland – but Britain, Belgium, and Spain held together for practical as well as emotional reasons. (Recipients of welfare payments or of official salaries, for instance, would rather rely for their benefits on long-existing nation-states than on new states with unknown financial credentials.)

Agreement on the future of the EU was therefore hard to achieve. The British, under John Major, would have preferred a European union which concentrated its energies on establishing free trade, while leaving the maximum of power to member states (a policy with which we personally sympathize). The British, in our view, also pursued a sounder labor policy than their European neighbors. Changes in British employment law made hiring and firing easier than on the continent. Having curbed the power of trade unions, the British experienced fewer strikes than before, and improved efficiency by changing work practices without hindrance. British firms reduced fringe benefits not included in the ordinary wage bill. Britain lacked a minimum wage law. Hence Britain's unemployment rate, though high (8.3 percent in 1995) was lower than the EU's average. Not surprisingly, London looked at Maastricht with skepticism. But even France and Germany, the EU's most devoted supporters and the closest of allies, failed to see eye to eye on fundamental issues. Helmut Kohl wished to give priority to the EU's eastward expansion, thereby fortifying Germany's traditional place in *Mitteleuropa*. The French, by contrast, desired the EU to give more attention and more money to the Mediterranean, especially North Africa where France would star as the premier power.

There was dissension also with regard to the powers of the legislature. Kohl wished the European Parliament to become the Union's key legislative body, with the Council of Ministers turning into Europe's Upper House, and the European Commission in Brussels as the *de facto* government. The French preferred real power to stay with the Council of Ministers where the member governments wielded effective control. Unlike the Germans, the French wished to preserve an individual veto on major decisions. As against Germany's federal vision, the French stuck to a union of nation-states.

Even more contentious was EMU, the proposed European Monetary Union. According to its advocates, EMU would facilitate trade and also restrict the ability of national governments to pursue inflationary policies. "One Market – One Money" went the EMU supporters' slogan. But, said the critics, Germany would be the strongest party in EMU. Germany would therefore have to insist on strong political leverage within EMU, even if all prospective members were to meet the stringent financial conditions set down under the Maastricht Treaty. Otherwise, Germany would be writing a blank check against its financial resources. Having experienced the trauma of two runaway inflations after two successive world wars, German citizens would be reluctant to substitute an untried Euro-currency for the trusted D-Mark.

Dissension was also loud in France. By 1995, something like 3,000,000 French were unemployed; another 2,000,000 were in dire financial straits, heavily dependent on support from the state. The extreme right had become influential (representing about one-fifth of the electorate), and the right bitterly opposed the mainstream parties' commitment to the EU. France, it appeared, would now find it almost impossible to meet the terms of joining EMU. France would have to reduce its budget deficit from 5.7 to 3 percent of the gross domestic product. But doing so would prevent President Chirac from pursuing some of his plans to create new jobs, such as lowering taxes. (Chirac's election to the presidency in 1995 was itself a blow to the federalist cause, as his Socialist opponent Lionel Jospin and Chirac's conservative competitor Edouard Balladur had both attacked the new president for his inadequate commitment to the EU and a strong France.)[6]

The Maastricht Treaty was, therefore, in deep trouble. Many Europeans had come to fear the power of Brussels, the potential controls of an EMU with a single currency and one central bank. Delors and company had gone too fast in trying to create an economic and political union with a socialist social charter. Citizens of the member states of the EU feared the loss of national sovereignty over the growth of a European superstate. For them,

6 Gail Russel Chaddock, "France's New Leader Chirac . . . ," *Christian Science Monitor*, 9 May 1995, pp. 1, 8.

Maastricht was illiberal, authoritarian, and interventionist. While Maastricht proffered a redistributive policy for the poorer members, it also restricted their freedom of action, as they had to comply with a high cost social charter and tie their interest rates, rates of inflation, and deficits to the Deutschmark. This also hurt states such as Britain.

The Maastricht Treaty raised equally troublesome questions in other European countries. Belgium insisted that the "convergence" criteria set out in the treaty should be relaxed. Italy suggested that the project should be postponed, presumably until such time as Italy would be ready. France rejected German proposals for tougher rules. Germany experienced quarrels between those who regarded financial orthodoxy as their highest priority, and those who desired the project to go forward for the sake of integrating Germany into Europe. Opinion was equally divided in Britain where pro-marketeers praised Brussels, whilst opponents denounced "The Rotten Heart of Europe."[7] Maastricht also entailed other kinds of interference with the rights of sovereign states. For instance, Maastricht would have given citizens of Italy working in France the right to vote in French local elections, or allowed the European Court in Luxembourg to impose high unemployment benefits on foreign workers in another state.

For EMU advocates such as Kohl, a common currency would create a common political consciousness, thereby firmly encasing Germany into Europe. But a common dollar in the US had not prevented civil war between North and South. Even in purely economic terms – Kohl's critics insisted – the EU does not need an EMU with one currency, one central bank. Except for reducing transaction costs with one currency, there are mostly hardships to having an EMU. The EU is too diverse in terms of the levels of economic development among the member nations to be regulated by one central bank. National economic policy should be written by those who know the local conditions and not by Brussels following the *Bundesbank*. The EU should rather implement in full the reforms of the Single European Act. The free movement of people, goods, services, and capital throughout the 12 states of the community would bring economic prosperity to all 300 million people (340 million if former EFTA states are added) and would make all of Europe more efficient and competitive. After the economies have converged, then implementing an EMU and EU can continue. The best future for Europe is a liberal, pragmatic, free-market customs union joining the EC, the former EFTA members, and some additional states – not a superstate with heavy control and interventionist policies ruled from Brussels.

In any case, pleads Martin Feldstein, one of the US's most distinguished economists, free trade between different countries does not require a single currency. (No one suggested that the US, Canada, and Mexico should give up their respective national coinage when they approved the North American Free Trade Agreement (NAFTA) in 1992.) The transaction costs entailed by separate currencies for transnational traders have greatly diminished as the result of sophisticated new banking methods. The advantages of a unified currency should be set against the disadvantages created for individual member states in losing the right to pursue an independent national policy. "An artificially contrived economic and monetary union might actually reduce the volume of trade between NATO members."[8] By 1995, moreover, only Germany and Luxembourg met

---

7 Bernard Connolly, *The Rotten Heart of Europe*, London, Faber, 1995.
8 Martin Feldstein, "The Case against EMU," *The Economist*, 13 June 1992, pp. 19–23. For another position, see Tommaso Padoa-Schioppa, *The Road to Monetary Union in Europe: the Emperor, the Kings, and the Genies*, New York, Oxford University Press, 1994.

the Maastricht criteria of low interest rates, low budget deficits, and low public debt. Not surprisingly, German finance minister Theo Waigel considered a currency union by 1997 to be "highly unlikely."[9]

Maastricht posed many more problems. How far, for example, should the powers of the European Commission be extended? The smaller countries looked to a strong Commission as an ally against the large states – Germany, Britain, and France. The large countries, by contrast, wished to clip the Commission's wings. Hence they welcomed Delors' departure from the presidency, and his replacement in 1994 by Jacques Santer. (Santer, formerly prime minister of Luxembourg, was a Christian Democrat, a practicing Catholic, a man of conciliatory disposition who lacked Delors' abrasiveness, and his delight in confronting the EU's largest partners.)

Other controversies hinged on economic issues other than EMU. Should, or should not, the EU attempt to pursue an industrial policy, whereby public authority would support favored industries at the taxpayer's expense?[10] Past failures in public planning provided strong arguments for those who questioned the public planners' ability to "pick winners." Equally controversial was the principle of "cohesion" whereby the rich regions should subsidize the poorest regions, a policy first proclaimed by the Single European Act. The EU's peripheral states – Ireland, Spain, Portugal, Greece, South Italy – naturally favored such development subsidies. So did poverty-stricken areas within the most developed countries, particularly those hit by industrial decay, or by declining farm incomes. (By 1993, something like one-quarter of the EU's budget went to so-called regional funds.) Tax-payers in developed countries were, however, loud in their complaints, particularly those in Germany which faced the burden of rebuilding the *Länder* formerly contained within the German Democratic Republic. "Cohesion" entailed bureaucratic warfare within contending directorates of the EU. There was waste and corruption. (The Court of Auditors, charged with detecting fraud, only had 80 investigators who lacked prosecutorial powers. Member countries had no incentive to police themselves. On the contrary, a country which reported its sins had to pay back the money lost. Those who reported nothing paid nothing.) Hence opposition to "cohesion" grew all the more adamant, as EU aid kept expanding year by year.[11]

Defenders of national sovereignty also found fault with the "European citizenship" created by Maastricht in tandem with existing national citizenships. Euro-citizens would be able to vote, not only for the European Parliament, but also in local municipal elections throughout the EU, wherever they lived and worked. Hence foreigners might

9 *This Week in Germany*, May 1995.

10 Bruce Barnard, "Confronting Industrial Policy: the View from Europe," *Europe*, October 1993, pp. 29–33.

11 Kyle Pope, "European Union's Aid to its Poor Nations Wasting Billions," *The Wall Street Journal*, 3 April 1995, pp. 1, 5. For a more general review of Euro-institutions, see Duignan and Gann, *The United States and the New Europe*; Leon Hurwitz and Christian Lequesne, *The State of the European Community*, vol. 1: *Policies, Institutions, and Debates in the Transition Years*, Boulder, Colo., Lynne Rienner, 1991; Alan W. Cafruny and Glenda G. Rosenthal, *The State of the European Community*, vol. 2: *The Maastricht Debates and Beyond*, Boulder, Colo., Lynne Rienner, 1993; Carolyn Rhodes and Sonia Mazey, eds, *The State of the European Union*, vol. 3: *Building a European Polity?* Boulder, Colo., Lynne Rienner, 1995; Desmond Dinan, *Ever Closer Union? An Introduction to the European Community*, Boulder, Colo., Lynne Rienner, 1994. The pro-European view is put most strongly by one of the EU's architects, Lord Cockfield, *The European Union: Creating the Single Market*, London, Wiley, 1994.

obtain a key vote in frontier towns and frontier villages, or in resort communities (in France the Maastricht provisions concerning the franchise for foreigners in local government elections necessitated a change in the constitution). Under the new dispensation, workers and professionals would be able to move freely in Europe (from 1995 onward also citizens of EFTA states). These new opportunities were welcomed by many, but also aroused opposition; for instance, Germans feared that Portuguese and Polish building workers would take over much of the industry because of their lower wages; the Swiss in particular dreaded an invasion of professionals from abroad, and also of land-buyers. The EU agreed in principle to a common visa policy, though asylum and immigration would continue to be determined by individual member states. This was an important provision for European electorates frightened of future mass immigration. During the prosperous 1950s and 1960s, newcomers had been welcomed. The mood changed when refugees flooded into Germany after the fall of the Wall and unemployment became rife (particularly in France and Germany), and immigrants appeared to threaten the jobs of native-born people, especially those without marketable qualifications.

Immigration created many new problems, even in the US where Americans at least assumed that legal immigrants would stay, and in turn acquire US citizenship. In Europe, by contrast, laws concerning citizenship were generally more restrictive. (For instance, a child born in the US automatically became a citizen − not so a foreigner's baby born in Germany. In the US, an alien with the right residential and related qualifications had a right to be naturalized. In Britain, by contrast, naturalization was a privilege accorded to the recipient at the Home Secretary's discretion.) To call oneself an Arab-American or a Greek-American or a Turkish-American did not sound peculiar in the US; few Germans, by contrast, would refer to a foreign neighbor respectively as an Arab-German, a Greek-German, or a Turkish-German, nor would an Irish immigrant or his children in Britain call themselves Anglo-Irish.

Popular opinion, of course, vastly overestimated the extent of the new influx. (In 1989, the percentage of foreign-born among the entire population stood at 5.7 percent in Germany, 4.4 percent in France, 3.3 percent in Belgium, 3.1 percent in Holland, 2.3 percent in Denmark, 1.8 percent in Britain, 1.2 percent in Greece, 0.4 percent in Italy.) But the immigrants were visible; they were widely concentrated in enclaves. They changed the ethnic composition of entire neighborhoods. (Berliners, for instance, stood aghast as Kreuzberg altered from a white working-class neighborhood to a semi-Turkish district, with its own peculiar sights, sounds, and smells.) Immigrants to northern Europe of an earlier era had mainly been Europeans − Sicilians, Portuguese, Spaniards. The new generation of immigrants, by contrast, included great numbers of Muslim people (North Africans in France, Turks and Kurds in Germany, Pakistanis in Britain). For the first time in history, Western Europe contained a substantial Islamic minority (estimated at some 12,000,000, with more practicing Muslims in Britain than church-going Anglicans).

The newcomers made new political and cultural demands. (For example, some called for separate Islamic education.) They brought to their new home old quarrels (for instance, the Turk–Kurd conflict to Germany or Islamic fundamentalism to France). The cultural élites in the European countries professed to welcome the new diversity. Not so the electorate at large. In both Europe and the US, anti-immigration sentiment therefore grew into a powerful political force. Such sentiments in particular favored extreme right-wing parties which, by the mid-1990s, managed to secure between 15 and 20 percent of the popular vote in countries such as France, Germany, Italy, and Austria. The burgeoning right in turn strengthened the anti-European camp in a manner unforeseen by the EU's founding fathers.

In theory, the European Parliament should have been able to meet the new challenges. Under the Maastricht Treaty, the European Parliament (EP) had won new powers, including the right to negotiate directly with the Council of Ministers, the EU's main policy-making body. In effect, the EP acquired a veto over Euro-laws. The EP assumed power to approve applications for new EU membership. Parliamentarians from different countries learned how to cooperate. The increase in the European Parliament's power was reflected in the growing number of Euro-lobbies ensconced in Brussels. (By 1995, about 400 trade associations, 300 or so large companies, 150 non-profit pressure groups, 120 regional and local governments, and 180 Euro-specialist law firms maintained lobbyists in Brussels.)

But the European Parliament suffered from numerous weaknesses. The Commission remained immune to any direct challenges from voters. Within the European Parliament, there were no genuinely pan-European parties – not surprisingly so since the electors mostly lacked genuinely pan-European commitments. "European voters see elections for the European Parliament as an opportunity to register a protest vote or send a whimsical or emotional message."[12] (The extreme right in particular suffered from this disposition.) Many members were chosen from party lists; hence they lacked close bonds to their constituents, a failing worsened by the lack of a Euro-consensus on broad policy. Matters were further complicated by the uneasy relations between Parliament and the European Commission, the latter supposedly a non-political civil service, yet endowed with the power to propose laws. In a more general sense, Euro-politics was affected by the same forces which modified national politics. Old and well-established parties suffered a relative decline; electors spent more time than in the past on new leisure activities unavailable to their forebears – from television to *concours d'élégance*. Voters increasingly became disillusioned with traditional politics: hence the striking diminution in the number of applicants for party membership cards.

Beset by such weaknesses, the European Parliament could not easily control the Euro-bureaucracy. Complaints concerning its size must, of course, be seen in perspective. By 1990, the EC's personnel numbered no more than 20,000, as compared with 50,000 employees on the payroll of the US Department of Agriculture alone. The EU, moreover, did not deal directly with ordinary citizens. It was the national bureaucracies which enforced the laws. But the Euro-bureaucracy was infinitely remote from ordinary people, its Euro-legalese hardly accessible even to experts. The bureaucrats formed a privileged body, remote from citizens at large. (A job at the EU headquarters in Brussels became one of Europe's most sought-after positions; in addition to ample salaries, Eurocrats received child allowances, household allowances, expatriation allowances, and other perks). In Brussels, the Eurocrats formed a social enclave in which Eurocrats mainly mixed with one another.

Not that the Euro-bureaucracy labored all in vain. By the mid-1990s the "single market" had gone a long way in assuring free trade within the EU. But the EU was much less open-minded in dealing with outsiders. On the contrary, the EU continued an elaborate system of traffic and discriminatory trade agreements, with duties on agricultural imports, steel, textiles, clothing – as the newly independent countries of East Central Europe would discover to their cost. Official favoritism for each country's national

12 "Capitol Hill Comes to Europe," *The Economist*, 15 April 1995, p. 46.

industries continued. (By 1995, for example, 95 percent of public works contracts were still awarded to domestic firms by the various national governments.)[13] The French *dirigiste* tradition went on to shape the bureaucracy which mistakenly believed itself capable of picking industrial winners. In 1986, the EC had received new powers, for instance, to strengthen the scientific and technological basis of European industry. "In practice, this meant spending millions of taxpayers' dollars developing French microchips that will never compete with East Asian ones on the open markets."[14] US firms already well established within the EU benefited from such arrangements, but not so American corporations operating from the US and seeking new markets in Europe.

Inside the EU, the bureaucracy attempted to create a level playing field for competition on equal terms. Brussels thus developed a mass of regulations laying down minute specifications for industrial processes and products. (The most absurd were Euro-regulations for a Euro-condom of prescribed length – 15.2 cm.) Harmonization was meant to simplify the task of producers who now only had to meet one standard within the EU instead of various national ones. But standardization, Euro-style, was also apt to make goods more expensive, and less competitive on the world market. In addition, the EU assumed power relating to environmental protection, health, and safety at work, and thereby increasingly imposed German-style costs on industries and services in Germany's neighbor countries. These costs fell in particular on small enterprises which had to pay disproportionately for monitoring equipment, and for inspection.

The Euro-bureaucracy also tried to apply German standards with regard to the social cost of labor. The welfare state created in Germany forced German employers to pay high wages, generous pensions, allowances for lengthy holidays, maternity leave, paternity leave, and other benefits. As a consequence, German labor costs were the world's highest. Naturally, the Germans sought to extend these privileges to the rest of the EU so as to protect the high-labor cost economies from competition employing cheaper labor. Socialists liked the new departure; so did high-cost employers of labor. But the expenses imposed by the Maastricht Treaty's social charter were apt also to damage the economy of poorer countries by imposing on them higher outlays on labor, as West Germany had done in East Germany after Germany's reunification. In the long run, even Germany might suffer by reducing the Germans' incentive to adapt their industries to worldwide competition or by forcing German employees to leave Germany for cheaper labor in neighboring states in Central Europe or elsewhere.

Maastricht's critics expressed equally strong reservations concerning the European Court of Justice, a body as remote from ordinary Europeans as the European Commission. True enough, the Court's powers were nothing like as great as those of the Supreme Court in the US. But in Europe, legal standards conflicted, as Roman law traditions clashed with English common law. National governments strongly resisted judicial domination from Brussels; but, even so, Maastricht's critics looked with dread on an even partial "judicialization" of Euro-politics. They likewise objected to the Court's determination that the Treaty of Rome should have direct effect in national courts. Euro-directives not yet legislated into national law were regarded as EU law, once they had passed the Council of Ministers. Worse still, the Court insisted that even in cases where no directive had as yet been issued, the Treaty of Rome and the Single European Act mandated certain forms of conduct.

13 "The Market Maker," *The Economist*, 17 June 1995, p. 74.
14 Noel Malcolm, "The Case against Europe," *Foreign Affairs*, March–April 1995, p. 59.

In their own defense, advocates of a united Europe insisted that bureaucratic and judicial interference was indispensable to eliminate remaining barriers on the free movement of persons, merchandise, and capital. Laws and regulations concerning the environment, job protection, and consumer regulation would have to be made compatible, otherwise the new Europe would never work. There would have to be an end to covertly excluding competitors by administrative regulations. (For instance, British fork-lifts had been banned for a time in Germany because they had not been tested by German authorities.) Eurocrats also began to stress the principle of "subsidiarity," whereby each problem should be dealt with at the lowest possible level, that is, closest to the man or woman in the street. But the principle remained ill defined, a bureaucratic convenience rather than a constitutional right which every Euro-citizen could understand.

Widening and Deepening

Looking to the future, Europeans also had to wrestle with a more fundamental problem, that of Europe's identity. As long as the Soviet Empire remained in being, East and Central Europe were simply regarded as part of the communist world. But what would happen to these countries, now that the Warsaw Pact and Comecon alike had dropped into the trashbin of history? Should Eurocrats give priority to improving cooperation between the existing Twelve (known as "deepening" in Euro-jargon)? Or should they "widen" the union by including new members? Despite partial failures, the EU had proved a success. If, indeed, the success of a club is to be measured by the number of candidates willing to join, the EU's record could not be bettered. The Single Market turned into the biggest and wealthiest trade association in history. Hence the EFTA states in particular reconsidered their position. As outsiders, the EFTA states continued to face an array of EU restrictions (for instance, through EU specifications on the size, quality, and composition of industrial imports). The EU was, however, essential for EFTA as a market. (In 1991, 58 percent of EFTA's exports went to the EU.) EFTA's population only amounted to 10 percent of the EU's. EFTA industrialists therefore had no wish to be left out in the cold. As we have seen before, Denmark and Great Britain had already left EFTA to join the EC in 1973. In 1994, Austria, Finland, and Sweden likewise agreed to adhere to the EU. Switzerland stood aloof as the result of a popular "no" vote taken in 1992.[15]

The decision to join the EU was nowhere uncontested. In Austria, the two Establishment parties, the conservative Austrian People's Party (ÖVP) and the Social Democrats (SPÖ) favored union, as against the new right represented by the Austrian Freedom Party (ÖFP), led by populist Jörg Heider. The new right, however, suffered a smashing defeat, as 66.4 percent of the Austrian electorate voted in favor of the EU and against Heider's demagogy. In the Scandinavian countries, there was a marked split between the big cities and the remoter rural (especially the Arctic) areas. The former favored union, the latter voted in opposition, as did feminists, ecologists, and many working-class people fearful for their welfare privileges. In addition, foreign policy considerations played their part. In Finland, 57 percent of the electorate voted for the EU – not surprisingly so, given Finland's traditional apprehensions concerning its powerful Russian neighbor. In neutral Sweden, accession was a near thing, with a majority of only 52.2

---

15 For a general survey, see John Redmond, ed., *Prospective Europeans: New Members for the European Union*, New York, Harvester Wheatsheaf, 1994.

Map 4 Economic links within Europe on 1 January 1993
Source: Peter Duignan and L.H. Gann, *The United States and the New Europe,*
1945–1993, Oxford, Blackwell, 1994, p. 247

percent. Norway alone decided to stand aloof (with 52.4 percent in a referendum voting against membership).

By 1995, the EU had acquired three new members, all prosperous, and all endowed with a long-standing tradition of social and ecological welfare. They would wish to strengthen the EU's social dimension. Given their neutralist tradition, they would be likely to go slow on security and defense cooperation. Ireland, Austria, Finland, and Sweden all claimed to be neutral. How could they be fitted into the security structure of the Western European Union or NATO? (In geopolitical terms, the EU for the first time had acquired a direct border with Russia, on the Finnish border, and with the Balkan peninsula, along the Austrian frontier.) Enlargement of the EU, moreover, threatened the relative standing of France and Germany both in the European Parliament and on the European Commission, where the smaller states were over-represented. Nevertheless, there were many additional applicants. Turkey had first moved to join the EC in 1987, but encountered bitter opposition from Greece. Cyprus and Malta applied in 1990. The breakdown of the Soviet Empire encouraged Poles, Czechs, Hungarians, and Slovaks to look to the EU for a freer and more prosperous future. Were Prague, Warsaw, and Budapest not part of historic Europe just as much as Athens or Madrid? (As part of an interim arrangement, the EU in 1994 concluded association agreements with Bulgaria, the Czech Republic, Hungary, Poland, Romania, and Slovenia.)

Kohl, in particular, wanted to extend the EU eastward so as to stabilize Germany's borderlands, while extending Germany's economic influence. (He particularly favored Poland, the Czech Republic, and Hungary, the "northern tier" states of the defunct Warsaw Pact.) (Astonishingly enough, after centuries of German–Polish hostility, 70 percent of Polish respondents to public opinion polls considered in 1995 that Germany was of all foreign countries the most friendly to Poland.)[16] But to bring in new members would create a host of new problems. The EU was already divided between big and small states, rich and poor countries, north and south, free traders and protectionists. How would the EU fare with new members burdened by as yet unsolved ethnic problems? (The accession of Hungary, for example, would involve the EU in the Transylvanian issue in Romania where a Hungarian minority felt oppressed by Bucharest.) How could a common agricultural policy be financed if, say, Poland and Slovakia were to join? How could the principle of "cohesion" be applied, when German, British, and French tax-payers had already become reluctant to subsidize poorer regions within the existing EU? How would the old member states cope with immigration from new member countries at a time of rising xenophobia all over Europe?

There were also administrative obstacles. To give just one instance, the European Commission, by 1995, already contained 20 members – too many for the efficient con-duct of business. What would happen if many more were added? Surely the machinery would break down? Moreover, complaints from the large states (particularly Germany) at being under-represented, would become even more vociferous than before. "Widen-ing" would also create new economic disputes, as well-established lobbies in the existing member states groaned at the prospect of competition from East Central European producers of iron, steel, textiles, footwear, and farm produce.

Further complications arose from the EU's relations with North Africa. The Muslim states on the southern shores of the Mediterranean in particular faced deep-seated econ-omic crises and civil unrest and militant Islamic fundamentalism. Eurocrats feared a future in which these states might disintegrate altogether through religious zealotry, terrorism, and corruption. In that case millions more Muslims would seek to join those of their co-religionists who had already settled in France, Spain, and Italy (between four and five million). Immigration, both legal and illegal, would further poison relations between the indigenous citizens and the newcomers, while promoting Muslim militance. France, Spain, and Italy thus insisted that the EU should not merely look to eastward expansion, but should take an equal interest in the southern and eastern shores of the Mediterranean. The EU therefore stepped up aid to its southern neighbors (reaching about six billion dollars in 1995–6). Association agreements were under consideration with Egypt, Morocco, Jordan, and Lebanon; a full agreement was signed with Tunisia, with Cyprus and Malta under consideration for full membership. Free traders looked to a future European–Mediterranean free-trade area, rivalling NAFTA. The cultural and

16 Interview with Polish President Kwasniewski, *Der Spiegel*, no. 48, December 1994, p. 157.

religious differences between the EU and Muslim North Africa were, however, even greater than those existing between the US and Mexico. The statesmen of the future would, therefore, confront a difficult task.

Cooperation proved equally hard in foreign and military affairs – a subject to which we return in the subsequent section on NATO. Europeans had a common interest in economic cooperation, and extending the rules of democratic conduct. Western Europeans successfully cooperated with the US in getting the Helsinki Final Act adopted in 1975. But each member also had, in foreign affairs, its own particular concerns not necessarily shared with its neighbors. Whatever theoreticians might say, Britons felt closer to Americans and Australians outside the EU than to Greeks and Portuguese inside. (Americans reciprocated by consistently putting Britain and Canada at the top in the list of preferred countries in public opinion surveys.) Similarly, Spaniards had more in common with Spanish-speaking Argentinians outside the EU than with Finns and Swedes inside.

Given such complexities, the EU failed to make a united response in the major crises of the 1980s and the 1990s. During the Falklands War, Britain received far more aid from the US, a non-European power, than from any of her European allies. The EU's reaction to Iraq's invasion of Kuwait in 1990 was unimpressive, even though the Europeans were heavy users of Middle Eastern oil. The bulk of the fighting was done by the Americans. Only the British, among the US's allies, sent both a sizeable and a useful force (as they had done in the Korean War). The Germans sent money. The less said about the other European allies, the better. Less effective still was the EU's response to the Yugoslav tragedy. "This is the hour of Europe," cried Jacques Poos, foreign minister of Luxembourg, when the Yugoslav army first opened fire in 1991. But foreign policy by consensus proved impracticable.

Prospects for a pan-European foreign policy worsened when, in 1995, Jacques Chirac assumed the French presidency. Chirac personally liked the US and got on well with Americans. (He had spent some time as a student at Harvard.) But Chirac was a neo-Gaullist, determined to look out for French interests, even at the expense of Franco-American and Franco-German relations. Chirac wished to modernize France's nuclear forces, even though this meant breaking an existing moratorium on nuclear tests. He desired to push for more trade with Iran and Iraq, even at the cost of affronting the US. Franco-German cooperation would be harder to achieve at a time when the Soviet threat had disappeared, and Germany increasingly looked to East Central Europe, whereas France emphasized its interests in the Mediterranean.[17] France, of course, was a European country. Nothing would work without France. But France was divided; even the ruling Rally for the Republic was split on the European question. Chirac would have to make a choice, but his hands were tied. According to his electoral promises in 1995, the fight against unemployment would be his government's first priority. But in order to create more jobs, the president would have to go slow on EMU. Chirac also annoyed his EU partners by his lordly Gaullist ways. (France in 1995 completely ignored all protests concerning French nuclear tests in the Pacific. France likewise rejected a Dane to lead NATO and consideration of a joint plan for creating a transatlantic free-trade area.)

To deal with such difficulties, Euro-theoreticians worked out a variety of designs for a "multi-track" Europe, or a "multi-speed" Europe, or a "Europe of concentric circles." (According to a policy document, "Reflections on European Policy," issued by a CDU

17 Philip H. Gordon, *France, Germany, and the Western Alliance*, Boulder, Colo., Westview Press, 1994.

Map 5   NATO member countries (France was a military member 1949–66,
remained a political member, but effectvely rejoined the military structure in 1994).
Source: Peter Duignan and L.H. Gann, *The United States and the New Europe,*
1945–1993, Oxford, Blackwell, 1994, p. 43

parliamentary group, Germany, France and the Benelux countries should form the core of the EU. These five countries should drive on the "fast" track while the other partners would proceed at a slower pace. The five "core" states would formulate basic policies.) Unfortunately for this and other plans, only a minority of Europeans really wanted the Maastricht Treaty (with Britain at the bottom of the list.) Dissensions concerning foreign policy are likely to grow rather than diminish now that Finland, Austria, and Sweden have joined the EU and imported their own neutralist and isolationist traditions. European cohesion would further dilute if former Warsaw Pact countries were soon to join the EU. The EU's problems continue to loom large. The fact remains that the EU has constituted the most successful attempt in history to assure cooperation between sovereign states. It is a success story vital also to the US which remains linked to its transatlantic partners both for security and prosperity.

NATO and its Neighbors

From its beginnings, NATO faced numerous troubles. Each of the allies had its own separate national interests, and its own military culture.[18] NATO's intelligence was deficient. The US spy-masters, in particular, gravely underestimated the proportion of the Soviet Union's gross national product devoted to armaments, while overestimating the Soviet Union's economic production. US intelligence had excessively high regard for the morale and striking capability of the Warsaw Pact force. But Western intelligence officers failed to understand the extent of ethnic rivalries within the Soviet Union, and of the social disintegration at work within the Soviet empire. "That, too, was an intelligence failure of major proportions."[19] There were numerous shifts in strategy both conventional and nuclear. Planning for conventional war veered from a cautious strategy of initial retreat to "forward defense" (to please the Germans). Nuclear strategy turned from initial designs for "massive retaliation" to graduated response.[20] But in the final analysis, no expert had any realistic idea of how a conventional war could be stopped from spilling into a nuclear encounter, and how a nuclear war itself could be fought successfully. Weapons proved hard to standardize; intelligence difficult to coordinate. There were all manner of disagreements on how the alliance should be led. (These culminated in de Gaulle's decision in 1966 to withdraw from NATO's military command.) There were political quarrels. (The worst were those between Turkey and Greece which disliked each other almost as much as they disliked the Warsaw Pact powers.)

Defense, Victory, and Reorganization

In terms of population and economic production, the NATO powers greatly outnumbered the Warsaw Pact states. But, for financial reasons, the NATO powers were never prepared to translate this superiority into military terms. The Warsaw Pact armies combined were

18 L.H. Gann, ed., *The Defense of Western Europe*, London, Croom Helm, 1987.
19 John Lewis Gaddis, *The United States and the End of the Cold War: Implications, Reconsiderations, Provocations*, New York, Oxford University Press, 1992, p. 101.
20 Beatrice Heuser, "The Development of NATO's Nuclear Strategy," *Contemporary European History*, vol. 4, part 1, March 1995, pp. 37–66; Stanley Kober, "Strategic Defense Deterrence and Arms Control," *Washington Quarterly*, Winter 1991, pp. 123–51.

thus considerably stronger than the NATO forces. In consequence, the NATO states were under persistent pressure to keep modernizing their forces so as to maintain a qualitative superiority. This was not an easy task, especially as the cost of equipment continued to rise, reflecting the ever-increasing complexity of modern weapons. Advanced armaments in turn required highly trained, hence expensive, personnel. Any yokel had been able to handle the rifle of World War II: a modern infantry-man, by contrast, had to be a highly trained specialist.

Above all, NATO had to cope with the perils of prosperity. Growing wealth diminished the lure of military life. So did the European peace movements, particularly popular among the young and the academically educated (especially in Germany, a country once renowned for its militarism.)[21] Declining birth rates lessened the number of eligible recruits; so did the growing popularity of "alternate civilian service" available to German and French conscripts in particular. In effect, the task of modernizing or rebuilding the armed forces fell, above all, on the officers of field rank, as a group the most flexible and most innovative men within the armed forces.[22]

NATO was continuously troubled by disputes over burden-sharing.[23] These reflected striking disparities between the relative military expenditure of the various partners as a percentage of their gross domestic product. The position in 1991, in descending order of percentage of GDP spent on the military, was as follows: US, 5.6; Britain, 3.9; France, 3.6; Germany, 2.8; Italy, 2.1; Canada, 2.0; Spain, 1.8 (according to The Economist, 25 December 1993, 7 January 1994). Why should rich Germans spend a much lesser proportion of their resources on the common defense than British, not to speak of US citizens? In their defense, Europeans such as Helmut Schmidt argued that statisticians under-represented the value of the European, including the German, contribution. (In terms of manpower, the European contribution to NATO's standing forces in Europe was as follows: manpower 91 percent, divisions 96 percent, tanks 86 percent, artillery pieces 95 percent, combat aircraft 82 percent, major fighting ships at sea in European waters and the Atlantic 70 percent.)[24] Americans, admittedly, supplied the bulk of nuclear weapons and command and control equipment. But existing arrangements gave to the US many obvious and not so obvious advantages. The US enjoyed undisputed primacy within the alliance: US troops were kept in a high state of readiness. Membership in NATO provided some consistency to American foreign policy at a time when the US public and US politicians kept vacillating between isolationism and interventionism.

For all its weaknesses, NATO worked. It was under the aegis of NATO that free institutions took root in Germany, Italy, Portugal, Greece, and Turkey. It was under NATO's auspices that old rivals – Britain, Germany, France, Italy, Turkey, Greece – cooperated in a military sense. NATO kept the peace. As Helmut Schmidt pointed out in "Defense: a European Viewpoint," this achievement rested on five principles. First came

21 David Gress, Peace and Survival. West Germany: The Peace Movement and European Security, Stanford, CA, Stanford University Press, 1985.

22 For a good summary of NATO's organization and doctrine, see Frederic N. Smith, "The North Atlantic Treaty Organization: a Brief Description," Defense and Foreign Affairs Handbook 1989, Alexandria, VA, International Media Corporation, 1989, pp. 1287–94; and Duignan and Gann, The United States and the New Europe, pp. 253–69.

23 See, for instance, John R. Oneal and Mark A. Elrod, "NATO Burden Sharing and the Forces of Change," International Studies Quarterly, 1989, no. 33, pp. 435–56.

24 Helmut Schmidt, "Defense: a European Viewpoint. Europe's Contribution Should not be Seen only in Terms of Military Spending," Europe, November 1986, pp. 13–14, 45.

deterrence. Whatever their intentions, the Soviets understood that a war of aggression would not be cost-effective. Secondly, the alliance maintained credibility. (The Cuban crisis was the first and last open nuclear confrontation.) Thirdly, the NATO leaders stuck to proportionality of means; there was not a touch of adventurism to NATO planning. Fourthly, NATO proved capable of constantly re-evaluating its performance. Overall, the NATO forces in Central Europe surpassed their opponents in technology and resources, flexibility and adaptability. Lastly, the alliance maintained a rough balance of security for both sides, and it did so for more than 40 years. In 1991, the Cold War ended with the communist defeat. The Warsaw Pact broke up (April 1) and eight months later Boris Yeltsin and Mikhail Gorbachev announced the forthcoming dissolution of the Soviet Union. The Soviet army was succeeded by the Russian army. The Soviet Union's empire disintegrated. For the first time in its history, NATO found itself without an enemy.

Revisionist scholarship in the West consider that *We All Lost the Cold War*.[25] Revisionists mean that the Cold War entailed an immense misuse of precious resources, and a coarsening of politics all over the West. Such arguments, however, overlook the enormous military strength that the Soviet Union had deployed. As late as 1991, by which time a number of major reductions had been made, the Soviet Union had in uniform a total of about 4,000,000 men, with another 9,000,000 in reserve. The Soviet Union's land forces were by far the largest in Europe; the Soviet navy ranked as the world's second; the Soviet ballistic missile forces and strategic aviation were formidable – between them they formed the most awesome aggregation of military forces ever assembled in peacetime. Even the German *Wehrmacht*, as deployed by the Third Reich before World War II, looked puny by comparison.

The Gorbachev revolution after 1985 at first made no difference in this respect. As Ambassador Richard F. Staar has pointed out, Soviet arms spending continued to rise, at disastrous cost to the Soviet civilian economy, the Soviet consumer, and, ultimately, to the Soviet system as a whole. (According to Sergei M. Rogov of the USSR Institute of the US and Canada, military expenditure was expected to go up from 26 percent of the Soviet budget to 36 percent in 1991.) The Soviets continued to deploy advanced versions of intercontinental ballistic missiles, but also silo-based and mobile ones. (The US had no weapons in that category.) The Soviets reportedly worked on new Delta ballistic missile submarines. The START treaty, signed between the US and the Soviet Union in July 1991, also permitted the Soviets to maintain a great array of defensive weapons against ballistic missiles, aircraft, and Cruise missiles.[26] Again, the US had no comparable counterforce. The Soviet Union also had accumulated a vast Strategic Grain Reserve that would have enabled the Soviet military to wage a lengthy war even in the event that domestic farm production had been disrupted. Given such massive armaments, given also the difficulties in verifying compliance with treaty obligations, caution was in order for the Western powers.

Would Moscow have ever used this force against Western Europe? The secret intentions of Soviet policy-makers will only be uncovered when the archives of the former Soviet Union become available to researchers – perhaps not even then. But the declared doctrines of the Soviet armed forces had stressed the importance of surprise, deception,

25 Richard Ned Lebow and Janice Gross Stein, *We All Lost the Cold War*, Princeton, NJ, Princeton University Press, 1994.
26 Richard F. Staar, "Soviet Arms out of Control," *New York Times*, 19 August 1991, p. 11.

and the strategic initiative. Theirs was not a defensive doctrine; they believed in the merits of a sustained offensive. Would Moscow have confined their military interests to safeguarding the Warsaw Pact from aggression? According to the Soviets' own statements, the answer to this question is "no." Soviet theoreticians had elaborated a doctrine of "proletarian internationalism" whereby the working class of one country might legitimately give support to revolutions in other countries. It was on these grounds that the Soviets had sent arms to Cuba and Vietnam, Cuban proxy forces had fought in Angola and Ethiopia, and Soviet troops had intervened in Afghanistan.

Would Soviet troops have intervened in Western Europe had there been no NATO alliance? We cannot be sure. We do know, however, that during the Portuguese revolution of 1974, the pro-Moscow Portuguese Communist Party briefly hoped to seize power in Lisbon, intending to install a communist dictatorship on the Eastern European model. There was nothing in Soviet doctrine or Soviet experience that would have prevented Soviet forces from supporting their communist comrades in Portugal – or for that matter in Italy or France, which also had large communist parties – without NATO's preventative armaments. NATO, however, had built an impressive deterrent force designed to contain any Soviet advance, and to prevent military blackmail at the conference table. In the end, NATO won without firing a shot.

NATO's bloodless victory was unique in history – as complete as it was unforeseen. For all its weaknesses, NATO effectively protected Western Europe from Soviet threats; the pessimists' fears were confounded; the optimists' hopes were more than fulfilled. In 1989, during its last year, the Warsaw Pact powers, for the first time, announced a defensive doctrine; they enunciated a somewhat ill-defined doctrine of "reasonable sufficiency." Within two years, the Soviet forces were preparing to withdraw from Eastern Europe, thus completely altering the strategic balance. In 1992, the former Soviet Union, by then reconstituted as the CIS (Commonwealth of Independent States), agreed that the member states would form their own separate armies. The former Soviet armed forces would therefore be divided. (Ukraine proceeded to form its own army immediately.) Belarus, Ukraine, and Kazakhstan publicly announced their intention of becoming nuclear-free states but as Graham Allison, an American expert, put it "do not count on today's preferences lasting as circumstances change or less responsible people become more influential."[27] The position as yet remains uncertain, with tensions between Russia and Ukraine over the future of the Black Sea fleet, the Crimea, and nuclear weaponry remaining in Ukraine as well as conflict continuing in several states in Central Asia and in Moldova and Georgia.

Imperial Breakup

Contrary to Marxist forecasts, it was the Soviet empire which broke, not NATO. The dissolution of the Soviet empire involved the most far-reaching act of decolonization experienced in modern history. Having unwisely preached decolonization abroad, the Soviet empire now suffered at home. Post-communist Russia (the Russian Federation) was smaller even than the rump state left by the Treaty of Brest Litovsk, imposed by victorious Germany on Russia in 1917. The Baltic states (Estonia, Latvia, Lithuania), Belarus, Ukraine, the southern Muslim states, most of the trans-Caucasus gone! Not

27 Graham Allison, "Nuclear Objectives," *Financial Times*, 31 January 1992, p. 8.

Map 6 The Commonwealth of Independent States (CIS)
at the end of 1992 (Georgia was not yet a member)
Source: Peter Duignan and L.H. Gann, *The United States and the New Europe,
1945–1993*, Oxford, Blackwell, 1994, p. 18?

surprisingly, the Russian armed forces had to cope with indiscipline, crime, poor living conditions, poor morale, and corruption. Overall performance deteriorated, as shown in the Russians' half-botched reconquest of Chechnya (1994–5), a dissident Muslim province of the Russian Caucasus. "The Great Patriotic War" (World War II) had helped to legitimize the Soviet regime half a century earlier; from the late 1980s, by contrast, wartime glory had tarnished in the eyes of successive generations. Instead, there was now a new gangsters' internationale which linked Russian syndicates with criminal organizations worldwide. Not surprisingly, experts feared that, in addition to conventional weapons, atomic, bacteriological, or chemical weapons might find their way into the arsenals of terrorists or of outlaw governments.

NATO therefore faced an entirely new set of challenges. NATO somewhat simplified its overly complex command structure.[28] The military forces in Central Europe thinned out. The border zone between NATO and the Warsaw Pact had once been the most

28 As of 1 July 1994, NATO'S northern flank was placed under Allied forces North West Europe (AFNORTHWEST); NATO's southern flank was headed by Allied Forces Southern Europe (AFSOUTH). Ill-fated attempts at peace-keeping in Bosnia were entrusted to a United Nations Protection Force (UNPROFOR), composed mainly of NATO troops.

highly militarized region in history, with something like three million men on both sides of the frontier, and a huge accumulation both of conventional and nuclear weapons. (Even a conventional clash between the huge opposing armored and mechanized forces, each with enormous firepower, would have devastated the region, and produced an ecological as well as an economic and demographic catastrophe.) On 19 November 1990, by the time the Soviet empire was faltering, the NATO and Warsaw Pact members signed an unprecedented Treaty on Conventional Armed Forces in Europe (CFE). (The treaty imposed equal ceilings on non-nuclear weapons located between the Atlantic Ocean and the Ural Mountains, limiting each side to 20,000 tanks, 20,000 artillery pieces, 30,000 armored combat vehicles, 6,000 combat aircraft, and 2,000 attack helicopters.) The treaty also imposed restrictions on where these forces were to be deployed.

While the CFE has been successful so far, in 1995 disagreements developed over the "flank zones." The treaty had put restrictions on forces in north-western Russia and in the Northern Caucasus Military District in south-western Russia. Because of unrest in Chechnya and other parts of the Caucasus, the Russians claimed that they could not comply with force restrictions in Article V of the Treaty. Failure of CFE would hurt European security and would damage Russian relations with its neighbors and the US. "It would adversely affect ratification of the START II arms control agreement by the Russian State Duma and US Senate while delaying . . . economic assistance to the Russian Federation, including Nunn-Lugar funding."[29] Further arms control negotiations would also be harmed if CFE failed. The OSCE (the former Conference on Security and Cooperation in Europe, founded in 1975) and many north and south Central European states and the Baltics would feel their security was at risk. This could lead them to demand immediate admission into NATO to protect themselves against a Russian threat.

Like all disarmament agreements, this accord proved hard to enforce. In 1995, moreover, the West agreed to extensive concessions in order to reduce tensions between NATO and Russia over the Chechnya and the Bosnian issues. (The West allowed Russia to deploy more weapons in the regions adjoining Europe than was permitted under the treaty – this at a time when the Russians needed massive troop concentrations to hold down Chechnya.) But when all is said and done, both the West and Russia profited from the dispersal of the huge arms concentrations on both sides of the Elbe river. NATO forces in Europe strikingly diminished in number (from 3,151.8 million men in 1985 to 2,753.6 million men in 1992, with further reductions thereafter. In 1993, Russia and the US signed an agreement known as START II (confirming a Joint Understanding between Presidents Bush and Yeltsin in 1992). The signatory powers pledged to make substantial reductions in their strategic warheads; they also promised to reduce their submarine-based missiles; they banned intercontinental ballistic missiles with multiple independently targeted re-entry vehicles. The agreement reflected the striking improvement that had taken place in US–Russian relations. But, like so many other disarmament agreements, the accord depended on the mistaken assumption that the intelligence services of one country could clearly find out the details of another country's armory: the number of its warheads, of its rocket-launching sites, and above all, their state of preparedness. Above all, accords must rely on mutual confidence and compliance – hard to attain when partners rapidly change their minds for reasons of internal politics.

29 "The Indivisibility of Arms Control: Saving the CFE Treaty," *The Atlantic Council Bulletin*, vol. 6, no. 9, 14 September 1995, p. 1.

(In 1995, Presidents Clinton and Yeltsin thus announced major plans for the exchange of nuclear data and weapons inspection. Less than a year later, the Russians essentially suspended the talks.)

The classic doctrine of "forward defense" gave way to a new concept that relied on smaller, more flexible forces. The military adjusted to the information revolution in the civil sphere, and elaborated new techniques of remote-sensing, precision-guided weapons, and communications. Their development would center, above all, on the US, now by far the biggest defense spender on the globe.[30] In Europe, battlefield nuclear weapons disappeared; medium-range nuclear weapons would stay in NATO arsenals, but no longer be constantly deployed on surface vessels and submarines. A much larger proportion of NATO forces than hitherto would consist of reserves. NATO likewise adopted a new crisis management strategy. This entailed a cut by two-thirds of the US forces in Europe, and the creation of a multinational Rapid Reaction Force (RRF, with its headquarters at Rheindalen, Germany). The new force would number 100,000 men. The RRF would be in a position to repel small attacks anywhere in Europe, and thereby acquired new flexibility.

Under the new dispensation, East Germany became part of NATO through fusion with West Germany. At the height of their power, the East German armed forces had numbered 170,000 men, part of the Warsaw Pact's military élite, and the last German stronghold of Prussian military discipline. Henceforth, the *Bundeswehr* took over about 10,000 East German professionals (all below the rank of colonel, and all obliged to enlist at ranks lower than their former position). The *Bundeswehr* successfully integrated East Germans into the German army, and therefore played a major, though little regarded, role in German unification. (Just as the US military had turned out to be the most successful of US public institutions in integrating whites and blacks, the *Bundeswehr* proved the most effective of German institutions in joining *Ossies* and *Wessies*.) At the same time, the *Bundeswehr* diminished in size, to 370,000 men, with further cuts to follow. Germany therefore was left with a defense force smaller than that of France – the *beau idéal* of French military planners since the creation of the Bismarckian Reich (1870). At the same time, progress continued in the "internationalization" of NATO forces through the creation of mixed corps (including the two US–German corps, a mixed German–French–Spanish corps, and a German–Dutch corps in process of formation).

Within the NATO alliance, the future role of the Western European Union (WEU) is of major importance to US geopolitical concerns. WEU originated in the Brussels Treaty concluded in 1948 between Britain, France, and the Benelux countries, and, at the time, Britain was by far the strongest power within this grouping. Its original object was to provide security against the resurgence of a vengeful and defeated Germany, as much as against Soviet ambitions. In 1954, the Brussels Treaty Organization admitted West Germany, as well as Italy, and the Brussels Treaty Organization was transformed into the WEU. WEU has its own parliamentary assembly, and its own secretariat. But all real work regarding defense was, however, done by NATO.

It was only from the mid-1980s onward that WEU's members decided to reactivate the organization, part of Europe's search for a new political and military identity. (It now includes all EU states except Ireland, Greece, and Denmark.) In 1987 an agreement

30 According to *The Economist*, 10 July 1995, "Survey of Technology," p. 7, defense spending (in billion dollars) stood as follows: US: 297.6; Russia: 113.8; China: 56.2; France: 42.6; Japan: 41.7; Germany: 36.7; Britain: 34.0; Italy 20.6.

Map 7   The Western European Union (WEU)
Source: Peter Duignan and L.H. Gann, *The United States and the New Europe,*
1945–1993, Oxford, Blackwell, 1994, p. 262

was reached on a "Platform of European Security Interests," and the WEU thereafter sought to extend its memberships in accordance with the Single European Act.

During the Gulf War, Europe's record was admittedly far from substantial. (The only major contribution came from Britain, which sent 45,000 men, but even this sizeable body constituted no more than 8 percent of the total allied forces involved.) Nevertheless, the WEU did some useful work in the Gulf, a region outside the direct defense area of Europe or NATO. WEU coordinated British, French, Dutch, and Italian naval forces in the Gulf. A precedent was thus set for joint European action in "out of area" conflicts. However, WEU's future role is as yet far from clear. France favors an independent European force to support an independent EU foreign policy. Germany wants the best of both worlds: WEU would form the future defense arm of the EU, but work in association with NATO. To Germany, this would be a way of drawing France (militarily a full member of WEU) closer to NATO, while preserving close links to the US. Britain, Italy, The Netherlands, Portugal, and Denmark put more emphasis on NATO; they want the WEU to remain subordinate to NATO rather than constituting the core of the EU's defense.

The collapse of the Soviet empire changed the military situation in many ways. Russia retained a mighty rocket force: the only power in the world able to annihilate the US in an afternoon. By contrast, the navy declined. So did the Russian army which saw a striking diminution in morale, efficiency, cohesion, and numbers. (In 1987, the Soviet Union had 5.2 million men under arms. By 1996 the Russian defense forces numbered only 1.4 million.) For the most part, these troops are poorly equipped, poorly accommodated, poorly paid. An army which had once terrified the world seemed incapable of putting down even a few Chechen rebels. Would Russia in future be able to contain militant Islamic movements in the south or the People's Republic of China in the Far East? (According to Russian black humor, Reagan and Brezhnev are resurrected in a hundred years' time. Both, first of all, want to see a newspaper. "Listen to this, Mr Reagan," gloats Brezhnev. "It says here that the chairman of the Communist Party of the US has just been elected to the US presidency." "Nothing much in my paper," replies Reagan, "except a short news item on the back page. Negotiators in Helsinki have agreed on minor modifications of the Sino-Finnish border.") So unpopular did the draft become in Russia that planners, including Yeltsin, looked to replacing the conscript army by an all-volunteer force.

There was likewise a shift in the West. On taking office in 1995, President Jacques Chirac fully reintegrated France into NATO. With some exceptions, the Western forces retained their efficiency. While the number of men and women under arms diminished, the proportion of regulars increased, even within those countries which retained conscription.[31] France went even further by ending the draft altogether (as from 1997). In doing so, France only followed the example of Britain, the US, Canada, Belgium, and – more recently – Holland (which had terminated conscription in 1996). German military men and German politicians by that time were also debating the advisability of converting the German armed forces into an all-volunteer force; so did Russian military men, anxious to improve the efficiency and morale among their own badly stricken and discontented troops. The age of mass armies seems about to end; the future seems to lie with the professional soldier.

NATO also faced a host of other decisions. Earlier, in the 1980s, NATO had transformed itself from a war-fighting body to a peace-keeping, cooperating body. Should NATO simply stand fast, or should the alliance extend eastward? "Expansionists" were most prominent in the US (which possessed a large "ethnic" lobby made up of immigrants from East Central Europe, Poles, Czechs, Croats, and others), and in Germany (linked to its eastern neighbors by historic ties of long standing). The primary candidates for admission to NATO were Poland, the Czech Republic, Slovakia, and Hungary, the "northern tier" of the East Central European states. These states were largely homogeneous in an ethnic sense (partly as a result of "ethnic cleansing" carried out during and after World War II, first by the Nazis, later by the postwar governments). Privatization had made considerable advance. (By 1994 the private sector accounted for 65 percent of

31 Of the NATO countries which, by 1996, still retained conscription, the proportion of conscripts to the total number of men and women under arms stood as follows: Turkey: 500,000 to 630,000; Germany: 160,000 to 340,000; Italy 176,000 to 321,000; Spain: 180,000 to 204,000; France: 188,000 to 394,000; Greece: 124,000 to 178,000; Portugal: 12,800 to 50,000; Norway: 20,000 to 33,900; Denmark 8,400 to 25,700. The British regular forces amounted to 226,000, the Canadian forces to 73,000, the Belgian to 45,000; The Netherlands army would number 71,000. In Russia, the proportion stood at 400,000 to 1,520,000 (*Der Spiegel*, no. 23, 1996, p. 25).

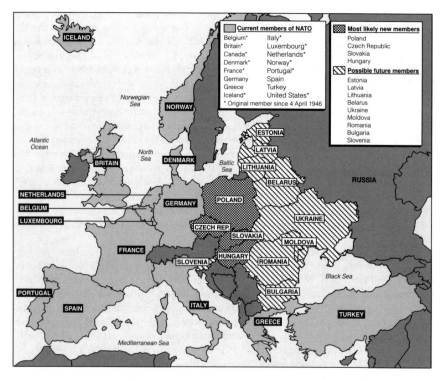

Map 8   NATO looks ahead
Source: The Washington Post National Weekly Edition, 31 July–6 August 1995

the gross domestic product in the Czech Republic, 55 percent in Hungary, Slovakia
and Poland, as against 50 percent in Russia and 30 percent in Ukraine).[32] The former four
countries all looked for Western support against a future resurgence of Russian imperialism. They also welcomed NATO membership as a means of maintaining internal stability. It was in the Western interest to strengthen democracy in the great border region
which separated NATO's existing members from Russia. And what better time was
there to extend the alliance than when Russia was weak, the Russian armed forces partly
disorganized, and engaged, moreover, in putting down internal risings (as in Chechnya)?
Russians might rail against NATO's eastward extension, but the Western powers could
not afford to conduct their foreign policy subject to Moscow's veto. Thus argued hawks
such as Volker Rühe, Kohl's able minister of defense, as did humanitarians within the
Clinton administration, such as former assistant secretary of state Richard C. Holbrooke.[33]

The advocates of caution took a different line. They had much support within the
US military, and also included retired soldiers such as John Galvin, formerly supreme

32 "After Communism," *The Economist*, 3 December 1994, p. 27.
33 Michael Dobbs, "NATO's Next Step," *Washington Post National Weekly Edition*, 31 July–8
August 1995, pp. 5–7.

allied commander in Europe, as well as foreign policy experts such as Paul Nitze and George Kennan, and politicians both Republican (Pat Buchanan, a right-winger) and Democrat (Sam Nunn, a moderate). In their view, NATO could not afford to make even more complex its already over-complex organization. To include Poles, Czechs, Slovaks, Hungarians in the decision-making process would make NATO unmanageable. NATO could not afford to inherit new quarrels. (What would happen if, say, Hungary and Romania were to clash over Hungarian minority rights in Transylvania?) What of NATO's moral cohesion? Would Portugal wish to fight for Poland, Spain for Slovakia? To extend NATO eastward would, moreover, offend Russia. Even well-meaning Russians would regard the eastward extension as a threat at a time when the balance of even conventional forces had decisively swung in the Westerners' favor. NATO's proposed eastward extension would alienate even Russian democrats – not to speak of Russian reactionaries.[34] Eastward extension of NATO might encourage Russia to reassert control over Belarus, Ukraine, and the Baltic states. Hence, Europe would in future be divided by a new boundary; it was folly to carry out a purely anti-Russian policy. On the contrary, Russia was needed as a great power by the West as a future counterweight against the People's Republic of China, and against militant Islam along Russia's southern marches.

At the NATO summit in January 1994, President Clinton, to mollify Russia, proposed the Partnership for Peace (PfP), as a substitute organization linked to NATO. Twenty-six states joined Partnership for Peace and 16 members had military representatives in the Partnership Coordination Cell (PCC) at Mons, Belgium. Partnership for Peace activities included military exercises, training programs, conferences/workshops, visits and other opportunities for dialogue. But, as yet, the NATO powers have not arrived at a hard-and-fast decision on enlargement. Such a resolution is all the more hard to reach because joining NATO would require enormous military expenditure on the part of NATO's prospective partners. All of them would have to update their military equipment, organization, and training at a time when they all face great budget constraints. (The Czech Republic has so far gone furthest in military modernization.) In any case, Western military influence advances eastward in an informal manner through Partnership for Peace. Poland, for example, has conducted joint military maneuvers with the German *Bundeswehr*. In 1995, additional joint exercises took place in Bulgaria, Romania, Hungary, and the Czech Republic.[35] More surprisingly still, the US, in 1995, for the first time carried out joint exercises with former reputed enemies and now members of Partnership for Peace, including Albania, Bulgaria, the Czech Republic, Croatia, Estonia, Hungary, Kirghizstan, Latvia, Poland, Romania, Slovenia, Ukraine, and Uzbekistan.

In the civilian sphere NATO in 1991 set up, in Brussels, a new institution called the North Atlantic Cooperation Council (NACC). NATO officials will consult with these various countries on a great variety of issues; by doing so they will meet halfway the desire of Poland, Hungary, and Romania to join NATO as full members. (NACC met for the first time on 20 December 1991.) Prime Minister John Major tactfully described such designs as "unsettling".[36] To push NATO to the borders of the Ukraine and Belarus might indeed be "unsettling" but necessary, nevertheless, if Russia falls under xenophobic

---

34 Pat M. Holt, "NATO Must Think First before Expanding East," *Christian Science Monitor*, 1 June 1995, p. 19.
35 *NATO Review*, July 1995, p. 8, provides a full list.
36 Cited by Scott Sullivan, Ann McDaniel and Pia Hinckle, "The Birth of a New NATO," *Newsweek*, 18 November 1991, p. 32.

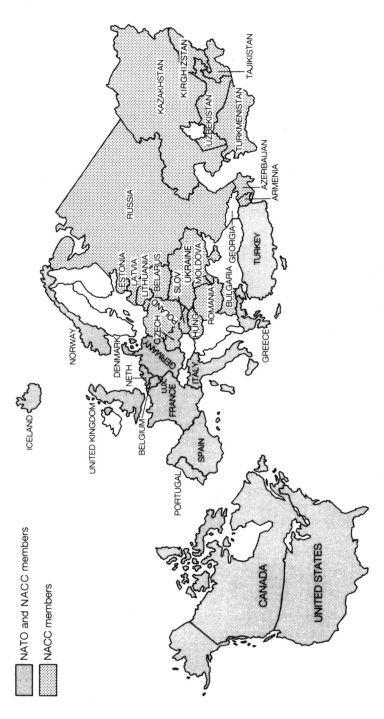

Map 9 The North Atlantic Cooperation Council (NACC), created in 1991.
NACC includes NATO countries; Georgia's formal membership is still pending.

Source: Peter Duignan and L.H. Gann, *The United States and the New Europe, 1945–1993*, Oxford, Blackwell, 1994, p. 259

NATO and NACC members

NACC members

nationalists and the military. NACC comprises the NATO countries and the members of the CIS, the Baltic States, the Czech Republic, Sweden, Poland, Hungary, Finland, Slovakia, Bulgaria, and Romania, providing them with new machinery for consultation.

According to former German foreign minister, Hans-Dietrich Genscher, the NATO council has four primary tasks: to put into effect the Treaty on Conventional Armed Forces in Europe; to ensure the security and speedy destruction of tactical nuclear weapons on the CIS's territory; to secure agreement for the Treaty on Non-Proliferation of Nuclear Arms from those countries which have not as yet signed; to furnish civilian opportunities for scientists formerly engaged in research on weapons of mass destruction. The NACC discussed the Nagorno-Karabakh dispute in Azerbaijan to try to get a peace accord. Violence has continued, however, between Armenians and Azeris.

Three additional organizations deserve to be mentioned in discussions concerning NATO's future. They include the CCMS (Committee on the Challenges of Modern Society), a body as yet little known to the public; the Organization for Security and Cooperation in Europe (formerly CSCE); and the Council of Europe. NATO, like the Warsaw Pact, was founded by men to whom a clear, smokeless sky over a factory town signified misery and unemployment, whereas black clouds pouring from factory chimneys meant work was once more returning to a city stricken by either an air raid or a disastrous slump. The growing ecological concerns of the 1960s also affected NATO. As early as 1969, the North Atlantic Council, then meeting in Washington, decided to give a new "social and environmental dimension" to NATO and set up the CCMS for the purpose. In 1990 the NATO summit in Brussels agreed to expand the CCMS's scope, and to invite experts from Central and Eastern Europe as well as from the Soviet Union to participate in the CCMS's work.[37]

More ambitious still in scope was the Conference on Security and Cooperation in Europe (CSCE, now known as the Organization for Security and Cooperation in Europe, OSCE). The CSCE had its origins in 1975 when the Helsinki Final Act endorsed fundamental principles concerning peaceful coexistence, human rights, and constitutional government. The CSCE, therefore, held periodic meetings to consider progress regarding particular aspects of the agenda ("Baskets") as defined in the Helsinki Final Act. Between major review meetings, there were formal discussions on matters such as economic cooperation, human rights, cultural cooperation, the reduction of conventional weapons, and so on. The CSCE's organization was at first loose and informal. Yet the CSCE exerted considerable indirect influence as Soviet and other Eastern European dissidents began to appeal to the principles laid down in Helsinki – much to the Soviet authorities' annoyance. In November 1990, the CSCE summit, held at Paris for the first time, adopted a Charter for a United Europe providing for permanent CSCE institutions.[38] In June 1991, the Council of Foreign Ministers met at Berlin; the Council would form the central forum for political consultation within the CSCE. The CSCE spanned the US, Canada, the EC, Yugoslavia, the former Warsaw Pact countries, and the successor states of the Soviet Union – potentially a powerful association. The CSCE provided not merely an international forum, but also a possible instrument for influencing public opinion. (For instance, in 1990, the CSCE, at a meeting in Bonn, recognized the link between a pluralistic democracy and a market economy.)

37 Deniz Yuksel-Beten, "CCMS: NATO's Environmental Programme . . . ," *NATO Review*, no. 4, 1991, pp. 27–31.
38 Duignan and Gann, *The United States and the New Europe*.

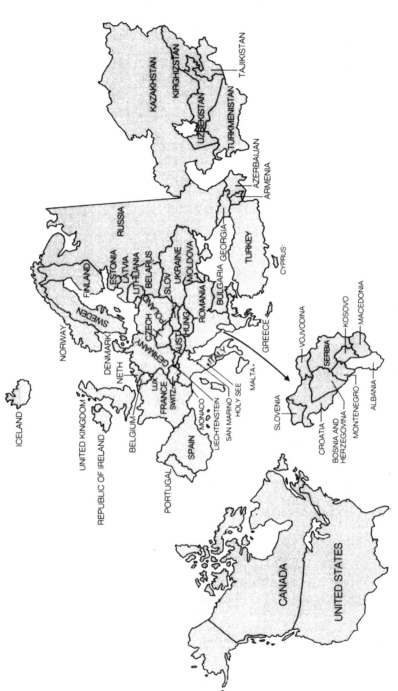

Map 10 The Organization for Security and Cooperation in Europe (OSCE) area

Source: Peter Duignan and L.H. Gann, *The United States and the New Europe, 1945–1993*, Oxford, Blackwell, 1994, p. 265

Map 11 The Council of Europe
Source: Peter Duignan and L.H. Gann, *The United States and the New Europe,*
1945–1993, Oxford, Blackwell, 1994, p. 268

There was yet another organization that also has been concerned with human rights in non-communist Europe. The Council of Europe was set up in 1949 in Strasbourg to work for European integration through strengthening pluralist democracy, to protect human rights, and to promote European cultural identity. The original members (10) were Belgium, Britain, Denmark, France, Ireland, Italy, The Netherlands, Luxembourg, Norway, and Sweden. The Council expanded to include all EC members (12) and EFTA's (6) plus Cyprus, Liechtenstein, San Marino, and Turkey. The Council remains a consultative body concerned with protecting human rights that can make no binding decisions unless ratified by member states. Nevertheless, the Council is not a mere talking shop; it favors European integration, it sponsors human rights and has issued over 120 instruments, such as the Convention for the Protection of Human Rights. A Court of Human Rights developed out of the 1950 convention. With the collapse of the Warsaw Pact and the Soviet Union, membership of the Council of Europe increased. (In 1989 and 1990, some communist states became "special guests" and then, in October 1990, Hungary became the first full council member. The Baltic States followed in 1991. Membership expanded to all 34 European states by 1992, and the Council called for an all-European parliamentary assembly.)

The Future of NATO

How has NATO responded to the changing circumstances of the new Europe? The central front has been "thinned out"; Germany no longer contains the greatest military forces ever assembled in peacetime. Tactical nuclear weapons were withdrawn at a time when a massive assault from the Warsaw Pact on Western Europe was no longer to be feared. Strategists therefore have had to answer several key questions. Assuming that NATO will continue, how great should be the US's commitment of military forces in Europe? Some Americans argued for a complete US withdrawal from NATO. Their desire reflected a revival of isolationism, evidenced by the preoccupation with domestic affairs during the 1992 presidential campaign. According to the neo-isolationists, NATO has served its purpose. Let Europeans build their own security system – linked, however, to the US in order to reassure Germany's neighbors.

European opponents of NATO, like their American counterparts, also derived from several parts of the political spectrum. Some of them held – as did numerous American intellectuals – that the US was on a downward slope, and that Europe must therefore break with US entanglements. NATO's opponents included the heirs of de Gaulle who hoped that Europe would one day include Russia; Europe would then stretch from the Atlantic to the Pacific: the one and only superpower of the twenty-first century. Others were more modest in their expectations; they stressed the merits of full Franco-German integration; France should resign herself to becoming part of the D-Mark block, station her nuclear *Force de frappe* on the Oder River in East Germany, and make sure that France did not end as a *Quebec européen*.[39]

Nevertheless, the future of NATO seems more secure than before. France has fully rejoined the alliance. US leadership remains undisputed. No European country wants the US out of Europe – not even France which, after all, required a transatlantic counterweight to balance the might of united Germany. Countries such as Poland, the Czech Republic, Slovakia, and Hungary are anxious to join the alliance. For all its troubles, NATO has remained a remarkable success.

Yugoslav Catastrophe

The worst of the new crises centered on former Yugoslavia (1991). On the face of it, Yugoslavia should have fared better than its eastern neighbors. Communism had not come to Yugoslavia in the conquering Red Army's baggage train, but derived from an indigenous resistance movement against German occupation in World War II. Marshal Josip Broz Tito (1892–1980) had broken away from the Soviet connection in 1948; his country had never belonged to the Warsaw Pact; Tito had steered a non-aligned course in foreign policy, and profited greatly from Western aid. Tito had ruled Yugoslavia with an iron hand, and had harshly suppressed competing national movements within the Yugoslav federation. The British historian, A.J.P. Taylor, had half-jokingly called Tito the last of the Hapsburgs. But Taylor was mistaken.

In the olden days, villagers in East Central Europe had identified themselves by their religion, their place of origin, and their extended family, rather than by their nationality. Modern nationalism was shaped by a new university-educated élite which created or elaborated resurgent national literatures, and built new states, in which ethnic affinity

39 Alain Minc, *La vengeance des nations*, Paris, Grasset, 1990.

itself became an instrument for advancement in public service – civil, military, or academic. On the face of it, Yugoslavs (meaning southern Slavs) should have managed to cooperate. Croats and Serbs speak essentially the same language (albeit using different alphabets, Cyrillic and Latin). Slovene is closely related to Serbo-Croatian. Muslims in Bosnia are a religious, not a linguistic, community. Slovenes, Muslims, Croats, and Serbs have much the same ethnic origins.

There are indeed differences. Slovenes had the highest per capita income, followed, in order, by Croats and Serbs. Slovenes and Croats are mainly Catholic; they were formerly subjects of the Austro-Hungarian empire and traditionally looked to Central Europe. Serbs are Eastern Orthodox and derive their culture from Byzantium. Croatian society was traditionally stratified. Serbian society rested on an egalitarian form of peasant proprietorship. Muslims were the descendants of Slav converts who formed part of the urban and land-owning ruling class under the Ottoman empire, whereas the Serbs had overwhelmingly been rural people. Such divisions might nevertheless have been overcome, as the various national groups had never been rigidly separate from one another. But Yugoslavia was then struck by two successive catastrophes. In 1941 the Nazis invaded Yugoslavia. Yugoslavia for a time disappeared from the map. Croatia was turned into a Quisling state which ferociously persecuted Serbs, Jews, and Gypsies, killing an estimated 600,000. There was a powerful resistance movement in Yugoslavia, but the various partisans were politically divided and ended by fighting one another with even greater rancor than they were fighting the Germans. A new wave of terror followed when, at the end of World War II, the communist partisans took over the entire country under Tito. The new rulers resorted to old-fashioned savagery in crushing all real or supposed opponents.

Tito added to Yugoslavia's troubles in other ways. A Croat-Slovene by origin, he regarded the Serbs with suspicion, and redrew Yugoslavia's provincial boundaries in such a way as to leave one-third of all Serbs outside Serbian boundaries (as opposed to about 22 percent of Croats in a comparable quandary). Albanians were favored over Serbs in Yugoslavia's Kosovo region, a site sacred to Serb nationalism. The Muslims of Bosnia-Herzegovina were recognized as a separate nationality, an odd move for a Marxist–Leninist state which proclaimed religion an outworn ideology.

Tito developed a mendicant variety of socialism, heavily dependent on Western loans, subsidies, and remittances from Yugoslav labor migrants abroad. The socialization of Yugoslavia's economy multiplied Yugoslavia's economic woes. Socialization also had the unintended consequences of accentuating existing ethnic tensions, as each economic decision turned into a political decision. Where to place a factory or a dam now involved ethnic rivalries. Tito's yoke somewhat lightened as the years passed, but he failed in his resolve of creating a Yugoslav nationality which would transcend existing ethnic affiliations.[40] The various republics increasingly acted as independent states, as their

---

40 Even in Bosnia-Herzegovina, a mixed region, only 250,000 citizens defined themselves as Yugoslavs, as opposed to 1,900,000 Muslims; 1,450,000 Serbs; 750,000 Croats. In Croatia, the respective figures were 400,000; 700,000; 3,500,000. For a complete breakdown, see Alex N. Dragnich, *Serbs and Croats: the Struggle in Yugoslavia*, New York, Harcourt Jovanovich, 1992, pp. 194–5. For the general background, see David A. Dyker, *Yugoslavia: Socialism, Development and Debt*, New York, Routledge, 1990; Monika Beckman-Petey, *Der Jugoslawische Föderalismus*, New York, Oxford University Press, 1989; Misha Glenny, *The Fall of Yugoslavia: the Third Balkan War*, London, Penguin, 1992.

respective leaders, especially Slobodan Milošević in Serbia and Franjo Tudjman in Croatia, switched from communism to nationalism. Resenting Serb pretensions to dominate Yugoslavia, Slovenia, in 1991, formally seceded. Under the terms of the international treaties that had established independent Yugoslavia in 1918, and also under the existing Yugoslav constitution, such fundamental changes should have been made by mutual agreement, entailing effective guarantees for minority rights and perhaps frontier rectifications. Slovenia, an ethnically almost homogenous state, presented no problems in this regard, and the Serbs soon agreed to let Slovenia go. Croatia, by contrast, had a large Serb minority (600,000). Conscious of the massive atrocities committed against Serbs in World War II, the Croatian Serbs established a secessionist government in Serb-populated Krajina. But the Croats were in no mood to make concessions. Neither were the Serbs who dominated the Yugoslav army, and who suppressed the Albanians in Serbia's Kosovo province, while demanding full civic rights for their own compatriots outside Serbia.

The NATO powers were at first divided. US President Bush initially feared the multiplication of small ethnic states; he had at first no more desire to see Yugoslavia break up than witness the dissolution of the Soviet Union. Britain, France, Spain, all had separatists at home: respectively, in Scotland and Northern Ireland; Brittany and Corsica; Catalonia and the Basque lands. Hence they were far from enthusiastic about Yugloslavia's threatened collapse. Germany, however, had different priorities. The ruling CDU (more particularly the CSU, the CDU's Bavarian sister party), sympathized with fellow Catholics in Croatia. Germans, of whatever religious persuasion, felt that the right of self-determination, so recently claimed by Germans in the German Democratic Republic, should not be withheld from Croatians or Slovenes. More particularly, Chancellor Kohl and his former foreign minister Dietrich Genscher, a Liberal Democrat, wished to reassert united Germany's might in Europe. Germany thus quickly recognized Croatia's and Slovenia's independence.[41] Thereafter, Macedonia broke away from Yugoslavia, followed at the end of 1991 by Bosnia-Herzegovina. In Macedonia, Macedonians uneasily coexisted with Albanians, Serbs, Turks, Bulgars, and Gypsies. But ethnic strife was contained, at least for the time being, and Macedonia received international recognition in spite of Greek opposition.

In Bosnia-Herzegovina, by contrast, secession led to bitter and prolonged hostilities. Had Bosnia-Herzegovina agreed to stay within the boundaries of rump Yugoslavia (now composed only of Serbia and Montenegro), war might have been avoided. But once Bosnia-Herzegovina had broken away, the Bosnian Serbs in turn sought independence from a Muslim-dominated government, and set up their own republic, supported by Serbia proper. The Bosnian Croats wavered between supporting and opposing the Bosnian government. The Serbs initiated "ethnic cleansing" but Croats followed suit, especially in the Krajina. All three combatants raised substantial armies, costly to equip, expensive to maintain, a burden for every economy. These armies resembled one another in their composition – regulars, genuine volunteers, more or less reluctant conscripts, and a motley crew of thugs who looted for profit and raped for fun. It was these underclass soldiers who committed the bulk of numerous atrocities. But, for the Serbs in particular,

41 For a discussion, see "Brennend nach Aktion: Haben die Deutschen den Balkankrieg angeheizt . . . ?," *Der Spiegel*, no. 26, 26 June 1995, pp. 38–41; Angelika Volle and Wolfgang Wagner, eds, *Der Krieg auf dem Balkan: die Hilflosigkeit der Staatenwelt. Beiträge und Dokumente aus dem Europa-Archiv*, Bonn, Verlag für Internationale Politik, 1994.

"ethnic cleansing" proved a disastrous mistake from the viewpoint of *realpolitik* as well as of morality. The Serbs would have vastly improved their case had they treated the Bosnian Muslims as Serbs of the Muslim faith. (Earlier Serb nationalists, old-style, had been quite willing to occupy territories with non-Serb as well as Serb populations. Nationalists, new-style, by contrast, insisted on deporting all such people, as Stalin had deported Volga Germans, Crimean Tatars, Poles, and others from regions to be "purified" for strategic reasons.)

According to international opinion, the fault overwhelmingly lay with the Serbs for having initiated hostilities first against Slovenia and Croatia, later against Bosnia. Serb nationalists, by contrast, considered their own people as victims of an international double standard, if not an international conspiracy. Why should Bosnia's borders be regarded as sacrosanct, but not those of Yugoslavia, a state created more than 70 years ago under international auspices, a founder member of the UN, a signatory of the Helsinki Accords? No Balkan nationality wished to live under alien rule. The Serbs in this respect in no wise differed from their neighbors. Bosnia did contain people willing to identify themselves as Bosnians. (These included mixed families, particularly in major urban centers such as Sarajevo. A minority of Serbs proved willing to take up arms against fellow-Serbs in defense of the Bosnian government.) But the majority of Bosnia's inhabitants did not describe themselves as Bosnians, but as Croats, Serbs, or Muslims.

Why then, argued Serb nationalists, should the West turn against the Serbs, allies of two World Wars? Why should the West back Croats in reconstituting a Greater Croatia, reminiscent of the Croat puppet state established under German auspices in World War II? Why should Serbs accept Bosnia's secession from rump Yugoslavia against the will of the Serb minority? Why should "ethnic cleansing" be regarded as a peculiarly Serb crime after it had been practiced on a much vaster scale – without international disapproval – by Turks against Greeks (after the Greco-Turkish War, 1921–2), and by Poles and Czechs against Germans (after World War II)? "Why should Serbs be satisfied, on Yugoslavia's dissolution, to leave one-third of their once liberated compatriots to the whims of other masters?"[42] Why should Westerners assume that a Greater Serbia would menace NATO?

The Bosnian crisis not only exacerbated traditional ethnic hostilities, but also reopened long-standing cleavages in international affairs. Germany, as we have seen, once more supported Croatia, formerly part of the Austro-Hungarian empire. (There were considerable Croat ethnic lobbies in Germany as well as the US.) Greece and Russia backed their fellow Orthodox believers in Serbia. Greece, for a time, imposed a blockade on Macedonia, whose very name supposedly formed a threat to Greek Macedonia, and Russia supported fellow Orthodox Slavs and defended Serbs against NATO and the UN. Turkey sided with Turkey's fellow Muslims in Albania and Bosnia.[43] So did Turkey's rival Iran, which supplied the Bosnians with weapons.[44]

The UN responded by sending a "peace-keeping" force to Bosnia. Its task was to protect minorities caught behind enemy lines, supply food to starving civilians, and

42 Dragnich, *Serbs and Croats*, p. 193.
43 Misha Glenny, "The Macedonian Question: Still no Answer," *Social Research*, vol. 62, no. 1, Spring 1995, pp. 143–63; and "Heading off the Southern Balkans," *Foreign Affairs*, May–June 1995, pp. 98–108.
44 Daniel Williams, "Bosnia Makes Strange Bedfellow," *The Christian Science Monitor*, 24–30 April 1995, p. 17.

Map 12   Bosnian settlement, 1996
Source: The New York Times 17 Novermber 1996

protect so-called safe areas. But, given the size of the contending south Slav armies, the UN force was too small and too heterogeneous to succeed. At long last, NATO stepped in with a large military deployment. The IFOR (Implementation Force) would be substantial in size: 60,000 men in all, mainly US, British, French, but also including some Germans. An agreement was signed at Dayton, Ohio, in 1995. This would allot 51 percent of Bosnia-Herzegovina to a Croat–Muslim federation, and 49 percent to the Bosnian Serbs within a federal state. Bosnia would remain an internationally recognized state, with its borders intact. But each of the two constituent regions would enjoy self-government, with its own constitution. Each region would be allowed to form "parallel special relationships" respectively with neighboring Croatia and Serbia. The NATO forces would stay for at least a year and separate the combatants from one another. Civil administration would be left to the Organization for Security and Cooperation in Europe (OSCE). Headed by Ambassador Robert Frowick, an American, the OSCE Mission would comprise an international staff of 250 persons. They would supervise elections, monitor human rights, facilitate arms control, and conduct negotiations on security-building, a Herculean task. Elections would be held, and for the time being NATO forces would keep the peace.

Unfortunately, the former belligerents by that time were in desperate trouble. An estimated 2,000,000 to 3,000,000 people had been driven from their homes. Misery was rife and so was violence, both official and unofficial. Nevertheless, there were both winners and losers. The chief winner was Croatia. Supported by the US, Croatia had built a strong army, and created a Greater Croatia. Among other territories, the Croats had reconquered the Krajina from the indigenous Serbs. (The Croats thereby set off a great exodus of refugees without, however, thereby incurring the same international stigma which beset the Serbs.) The Muslim–Croat federation, created within Bosnia at US urging in 1994, seemed a fragile entity. To all intents and purposes, its Croat component joined Croatia.

The Serbs had done much worse. War had failed to pay. Extensive regions once populated, or largely populated, by Serbs had been lost: the Krajina, parts of northern Dalmatia, Banija, Western Slavonia. Serbia proper had been forced to accommodate a huge number of refugees. Serbia's economy lay in ruins. Internecine hostilities had magnified. All too many youngsters had been demoralized by war and the prestigious example of the newly rich – smugglers, speculators, looters, whores. Serbia, moreover, continued to be burdened with the problem of Kosovo where a discontented Albanian majority hoped to end Serb supremacy.

The Yugoslav disaster also illuminated the weaknesses inherent in international "peace missions." The old-style colonial powers (including the Austro-Hungarian monarchy which had run Bosnia-Herzegovina from 1878 to 1918) had claimed legitimacy on three grounds. Colonial rule had the (often unintended) effect of transferring to backward regions of the world new means of production, distribution, and exchange. Colonial rule spread abroad new forms of administration; colonial governance diffused new skills, new knowledge. Colonialists, old-style, had been able to carry out these functions because they could rely on a permanent administration, permanent technical services, a permanent police, on professionals willing to look upon work in the colonies as a permanent career.

The peace-keeping missions later sent to countries such as Somalia, Haiti, or Bosnia were different. To impose upon them the task of nation-building was absurd. They lacked a permanent administrative infrastructure and permanent courts. They even lacked linguists familiar with local tongues. Worst of all, the planners responsible for these missions confused the role of an army and a police force. Armies are designed to fight an identifiable foreign enemy, and impose on him the victor's will. A police force, by contrast, has a civic role. Its task should be to identify a suspected evil-doer, arrest him or her, and bring the offender before a recognized court of law. To carry out these tasks, a police force requires familiarity with local conditions and local languages, a familiarity which an occupying army or a "peace mission" necessarily lacks. Peace missions, therefore, face enormous unrecognized obstacles; they are apt to fail in the long run, while demoralizing the troops involved. (In 1993, Canada thus withdrew its peace-keeping forces from Cyprus. In 1996, the Canadian government announced that after its year-long IFOR commitment expired, Canada would withdraw its military from Europe.)

As regards the Bosnian imbroglio, many other questions remained unanswered. How far could NATO afford to multiply future peace missions? What would happen once the peacekeepers departed? Would the Serb Republic constituted within Bosnia's federal framework not seek to join rump Yugoslavia, if necessary by small steps? Would the Croat–Muslim federation within Bosnia not splinter into its two constituent parts, leaving the Bosnian Croats free to rejoin Croatia? How would the US, in particular, play the role of a neutral peacekeeper while at the same time training and arming the Muslim side? Supporters of such a dual-track policy argued that the US must create a balance of military power so as to keep peace between the contending factions. But what kind of balance? Not enough to build a balance between Muslims and Bosnia Serbs – the latter would ultimately receive support from rump Yugoslavia. To set up a Muslim army equal to Yugoslavia's would be a huge task requiring US assistance on an enormous scale. To build a Muslim force equal to Yugoslavia's and Croatia's combined would be an even harder assignment. And to come to an even more immediate issue, how would the peacekeepers assure the return of refugees to their respective homes?

Whatever solution would be finally accepted, the Yugoslav conflict had unfortunately resolved several international issues of major importance. The European Union had shown itself incapable of conducting an effective foreign policy; the Union's inability to do so boded ill for the advocates of a European superstate. Even more dubious were the claims of the UN to serve as a global peace-maker. By 1993 already, the UN had spent some $5.27 billion in peace-keeping operations alone. The scope of UN intervention, moreover, enormously increased from 1991 when Boutros Boutros-Ghali, an Egyptian diplomat, took over as UN secretary general. (Within two years of his appointment, the UN's expenditure on peace-keeping operations had grown by 7.5 times; the number of troops employed had quadrupled.) Yet little had been achieved in such strife-torn countries as Somalia, Cambodia, and Bosnia. The UN's reputation was further besmirched by widespread charges of administrative inefficiency and corruption. Not surprisingly, the UN's prestige began to slump, especially in the US where right-wing isolationists envenomed functional critiques of the UN with wild conspiracy charges. Only NATO had emerged with some credit from the Balkan tangle, but even NATO's future role in the Balkans seemed far from assured.

17

The Cold War: End and Aftermath

Ideology: Reality and Practice

In 1987 the Soviet Union celebrated the Seventieth Anniversary of the October Revolution. Regiment followed regiment on parade in Moscow's Red Square, impressing onlookers and television viewers by their discipline and splendor. The Soviet Union remained the world's mightiest land power; its might stretched from the Elbe to the Pacific. During the 1970s, the Soviet Union also had turned into the world's second mightiest naval power. The Soviet Union had acquired new allies in the Third World – Angola, Mozambique, Ethiopia, Nicaragua, Afghanistan, Vietnam, Laos, Cambodia – which, at least on paper, supported the Marxism–Leninist cause. Soviet progress was imagined to be irreversible; the tide of history would inevitably sweep Marxism–Leninism to worldwide victory. (*Vorwärts immer, rückwarts nimmer*, "Always advance, never retreat," as the East German slogan had it.) The Soviet Union was the workers' fatherland; to learn from the Soviet Union was the way to victory. But within four years it was all over: the Soviet Union dissolved, the Communist Party of the Soviet Union vanished, the eternal truths of Marxism–Leninism forsaken by most of their former adherents. No Western government, no intelligence organization, no research foundation, had foreseen such a rapid denouement.

There were exceptions. A handful of scholars such as Adam Ulam, Richard Pipes, Walter Laqueur, Marshall Nutter, Robert Conquest (whose classics on Stalin's terror were secretly translated in the Russian underground press) had written on the *nomenklatura's* cruelty, greed, corruption, and incompetence. Andrei Amalrik, a Soviet dissident living abroad, had predicted in 1970 that the Soviet Union would not last (in a remarkable book entitled *Will the Soviet Union Survive until 1984?*). A group of scholars assembled at a conference in Geneva in 1985 had investigated the consequences of a possible breakdown. A handful of academic bodies, such as the *Institut für Wirtschaftspolitik* at Cologne University, the *Institut für Systemvergleich* at Zürich, and the Institute for Policy Studies, had demonstrated communism's inherent weaknesses. But, in general, forecasts concerning the future breakup of the communist system were at a discount, associated with professional Cold Warriors, émigrés with an axe to grind, or elderly ladies wont to foretell the future from the *Book of Revelations*.[1]

---

1 Andrei Amalrik, *Will the Soviet Union Survive until 1984?*, English trans. published New York, Harper and Row, 1970; Alexander Shtromas and Morton A. Kaplan, eds, *The Soviet Union and the Challenge of the Future*, 4 vols, New York, Paragon Press, 1988–9. We contributed to this debate in L.H. Gann, "Would the Marxist–Leninist Regimes in Africa Survive the Collapse of the Soviet Union?", in Shtromas and Kaplan, eds, *The Soviet Union and the Challenge of the Future*, vol. 4, pp. 286–408; L.H. Gann and Mikhail S. Bernstam, "Soviet Vulnerabilities: What if the Battle for Succession after Brezhnev's Death Leads to a Breakdown of the Soviet Communist Party . . . ?,"

The Soviets had attempted to create a system in which the ruling party would "penetrate into the smallest corners of society in order to manipulate, control or transform it, in conformity with the dictates of Communist ideology."[2] Their creation seemed durable. Hence, the bulk of Western policy-makers and academics insisted that the Soviet Union's permanence must be accepted. According to one school of thought, Western democracy and Soviet communism would ultimately converge. According to a second school of thought (represented, for instance, by Hugo Gollwitzer, a German theologian of impeccably anti-Nazi conviction), the Soviet Union by its own inner logic would turn into a social democracy. A third school (represented by Jerry F. Hough, a US expert) claimed that the Soviet Union would liberalize to assure its own survival. Socialism's achievements were supposedly irreversible. Bookshelves in Western university libraries stood full of tomes indicating how and why capitalist should be transformed into socialist systems. By contrast, almost no scholar considered the alternative question of how to transform socialism into capitalism. Not surprisingly, the West was intellectually unprepared for the Soviet system's sudden collapse.

Generalizations concerning communist systems, of course, require caution. The record of the socialist economies was not uniformly bleak. However ill conceived, industrialization advanced in all the formerly communist countries; urbanization proceeded apace; so did formal education. Within each communist economy, there were islands of efficiency. (In World War II, for instance, the T-34 tank was for a time the finest produced by any belligerent power.) The communist countries, moreover, differed considerably among themselves. Yugoslavia, alone among its communist neighbors, attempted to introduce worker management into industry. Bulgaria placed more emphasis on agricultural, as opposed to industrial, development than did the other Warsaw Pact states. Romania, under Nicolae A. Ceauşescu, indulged in a personality cult that would have embarrassed Erich Honecker in East Germany. But Romania gained a certain independence in its foreign policy and, contrary to socialist theory, permitted Jews and ethnic Germans to depart in return for hard cash. Hungary, under János Kádár, took a softer line than its neighbors; Hungary's "goulash communism" gave more scope to consumers than any other communist state. Poland alone permitted an independent peasantry to exist, albeit subject to countless restrictions and disabilities.

Nevertheless, the communist leaders shared certain characteristics. They were tyrants who wished to reshape society. Even Ceauşescu was not merely a traditional Balkan despot, but a fanatic who wished to recast Romanian society by forced urbanization and the destruction of traditional rural society (the dialectical opposite of Pol Pot who desired to wipe out cities and "ruralize" Cambodia). All communist leaders attempted to use ideology as a substitute religion, with its martyrs, processions, and hallowed scriptures. Communists shared with Nazis this sense of fighting history's last struggle. ("Comrades, come rally, the last fight to face" rang out the Internationale, the communist's anthem. "For the last time, the rally sounds, as we stand ready for battle,"

National Review, 20 August 1982, and *Will the Soviet Union Stay Communist?*, Stanford, CA, Hoover Institution Reprint Series, Spring/Summer 1984, no. 71. See also Raymond L. Garthoff, *The Great Transition: American–Soviet Relations and the End of the Cold War*, Washington, Brookings Institution, 1994.

2 Charles Hoffman, *Gray Dawn: the Jews of Eastern Europe in the Post-Communist Era*, New York, HarperCollins, 1992, p. 7.

zum letzten Mal wird zum Apell geblasen, zum Kampfe stehn wir alle schon bereit, echoed the *Horst Wessel Lied,* the Nazi party song.)

In theory, communists stood committed to the philosophy of dialectical materialism which interpreted history in terms of economic conditions and resultant class struggles. In practice, communists widely explained conflicts in conspiratorial terms. The Nazis had explained the world's ills by reference to the supposed machinations of International Jewry. Communists, by contrast, blamed Western monopoly capitalists, their lackeys and their dupes. To free mankind from this scourge, and also to advance their own careers, communist leaders put their hope in disciplined cadres, trained in the theory and practice of Marxism–Leninism. The doctrines of Marx, more particularly those of Lenin, insisted that the class struggle was inevitable and revolutionary terror indispensable. The workers' victory was always to be followed by the extirpation of the bourgeoisie, and the creation of a revolutionary dictatorship. Each and every one of these dictatorships must be run according to Lenin's principle of "democratic centralism," that is to say, the absolute rule of the communist party, which itself should be run like a disciplined Guards Regiment. The socialist states must work together. According to the precepts of "proletarian internationalism," the working class in the socialist countries had both the right and the duty to assist by all means the struggles of the proletariat in less favored lands – if necessary and convenient, even by force of arms. Moscow must necessarily play the leading role in the world revolution.

Not that Gorbachev's predecessors had wanted for tactical flexibility. Soviet policymakers had always been capable of making rapid shifts in their alliances. For example, the Soviet Union first supported Israel (1947–50), and then switched to the Arab cause. The Soviets originally backed Somalia against Ethiopia, and then turned on their former allies to support Ethiopia when the Ethiopian monarchy fell (1974). Soviet policymakers were likewise willing to conclude temporary ceasefires in the struggle against what they regarded as global monopoly capitalism. But, in their view, permanent coexistence between socialism and global capitalism was impossible. Stalin had predicted that the capitalist and socialist camps must ultimately clash in a conflict of an apocalyptic kind. His predecessors modified this harsh prophecy. "Peaceful coexistence" could not last between different social systems; on the contrary, "peaceful coexistence entailed the intensification of that mighty international class struggle in which the Soviet Union represented the world's proletariat, while the US spoke for global monopoly capitalism."[3] These doctrines were abandoned only by Mikhail Gorbachev. Soviet ideology enjoined revolutionary strategists to strike at weakness and outflank strength. As President Boris Yeltsin put it in a major speech to the US Congress in 1992, communism therefore had "spread everywhere social strife, animosity, and unparalleled brutality, which inspired fear in humanity."[4]

3 See entry on "Friedliche Koexistenz" in *DDR Handbuch,* Köln, Verlag Wissenschaft und Politik, vol. 1, 1975, pp. 482–3.
4 Cited by Richard Pipes, "Misinterpreting the Cold War," *Foreign Affairs,* vol. 74, no. 1, p. 156. See also Richard Pipes, *Survival is Not Enough,* New York, Simon and Schuster, 1984. For a different viewpoint, see Garthoff, *The Great Transition*; Martin Walker, *The Cold War: a History,* New York, Henry Holt, 1994; Martin Malia, *Soviet Tragedy: a History of Socialism in Russia, 1917–1991,* New York, Free Press, 1994. We have gone into greater detail in Peter Duignan and L.H. Gann, *The United States and the New Europe, 1945–1993,* Oxford, Blackwell, 1994.

Crumbling Bastions

Despite its apparent strength, the Soviet Union, during the 1970s and 1980s, already faced a serious crisis. The economy was in disarray; there was massive crime. There were ecological disasters on a scale unparalleled in the West, including the nuclear catastrophe at Chernobyl (1986) which shook confidence in the safety of all nuclear reactors constructed within the Soviet sphere of influence.[5] The cult of Lenin increasingly came to be seen for what it was – a blend of idolatry and kitsch. Nikita Khrushchev (general secretary of the Communist Party of the Soviet Union, 1953–64) had delivered his secret speech on the crimes of Stalin (1956), indifference had grown *vis-à-vis* the supposed verities of Marxism–Leninism. Not that Khrushchev's reforms had gone far. The party's propaganda machine had continued; so had the secret police; so had the forced labor camps.

Nevertheless, terror lessened; discipline eroded. Even within the armed forces there was no longer the total unblinking obedience of Stalin's day when generals and marshals were shot without a qualm – not to speak of lower ranks accused of disloyalty or cowardice. ("It takes a brave man not to be a hero in the Soviet Army," Stalin grimly commented when a Western visitor congratulated him during World War II on the courage of Soviet fighting men.) Dissent extended even into the highest ranks of the *nomenklatura* (who now increasingly preferred to direct their own sons and daughters into jobs connected with the arts, sciences, or academic pursuits, rather than into employment with the Party). Dissenting opinion was spread through unofficial discussion groups and through *samizdat*. Anti-communism became a popular creed in every republic of the Soviet Union, mingled with contempt for the Soviet Union's revolutionary allies abroad. At its most unsophisticated, this derived from hostility to supposedly ungrateful Third World peoples who supposedly lived high on the hog by means of foreign aid supplied at the Soviet consumer's expense. (In this, as in so many other respects, the Soviet's own propaganda with regard to their foreign assistance program misfired.)

By the 1980s, the mass of the Soviet people was well aware that the regime was bankrupt morally as well as financially. (By 1991, the Soviet Union's foreign debt had risen to more than $70 billion; the country suffered from hyperinflation; the national budget deficit had jumped by 230 percent over the previous year.) The Slavic (as opposed to Asiatic) nationalities of the Soviet Union suffered from a demographic crisis, worsened by inadequate medical facilities, and by widespread infertility among women who repeatedly used abortion as a means of birth control.

The Soviet Union and its allies were both spy states and warfare states. All maintained a huge intelligence apparatus. (The East German secret police alone maintained some six million files on East German, and two million files on West German, citizens. These held reports from an army of informers – spouses, friends, pastors, colleagues – whose unremitting labors caused citizens to distrust their neighbors, belying those analyses which considered East German society a *Nischengesellschaft* whose members could find safe "niches" of privacy within the communist structure.) But the very size of these intelligence machines conflicted with their efficiency; the mass of intelligence became so huge as to be unmanageable.

The expansion of the "knowledge industries" weakened the communist dictatorships in a more subtle sense. All tyrannies depend on the strict control of information. In

5 Murray Feshbach and Alfred Friendly, *Ecocide in the USSR*, New York, Basic Books, 1992.

theory, the computer should have strengthened central authority through the computer's incredible capacity for storing, and making available, information. The computer came to the Soviet Union far more slowly than to the West. But come it did – indispensable alike for space travel, rocketry, and a host of other pursuits. In practice, however, the computer damaged central authority by allowing information to spread far beyond the ranks of the *nomenklatura*. In a more intangible sense, the computer created a new international language which spanned the globe, the meta-language of machines, with its own metaphors, its own analogies, its own verbal inputs and outputs, new thought patterns that could in no wise be forced on to the Procrustean bed of Marxism–Leninism.[6]

More burdensome still was the weight of military expenditure. The Soviet Union spent a huge part of its gross national product on defense. But Moscow could not maintain the pace. The massive rearmament under way in the US during the last years of the Carter administration, and thereafter under the Reagan presidency, increasingly threatened the Soviet position. So did the development of "high-tech" warfare, in which the West had an evident advantage, as demonstrated first in the Gulf War. Thereafter, came even more sophisticated innovations which made even the Gulf War technology seem out of date. In the military, as in the civilian sphere, communism failed to match capitalism. Above all, communist rule never won over those toiling masses whom the communist rulers constantly eulogized. Given the size of the Soviet underground economy, there was a widespread belief that poverty would lessen if socialism were to end.[7] The mass of the population had tired of socialist propaganda; Marxism–Leninism failed to hold its own against resurgent religions – Christianity, Judaism, and Islam. (By contrast, race, class, and gender, regarded by American multiculturalists and feminists as the three keys to history, played a negligible part in the destruction of the Soviet Union, or in the struggles that rent communist successor states.)

Three Crises

None of these troubles would have stopped the Soviet dictatorship on their own, but their effects were multiplied by additional factors. These included ethnic nationalisms within the "inner empire" (that is, within the Soviet Union itself); diverging ethnic nationalisms within the "outer empire" (that is, within the captive states of East Central Europe);[8] Western resistance to the expansion of the Soviet Union and its allies; and Western (specially US) pressure on the Soviet Union itself. These crises interacted, and their effects multiplied in consequence.

Consider each of them in turn. The Soviet Union was a multinational empire. Soviet theoreticians proclaimed that the various ethnic communities would ultimately fuse into one transcendent Soviet nationality. For a time, the Soviet Union's prestige recovered during World War II when the Soviets battled against Nazi tyrants who considered

6 Barbara Wallraff, "The Literate Computer," *The Atlantic Monthly*, January 1988, pp. 64–71. Procrustes was a fabled Greek robber who fitted his victims on to his bed by forcible stretching or mutilation.
7 Leslie W. Bowden, *Perestroika in the Soviet Union and Western Involvement,*, Washington DC, The Atlantic Council, 1989, p. 44.
8 See, for instance, Janusz Bugajski, *Ethnic Politics in Eastern Europe*, London, M.E. Sharpe, 1994.

Slavs to be *Untermenschen* (sub-humans). But World War II no longer meant to succeeding generations what it had meant to their fathers and grandfathers. Nor did Marxism–Leninism, whose slogans increasingly appeared stale, tired, and dated. Instead, ethnic nationalism overcame "Red" loyalties, and weakened the foundations of Soviet might: army, party, civil administration, secret services. Communist morale declined as the senior functionaries' own children commonly no longer wished to take up their respective fathers' political party career. Discipline weakened, especially in the army. Corruption – endemic in the Soviet system from the very start – grew to such an extent as to affect the performance of every government agency, factory, and farm. By the early 1980s, the Soviet empire was in serious trouble – a fact understood with exceptional perspicacity by President Reagan. (In a major speech at Notre Dame University in May 1981, the president dismissed the whole communist experiment as "a sad, bizarre chapter in human history whose last pages are even now being written," and promised that the West would not "contain but transcend communism.")[9]

Within the Soviet Union, the first great fractures appeared in the southern borderlands. In 1986 fighting broke out between Kazakhs and the police in the city of Alma-Ata, a landmark in the Soviet Union's march toward dissolution, according to a classic written by Helen Carrère d'Encausse, a leading French historian.[10] By this time Mikhail Gorbachev had succeeded Konstantin Chernenko as secretary general of the Communist Party of the Soviet Union and head of the Soviet state (1985). Gorbachev was a product of the communist system. He had begun his career as a convinced Marxist–Leninist who looked to the world revolution. Nor did he intend to dismantle the Soviet empire. (As late as December 1989, he told the CPSU's Central Committee that the existence of two sovereign German states had to be accepted.) At home Gorbachev wished to mend communism, not end it, to render the state more efficient, more humane, and more acceptable to the citizenry. Reform was to be administered in homeopathic doses; some critics even drew comparisons between Gorbachev's "New Thinking" and the approach of those Czarist police officers who organized official trade unions for the purpose of channeling and controlling the workers' wrath. But, faced with a troubled economy and widespread discontent among workers, intellectuals, and ethnic minorities, Gorbachev soon went much further than he had meant to go. He resolved to end the terror, terminate the Cold War, and create "socialism with a human face."

None of this was inevitable. Gorbachev might not have been advanced to the party's secretary generalship in the first place. Having attained supreme power, he might have been toppled, had the orthodox been united under some other strong man's leadership. But Gorbachev maneuvered skillfully, despite opposition from realists who assumed, correctly in our view, that both the Soviet empire and the *nomenklatura's* personal privileges could only be preserved by naked force. Gorbachev's reputation later slumped. In 1991, he only narrowly escaped being thrust from power by a "red–brown" coalition (uniting hard-line communists and hard-line Russian nationalists). Boris Yeltsin was

---

9 Cited in Pipes, "Misinterpreting the Cold War," p. 157.
10 Helen Carrère d'Encausse, *The End of the Soviet Empire: the Triumph of the Nations*, New York, Basic Books, 1993; and her *Decline of an Empire: the Soviet Socialist Republics in Revolt*, New York, Newsweek Books, 1979. See also Jack F. Matlock, *Autopsy on an Empire: the American Ambassador's Account of the Collapse of the Soviet Union*, New York, Random House, 1995; Archie Brown, *The Gorbachev Factor*, Oxford, Oxford University Press, 1996; David Remnick, *Lenin's Tomb: the Last Days of the Soviet Empire*, New York, Random House, 1993.

chosen president of the Russian Federation in Russia's first free election (1991) since the communists achieved power (1917). But it was Gorbachev who turned out to be the grave-digger of communism, one of this century's most significant statesmen.

In the meantime, unrest in Kazakhstan intensified, followed by what d'Encausse has called "the Lebanonization of the Caucasus." By 1989, the trans-Caucasus had partially slipped out of Moscow's control. The three Baltic republics used constitutional methods, but likewise aimed for independence. So eventually did Ukraine which, like the Baltic republics, had been decimated by Stalinist terror. The national revolutionaries' task was facilitated by the unintended consequences of earlier Soviet policy decisions. Stalin had insisted after World War II that the Ukraine and Byelorussia (Belarus) should have separate representation in the UN, but Stalin's policy now strengthened the nationalists' case within the Soviet empire. The Soviet Union had denounced Western imperialism, and called for the dissolution of the Western colonial empire. But arguments applied against Western rulers now seemed applicable also against Soviet overlords. Perhaps worst of all from the Soviet viewpoint, the Soviets in 1975 had signed the Helsinki Accords. Moscow had intended this agreement to secure implicit recognition of their predominance in East Central Europe. But the Helsinki Accords had also proclaimed human rights, and thereby gave a legitimate weapon alike to foreign and domestic critics of the Soviet system.

From the former all-Union standpoint, the departure of these smaller republics made only a minor difference. Decisive was the decision taken by Ukraine in December 1991 to seek complete independence. Ukrainian industry and mineral wealth had been important to the Soviet economy; Ukraine had also been one of the Soviet Union's great bread baskets. (In 1987 it accounted for 18.2 percent of Soviet consumer goods and 22.3 percent of its agricultural output.) Ukraine's population was larger than Poland's and Czechoslovakia's combined, and nearly as large as that of France (51,740,000 as against 56,400,000), but with a considerably larger land area at the Ukrainian people's disposal.

Like Russia, Ukraine is culturally varied. About 90 percent of its people worship in Ukrainian Orthodox churches, others are Uniates (Catholics with a Slavic rite). Ukraine's frontiers, like those of the other republics, were drawn by imperial overlords. After World War II, Ukraine greatly enlarged its territory as a result of the Soviet victory. Ukraine acquired Eastern Galicia and Volhynia from Poland (the so-called Western Ukraine). Czechoslovakia ceded Sub-Carpathian Ruthenia. Romania yielded Northern Bukovina and part of Bessarabia (Moldova). Most important of all, Ukraine in 1954 gained the Crimea from Russia as a "gift" from Nikita S. Khrushchev.

But unrest remained. There was a variety of nationality problems. (About two-thirds of the Crimea's population consists of ethnic Russians, Ukrainians one-quarter; other minorities comprised Poles, Jews, Byelorussians, Moldovans, and others.) Ukrainians and Byelorussians are kinsfolk of ethnic Russians. But there were also striking differences. Ukrainians and Byelorussians alike had much shorter experience than ethnic Russians of three crucial institutions that had shaped the lives of ethnic Russians: patrimonial autocracy, serfdom, and communal landholding.[11] Ukrainians on the whole farmed better land than the ethnic Russians; Ukrainian farmers were wealthier, and resented with particular bitterness the socialization of private land. Above all, the Ukraine had

11 Richard Pipes, *Russia under the Bolshevik Regime*, New York, Vintage Books, 1994, p. 142; John Keep, *A History of the Soviet Union*, New York, Oxford University Press, 1995; David Sutter, *The Decline and Fall of the Soviet Union*, New York, A. Knopf, 1996; Remnick, *Lenin's Tomb*.

a history of exceptionally brutal exploitation. The Nazi invaders plundered the country in World War II, widely treated Ukrainians as *Untermenschen*, and murdered every Jew and Gypsy they could find – part of a continental murder campaign. Even after being widely greeted as liberators on their arrival, the Nazis, through their destructive acts, sacrificed the opportunity to mobilize Ukrainians, Russians, Jews, and others against their Soviet oppressors; not surprisingly, Germany lost the war. Nazi tyranny, however bloodstained, lasted for only a few years. Except for the Western Ukraine, Soviet domination endured from 1917 – this despite bitter and prolonged resistance in Ukraine as well as in other parts of the Soviet Union. The demographic results of communist and Nazi cruelty combined were shattering.

Reacting against oppression, Ukrainian nationalism became a powerful force which animated not only a variety of opposition groups, but also penetrated into the Communist Party. Under the leadership of Leonid Kravchuk, the former communist republic's first secretary, Ukraine asserted its right to a national destiny, separated both from the Soviet Union and from neighboring Russia. (Ukrainian nationalists also stressed the ecological disasters brought about by Soviet rule, including the catastrophe engendered by the Chernobyl nuclear disaster.) Kravchuk's regime rested on a compromise between the old apparatchiks and the nationalists; reforms remained largely on paper; the old bosses largely kept their jobs; but at least Ukraine achieved independence from Moscow in 1991. This was the end of the Soviet Union. Then Ukrainian, Russian and Byelorussian leaders founded a new association, the Commonwealth of Independent States (CIS). But the CIS failed to become an effective force. Once Ukrainian independence had been consolidated, Russia was even smaller than the rump Russia constituted just over 70 years ago under the terms of the Brest-Litovsk treaty, forced on the Bolsheviks by Germany in 1917. In territorial terms, it was a disaster of a kind no empire had ever sustained without a preceding period of catastrophic war.

Weakening of the "inner empire" was paralleled by disintegration within the "outer empire," all the more so as Gorbachev was now clearly unwilling to use armed force. A particularly important role in the process of imperial dissolution was played by Poland. At the end of World War II, the German Reich had been bisected, the western half occupied by the Western allies, the eastern half taken by the Soviet Union. Stalin faced the choice between playing the German and the Polish card. He might have rebuilt a Red Prussia at least as powerful as West Germany. Instead, Stalin chose to give to Poland a large portion of former East Germany, including East Prussia, Pomerania, and Silesia from which the Germans were expelled. (As a compensation to the Soviet Union, Poland lost its eastern provinces to the Soviets who drove out the Polish inhabitants.) The new Poland created by this westward shift differed strikingly from prewar Poland with its numerous Jewish, Ukrainian, and Byelorussian minorities. The new Poland was ethnically homogeneous. It was also overwhelmingly Roman Catholic; hence Marxism–Leninism fell on stony soil.

Poland was also unique among communist countries in that an independent peasantry survived, despite the rulers' prejudice against "kulaks." Poland was in some sense a pioneering land. (Polish people, especially expellees from eastern Poland, settled the new West, without, however, abandoning their anti-Russian sentiments.) Poland, lastly, had a long tradition of resistance against foreign rule. During World War II, Poland had developed the largest underground movement in Nazi-occupied Europe relative to its population. Poland's very national anthem *jeszcze Polska nie zginela* proclaimed that Poland was not yet lost.

Poland was unusual in other ways. Large numbers of Poles had settled abroad, especially in the US. Next to Jewish, Greek, and Irish-Americans, Polish-Americans formed one of the most numerous and best-organized ethnic lobbies. Like other immigrants from East Central Europe, Poles concentrated in electorally significant states in the Mid-West and North-east. Hence Polish lobbyists obtained a respectful hearing both in Congress and the White House – it was an asset that Poles used to good effect. Overall, contacts with the West remained close, no matter what Warsaw ordained.

Poland also took pride in the election of a Polish Pope, John Paul II (born Karol Jozef Wojtyła, elected Pope in 1978, the first non-Italian Pope since the sixteenth century). The new Pope played a crucial part in modern history. His visit to his native country in 1979 marked the beginning of a new era. As Timothy Garton Ash, an insightful British observer put it, "the Pope's first great pilgrimage to Poland was the turning point. Here, for the first time, we saw that massive, sustained, yet supremely peaceful and self-disciplined manifestation of social unity, the gentle crowd against the Party state which was both the hallmark and the essential catalyst of change."[12] As Andrei Gromyko, the Soviet foreign minister saw it, the Pope's visit entailed "a psychological earthquake."[13]

Poland also created the first independent political movement within the Soviet bloc. This was "Solidarity," a trade union founded in 1980 against bitter official opposition. Led by Lech Wałęsa, Solidarity was in fact a national front which united workers, farmers, intellectuals, churchgoers, and disappointed communists. The communist party weakened; its membership declined; its authority eroded. The leadership called upon the army as an instrument of stabilization. General Wojciech Jaruzelski (prime minister 1981–9) first tried a hard line by proclaiming martial law and arresting Wałęsa. He then switched to a reformist cause – but nothing worked. Poland (like East Germany and the Soviet Union) took up huge loans from the West, but this infusion of foreign capital augmented, rather than diminished the recipient's economic problems. In 1989 Jaruzelski agreed once more to legalize Solidarity, and introduce far-reaching constitutional reform. Solidarity gained control of the new parliament. Tadeusz Mazowiecki, a leading Catholic intellectual, and one of Wałęsa's most trusted advisers, became prime minister, the first non-communist premier in East Central Europe since 1945. In 1990, the Polish Communist Party disbanded. Poland, the first of the Soviet satellites to be subjugated, was the first to be freed.

12 Timothy Garton Ash, *The Magic Lantern: the Revolution of '89 Witnessed in Warsaw, Budapest, Berlin and Prague*, New York, Random House, 1990, p. 133. See also Timothy Garton Ash, *The Uses of Adversity: Essays on the Fate of Central Europe*, New York, Random House, 1989. Other general works include Stephen R. Graubard, ed., *Eastern Europe–Central Europe–Europe*, Boulder, Colo., Westview Press, 1991; Gale Stokes, ed., *From Stalinism to Pluralism: a Documentary History of Eastern Europe since 1945*, New York, Oxford University Press, 1991; Reiner Weichardt, ed., *The Central and East European Economies in the 1990s: Prospects and Constraints*, Brussels, NATO Economic Directorate, 1990; Paul M. Johnson, *Redesigning the Communist Economy: the Politics of Economic Reform in Eastern Europe*, Boulder, Colo., Westview Press, East European Monographs, 1989; Richard F. Staar, ed., *East-Central Europe and the USSR*, New York, St Martin's Press, 1991; Andre W.M. Gerrits, *Failure of Authoritarian Change: Reform, Opposition and Geo-Politics in Poland in the 1980s*, Aldershot, Hants, Dartmouth, 1990; Roman Laba, *The Roots of Solidarity*, Princeton, NJ, Princeton University Press, 1991; Adam B. Ulam, *The Communists: the Story of Power and Lost Illusions, 1948–1991*, New York, Charles Scribner's, 1992.
13 Sabrina Petra Ramet, "Priests and Rebels: the Contribution of the Christian Churches to the Revolutions in Eastern Europe," *Mediterranean Quarterly*, vol. 2, no. 4, Fall 1991, pp. 96–110.

Map 13   Democratic movements in Eastern Europe, 1989–1991
Source: Michael Schaller, Virginia Scharff and Robert D. Schultzinger,
Present Tense: The United States since 1945, Boston, Houghton Mifflin, 1992, p. 588

From the communist hard-liners' viewpoint, Poland set a terrible example to its neighbors – East Germany and Czechoslovakia, both ruled by hard-liners (Erich Honecker in the German Democratic Republic, and Gustav Husak in Czechoslovakia.) We have already dealt with the breakdown of the German Democratic Republic in chapter 12. Sufficient to say that change came peacefully: without Soviet support, the communist regime in East Germany was helpless. Hungary and Czechoslovakia likewise effected a peaceful transition. There was violence only in Romania where Nicolae Ceauşescu and his spouse Elena tried to hold on by armed force, only to meet their death by firing squad (1989). The disintegration of the Soviet Union's "outer empire" was followed by the "inner empire's" breakup. In April 1991, the Warsaw Pact was officially dissolved.

Five months later, the Soviet Union followed suit. In a declaration issued at Minsk, the respective heads of the Russian Federation (Boris Yeltsin), Ukraine (Leonid Kravchuk), and Belarus (Stanislav Shushkevich) proclaimed that the Soviet Union had ceased to exist.

The fall of empire was speeded by foreign as well as domestic forces. Decaying empires commonly seek to quiet discontent at home by winning victories abroad. In this respect, the Middle East had been of particular importance. The Soviet Union's chief enemy in the Middle East was Israel. According to the Soviets, international Zionism and US monopoly capitalism were linked in a malignant alliance; the worst charge which could be levied against a Jew within the Soviet sphere was the accusation of being a "Zionist."[14] The Soviet Union and its satellites thus resolutely supported the PLO (Palestine Liberation Organization), and also Egypt and Syria in their former aim of destroying Israel. But the Israelis won three major wars (the 1956 Suez War, the 1967 Six Days War and the 1973 Yom Kippur War). Thereafter, Egypt concluded peace with Israel (1979), a major defeat for Soviet policy. As Polish Gentiles put it with a grin, "*our* Jews whipped *their* Arabs."

The Soviet cause did no better in the so-called Third World. Pro-Soviet regimes, set up with dubious Marxist–Leninist credentials as far afield as Angola, Mozambique, Ethiopia, and Nicaragua, all met with bitter internal opposition. (In the case of Angola and Mozambique, this enjoyed strong support from South Africa's as yet unreformed Afrikaner regime.) But Marxism–Leninism's worst defeat occurred in Afghanistan. In 1979 Soviet troops invaded Afghanistan – not by proxies, but with their own troops. The Soviets, however, proved no more able to defeat Afghan mountaineers than the British had been in the nineteenth century. The Afghans were supported by US cash and US weapons (especially ground-to-air missiles capable of destroying Soviet helicopters): the Soviet army faltered. The Soviet army, trained to wage a mechanized war in Europe, was ill designed for guerrilla war in mountainous country. There was widespread demoralization, and, in 1989, the last troops left in a mood of bitterness, which spread into Soviet society at large.

What of the part played by the US, more particularly, by President Reagan, in the destruction of the Soviet Union, the downfall of communism, and the end of the Cold War? The disruption of the Soviet Union itself was never a US objective. US global strategy necessitated a counter-weight against the People's Republic of China along the Soviet Union's eastern border, and against militant Islam along the Soviet Union's southern frontier. US policy-makers, moreover, feared "Balkanization"; President Bush in particular, therefore, wished to preserve a liberalized version both of the Soviet Union and Yugoslavia (1991).

President Reagan, on the other hand, had condemned communism, hoping to roll back the "evil empire" in East Central Europe, and the Third World. According to his critics, his endeavors counted for little. The donkey brayed and the sun went down. But only fools would imagine that one caused the other! Scholars such as Raymond Garthoff thus argue that US policy was almost irrelevant; in any case, no one could have foreseen in the early 1980s that within a decade the Soviet Union and the Cold War would both have ended.[15] Carrère d'Encausse, in her work, does not even refer to Reagan.

---

14 Hoffman, *Gray Dawn*, p. 6ff.
15 Garthoff, *The Great Transition*; Pipes, " 'Misinterpreting' the Cold War," pp. 154–60; Walter Laqueur, "Gorbachev and Epimetheus," *Journal of Contemporary History*, vol. 28, 1993, pp. 388– 419, "Russia – Beyond Brezhnev," *Commentary*, August 1977, pp. 39–43.

We have already dealt at length with Reagan's foreign policy in chapter 10. We shall here limit ourselves to recapitulating the main points. Reagan realized that the Soviet Union's apparent military superiority rested on weak foundations. Both in demographic and economic terms, the US and the European Union were vastly stronger than the Soviet Union; the Western allies had merely failed to translate their overwhelming economic superiority into overwhelming military strength. Had they done so, the Cold War would never have been waged as a competition between equals. Reagan vastly expanded the rearmament program begun by President Carter during the end of his presidential term when he gave up "disarmed diplomacy." Reagan also initiated the anti-ballistic missile SDI (Star Wars) program. No one knows whether the program could have worked, but the Soviets believed that the system might function – a terrifying prospect. Not surprisingly, former Soviet foreign minister Aleksandr Bessmertnykh insisted thereafter that programs such as SDI accelerated the decline of the Soviet Union.[16]

The Reagan administration injured the Soviet Union in other ways. Peter Schweizer, in his book *Victory*, thus explains how CIA director William Casey, in 1982, persuaded Saudi Arabia to cooperate with the US to lower oil prices. These moves reduced Soviet hard currency earnings, which heavily depended on oil exports, and damaged the entire economy. In a more general sense, Marxist–Leninist revolutionaries now met with decisive resistance throughout the world; US arms and money backed anti-Soviet forces in Afghanistan, Angola, Mozambique, Ethiopia, Nicaragua. Reagan also took seriously the massive intellectual backlash of the 1980s against Marxism–Leninism; bodies such as the Hoover Institution and the American Enterprise Institute helped to delegitimize the Soviet Union's intellectual foundations. Hence, according to Oleg Kalugin, a former KGB general, "American policy in the 1980s was a catalyst for the collapse of the Soviet Union."[17]

Stricken, also, were the communist parties of Western Europe. The French Communist Party stuck to its guns longest. (The party's leadership maintained the Leninist principal of democratic centralism until 1993.) But the party was reduced to a remnant. The Italian Communist Party, long inclined toward reform, changed its name and ideology (1990).[18] The SED, the former East German ruling party, altered its designation to Party of Democratic Socialism, and ended by claiming victim status. It was a débâcle without parallel.

Who had been most responsible for ending the tyranny? According to Timothy Garton Ash, a well-established expert, "The politics of the revolution were not made by workers or peasants. They were made by intellectuals."[19] On the face of it, Ash was right. The list of revolutionary leaders reads like an extract from an authors' and artists' *Who's Who*. But, for all their distinction, these intellectuals would have counted for nothing had the communist regimes not been hated by the great mass of the people. It was the people who had disbelieved their own government's propaganda and tuned in

16 Peter Schweizer, *Victory: the Reagan Administration's Secret Strategy that Hastened the Collapse of the Soviet Union*, New York, Atlantic Monthly, 1994, p. xi; George P. Shultz, *Turmoil and Triumph*, New York, Charles Scribner's, 1993; Michael Beschloss and Strobe Talbott, *At the Highest Levels*, Boston, Little, Brown, 1993; Matlock, *Autopsy on an Empire*.
17 Schweizer, *Victory*.
18 Martin J. Bull and Paul Heywood, eds, *West European Communist Parties after the Revolutions of 1989*, London, Macmillan, 1994.
19 Ash, *The Magic Lantern*, p. 136.

to Western radio and TV stations; they had resisted communist indoctrination; they had sabotaged official plans by working to rule, by going absent without leave, by turning a blind eye to infractions at work, by fiddling on the black market. ("They pretend to pay us and we pretend to work" sneered Soviet workers everywhere.) Unlike the intellectuals, these anonymous citizens had lacked access to the international media; but it was the man and the woman in the factory, the office, the home, who had caused communism to die the death of a thousand cuts.

Even in defeat, communism left behind a substantial legacy, a legacy much greater than Nazism. The Nazis, in 1945, had surrender unconditionally. Communism ended through a negotiated transfer of power; ex-communists remained in charge, or regained governmental powers as far afield as Russia, Poland, Croatia, and Serbia. Communism, in defeat, left behind a vague nostalgia. The Cold War, the argument went, had at least assured an international equilibrium. For all its ills, the communist system had kept ethnic antagonisms from breaking out into open warfare. When the communist empire broke down, longstanding ethnic, cultural, and political problems, dormant since the end of World War II, once more dominated politics. Disputes intensified over fundamental issues such as national identity, national self-determination, the legitimacy of existing boundaries, the status of national minorities, the place of religion in public life. In Third World countries, such as Angola and Afghanistan, guerrilla and counter-insurgency warfare left a dreadful inheritance of gun-running, drug-running, and civil war, a legacy unforeseen by those who earlier had eulogized the armed struggle as an instrument of social revolution. In Europe itself, Yugoslavia broke up (1991), its dissolution followed by three-cornered warfare between Serbs, Croats, and Muslims. In the Russian Federation, the Soviet Union's most powerful successor state, bloody strife erupted, as Chechnya unsuccessfully attempted to secede (1994–6), and as the Russian military became engaged in Georgia and Moldova and elsewhere. Official terror ceased, but private crime flourished as never before.

These observations are perfectly true. But they underplay the evils of the Cold War. The international system had by no means been stable. The world always stood near the brink of disaster, as local disputes threatened to widen. (For example, the East German government, as we have mentioned, had contingency plans for suddenly seizing West Berlin, an enterprise which, if completed, would have set off World War III.) Civil War in Yugoslavia was bloody enough, but not as bloody as the two Balkan Wars that preceded World War I. Other conflicts – say between Hungary and Romania, Russia and Ukraine, Bulgaria and Serbia – were happily avoided. The breakdown of the Western colonial empires in Asia and Africa had been followed by conflicts considerably more ferocious than those which beset the post-communist states once comprised within the Warsaw Pact.

In a wider sense, communism had begun as a secular religion which, for a time, inspired deep and lasting devotion among true believers. The volunteers who had fought in the International Brigades during the Spanish Civil War, or had spied for the *Rote Kapelle* (a communist espionage ring in Germany) during World War II, had risked (and often lost) their lives for socialism. By the 1980s, this faith had largely evaporated, with few believers left outside old-age homes and lunatic asylums. There was also an end to Marxism–Leninism as a self-professed science. According to Marx himself, the originality of his system consisted in his scientific demonstration that capitalism must inevitably lead to communism; communism would free the liberated economies from the shackles that had impeded them under capitalism; socialism would bring prosperity and a classless society. This had not happened anywhere. Why? Marxist–Leninists put the blame on "Stalinist deformations." But this was a dangerous argument from the Marxist–Leninists' own perspective. For if one wicked man, or even a clique of wicked men, can wreck the course of history, what becomes of Marx's materialist interpretation of history? If terror had all been Stalin's fault, why had terror also existed in communist countries where Stalin had never ruled? And why had Marxism–Leninism been unable to predict its own demise?

In fact, Marxism–Leninism had always created a counter-reality. Everywhere Marxist–Leninists had fabricated statistics and falsified history. All over East Central Europe ordinary people had learned how to speak two separate languages: one for public discourse, another for private communication. Citizens came to lie as a matter of habit; some even internalized the censorship imposed from outside in a surrealist world of double-think and double-speak. Wherever they had ruled, the communists had insisted on rigid obedience to the party line. Always and everywhere, experts and technicians had been subordinated to "partocrats"; the party's needs had universally taken priority over technical requirements. Work habits had been disrupted. Managers and workmen alike had become habituated to meeting quotas, compulsory targets, but quality was of small account, except for military merchandise. Absenteeism had been rife in industry, not only because workers were lazy or drunk, but also because they required time to stand in line for buying merchandise in short supply. Theft of state property had been rife, despite heavy penalties, for state property was widely regarded as nobody's property – *res nullius*. This was not a good preparation for developing private initiative.

There was more bad news. Even before the communist takeovers, the state had already played a major part in the economies of all East Central European countries (except Czechoslovakia). The communists thereafter assumed control over all "commanding heights of the economy." Entrepreneurs were wiped out or driven underground. Entrepreneurial ability was defamed by agitprops, poets, and professors. Not that private enterprise disappeared. In so far as the official economy worked at all, it did so because it was sustained by a huge "second economy" in which buyers and sellers traded in a chiaroscuro of sanctioned illegality. There were entrepreneurs aplenty, but there was a touch of the protection racket and the football pool to their enterprise, not a prescription for turning out a self-reliant and self-respecting bourgeoisie. (Almost 40 percent of Russian businessmen surveyed after the downfall of communism by the Russian Union of Producers and Entrepreneurs admitted that they had been active in the Soviet underground economy. "The initial criminalization of Russian business virtually predetermined development for many years to come.")[20]

The moral foundations of society were further weakened under communism by the near-universal habit of tale-bearing. Neighbors spied on neighbors, colleagues on colleagues, children on parents, pastors on parishioners. The communists carried this practice to even greater perfection than the Nazis. Supposedly, one-fifth of the German Democratic Republic's population worked for the state security service. As a Berlin taxi driver put it to visitors, the acronym DDR (*Deutsche Demokratische Republik*) should have read *Deutsche Denunzianten Republik* (German Stoolpigeons' Republic).

In purely economic terms, moreover, the communist states did not sufficiently develop modern industrial skills. The fault was not the educators', many of whom continued to do an excellent job. The problem derived rather from deficiencies in planning, state

20 Vladimir Buyev, "Generation of Criminals," *The Moscow Times*, 19 March 1995, p. 22.

ownership, and the widespread use of obsolete machinery. An East Berlin motor mechanic trained only to repair a *Wartburg* car did not perform well on a modern Mercedes. In countries such as West Germany and the US, consumerism itself developed new skills as a workman might also profit from his leisure – he might construct model planes or repair his own swimming pool. Such incentives did not operate in the communist world where status (through affiliation to the regnant *nomenklatura*) counted above all else.

The communist economies had suffered from numerous endemic ills. Communist planning had inadequately provided for repairing infrastructures: buildings, factories, roads, bridges, railroads. Buildings went unpainted; roofs were not re-tiled; drains smelled; housing stock rotted away. The communists took extraordinary pride in the extent of their capital investments. But most of these investments were ill planned, outdated already at the time when they were made. Too many workers produced too many shoddy goods with obsolescent machinery. The communists were left with a huge array of antiquated steelworks, superannuated shipyards, out-of-date factories. Western countries, of course, also suffered from industrial obsolescence: by the 1980s, cities such as Belfast and Liverpool had to cope with problems resembling those of Rostock or Greifswald. But no Western country had ever experienced the depreciation of industrial capital on such a huge scale as the communist countries. Half a century's industrial investment had been uncompetitive, military products apart; few "Eastern" products could hold their own in a free market. To make matters even worse, the communists had taken no notice of ecological problems. In East Central Europe, in East Germany, in the Czech and Slovak republics, in Poland, and in Romania, these assumed catastrophic proportions – with enormous damage done to army sites, rivers, lakes, and farming land, and with unsafe nuclear power stations posing the risk of future disasters.

Not surprisingly, communist rule proved a universal failure. Czechoslovakia, by 1989, was much less prosperous or economically developed than Austria, a neighbor with which it might reasonably be compared; North Korea was in much worse shape than South Korea; Estonia than Finland. East Germany, in particular, had turned into Germany's equivalent of the *mezzogiorno*. Not surprisingly, the collapse of the Soviet Union and its satellites also sealed the fate of orthodox communist parties in the Western world. We have already dealt with the French and Italian communist parties in chapters 13 and 15, but minor parties such as the CPUSA (Communist Party of the United States of America) also deserve mention. As a recently published documentary collection shows, in detail, the CPUSA had received funds and accepted directives from Moscow. The CPUSA spread propaganda and disinformation for Moscow's benefit. The party provided opportunities for recruiting spies. (It was Mikhail Gorbachev who broke the partnership by stopping Moscow's subsidy in 1989.) The notion that the American Communist Party was a homegrown assemblage of amiable but impracticable eccentrics, friendly to Moscow but not connected to Moscow, is a lie, "methodically deceptive, historically false."[21]

Aftermath: East Central Europe

The newly independent states of East Central Europe all faced difficult problems. Liberation was expected to bring alike liberty and prosperity. But even before the communists

21 Philip Terzian, "The Secret World of American Communism" (review of Harvey Klehr, John Earl Haynes, and Fridrikh Igorevich Firsov, *The Secret World of American Communism*, New Haven, Yale University Press, 1995), in *The American Spectator*, June 1995, p. 68.

had seized power, the East Central European states had, in general, been more backward than those of north-western Europe. Likewise, parliamentary institutions had been weaker in the successor states of the Hapsburg, Czarist, and Ottoman empires than they had been in north-western Europe. (Czechoslovakia had been the main exception to both generalizations.) The post-communist governments faced an evil economic legacy: obsolescent industry, neglected infrastructure, massive unemployment, extensive foreign debt, flight of capital. The bourgeoisie had been deliberately destroyed. Capitalism, new-style, thus widely depended on former members of the *nomenklatura* who used their skills and connections to build private fortunes. (Leon Trotsky, Stalin's great rival, had been one of the few to foresee the ultimate emergence of "*nomenklatura* capitalism.")

Except for East Germany and the Czech Republic, former communists also held on to an important share of power. (In Romania, for instance, it was seven years before communists lost the presidency, assumed by Professor Emil Constantinescu, after the 1996 elections.) More important still, the post-communist governments now all had to deal with resurgent nationalisms. During the communist era, these had for long been deliberately distorted. Thereafter nationalism assumed new forms, and all too easily served as a salve for injured collective vanity, or as an alibi for national failure. One's own national group may have failed to succeed in business or politics, but look at its deep spiritual qualities, its splendid cultural legacy! This form of collective self-deception both misrepresented the present and falsified the past. Great cultural centers such as Vienna, Prague, Budapest, and Vilnius had always drawn their vigor from the ethnic diversity that had distinguished them in the past. Prague had once been a German and Jewish as well as a Czech city. *Don Giovanni*, Mozart's masterpiece, had first been performed in Prague – not in Vienna. It was a dangerous piece of self-deception for Czechs to commemorate the occasion when the real Mozart and his wife would have been expelled from the city as Germans had they chanced to live in Prague in 1945.

Troubled by such irrelevant considerations, the new authorities had to rebuild their respective countries, and they had to do so with little aid from abroad. (Only East Germany had a rich uncle in Bonn, able to finance huge cash transfers from West to East.) Two states broke apart under the pressure: Czechoslovakia and Yugoslavia, both creations of Wilsonian diplomacy and the post-World War I settlement. (Czechoslovakia dissolved by peaceful arrangement, 1992; Yugoslavia perished in bloodshed.) Elsewhere the political map of the former Warsaw Pact states remained unchanged, and – given their difficulties – the liberated states performed better at least than many Western media accounts would indicate.

Considerations of space prevent us from giving equal attention to all members of the former Warsaw Pact. Suffice it to say that a crucial part was played by Poland, by far the most populous of the Soviet Union's ex-allies, and the most important among the new applicants for EU membership.[22] Poland's performance was all the more remarkable as Poland had endured exceptional suffering, even by the standards of the twentieth century. The Nazis had murdered most of the Polish Jews (three million), and an equal number of Polish Christians, especially those whom the Nazis considered to be potential leaders. Then came the Red Army and its Polish communist allies; the latter continued the persecution of middle-class people and of independent-minded dissidents of every

22 Poland, in 1994, had an estimated population of 38,600,000. Romania, in 1992, 22,800,000. The Czech Republic and Hungary, in 1994, each 10,300,000; Bulgaria 8,400,000; Slovakia 5,200,000.

kind. Countless Poles fled abroad; no country suffered from the brain drain more than Poland. Poland also faced difficult relations with its new neighbors. As long as Poland had formed part of the Soviet empire, Poland was at least shielded from disputes with adjoining states. Once the Soviet empire collapsed, there was a striking change in Poland's geopolitical situation. Instead of a weak and discredited German Democratic Republic, Poland in the West now faced a strong and united Germany. But Germany had renounced all claims to those territories taken from Germany by Poland at the end of World War II. Germany was now Poland's best friend. German and Polish troops joined in maneuvers. And Poles were foremost among those Eastern Europeans who looked alike to the EC, NATO, and to the US to maintain a new balance of power in foreign affairs.

By contrast, Poland faced serious internal problems. Poland had been the first to modify the communist system; Poles did so by a series of compromises which at first left the communists with greater residual power than they would enjoy in East Germany and Czechoslovakia. The Polish communists, moreover, had an early start in the creation of *nomenklatura* capitalism. The process began in the late 1980s when Poland took steps for the limited privatization of state enterprises and the creation of joint state–private companies. The head of the state enterprise, a communist, would often thereafter become president of the private company, enriching his own enterprise at state expense. The communist successor parties, moreover, inherited much of the former Communist Party's property; hence, communists retained a considerable stake in the new economy. "Clean" capital, locally engendered, was hard to find – a problem that beset every country formerly under communist rule.[23] In post-communist Poland, the anti-Soviet solidarity of the communist era disappeared. There was disillusionment and alienation as a result of massive initial inflation and massive unemployment. As in prewar Poland, a multiplicity of parties battled in parliament, but political enthusiasm had largely disappeared. The long-expected prosperity failed to come, as Polish living standards lagged behind Chile's and Portugal's.[24] (In the presidential elections of 1995, Lech Wałęsa, hero of the Solidarity movement, was replaced by Aleksander Kwasniewski, a former communist turned democrat.)

For Kwasniewski's critics, his victory represented the resurgence of the *nomenklatura* transmogrified into capitalists: ex-party secretaries turned bankers, ex-agitprops into public relations experts. In this respect, Poland followed the other ex-communist countries (with the exception of the Czech Republic and East Germany, both of which placed restrictions on the rehabilitation of yesterday's senior office-holders). But at least the born-again democrats now had too great a stake in the new order to strive for the restoration of the old. In Poland, as in other formerly communist countries, there was a striking rise in private crime. But this was balanced by the decline of public crime carried out by government agencies behind a curtain of legality.

In fact, fortune favored Poland. Poland's economy rapidly expanded. By 1993 already, more than 80 percent of her industry was in private ownership through investment funds distributed to workers, or through corporate shares nominally owned by the

23 Duignan and Gann, *The United States and the New Europe*, pp. 144–8.
24 In terms of the UN's "human development index," Poland's living standards ranged, in order, behind Greece, Argentina, South Korea, Chile, Portugal, the Czech Republic, Venezuela, and Hungary. Poland in turn was followed, in order, by Russia, Mexico, Columbia, Brazil, and Turkey (*The Economist*, 26 August, 1995, p. 90).

treasury but available for purchase. The Warsaw Stock Exchange (set up in 1991) had become a power in the economy; many new jobs had been created in private enterprises. Foreign capital investment was on the rise – albeit slowly. The expansion of small business had altered alike the physical appearance of cities and the shape of politics. Poland's problems remained enormous. But Poland was ethnically homogeneous. The Catholic Church provided common cultural standards as well as a common religion and a host of voluntary social services, and, in a broader sense, those moral foundations essential to capitalism. For all its troubles, Poland had one of Europe's fastest recovery rates.[25]

Equally striking, in relative terms, was the success of the Czech Republic, the second most important among the new applicants for EU membership. As a result of Czecho-slovakia's (more properly, by then Czecho-Slovakia's) "velvet revolution," power fell to remarkable men. The new president was Václav Havel. Havel, a playwright, was one of those remarkably courageous intellectuals who led the resistance against communism: Tadeusz Mazowiecki, an editor, in Poland; Kurt Masur, a conductor, in East Germany; János Kis, a philosopher, in Hungary; Petre Roman, an engineer, in Romania. Havel's minister of finance and namesake was Václav Klaus, an economist, and an admirer of Milton Friedman. Under Klaus's energetic leadership, the Czech state embarked on a bold program of modernization and privatization. (By 1995, there were 1,700 domest-ically listed companies. The large number of Czech companies derived from a program by which most state enterprises became private ventures and millions of Czechs became small stock owners.) Klaus equally valued foreign capital and foreign connections. Not for him a "third road" between capitalism and communism. ("The third road leads to the Third World.") Thereafter, German economic influence became predominant. (By 1992, pledged foreign capital amounted to 80 percent of all foreign capital.) German remained the most widely known foreign language. Czechs might feel ambivalent about the country's threatened "Germanization"; nevertheless, most Czechs approved of a German–Czech friendship treaty prepared by Kohl and Havel in 1992. Having endured the miseries of what Czechs now called "the missing half-century," Czechs now wanted to rejoin the West, and participate in the EU.

In a certain sense, the Czech reformers' task was made easier by the breakup of Czecho-Slovakia in 1993. Slovakia achieved independence. The Czech Republic thereby lost its *mezzogiorno*, burdened by a backward agriculture, and by huge iron, steel, and arms industries, a region which had always drawn large subsidies from the Czech lands. Slovakia's modest record of economic achievements weakened the argument of those who preferred reform by homeopathic doses to shock therapy. The Czech Republic enjoyed the advantage of only having friendly neighbors. Not so Hungary. In the south, Hungary adjoined Croatia and Serbia, both neighbors with whom it was hard to live. In the east, Hungary shared a common frontier with Romania. Romania contained a substantial Hungarian minority in Transylvania, and Hungarians claimed, with much justification, that their compatriots were widely denied civil rights. Hungary, on the other hand, enjoyed extremely amicable relations with Austria; Vienna and Budapest resumed the age-old partnership which had once stabilized the Austro-Hungarian empire.

Hungary's task was hard. When communism fell, the country's economy was in serious trouble and inflation was rampant. Hungary lacked a national organization such

25 Between 1994 and 1995, Poland's gross domestic product grew by 5 percent; the Czech Republic by 3.9 percent; Hungary 2 percent; Russia –5.0 percent (*The Economist*, 5 August 1995, p. 98).

as Solidarity. In Hungary, as elsewhere, there was, moreover, a revival of traditional nationalism, complete with traditional chauvinism and anti-semitism. Alone in Nazi-occupied Central Europe, a fairly substantial Jewish minority had managed to survive the Nazi persecution. Jews were well represented in journalism and academia. Jews overwhelmingly lived in Budapest, the capital; they were traditionally associated with "liberalism" and "cosmopolitanism." The infighting between organizations such as the Hungarian Democratic Forum and the Free Democrats sometimes had an ethnic edge, when Free Democrats, especially its Jewish members, were accused of lacking the true Hungarian spirit. Alone, in East Central Europe, Hungary had experienced an extended period of "goulash communism" (a more consumer-directed form of communism) before communism's collapse. Psychologically, the change-over came more easily to Hungarians than to Czechs or East Germans. Hungary thus made substantial progress. (By 1993, the country was the largest recipient of direct foreign investment in East Central Europe.) Hungary lived at peace with its neighbors. At least, the future would be better than the past.

Aftermath: Russia and Ukraine

Russia posed the greatest question mark of all. The Russian reformers' difficulties were even greater than those of their colleagues in Hungary, Poland, or Romania. These countries all had maintained their territorial integrity. In Russia, by contrast, the breakdown of communism had gone with the dissolution of the Soviet Union. Russia's territorial losses had been even greater than those sustained by Russia through the disastrous Brest-Litovsk Treaty, forced upon Russia by the Kaiser's Germany in 1917. From being a superpower, Russia seemed to have declined to a huge, Third World country – "Upper Volta with rockets," as the critics scathingly put it. There were other problems. In East Central Europe the communist successor states were fairly homogeneous (with Yugoslavia the chief exception). By contrast, the Russian Federation was itself an empire, a national hodgepodge (minorities numbered some 18 percent of the population). Worse still, something like 25,000,000 Russians lived outside Russia's new borders. (During the Soviet era, the number of Russians dwelling beyond the boundaries of Russia grew from 6.7 to 17.4 percent.)[26]

There were also psychological problems concerning Russian identity. Had ethnic Russians been overlords or victims of the Soviet empire? In East Central Europe, opposition to communism had drawn on a strong sense of nationalism and hostility to the Soviet occupiers; memories of prewar parties and the prewar state survived. Czechs, Slovaks, Hungarians, Poles had all desired that their respective countries should "return to Europe." In Russia, by contrast, there was no common agreement regarding the meaning of Russian nationalism. In the past, Russian and Soviet nationalism had been confused; moreover, the age-old debate between Slavophiles (that is to say, cultural isolationists) and Westerners remained unresolved, having been suppressed during the long years of communist tyranny.

26 Vladimir Shlapentokh, Munir Sendich and Emil Payin, eds, *The New Russian Diaspora: Russian Minorities in the Former Soviet Republics*, Armonk, NY, M.E. Sharpe, 1994, pp. 31–2. Russia's population in 1994 stood at 147,800,000.

In Russia (and also in other successor states such as Ukraine and Belarus) communism had lasted longer than in East Central Europe.[27] For nearly three-quarters of a century, Russians had been taught that to spy on their neighbors was patriotic, that success in private enterprise was despicable, that a successful speculator was an enemy of the people. (According to Russian black humor, a Frenchman, an Englishman, and a Russian find a bottle by the seashore. They open the bottle. A good djinni comes out, and promises to grant one wish to his three respective rescuers. The Frenchman wants to own the finest vineyards in France. "Granted, Monsieur," says the djinni. The Englishman wishes to become a peer of the realm. "May I congratulate your Lordship on your new title," the djinni responds. Insists the Russian, "My neighbor Sergei has a cow. I don't have a cow. Kill the cow.") It was an evil legacy.

The resultant crisis took many forms. The Russian state and its various agencies were in disarray. There were problems with overlapping jurisdictions; a weakened central government could not easily enforce its will on a great network of local authorities. There was ethnic discontent aplenty. (Russian forces had to reconquer by force of arms the federal republic of Chechnya, a Muslim state.) Russian entrepreneurs had to cope with high taxes and inflation, set almost at a confiscatory level, ill-defined property rights, ill-defined legislation, burgeoning bureaucracies, and a criminal class of extortionists.

There were laws, but there was no effective constitution. Corruption was rife on every level of government. Organized crime developed on a scale that would have astounded Al Capone.[28] As punsters put it, *glasnost* (openness) and *perestroika* (reconstruction) had been replaced by *naglost* (brazen insolence) and *perestrelka* (shoot-outs). The economy continued to be weighed down by a huge and unproductive military–industrial complex embracing, in particular, state-owned heavy industries and arms manufacturers and collectivized farms. "The usual estimate is that three-quarters of the industrial output of two of the country's largest cities, St Petersburg and Moscow, comes from the military–industrial complex. On a conservative estimate it accounts for over a third, and perhaps as much as half of the Soviet Union's total industrial output."[29] The switch to a peacetime economy, let alone a market economy, would be extraordinarily difficult. Having escaped from a dictatorship, Russia, oddly enough, lacked a strong state. For no market economy could function without a well-organized central bank and legal system, an incorruptible judiciary and an efficient and honest police to enforce the rule of law. A market economy likewise required a sound currency and banking system, effective social service agencies, a competent internal revenue service able to collect taxes, a reliable

27 For the transition in Russia, see John R. Dunlop, *The Rise of Russia and the Fall of the Soviet Empire*, Princeton, NJ, Princeton University Press, 1993; and *The Faces of Contemporary Russian Nationalism*, Princeton, NJ, Princeton University Press, 1983; James H. Billington, *Russia Transformed: Breakthrough to Hope*, New York, Free Press, 1992; Moshe Lewin, *Russia, USSR, Russia*, New York, New Press, 1995; Edward P. Lazear, ed., *Economic Transition in Eastern Europe and Russia: Realities of Reform*, Stanford, CA, Hoover Institution Press, 1995; Richard F. Staar, ed., *East-Central Europe and the USSR*, New York, St Martin's Press, 1991; Adam B. Ulam, *The Communists: the Story of Power and Lost Illusions, 1948–1991*, New York, Charles Scribner's, 1992; Heyward Isham, ed., *Remaking Russia*, New York, M.E. Sharpe, 1995.
28 Barbara von der Heydt, *Corruption in Russia: No Democracy without Morality*, Washington DC, Atlantic Council, 1995, p. 4; Stephen Handelman, *Comrade Criminal: the Theft of the Second Russian Revolution*, London, Michael Joseph, 1994.
29 "The Lords of Misrule," *The Economist*, 6 April 1991, p. 20.

census bureau, and many other official agencies whose performance Western business-men and economists take for granted. These foundations remained to be built.

The Commonwealth of Independent States (CIS) worked badly, as each member pursued its own interests. The Russian armed forces suffered from an equal malaise. They remained powerful in terms of numbers and weaponry. But they were organizationally divided (with special formations remaining under the control of agencies such as the Ministry of Internal Affairs and the KGB). Generally speaking, the armed forces remained beset by poor morale, divided loyalties, and uncertainty concerning their mission, career prospects, accommodation, and pay. There was widespread alcoholism and drug abuse. The war against rebellious Chechnya was fought by the army with an incompetence that matched its cruelty. Despite the army's image of a national institution transcending politics, it was riddled by corruption and political favoritism.[30] Worst of all, Russia remained a great nuclear power, armed with an enormous array of nuclear weapons. Who would guard them against diversion into the hands of rogue governments or terrorists?

Russia's political institutions likewise needed reconstruction. Of parties there were many: 43 blocs competed in the 1995 parliamentary elections. But most of them were small, with fluctuating membership, puny financial resources, and weak organization. Only the Communist Party remained well organized and rich. Their core supporters varied: ex-communists, communists, bureaucrats, regionalists, pensioners, farmers, nationalists of various persuasions, blue-collar workers, housewives. Politicians faced distrust as a group; there were likewise striking ideological cleavages between reformers, centrists, and hard-liners (often mistakenly referred to as conservatives by the Western media). Russia, moreover, shared another weakness with the remaining successor states of the Soviet empire. All adopted systems of proportional representation, instead of the Anglo-American system of plurality voting. Whatever its theoretical merits, proportional representation tends to fragment parliamentary parties, and gives undue influence to extremist groups, a generalization applicable to countries as varied as Russia, Poland, and Israel.

The hard-liners rejected reform, calling for the restoration of Russia's armed might and the recovery of Russian leadership over the former member states of the Soviet Union. (Even moderates widely considered that Russia should at least seek a much closer form of association with Ukraine and Belarus.) The hard-liners blamed Jews, foreigners, as well as home-grown evil-doers, for Russia's ills. Fanatics such as Vladimir Zhirinovsky looked to new conquests abroad: Iran, Turkey, Afghanistan, the Baltic, Alaska, the world. Hard-liners, but not only hard-liners, associated the West with spreading crime, drug addiction, prostitution, a raucous youth culture, and contempt for authority in general. The reformed Communist Party (claiming to have shed the Stalinist legacy) did better in elections and public opinion polls than any of its numerous rivals, admittedly not much of an accomplishment. The Communists were well organized, whereas their opponents lacked discipline. The Communists had inherited from the *ancien régime* disciplined cadres, ready to ring central and turn out the voters; hence, Communists did particularly well in outlying districts. (In the parliamentary elections of 1995 the Communists, led by Gennady Zyuganov, scored 22.3 percent of the vote, followed by Zhirinovsky's ultra-nationalists with 11.1 percent. Prime Minister Viktor Chernomyrdin's pro-government party obtained 9.9 percent, and Grigory Yavlinsky's reformist Yabloko movement, only 6.9 percent.) The Communists – like the nationalists – wished to

30 Richard F. Staar, *The New Military in Russia: Ten Myths that Shape the Image*, Indianapolis, Md, Naval Institute Press, 1996.

restore the old Soviet Union, voluntarily of course. The Communists promised once more to end privatization, regulate food prices, and help the poor in other ways. The Communists, in particular, therefore derived support from aged people who looked with regret to the olden days, at a time when inflation kept reducing the value of pensions. Forgotten were the realities of former communist days: the unmet rations, the interminable lines outside state shops, the host of informers, the Gulag Archipelago. The Communists, in fact, enjoyed a good deal of support from workers in now endangered heavy industries, from military men, and from bureaucrats – from a great army of discontent whose members might opt for a "Red–Brown" (communist–fascist) alliance. Boris Yeltsin's popularity, by contrast, slumped.

Foreign investment in Russia lagged far behind foreign investment in other postcommunist countries such as Poland and Hungary. Foreign investors feared Russia's erratic as well as heavy taxation, cross-cutting bureaucratic jurisdictions, red tape, uncertain property rights, crime, and remaining hostility toward foreign entrepreneurs allegedly resolved to buy the Russian motherland for a song. Distrustful of their own government, Russian financiers massively sent capital abroad. Worse still, Russia suffered from a massive brain drain as specialists looked for better-paid jobs in foreign countries. Public discontent remained widespread, especially among former party officials now without jobs, ex-officers without promotion, and a great mass of ordinary people – collective farmers, blue-collar workers, housewives. Official salaries might remain unpaid for months. Russians were irked by high unemployment, high prices, by the prestige accorded to whores plying their trade for hard currency, or by the sight of grim-faced men who drove in unmarked luxury cars, parked their vehicles illegally whenever the drivers pleased, and were assiduously saluted by police officers. Reformers shared the hard-liners' discontent as old *nomenklatura* members made new fortunes. And what of Russia's reputation as a great power? The West defied her with impunity in Bosnia. She was even defied by a small breakaway republic such as Chechnya. Not surprisingly, Boris Yeltsin and his associates had, by the mid-1990s, lost much of the confidence that they had initially inspired. Politicians faced distrust as a group – much more intensely even than in Western Europe or the US. Pessimists therefore feared that the new Russia might share the fate of the Weimar Republic. Hard-liners might seize power (as they had unsuccessfully tried to do in 1991). Fascism would then prove the last and highest stage of Soviet communism – as Trotsky had predicted two generations earlier.

Fortunately, there were also grounds for optimism. The parliamentary elections of 1995 by no means constituted an irretrievable disaster for the cause of reform.[31] Zyuganov's rhetoric certainly invited apprehension: "Socialism with a fascist face", as Adrian Karatnycky, an American scholar, starkly put it. Zyuganov now stood for a patriotic form of communism: no truck with foreigners such as Trotsky, a Jew, and Stalin, a Georgian. Zyuganov supported a state-dominated economy, an anti-Western foreign policy, and a restoration of Russian military might.[32] But even Zyuganov would no longer reverse all privatization, and no longer claimed for the Communists a monopoly of power. Whether hypocritical or honest, his protestations reflected the mood of a country from which the fanatical enthusiasm of Stalin's time had fled. The Communists' strongest support, moreover, came from older people, not from the young. In the presidential elections of 1996, Yeltsin, with Lebed's support, won a striking victory. (In the

31 Michael McFaul, "A Communist Route?" *New York Times*, 20 December 1995.
32 Adrian Karatnycky, "Socialism with a Human Face," *Wall Street Journal*, 19 December 1995, p. 18.

second-round run off, Yeltsin gained 53.7 percent of the vote, as against 40.4 percent.) Tough, capable, magnificent in crises, though ill suited for the daily grind of administrative routine, Yeltsin has a chance to build the future if his health holds up.

Yeltsin's Russia stands comparison with the German Weimar Republic (1918–33); both states were or had been endangered by massive unemployment, by extremism both on the left and the right, and by real or imagined humiliation on the international stage. But there are also striking differences. In Russia, the Communists sought support from traditional chauvinists but they did so in a country whose people had no stomach for foreign wars. In Russia, the opposition lacked a charismatic leader. There were no stormtroopers in the streets. Communism, like Nazism, would no longer inspire the fanatical enthusiasm that totalitarian creeds had aroused in the days of Hitler and Stalin. For all the ills suffered during the Soviet empire's breakup, its dissolution had occasioned much less bloodshed than decolonization in British India, in Algeria, or in the former Portuguese colonies. A military takeover was unlikely, given the divisions within the armed forces themselves. Moreover, Russian officers, though respected, had never commanded the same prestige their colleagues had once enjoyed in Germany and Japan. The army had not performed well in Chechnya – a territory no larger than New Jersey, with a population of less than 1,000,000 people. Of martial enthusiasm there was none. But Russia's relations with its neighbors were reasonably correct. (For instance, Russia made no effective attempt to reclaim the Crimea which had been transferred from Russia to Ukraine at Khrushchev's frivolous whim.)

As for the economic record, Russia's human wealth and physical resources remained enormous. So was Russia's capacity for unexpected recuperation (shown after every major war in Russia's past). There were, moreover, good reasons for distrusting Russian statistics, both past and present. In the Bolshevik days, statistics had grossly overstated production so as to please the planners. In post-communist Russia, statisticians erred in the opposite direction. They did so because a great deal of economic production derived from clandestine enterprise – both state and privately owned – whose directors naturally wished to avoid attention from census-takers and tax-collectors.

Contrary to widespread misconceptions, the Russian people were not starving. Private enterprise revived; shoemakers, barbers, jewelers, carpenters, once again went into business. Private restaurants once more opened their doors – not just luxury establishments for the élite, or foreign-owned chains such as McDonald's, but also low-cost indigenous enterprises such as Russkoye Bistro where a Muscovite could order for an affordable price, a cup of mushroom soup, meat piroshki, and a glass of kvass, the traditional fermented brew. Consumer goods once more became available for those with money to spend. A substantial portion of Russian industry went into private ownership. (By 1995, vouchers had been issued in 15,000 companies.) There were new entertainment industries; there were new, vibrant, and iconoclastic media, a new public opinion which governments could no longer simply ignore. Inflation sharply dropped (from 17.8 percent in January 1995 to 6.7 percent in June.) By 1995, reforms had gone too far to be reversed; Russia had developed functioning markets for goods and capital. Marxist–Leninist ideology had insisted on treating the petty bourgeoisie as a dying class. On the contrary, however, the petty bourgeoisie reformed in all post-communist countries with astonishing speed: butchers, bakers, hairdressers, restaurant owners, shopkeepers – a great army of hard-working men and women.

In addition, Russia rebuilt an entrepreneurial élite. The foreign press (and Russia's own left-wing press) made much of the new *mafiosi*. But, in addition to this criminal element, Russia once more developed a new class of civically minded capitalists. Like the Tretyakovs and Riabushinskis of Czarist days, these magnates gave massive support to churches and cultural organizations, thereby changing Russia in a sense no Marxist–Leninist could have anticipated. Russia by now had opened to international trade; imports had become essential both to industry and ordinary consumers. These changes had produced powerful new lobbies with a stake in maintaining reforms – this at a time when even the Communists had lost the old Leninist discipline. Far from contemplating foreign aggression, the Russian Federation faced the danger of breakaway movements in several of its constituent parts. (Of these, Chechnya was only the foremost.) From the Western viewpoint, it was a success story which, at the end of World War II, no prophet could have foreseen and which no statesman could have bettered.

Index